Freedoms Won

Caribbean Emancipations, Ethnicities and Nationhood

Hilary McD. Beckles

Verene A. Shepherd

CAMBRIDGE
UNIVERSITY PRESS

CAMBRIDGE
UNIVERSITY PRESS

University Printing House, Cambridge CB2 8BS, United Kingdom

One Liberty Plaza, 20th Floor, New York, NY 10006, USA

477 Williamstown Road, Port Melbourne, VIC 3207, Australia

4843/24, 2nd Floor, Ansari Road, Daryaganj, Delhi – 110002, India

79 Anson Road, #06–04/06, Singapore 079906

Cambridge University Press is part of the University of Cambridge.

It furthers the University's mission by disseminating knowledge in the pursuit of education, learning and research at the highest international levels of excellence.

www.cambridge.org
Information on this title: www.cambridge.org/9780521435451

First published 2006
20 19 18 17 16 15 14 13 12 11 10

Printed in the United Kingdom by Latimer Trend

A catalogue record for this publication is available from the British Library

ISBN 978-0-521-43545-1 Paperback

Dedication

This book is dedicated to Norma Joy Lazarus (d. 1982)

and to

the people of the former British-colonised Caribbean on the occasion of the bicentenary of the final abolition of the trans-Atlantic trade in Africans (1807–2007)

Contents

Introduction

....

'*Emancipate yourselves from mental slavery; none but ourselves can free our minds …*'
(Bob Marley)

Freedoms won: Caribbean emancipation, ethnicities and nationhood, like its companion volume *Liberties lost: Caribbean indigenous societies and slave systems*, is designed primarily for secondary level students writing the CXC (Caribbean Examinations Council, C–SEC) or equivalent examinations. It should also be of interest to the general reader, year one college level students and those who require background reading for the CAPE (Caribbean Advanced Proficiency Examination) and the 'A'-Level Caribbean History Paper administered by the University of Cambridge, Local Examinations Syndicate.

This present text aims at setting out the essential details of the social, economic and political experiences of Caribbean people as they emerged out of their enslavement, indentureship and other forms of unfreedom, and sought to actualise their liberty and create their own societies in the period 1838 – ca. 1985. A focus on post-slavery societies is crucial to any study of Caribbean civilisation as one cannot simply leave the scene of action at the moment of legal freedom, but should focus on long-range reflections.

As *Liberties Lost* showed, from the moment of capture and enslavement, Africans in the Caribbean, as elsewhere, signalled their intention to resist the plantation system. Resistance forced structural changes in the internal relations of Caribbean societies. While antislavery forces were not all internal, acts of self-liberation, most notably those in French St Domingue (now Haiti) where a revolt of those enslaved in 1791 brought down slavery, illustrate that those enslaved there were first to implement sustainable emancipation schemes within the hemisphere. Between the Haitian revolution and the last quarter of the 19th Century, the system of enslaving Africans in the Caribbean ended in a drawn-out programme of legislative emancipation.

Emancipation came about at various dates in the different Caribbean territories. In a sense, the enslaved peoples of the French-colonised Caribbean territories had achieved emancipation earlier than other enslaved peoples, those in Haiti having won their freedom by revolutionary means in 1794. For a short while after the Haitian revolution, slavery was also declared abolished in the other French-colonised Caribbean territories, but by 1802 it had been re-imposed by orders of Napoleon Bonaparte. The Haitian army led by Toussaint tried to free enslaved people in neighbouring Santo Domingo.

President Boyer succeeded in 1822, despite several efforts by European powers to delay this process. It was not until 1848 that enslaved peoples in the other French-colonised territories of Guadeloupe, Martinique and French Guiana, now referred to as Guyana, were freed.

In 1834, by an Act of Parliament of 1833, 668,000 enslaved people were freed in the British-colonised Caribbean territories. But Emancipation Acts did not signal the end of systems of domination. With the exception of the French Caribbean, Antigua and Bermuda, forms of new slavery, whether euphemistically called Apprenticeship, Free Birth/Free Womb, *regimen de contratación* or *patronato*, were introduced to the Caribbean as a means of replacing old forms of slavery. Intended to last from 1834 to 1840, the Apprenticeship System in the British-colonised Caribbean collapsed in 1838 in the face of the anti-slavery activities of humanitarians and apprentices, and the inefficient systems of implementation. After 1838 all formerly enslaved adults were freed.

The ending of the Apprenticeship System in the British-colonised territories, as indeed the ending of the other transitional systems, terminated the brutal slavery regime that had characterised the history of the region for over four centuries. The analysis of the Apprenticeship System revealed that it simply continued the project of labour control which began in the 15th Century. It was no wonder that the apprentices, especially the women, whose continued brutalisation became an issue of anti-apprenticeship activism, fought to end the new slavery system.

A somewhat different sequence of events took place in the Cayman Islands, Antigua, Barbuda and Bermuda. Both Bermuda and Antigua rejected the Apprenticeship system, and implemented immediate emancipation in 1834. Antigua did not bypass the Apprenticeship system because of moral or humanitarian reasons but for economic reasons. The Antiguan planters believed that full freedom would be cheaper than a delayed emancipation and that as a full plantation colony, alternatives to non-estate labour were limited; and so they had little fear that the formerly enslaved people would not return to work on the estates.

Barbuda was the private property of the Codrington family, owner of estates in Antigua and Barbados at the time of emancipation. It had no colonial government to pass an Emancipation Act and the framers of the Emancipation Act in Britain had not even mentioned the island by name. Technically, of course, Barbuda fell under the British Crown, and so it was expected that emancipation would apply to Barbuda also. The years after 1834 posed problems for the Codringtons, the formerly enslaved people and the British Government. In the Cayman Islands (which came under the governorship of Jamaica), because the technicalities of registration of those enslaved laid down by the 1834 Emancipation Act had not been followed, emancipation took place by proclamation on 3 May 1835; and in 1837, by order of the new Governor of Jamaica, the Marquis of Sligo, those formerly enslaved were discharged from the remaining terms of their apprenticeship. In the Bahamas, the Acts to implement emancipation and the Apprenticeship System were on the statute books well before 1 August 1834.

The abolition of slavery came later in the other Caribbean territories – Santo Domingo in 1844, the Danish-colonised territories in 1848, the Dutch-colonised territories in 1863, Puerto Rico in 1873 and Cuba in 1886. Within the Americas, the Portuguese-ruled territory of Brazil was the last to abolish slavery in 1888; so the Iberian powers had been the earliest to establish slavery in the region and the last to abolish.

Individual enslaved persons had, of course, obtained freedom through marronage and self- or gratuitous manumission even before the slave systems officially ended: but, for the majority of enslaved people in the Caribbean, freedom came by legislation in the 19th Century.

The ending of the system of slavery was a major event in all of the Caribbean. All freed people had high hopes of emancipation and citizenship, and expected a changed life. Skilled wage workers in rural and urban areas wanted greater bargaining power and better working and living conditions. Those who wanted to live independently of the estates as farmers wanted land on which to grow crops for subsistence and sale. The ownership of land was also a route to political enfranchisement and was important. But various obstacles were placed in the way of the fulfilment of these far-ranging hopes. Thus the post-slavery period was conflict-ridden as former owners and those formerly enslaved each struggled to realise their own expectations of the new order. In the case of the former slaveholders, they were intent on preserving their wealth and social status and wanted the freed people to continue to provide the labour which would allow them to do this. The freed people were equally bent on making their own conditions of labour – even to make a life for themselves if necessary

outside of the boundaries of their former work places. A class struggle naturally ensued, and one result was the frustration of the peasantry in many places.

Furthermore, the importation of unfree immigrant labourers, in places, frustrated the independent action of the newly freed who, particularly in the larger colonies, were intent on settling in free villages and working on their former masters' and mistresses' properties only part-time, if at all. Many people believed that some of the colonies did not need to import bonded immigrants as they experienced a declining sugar industry and even had to begin to grow crops other than sugar cane; and alternative crops which replaced sugar-cane did not need as many full-time labourers. In the end, though, despite the pros and cons of immigration, bonded immigrants contributed greatly to the social and economic development of the Caribbean; and the descendants of immigrants who settled in the region have played fundamental leadership roles in Caribbean society. Like enslaved Africans, the majority of bonded Indians had been relocated to the Caribbean against their will by British colonialism, but struggled to free themselves from the legacies of indentureship.

African and Indian women encountered gender-specific obstacles as they sought to actualise their freedom. The workforce became increasingly male after the abolition of slavery and African women's lack of education confined them to low-paying jobs. In many cases the use of indentured labourers displaced them as agricultural labourers and smaller properties no longer demanded their labour. Indentured Indian and Chinese women themselves, despite their tremendous effort, experienced multiple forms of oppression under the system of indentured servitude. Women of all ethnic groups experienced the effects of patriarchy and male dominance. The gender order enabled men to occupy the public sphere of wage labour while women were to confine themselves to the home, the 'private sphere'. Those who braved the odds and remained as labourers were given the less remunerative tasks.

Except in Haiti, the governments of the Caribbean territories were controlled by the traditional planter elements, most of whom did not play a liberating role in shaping the new society to fulfil the expectations of the newly freed. Their allies, European officials, believed that African and Indian people should provide cheap labour for the estates. The elite land-owning class and its imperial supporters joined in oppressing the freed and bonded people and made inadequate provisions for their health, housing and education. Education was a route to upward social mobility and non-plantation occupations; the elite class did not want any democratic obstacles in the way of its economic interest. The right to vote continued to be restrictive in most post-slavery societies well into the 20th century; and so the mass of African and Asian people were denied an active role in government. The refusal of colonial governments and land-owners to implement policies to help the formerly enslaved people and newly bonded, combined with continuing economic crises and failing economies, caused protest and anti-imperial struggles in all territories. For example, less than 30 years after the implementation of the Emancipation Act, the 'Vox Populi' protest erupted in St. Vincent (1862). Following close on the heels of that 1862 protest were the 1865 Morant Bay Rebellion in Jamaica, the 1872 'Bridgetown Riots' and the 1876 'Confederation Riots' in Barbados.

The early 20th Century was as conflict-ridden as the 1840s and 1850s. By the mid 20th Century, Caribbean people struggled to throw off the colonial yoke. In the British-colonised territories, they first tried to do this collectively through the creation in 1958 of an independent political federation. This federation collapsed in 1962, resulting in the movement to independence as separate countries. Jamaica and Trinidad and Tobago were the first to seek independence, achieving this on August 6 and 31, 1962 respectively. Barbados, and colonial Guyana followed in 1966; Dominica, St Lucia, St Vincent, Montserrat, St Kitts-Nevis, Anguilla and the Cayman Islands continued for longer under imperial rule. By 1985, however, many more former British-colonised territories had thrown off the imperial yoke.

For the French-colonised Caribbean territories like Martinique and Guadeloupe, and a few British-colonised Caribbean territories like Bermuda, the Cayman Islands, Montserrat and Anguilla, independence still has not become a reality; though forms of anti-imperial struggles continue. Martinique, Guadeloupe and Guyane are overseas departments of France. Up to 1985, independence had still not been achieved for the Dutch-colonised Caribbean territories with the exception of Suriname.

Political independence may have been attained by some, but this did not bring economic independence. Reliance on external sources for loans and investment created the environment for increased United States and European power in the region, supported as they were by their own political agenda in the face of the Cold War. Haiti and the Hispanic Caribbean were particularly affected by United States military interventions.

As this text shows, despite these difficulties, the Caribbean people have been able to carve out a life for themselves. They have used their dynamic freedom culture to help them to bear their social and economic difficulties. Others have resorted to emigration as the route to economic betterment; and their remittances have done much for the development of the region.

Hilary McD Beckles and **Verene A Shepherd**

Acknowledgements

This book could not have been completed without the assistance of several people. First of all, we acknowledge the research assistance provided by the following graduates of the University of the West Indies: Jaset Anderson, Dalea Bean, Symone Betton, Eldon Birthwright, Cavell Francis, Shanette Geohagen, Karen Graham, Tannya Guerra, Georgia Hamilton, Natalie McCarthy, Kerry-Ann Morris, Arthur Newland, Michele Salmon, Nicole Plummer, Coral Purvill, Ahmed Reid, Mitzie Reid and Vernon White.

We recognize the invaluable help of Dalea Bean, Cavell Francis, Shani Roper and Maxine McDonnough with the photo search, and thank the reviewers for their close reading of the manuscript and useful comments, which helped us to improve the final product. The students and teachers who participated in workshops and seminars, at which some of the themes in the text were debated, must also be thanked.

The hospitality and assistance of colleagues, friends and family in London must also be acknowledged. Specifically, Angella and Jason Lazarus, and Annette, Janice and Philip Brade went beyond the call of duty to offer accommodation and technical support to Verene during summers of research and writing of early drafts.

We owe a huge debt of gratitude to the editors and production team of Cambridge University Press, Africa and the Caribbean, who exercised patience and understanding throughout the process of writing, re-writing, editing and proof-reading.

Finally, we are grateful to our families for their patience and support and thank the following for permission to use important lines from their songs and to reproduce photographs and illustrations from their works and holdings:

Courtesy of National Library of Jamaica: 1, 3, 5, 7, 11, 12, 13, 21, 24, 26, 32, 33, 38, 40, 44, 45, 46, 47, 48, 53, 57, 63, 66, 69, 71, 73, 76, 82, 85, 86, 87, 91, 98, 104, 106, 109, 110, 115, 116, 117, 120, 124, 127, 128, 130, 131, 138, 154, 155, 165, 166, 168, 171, 176, 182, 185, 187, 201, 203, 206, 212, 214, 217, 220, 223, 237, 238, 264.; www.gettyimages/GalloImages: 143, 211, 213, 247, 267, 268; INPRA: 99, 111, 119, 132, 139 (right), 142, 145, 147, 151 (left), 152, 153, 154, 155, 157, 158 (left), 162, 170, 173, 176, 201, 218 (right), 262, 265; iAfrika: 70, 195, 239, 242, 251, 258, 263; John Carter Brown Library: 4.

Authors: 139 (left), 151 (right), 158 (right), 178, 186, 193, 199, 202, 205, 215, 218 (left), 224, 225, 226, 227, 228, 229, 230, 231, 232, 233, 234, 235, 243, 245, 253, 255, 265, 270, 276.

Maps by Ann Westoby: 6, 8, 17, 19, 26, 41, 60, 64, 74, 100, 150, 248, 259.

Songlines: for the songlines by Bob Marley that preface chapters 2, 4, 6, 8, 9, 12, 14, 17 and 18, we gratefully acknowledge permission from the Bob Marley Foundation; for the songlines by The Mighty Scraper, we thank Stephen Gay.

Toussaint L'Ouverture

Chapter 1

The limits of emancipation: freedom contained in Haiti: 1804–1844

'Bon pawol pale, the truth speaks, children come listen,
listen to me, a revolution is truly starting.'
(Boukman Eksperyans)

Introduction

On 22 August 1791 Boukman Dutty and other enslaved
people in St Domingue launched the greatest revolt for
freedom from slavery known in the Americas. Following
this, the revolutionary government of France at its 1794
Convention passed an Emancipation Act, abolishing
slavery in its Empire. From 1794 onwards all European
governments with Caribbean colonies passed
Emancipation Acts, making it illegal for anyone to own
people as property. The last European country with
colonies in the Caribbean to pass emancipation legislation
was Spain in 1886.

These abolition of slavery Acts did not immediately
grant the newly freed people the same civil rights and
liberties as the European community. They also did not
put the emancipated African people on an equal social
standing with formerly free minority groups, such as Jews
and propertied mixed-race people.

In the British colonies the Abolition Act of 1833 only unconditionally freed children under six years old. The majority of 'freed people' went through a further period of bondage. The British and Dutch officially called this period 'the Apprenticeship'; in Cuba it was called the *patronato*; in Puerto Rico the *régimen de contratación*; and in the territories ruled by Denmark, it was called 'free birth' or 'free womb'.

In the French-colonised Caribbean there was no formal period of partial emancipation. However, before 1804 in Haiti (the former St Domingue), the newly emancipated people still had to work on a contract basis for their former enslavers.

In this chapter we will learn about:
1 Freedom and bondage in revolutionary Santo Domingo and Haiti under the regime.

This timeline will help you to organise information around the dates of important events:

Timeline

22 August 1791	Start of Haitian Revolution
1794	Revolutionary government of France passed Emancipation Act; implemented in Haiti
1795	Toussaint takes over Haiti as ruler
1801	Workers' rebellion in Haiti led by Moise
1802	Toussaint captured
	Napoleon re-imposes slavery in the French-colonised Caribbean
1803	Toussaint dies at Fort de Jour
1804	Dessalines declares Haitian Independence
1806	Dessalines killed and Christophe takes over
1818–1843	Boyer rules Haiti
1833	Emancipation Act passed, British-colonised territories
1838	End of Apprenticeship, British-colonised territories
1844	Independence in Santo Domingo
1848	Abolition of slavery – French-colonised Caribbean
1886	Emancipation in Spanish-colonised Cuba

1 Toussaint's rule

In 1793 the former enslaved population in St Domingue defeated the French and their allies, Spain and Britain. By 1795 Toussaint L'Ouverture was in political and military control of St Domingue. He was anxious to rebuild the economy and to restore trade and production levels. The question was whether he could rebuild the economy with free rather than bonded labour, especially as there was huge opposition to the use of bonded labour from all the European and American enslaving nations.

Toussaint developed an agricultural policy to help rebuild the plantation sector. This policy returned many properties to the families who had owned them during slavery. It also encouraged foreign trade with European merchants, and tried to attract investments from Europe and the United States. Toussaint believed that this policy was the key to economic restoration, as well as to political and social stability. Not all freed people supported this policy. They did not warm to his idea that they should return in large numbers to work on the large coffee and sugar estates. Neither did they readily accept his vision of them as a service labour force needed to rebuild an economy based on exports.

After the revolutionary abolition of slavery, workers throughout St Domingue continued to resist and rebel when forced to return to work on the large estates. Many fled to the hills to live as peasants or to join the Maroon communities. Others migrated to the towns in search of work that was not linked to plantation slavery. In the rural villages people preferred to be independent farmers and peasants rather than labourers on former estates. The rural people associated the old economic system with plantation slavery. For them liberty meant not working on the plantations under a system that controlled their social, economic and political life.

Toussaint was faced with a dilemma – how could he supply labour to the plantations restored to former owners? Workers would work on the plantations only if they were forced to do so. Toussaint's answer was to use the law to force people to work on the plantations, backed up by the courts. The government issued an order that stated that:
■ All freed people who were plantation labourers must return to the plantation on which they lived before the abolition of slavery.
■ Those who did not return to the plantations would be arrested and placed at the disposal of the army.

Chapter 1 | *The limits of emancipation: freedom contained in Haiti: 1804–1844*

- Those who refused to work or who left the plantation without permission would be reported to the military commanders, so that legal action could be taken against them.
- In return for their labour, workers would receive a quarter of the crop produced, or a quarter of its net value. The other three-quarters belonged to the landowner. They would also be given provision grounds, which they could cultivate for themselves.

Government also introduced new labour laws, known as the rural code (see page 5 for description) to protect the labourers from abuse and injustice at the hands of landowners. For example, the landowners were not allowed to use a whip or any other form of corporal punishment. Another example was that the code said the working day could only last from 5 a.m. to 5 p.m. However, many of these measures simply helped to bring back elements of the forced labour system of the plantations against which the workers had fought and died in large numbers.

Worker's rebellion of 1801

It was anticipated that there would be popular opposition to Toussaint's rural development policy. In 1801 a workers' rebellion broke out in the Northern Department against Toussaint's government. It was led by one of the more radical leaders, General Moise. He was in favour of breaking up the large plantations and making land available to the freed people. This policy was in direct opposition to Toussaint's policy. The workers aimed to prevent the French community from regrouping as an elite, to unite the mixed-race and African people, and to declare the independence of St Domingue. The revolt was severely suppressed by Toussaint's army which executed over 1,000 workers. Moise was arrested, condemned as a traitor, and shot.

Napoleon tries to re-impose slavery

Moise's revolt was not the only serious challenge that Toussaint and his government had to face. Napoleon's government was determined to overthrow the revolution and re-impose slavery in St Domingue. So, workers had to support Toussaint to protect their freedom, but at the same time they opposed his economic policies. The major challenge Toussaint faced was to lead people who had high expectations of freedom and who supported his military strategies, but who opposed his economic policies. He lived in constant expectation that someone within his own ranks would betray him.

Napoleon's top priority was to capture Toussaint. He believed that if he could cut off the 'head of the revolution',

then the 'body' would 'fall and die'. In 1802 he succeeded in cutting off the 'head' through a deceitful plot. Toussaint was invited to a meeting with French officials in Port au Prince supposedly to discuss the future relations between his country and France. Here he was kidnapped and taken to France. In France he was imprisoned high in the French Alps at Fort de Jour where he died on 27 April 1803.

Fig 1.1 Napoleon Bonaparte

Dessaline's rule

The officers of Toussaint's army had not supported his policy of negotiation with the French because they did not trust the intentions of the French government. Once Toussaint was captured, his officers were determined to resist Napoleon's attempts to restore slavery. They also resolved to step up the war for independence.

Jean-Jacques Dessalines emerged as his replacement to lead the armed forces. Dessalines and Henri Christophe, another of Toussaint's top military commanders, revived the struggle against the French and they succeeded in defeating the French army. In 1804 Dessalines named himself Jean-Jacques 1, Emperor of Haiti. He expelled the rest of the Napoleonic army and declared St Domingue independent of France. He renamed the country 'Haiti' after the Taino word meaning 'mountainous'. He also positioned Haiti as a safe haven for hemispheric Africans fleeing enslavement.

Dessalines's economic policies, which were similar to those of Toussaint, resulted in even harsher measures taken against workers. The idea of meaningful freedom was becoming less and less of a reality to workers.

Fig 1.2 Jean-Jacques Dessalines

Dessalines imposed a military dictatorship on the newly independent country. He brought a large percentage of land under the control of the state. He planned to rebuild agriculture by establishing a number of large agricultural projects and by using the plantations. But first he had to rebuild the large plantations, which had been ruined in the war of liberation. This required the mass mobilisation of labour. Second, he had to tackle the task of producing in workers a commitment to high productivity.

Dessalines declared that all Haitians, except soldiers, must be available for work to cultivate the plantations. Women could not join the army even though at independence in 1804 they outnumbered men 3:2. So women formed the majority of the labour force. They took on the greater share of the hardship associated with this policy of compulsory plantation labour. Women protested against the injustice of this. They had fought alongside the men in the war of liberation. Now these economic and social policies put them in an inferior position to men; while men were promoted as the more privileged citizens.

Labourers were treated like serfs. They were forbidden to leave, without permission, the plantations to which they were assigned. But overseers, mostly soldiers, were told not to whip the labourers; most of them still did so. Government officials at the local level kept a daily record of the work done by each labourer. Those labourers, who were said to be idle or lazy were made to build public roads. Workers resented these measures in the same way as they had resented Toussaint's measures. There was widespread public protest, which divided the army that was called upon to suppress the opposition: some soldiers supported the workers, while others did not. This situation bred rebellion amongst officers. So Dessalines' government experienced diminishing popular support. He was eventually assassinated in 1806.

Henri Christophe's rule

The mixed-race community had settled mainly in the south. They saw themselves as a separate political group, with its own interests. They had made a bid to replace Dessalines with one of their own leaders. It was generally believed that they were responsible for creating the circumstances in which Dessalines was murdered. They had opposed him and were determined to overthrow his government. However, despite this aggressive political campaign of the mixed-race people the Haitian general, Christophe, emerged as President to succeed Dessalines. He had established his own political base in the north of the country. The bitter struggle between the African and mixed-race elite for political leadership grew stronger. It ended in Haiti being divided into two separate 'countries':

Christophe ruled in the north while Pétion, the leader of the mixed-race people, governed in the south.

Just like Toussaint and Dessalines, Christophe tried to revive the large sugar and coffee plantations using forced labour. Women, who were the majority of workers, worked from dusk till dawn in the fields, often with their children. For these women there were many similarities between slavery against which they had fought and the new conditions of work. Those women who were not strong and healthy were expected to do so-called 'lighter work' around the estate and to look after the children of field labourers. This was to make sure that ill-health was not used as an excuse to avoid work, a practice that was common during slavery.

Christophe's labour arrangements in the north were very different to what was happening under Pétion's leadership in the south. Pétion's policies were more advantageous to peasant farming and to helping workers get land. The result of this policy difference was that people thought that Pétion's republic was more favourable to Haitian workers than Christophe's kingdom. So it was normal to find Haitian workers crossing the border in flight from Christophe's kingdom to Pétion's republic to seek a better life for themselves.

Fig 1.3 Henri Christophe

Jean-Pierre Boyer's rule

Jean-Pierre Boyer took over the government of both the north and south of Haiti after Pétion died in 1818 and Christophe died in 1820 and so united the country once again. In 1826 he introduced the dreaded *Code Rural* which was designed to re-organise the agricultural economy of Haiti. The *Code Rural* was based on the principle that peasants were obliged to work on plantations and if they refused to they would be punished. The objectives of the code were:

■ To make it possible for the Haitian economy to recover the levels of productivity achieved under Dessalines.
■ To make sure that there was a constant supply of labour, which was sometimes short because peasants had a tendency to evade work and leave the plantations to cultivate their own land.

Terms of the Code Rural

The main terms of the *Code Rural* were as follows:

■ No one was excused from working on the land, except for government servants and professionals.
■ Landowners could not abandon the plot on which they lived and to which they would be attached from then onward, without prior permission from the local justice of the peace or military chief.
■ Children of agricultural workers were not allowed to attend school without the permission of the authorities, if it meant they would be abandoning their parents' plots.
■ Workers could not leave the countryside under any circumstances to engage in business.
■ Workers could not build their own houses and leave the plantations on which they were supposed to be working for a living.
■ Workers were not allowed to spend more than eight days outside the plantation even with permission from the plantation owner.
■ A fine or imprisonment would result if a worker failed to stay for three years with one employer.
■ Vagrancy was forbidden.
■ Pregnant women had to work up to their fourth month of pregnancy.
■ Women had to return to work four months after the birth of their children.
■ Soldiers were assigned to each plantation to make sure that the code was obeyed.

The *Code Rural* did not achieve its objectives for the following reasons:

■ There was worker resistance to this form of enforced labour.
■ The army could not enforce the regulations.

- When the army no longer feared a French invasion it relaxed military discipline.

It was not only in Haiti that Boyer's policies were unpopular among the people. They were also unpopular in Santo Domingo.

Santo Domingo

In 1822, President Boyer, feeling secure that Haiti was united, boldly invaded the neighbouring Spanish colony of Santo Domingo. He reached his objective by taking control and abolishing slavery there.

Toussaint had already attempted this in 1801, but at that time the Spanish forces were backed by French enforcements, and they managed to stop Toussaint's efforts to abolish slavery. Haitians remained determined to remove slavery from the entire island of Hispaniola. Toussaint's occupation of St Domingo was, therefore, shortlived.

Fig 1.4 Hispaniola

Toussaint had also in the short period tried to change the agricultural land policy in Santo Domingo and to reorganise the system of labour. As in St Domingue, he tried to bring in an export-oriented plantation system based on forced labour rather than a traditional economy based on small-scale livestock farming and subsistence agriculture. In this respect Boyer's regime was similar to Toussaint's. He selected military commanders to govern Santo Domingo and to make sure that production for export was continued under the *Code Rural*. He passed laws to force freed people to grow only export crops. People were not allowed to own large tracts of land.

Boyer's occupation of Santo Domingo, in contrast, lasted for 22 years. In this time there was increasing Spanish colonial opposition to Haitian rule of the country. The Spanish government had criticised the invasion of its colony. The Haitians responded by saying that invasion was necessary to bring freedom to the enslaved, to secure the borders of Haiti, and to unite the country in its opposition to slavery and colonialism. But the liberated workers also opposed Boyer's land policy and the stringent policies of his government, just as the workers had done in St Domingue under Toussaint. Boyer's overthrow strengthened anti-Haitian sentiments in Santo Domingo and this led to separatist agitation. This was successful since, in 1844, Santo Domingo declared its independence from Haiti.

To sum up

Slavery had ended in Haiti and Santo Domingo, but the newly emancipated did not experience complete liberation. Consequently they resisted autocratic regimes and all systems of reformed-slavery, such as the new labour codes.

Revision questions

1 Read the extract and answer the questions that follow:

The abolition of slavery in St Domingue through slave revolution and warfare against the French and their allies, and the achievement of independence in 1804, left the Haitians free of Imperial rule. Several rulers from among the people of Haiti came to power between 1795 and 1804. Their policies at times antagonised the freed people.

a Name two rulers who came to power in Haiti between 1795 and 1804.
b State four reasons why the rulers in Haiti 'antagonised the freed people' between 1795 and 1804.
c State three ways in which Haitians resisted the policies of their rulers in the period 1795–1804.

2 Explain the importance of Haitian independence in your life.

Treadmill

Freedom without liberty: 1833–1886

'Let's get together to fight this Holy Armageddon.'
(Bob Marley)

Introduction

Unlike the French, the British forced the majority of the newly emancipated to go through a further period of bondage after the abolition of slavery. This was called the Apprenticeship System. Its major aim was to guarantee former enslavers, who were mostly planters, an effective supply of labour. This was until a free market system was up and running which would help to secure a reliable and adequate supply of labour. The Apprenticeship System also aimed to make sure that the plantation system would continue as the main economic system and with it the continued rule of elite landholders.

In this chapter we will learn about:
1 Apprenticeship in the British-colonised Caribbean
2 How Apprenticeship came to an end
3 'Free Birth' in the Danish-colonised Caribbean
4 Apprenticeship in the Dutch-colonised Caribbean
5 *Contratación* in Puerto Rico
6 *Patronato* in Cuba

1 Apprenticeship in the British-colonised Caribbean

On the whole, the British planters in Jamaica, Trinidad and colonial Guyana (British Guiana) were anxious that if the Apprenticeship systems were not established, then freed people would desert the estates and settle on the large tracts of uncultivated land that existed. This would ruin the sugar industry on which class and racial domination was largely based.

These fears were not as pronounced in those colonies where there was no land for freed people to access, or where there were no Maroon communities in the hills and

KEY

British colonies that implemented the Apprenticeship System

ANTIGUA British colonies that did not implement Apprenticeship System

Fig 2.1 British colonies that implemented the Apprenticeship System and those that did not

Chapter 2 | *Freedom without liberty: 1833–1886*

forests which they could join in opposition to the plantation sector. The Caribbean planters described these kinds of colonies as having no frontier. In other words, they did not have places where new, independent communities could be established beyond the reach of estate owners.

Two colonies that did not implement the Apprenticeship System were Antigua and Bermuda. Landowners in those territories believed that they had effective control over the landspace and work force that was available in the colony. Antiguan landholders argued that it was more economical to go straight for complete emancipation from slavery. One advocate of complete emancipation was Samuel Otto Baijer. He noted that free labour would cost a third less than enslaved labour. The deciding factor in this case was that Antigua did not have large areas of uncultivated land on which freed people could settle. Also, landowners did not fear the possibility of workers emigrating from the colony.

Terms of Apprenticeship

In those British-colonised Caribbean territories where the Apprenticeship System was used, the main terms were as follows:

- Children under six were freed unless their mothers could not provide for them. In this case, the children served indentureship on the estate on which they lived until they reached the age of 21. This meant that they were contracted to work as apprentices on this estate.
- All apprentices over six years were classified as either agricultural apprentices (praedial) or domestic/artisan apprentices (non-praedial), depending on the type of work they did twelve months before the Abolition Act was passed. An exception was in the Bahamas where no child under twelve could be classified as praedial.
- Agricultural workers were to serve a six-year apprenticeship and would finally be freed in 1840. In the Bahamas another term was that no praedials could be removed from the soil without the permission of the magistrate.
- Domestic servants and all non-praedials were to serve a four year Apprenticeship and would be freed in 1838.
- Apprentices could be valued and could buy their freedom before these dates if their owner agreed. The Act said that owners had to accept a fair payment for the apprentice's freedom. The amount charged for an individual's freedom was determined by an objective evaluation of how much the apprentice's labour was worth.
- A tribunal consisting of Stipendiary Magistrates (SMs) and planters did the evaluation for the purposes of selling freedom.

- During the Apprenticeship System all employers had to continue supplying legally established allowances of food, clothing, lodging and medical attendance to the apprentices. In the Bahamas, employers could choose not to supply food and clothes, but instead to supply good land if they reached an agreement with the freed people. The sick and aged continued to be the responsibility of the landowners.
- Apprentices worked for $40\frac{1}{2}$ hours of unpaid labour per week for their former owners. Any labour done outside of these hours was paid for.

In the Bahamas, new legislation provided that there could be labour contracts. In other words, workers could be contracted to work for the landowners, but these contracts could only last for two years. The contracts had to be witnessed by two people who could show that they understood the terms of the contract. Each employer was to keep a record of all contracts, which Stipendiary Magistrates could inspect. Finally, workers could not work on Saturday and Sunday, i.e. weekends were considered 'free time' for workers.

Other terms of Apprenticeship were:

- 100 Stipendiary (or Special) Magistrates would be appointed to supervise how the Apprenticeship worked.
- In colonies that were not Crown Colonies the legislature in the colony was to pass its own Emancipation Act, which had to be approved by the Crown.

These Acts had to provide for the following:
- How the apprentices would be classified.
- How they would be valued if they wanted to buy their freedom.
- How discipline among apprentices would be maintained.
- How laziness and vagrancy would be prevented. These terms would be defined by those in power.
- How the former owners should conduct themselves toward apprentices.
- The kind of punishment employers would receive for acts of cruelty against apprentices.
- The continued provision of customary allowances by the former owners.
- How the employers would observe the limit on the free labour time of the apprentices.
- How the sale of apprentices would be prohibited unless the estate on which they were serving their apprenticeship was being sold.

A Crown Colony had legislative Acts sent down from Britain. Those colonies that were not Crown Colonies passed their own Acts, subject to approval by the Crown.

The terms of the Emancipation Acts were adapted to suit local needs. For example, in 1835 the Bahamas allowed praedial apprentices to become more independent under certain conditions. Usually praedial apprentices worked five days for their employers, who would supply the apprentices with clothes and provisions. Non-praedial apprentices were allowed to cultivate a plot of land for their own support and maintenance for $2\frac{1}{2}$ days of the week. Apprentices engaged in sea-going activities were only partly maintained by their employers, and also had to give two-thirds of their earnings to their 'owners'. In Barbados, planters would not provide children under six with the customary allowance if parents refused to indenture their children; and in St Kitts, estate owners allowed the freed people to cultivate idle land instead of giving them allowances.

Freed people react to the Apprenticeship System

Although the emancipated workers resisted and criticised the system of delayed freedom, they did not greet Emancipation day with the large-scale military assault on slave owners that pro-slavery advocates had argued they would. In most colonies the day itself passed peacefully. Joseph Sturge and Thomas Harvey, two anti-slavery advocates who visited the Caribbean during Apprenticeship, reported in 1838 that many freed people went to church to give thanks for the legal recognition of freedom.

Despite this, the British put many oppressive measures in place in its territories. For example, they gave police extended powers over the freed population, they brought in military reinforcement, and then passed Vagrancy Laws to restrict movement. In the Bahamas, the British anticipated protests and so sent their troops to Exuma and Turks, leaving Nassau largely unprotected. Generally, the Barbados elite did not expect any major confrontation with workers and they also felt protected because of the presence of British regiments garrisoned at St Ann's Fort. Nonetheless, to counter any potential protest, the legislature immediately established a police force which could cover the island through a series of district stations.

In several territories Trespass Laws, Vagrancy Acts and other restrictive legislation were also passed. The Bahamas passed Vagrancy Laws that tried to address

notions of 'idleness, loitering and carousing'. The colonial legislature also kept corporal punishment in law, stipulating that runaways were to be returned by force.

Did you know?

Runaways were not simply those who were absent for short periods, but those who did not have permission to be absent and had been so for one month or more.

The Jamaican government passed a Vagrancy Act in 1833. Under this Act anyone who simply threatened to run away from estate labour could be charged. In Dominica the Vagrancy Act categorised any apprentice who made too much noise in the streets as a vagrant. In St Kitts, the Vagrancy Act of 1835 labelled a vagrant as any person 'knowingly spreading any false report to the commission of any act of subordination'. A person found guilty of this could receive as many as 60 lashes or six months in prison. Barbados passed a Trespass Act in 1837. In 1844, Antigua also passed a Vagrancy Act that made 'vagrancy, vagabondage and begging' an offence. Vagrancy Acts were also passed in Trinidad, Tobago and colonial Guyana.

Restrictive legislation did not prevent protest by the freed people over the delaying of full freedom. Freed men and women on many estates in St Kitts refused to return to the estates after 1 August 1834. They had to be forced to do so by the militia. On 2 August 1838, the militia in Trinidad had to quell a protesting crowd of about 200 people, mostly women. They were demanding full freedom. They had gathered in front of the governor's house chanting, 'no six years, we are free, the king made us free'.

On the Essequibo coast in colonial Guyana, the freed people withdrew their labour and engaged in violent protest against their delayed freedom. The ringleaders were usually rounded up, arrested and charged.

Similarly, in Jamaica, the last months of 1834 were a period of protest as freed people, individually and collectively, opposed the implementation of the system of Apprenticeship. This was despite the attempts made by Governor Sligo, planters, missionaries and magistrates to explain to the apprentices the terms of the Abolition Act and their responsibilities under the new system. On several estates in the parishes, notably in St Ann and St Thomas-in-the-Vale, apprentices refused to return to work unless wages were to be paid not just for part of the week, but for every day of the week. The apprentices distrusted the landowners so much that they insisted on being paid every evening.

We learn from Swithin Wilmot's research that these actions caused Governor Sligo to call out reinforcements of the troops and police. They arrested those who resisted going back to work. The ringleaders were tried and sentenced to be publicly flogged as an example to the others who might have planned to continue resisting. While the governor managed to crush the protest in St Thomas-in-the-Vale and nearby parishes, strikes and protests in St Ann continued until 9 August 1834. The most determined resistance was in the eastern districts of the parish on estates such as Shaw Park, Drax Hall, Roaring River and Boyd. In all cases workers demanded wages. Their resistance was suppressed by the police and military, who were called out by the Governor. Over 24 properties were involved in the protest.

In anticipation of social unrest, Governor Smith in Barbados dispatched several units of imperial soldiers to Bridgetown on Emancipation Day. He told the newly freed that 'the law is strong' and all those who did not work 'the law will punish'. While there was no large-scale violence, the apprentices still found non-violent ways to express their disapproval of the delayed freedom. In Trinidad, there were protests in Port-of-Spain as Africans opposed the delay in 'full free'. Threats of protests were also reported in colonial Guyana and St Kitts.

In Dominica and Montserrat many landholders found it difficult to persuade the apprentices to return to the estates after 1 August 1834. Property-holders in Montserrat had difficulties in getting labour as the freed

Fig 2.2 Governor Sligo

people were reluctant to work on planters' terms. The property owners had to call out the troops to get the apprentices to go to work. In St Lucia and Tobago there were reports of high instances of restlessness, threats of desertion and insubordination. There were many examples, in places such as Grenada, of penalties, whipping and imprisonment of apprentices for actions seen as acts of insubordination. In Nevis, there was dissatisfaction but little open confrontation between apprentices and employers.

Apart from collective resistance there were cases in which individuals resisted the implementation of Apprenticeship. Good examples from Jamaica are those of the former slave driver on Mt Goshen in St Catherine who was imprisoned in 1834 for 'disorderly conduct'. John Minot of Friendship Hall in St Andrew was sentenced to 14 days at hard labour and John Graskell of Mt Sinai in the same parish was found guilty of insubordination and attempting to get other apprentices to resist.

The working of the system

The Apprenticeship System did not work to anyone's satisfaction in these colonies. Former enslavers were only prepared to carry out their part of the arrangement with the help of force. They tried to exercise their usual power over the freed people. For example, many employers did not have enough finance to provide for the maintenance of the apprentices, which was their responsibility. They refused to pay fair wages for work done by the apprentices outside of their hours of compulsory labour. Many paid wages late and imprisoned and punished workers for alleged breaches of the terms of Apprenticeship. The treadmill became a common method of punishment used by employers.

Employers also refused to allow the apprentices ordinary privileges such as the pasturing of their animals on the estates and giving time off work during periods of heavy rainfall. Other problems developed over whether apprentices should work for eight or nine hours a day for four and a half or five days per week. The eight-hour day prevented them from starting their independent work on Friday afternoons. There were also disputes over employers' attempts to use the labour of free children on the estates. Equally contentious was the attempt of employers to reclassify apprentices so that those who were formerly nonagricultural were now categorised as agricultural.

Other conflicts included employers' extremely high valuation of workers when workers wanted to buy their freedom; employers sending women back into the fields who had over six children and had previously been excused from the field; and the use of the hospitals as places of punishment. Workers could be detained for punishment in hospitals because the hospitals were outside of the control of the Special Magistrates.

Fig 2.3 Ruin of Kellits Hospital, Jamaica, where workers were detained

The matter of over-valuation of apprentices to discourage them from purchasing their freedom was noted in several territories. St Vincent apprentices, for example, paid at least a third more than they should. The case of Sally from Jamaica is also instructive. Sally was 35 years old and in 1836 applied to be valued so that she could buy her freedom. Her owner valued her at £41.10/-. Stipendiary Magistrate Gurley said that this value was a complete outrage as Sally had five children, was expecting a sixth, and was not a primary worker. She worked in the second gang and during slavery would have valued less than £20. In Barbados, freed people willing to purchase their freedom during the first year of the Apprenticeship were often forced to resort to all manner of trickery so as to obtain a low evaluation from Justices – at times by faking illness and old age. Also noted were efforts to obstruct the process whereby apprentices could purchase the un-expired portion of their Apprenticeship.

However, apprentices were not deterred. Between 1834 and 1836, in Jamaica alone, 1,480 apprentices purchased their freedom or successfully negotiated the un-expired portion of their Apprenticeship. By August 1836, Special Magistrate Ryan in St Lucia was forecasting that the present rate of self-purchase would cause the abandonment of sugar cultivation in St Lucia within two years. In February 1838, the desire for self-purchase was reported as 'strong to universal' in St Lucia, and between mid-May and the end of July 1838, the Special Magistrates were inundated with applications for valuation. In reality, probably no more than 10-15 per cent of apprentices (the majority women) managed to purchase their freedom in the Windward Islands. The number freed in Barbados during Apprenticeship was also low, numbering just about 907 in the first year, with only about 40 being through self-

purchase. Most of those freed – 70 per cent – were in Bridgetown, an indication that the plantation sector proved relatively more rigid in its response to emancipation.

On account of the expected two-tiered timeline for the termination of the Apprenticeship System – in 1838 for non-praedials and 1840 for praedials – some employers tried to re-adjust workers' classification. For example, in Grenada, planters were classifiying all apprentices as praedial in December 1837. In Tobago, the Privy Council was still insisting in March 1838 on classifying all domestics as praedial. In St Lucia, the Lieutenant-Governor discovered several cases of false classification; and in St Vincent Special Magistrate Colthurst reported an example of what he termed 'cool classification'. Apparently a planter had returned all his 150 apprentices as praedial with the ingenious explanation that the domestics had been counted among the 'field negroes' because they often worked in the field. Inaccurate classification was the subject of formal appeals to the Special Magistrates and to the courts, particularly as the date for the emancipation of the non-praedial apprentices approached. Special Magistrate Colthurst was presented with numerous cases of appeal against the registry that dealt with classification; and apparently he felt that 100 out of 163 appeals from 18 plantations could be sustained.

The Apprenticeship was also marked by conflicts over task versus day labour. Task work was an issue in Grenada and St Vincent where the adoption of a Scale of Labour in 1836 had facilitated the spread of the practice. These conflicts were greater on sugar estates than on properties that engaged in alternative activities. Generally the type of production these owners expected could be done within the stipulated hours of compulsory labour. This difference was reflected in the reports of the Stipendiary Magistrates from the livestock-farming regions of Jamaica. Magistrate Laidlaw, who was assigned to the parish of St Ann, said that, 'there has been very little need in the pen [livestock farm] parishes for extra labour'. He further added, 'the time allowed by law being in general amply sufficient for the species of cultivation required'.

On the other hand sugar planters needed extra labour for harvest time. They experienced labour shortages if they treated labourers unreasonably, or if labourers preferred to work on their own grounds during the hours of non-compulsory labour. The disputes which developed over these issues caused Governor Sligo of Jamaica to admit to the Secretary of State in October 1834 that, 'I cannot, after two months trial of the New System report to you that it is working at all in a satisfactory manner'.

In conflicts over wages and allowances the apprentices knew that they had the upper hand. This was especially so in territories like Jamaica where there were many different jobs so that freed people had many alternatives to sugar estate labour. For example, sugar estates that were near pimento farms or good provision lands suffered the most. Without the extra labour during crop time, the harvesting and manufacture of sugar could not go on. Unless workers were paid more than they could get by attending to their grounds, they were unlikely to work beyond the specified 40½ hours. A Special Magistrate reported from the parish of Clarendon in Jamaica that the apprentices there would not work for hire. One worker, according to the SM:

> … made more money by working his own ground than any sum of money his overseer or manager would give him …
> Four Paths market is well stocked every Saturday with the finest provisions.

On the one hand the employers wanted cheap labour. On the other hand the apprentices wanted fair and adequate wages. These opposing wishes could not be reconciled.

The Stipendiary Magistrates

Apprentices in many territories also saw the Stipendiary Magistrates as part of the problem of the Apprenticeship System. They were appointed to visit the estates and settle disputes between employers and apprentices, and generally to make sure that the labour system ran properly. They worked on two-year contracts and could be dismissed if they were inefficient. But there were not enough Stipendiary Magistrates in each territory to make the system work well. There were only 150 for the British-ruled Caribbean territories, with 60 of these stationed in Jamaica. In the Bahamas, three were appointed in 1834 for New Providence, Eleuthera and Turks Islands. By 1838 three more were appointed.

In some territories the local justices of the peace (JPs) assisted Stipendiary Magistrates. Some of these JPs were of mixed race, like Richard Hill of Jamaica, and this complicated arrangements because some British employers did not wish to relate to mixed-race people in this way. Some British JPs themselves also used apprentice labour and did not want mixed-race people employed as JPs. Governors, like Colebrook in the Bahamas, also employed apprentices and indicated their difficulty with the use of mixed-race JPs as assistants to SMs. Colebrook opposed their appointment in the Bahamas.

Also, many magistrates came from the planter-class or were pro-planter in their thinking, and so could not function as objective and neutral negotiators in disputes. Some found the task of visiting the numerous estates difficult, especially in a large island like Jamaica. Many died from health-related illnesses during the first year of

Fig 2.4 Richard Hill – mixed-race Stipendiary Magistrate of Jamaica

their service. They considered the initial salary of £300 grossly inadequate. This was later increased to £450. It was widely understood that this low salary made them likely to accept bribes from employers. In addition, as the magistrates did not have any control over plantation discipline, the owners could quite freely administer punishments. If the apprentices refused to work and had to be brought before the courts, the magistrates had no control over the legal process. The result was that apprentices were systematically victimised by the legal system.

Some historians have argued that despite these many difficulties, on the whole the magistrates did the best they could and performed well within the constraints that existed. There were even fewer complaints against them in the Bahamas and the British Virgin Islands. They functioned in this capacity well into the 1870s, long after the end of the Apprenticeship System. According to historian, W L Burn, a 'good' magistrate was one who:

> … tolerated neither undue laziness on the part of the apprentices nor undue severity on the part of the masters; kept their districts in order, tried to work with the governor and (while courting neither the favour of the planter nor that of the 'negrophilists' [sic]) tried less to impose a system upon the community than to engage the community in the task of living contentedly within the system.

According to Woodville Marshall, Special Magistrate John Bowen Colthurst, who worked in Barbados and St Vincent, was a diligent officer who insisted on 'ample justice to all'. Colthurst was aware of the planters' tendencies to bribe magistrates and so he tried not to socialise with them or accept their hospitality. His attention to his duties earned him a reputation as a conscientious, efficient and fair minded Stipendiary Magistrate.

Other SMs who gained good reputations were Captain James Grady who was stationed in colonial Guyana, William Oldery, William Ramsey (Jamaica), Colebroke and EB Lyon. All these SMs realised the difficulties of their jobs and the possibility of planters bribing them. In fact, Brady resigned rather than come under planter control. Burns reports that Ramsey, who was also an Inspector-General of police in Jamaica, was regarded as Jamaica's Governor Sligo's 'right-hand man'.

2   Apprenticeship comes to an end

The Apprenticeship System in the British-colonised territories failed because it was plagued by poor labour relations and by attempts by the landowning class to keep its traditional power and racial dominance over the apprentices. In a sense it also failed because the different parties to it had different ideas and expectations of the system.

On the one hand the British government and the supporters of emancipation saw this time as a period of labour change or transition. In this time the labourers would be guided along the paths of social and economic compliance toward full freedom, which they would get in 1840. On the other side were the landowners and managers who saw the Apprenticeship System as a part of their compensation for the loss of money that their enslaved labourers represented.

Then there were also the apprentices to whom all of this was completely unreasonable and unacceptable. They were used to working hard, already knew how to earn, spend and save money, and knew how to live very well as free people as long as no obstacles were put in their way. There was no practical way in which these conflicting opinions could be reconciled.

By 1837 it was clear to all parties that the Apprenticeship System was disastrous and should be abolished. Not only had it failed in its objectives but opposition to its continuation was increasing on all fronts – in Britain and in the colonies.

Internal opposition to the Apprenticeship System in the British colonies

Internal opposition basically included the struggle of the apprentices to bring the system to an end. They received some support from anti-Apprenticeship activists in Britain.

The apprentices were aware of the importance of this support and adjusted their strategies accordingly. Field labourers and artisans agitated for full freedom along with urban and other non-praedials, who were promised freedom ahead of others. Remember that non-praedials included all other workers who were not agricultural workers.

Apprentices opposed the continuation of the Apprenticeship System by increasing their efforts to buy legal freedom, by increasing their acts of social insubordination, and by widespread refusal to work. Just as in the times of slavery, women were also in the forefront of acts of resistance. Many of them were imprisoned for their activism and sentenced to punishment on the treadmill, which was an instrument of torture. The images of women on the treadmill fired anti-apprenticeship agitation in Britain. They saw in it the worst evidence of slavery with respect to how women were treated, which they considered barbaric.

External opposition to the Apprenticeship System

By 1837 public opinion in Britain was against the Apprenticeship System. Anti-slavery societies were revitalised, for example, the Committee for the Abolition of the Slave Trade. These pressure groups held large public meetings, many of which sent petitions to Parliament. There were many reports about how the Apprenticeship System was being abused in Jamaica, and there were also reports about the specific actions of magistrates in St Kitts. This fuelled the anti-apprenticeship movement. The House of Commons formed a committee to investigate the abuses. It was made up of 15 members representing the planter class and anti-slavery activists.

The findings of this committee were not conclusive; but when evidence was later supplied by Sturge and Harvey, the weight of evidence became stacked against the continuation of the Apprenticeship System. In 1836 a Quaker humanitarian, Joseph Sturge, visited Jamaica and reported on the cruelties of the workhouses and other negative aspects of the system. The result of these investigations was the publication of an influential book, *The West Indies in 1837*, by Sturge and Thomas Harvey. They had also collected evidence of abuse in colonial Guyana and islands in the Eastern Caribbean, while they were part of a four member investigating team. They also used evidence collected by the two other members of the team, John Scoble and William Lloyd.

The House of Commons Committee found that:
- Freed people in Dominica had gained no benefits from apprenticeship.
- The system had been a disaster in Montserrat.

- The system was severe in Barbados where Stipendiary Magistrates were said to be corrupt.
- In Jamaica, the magistrates forced freed people to work and maintained European dominance.
- Despite the prohibition against whipping, 350,000 lashes had been administered to apprentices in Grenada, colonial Guyana, Jamaica, and St Lucia during the first 22 months of the system.

As a result of Sturge and Harvey's report, the Abolition Society increased its agitation for the end of the system. In November 1837 it sent a petition to Parliament demanding the immediate end of Apprenticeship. The Central Negro Emancipation Committee also held public meetings and distributed pamphlets on the evils of the system to win

WEST INDIES

IN

1837

BEING THE

JOURNAL OF A VISIT TO ANTIGUA,

MONSERRAT, DOMINICA,

ST LUCIA, BARBADOS AND JAMAICA;

UNDERTAKEN FOR

THE PURPOSE OF ASCERTAINING THE ACTUAL

CONDITION OF THE

NEGRO POPULATION OF THOSE ISLANDS.

BY

JOSEPH STURGE AND THOMAS HARVEY

LONDON

HAMILTON, ADAMS & CO. PATERNOSTER ROW.

PRINTED BY B HUDSON, BIRMINGHAM

MDCCXXXVIII

Fig 2.5 The cover of Sturge and Harvey's influential book

support for its cause. This Committee had the support of Lord Brougham who spoke on its behalf in the House of Lords in 1838.

The result of this campaign was that the Committee sent several further petitions to Parliament. Petitioners wanted to reform and regulate the system so that it was in line with the government's policy to improve the lives of apprentices, rather than to abolish the system altogether. Parliament passed an Act to amend the Apprenticeship System. This Act ruled that the flogging of females was to be stopped. It outlawed punishment on the treadmill and authorised governors to supervise the workhouses more closely.

The Act also proposed giving more power to the Stipendiary Magistrates at the expense of the Assemblies and the planter Justices. On account of this, planters did not support the reform. Planters believed that, tactically, it was better to support the abolition of the Apprenticeship System rather than be investigated all the time and rather than the SMs having more power over them. The governor-in-chief of the Windward Islands, for example, successfully got the approval of the Assemblies for complete abolition.

With these kinds of developments the British government was forced to recommend abolition of the system. However, just as in 1834, the government was still concerned that full freedom in 1838 would be accompanied by mass riots in the colonies. In 1838, Lord Glenelg, a senior official in the Colonial Office, wrote to the colonial governors urging them to end the system before 1840. He told them that public opinion in Britain was so strongly against the system that agitation would only increase.

The end of the System was also associated with considerable controversy over the status of artisan apprentices (non-praedials). Their labour was crucial to the technological maintenance of the estates. Artisans seeking to maintain their traditional privileges over unskilled workers, insisted that they should be free at an earlier stage. They argued for their full freedom to begin in 1838, if the praedials were to be freed in 1840. This proposal was so controversial that, in the end, it caused the complete freeing of all apprentices in 1838. Planters accepted that they could not run the estates without the artisans. But they also needed the services of fieldhands. They wanted to appease the artisans and non-praedials, but they anticipated that freeing one group of apprentices before the other would cause so much conflict, that it was not a wise action.

The planter-class opposes the ending of Apprenticeship

Predictably, there was some opposition from the planter-class about ending the system earlier. For example, in the Bahamas the House of Assembly opposed the ending of the system. In July 1838 they petitioned Governor Cockburn to continue the system for its full term. But this kind of opposition was not widespread in the Bahamas because there was no shortage of cheap labour there. Also, in most of the islands outside Providence, plantations had already been broken up. Many freed people were already independent farmers or squatters, or eager to sign contracts for whatever work was available.

Opposition to ending the system came from Governor James Smyth of colonial Guyana who wrote to the Colonial Office in 1836. He spoke on behalf of the Guyanese planters who were opposed to ending the system when he said:

> I assure your Lordship [the secretary of state for the colonies] that I should much regret and lament the doing away of Apprenticeship.... The permanent well-being of the labourer would [not be] accelerated by any immediate change in the system.

He argued that the system was working well in his territory and had not been accompanied by any acts of cruelty or abuses.

Objection to the ending of the system also came from sections of the European community in Jamaica, Trinidad, Tobago and St Lucia. In 1837, the Jamaican House of Assembly had passed a motion that it was '...highly inexpedient to entertain any measures having for its object the abbreviation of the period of Apprenticeship as fixed by the Abolition Act'. When abolition came, the Assembly issued a statement to Governor Smith demanding 'indemnity for abandoning the apprenticeship'. In other words they wanted to be compensated for the ending of the system.

Jamaica was not the only place where compensation was demanded. In Belize, employers also claimed that they should be promptly and properly compensated for the loss of their property. In territories like Trinidad, Tobago and the Windward Islands, restrictive legislation was passed to prevent freed people from progressing. This legislation showed how the planters felt about the ending of the Apprenticeship System.

And some planters support …

But some planters also supported the early ending of Apprenticeship. The main reason for their support was that they believed that they could reduce their expenses by no longer having the direct financial responsibility for maintaining children, the aged and infirm on their estates. They also believed that they could have better labour relations once the unpopular system was abolished. In the St Vincent House of Assembly, there was considerable support for the early ending of Apprenticeship. In an address to the governor, these members said:

> We do solemnly protest against it [the Imperial Abolition Act] as establishing a ruinous system, which not only renders its imperative upon the owners to continue, in their fullest extent all the privileges, indulgences and allowance which his slaves had hitherto enjoyed but gives to his apprentices an unreasonable portion of time as will render it impracticable for his master to continue the practicable cultivation of the soil.

The Jamaican Assembly was the first to pass legislation to bring about emancipation (called an Act-in-Aid) in March 1838, showing its intention to end Apprenticeship. The Jamaican Act was quickly followed by a British Act to amend the Act for the Abolition of Slavery. In May 1838 came accounts that Barbados, Nevis, Montserrat and Tortola in the British Virgin Islands had all passed acts of general emancipation releasing all apprentices on 1 August 1838. Also that St Kitts, Grenada, St Vincent, Dominica, Tobago and St Lucia intended to do likewise.

3 'Free Birth' in the Danish-colonised Caribbean

As a result of the emancipation policy of the British in 1838 and the 1840s protests in Martinique, the struggle to abolish the system of 'Free Birth' increased in Denmark and the Danish-colonised Caribbean territories. On 28 July 1847 Denmark finally freed the enslaved people in St Thomas, St Croix and St John/Jan. However, this was not full freedom. Only children born after July 1847 were to be free under a policy called 'Free Birth' or 'Free Womb'. This literally meant that the 'wombs' of African women would no longer be used to produce children to be enslaved. Enslaved adults were required to serve a 12-year apprenticeship period, which would end in 1859 with complete emancipation.

But the enslaved objected to this delay. They regarded this period between full slavery and full freedom as a servitude they were being asked to endure patiently. The attitude of an enslaved man named Edward from Rosenhill Estate reflected their common feelings. He told his owner, 'Mr van Brackle, here is your hoe and your cutlass. I will no longer work for you and if I work I will buy them myself.'

Protest increased among enslaved people in the Danish-colonised Caribbean. From 2–3 July 1848 there was a great protest by the 25,000 enslaved people in St Croix. The main leaders were said to have been Martin King and General Buddhoe who encouraged all the enslaved to leave their places of work and demand emancipation.

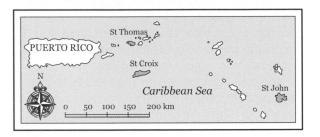

Fig 2.6 *The Danish Caribbean*

The enslaved workers attacked the houses of several citizens, including those of the police chief, the judge and a merchant who had asked for the suppression of the rebels. In early July 1848 the island was already in the hands of the rebels. Women like Rosaline, Mathilda (from Frederiksted), Sey and Sara were among the rebels. They were described as being more aggressive than the men in the various acts of resistance, including arson and destruction of property. So on 3 July 1848 Governor von Scholten proclaimed full freedom in St Croix. Some sources suggest that Anna Heegard, a free mixed-race woman who became Governor Von Scholten's mistress, knew Buddhoe and influenced the governor to listen to his demands. Emancipation was then effected in the rest of the Danish-colonised territories. Ringleaders were nevertheless imprisoned and, in the case of Buddhoe, deported, from the island.

According to the emancipation settlement, the enslaved people who were freed were allowed to remain in their houses and provision grounds for three months after 3 July 1848. After that period, landholders tried to force the formerly enslaved back into a position of dependence with the help of various coercive measures from the colonial state. For example, a decree of 1849 obliged all those who wished to continue to live on plantations and to work their provision grounds, to enter labour contracts with the planters.

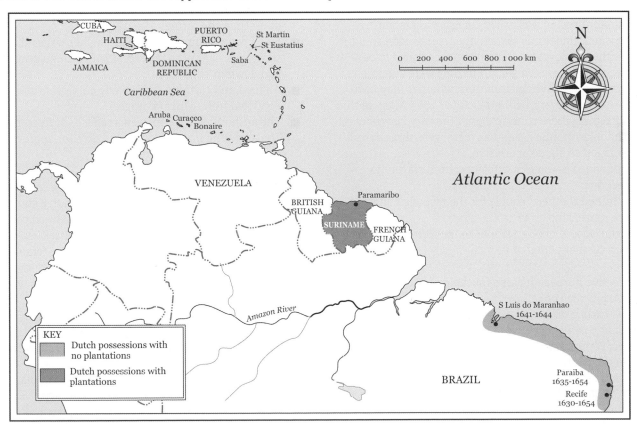

Fig 2.7 *The Dutch Caribbean*

4 Apprenticeship in the Dutch-colonised Caribbean

There was a similar movement for emancipation in the Dutch-ruled territories. There was a revolt among the enslaved in St Eustatius. In St Maarten, the enslavers feared a similar revolt, so they petitioned the governor to move to immediate freedom. Emancipation became law for the 45,275 enslaved people in the Dutch-colonised Caribbean territories on 1 July 1863.

As in the British- and French-colonised Caribbean territories, the owners in the Dutch-colonised Caribbean received compensation for the loss of their chattel property. They received 300 guilders per enslaved person. This was reduced to 200 guilders per enslaved in some of the islands. In St Maarten, the rate was at first lowered to 30 guilders per enslaved, but raised to 100 when owners protested that this was too little for their 'property'. The original rate was maintained in Suriname where it was argued that the enslaved were of a higher value.

Just as in the British-colonised territories, the freed people in the Dutch-controlled Caribbean who were between the ages of 15 and 60 had to serve a period of apprenticeship at a minimum wage for a further ten years. This apprenticeship was called *Staatstoezicht* (state supervision). Under this system, the freed person could choose the employer to whom he or she wished to be contracted for these ten years. But they were supposed to sign contracts with their employers, whether they were new or old employers, before 1 October 1863. Many of them put off signing these contracts until the very last moment. The Dutch authorities said that there were three so-called 'advantages' to state supervision:

■ It provided a peaceful transition from slavery to freedom.
■ It trained the freed people for the responsibilities of free citizenship.
■ It guaranteed enough labour to the former enslavers for a further period of years.

So, effectively, freedom came for the majority of the enslaved in 1873 only.

This extra period of slavery did not go smoothly. There were many conflicts between freed people and former owners. Former owners were dissatisfied as many freed people chose other employers. So even though 1863–73 was designed to continue to provide the plantations with workers, many plantations lost their labourers. There were no major rebellions against the contract system, but workers found ways around the system. Some signed fake contracts, some escaped to French Guiana and Colonial Guyana and others refused to return to the plantations.

5 *Contratación* in Puerto Rico

In 1870 the partial abolition of slavery in Puerto Rico was declared by the Moret Law. By this law, all newly born enslaved people and all the enslaved over 60 years old, on or after September 1868, were freed. Altogether 10,000 enslaved persons were freed.

The other 31,000 were legally freed in March 1873. This regulation was approved in Madrid on 26 March 1873 and published one month later in Puerto Rico.

The abolition law provided for enslavers to be paid 7 million pesos as compensation and to be assured of the compulsory labour of the *libertos* for three more years.

The name given to this three-year period of compulsory labour in Puerto Rico was *contratación*. The authorities hoped that this system would guarantee the continuation of the production on haciendas for a further three years.

The main terms of *contratación* were that:

■ All freed people were to enter into contracts with their former enslavers.
■ Freed people could choose to contract with someone other than the former enslaver.
■ Freed people could not demand higher wages than those existing at the time the contract regulation was laid down in 1870.
■ All food and clothing supplied by employers should be deducted from workers' wages.
■ The authorities were to keep a register of freed people. The authorities were also responsible for approving the contracts to guarantee their legality.

Contratación ended in 1873. At the end of 1873, 21,594 freed people were working under contract. About 818 could not be accounted for. The balance of the 31,000 freed people who were supposed to be affected by *contratación* were over 60 or under twelve. Of the 21,594, 10,120 were females. About 5,415 of these females had remained with the same employer. The rest had changed employers. Many were rural workers.

6 *Patronato* in Cuba

As in Puerto Rico the Spanish authorities put in place a plan to delay full freedom in Cuba. In February 1880 the Spanish parliament abolished slavery in Cuba and announced the impending apprenticeship or *patronato*. This system was to come into effect on 8 May 1880 and was supposed to end in 1888. But it came to an end on 7 October 1886 by a royal decree after a parliamentary resolution. This premature end was linked to a decline in the population of *patrocinados* as manumission increased.

One of the main reasons for the introduction of the *patronato* was to give landholders time to find substitutes for the decreasing enslaved labour force. Another reason was that the landowners and the Spanish government wished to satisfy the pro-slavery planters who wanted to keep the slave relations of production a while longer. *Patronato* also tried to satisfy anti-slavery activists, urging abolition.

The 1880 Spanish parliamentary decree contained the following clauses:
- All the enslaved were to be called *patrocinados*.
- All *patrocinados* were to work for their former enslavers until they were totally freed.
- Employers had to pay 1 to 3 pesos monthly to freed people. Under slavery only irregular bonuses had been paid.
- *Patrocinados* could buy their freedom for a set price
- Beginning in 1885, one-quarter of the remaining *patrocinados* were to be freed each year, in descending order of age, until the system came to an end in 1888.

The law granted some rights to the *patrocinados*. For example, the *patrocinados* had the right to charge their employers if they broke the set regulations of the *patronato*. If the *patrocinado* won the case, then he/she would get freedom as a reward. On the other hand, the former enlavers still had control over the movement of the *patrocinados*. They could set labour hours and conditions of labour. Until 1883 they kept the right to use corporal punishment on *patrocinados*.

At first the *Patronato* system did not bring about any marked changes on Cuban sugar plantations. Unlike in the British-colonised Caribbean territories, Cuban planters did not take away the usual maintenance and other allowances they owed the *patrocinados*. They maintained the traditional holidays and rewards given to freed people. The *patronas* (ex-enslavers) appeared to be more anxious than the British-colonised Caribbean ex-enslavers to disrupt plantation routine as little as possible and maintain the current production levels. Of course, now the planters needed more cash to pay the required wage to their workers, so some continued to exploit the workers during crop time, and ignored the arrangement of free Sundays.

Although the former enslavers tried to continue with some of their usual exploitation, by 1882-83 Cuban plantations began to feel the effects of the new system. *Patrocinados* began to buy their freedom. The money from these sales helped the *patronas* to pay the wage bill, but the *patrocinados* who left had to be replaced by hired hands or they had to be paid higher wages to remain. *Patrocinados* also began to demand prompt payment of wages and to take abuses before the courts.

It was not unusual for *patrocinados* to win such cases and to obtain their freedom. The freedom of *patrocinados*, either by order of the courts or by self-purchase, meant that the population of *patrocinados* on Mapos fell from 277 to 135 by 1884. Between 1880 and 1886, 113,887 *patrocinados* had gained their freedom despite attempts by employers to put obstacles in the way. By 1883 the number of *patrocinados* in Cuba was only 99,000, half of what it had been in 1880. As a result of the declining numbers some employers tried new, positive measures to keep the labourers on their plantations. Some freed their workers,

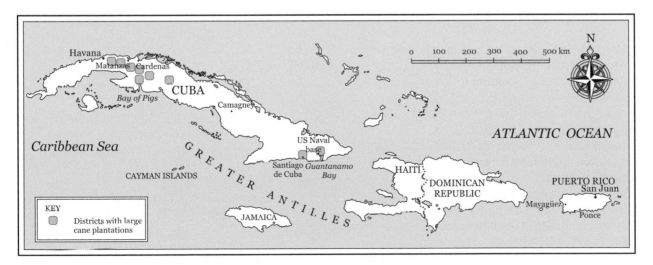

Fig 2.8 *Map of the Greater Antilles area, highlighting islands colonised by Spain*

some paid prompt wages while others introduced prizes for good work.

Remember that by 1885, one-quarter of the remaining *patrocinados* were to be freed each year, in descending order of age, until the system came to an end in 1888. But by 1885 employers had already increased wages to hired hands, many of whom were *ex-patrocinados*. Employers paid 20 pesos per month for men and 18 for women. They also hired Chinese contract workers at lower wages and were employing other hired hands on a seasonal basis. It was clear that the temporary arrangement of delayed full emancipation could not last. It officially ended on 7 October 1886, two years before the scheduled time.

To sum up

Despite the Abolition Acts in the Caribbean from the late 18th to the late 19th Century, former enslavers were generally reluctant to release the enslaved. Most territories tried to delay full freedom by bringing into being transitional periods. In the end, the landholders had to agree that only full freedom would satisfy the African masses and prevent more protests and rebellions in the region.

It should be noted that most former enslavers received compensation for the loss of their 'human property'. The enslaved people received nothing. This is why many descendants of enslaved people are claiming reparation for slavery from countries that had participated in the enslavement of Africans. Haiti, which had to pay France 150 million gold Francs to recognise its freedom, leads the call for reparation.

Revision questions

1 a Match the 'transitional period' in Column A with the appropriate territory in Column B.

Column A	Column B
Patronato	British Caribbean
Free Birth	Cuba
Apprenticeship	Puerto Rico
Contratación	Danish Caribbean

  b State two differences between '*patronato*' and 'apprenticeship'.

  c State three ways in which the newly freed showed their opposition to the system called 'Free Birth'.

  d State two results of the freed people's opposition to any two of these 'transitional systems'.

2 Compare the '*staatstoezicht*' in the Dutch-colonised Caribbean with the 'Apprenticeship System' in the British-colonised Caribbean.

Chapter 3

New rights – old wrongs: 1804–1890

'I want to rule my destiny.'
(Buju Banton)

Introduction

The ending of the Apprenticeship and other transitional slave systems in the Caribbean colonies and the coming of full freedom meant that freed people had total control over their social movement for the first time. They also had greater bargaining power over their working conditions. Some even exercised their right to move into new communities and to bargain for better working conditions. Most of the former enslavers, however, did their best to limit the rights of workers and to reduce their bargaining power.

This chapter examines how, when and why freed people exercised their liberty as well as the problems they faced in doing so. It also examines why large-scale landholders complained that they had a labour problem and what some of them did about it.

In this chapter we will learn about:
1 Why workers moved to new communities
2 The 'labour concerns' of the landholding class
3 Labour scarcity: the Spanish-, French-, and Dutch-colonised territories
4 Landholders' solutions and alternatives

Higgler in Barbados

1   Worker migration to new communities

There is an on-going debate among historians who study the post-slavery period, particularly in British Caribbean history, about how many freed people left the plantations and other slave locations when full freedom came, and whether this movement was gradual or immediate. Historians frequently ask questions like: did freed people move because of their memories of the horrors of slavery? Did they leave because they wished to be unproductive, as some Europeans claimed? Did they leave because of the negative actions taken against them by planters? Was it because of their desire to emigrate to other territories to seek higher wages? Or was it because of the real possibility of being employed in non-plantation activities, particularly in free villages and urban centres?

Did freed people move because of the memories of the horrors of slavery?

For most freed people the plantation was the main 'scene of the crime' of slavery. The plantations held horrible memories for freed people from which they wanted to distance themselves. But the plantations were also the places where the results of their hard work, domestic lives and culture could be seen. So for most freed people there were two sets of reactions: those that were of a negative emotional nature, and those that reflected rational economic thought. Freed people had to support themselves and their families and so they stayed on the plantations as long as the wages were fair, the working conditions acceptable and the employers reasonable. As Douglas Hall puts it:

> The movement of the ex-slaves from the estates was not a flight from the horrors of slavery. It was a protest against the inequities of early freedom. It is possible that, had the ex-slaves been allowed to continue in the free use of gardens, house and grounds, and to choose their employers without reference to that accommodation, there would have been very little movement of agricultural labour at all from the communities apparently established on the estate during slavery.

Coercive strategies used by landholders

Many employers made no effort to encourage positive labour relations or maintain a reliable labour force. They did not try to negotiate fair wages and adequate working conditions with workers. Instead, they chose to use different kinds of coercive strategies against their workers to force them to remain on the plantations. This resulted in many freed people choosing to leave the estates. Too often, employers did not support freed people's right to choose where they wanted to work, what job they wanted to do, how long they wanted to work and for how many days. It was not easy for freed people to choose to leave the estates. For example, when women moved to another estate, they did not always remain on that estate permanently. They often moved back to their original estate when they needed more money. Landholders could not tolerate this freedom of choice.

The following are some coercive strategies that landholders used in British-colonised territories and which created disaffection among the workers:

- They used the magistrates and police as agents of labour discipline.
- They increasingly used the schools, churches and missionaries to get freed people to believe in the so-called virtues of humble work, social order and good manners, and obedience to authority.
- Many landholders refused to switch to the task work system, as they preferred to hold on to the day labour system. On some Jamaican livestock farms, for example, the farmers refused to allow freed people to work and be paid by the task, a change that had long before been made on sugar plantations.
- Landholders charged workers rent for tools, pasture, houses and grounds.
- They tied the rents to the workers' wages.
- Landholders evicted workers if they did not pay their rents.
- They tied workers' accommodation on their plantations to actually working there. This was to prevent workers from choosing their employers freely, living in one place while working on another.
- They tried to bind freed people to their former workplaces through contracts – a strategy which the workers and their supporters resisted strongly.

Labour contracts

In Belize, during slavery, there was a system of labour contracts that landholders used with free labourers. This system was extended in 1846 to control all of the work force. These contract laws allowed employers or their agents to arrest and imprison a worker without a warrant, and to forcibly remove the worker to his/her place of work. Workers who did not perform according to the terms of the contract were treated as common criminals and often imprisoned for three months hard labour.

The truck system

Another system that was used to tie workers to the plantations was the truck system, which was used for example, in the Bahamas and in Belize. This system was designed to make workers feel indebted to their employers. In Belize it worked like this: employers gave their workers goods or money advances on their wages when they signed a contract at the start of the season. This was usually around Christmas. Once the workers had used the goods or spent the money, they had to get credit from a 'truck shop' in the forest when they went back to work. Usually their wages could not pay off the loan and meet their expenses, so they had to work to pay off their debt. The worker then had to sign another contract for the next mahogany-cutting season, thus becoming trapped in a cycle of debt.

Taxes

In the French-colonised territories, the state imposed a tax on the freed people to make sure that the colonies were not ruined economically from emancipation. This tax was higher for urban workers because the state tried to discourage rural workers from moving to the urban areas, thereby depriving the estates of labourers. This tax was 10 francs 50 centimes per year in Pointe-a-Pitre, but in 1849 jumped to 15 francs. It was also raised in other parts of the French-colonised territories.

Workhouses

In 1848 workhouses were created in the French-colonised territories to control workers. All persons who were considered by the state to be beggars or vagabonds were put in workhouses. The inmates of workhouses were supposed to work on the construction and upkeep of roads, canals, rivers, etc. The workload and discipline of these *ateliers de discipline* (workhouses) closely resembled those in slavery. The only exception was the absence of the routine whip. To make workers even more controllable, they got religious instruction.

Controlling the cultivation of certain crops

To further control labour, French Antillean governments tried to prevent or discourage workers from cultivating crops other than the major staples of sugar and coffee. They imposed a tax of 20 francs per hectare on land that was not producing sugar and coffee. This tax was intended to stop the provision grounds expanding. They also charged all freed people a tax which the government claimed was for the upkeep of roads.

Other controls

Further controls in the French-colonised territories included:

- Workers over sixteen years needed a passport to travel even within the colonies.

- The police force was enlarged and expanded to track down vagrants and domestic passport offenders.

The pass system

In 1852 the French-colonised territories introduced the pass system to force freed people to accept contract labour. The law stated that, 'Every individual working for a salary or a daily wage, or every holder of a work contract of less than one year, should possess a pass'. If freed people did not have a contract, they were considered to be vagabonds or they were forced to have a pass.

There was a charge for each pass. The pass holder had to renew the pass each year at the cost of a one franc stamp. If the person did not travel with a pass or a domestic passport, he or she could be imprisoned or fined.

All those who could not pay fines for any offences they committed were transported to the workhouses where they had to work out their fine. People could only serve their work sentences in the workhouses on rural plantations. Employers who broke the labour laws did not receive any similar penalties. In 1858 only two employers of the 261 disputes heard in Guadelope were found guilty.

A gradual movement or an exodus?

The fact that the movement of workers to other areas was not an exodus or an immediate mass flight, proves that they moved in response to the actions of planters. There are detailed journals of a property called Fort George Pen in Jamaica which clearly show that workers left gradually – some only after they were evicted by the landowner. Some left when they could no longer pay rent or as a protest to paying rents.

Did workers leave because they wished to be unproductive?

Stephen Harmer was overseer of coffee properties in Manchester, Jamaica. In 1840 he wrote to his brother in England:

> I regret to say that this once fine country is going fast to destruction through the want of continuous labour. One half of the negroes have scarcely done anything since they were made free and them that do work demand very high wages from 4/- to 5/- per day and then they will not do even half a day's work for that.

Harmer stressed erroneously that freed people had few wants, were easily satisfied and 'will lay down under their plantain trees and sleep sounder than work for fair wages'.

Other views like this were expressed by Thomas Carlyle, the English political commentator, who wrote a paper called, 'Discourse on the Nigger Question' in 1849.

What we could refer to as 'Harmer's lament' was the typical attitude of many Caribbean landholders. They resented the fact that freed people could exercise choice. However, it was the labour of these African people that created the profitable sugar industry and the wealth of many Europeans. The late Prime Minister of Trinidad and Tobago, historian Dr Eric Williams, as well as the historian C L R James, have shown that profits from colonial trade and production developed and sustained many industries in England and France. (See Vol.I.)

Nineteenth-century visitors to the Caribbean wrote about the tension between the idea of freedom and the idea of forced labour. In 1840 Nancy Gardner Prince, an African-American woman who visited Jamaica, informed Jamaican workers that Americans were told that the Jamaicans were not productive workers. She told a crowd of about 200 freed people, 'I heard in America that you are lazy and that emancipation has been of no benefit to you, I wish to inform myself of the truth respecting you, and give a true account on my return'.

At the end of her visit she had come to a different conclusion. After she saw the bustle of the goods markets in Kingston she observed:

> … they are not the stupid set of beings they have been called, here surely we see industry, they are enterprising and quick in their perceptions … and quite capable of taking care of themselves.

Did they move because of off-estate opportunities?

Many freed people left the estates because they either wanted to live in their own villages and offer part-time work on the estates, or because they wanted to explore

Fig 3.1 A wayside market

other opportunities for making a living. African workers frequently accused African and mixed-race owners, especially women, of being harsher employers. So, they might have had greater difficulty in getting workers.

Among the first ex-apprentices to leave the estates were field-women, children and skilled men and women. Skilled people like masons, carpenters, laundresses, seamstresses, cart builders and wheelwrights believed that new opportunities and higher wages could be found in the towns. So that is where they looked for jobs. However, many workers, especially field women, chose to work part-time on the estates. This was not always easy to accomplish, as planters wanted only those workers who would work full-time.

Some workers moved completely away from the rural areas and established new lifestyles in the towns. Here they competed with workers who had been based in the urban areas during slavery. Domestic and service jobs in towns were prized jobs, even though migration into strange, unknown towns was a risky business for country folks. Many nevertheless took the opportunity because they were determined to seek a new life outside the plantation sector.

Some ex-apprentices became peddlers, petty traders/retailers and shopkeepers. They were an important part of the development of the commercial sector in their countries. Those who remained in agriculture chose between work on large and small properties, and between familiar and new employers. Some became higglers or hucksters in the towns, often selling goods, which they usually bought from rural provision growers in the markets.

Nancy Gardner Prince remarked on these markets in Kingston:

> I called … at the market and counted the different stalls. For poultry and vegetables 196, all numbered and under cover; besides 70 on the ground; these are all attended by colored [meaning black] women. The market is conveniently arranged, as they can close the gates and leave all safe.

She observed that the African-Jamaican men and women also sold fresh fish, pork, beef and turtle in the market.

Intra-Caribbean migration

Not all freed people remained in rural agriculture or sought work in the towns. Some moved out of their own country to new territories to look for better paying jobs and in search of family members. In the Apprenticeship period, the British government had a consistent policy that the apprentices should not move between colonies.

However, once they were freed they moved around the Caribbean in large numbers. (We will deal with this in more detail in Chapter 6.)

2 The labour concerns of the landholding class

Landholders complained that they had a 'labour problem' because freed people moved off the agricultural properties to which they had been attached, or out of individual territories; and because they bargained for higher wages and improved labour conditions. What the landholders usually meant was that they had lost their tight control over workers' lives and that they did not have enough, full-time workers, working under labour conditions which the landholders set.

Complaints of labour shortage came more consistently from sugar planters in Trinidad and colonial Guyana, which had developed late as sugar colonies. They had not had the opportunity to import enough enslaved Africans to help the industry grow before the British trade in African captives was abolished in 1807. In 1838 in Trinidad there were 16,000 freed people on the estates. In 1847 there were 10,000 and by 1851 it was said that only 3,116 of these workers were at work regularly.

In colonial Guyana there were 38,000 freed people still on the plantations in the mid-1840s. This was 43 per cent of the workforce at the time of emancipation.

In Jamaica it was estimated that in 1860 only 9 per cent or 40,000 of the total population worked on the estates whereas the island had had over 300,000 enslaved people in 1834. Some people in the island were reluctant to describe the situation as a 'labour crisis'. The American journalist William Sewell, who visited Jamaica in 1860, noted that there were labourers everywhere in Jamaica and that it was only on the estates that he heard of a labour shortage. The Baptist missionary Tinson argued that the people were willing to work, but many complained that they could not get work. In an unusual petition to the House of Assembly several labourers from the parish of Westmoreland in Jamaica complained that they could not get work. William Wemyss Anderson wrote to the Colonial Standard in 1850 that he could readily get workers for work in the field at one shilling per day.

By the 1860s when the sugar sector had deteriorated in Jamaica, it was clear that there were far more people available for work than the work that was available on the estates. The real problem was the conflict between workers' demand for adequate wages paid on time and fair conditions of labour, and the landholders' desire for complete control over the labour force. The Rev Hope

Waddell, who visited Jamaica in the 1840s, agreed that unfair wages were a factor contributing to the 'labour problem' of the landowning class. However, he also seemed to suggest that the workers' love for imported goods meant that hardly any wage rate would satisfy them:

> Eager for money, they would do double daily work if sure of getting double wages; and [they] came to have so many real wants that no possible wages, it was said, could satisfy them. Their provision grounds, so far from engrossing their attention were partly neglected for the sake of foreign food, till the scarcity of native breadstuffs enhanced their value. It was shipbread, flour and rice, and cornmeal they wanted, with saltfish and saltpork, luxuries before, but now in daily demand.

In the immediate post-slavery period, there were fewer complaints of labour shortages in territories like Barbados, Belize and Antigua. Here the landholders' control over the land was effective and there were not as many alternatives to non-estate jobs as there were in Jamaica, colonial Guyana and Trinidad. Complaints of labour shortage were also few in Caribbean territories where there was not a strong plantation economy or the plantation economy had declined and colonists had turned to other ways of making a living such as fruit-growing, salt-raking and fishing and ranching.

3 Labour scarcity: the Spanish-, French-, and Dutch-colonised territories

There were not only complaints about labour scarcity and changed labour relations in the British-colonised Caribbean. The Spanish, as well as some Dutch and French Caribbean territories, also said that the labour supply was not enough to continue the plantation system.

Santo Domingo
By the late 19th Century, employers in Santo Domingo were complaining that the labour supply was not enough, especially during the *zafra* or harvest. To attract more labour, they first tried to force the local labourers to provide continuous, on-going labour. The state passed Vagrancy Laws which stipulated that all people who were considered to be vagrants were to be forced to work. An official was put in charge of identifying people who had no visible means of making a living and who formed part of the population described as 'disorderly'. These people

Fig 3.2 *Fruit vending in Barbados – an alternative to plantation work*

were handed over to the relevant authorities, who would find work for them to do. Gambling, cock-fighting and other forms of amusement were forbidden. Efforts were also made to recruit and contract Dominicans on terms similar to foreign workers.

These efforts failed to solve the shortage of labour in Santo Domingo. It was clear that neither force nor persuasion nor recruitment increased the numbers of local labourers. Yet, landholders refused to increase wages, which would have attracted more labourers. Ever since 1884 landholders had insisted that wages be allowed to rise and fall with demand and supply. The Dominican planters were also determined to keep wages down to make sure that the sugar industry was more 'viable' than the industry in Cuba. In 1884 Dominican workers struck for more wages. Their complaint was that the wages they received could not even buy basic necessities like butter and mackerel.

Demand and supply factor affected the labour supply and the ratio of wages. When there were many labourers, wages tended to be low, when scarce, wages went up.

The French-colonised Caribbean

In the first two months of freedom, many labourers moved off the plantations in Guadeloupe and Martinique. Immediately after the abolition of slavery, the labour force in Guadeloupe declined to 18,739, half of what it was in 1848. In those months sugar production declined. Freed people left the estates and acquired land to form a

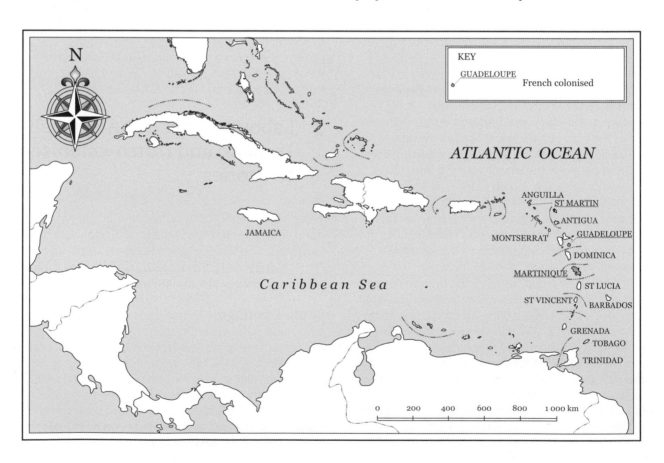

Fig 3.3 *French colonies in the Caribbean*

Chapter 3 | *New rights – old wrongs: 1804–1890*

peasantry. Some women stayed at home and looked after their family, others pursued fishing or moved to the towns to seek jobs as dockers and porters.

By 1853 it was claimed that more than one-fifth of the sugar workers in these French-colonised territories had abandoned plantation work altogether since abolition. Of course, to meet their increasing expenses, some freed people continued as plantation workers. Some exchanged several days of wage labour for the free use of huts and provision grounds. This type of worker, seeking on-estate huts, increased after 1870 when landholders had a number of abandoned immigrant houses in which to house them.

The labour relations in these colonies were affected because the landholders refused to pay workers in cash, partially because of their financial crisis and indebtedness. Both Governor Braut of Martinique and Governor Gatine of Guadeloupe indicated that workers preferred to be paid in cash instead of in kind or according to the *metaire* (also referred to as the metayage system) arrangement. By 1870 in Martinique this demand for wages in cash was one of the dominant labour relations issues.

In French Guiana (Guyane), freed people immediately turned away from estate labour as there was plenty of land to occupy and farm. After 1848 most of the remaining workers left the plantations on a full-time basis, though they worked seasonally at times.

The Dutch-colonised Caribbean

When the Apprenticeship System ended in the Dutch-colonised Caribbean territories, these colonies faced stiff competition from new Dutch colonies in the East Indies. In the East Indies, 'free' labourers were used to cultivate sugar. In the mid-19th Century the Dutch-colonised Caribbean territories also faced competition from European beet sugar.

One of the worst affected Caribbean colonies was the main plantation colony of Suriname. The Surinamese planters had needed more labour than they could get during the period of slavery. This was because they were still expanding cultivation at the time the trade in African captives was abolished. By the late 19th Century they were complaining of a labour shortage. The freed people had migrated to the towns to seek better paid jobs, just as they had done in the other Caribbean territories. If they remained as plantation workers, they demanded higher wages. The Dutch Antilles were not developed as plantation colonies and so complaints of labour shortage there were not as widespread as in Suriname.

Puerto Rico

Contratación had assured the *hacendados* or landholding class in Puerto Rico continuous labour for an additional three years. After 1873 the landholders made attempts to contract *libertos* or freed people.

Regulations regarding freed people, which were approved by the overseas minister in Madrid, directed that freed people in Puerto Rico should:
- Contract with a new or their former employer. The contract should be for three years, though all three years did not have to be with the same employer.
- Accept the going wage rates and not demand any higher rate.
- Have the cost of any food or clothing taken out of their wages.

The regulations also said that a registration of freed people should be kept. The authorities should be responsible for approving contracts to guarantee their legality.

Despite this attempt to guarantee continuous labour after the abolition of slavery in Puerto Rico, these measures did not satisfy the landholders. *Hacendados* still complained that they could not get a regular supply of labour. They said that some of the formerly enslaved refused to return to work unless the employers agreed to pay a daily wage in cash. Other freed people abandoned the *hacienda* as soon as they learnt of abolition. Those who did sign contracts changed their employers on a competitive basis. *Hacendados* further complained that:
- The fact that workers could move around in search of the best terms of labour caused instability in the labour force.
- Workers lacked regular and disciplined labour.
- Some *hacendados* had to abandon their *haciendas* because of shortage of labour.
- They could not increase productivity as they needed cash to attract free labour.
- They could not stabilise the demand for workers and therefore they could not do the technical innovations their *haciendas* needed.

Freed people had the upper hand in April 1873 as they knew that they could demand high wages. In two or three days of the week, some freed people could earn enough to pay for their subsistence. Consequently, some refused to work for the whole week. The employers appealed to the government to force the freed people back to work. But the government held that the freed people had every right to negotiate the terms of their labour contracts.

Cuba

Cuba had a long colonial history of labour shortages. This was made worse after 1817 by the Anglo-Spanish Treaty, which banned the trade in African captives, and again in 1835 when a new treaty tried to make the ban of the trade more effective. British ships patrolled the seas capturing illegal Spanish slavers and 'freeing' the captives. The demand for labour after 1845 continued to be higher than the slaves that could be supplied, as Spain took active steps to stop illegal trading in African slaves.

After the abolition of African slavery and the end of the *Patronato* in Cuba, planters spoke in terms of a labour shortage or a 'labour problem'. In fact, they were trying to get the state to meet part of the cost of immigration or to pass laws to restrict workers' rights. In real numbers there was no alarming shortage of workers. Many remained and hired themselves out as wage labourers. Yet landholders in Cuba, as in all post-slavery societies, complained that freed men and freed women spent too much time in leisure or domestic occupation. They complained that workers spent too much time working on their own provision grounds. They especially complained of the shortage of full-time female workers on the plantations. They regarded female workers as the most constant and effective labourers. But the complaints of 'labour shortage' in Cuba, as elsewhere, were simply a reflection of the employers' desire for a larger work force to drive down the cost of labour. These complaints were part of their unwillingness to offer higher wages than 20 pesos per month for males, and 18 pesos for females, exclusive of rations.

It is true that when slavery ended there were changes in the kind of work freed people in Cuba did and the way they earned money. Many of them migrated internally, looking for the best working conditions and the best wages. They moved from gang to gang or from estate to estate when there were changes or variations in wage rates. Young children were withdrawn from estate labour by their parents; women shifted back and forth from estate to household as their money needs changed. Some women only worked if they were paid the same as male workers. Some freed people joined *caudrillas* or work gangs or hired themselves out individually. Others migrated to towns where women did domestic jobs and men worked on nearby agricultural units. There was also a significant movement out of plantation areas to eastern Cuba. Matanzas, for example, lost 32 per cent of its Black population between 1887 and 1899. Eastern Cuba was not a sugar-dominated area, and the freed people believed that they had a better chance of acquiring land there. Finally, some left Cuba entirely for work in South and Central America and the USA.

4 Landholders' solutions and alternatives

We have already shown how landholders used negative measures to stop the flow of labour from the plantations and other locations. This tactic backfired and acted as a push factor, with many freed people migrating to the towns or free villages or leaving their individual territories altogether. Once employers realised that emancipation had come to stay and that they could not prevent the movement of labourers through negative, coercive means, they began to look for alternative solutions.

Conciliatory measures

The more sensible planters in the Caribbean adopted a variety of positive strategies to encourage the labourers to remain on the estates. At first British colonial Guyanese and Trinidadian planters competed with each other in the labour market by paying labourers higher and higher wages. Their attempts to outdo each other wore down their unity. It also led to uncertain labour supply on the plantations because labourers moved to wherever the wages were highest. Laws that were passed to force labourers from moving had little effect. In colonial Guyana with a population of 100,000 and a land area of 83,000 square miles, landholders saw the loss of the labour force as disastrous for further agricultural development.

In the French-colonised islands, like in some of the British-colonised Windward Islands, the *metaire/metayage* system and a rent-free tenant system were tried out to persuade labourers to remain. Task work also replaced daily labour on many estates. Landholders established work fêtes where workers got prizes for good work. In Martinique it was decided that each year four gold medals, 25 first class silver medals, 25 second class silver medals, and 70 awards of 20 francs each would be distributed to deserving labourers. On one side of the medal was the likeness of Napoleon. Medals were also awarded to students who excelled at agriculture in schools.

Labourers were not persuaded by the system of rewards/medals to get them to work and the labour laws increased their determination to leave the estates. They revolted against the pass laws. Some labourers attacked policemen who tried to implement the harsh labour laws. Those labourers who were forced to accept passes or forced to work, used various strategies to resist the labour laws such as malingering (go slow). Above all, the labour laws did not increase the work force. The number of Black Martiniquan labourers dropped from 26,865 in 1848 to 23,840 in 1874. In Guadeloupe the number only rose slightly from 25,755 in 1849 to 27,310 in 1874. The combined figures for both islands were lower than their combined enslaved populations in 1847.

Technological improvements
Some planters tried to reduce the need for labourers by bringing in machines, such as steam engines. But these measures could not work unless they could find a way to reduce the need for labourers in the field operations. Mechanisation was only part of the solution. They also needed to improve the supply of labourers. In fact a large and regular labour supply would help the mechanisation to crush canes faster and extract more juice.

Metaire/metayage system
Since the economic depression of 1846–1855, planters were short of money and so could not import extra labourers to continue sugar production or to pay higher wages. So Windward Island planters, like those in Tobago and the British Virgin Islands (BVI), began to explore the metayage (*metaire*) system. This was a system of share-cropping, which had been used during the French occupation of those islands. It had many similarities to the share system already used in the Bahamas.

In the Bahamas planters did not complain of a labour shortage. They used the share system to solve their serious capital or money shortages, which among other things also affected the payment of workers' wages. By the 1880s this share system was crucial on pineapple plantations. However the pineapple industry began to decline and so the merchant-landlords did not need so much labour. By the 20th Century the share system was no longer an important form of land possession in the Bahamas.

The terms of the metayage system
Under the metayage system, the planter supplied about one acre on which the labourer had to grow cane in the case of sugar. The planter also supplied manure, in some cases, the plant canes, and the stock and machinery. The worker was responsible for clearing the land, planting and reaping the crop. On sugar estates, workers had to cut and haul the canes to the factory using the planters' carts, factory and draft animals. Estate owners supplied the manufacturing facilities, supervised the manufacturing process, and marketed the sugar. Metayers or workers received half of the sugar from canes planted on their land. However, if they had received a field of ratoons from the planter, then they only got one third or one fifth of the sugar. In general, the workers had to wait until the estate owner sold the sugar and took off expenses for production before they could get any money from the sale. But, in

some cases they could sell the sugar themselves. The planters usually kept all the rum and molasses from the sugar crops. However, in Tobago and Grenada the rum was shared, a gallon of rum for every barrel of the worker's own sugar. In the BVI, when the sugar was manufactured, the sugar and sometimes the molasses were divided in fixed amounts between planters and labourers.

Did you know?
Cane could grow after cutting to be harvested more than once. The secondary crops from this were called ratoons.

These terms of the metayage system were usually agreed upon by vague contracts, mostly verbal. There were a few signed contracts, for example, in the BVI and St Lucia where the Stipendiary Magistrate was called on to certify them. But these contracts were one-sided, as they gave the landholder more security than the worker. The contracts did not mention ending the contract, they did not mention how metayers would be compensated if they were forced to surrender land with a crop on it, and they did not stipulate the extent of the metayers' responsibility for damage to the planter's stock, carts and machinery.

Above all, contracts offered no firm guarantee to metayers of their rights of possession, security of tenure, and a clear claim to a share of the crop. The Stipendiary Magistrates had no real political or legal power over metayage agreements.

Why was the system introduced?
The main reasons for the implementation of the metayage system, particularly in the British-colonised Caribbean territories, were as follows:
- There was a loss of the protected market for sugar in Europe from 1848–1854. This meant that Caribbean sugar had to be sold on the open market and not in guaranteed English markets.
- There was a fall in sugar prices between 1848–1854, which caused a serious shortage of capital or money and increased planters' debts.
- Planters feared that they would now have to abandon their estates as they could not find the cash to pay wages. Above all, they would lose social status and control over the labour force.

It was hoped that through metayage, landholders would:
- keep ownership of their estates
- still secure some profits from their land
- keep some control of the workers even if this decreased

- solve their cash flow problems and pay wages in kind rather than in cash
- share some of the risks of cultivation with the workers
- delay the expansion of the peasantry and the movement of freed people away from the estates.

The freed people also hoped to benefit through metayage. If it worked as it was supposed to, the system would fulfil some of their social hopes for getting land. Up until then the workers had accessed land through squatting and rental, and through buying land. Freed people also expected the following benefits from the metayage:

- They could stop using emigration, or rural-urban migration, as a solution to their economic problems.
- They would not be evicted from their land without reasonable notice (usually six months) and not without the opportunity to first reap their crop.
- They could maintain their houses and grounds.
- They could have secure employment and return for their labour and still have time to work on their grounds.
- They could avoid all the risks of production.
- They could have a guaranteed market for their sugar.

The metayage or *metaire* was used in St Lucia in the early stages of the development of the cotton and coffee plantations. The system was extended to the sugar plantations in 1840. By 1848 one-quarter of the sugar cane cultivation in St Lucia was done by the metayage system. St Lucia continued the system until 1861 on estates such as Beau Sejour, Anse Canot and Mt Lizard.

St Vincent and the Grenadines used the metayage system on sugar, cotton and provision estates. The planters were reluctant to use the system because of their feeling of loss of power over their labour force. However, the majority of the 95 estates in Grenada were forced to use the system because of the depressed financial circumstances and they only stopped using it on sugar, cocoa and coffee estates in the 1850s.

In Tobago the system was first introduced in 1843. From this time onwards it proved essential because of a series of problems, such as financial problems, a constitutional crisis in 1846–1847, and a devastating hurricane in 1847. By 1853, in one Tobago district alone, the number of metayers had increased from 208 to 500. Tobago planters could not pay for immigration or pay cash wages to ex-slaves and so they continued using the metayage system up to 1897, long after others had abandoned it.

The system was adopted in the BVI during the depression of the 1840s and by 1846 there was hardly an estate in the BVI which did not use the system. In 1847 the major sugar company, Reid, Irving and Co., collapsed.

Planters then found it difficult to continue wage payments. So they saw metayage as a way to save the sugar plantations from complete disappearance.

The results of the metayage system

Metayage had some success. In some territories, the decrease in sugar production was stopped. In fact, in some cases sugar production increased and some profits were made. In 1846 Grenada, St Lucia and Tobago exported 8,966 tons of sugar to the UK. In 1850 these exports rose to 9,552 tons and in 1852 to 13,342 tons. Finally, metayage helped keep the major staple crops going.

However, the results were not all positive. The planters were not committed to metayage on any long-term basis. They did not want it to become a form of land possession and a route to independence for freed people. So the implementation of the system was riddled with confrontation and conflict. Planters were unfair in their dealings, especially when they bought the workers' share of the crop. In fact, the planters did not always tell the workers the truth about how much they had sold the sugar for. Also, workers did not always have time to work on their own plots; and so they could not support themselves between sugar crops. Because of this they had to take advances from the planters and accumulated heavy debts.

Petition to the House of Commons

Planters turned to the government for help when their own measures did not have the desired effect of keeping the freed people's labour on terms that they could control. For example, in the British-colonised territories, the planters' complaints about labour shortages were presented in the form of evidence before a Committee of the House of Commons in 1842. The main planter complaints can be summarised as follows:

- Colonial Guyana and Trinidad had long suffered a labour shortage. This became worse with the abolition of slavery. So they definitely needed extra labourers.
- The work force was much smaller now that women and children were withdrawn from it and because men looked for non-estate occupations.
- Those workers who remained gave irregular and inefficient labour.
- Workers demanded unreasonably high wages.
- Colonial governments could not control the expansion of the peasantry, which competed with the estates for workers' time.
- Expensive equipment in field and factory required the maintenance of large agricultural establishments so as to be cost-effective. A regular labour force was vital to

make good use of the new technology on the sugar estates.

■ Workers could now bargain with employers.
■ Between 1838 and 1841 sugar exports had fallen by around one-third in many territories, with the industry doing well only in territories like Barbados.

The planters wanted to import labourers as a solution or 'antidote to emancipation'. They argued that this was necessary especially as the full-time labour force was becoming smaller because of the peasantry expanding and African-Caribbean workers moving away from their own countries to other territories inside and outside the region. Eventually many plantation owners were forced to spend a lot of money on imported labourers to work on their estates.

To sum up

When the transitional periods between full slavery and full freedom in the Caribbean ended, the landholders tried different tactics to secure a labour force from the freed people. Despite the horrible memories of slavery, many of the freed people would have worked for their former employers, if the employers had showed them respect and offered them fair wages and working conditions. However, many employers used force to make the freed people remain on the plantations. Many of the freed people, especially the women who got lower wages, moved to the urban areas or looked for other work which would give them more independence and dignity. The employers did not like this new independent attitude. They were used to having the advantage in work relations. So they began to complain of labour shortages and saw the immigration of outside workers as a solution to their 'problems of emancipation'.

Revision questions

1 Read the extract below and answer the questions that follow:

With the termination of the various apprenticeship-type systems of semi-slavery, freed people were free to bargain for wages and establish their working conditions. Many male and female property owners resented the new bargaining power of the newly freed and put obstacles in their way.

a State three ways in which the newly freed tried to 'establish their working conditions' after the complete abolition of slavery.
b Give two reasons why 'male and female property owners resented the new bargaining power of the newly freed ...'
c Discuss the 'obstacles' which the property owners put in the way of the freed people in either the French- or the British-colonised Caribbean territories.

2 With the use of suitable examples, discuss fully how racism and sexism were apparent in Caribbean societies after 1838.

3 Read the extract then answer the questions that follow:

The movement of ex-slaves from the estates was not a flight from the horrors of slavery. It was a protest against the inequities of early freedom. It is possible that had the ex-slaves been allowed to continue in the free use of gardens, house and grounds, and to choose their employers without reference to that accommodation, there would have been very little movement of agricultural labour at all from the communities apparently established on the estate during slavery. (Douglas Hall)

a Give four examples of the 'inequities of early freedom'.
b State four ways in which the former slaves protested against the 'inequities of early freedom'.
c State three effects of the freed people's protest against the 'inequities of early freedom.'

4 Read the extract and answer the questions that follow:

... they are not the stupid set of beings they have been called, here surely we see industry; they are enterprising and quick in their perceptions ... and quite capable of taking care of themselves. (Nancy Gardner)

a Give two examples of early writers who suggested that the freed people were a 'stupid set of beings'.
b Explain fully why Nancy Gardner Prince did not agree with the description of the freed people in Jamaica as a 'stupid set of beings'.

Chapter 4

The African-Caribbean peasantry

'Come out a mi lan'.'
(Peter Tosh)

'I an' I built a cabin, I an' I plant di corn.'
(Bob Marley)

Introduction

Land is used for economic survival, social status, and political power. But colonisation drove the indigenous Caribbean people out of their land. Before the abolition of slavery only a few freed African and mixed-race people owned their own land. The majority who were enslaved Africans could not own land. Some enslavers gave the enslaved land to use for provision grounds. When slavery was abolished, the freed people made a combined effort to acquire land that would not be controlled by their former enslavers.

In the next two chapters we will examine the struggle over land between the freed people and the former enslavers. We can see from William Sewell's 1861 comment, 'If any one doubts that a very ... astonishing number of the emancipated labourers have become independent proprietors, let them look at the scores of villages built up since abolition and so thickly scattered throughout the cultivated districts of Trinidad ...' that many freed people were successful in acquiring land.

However, as the Jamaican pan-Africanist Marcus Garvey indicated, even where progress was made, the large landholders still held on to most of the land way into the 20th Century. So we can say that the history of the African-Caribbean peasantry has been one of 'contested terrain'. He said in 1929, 'Everybody in Jamaica knows that the land of this country is really in the hands of a few large land proprietors. We have a population of nearly one million people, and out of that number, not five per cent can find land to settle on.'

In this chapter we will learn about:

1 Trends towards peasantry before and after the abolition of slavery
2 The profile of the Caribbean peasantry
3 How the peasantry became established
4 Obstacles to the development of the peasantry.

1 Trends towards peasantry before and after the abolition of slavery

Before emancipation

The Caribbean during slavery created a peasantry. However, before the abolition of slavery not many African people were peasants. Most of the peasants were known as 'poor-Whites'. However, some freed African and mixed-race people did own small units of land on which they planted crops, either for subsistence purposes or to sell. Maroons in the mountains and in the forests also practised peasant farming.

Did you know?

Peasants are usually small-scale farmers who own their land, on which they produce most of their own food; and they also produce items for sale.

Before the development of sugar plantations in the Spanish-colonised territories, it was common for different groups to establish small farms in the interior of Hispaniola, Cuba and Puerto Rico. These groups included escaped Africans, poor European settlers, free mixed-race people and military deserters. This was also the case in Jamaica before the English captured it. The land that the Spanish settlers farmed was captured from the Tainos.

Before the onset of the sugar revolution in the French- and English-colonised territories in the Eastern Caribbean, a peasant class developed out of the system of White contract workers. In Martinique, Barbados and elsewhere, the officials made an effort to honour a policy that was developed in the 17th Century of granting land to ex-indentured workers. But this was not always possible because of the sugar revolution, which was associated with the expansion of the sugar plantations and the need

to discontinue the partition of land into smaller parcels. The European peasantry grew tobacco, indigo, cocoa, coffee, cotton and other crops, and reared cattle. They lived very well on this. However, they just about disappeared after the development of the large plantations and farms. This was the case except in the Hispanic Caribbean and, to an extent, in Barbados where they continued to survive on marginal land in non-sugar areas.

Did you know?

Enclosure movement: in the enclosure movement, properties were being fenced to create boundaries.

The enslaved did have some access to land, but they were not given ownership. Most African people were enslaved and under the law all enslaved people were legally defined as property. Property could not own property. So the enslaved were allowed to use land but not to own it. The enslaved were allowed to develop provision grounds on their owners' land on which they could grow food for themselves or sell any extra or surplus at local markets.

Fig 4.1 A peasant family

Did you know?

Proto means 'the original' or 'first'. So, proto-peasantry was a term used by Sidney Mintz to describe enslaved people who had access to and use of land, but they did not own this land. A peasant, however, was a free person who owned, rented or leased or squatted on land.

The anthropologist Sidney Mintz has described the enslaved who work the provision grounds as a proto-peasantry. Once the various slavery regimes ended, African people – and later contract servants mostly from India and China – became an important part of the peasantry. The peasantry developed faster in some territories than in others. For example, in the late 19th Century in Cuba, the sugar industry was so profitable that official policy favoured the increase of agricultural workers but did not favour the creation of a African peasantry. It encouraged European small-landholders rather than African peasants.

The peasantry developed in all Caribbean territories, including independent Haiti, and the British-, Spanish-, French-, Dutch-, and Danish-colonised territories.

After the abolition of slavery

After securing their freedom an important factor in freed peoples' lives was to own their own land. One way to establish their freedom was for them to move onto peasant property and to show planters that they were dissatisfied with insecure jobs on the farms and plantations. In a situation in which planters were using coercive tactics and still had political domination, land ownership was the main route to individual freedom and independence, especially for freed men.

So the formation of a Caribbean peasantry was in fact a form of resistance to colonial domination. It had implications for the social, cultural and economic status of African people. The planters, on the other hand, saw peasant development as a barrier to plantation security and so the colonial elites did not encourage its development. The colonial and imperial agenda for emancipation was to give effect to a landless freedom for the African community. Landlessness for Africans was considered the principal method by which the European community could maintain its monopoly hold on the economy, the political process, and to assure European social elitism. Planters believed that to encourage a peasantry would be to contribute to a decrease in their labour force. It was within this context that the land-owning elite tried everything in its power, especially in Barbados, to secure a landless emancipation. But their intention was defeated in some territories. In some colonies, therefore, plantations and peasant holdings existed alongside each other and were at times dependent on each other. In the long term, though, this relationship was always unstable and occasionally hostile.

2 Profile of the Caribbean peasantry

In many cultures, peasants are small-scale farmers who produce much or most of their own food as well as generate a surplus for sale. They would not work full time for wages on anyone else's land.

However, in the Caribbean, peasants often had to work for wages on plantations in addition to working and earning from the land they cultivated. Part of the reason was the precarious access to land. Some Caribbean peasants owned their land but others rented, leased or squatted on Crown or other lands. Most Caribbean peasants produced for the internal markets, but some were able to produce a large enough surplus to enable them to tap the overseas markets. Peasants used mostly family labour to grow cash crops such as coffee, sugar, bananas, ginger, citrus, rice, and ground provisions. Unlike the peasants, the small farmers usually owned their land, produced more surplus for the market and made larger profits from agriculture.

3 Ways in which the peasantry became established

Many different factors together helped the Caribbean peasantry to develop. First, when the Emancipation Acts were passed and the different apprenticeship systems ended, there was a freer climate in which proto-peasants could become peasants. Other factors included the freed peoples' own determination to overcome planter resistance to their access to land, missionary help and eventual planter fragmentation in their attitude to peasant development. Indeed, some planters, even if reluctantly, sold land to aspiring peasants; and, in some territories, Crown or other undeveloped lands were also released. The decision to sell, lease or rent was made because some planters had huge debts and one solution to this was to dispose of land. This was especially urgent in English colonies after 1847 and the passing of the Sugar Duties Equalisation Act (see Chapter 10).

Did you know?

Crown land was land that was not owned by private landholders in the Caribbean, but was technically controlled by the British government.

There were some territorial differences in the ways freed people established themselves as peasants or gained access to land for food production. Some of these ways were:

- They bought Crown lands where these were offered for sale.
- They squatted on Crown lands.
- They reluctantly subjected themselves to the Tenantry system in Barbados.
- They established free villages by working together.
- Individuals bought land from planters by using money saved during the Apprenticeship System.
- They rented or leased land from landholders.
- They received help from church/missionary groups, e.g. the Baptists.
- They received help through the metayage system.
- They used land left by planter sponsors.

Did you know?

Free villages were communities of freed people who left the plantations to live on other land.

The issue of squatting was highly contentious. Squatting is defined as the illegal occupation of someone else's property. But the newly freed community believed that they had a moral claim to land. This has been called a 'moral' economy right. In other words, the freed community claimed they had a right to use the land that they had worked on for generations and they had a right to survive from the fruit which it bore. Also, freed people and would-be peasants believed that former enslavers, and the governments that had backed them, had a moral obligation to provide for their subsistence and welfare. There was no planter agreement on these issues.

4 Obstacles to the development of the peasantry

As a result of the concern over the supply of labour to the plantations and the need to deny social freedom to Africans, it was not easy for the freed people to establish themselves as a viable peasantry in the colonial Caribbean. Many obstacles were placed in their way. Some of these obstacles are detailed below.

Obstacles in Belize

In Belize ex-apprentices never managed to establish a viable peasantry, despite the fact that there was a lot of land in relation to the population. Before the 1800s, European settlers had claimed most of the lands within the country. These European landholders did not want freed people to have access to private land.

Lord Glenelg was the English Secretary of State for the Colonies. In his despatch in 1838, he forbade ex-apprentices to squat. He allowed ex-apprentices to buy Crown lands, but not for less than £1 an acre. This strategy of keeping Crown lands away from the freed people was successful and, up to 1868, very little Crown land was sold.

In Belize land was cheaper than in many other British-colonised Caribbean territories, but Crown lands were not in the best position. They were far from the only market in Belize town, so the freed people were not interested in buying such lands – even at £1 an acre. Also, while the sugar industry was declining in the other British-colonised territories, Belize's main export, which was mahogany, was experiencing better times. Landholders needed all the labour they could get for the timber industry and so they actively discouraged the rise of a peasantry. Sometimes they even paid wages so as to tie the labourers to the estates.

Obstacles in the British Virgin Islands (BVI)

There were also obstacles to peasant development in the British Virgin Islands. Here most of the land was legally owned even if it remained unfarmed. A number of estates were in Chancery Court, which hears cases dealing with property, and the ownership of these estates was in dispute. African people were unwilling and unable to buy land where ownership was not clear and so the land could not be divided up and sold to ex-apprentices. Also, squatting was discouraged and laws were passed to forcibly remove squatters. All landholders who cultivated their land with crops that were not for export, had to pay a tax of 20 shillings per acre. Export crops included cane, indigo, and cotton. This tax was designed to limit the size of peasant holdings and reduce the rewards of small farming. Peasantry was also discouraged on the Virgin Islands because the price of land was so expensive.

Obstacles in the Bahamas

In the Bahamas, Lord Glenelg brought out an order in 1836 that no Crown land was to be sold for less than £1 an acre. In 1839 he declared that 40 acres was to be the smallest size of land to be sold to individuals. This was a clear anti-peasant legislation, as few freed people could afford to buy or develop such a large piece of land. In 1840 planters were allowed to sell lots of 20 acres for 12 shillings an acre, but even this reduction in acreage did not result in many African people being able to buy the land.

Obstacles in Antigua, St Kitts and Barbados

In Antigua, St Kitts and Barbados, there was little change in the system of land possession after 1838. In these territories there was very little Christian missionary help in the formation of free villages, unlike in Jamaica. The plantations continued more or less as before. Sugar production even increased in Barbados, where the Tenantry System was entrenched and the plantation sector owned most of the land. In 1842, 441 of the 508 estates controlled 81 per cent of the island's 106,000 acres.

The planters tried not to sell land to the freed people. There were no extensive Crown lands for squatting in Barbados as there were in territories like Jamaica. The price of land was high so that most people could not save enough to buy land. Their wages were also among the lowest in the region. Furthermore, the government was not committed to the development of the peasantry. For these reasons it was difficult for a peasant class to form in Barbados and many Eastern Caribbean territories. A Stipendiary Magistrate in the parish of St Michael in Barbados was forced to concede in 1842 that:

> Little progress has been made by the labourers in establishing themselves as freeholders, not from any disinclination on their part to become so, but circumstanced as our island is there is little probability of any great number being able to obtain freeholds. The reason is obvious: there is not in the whole island a spot of waste land fit for cultivation; and as the land is principally divided into plantations, the proprietors are not likely to sell off small plots for that purpose; and there being no public lands available, it's plain that freeholders to any extent cannot be established in this country.

Obstacles in colonial Guyana, Jamaica, Trinidad and Tobago

Obstacles to peasant development were also present in the larger territories like Colonial Guyana, Jamaica, Trinidad and Tobago. Planters were unwilling or reluctant to sell land, the government refused to survey Crown lands, and there were problems over titles or ownership. In Jamaica high land prices and low wages continued.

Guyana had even larger tracts of undeveloped land, but the influential planter-class persuaded the governor to pass laws to limit the development of the peasantry and free villages. For example, in 1852 the government passed an Ordinance that banned the purchase of land by a group of more than 20 people. Ordinance 33 of 1856 reduced this to 10 or fewer people.

This law also said that each member of the group had to pay cash towards the upkeep of drains, dykes, roads, etc. But it was too expensive for individuals to afford the land and to afford to maintain these things. In fact, they now needed far more people in the group to contribute the cash. So the planters succeeded in preventing the growth of communal villages. Some of these villages had to be broken up and sold. This resulted in the collapse of some of the villages. The African-Guyanese either had to return to the estates or squat on land in the interior.

Did you know?

Communal villages were those formed through the pooling of resources by several freed people.

From as early as 1838 in Trinidad an Order-in-Council gave Stipendiary Magistrates the authority to evict squatters who had occupied land for less than a year. The squatters could be imprisoned if they failed to move. However, some planters did not co-operate with the magistrates by telling them where squatters were. For example, Lewis Pantin, the owner of plantation Bon Aventure, said that he would never inform on a settlement of 50-60 squatters in his neighbourhood. He needed their labour and if they moved another planter would benefit.

Table 4.1 Landholdings Under Fifty Acres 1880 – 1930, Jamaica

Year	Under 5 acres	5 – 49 acres	Total holdings under 50 acres
1880	36,756	13,189	49,945
1895	95,942	16,015	111,957
1899	60,671	16,160	76,831
1902	108,943	24,226	133,169
1930	153,406	31,038	184,444

Source: Eisner, Gisela. *Jamaica, 1830 – 1930: a study in economic growth*. London: University of Manchester Press, 1961, p.220.

Freehold Settlement over Fifty Acres in 1845 Jamaica (by county)

County	50 – 99	100 – 249	250 – 499	500 – 749	750 – 999	1000 and over
Surrey	123	151	130	55	55	106
Middlesex	303	330	274	155	95	292
Cornwall	690	689	538	300	243	651

Source: Hall, Douglas. *Free Jamaica 1838 – 1865: an economic study*. Yale University Press, 1959, p. 160 – 162.

Obstacles in Haiti

As we saw in chapter 1, in Haiti the planter-class had been militarily defeated, but Toussaint and other leaders believed that for economic reasons the plantation system should remain in place. Only Pétion encouraged the rise of the peasantry. The freed people chose an alternative developmental model to the plantations, based on subsistence farming and small-scale agriculture. But the revolutionary leaders tried to impose the plantation-model based on export agriculture. The freed people resisted this policy. They tried to develop themselves into a new peasantry and, in this way, create an alternative way of life that reflected their most immediate interests: the desire for land and self-sufficiency.

This desire of the freed people to become farmers meant that large-scale production was not possible because the plantations did not have an adequate labour force. Toussaint's government was depending on an export drive to rebuild the economy in Haiti, but this needed large-scale agricultural production on the plantations. So the hopes of the Haitian masses and the plans of the new leaders were in conflict. The government therefore imposed coercive measures to tie freed people in Haiti to the large estate. This limited the growth of the peasantry – but only for a time.

Obstacles in Santo Domingo

When Boyer took over Santo Domingo he wanted to give state land to the newly freed. He wanted to turn them into *campesinos* or peasants – owning and cultivating their land. However, Spanish land ownership laws did not support private ownership of land by the masses. Also the large landowners were hostile to the plan. So it was difficult for Boyer to put his vision into action and to fulfil the promise to the newly freed.

Obstacles in St Vincent

In St Vincent land prices were sometimes as high as £30 an acre. This restricted freed people from buying land. Also, the land was often unsurveyed land and, as such, could not be sold. The fertile areas were owned by planters. Forty three per cent of the land was not suited for cultivation. In 1844, small landholders had to pay high taxes of £1 and lease-holders had to pay 10 shillings. This was later lowered to 5 shillings for land worth less than £100 and 10 shillings for land worth more than that sum. In 1850, small holders and leaseholders with plots of fewer than two acres paid 5 shillings.

To sum up

The ability of African-Caribbean people to secure their freedom with the ownership of land was limited by several factors. These were common to most territories:

- The politically dominant planters had a monopoly of land rights.
- Many planters did not want to sell or rent land to those they had enslaved.
- In some colonies there were no large tracts of Crown Lands on which the ex-enslaved could squat. Also landholders still controlled these Crown lands.
- Restrictive legislation was passed to stop squatting.
- Landholders insisted that freed people should remain a dependent wage-earning population. Related to this was that the wages workers earned did not allow them to afford to buy land.
- The governments refused to survey Crown lands, which was necessary for the distribution of these lands.
- Prices for the rent or sale of land were increased. Prices ranged from £20 an acre in some territories to as high as £200 in a few cases.
- Landholders tied the access to land to estate labour/residence.
- Heavy licences were imposed on the sale of small quantities of sugar, coffee, etc. This was designed to discourage small producers.
- Laws were imposed to limit the number of people who could together buy land. In some territories only a minimum amount of land would be sold – this was usually large.
- There were high land taxes.

Revision questions

1. a State one way in which the Caribbean peasantry differs from the peasantry elsewhere in the world.
   b Give four reasons why the planter class did not want a peasantry to form in the Caribbean.
   c Describe four ways in which freed people formed a peasantry, despite planter opposition.

2. Explain the differences between a 'peasantry' and a 'proto-peasantry'.

3. Choose a community in your territory that started out as a Free Village and write its history. You may need to interview the older inhabitants in this community.

Picking coffee

Chapter 5

Peasants and production

'Well the oppressors are trying to keep me down ... But as sure as the sun will shine, I'm gonna get my share.' (Jimmy Cliff)

Introduction

In the previous chapter we saw how the elite landholding class tried to put obstacles in the way of the establishment of the Caribbean peasantry. Despite this, freed people in most Caribbean territories found ways to overcome some of the obstacles of owning land and expanding the peasantry. Over time the peasant plots became the basis of upward social mobility and a means toward political participation, especially for African men.

In this chapter we will look at the extent of peasant development in different Caribbean territories. We will look at some examples of territories in which a peasantry was established and at the economic, social, cultural and political value of the peasantry to the Caribbean.

In this chapter we will learn about:
1. The extent of peasant development in Haiti
2. The extent of peasant development in Santo Domingo
3. The extent of peasant development in the French-colonised Caribbean
4. The extent of peasant development in the Dutch-colonised Caribbean
5. The extent of peasant development in the British-colonised Caribbean
6. The importance of the peasantry to the Caribbean

Timeline of the development of the peasantry in different Caribbean territories:

HAITI

1789	Hardly any land in peasant development Most of the land in plantations. Agriculture. on about 8,000 plantations
1807	Pétion allowed freed people with land to keep it, but allotted no new land
1818	Around 100,000 hectares of land in hand of the peasants
1842	46,610 small landowners (or one-third of the Haitian population). One-third of the rest squatted on others' land

SANTO DOMINGO

1824	Start of policies under Boyer's law to encourage peasantry

FRENCH-COLONISED CARIBBEAN

1847	1,128 market gardens in Guadeloupe
1848–1870	Expansion of peasantry in Guadeloupe and Martinique
1849	2,170 market gardens in Guadeloupe
1859	3,467 market gardens in Guadeloupe

BRITISH-COLONISED CARIBBEAN

Antigua:	3,600 people living in free villages; in 1846, 9,000; in 1858, 15,600
Barbados:	2,674 freeholds; in 1897, 8,500 peasants owned 10,000 acres of land
St Vincent:	3,664 people in free villages; in 1857, 8,209
Grenada:	1860, 3,600 freeholds; in 1911, 8,000
Jamaica:	1835 – first free village (Sligoville) formed; in 1842, 200 free villages with a total of 100,000 acres
Trinidad:	in 1849, 7,000 smallholders of land, in 1861, 11,000 smallholders of land; in 1866–1870, tremendous growth of the peasantry under Governor Gordon

1 The extent of peasant development in Haiti

Between the Haitian revolution in 1791 and the death of Henri Christophe in 1820, Haiti was transformed from a plantation economy to a republic of peasant farmers. In 1789 there were 8,000 plantations which produced sugar, coffee, indigo and cotton. By 1820 these had virtually disappeared. By 1818 it is believed that more than 100,000 hectares of government land was redistributed to small holders.

African-descended Haitians wanted to follow the example of Maroons and previously freed people and become independent farmers. They wanted to farm the hilly lands in their mountainous refuges, the uncultivated plots on the edges of the plantations, or the redistributed lands of their former enslavers – especially the abandoned coffee estates. Haitian peasants simply took over some of the abandoned estates. They declared that the properties belonged to them by right, in the absence of the owner. Some Haitians people tried to buy their own land from planters who were willing to get rid of land. Those with enough cash bought land for themselves. Those without enough cash pooled their resources and bought land collectively.

Most Haitian peasants engaged in subsistence farming, but some produced coffee and other crops which they sold in rural markets. Many of the farmers in the mountainous lands produced coffee – this marked the explosion of coffee production among small independent farmers, a pattern that increased in the 19th Century. Peasants also cut down trees and used the wood to burn charcoal for sale, build their houses, or they exported the wood.

Peasants kept small gardens near their houses, which they fenced in with bamboo, logwood or aloe hedges.

Family members or friends worked on the plots. Farming was at a subsistence or survival level as people had very simple tools and few fertilisers, and the amount of crop they could produce was limited. Crops grown included yams, plantains and bananas. Also peasants kept animals like cows, horses, pigs and goats. They killed animals, sold the meat and used the money received to buy goods they did not produce.

In 1807 Pétion had passed a law stating that freed people who already possessed land – no matter how small – were allowed to keep it as long as they cultivated it. Although the government would not allow any new smallholdings, to keep soldiers loyal they were allowed to get land. The mulatto soldiers later left for the towns and sold their land to Haitian peasants. So the rural masses tended to develop into a peasantry, while the trend was for the mulatto elite to become urban dwellers.

By 1842 government officials noted that 46,610 small plots were 'under fair cultivation'. This represented only about one-third of the African-Haitian population. Another one-third had access to land through squatting. The remainder shifted from wageworkers to peasants, except the town dwellers. Some wageworkers had access to land through share-cropping, which as a system failed in Haiti, just as it failed elsewhere in the Caribbean.

2   The extent of peasant development in Santo Domingo

It was only in 1824, with Boyer's Law, that some of the land ownership difficulties were eventually settled in Santo Domingo. This cleared the way for the development of the peasants or *campesinos*.

Boyer's Law stated that new owners could not own land of less than 15,5 acres. In addition they had to use the land to grow export crops. Farmers who could not keep all their units of land in production had to surrender it to other landowners. Also, the law said that farmers needed 75 acres of land to rear livestock profitably. Predictably there was opposition from the large landowners to this policy, for while it practically did away with state land and tried to encourage private ownership, it also tried to increase landholding among the peasants. This threatened large landowners and they believed they were in danger of losing land to peasants and small farmers.

The peasants or *campesinos* also objected to the policy because Boyer wanted them to grow coffee, cotton, cocoa, sugar cane, tobacco and foodstuffs for export. They wanted to continue cutting mahogany, growing tobacco and raising livestock, as they had done before.

3   The extent of peasant development in the French-colonised Caribbean

Emancipation gave rise to the growth of small landownership in the French-colonised Caribbean territories of Martinique and Guadeloupe. Workers wanted land so that they could pursue independent economic activities. So they cultivated more and more provision grounds. In the period from 1848 to 1870, freed people used many different methods to acquire these properties. They squatted on available land, bought small lots, 'captured' abandoned estates, rented land and bargained

Fig 5.1 Yams

with planters for small estate land in return for labour. Some also kept using plots on the edges of estates while continuing to work for the plantations. They used plantation wages to buy land outright or to pay off for land on a yearly basis.

On their plots the peasants grew sugar cane which they sold to the factories. Some also did provision farming and reared small stock, which they sold in the markets and towns. The peasantry was more established in Guadeloupe than in Martinique where there was less land suited for sugar cane cultivation. In Guadeloupe, the number of market gardens grew from 1,128 in 1847 to 2,170 in 1849. By 1859, the number had grown to nearly 3,567.

4   The extent of peasant development in the Dutch-colonised Caribbean

With emancipation in the Dutch territories in 1863, many planters deserted their estates, especially those that were not profitable. Some of this land was taken over by freed African people and a few Dutch people for the growing of food. After the abolition of slavery planters in Suriname complained of a labour shortage on the country's 400 plantations. Many freed people deserted the plantations – some for the city, Paramarabo. By 1900 fewer than 100 estates were in operation. The government tried to prevent the collapse of the estates by granting small plots of land to encourage family farming.

The government made some land available to the emancipated even in former non-plantation colonies such as Aruba and Bonaire. In 1867, the land at both ends of the island of Bonaire was sold in zones to freed people. This allowed them to develop as small peasant landowners. The government eventually also rented the central district to small farmers. The peasantry in other islands remained very small. Ex-slaves emigrated to Cuba and Puerto Rico in search of better jobs and higher wages. The women became involved in food growing and marketing.

5 The extent of peasant development in the British-colonised Caribbean

Cayman Islands and The Bahamas

In the Cayman Islands many of the newly-freed workers took to the unsettled lands in the north of Grand Cayman.

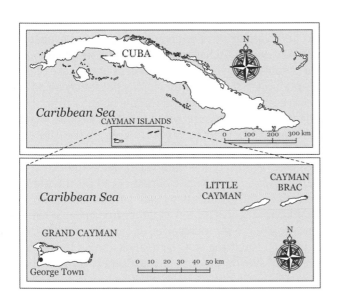

Fig 5.2 Cayman Islands

In the Bahamas a peasantry had developed during slavery. By 1784 this peasantry had developed among freed Africans. In Eleuthera, in the Bahamas, liberated apprentices bought Crown lands at the settlement of Pimman's Cove in 1835. They bought this land for an average price of £5 sterling and they became involved in the profitable business of producing pineapples for export. In 1838, Sandilands Estate in eastern New Providence was divided among the newly emancipated. In Exuma, Lord John Rolle gave his extensive lands in Exuma to the enslaved and their descendants. After this the villages of Rolleville, Rolle Town, Mt Thompson and Ramsey were formed. In 1840 freed people bought 6,000 acres of land for $1,000.

The Northern Leeward Islands and Barbados

Conditions in Barbados and the northern Leeward Islands were not as favourable to peasant development as in the Greater Antilles. But even in these territories peasantries were established despite major obstacles.

In Antigua, the governor, Sir William Colebrooke, encouraged the development of villages even though White landowners were reluctant to do this. However, after the 1840s and the crisis of the Sugar Duties Act, some owners, like the owners of Drew's Hall, Weirs, Buckleys and Sweets Estates, were more willing to sell their land. They found they needed whatever money they could earn from the sale of their land to freed people.

Did you know?

The Sugar Duties Act was a measure that removed discriminating duties or taxes on sugar entering Britain from non-British colonies.

They sold wasteland for as much as £120 per half hectare. By 1842, there were 27 independent villages in Antigua containing 1,037 houses and 3,600 dwellers. By 1846, over 9,000 freed people in Antigua were living in free villages. By 1858, 15,600 Antiguans lived in independent villages and could at least bargain for better wages. These African-Antiguans managed to get freehold ownership of small parcels of land or rented land. There was some missionary help in Antigua where the Moravians sponsored a village in 1842. But these plots were so small that their owners still had to work on the estates – even if only part-time.

In Barbados some landowners were generous and this allowed for the rise of some free villages. Reynold Elcock was the owner of the 620 acre Mt Wilton Estate in the parish of St Thomas. In 1821 he died and the freed people on his estate were allowed money to buy land. He had said in his Will that each enslaved person should get £5 each year. But the workers did not get the money left by Elcock until 1841. They then used this money to buy land in the parish. They bought part of Rock Hall Estate, and this formed the basis of the village of Rock Hall. In 1856 the owner of Workman's Estate – Peter Chapman – divided up 102 acres of the estate into 1 to 2 acre lots. These he sold to the workers in instalments. This is how Workman's village in St George parish came into existence.

Other freed people who owned land were usually artisans or other skilled people who could command a good wage. The tenantry system, despite being a system to maintain slave-like control over the African-Barbadian labouring population, tying workers to the estate in exchange for low wages and estate accommodation, did also allow African-Barbadians some access to marginal estate land. Overtime, it also allowed them to become leasehold users of land without offering their labour to the plantations. But this development should be distinguished from the socio-economic implications of owning land by freehold; and there was limited success in this area. By 1860 the number of freeholds in Barbados stood at 2,674. In 1897 there were about 8,500 independent peasants who had legally acquired 10,000 acres, while another 4,500 rented lands. Not all of the small landholders in Barbados were newly freed people. Some were poor Europeans, free mixed-race and African-Barbadians already free before 1838. These people who could find the money bought or rented land varying in size from a quarter acre to two acres, a few even larger acreages in some instances. Barbadian peasants grew vegetables, fruits, sugar cane, and food crops like yam and potatoes, cotton, ginger, aloe and arrowroot.

Landholders in Montserrat, Nevis and St Kitts also made land available to the freed people. This was because they feared the effect of freed people's continued emigration to Trinidad, colonial Guyana, Cuba and Puerto Rico. Planters, like Mr Parsons of Sadlers Estate in St Kitts, rented out some of his 200 acres to freed people, because he hoped that the workers would stay and offer even part-time work on the estates if they had access to land. Territories like St Kitts had no Crown lands. Also this island was mountainous. These islands used a system called the Tenantry System, which allowed some freed people some access to land.

Under the Tenantry System, planters made small estate lands available to estate workers, but not as owned property. Later a few freed people managed to lease these lands without the obligation to work on the estates. In 1856, Nevis had a population of 9,571 persons of which 2,000 lived as peasants in free villages. By 1897 about 8,500 of these small landowners had legally acquired about 10,000 acres of land, while another 4,580 acres were rented by the workers in these islands.

In the British Virgin Islands, the freed people squatted or pooled their resources to buy land. In the Danish Islands (now the USVI), they were helped greatly because the value of estate land had declined. They were also helped by government actions and the cancellation of the Act of 1841, which had put 20 shillings an acre on land that was not used for export crops. The government itself held large acres of land which were either useless or were causing financial loss. They parcelled these out to freed people at reasonable prices. Landholders who were afraid that their estates would lose more value, were also willing to sell their land, for example, Enfield Green and Lower Love.

At first land sold to freed Blacks ranged from 1 to 10 acres. Later peasants were given good terms to buy land of

between 8 and 28 acres. By the end of the 19th Century, the BVI consisted mainly of small peasant holdings. By 1879, there were 291 landholders with land of under 20 acres. The peasants on St Croix planted sugar cane on former government lands that had been parcelled out. They delivered cane to co-operative factories for export.

The Windward Islands

In the Windward Islands freed people had some access to land although this was limited. In 1848 there were 8,200 small farmers in St Vincent and Grenada and St Lucia had about 2,500 small landholders – even though these plots were tiny. By 1861 these islands together had 10,000 landholders. The number of residents in Grenada and St Vincent was 20,000 in total. Where the *metayage* system was adopted it provided tenants with some access to land. (See Chapter 4 and below for more on *metayage*.) Freed people also took the initiative to acquire holdings and this was very important.

At first planters were reluctant to make land available for rent, lease or purchase. In addition, the mountainous state of some of the islands (43 per cent in the case of St Vincent) limited the extent to which a peasantry could develop because there was little fertile land.

Planters in Dominica reported that they needed 300 to 400 imported labourers each year to keep up the estates that had been deserted by freed people. But only a few Portuguese went to that island. The coffee farmers, especially, were facing financial ruin. So, to get the workers to remain on the estates they made land available for peasant farming on easy terms. Other freed people had already started to set themselves up in villages. They did this through squatting on Crown lands and on lands on the leeward side on the strip of coastland known as 'The Queen's Three Chains'.

According to the report of one Stipendiary Magistrate, by 1846 in Grenada the number of persons living in Free Villages was 2,000. In 1860 the number of freeholds was 3,600 – this increased to 8,000 by 1911. The size of their lots varied from $2\frac{1}{2}$ acres to 10 acres. Grenada's significant cocoa exports by 1896 were due largely to the efforts of the peasantry.

In St Lucia about 60 freed people were already freeholders by 1841. The peasants settled in the Soufriere area in Morne Belaire, St Jour and Hermitage. They built about 26 houses in the Morne Belaire area and grew coffee on 3 to 10 acre lots, which were leased to them by Mr Tinsnes. At St Jour by 1841, peasants grew coffee, provisions, spices and other produce. Eighty-four villages lived off these crops. A Stipendiary Magistrate's report in 1845 gave evidence to the expansion that had taken place among the peasantry in that island:

I have already had occasion to notice the fondness of home, causing many of the negroes to establish themselves on small lots of land in the vicinity of estates on which they had formerly been slaves. The settlements augment everyday, and many of them assuming the character of small sugar estates …

William Sewell recorded that there were 2,045 African-descended freeholders in St Lucia by 1857, despite the tremendous difficulties of taxes they had to pay on cultivated land, export crops and houses, and land titles.

Sales of house plots and small estate lands started as early as 1839 at Layou in St Vincent, despite the difficulties. Sales for Victoria Village, which was close to Calliaqua in St George, were registered in 1843. These sales were followed in the mid-1840s by the sale of plots to form villages on Career Estate and Gomiers. By 1845, 315 sales of land to peasants were recorded – many for less than one acre. Some buyers were women, for example Maria Coulter who bought 18 acres of land in St Andrew near Campden Park Estate for £420. She then resold this land as house plots of 1/10th of an acre to local labourers, each paying between £30 and £40.

By 1846 about 3,664 freed people were living in villages. More land sales in the 1850s meant that more Free Villages were developed at Westwood, Spring and the Grove. By 1857, 8,209 people were in their own houses and by 1860 some 10,000-12,000 acres of land were being cultivated by small landowners, each of whom owned 1-5 acres.

By 1861 there were 507 freehold properties in the leeward parishes of St Vincent, as well as two Kalinago villages. By 1897 only 1,386 of these properties were smallholdings of under 20 acres. The peasantry in St Vincent was helped by the downfall of the sugar industry.

Peasants in St Vincent grew ground provisions and export crops such as arrowroot, cotton, limes, spices, logwood and coconuts. They also raised cattle. Before emancipation the export of arrowroot was at a low of 60,000 lbs, but by 1847 arrowroot became the major export after sugar. By 1857 around 1,353,250 lbs of arrowroot were being exported. This was valued at $750,000.

Did you know?

Arrow root is a starchy root-tuber from which byproducts such as flour, biscuits and starch are derived.

Jamaica

The first post-slavery Free Village in Jamaica was formed in 1835 at Sligoville in St Catherine. The number of freeholds that were less than 10 acres increased from 883 in 1840 to 20,724 in 1845. In 1842 the island had 200 free villages with a total of 100,000 acres.

By 1846 the number of workers living on the estates was only one third of what it had been in the final years of slavery and by 1861 the number of peasant property had increased to about 50,000. By this date there were more peasant landowners in Jamaica than casual estate workers.

Peasant development was greatly helped by missionaries and the anti-slavery society. In the late 1830s and in the 1840s Christian missionaries acquired most of the land for Free Villages. They acted as a financial mediator or neutral party between the planter-class and the newly freed people. Where planters did not wish to sell land to freed people, the European missionaries bought the land and then sub-divided and sold it to them. The Baptist missionaries led the establishment of post slavery free villages and the establishment of the peasantry. By 1842 it had established over 8,000 freed people in villages.

In 1829 the Baptist missionary, Rev Phillippo, bought the 195 acres of Scots Hall Plantation. In 1835 he bought another 25 acres in Sligoville to establish a Free Village after emancipation. Scots Hall became the village of Kitson Town, which opened on 3 July 1841. Sixty-four acres of land were sold, with between 16 and 20 cottages built or under construction. Some 50 people lived there. Another Baptist missionary, William Knibb, arranged for a loan of £500 to buy a village at Birmingham and a friend offered him £10,000 to buy more land. By January 1839 Knibb had helped about 70 families with money to buy and to build the town of Birmingham.

In the first four years of freedom in Jamaica, the Baptist Western Union established 3,300 freeholders on the land, at a cost of £38,450. John Clarke of the Jericho Baptist Station bought 142 acres of land. He paid for half and gave a note for full payment of the rest within a year. Other villages were Sturge Town, Wilberforce, Buxton, McCauley, Normanby, Vale Lionel, Gurney, Brougham, Kensington, Stepney and Harvey. Sturge Town was bought by missionaries for £1,250; Clarksonville for £2,400 and Stepney for £700. Members of the anti-slavery society gave £50,000 for use in Jamaica.

The Presbyterian settlement in Goodwill came into existence when Rev George Blyth bought the land and sold it to his parishioners. Two acres were set aside for a minister's residence and a half an acre for a church. There were other ways in which missionaries helped. For example, the land had to be surveyed and sub-divided, and they saw to this. They managed the construction of

Fig 5.3 The Baptist missionary, Rev Phillippo

roads and streets and offered help in the building of houses and the development of provision grounds. Above all, they assisted the freed people in getting land titles. However, we need to note that the missionaries did not intend for the newly freed to be completely independent of the planter estates. They supported the continuation of the large plantations and the society which resulted. So the land they made available to the peasants was just enough for them to subsist on and to use to bargain for higher wages on the estates.

Land for peasant development became available in several other ways, for example, whole properties or smaller parts of the properties were sub-divided and sold or rented to freed people. In the period after 1838, 19 livestock farms sold or rented land to freed people. Among them was Belmont Pen in St Ann, which rented 20 acres to workers in 1838. Lloyd's Pen in St David was made up of 433 acres; 63 acres were sold to 15 workers. Rooksby Park Pen sold 24 acres, 28 perches of land to 8 small settlers; and Kelsal Pen in St Catherine rented 38 acres of its 206 acres to freed people. Bonny Pen in St Mary sold its entire acreage to freed people because of ongoing economic decline. Johns Hall Village came into being after the owner of Dorothy Pen sold 255 acres of pen land to ex-apprentices.

After the 1880s, the expansion of the peasantry was restricted by the revival of the large plantations. These large plantations took back a lot of land and forced many ex-slaves back on to the estates as wage labourers or out of the island altogether. Unlike Trinidad and colonial Guyana, after the 1880s the Indian peasantry in Jamaica did not grow significantly.

Colonial Guyana

In colonial Guyana Free Villages started during slavery when runaway slaves established their own communities in the interior. In the post-slavery period in colonial Guyana, emancipated people had a great demand for land. Many freed people established peasant holdings on land on which they squatted or on rented land. But some freed people could buy land out of their savings as the price of land in Guyana ranged from £4 to £50 in comparison to the high prices in the Leeward Islands.

As early as 1839, Governor Light documented that people were buying land for £15 an acre, and they were spending from £40 to £50 on the construction of homes. In 1842 in Berbice and Demerara, there were 4,000 freehold properties covering some 22,000 acres of land at a cost of £70,000. By 1848 some 32,717 people lived on freeholds with their own titles. And by 1852, 11,000 people in Berbice and Demerara alone owned freeholds. One important suburban settlement was Albert Town. By 1850, 42,000 Guyanese out of a total of 82,000 had managed to buy land off the estates. By 1851, 46,368 people lived in villages that had been formed since 1838. Still about 45 per cent of the emancipated population worked on the estates.

African-Guyanese bought proprietary villages on small estate lands in which freed people held individual titles. They also pooled their money and bought whole plantations. The villages that were formed out of this collective effort were called communal villages.

In 1839 Northbrook Estate was bought in this way and then divided among 63 African-Guyanese – many of them former headmen – for $10,000. In the same way, four headmen bought Plantation Den Amstel on behalf of 70 fieldworkers for $25,000. Good Hope was bought in a similar way for $50,000. Other estates which were bought up by groups of freed people were:

- Plantation Friendship (202 hectares sold for $80,000)
- Plantation New Orange Nassau (Buxton Village for $50,000)
- The 162 hectare Plantation Beterverwagting for $22,000.
- By 1850, there were more than 25 Guyanese co-operative villages, which had land valued at over one million dollars.

Chapter 5 | *Peasants and production*

Peasants in the interior were involved in timber cutting and the sale of wood. Those on the coast grew rice, food crops, vegetables; and they reared cattle. They supplied the market in Georgetown. Floods constantly threatened the villages that were established on the coastal plains or along the riverbeds. But all these villages, including the communal villages, could not afford drainage and irrigation expenses. Because of this many communal villages failed.

Between 1850 and 1891 the number of independent peasants more than doubled in colonial Guyana. The major reason for this was not the growth of the African-Guyanese peasantry but the rise of the Indian peasantry. As chapter 6 will show, the government in colonial Guyana encouraged 'time-expired' Indians to settle on the land by offering them the land rather than sending them home. By 1891 there were already 28,412 Indians living in villages throughout colonial Guyana. These villages had names such as Barrackpore, Calcutta, Madras, Malabar, Simla. The Indians there produced rice and raised cattle.

Trinidad

At the time of emancipation, Trinidad had over a million acres of Crown lands. Also, most of the land that was privately owned was still uncultivated or under-cultivated.

With such a huge amount of undeveloped land, it was impossible for the state and the landowners to prevent the development of a peasantry in Trinidad, despite their efforts to do so. In fact, by 1847 the labouring population had decreased by 40 per cent. By 1849 there were about 7,000 smallholders. In 1851, only 3,116 labourers were working regularly on the estates.

By 1861 the island had about 11,000 small farmers and fewer than 5,000 labourers worked on the estates. After 1845 the peasantry grew with the arrival of the Indians and land being offered to them instead of being sent back to India. The peasantry also grew under Governor Gordon's administration from 1866 to 1870. An 1869 law said that the price of Crown lands would be reduced to £1 an acre, and that the minimum lot was 5 acres. This was instead of the 340 and 680 acres of the 1830s and 1840s. Legal fees were reduced and land surveying made easier.

Gordon's regime also helped squatters to legalise their status to landholders on reasonable terms. Between the time when Governor Gordon left office and Sir William Robinson became governor, the sale of Crown lands slowed down because of changes in the official policy. As peasants were encouraged to grow other crops because of the sugar crisis of the 1880s, the peasantry continued to grow.

Fig 5.4 Indian peasant family

Squatting was a popular way of gaining access to land in Trinidad, even though the authorities tried to stamp it out. By the mid-1860s squatters included cocoa farmers. Some of them owned thousands of trees, especially in the Northern Range, in the districts east of Arima and in the Montserrat area. In fact, we can say that the Trinidad cocoa industry was established and built up by the peasantry. Villages were established in such areas as Arouca, Tacarigua and D'Abadie. Within five miles of San Fernando, the villages of Rambert and Victoria were established.

6 The importance of the peasantry to the Caribbean

As far as most plantation owners were concerned, the development of the peasantry adversely affected the labour supply to their properties. Only a few owners saw it as an advantage to have peasant settlements close to their properties and encouraged their formation. At first most planters tried to stop peasant villages from developing. But in the end they realised that they could not stop the freed people from acquiring land. Caribbean peasants contributed to the economic, social, cultural and political development of the Caribbean.

Economically, the peasants helped the Caribbean people to reduce their dependence on imported food as they grew food crops for the local market and for their families. Their goods consisted of mostly fruit, vegetables and ground provisions. These they sold at the local Saturday or Sunday market for cash. A complex system of direct trading and middlemen trading developed in places like Jamaica, where not all the peasants who produced came to market. Farmers in the mountainous eastern parishes sold their produce to coastal traders who carried them to the southwest where many wage-earners still worked on sugar plantations. Other peasants sold goods to those who were going to market in Kingston and Spanish Town. Some in the eastern Caribbean traded with other islands for provisions. For example, Montserrat small farmers sold food to people in St Kitts, Nevis and Antigua. Small farmers were also involved in the export market. They used the cash they earned to buy luxury items and to educate their children. In St Vincent, small growers exported 61,338 kilograms of arrowroot. Small farmers in Grenada exported coffee, cotton, cocoa, copra, honey and beeswax. In Trinidad, squatters on Crown Lands sold timber for charcoal burning and boat building. Later they exported coffee and cocoa. In colonial Guyana, peasants only earned money when they started cultivating rice because their land was too wet and swampy and not suitable for cultivating the crops grown by other peasants in the rest of the Caribbean. They were also off the main trade routes and could not attract buyers of food crops. In Jamaica, in 1832, the production of ground provisions was 27 per cent of all agricultural products. This increased to 55 per cent in 1890. This was because of the efforts of the peasants.

By exporting some of their produce – spices, ginger, logwood, cotton, cocoa, sugar, rum, coffee, arrowroot, citrus, pimento, lime juice and coconuts – the peasants also contributed to the money earned by the region. They exported their goods to Central America, for example, where Caribbean migrants had gone to look for work. In Jamaica, the value of the trade in ground provisions increased from £577 in 1874 to £16,000,000 in 1887. In 1850 in Jamaica, small settlers contributed 10 per cent of the value of exports. By 1890 this had increased to 39 per cent. In 1850 peasant production had consisted of 83 per cent of ground provisions and 11 per cent of exports. By 1890 it was 74 per cent of ground provisions and 23 per cent of exports.

The development of the peasantry helped to make sure that a variety of different types of crops were grown in the region. In the Eastern Caribbean, the peasantry changed the pure plantation economies which was based on growing just one crop. In Tobago by 1898 only peasants grew sugar cane. During slavery, Manchester in Jamaica was not a sugar parish, but peasants started growing sugar there and they took over sugar cultivation from other parishes like Portland. In fact, by the end of the 19th Century, there were no large sugar estates in Portland. In Manchester they made sugar and sold it locally. In Jamaica,

Fig 5.5 Cassava plant

at first the peasantry dominated the cultivation of coffee and bananas. They put money in the bank as they were becoming more and more interested in saving. In Trinidad, rice and cocoa cultivated by peasants helped to make sure the economy branch out.

The peasants themselves benefited from their new status as they now had an alternative to full-time work on the plantations. By 1861 about 120,000 Jamaicans, for example, were earning their living away from the large plantations. Sixty-five thousand of them owned small farms, which together made up over 143,264 hectares. Two hundred independent villages had been built.

Fig 5.6 Cocoa pods

To sum up

The peasantry helped to change the way people saw and thought about the economy in the Caribbean. Before emancipation, the plantation economic thought could be described as plantocratic and elitist. The economy existed because of the forced labour of Africans. In some territories there was some variety in the economic activity. But this was not enough to change the way people saw the economy. The other economic activities supported the estates and were not in competition with them. Now after emancipation there was a challenge to the established economic system; and by the group who had no interest in the survival of sugar or even in producing staple crops.

Peasants founded villages and markets. These became centres of social, cultural and economic activity. They promoted cultural events, some of which helped to keep African and Indian culture alive in the Caribbean. The peasants laid the foundation of modern Caribbean society by building schools and churches in their villages, by campaigning for roads and streets, and for improved medical and educational facilities. They started local cooperatives as early on they pooled their resources for communal purposes.

The peasants helped to develop Friendly and Benefit Societies, and to develop agricultural societies and co-operative banks. The vote for all adult men and women only came to the British-colonised Caribbean after the 1940s. Up until that time the money peasants earned from small-farming, provided some freed African men with the means to qualify for the vote and to participate in the political life of the region, even if only on a small scale.

Before the large scale importation and indentureship of Asians, Caribbean planters tried to solve their labour problems through the use of immigrant labourers from Europe, North America and Africa.

There was also significant movement of Caribbean labourers within the region. The subject of immigration, labour mobility and the benefits of imported labour generated heated debates, even opposition. But as the next chapter will show, labour migration continued up to 1917 as a strategy for coping with the post-slavery economic woes of the planter class.

Revision questions

1 Write an essay on the benefits that the Caribbean has derived from the existence of a peasantry.
2 Examine the role of the missionaries in the emergence of Caribbean peasantries.
3 How did the rise of the African-Caribbean peasantry differ from the rise of the Indian-Caribbean peasantry?

Chapter 6

Immigrant labourers: new terms of bondage

'My feet is my only carriage, so I got to push on through.'
(Bob Marley)

Introduction

After the abolition of slavery, the employer classes in many Caribbean territories decided to import bonded labourers from abroad. There were many reasons for this, some of which were discussed in previous chapters:

■ The emancipated people could move around and choose employers, as well as where, when and on what terms they should work.
■ Many freed people refused to enter into an employment relationship with their former enslavers.
■ Many of the freed people became part of a peasantry which grew and developed.

The planter class especially found it difficult to get labour on an ongoing basis and on terms that it could dictate. In the next three chapters we explore the circumstances under which different ethnic groups were imported to the Caribbean after slavery was abolished, their experiences and how they contributed to the region.

Immigrant ship in heavy seas

In this chapter we will learn about:
1 Complaints of labour shortages
2 Two phases of labour immigration
3 Opposition and support for immigration
4 The aims of immigration
5 Inter-territorial migration
6 Various schemes of immigration to the Caribbean

1 Complaints of labour shortages

Sugar planters, especially, continuously complained of a labour shortage, especially in the British-colonised Caribbean. In 1842 this led the British House of Commons to pass a resolution that said that the only way to compensate employers for their loss of control over the labour force was to help them import bonded labourers.

There was an official view that imported labourers would solve the 'problems' associated with the emancipation of enslaved people in the Caribbean. Once the imperial government and colonial elites had agreed on cost issues, they began to look at different sources and design different ways to get immigrant labour. The major sources they looked at were Africa, the Azores, China, Europe, India, Java, Madeira, Malta and North America.

Between 1834 and 1917, close to 750,000 immigrants were transported to the region, largely as contract or indentured servants. Approximately 536,378 of these labourers were Indians. There was also a large migration of Caribbean people between territories, with people from the Bahamas, Barbados, Jamaica, and the Leeward and Windward Islands seeking jobs in colonial Guyana, Cuba, Trinidad, Suriname and elsewhere.

2 Two phases of labour immigration

There were two broad phases of labour immigration schemes:
- Those undertaken even before the final abolition of slavery. This was because planters anticipated a labour shortage and wanted to prevent it.
- Those immigrations that were undertaken because of a real or perceived labour shortage after the final abolition of slavery.

The first phase involved the immigration of Europeans, Africans, Mayans (to Cuba), Chinese, the Canary Islanders and Portuguese Atlantic Islanders, other Caribbean Islanders, and North Americans. Some Europeans were also imported, but the main schemes involved Africans and Asians. Intra-Caribbean migration also continued in response to the growing demand for labour in the larger colonies.

The early post-emancipation immigration schemes operated largely through the bounty system or private financing. For example, John Gladstone, who led the way in Indian immigration to colonial Guyana in 1838, funded the immigration project between himself and the planters. Later in the 19th Century the government imposed taxes on colonial importers to help planters pay the cost of immigration.

3 Opposition and support for immigration

There is ongoing debate about whether or not planters should have resorted to immigration, especially as there was internal and external opposition to it. There was opposition to immigration in most colonies as well as in Europe and source countries. In the British-colonised Caribbean, there was more obvious opposition in Jamaica than in colonial Guyana and Trinidad. As early as 1847 letters appeared in the Jamaican newspapers criticising the importation of Indians. One 'Publicola', in a letter in the *Morning Journal* of 1847, opposed Indian immigration:

> *… which tends to demoralize our peasantry without benefiting any party. If we must import human beings let them be Africans who have already demonstrated to the West Indian planters that they are more capable than any other race to carry out the object required, namely, good and cheap cultivation of the soil.*

The leadership of the Baptist missionary church in Jamaica also opposed immigration on what they called 'moral' and economic grounds. They believed that Indians in particular would not only compete with newly freed people in the labour market, but would also have a negative effect on their socio-cultural life. In other words, they would introduce what the Baptists considered to be a 'pagan' culture to the newly freed people and undo the 'civilising' efforts of Church missionaries. In Trinidad, from the mid-19th Century, Indian immigration was attacked on the same basis. Missionaries criticised immigration on financial and moral grounds. In Santo Domingo, the mulatto community openly demonstrated against the immigration of Africans on racial and cultural grounds. The anti-slavery society in England also opposed African immigration. In Africa opposition was raised.

In Sierra Leone, Christian missionaries feared the loss of converts, and employers, such as timber merchants, feared the loss of labour. Both groups actively discouraged the emigration of the Kroo people. The missionaries wanted their converts to remain in Africa and help spread the gospel there.

Did you know?

The Kroo people: The Kroo people are from Kru Coast, three hundred miles south of Freetown in Sierra Leone.

Despite this opposition, immigration schemes went ahead because local and foreign governments supported them in order to pacify planters. These powerful interest groups believed that immigration was the solution to emancipation. The main problems in the post-slavery period were, however, linked to poor labour relations. These were brought on because employers were reluctant to meet the labour expectation of the freed people, who refused to continue in the old exploitative relationship with planters.

Instead, planters saw immigration as the major solution. They wanted to get back their traditional control over the labour force, limit freed people's mobility, and set their own terms of work and wages. Immigration was considered just as important in territories like Trinidad, Suriname and colonial Guyana where the areas to be cultivated were beyond the capacity of the available labour supply, in the Windward Islands where metayage had failed to achieve its worthy objectives, and in places where the movement of freed people had created an absolute scarcity of labourers.

Europeans were committed to keeping the plantation society with their ethnic dominance, supported economically by a largely one-crop export system (sugar). There was no place in the imperial and plantocratic scheme for political and economic power to pass into the hands of the emancipated Africans. Planters knew that this could happen if the peasantry developed. Governments were sympathetic to the demands of the landholding elite for full-time, resident, contract labourers.

There was lukewarm support, or no support at all in the early stages, for immigration in the Leeward Islands, Belize and Barbados. This was because there was either a forced labour system that kept the majority of freed people tied to the estates; or the supply of labour was more than the demand. However, by the late 19th Century, even Leeward Islands like Antigua, St Kitts and Nevis were calling for immigrants and Antigua continued complaining about a labour shortage up to the early 20th Century.

In 1920 Mr A P Cowley, chairman of the Agricultural and Commercial Society in St Johns, Antigua, informed the British government:

Both the Government and the planting community experience the greatest difficulty in obtaining the necessary labour for road developments and improvements and for general agricultural operations, and it is too well known that these islands [Leeward] are in a similar position as regards shortage of labour as colonial Guyana.

Cowley's reference to colonial Guyana was because that colony was considering recruiting Leeward Islanders after Indian immigration had ended.

4   The aims of immigration

The employer class and its imperial allies hoped that immigration would:
- balance the African-European ratio, if they could encourage European immigration, e.g. from Germany
- provide immigrant labour to work land in colonies where there was unused land. This would correct the unfavourable balance between population and land
- build up an extra supply of labourers
- lower wages by setting up competition for jobs
- provide planters with a steady core of continuous labourers and restore the planters' control over labour
- keep the sugar economy as is, or even expand it and increase output.

However, in order to realise these aims, planters needed to import immigrants in large numbers. Immigrants would need to work under long contracts, be available on the estates throughout the year, be affordable, be paid low wages, be controllable, and finally, be isolated from local labourers to limit opportunities for class solidarity.

5   Inter-territorial migration

Some planters tried using labourers from other Caribbean territories before they started importing immigrant labourers on a large scale from outside of the Caribbean. By 1837 the inter-territorial migration was significant. Many labourers were moving southward from the Northern Leeward Islands of Antigua, Nevis, Montserrat and St Kitts. Others were moving from the Windward Islands – Grenada, St Lucia, St Vincent and Dominica – and the Turks and Caicos Islands, to Trinidad and colonial

Guyana. Bahamians went to colonial Guyana from as early as 1838. Colonial Guyana imported about 40,656 workers from the Caribbean islands by 1893, mainly from Barbados.

Barbadian workers emigrated to other territories, including Cuba and Suriname. Large numbers of Grenadians went to Trinidad. By 1847 an estimated 2,600 British Caribbean workers were located on the sugar estates in Trinidad. Caribbean migrants made a huge contribution to the survival of the estates in Trinidad and colonial Guyana. Freed people from the Leeward Islands, the British Virgin Islands and the Windward Islands migrated in the sugar harvest to Dominica. Labourers from Anguilla, Nevis, Montserrat and St Martin also went to cut cane in St Kitts during the harvesting season. Workers from the BVI moved to Guadeloupe. Leeward Islanders also moved to Bermuda in the early 20th Century to work in the dockyards and military installations.

Why did freed people move from one part of the Caribbean to the next? First, they knew they could get higher wages outside their own territory. Trinidad and colonial Guyana offered between 24 and 32 cents a day compared to 12 to 13 cents a day offered in the Leeward Islands. Second, they were influenced by geographical factors such as the fact that the territories they went to were relatively close to their own countries and it was fairly easy to get there.

Not all landholders liked the immigrants. Some complained that the immigrants joined the peasantry as soon as they could and that they were not submissive.

The inter-territorial migration was limited because contracts could only be settled inside the importing colony, and source countries put many obstacles in the way of migration. The landholders in the source countries obviously did not want to lose labourers and passed laws opposing the labourers from migrating. For example, the BVI did not want their labourers to leave. In 1837 they banned all the activities of the recruiting agents from colonial Guyana and Trinidad who were trying to recruit BV Islanders. The ban was lifted in 1838 at the end of Apprenticeship. By 1848 BV Islanders were emigrating to nearby Vieques, and St Thomas in the Danish Virgin Islands. Landholders in Jamaica tried to recruit labourers from Barbados, but they were not very successful, as few Barbadians would work for the low wages offered in Jamaica.

Puerto Rico

After *contratación* ended in Puerto Rico, planters had to rely heavily on other Caribbean immigrants to service their sugar industry. This was because the rewards planters gave their own freed people to get them to remain on the estates, did not work. The *hacendados* in Puerto Rico, for example, provided their labourers with houses, provision plots, free pasturing of animals, the rights to collect forest wood for cooking, the sharing of special crops of sugar, as well as sharing rum and molasses among the workers. None of this worked. There were also some negative measures that planters used: for example, making labourers spend their money only in the estate store. So the end of *contratación* saw the *hacendados* calling for extra labour.

Before 1873, labourers from Antigua and BVI went to Puerto Rico to work, in Poncé, Humacao, Loiza and Carolina. Indeed, some 100 Antiguans were contracted to work in Loiza. They were recruited by agents who had been sent to the Eastern Caribbean. These labourers worked on annual contracts. They lived on the estates; received a daily wage that was different according to age and gender; and were paid extra wages for night work, work done on week-ends and in the factory.

Labour relations between contract workers and employers in Puerto Rico were affected by several problems. In most cases, the contracts were written in Spanish and needed to be interpreted to workers. However, workers were never sure that the terms explained to them were what actually had been written down. Some employers took advantage of the language barrier to slip in harsh terms of labour, for example the requirement that labourers had to work at nights and on Sundays.

Employers complained that the contract workers in Puerto Rico were difficult to control and that they often challenged the authority of the police. In 1874 a group of contract workers from Playa Grande challenged the police. One from Nevis was killed, 37 were arrested and two were injured. In the same year over 100 workers from Campo Asilo set fire to the canes. They threw stones at the authorities to prevent them from putting out the blaze.

Dominican Republic

The Dominican Republic imported immigrants from the British-colonised Caribbean territories and nearby Haiti. From 1879 labourers began to spontaneously emigrate from the British Caribbean territories. A few artisans and fieldworkers had entered the Dominican Republic before that date. There was no widespread support for the importation of African workers, especially those from Haiti, and laws were passed to prevent or limit the importation of Africanised non-Hispanic workers.

Dominicans preferred to import European immigrants and tried to attract Canary Islanders. Some even suggested using Asians, but the British Foreign Office turned down their request.

Some immigrants were employed in the cocoa industry in Samaná. Some worked as lightmen and boatmen in Puerto Plata. In San Pedro de Marcoris, a number became established tradesmen and moneylenders. By 1916 around 4,000 immigrants from the British Caribbean had settled in the Dominican Republic. They were called *cocolos*. Those on sugar estates worked as cane-cutters, millhands and engine drivers. Some were fishermen and wharf-labourers. It is said that the *cocolos* were 'troublesome' as they did not accept unfavourable terms of labour but struggled for better wages. In addition to these 4,000 immigrants, another 2,000 to 2,500 came each year for the harvest from December to June. These seasonal workers were mainly cane-cutters and were paid by piece-work.

By 1917 about 900 or 10 per cent of the population of the town of Puerto Plata were from the British-colonised Caribbean, mostly from the Turks and Caicos Islands. In 1917, between 17.5 per cent and 20 per cent of the population of Montechristey were British Caribbean immigrants. In Sanchez, the site of the terminus of the British railroad, there were about 600 British Caribbean immigrants. In 1891 there were about 200 immigrants in Samaná working as artisans, mechanics, farmers and shopkeepers. Though the majority settled in and around the sugar-growing areas, a significant number settled at some of the main commercial centres.

In addition to Haiti, the Turks and Caicos Islands, the immigrants came from St Kitts, Nevis, Anguilla, colonial Guyana, Dominica and Barbados. Some Virgin Islanders emigrated as labourers from around 1912. About 90 per cent of the population of Anguilla migrated on a seasonal basis to the Dominican Republic. Immigrants also came from the Dutch Antilles of Curaçao, Aruba, Saba, St Maarten, Bonaire and St Eustatius. They came to Suriname and the Hispanic and larger British Caribbean territories.

Among the first immigrant workers introduced to the French-colonised islands were those from the nearby British-ruled territories of St Lucia and Dominica. About 150 of these workers landed in Guadeloupe in 1848. By the end of November 1848, there were 266 African workers from the British-colonised Caribbean in Guadeloupe. None seem to have gone to Martinique.

6 Various schemes of immigration to the Caribbean

a The North American immigration scheme since 1783

The Caribbean territories tried to recruit African-Americans and African-Canadians. Richard Hill, the mixed-race Special Magistrate of Jamaica, had gone to Haiti and seen African-Americans there working well. He thought that if some could come to Jamaica, they would be an example of hard work to the newly freed people.

Governor Metcalfe sent Alexander Barclay – the Immigration Agent – to the United States of America (USA) to try to persuade African-Americans to come to Jamaica. Barclay met with leaders in Georgia, Philadelphia and Virginia in the southern United States and handed out pamphlets on Jamaica. However, African-Americans were not too attracted by the economic reasons for going to Jamaica. They went to Trinidad, though, where wages were higher. Jamaica's only attraction for the African-Americans was that it was not a slave society. The people from the USA wanted to escape racial discrimination and the poor economic conditions of freed people in their own country.

The first group of 216 African-Americans arrived in Trinidad in 1839. The government of Trinidad paid their passages. By 1847 about 1,307 had arrived in Trinidad from Delaware, Maryland, New Jersey, New York and Pennsylvania. By 1848 only 148 were still on the estates, they really preferred non-agricultural, artisan jobs. They found wages in Jamaica and other territories low. By 1860 there were fewer and fewer immigrants from North America because of the more successful Asian immigration. (We will discuss this in Chapter 8.)

African-Canadians were reluctant to go to the Caribbean for the same reasons as discussed above. Jamaican and other agents tried to interest runaway slaves from Canada to work in the Caribbean. Only 169 came to Jamaica between 1841 and 1845. As they were all skilled workers and not the type of workers Jamaica needed, many soon returned to Canada because the working and living conditions in Jamaica did not meet with their expectations.

Slave owners and abolitionists in the USA and Canada opposed the emigration of their workers to the Caribbean. Abolitionists wanted to send free Africans back to Africa. The emigrants themselves wanted land, not field labour. Or, if they had to do field labour, the wages had to be good enough to enable them to buy land. Britain was also reluctant to recruit immigrant labourers from slave societies as it was afraid of world opinion. So only a handful of Canadian and African-American people emigrated as workers to the British-colonised Caribbean. When Nancy Gardner Prince visited Jamaica in 1840, she commented on how unhappy the African-Americans seemed to her. She said they all complained to her that they had been promised free return passages but none had received them.

b European immigration: Europe and the Atlantic Islands

After the abolition of slavery, the British-colonised Caribbean territories also imported European labourers. The first group consisted of Portuguese from the Azores. They went to Trinidad in 1834. In 1835, Jamaica followed. They sent recruiting agents under a government bounty to Europe to secure Germans to be settled in places like Seaford Town.

Fig 6.1 Priest blessing Irish immigrants, 1851

THE BRITISH-COLONISED CARIBBEAN

Some Portuguese started to emigrate from Madeira in 1835. They first went to colonial Guyana and later to other territories. In 1836 immigration was banned by the authorities in Madeira, partly because of the high mortality rates of Madeirans in the colony, but reopened again in 1841. But the death rate of Portuguese in the colonies was high. So in 1842, the government once again withdrew permission to recruit them. A famine in Madeira in 1846 once more caused emigration to be allowed, but when the famine ended in 1847, the flow of emigrants slowed down.

Immigration was also tried from among the Maltese, as some landowners believed that the Maltese were superior to other European labourers from southern Europe and that they would withstand the heat of the Caribbean. In some territories, like Grenada, the planters made efforts to attract Maltese one year after the Apprenticeship system ended.

European labourers were also recruited from the Canary Islands, the Azores, the Cape Verde Islands and various countries in western Europe. European immigrants were expensive and there were also not enough of them. While the Maltese were mostly imported under private arrangements, Madeiran immigration was financed by the state. In some territories, the tax imposed by the government on rum paid for the importation of Madeirans.

After much effort and cost, Jamaica, Trinidad and colonial Guyana could attract only 4,500 European immigrants, Trinidad 1,500, and British Guiana 1,000 from the Azores, Madeira, Britain, Germany, France and Malta. Europeans generally did not like contract labour in the Caribbean. This caused some agents to use fraudulent ways to increase the number of Europeans shipped.

Colonial Guyana imported a significant number of Portuguese, namely 4,312 in 1841. By 1882, 32,000 Portuguese reached colonial Guyana; 2,500 reached Antigua; 2,100 St Vincent; 2,100 St Kitts-Nevis, and 1,000 Trinidad. Madeiran emigration to St Vincent started in 1845 when 254 immigrants arrived and were assigned to James Porter, a merchant and council member. It ended in 1848. Other territories that imported Madeiran Portuguese were Dominica and Grenada. According to Edward Cox, the first shipment with 165 Madeirans to Grenada landed from the ship *St Vincent* in 1846. The following year 438 arrived in four separate shipments. In 1851 another 10 arrived on the ship *Cockermouth Castle*, making a total of 613. Between 1835 and 1881, around 40,971 Madeiran Portuguese entered the Caribbean, with the largest numbers going to colonial Guyana.

THE FRENCH-COLONISED ANTILLES AND CUBA

The French-colonised Antilles and Cuba also recruited European immigrants. The Governor-General of Martinique set aside 100,000 francs to import European immigrants. Between 1848 and 1859, 300 Madeirans and about 200 immigrants from France were imported to the island. In 1852 French prisoners were transported to Guyane. Railway contractors in Cuba brought their own European labourers with them. Between 1834 and 1839 many thousands of European labourers arrived from Spain, the Canaries and the United States of America. Cubans made a determined effort to import only European immigrants.

Most of the European labourers refused to work alongside enslaved workers and withdrew from the estates. Some mutinied, others complained about the hot climate, poor treatment and low wages. More success was achieved in the 19th Century with post-slavery European immigrants. For one, they no longer had to complain about working alongside the enslaved. The government paid their passages, improved their working conditions, and between 1882 and 1895, increased their wages. Eighty thousand Spaniards arrived in Cuba. But the continued arrival of labourers made wages fall again in 1886. In 1898, the US abolished contract labour in Cuba. But in the 20th Century immigration once again became significant for the Cuban sugar industry. This time free European labourers immigrated to Cuba.

DUTCH-COLONISED CARIBBEAN

The Dutch colony of Suriname also tried to attract European farmers and workers. In 1860, 348 Dutch farmers were recruited and settled on an abandoned estate. Just like the Germans in Jamaica, many of the Dutch died from diseases, others emigrated to the town and others returned to Europe. Between 1822 and 1872, the Dutch were using Madeiran immigration. About 480 Madeirans were attracted to Suriname.

GENDER BALANCE AMONG MADEIRANS

There was a consistent policy to have a balance between men and women among the Madeiran immigrants, even though more males than females eventually still emigrated. The first batch of immigrants to St Vincent consisted of 136 males and 118 females. It included 60 families and 12 unmarried men. Of the 387 who arrived in Grenada in 1847, 53 per cent were males and 47 per cent were females. This is still a more balanced sex ratio than early Asian immigration. In the 1880s, family emigration from Madeira was encouraged, and again there was a policy to keep a balance between men and women.

REASONS FOR EUROPEAN IMMIGRATION NOT MEETING ITS AIMS

European immigrants did not all satisfy the landholders' desire for reliable, adequate and controllable workers. There were some territories like Grenada that considered Madeirans absolutely valuable to the cocoa plantations on which they were located. Those who used Madeirans as farmyard servants on sugar plantations gave favourable reports. However, for the most part, there were not enough European labourers in the region to have an influence on the peasantry as some had erroneously hoped. Only in some territories, like Grenada, did they establish themselves as a peasantry, cultivating provision grounds for themselves.

European immigrants also did not affect the land/labour ratio in any major way. Some owners had hoped erroneously that they would be 'an example of hard work' to the newly freed. This too was not the case. Many did not fulfil their contracts and deserted field labour for non-agricultural enterprises in the towns. Some emigrated to the United States of America. The fact that many immigrants saved up money to return to their homeland shows that immigrants did not all like their stay in the Caribbean.

In 1864 there were only 78 Madeirans on estates in St Vincent. Often immigrants deserted or emigrated because they disliked the terms of their contract. In most territories Madeirans at first were employed on one-year contracts, although planters tried to bring in two-year contracts. The Maltese recruited for Grenada had five-year contracts. Adults received 8 pence a day and children 5 pence. The medical treatment and material welfare they received did not always satisfy them.

Maltese complained that there was a great discrepancy in what they were promised when they were recruited, and what they actually experienced in the Caribbean. On recruitment they were promised free passage, free rations and maintenance in the colony, reasonable hours of work and rest, free cottages, adequate wages, land, etc. Some of the Portuguese were good workers and those who survived the hardships of the voyage and the many diseases, were good fieldworkers. But they preferred the retail trade and shopkeeping to agricultural labour.

By 1882, 99 out of every 100 shops/stores in colonial Guyana were owned or managed by Portuguese. In Jamaica, employers saw many Portuguese in St Catherine and St Ann as troublesome. Many died from diseases such as malaria and yellow fever. There were varied reasons for this:

- Inadequate provisions were made for their health and housing.
- They did not get used to the climate quickly.
- They arrived in a poor state of health after their long voyage.
- They arrived at an unseasonable time of the year.
- They drank too much rum.
- The damp unhealthy environments on estates such as Tivoli and Conference in St Andrews, Grenada, took their toll on the immigrants.

Some estates experienced particularly high death rates. Within six months of their arrival, twelve of the 32 migrants on Mt Gay estate in St George's in Grenada died. So did ten of the 20 who went to Hook's Bacolet in St Andrew's.

c The African immigration scheme

The importation of free West Africans to the Caribbean was also numerically significant. The Bahamas were among the earliest importers of West Africans. The scheme lasted from 1811 to 1860, by which time about 6,000 people had been imported. The West Africans were settled in areas such as Highborne Cay, Carmichael,

Adelaide and Headquarters in New Providence. They also established settlements at Williamstown, Victoria in the Berry Islands, Bennett's Harbour on Cat Island, the Bight and Great Harbour on Long Island and on Rum Cay and the Ragged Islands. In addition to Liberated Africans, Chinese, Greeks, US nationals and British Carribean settled in the Bahamas. However, these people did not enter as labourers as labour migration was not huge in the Bahamas.

Other early importers of West Africans were colonial Guyana, Trinidad and Grenada. The first batch of 337 'liberated Africans', were initially bound for Cuba. They arrived in Grenada in 1836 on the Portuguese ship *Negrinha*. The *Vestal* brought in another 486 in the same year. About 50 per cent of Grenada's African indentured workers arrived before the end of Apprenticeship in 1838.

In the 1840s African immigration to the rest of the Caribbean started. This involved the so-called 'liberated' Africans, as well as Africans from Sierra Leone, Liberia, Gambia, St Helena and the Kroo Coast. After the abolition of the British slave trade in 1807, British men-of-war patrolled the Atlantic Ocean trying to stop illegal and foreign slave traders. Africans captured in this effort were sent to chosen entrepôts of St Helena and Sierra Leone. They were later taken to the Caribbean. Here they could become 'liberated' Africans, or sent directly to the West Indies as indentured labourers. The yearly importation of immigrants from Africa was always low.

Between September and December 1841, six shipments arrived in Jamaica alone. Here they were mainly used in the parishes of St Thomas, St Mary and Westmoreland. Immigration was under the bounty system up to 1842. After this the government assumed direct responsibility for immigration until the schemes were finally abolished in 1867.

The French-colonised Caribbean had more success with West African immigration than with European immigration. They imported around 16,000 African immigrants, but these were not truly 'free labour'. Rather they were Africans captured in French armed missions in the Congo where France later built a colony. These Africans were given their freedom when they landed in Martinique and Guadeloupe. About 17,000 Africans went to the French Caribbean after emancipation. Up to 1859 Guadeloupe had received 6,126 Africans, Martinique 10,659 and French-colonised Guyane, 1,500. This scheme was officially stopped in 1871.

Gender balances in African immigration

Like all the other schemes of labour migration, in African immigration there were also more males than females. This happened despite the efforts of the authorities to create an acceptable male-female ratio on each immigrant ship. For example, to avoid the same sexual imbalance of the trade in African captives, the Jamaican Immigration Act specified that one-third of the African immigrants must be female. But the shipments always had more men, except for the very first shipment in which 106 of the 265 passengers were female. They were mainly Maroon women and soldiers' wives.

In most of the shipments to Grenada and St Vincent there were about 60 per cent males to about 40 per cent females. One ship bound for Grenada, the *Athletoe*, carried males only. In general, African women did not want to cross the salt water. They also had horrible memories of the trade in African captives and how slowly those who had gone before, had returned home. Many would only agree to emigrate if they were given guaranteed return passages. This guarantee was hardly ever given and so recaptives or 'liberated ' Africans were not allowed to return home.

WORKING CONDITIONS

Until the time when large numbers of Asians were imported, it was the African contract worker who helped to prop up the sugar industry where it was falling. They were also employed on cocoa estates in the Windward Islands and Trinidad. When they left the estates they became involved in small farming and helped the peasantry grow. This made planters complain that West Africans under contracts did not solve their 'labour problem'.

About 63 estates in Grenada hired Africans from the 463 who arrived on the ship *Brandon*. They worked on one-year contracts that could be renewed. Some territories imposed a three-year contract on children. The Africans received low wages, as low as 5d a day in Grenada in the first year, 10d in the second year and 1/3d in the third year. Planters assumed that over time the Africans would become better and more valuable workers who could demand higher wages.

The general welfare of African contract workers and their death and birth rates varied from territory to territory. St Vincent had a higher death rate than Grenada, for example. The death rate was not only high on some plantations but also on the ships, even though there were ship doctors.

The estates in Grenada and St Vincent who received Africans were supposed to provide them with certain facilities and resources: free housing, land on which to grow food, weekly rations, medical attention, medicines. On both islands, Stipendiary Magistrates had final legal responsibility over the immigrants. It was their responsibility to see to it that estates honoured the terms of the contracts. The Africans themselves often forced the planters to obey the terms through their resistant behaviour. Some who could not cope with the harsh plantation system deserted. The settled Creole population hid the African deserters and so it was not as easy to capture and return them to the estates as it was with later Asian deserters.

CONTRIBUTIONS

West African immigrants contributed economically to the region through their work on estates. They also contributed to the peasantry. They helped to sustain – and in some cases revitalise – African culture in the Caribbean. For example, the 'liberated' Africans in Trinidad and Grenada formed communities in which the Yoruba language was spoken and parts of Yoruba culture practised, including kinship elements and rites. The mixture of Roman Catholicism and Yoruba nation dance resulted in the Shango form of religious ritual. In the 1880s when King Ja Ja of Opobo arrived in exile in Grenada and St Vincent, he also contributed to the survival of the Yoruba culture and identity.

Did you know?

Shango is a part of the Yoruba religion which celebrates the deity called 'Shango', God of Thunder and Lightning.

To sum up

Before the large-scale importation and indentureship of Asians, Caribbean planters tried to solve their 'labour problems' through the use of immigrant labourers from Europe, North America and Africa. There was also significant movement of Caribbean labourers within the region. The subject of immigration, labour mobility and the benefits of imported labour generated heated debates, even opposition. But as the next chapter will show, labour migration continued up to 1917 as a strategy for coping with the post-slavery economic woes of the planter class.

Revision questions

1   Explain why European immigration did not fulfil its aims in the British Caribbean.
2   Discuss the ways in which African immigration was useful to Caribbean planters.
3   Explain why African and European migration schemes were male-dominated.

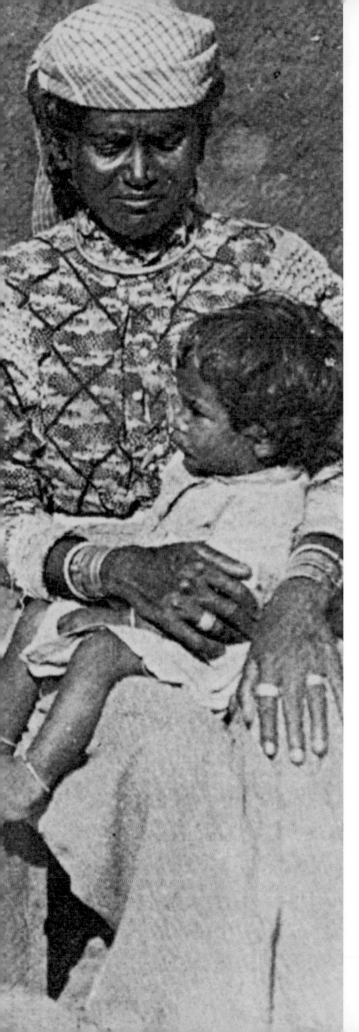

Chapter 7

Indian arrival

'I don't have nothing right now in mi han, come let we go, dudu, come let we go ...'
(Nisha Bissabhar)

Introduction

The most significant immigration schemes in terms of numbers involved the Indians, Chinese and Javanese. Planters also imported a few Japanese and Annamites. Indian immigration proved more regular, continuous and larger in numbers than all the other schemes. Once the Indians started to be imported in large numbers, most of the other schemes were discontinued.

In this chapter we will focus on Asians who formed the majority of imported workers in the Caribbean.

We will learn about:
1 The early experiments with Indian immigrants
2 Why Indians left India
3 How immigrants were recruited
4 The gender differences in Indian immigration
5 Castes and religion of Indian immigrants
6 Post-recruitment experiences
7 The passage to the Caribbean
8 Immigration laws in the Caribbean
9 Immigration and indentureship
10 How employers disobeyed the terms of the law
11 Indian resistance
12 The end of Indian immigration and indentureship
13 Post-indentureship
14 Emigration to third countries

Indian mother and child

1 The early labour experiments with Indian immigrants

The Gladstone experiment

The first group of immigrant Asians in the Caribbean were the 414 Indians who arrived in colonial Guyana in 1838 on the ships *Whitby* and *Hesperus*. This arrangement was called the 'Gladstone experiment', because the immigrants were privately imported by John Gladstone, a large landholder in colonial Guyana, together with a company in Calcutta. The Indians were imported on five-year contracts for six sugar estates. Their treatment was so poor and the death rate so high on the estates of Belle Vue (the property of Andrew Colville), Vreed-en-Hoop and Vreedenstein (the properties of John Gladstone) that the state imposed a ban on future importations.

Stops and starts

The British Anti-Slavery Society, especially, opposed further importations of Indians. It got the British government to appoint a local Commission to investigate the treatment of immigrants. In 1843, the government banned importations until the Indians who had survived their indentureship in colonial Guyana were repatriated to India. The ban was lifted in 1844, and in 1845, colonial Guyana, Trinidad and Jamaica once again started importing Indians. The first group of 226 Indians arrived in Trinidad in 1845 on the ship *Fatel Rozack*. The first group of 261 arrived in Jamaica in the same year on the ship *Blundell Hunter*.

Landholders in Trinidad, colonial Guyana and Jamaica were positive about the contribution that Indians made to their economies. So in 1846 they requested that a further 29,000 be imported – 5,000 for Jamaica, 4,000 for Trinidad, and 10,000 for colonial Guyana. But before their requests could be filled, the Sugar Duties Equalisation Act was passed. This Act, which removed the preferential duties on sugar imported to Britain from the British-ruled Caribbean, deepened a commercial and financial crisis in the sugar industry as landholders cancelled their orders for immigrants. This meant another short-term stoppage of immigration from 1847 to 48. After the British government received a report on the economic conditions of the landholders, it decided to help them with a loan of £500,000 to be shared among Trinidad, Barbados, colonial Guyana and Jamaica. At first Jamaica refused the loan. Trinidad and colonial Guyana used their share to start up immigration again in 1850 and 1851.

Jamaica did not start immigration again until 1860 and then continued irregularly to 1916. Later in the 19th Century, Indians were imported to Nevis, St Kitts, St Lucia, St Vincent, Grenada, Martinique, Guadeloupe, St Croix and Suriname. By the 1890s Indian immigration had been discontinued in the Leeward and Windward Islands.

Did you know?

The Sugar Duties Act provided that all sugar entering the British market would pay the same amount of duty.

2 The reasons Indians left India

Long-range emigration was not new to Indian society. In fact, it was well-established. Long before they were imported to the Caribbean, Indians had emigrated to other countries in South East Asia and Australia. The emigrants came to the Caribbean for various reasons. Some left to escape economic distress, especially during times of famine. Some left hoping to earn higher wages, others to escape their debts. Many left because they had lost property and status due to the unfavourable British land policies in India. Some left because Western industrialisation had undermined their industries, such as the cloth industry.

In addition, some women emigrated to escape oppressive marriages or home conditions and to seek a more independent life. For many, emigration offered a new adventure. Chandra Kumari, a young female emigrant to Jamaica, asked in 1891 to be released from her contract and returned to India before even trying to fulfil her contract. When asked for a reason for her attitude, she explained that she had left for Jamaica in search of adventure and because she was curious. She had claimed that she was from a royal family and that was why she asked to return to India, but this was later found to be false.

Let us look at the relationship between famines and emigration in more detail. Famines and their hardships alone did not cause Indians to emigrate to the Caribbean, although the famines made it easier to persuade more people to emigrate. But, in the end, it was the extent of the demand of Caribbean planters for labourers rather than displacement from famines which determined the number of people exported from India.

Table 7.1 Number of Indians imported to the Caribbean, 1838-1917

Territory	Years	Numbers imported
Colonial Guyana	1838–1917	238,909
Trinidad	1845–1917	143,939
Suriname	1873–1918	34,024
Guadeloupe	1854–1887	42,595
Jamaica	1845–1916	38,681
Martinique	1848–1884	25,509
St Lucia	1858–1895	4,354
Grenada	1856–1885	3,200
St Vincent	1860–1880	2,472
St Kitts	1860–1861	337
French Guiana	1853–1885	19,296

Sources: K. O. Laurence, *Immigration into the West Indies*; G. Eisner, *Jamaica 1830-1930*, 144; C. Seecharan, *Tiger in the Stars*, 4; V. Shepherd, *Transients to Settlers*.

Table 7.2 Immigrants introduced to Guyana, mainly under indenture, 1834-1917

Source	Period of Immigration	Numbers
India	1838-1917	238,909
Madeira	1835-1881	32,216
Africa	1834-1867	14,060
China	1852-1884	13,533
Europe	1834-1845	381
Other	1835-1865	1,868
TOTAL		300,967

C. Seecharan, *Tiger in the Stars*, p. 3, G. W. Roberts & J. Byrne, 'Summary statistics on indenture and associated migration affecting the West Indies', *Population Studies*, Vol. 20, Pt. 1(1966), 127.

3   Methods of recruitment

Once landholders in the Caribbean decided on how many immigrants they needed, they sent an application to a central agency in the colony. Advertisements put out by each colony's Immigration Office inviting applications for immigrants also appeared in the colonies' newspapers. The Immigration Officer processed all applications and then sent the requests for total numbers to the Colonial Office in London. The Crown agents in London in turn passed on requests to the Emigration Office in Calcutta or Madras. Recruiting operations then started.

The Protector of Emigrants appointed recruiting agents. The agents in turn appointed sub-agents to do the actual recruiting. All recruiters had to be licensed even though unlicensed ones operated without being found out. Appointed assistants called *Kutty Maistries* in Madras and *Arkatias* in Calcutta travelled around the villages to get recruits. They were supposed to be truthful about the places to which the people would emigrate and the conditions of immigration. But of course not all recruiters were honest and many Indians agreed to emigrate on the basis of false promises.

Some people were also kidnapped. The recruiters were paid a certain sum for each person they persuaded to leave India and that is why some went to all lengths to get recruits. For example, the recruiters had a hard time filling the required number of Indian women. So at times they tricked the women they found at bazaars, markets and temples into migrating. Recruiters were paid more for females than male immigrants in order to encourage them to recruit more females. In Suriname, recruiters were paid 25 rupees to recruit an Indian man and 35 rupees for each female because they were harder to find.

Planters also told the recruiters to recruit women in the age group 25 to 30. The minimum age was 16 for children being recruited on their own and the maximum age for men could be from 30 to 35. In reality, recruiters often deliberately lied about the ages of the immigrants. Because it was difficult to get suitable recruits, especially female, they passed off quite old people as young men and women. Mr A Culver-Jones was Surgeon Superintendent of the ship *Robert Lees* which left Calcutta for Jamaica in January 1875. He complained that:

> *I am sure that many of the coolies have their ages wrongly stated. Both of the men who died of apoplexy were grey-headed and at least 50; yet their ages are stated as 29 and 39. The same is the case of others on board. Recruiters shaved the heads of the old men so that they would look younger. But their hair and beard grew back on the voyage and showed their age.*

Areas of recruitment

In the 1840s recruits came from among the Hill people of the Dhangar ethnic group, from the Chota Nagpur division of the Bengal Presidency. By the late 19th Century the main recruiting areas were the North West Provinces, Bihar, Orissa, Rajputana and the United Provinces of Agra and Oudh. Districts of recruitment included Fyzabad, Lucknow, Gonda, Basti, Sultanpore, Allahabad, Sitapore, Benares, Gorakpore and many others. Indians also came from Nepal, Central India and the Punjab.

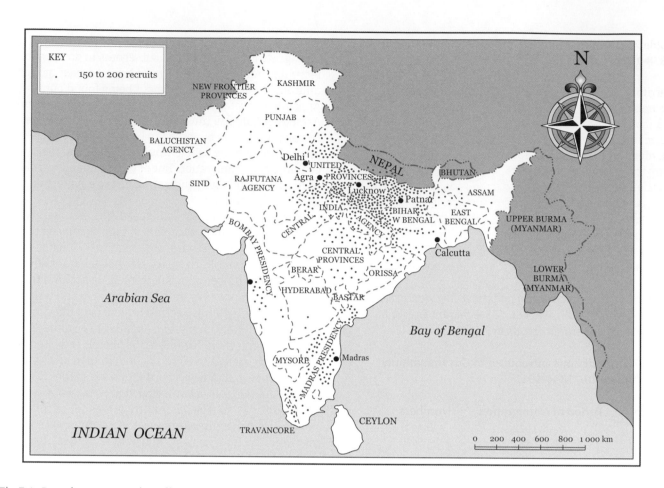

Fig 7.1 Recruitment areas in India

About 86 per cent of Indians recruited for colonial Guyana came from the Bhojpuri-Hindi speaking United Provinces (now Uttar Pradesh) and western Bihar. Only about 5 per cent came from Madras, mainly from among the Tamils, in South India. British-colonised Caribbean planters did not like these recruits and called them troublesome. Of course the workers from Madras worked well, but they tended to stand up for their rights and some planters did not like this. However, Cuban planters preferred Indian Madrasis from South India and Mauritius. They imported 68 per cent and 32 per cent Madrasis from these areas respectively. It should also be noted that South Indians themselves did not view the Caribbean as the best destination for migration. They preferred to go to countries like Ceylon, Burma and Malaysia as it was easier to return to India from these countries, closer to India than the faraway Caribbean.

The French who had owned trading stations such as Pondicherry and Karikal in South East India at first recruited workers in that area. The suppliers of these emigrants were the commercial houses of Pondicherry and, after 1856, the Emigration Society of the same town.

French recruiters also recruited from Madras, Bihar, Central Provinces and Hyderabad. But as it was easier to recruit from the more populated northern plains, they agreed with the British in 1861 to recruit there. This arrangement caused many conflicts. Firstly, the Anglo-French Convention provided that French agents could only recruit in the areas of Salem, Arcot du Sud, the provinces of Madourai and Tannevely, and the districts of Tritchinopoly and Tanjore. Bengal was tapped in times of famine when more people were willing to emigrate.

The emigrants for Suriname were recruited from the same general areas as those for the British territories. In fact the Dutch had to ask the permission of the British to begin recruitment.

4 The gender differences in Indian immigration

There were far more Indian men than women in the shipments to the Caribbean and officials moved slowly to correct this difference. In the 1850s and 1860s, the French colonies stipulated a ratio of 25 women to every 100 men. They increased this ratio in the 1860s. In 1854, only 16 per cent of the Indians shipped from Calcutta were females. In 1857 colonial Guyana had a ratio of 35 women to every 100 men and by 1860 it was 50:100. By 1855 the usual ratio set by the authorities in India and England was 33:100. After 1860 this was increased to 40:100. Despite these increases in the ratios Indian women were still outnumbered.

In 1845, there were only 28 women (15 per cent) of the 261 passengers on the first ship to Jamaica, the *Blundell Hunter*. A survey of the other ships which arrived in the British-colonised Caribbean territories after the 1880s shows that the ratios improved with there being even more females than males in some years.

Table 7.3 Legally stipulated ratio of females to males among Indians shipped to the Caribbean. (Note that the recruiters were hardly ever able to honour these ratios.)

Year	Colony	Females for every 100 males
1850s & 1860s	French Colonies	25
1855	British Colonies	33
After 1860	British Colonies	40
1872	Suriname	50 later lowered to 40

Year	Colony	Actual Female/ Male ratio
1857	colonial Guyana	35:100
1860	colonial Guyana	50:100

In Suriname, it was also noted that there were far more male than female immigrants. The 1872 treaty between the Dutch Parliament and Britain on emigration from India said that a 50:100 female-male ratio must be maintained. This was later lowered to 40:100 because it was too difficult to meet the 50:100 ratio.

Why were recruiters unable or unwilling to recruit more women?
- Planters felt that importing women was uneconomical and they did not want the added expense of childrearing.
- Planters believed that only men were 'able-bodied' labourers, despite the example from slavery where African women outnumbered men in the field gangs.
- Agents were penalised if they recruited women who were not widows or women who had run away from their husbands.
- The insistence on filling the female quota delayed ships. Women, especially married women, usually had several children with them. This usually meant more costly medical care and the threat of epidemics.
- Some agents were reluctant to take on single women. They showed a preference for those travelling as part of a family.
- Reports from India indicated that one reason for the imbalance between male and female immigrants was that it was more difficult to persuade women to emigrate. This was not necessarily because of any complaints about the indentureship system but because there were few unattached women available for emigration from India. Also, as one official put it, 'there is an objection among the vast majority of the Indian races to permit their women-folk to emigrate...'
- Usually Indian women moved only when the whole family moved.
- Indian men objected to the type of medical examination given to women at the recruitment depot in India.

5 Castes and religions of Indian immigrants

The majority of emigrants were Hindus, but there were also Muslims and Christians. Among the Hindu castes of the immigrants were Ahir, Brahmin, Chamar, Chattri, Gour, Gowala, Jat, Kahar, Rajput and Lohar. Hindu society was based on castes and each caste represented specific occupations, even though the emigration records listed the occupation of all the immigrants as 'agricultural labourers'. The Indians were goldsmiths, leatherworkers, cattle breeders, graziers, butchers, etc. Some were from the higher castes, some from the lower castes. Thirteen per cent of those who were shipped to Jamaica in 1897 were high caste Brahmins. Eighteen per cent of those who went to Trinidad between 1876 and 1885 were from the high social castes, e.g. Brahmins.

Some of the French Caribbean Indians came from the South East Tamil country and the centre of the Indo-Gangetic plain.

Did you know?
The Indo-Gangetic plain is a rich fertile land in northern and eastern India and parts of Pakistan. The plain is named after the Indus and Ganges rivers.

Some of these Brahmins said they were promised non-agricultural work when they agreed to go to the Caribbean but on arriving were expected to work in the fields. They objected and asked to be released from their contracts. Sometimes their wishes were granted. In 1913, for example, Mohabir who came to Jamaica on the ship *Indus*, complained to the Protector of Immigrants that he had been forced in India to say he was of the Kahar caste, but he was not. He asked to be released from agricultural work. The Protector agreed to do so saying that Mohabir's hands were too soft for him to have done any agricultural work previously.

6 Post-recruitment experiences

Recruits, accompanied by men called 'messengers', were taken to depôts in the areas of recruitment. They then went by train to embarkation depôts at Madras or Calcutta. Here they were medically examined to make sure they were fit for the journey to the Caribbean and for agricultural labour, before boarding ships for the journey. The women were not given as detailed an examination as the men. The surgeon superintendent of the ships often complained that this was why some women who were not healthy and fit for agricultural labour were put on the ships. Some of these doctors lamented the absence of female doctors to conduct the examination, especially as Indian men were opposed to strange male doctors examining women. Emigrants were vaccinated or revaccinated and given a certificate of emigration. They signed contracts before leaving India. In the later years of emigration, female doctors examined female recruits at the depôt in India.

7 The passage to the Caribbean

The men and women were put on board the ship once the agents were given the go-ahead to undertake the voyage and everything was ready for the ship to sail. Men and women were accommodated in different parts of the ship. Married people were separated from the single, and males separated from females. Single women were placed in the rear, followed by married people, with the single men forward. The agents tried to make sure that the ships had adequate crew, medical personnel, sweepers (called topazes) and cooks. They also tried to make sure that the crew looked after the welfare of the emigrants.

In the early years of Indian emigration, the topazes were African and African-Caribbean people. By the 20th century they were replaced by Indian topazes because of the racial tensions between African topazes and Indians.

Crew and emigrants were not allowed to mix, although this rule was not strictly enforced. There were complaints from time to time that some of the crew (African, European, Asian) sexually abused female emigrants. Between 1854 and 1860 there were also complaints against several surgeon superintendents of sexual harassment of female emigrants. These complaints included those made against Dr Wilkinson on the ship *Bucephalus*; Dr Galbraith on the *Devonshire*; Mr Simmonds on the *Royal George*; and Dr Cook on the *Assaye*, all ships bound for colonial Guyana. It is reported that the captain of the *Thetis* said that he would not bother crew who wanted to form relations with the women on board. The complaints were not only against the high-ranking officials. On the ship *Moffusilite* from Calcutta to Jamaica in 1875, George Martin, the dispenser, was suspended from duty 'for having connection with the women on board'. On the voyage of the *Sutlej* to colonial Guyana in 1912, there was a complaint that a 'young purser in service of Messrs. James Nourse (the shipping agents), failed to conduct himself properly'; that he had 'misconducted himself with one of the female emigrants on board'.

A most bizarre case was that of the 20-year-old Maharani who died on the journey from India to Guyana on the *Allanshaw* in 1885 supposedly because of the sexual abuse she suffered at the hands of sailors. There was a nine-day inquiry into her death, with 22 witnesses called. In the end no one was found to be criminally responsible.

Planters tried to make the journey more bearable by paying attention to the emigrants' medical care, accommodation and entertainment. Musical instruments were allowed on board. The emigrants were provided with combs, and the crew sometimes gave those who wanted it, rum mixed with lime and special types of pipes called chillum pipes. At times there were not enough chillum pipes and combs for the people who wanted them. In 1874 one surgeon superintendent reported that,

> *… they suffered much from want of chillums although 300 were sent on board; these things are easily broken. I tried making tin ones but they did not answer at all. They are cheap in India so more should be put on board.*

A similar complaint was made about the combs. Only 24 combs were put on board the *Chetah* on its journey to Jamaica in 1876. The Chinese carpenter on board had to make an extra 69 combs from expensive sandalwood – to the delight of the women.

Fig 7.2 The immigrant ship Allanshaw *in heavy seas*

The ships

Emigrants were shipped from the North Indian port of Calcutta in Bengal and from the South Indian port of the Madras Presidency. The route took emigrants through the Indian Ocean, around the Cape of Good Hope into the Atlantic. They entered the Caribbean from the south. Ships picked up fresh food and provisions at St Helena, Natal or the Cape Colony.

In the 19th Century the journey on sailing ships could take up to three months, while steam ships could make the voyage in one to two months. For example, the barque *Silhet* took 96 days to reach Jamaica from Calcutta in 1878. By contrast, the steam ship *Indus* left Calcutta on 27 November 1912 and arrived in Jamaica, via Trinidad, on 12 January 1913. This journey took about one-and-a-half-months.

The death rate for the voyages from India to the British Caribbean was more or less 17.8 per cent for the period 1858 to 1873. The death rate was higher on the more crowded ships sailing from Calcutta than on those sailing from Madras.

At the beginning of the 20th Century steam ships owned by the company of Messrs Nourse Ltd were used. These ships reduced the length of the journey and therefore also on the death rate on board the ships. By the 1890s the death rate for Jamaica was lower and ranged from 1 to 4 per cent. It was seldom more than 3 per cent.

The causes of death were recorded by the surgeon superintendent of each ship. The causes were hardly ever gender-specific, except in the case of suicides and deaths associated with childbirth. Pregnant women suffered from seasickness, which caused them to lose their babies. But the data show that men were more likely to commit suicide on the journey.

The more usual causes of deaths were dysentery, mumps, diarrhoea, pneumonia, phitisis and bronchitis. The surgeon superintendents suggested that infants sometimes died from maternal neglect and that some mothers were not keen to let their babies live. The report on the voyage of the *Silhet* to Jamaica shows that a nine-month-old girl was 'ill before embarkation and [was] very carelessly nursed by [her] mother', and eventually died

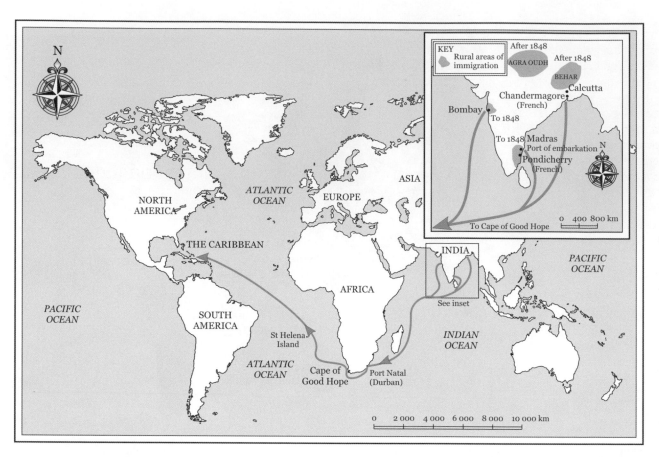

Fig 7.3 Sea route from India to the Caribbean

from dysentery. The same report said that a five-month-old baby boy, Beharer, died from dysentery also; but added: '... mother appeared to wish for death'.

When they landed in the Caribbean, immigrants were again given a medical examination. Those who were too ill to work on the estates were sent to the hospital. Those who were considered to be unfit to do agricultural labour were let off their contract and later sent back to India. The others were distributed to the plantations.

8 Immigration laws in the Caribbean

All colonies drew up immigration laws to control the conditions under which Indians were contracted, and appointed officials to supervise the system. The titles of the officials were different in different territories and, in some cases, changed over time. At first the officials were called 'Coolie' Magistrates; then Agents General of Immigrants, or Inspector of Immigrants; then Protector of Immigrants.

The laws stated that immigrants had to obey the terms of their contracts. These included that they should not drink liquor while on the estate; they should be respectful to employers; obey all orders of the landholder, not participate in resisting or rioting; and complete work which employers felt was not well done. The laws were more in favour of employers than labourers, and the contracts were not really agreements between equal parties. The law did mention the employer's responsibilities towards labourers. This included giving labourers rations, housing, medical care, wages, medical treatment and paying for repatriation.

Trinidad

The main law in Trinidad was passed in 1854. For the first ten years of immigration, Trinidad had experimented with different laws, which regularly changed. By 1850 all parties felt that certain aspects of the law had to be standardised. Landholders were not carrying out their part of the immigration laws; the death rate among the Indians was high; many deserted or became vagrants; and Britain and the local government in India were not satisfied with how the system was working. The landholders also wanted a regular system and new laws around contracts.

Trinidad had tried in the past to lay down laws, for example the 1846 Ordinance. This law was opposed by the Anti-slavery Society. Another example was Ordinance 9 in 1847. Five other Ordinances were passed between 1850 and 1853 but all lacked support from the British government. The 1854 Ordinance had more support. Perhaps this was because in this year the British government removed all protection for sugar in the British market. Britain then brought in more labour measures to help the sugar growers. The terms of the 1854 Ordinance were as follows:

- Five-year contracts with a single employer; and another two-year contract with other employers.
- Jail term for breaking the law.
- Time spent in jail was added on to the contract period.
- Labourers needed 'tickets of leave' to leave the estates during work hours. In Trinidad, leaving the estate without a pass was punishable by a fine of £5 and two months in jail.
- People whose contract time had expired always had to carry their certificate of industrial residence with them to prove they were not contracted.
- Repatriation after ten years of continuous stay in the colony except for those imported before 1 January 1854 who could still return to India after five years.
- A jail term for those supporting deserters. The Jamaican Law defined a deserter as 'any immigrant who at any time except on Sundays or on holidays or festivals is found during the ordinary hours of work at a distance of more than two miles from the estate on which he is indentured and fails to produce a certificate or exemption or a written ticket of leave signed by his employer'.
- After the first five years, labourers could sign a new contract with the same or another employer. (Jamaica abolished this in 1891.)

Jamaica

Law 23 of 1879 sought to control immigration and indentureship in Jamaica. This law improved on earlier laws and with a few changes it continued to the end of immigration. The terms of this law were closely modelled on the Trinidad and Guyanese laws. Other colonies also did this.

Suriname

Laws passed in Suriname provided that husbands and wives or parents and children (under 15) must not be separated, rather should be contracted as families. All laws provided that wages for women and children must be lower than those for male workers. Women earned an average 9d per day for a nine-hour day; men earned 1s to 1s.6d per day. Employers did not always carry out the terms of these immigration laws. The immigrants ,too, did not always keep to the laws. This was often seen as resistance to the system, which has been described as a new form of slavery.

9 Immigration and indentureship

Indian immigrants served their indentures in colonial Guyana, Belize, Grenada, Guadeloupe, Jamaica, Martinique, Guyane, St Kitts, Nevis, St Lucia, St Vincent, Suriname and Trinidad. They were contracted to those owners who had requested their services and who had partly funded their importation. The Protector or Agent-General explained the terms of their contract to them. They also saw to it that the employers signed the indenture certificate before the proper authorities and gave a written guarantee that the immigrants would receive medical care and housing.

The Indians were located on sugar plantations. In Jamaica they were also on banana plantations and in Trinidad on cocoa and coconut estates. Most of the estates were in rural areas, and so for most of the 19th and 20th Centuries the immigrant population remained rural. In Trinidad, there were immigrants in the areas of Arima, Barrackpore, Caroni, Couva, Diego Martin, Mayaro, Naparima, Princes Town and Fyzabad. In colonial Guyana, they were in Berbice, Demerara, the upper Corentyne district, New Amsterdam and areas near the Essequibo.

In Martinique, Indians settled in Saint Pierre, Basse-Point, Lamentin and Saint-Espirit. In Guadeloupe, they settled around Baillif, Moule, Basse-Terre and Capesterre. In Suriname, Nickerie was an early location of Indians.

Table 7.4 Return of Indian immigrants in the Presidency of Nevis, 1878

Estate	Employer	Number of Indians		
		Male	Female	Total
Clifton	Bovell & King	13	4	17
Spring Hill	Joseph Connell	17	10	27
Round Hill	Sir T G Briggs	29	10	39
Hamilton	Sir T G Briggs	20	9	29
Stony Grove	Sir T G Briggs	21	8	29
Tower Hill	Sir T G Briggs	22	10	32
Old Manor	Sir T G Briggs	20	6	26
Fothergill	Sir T G Briggs	19	3	22
Farm	T H Hutchinson	10	11	21
	Total	171	71	242

Table 7.5 Distribution of some of the Indians who arrived in Trinidad on the ship *Mutlah*, 1913

Proprietor	Estate	Men	Women	Boys	Girls	Infants
Tenants	Bienvenue	4	1			1
Estates Ltd.	La Fortune	4	1		1	
	Hermitage	10	4			
T'dad Estates	Caroni	13	5			
Co. Ltd	Berchin					
	Castle	12	4			
Kleinvert,	Waterloo	10	4			1
Sons & Co.	Exchange	14	5			
E.A. Robinson	Non Pariel	13	5		1	3
W.I. Estates Ltd.	Orange					
	Grove	15	5	1		

The Indians worked under contracts in all territories in which they were imported. The Dutch colonies, for example, used the same contract terms as the British. In the 1840s Indians served one-year contracts. They could re-contract after the first year, but most did not. So employers called for longer contracts. By the 1850s there were three-year contracts with the first employer and by 1862 five-year contracts with the first employer were introduced. Some landholders wanted seven-year contracts.

Indians could buy out the part of their contract that was not yet over if they wanted, but few could afford this. Initially immigrants were guaranteed fully paid return passages at the end of their contracts. At first this was after five years but later after ten years of continuous residence. Later, they had to pay a part of the cost of repatriation. Immigrants could also accept a cash or land grant instead of repatriation.

Fig 7.4 Indian immigrant family

Housing

Immigrants in some territories were housed on the estates in barrack ranges. These were long buildings divided into rooms of 120 square foot each, with a covered veranda five foot wide. The buildings had dirt floors. The houses were similar to those of slavery in Trinidad. In Jamaica some Indians lived in detached huts.

Clothes

After adjusting to the Caribbean, Indian labourers worked for nine hours a day, six days a week. Employers gave them working tools, cooking utensils and clothing. Males were given trousers made from the material Osnaburgh and shirts out of the fabric striped Holland. Females were given clothes made out of brown calico and striped Holland. In 1870 a new immigration law was passed in Jamaica. It provided that instead of each employer giving each male six yards of brown calico and each female seven yards in their first three months, they should now give a shirt and trousers of Osnaburgh to each man and boy and a jersey with sleeves and a petticoat to each girl and woman.

For the first three months the employers gave labourers rations. But after that they had to buy their own food out of their wages. Once the Indians received better medical treatment and their death rate declined, they proved beneficial to Caribbean employers who used them.

Work

At the start of the system immigrants did fixed-hour day labour. By the late 19th Century they were employed on a task-based system. They worked alone or in gangs, depending on the crop or activity; for example, field labour on the sugar estates used gangs. The hardest work was done on the sugar estates. In crop time, men and women could work up to 15 hours a day. African-Caribbean or Indian headmen, called sirdars, supervised gangs. Immigrants were placed in gangs according to age, gender and physical condition/ability.

In Jamaica, landholders gave African-Jamaicans the higher paid jobs in the field and the factory. Women and children weeded. Or, if they were very old or very young, they were placed in the invalid/convalescent 'small' gang. Indian men prepared the land for planting the crop, planted, reaped and in some cases helped in the manufacturing process of the cane. On sugar estates, women weeded and manured the canes. On banana plantations, women hoed, used machetes to weed and cut grass, forked, trenched, and carted bananas to the wharf. They also pruned the banana trees, manured, and weeded the land. Some were domestic workers on the estates.

Wages

Wages varied by territory. In the British-colonised territories, the highest wages were paid in Trinidad and colonial Guyana. In the 1840s wages in Trinidad were two shillings one pence a day, sometimes more. However, in years after this they fell due to the economic crises after the Sugar Duties Act of 1846. In the 1840s in colonial Guyana wages ranged from between one shilling four pence and two shillings per day. In the 1870s colonial Guyana and Trinidad set a minimum wage for each task, but many labourers still earned below this wage. In the 1890s in Trinidad some earned only six pence.

Planters calculated out the payment of wages by dividing work into 'heavy' and 'light' work. They gave light work to women and paid less for it. Adult male workers received more pay than adult females and children. This difference in the rate of pay according to gender was based on the misguided view that women were not equal to men and could not work as hard. This was despite the fact that women were placed in the field to do work alongside men. Men were also more likely to get skilled and supervisory positions, which paid more. So, overall, women earned less in all the colonies, generally about two-thirds of the wages earned by men.

This difference in wages for males and females was not unique to the Caribbean. In India itself, male workers were paid more than female workers. But generally the wages paid in India to agricultural labourer were lower than in the Caribbean.

At the end of the first three months of their contracts, workers and employers could agree to task and not day labour. This meant that if workers could finish more than one task in a day, they could earn higher wages.

In some territories, for example in Suriname, wages on sugar estates were lower than on other types of estates. Around 1920 wages for immigrants in Suriname rose to 80 cents for men and 60 cents for women. Women and children often had to join the weeding gangs and so their wages were low.

All wages had to be paid in cash, not in kind, and employers could not make any deductions, except for rations. The law said that if employers did not pay the wages or paid them late for any reason, they would be fined not more than £5. But there is evidence that wages were not always paid on time, and that employers were not fined for this. There is also evidence that workers did not always get the minimum wages fixed by law. For example, in 1909, Ramadhin of Bog Estate in Jamaica wrote to the Protector of Immigrants as follows:

> I send to make you know that I can't even make 3/-per week. Then how must we live dear sir?

The Protector of Immigrants was warned that an investigation must be undertaken and improvements made otherwise, 'it will bring some great trouble'. To avoid paying them full and proper wages employers used the excuse that the immigrants were lazy. In 1913, two Indian officials, sent to investigate working conditions among Indians, confirmed that many immigrants in Jamaica were paid below the minimum rates.

Re-indentureship

One feature of the indentureship system was re-indentureship. Many workers signed new five-year contracts after the expiration of their first contract, although not always with the same employer. Many landholders preferred to hire ex-indentured workers as they had already been trained. Employers also hired workers whose contracts had expired but who did not wish to sign new contracts. These workers were called time-expireds. The Protector of Immigrants for Jamaica noted in 1910/11 that:

> There is great demand for his services when he has completed his five year's indenture and becomes an experienced agricultural labourer, and he is always able to find suitable and remunerative employment without entering into any further period of indenture.

To encourage the ex-contract workers to settle and work near the estate, planters in Trinidad and colonial Guyana sold them small plots of land when their contract ended. This was the beginning of the development of the Indian peasantry as well as of Indian villages like Fyzabad, Madras and Amity in Trinidad. In these villages the Indians rebuilt parts of their culture. This system never developed as well in Jamaica and Windward Islands.

10 Employers disobey the terms of the law

Employers did not always keep to the laws that set out their responsibilities towards the immigrants. We have seen how employers tried to escape their responsibilities towards the Indians in terms of their work load and wages. They neglected the immigrants' medical care and they did not always give them adequate housing. This led to a high rate of illness and death.

Immigration officials or legal personnel tried to make sure that the immigrants' welfare was looked after, but employers often harassed them. This happened to James Crosby, a magistrate, William Des Voeux and the Chief

Justice Joseph Beaumont – all of colonial Guyana who complained of the poor treatment of the Indians.

The Governor transferred Des Voeux to St Lucia and Beaumont lost his position. Crosby's allowance was stopped.

However, from time to time there were attempts to improve the labour conditions and the terms of the relevant laws. For example, after 1870 employers who were convicted of offences against the immigrants had to pay a fine. At the same time, workers' fines were reduced significantly.

There were also sensitive officials who tried to discipline uncooperative employers. Uncooperative employers also included female estate owners. For example, Mr Havelock, Administrator of St Lucia, was forced to remove 17 Indians employed on Ms Augier's estate because she had neglected their welfare. In his letter to her dated 8 November 1878, Havelock wrote:

> Madam,
> I regret to state that during the last three months I have received frequent reports both from the Protector of Immigrants and from the Medical Officer of the District of your neglect to comply with the necessary requirements as to the providing of suitable quarters in a healthy site for the Indian coolies indentured on Chue estate.

Other reports showed that Ms Augier's neglect had caused long periods of hospitalisation of the Indians at the public expense. Reports also said that some Indians 'are frequently to be seen at all hours of the day wandering about the public roads and even begging'. The Secretary of State approved of the removal of Ms Augier's workers by the Administrator and the Protector of Immigrants.

There were other immigration officials in the colonies who tried to be fair to the Indians and see that the neglect of the managers and employers did not go unnoticed. Major James Fagan of Trinidad and Robert Duff of colonial Guyana were known for their criticism of planter neglect of the Indians. And in 1897 Commander Coombs of Trinidad charged an influential manager, Peter Abel, for the physical abuse of six Indian labourers. He had tied them together with a rope as a disciplinary measure. Abel was found guilty and fined £60.

11 Indian resistance

Indian men and women did not accept estate abuses and the breaking of the laws without putting up some resistance. They resented the almost total control that employers had over them. They also resented the laws that were biased against them, for example the strict pass laws; how the employment contract made them into criminals rather than an equal party; the poor wages; the late payment of wages; the sexual and physical abuse; the delayed repatriation; and the inadequate provisions for their welfare.

Indians used different resistance strategies to show their dissatisfaction. These strategies included sabotaging and undermining plantation production through strikes and other forms of non-violent resistance. They deserted the estates, failed to honour work regulations, criticised the indentureship system openly, pretended they were ill, committed suicide, bought themselves out of their contracts, demonstrated, and went on strike. Some physically assaulted estate personnel who abused them.

As early as 1847, just two years after the first group of Indians arrived in Jamaica, they went on strike for improved wages and working conditions. There were eighteen strikes in Jamaica between 1847 and 1921. One of the more notable strikes was in 1907 on Moreland Estate in the parish of St James. It was caused by the fact that employers illegally deducted money from workers' wages. All the contract servants stopped working and attacked the estate personnel with sticks, stones and whatever weapons they could find. The Protector was called in to settle the strike.

The Leonora Estate protests in August 1869 in colonial Guyana are well-documented. Protests and acts of physical violence also spread to Plantations La Jalousie, Malgre, Tout, Enterprise and Mahaicony. Armed police and military personnel were sent in to stop the protests. A Commission of Enquiry led by Sir George Young was appointed. It recommended several changes to the indentureship system after 46 witnesses had given evidence about the many negative aspects of it.

There were also strikes in Trinidad. It is estimated that between 1870 and 1901 there were 52 strikes, with seven happening in 1882, six in 1883 and twelve in 1884. As in other territories the main causes of these strikes were grievances about too many tasks, forced labour on holidays and reduced wages. These strikes were confined to the estates and so did not involve an armed struggle with the police. The 'Hosein riots' in 1884, which involved a clash with police, started as a religious procession. Strikes and other forms of resistance continued until the end of the immigrant system.

There were eight strikes in 1916: three at Orange Grove, two at Non Pareil and one each at Waterloo, Camden and Caroni. In 1917, the last year of importation to Trinidad, a strike took place on Plantation La Bonne Intention. David Clarke, manager of the estate, wrote in a letter to the Agent-General of Immigration, RP Stewart on Feb. 10, 1917:

Sir,
As you are aware, a strike amongst the indentured immigrants occurred here towards the latter part of September and beginning of October which, when at an end, still made itself felt by a continuance amongst several members of the striking community of an utter disregard to order and discipline.

In the French-colonised Caribbean territories, the immigrants also resisted. Indians deserted the estates, refused to work, set fire to the estates, and went on strike for better conditions. In 1861, four Indians in Guadeloupe burned the bagasse hut and a piece of cane land. They then tried to burn down the purifying plant. In 1869 the Attorney General for Guadeloupe reported that out of 31 accusations for arson, eight were Creoles and 23 were Indians.

There were other ways in which immigrants dealt with indentureship. Some people, mainly males, committed suicide because of the conditions of indentureship. Barachue from Orange Hill State in Jamaica took his life because of 'despondency owing to money losses and prosecution before the resident magistrate for malingering'.

Indians also took employers to court, but it was more likely for immigrants than employers to be convicted as the courts worked in favour of employers. Dutch historian Pieter Emmer records that in the period 1873-1916, only 10 per cent of employers charged with breaking the immigration law were convicted. We can compare this to 71.4 per cent of workers who were convicted in Suriname for alleged misdemeanors.

12 The end of Indian immigration and indentureship

By 1917, all Caribbean territories had discontinued Indian indentured labour migration and by 1922 all Indians were free of their indentured contracts. The last shipments of immigrants reached colonised Guyana and Trinidad in 1917, but some territories had ended this system sooner: St Vincent in 1880, Grenada in 1885, St Lucia in 1893, and Jamaica in 1916.

There were several reasons why the system ended. One reason was that the sugar estates continued to decline in the Windward Islands. Other economic activities were undertaken and this removed the need for imported plantation labourers.

In addition, during the World War I (1914-1918), which Barbadian scholar George Lamming calls the First European Civil War, the navy needed the immigrant ships,

and, as a result, few ships with contract labourers reached the Caribbean. In any case, war conditions made any transatlantic voyage dangerous. Another reason was that Indians were recruited to serve in the war effort. Yet another reason was that planters expected costs to rise after World War I, making it more expensive to recruit, ship and maintain the depots and the agencies in India. Recruiting costs had already increased from just over £3 per head in 1903 to £7 in 1915. Shipping rates were to go to £18 per head after the war; and planters would have to pay as much as £29 to import each adult Indian. Most planters were not prepared to pay these costs.

There was also increasing opposition in India and in the colonies against the continued exportation of its people for labour. Opposition came from Mahatma Gandhi and other influential leaders, as well as from other sections of the Indian population. From the 1870s to 1913, Surgeon Major Comins, Chimman Lal, James McNeil and the Sanderson Commission had investigated the conditions of the Indians in the Caribbean. None of them recommended abolition of the system, but had suggested improvements.

The anti-slavery society in Britain, Indian officials in India and local church and secular groups in the colonies had also called for the end of immigration and indentureship, which they labelled 'a new system of slavery'. The anti-slavery society was outraged by the abuses of the early immigrants on Belle Vue Estate in colonial Guyana – part of the Gladstone experiment; the conditions of poverty of the ex-indentureds in Jamaica; and the low status of workers. They criticised indentureship and saw it as slavery revived. They argued that the living and working conditions, and the recruitment and shipment of Indians was similar to that of the slave trade and slavery. They said that the way people lived and worked, and their lack of access to power was the same as a slave society. How true were these accusations?

The Indian National Congress and opposition from India

The Indian National Congress was formed in 1885 to press for greater self-government by the people of India. Their work, and the work of C F Andrews, W W Pearson, Mahatma Gandhi and Gopal Gokhale, was important in ending immigration, indentureship and in some cases repatriation. The Congress especially fought for the end of indentureship and repatriation. In fact, the state of the returnees convinced Ghandi and others that immigration should end. They felt that Indians in the Caribbean should receive land grants and be helped to settle on the land in the Caribbean.

Fig 7.5 Mahatma Gandhi

The government of India was particularly opposed to the repatriation of the ill, disabled and poverty-stricken Indians. These people had no means of support in India and could not last long on the 50 rupees each that the government gave them when they arrived. E G Turner of the India Office, writing to the Under-Secretary of State in the Colonial Office stressed in 1933 that:

> ... it will be observed that the Government of India consider that if possible steps should be taken to discourage the return of emigrants who though entitled to government assistances regards their return passages have neither sufficient resources to support themselves nor can give satisfactory evidence that they have relatives or friends in India willing to look after them.

The government and people of India were particularly opposed to the emigration of women unless they were going as part of a family.

Such opposition as well as the failure to improve the emigration system after the end of World War I meant the end of the system. After this the majority of Indians settled in the Caribbean, leading productive lives and contributing greatly to the economic, social and political development of the region.

A new system of slavery?

Joseph Beaumont was Chief Justice of colonial Guyana from 1863 to 1868. He was removed from office because of his empathy for the cause of the Indians. In 1871, he wrote 'The New Slavery'. Hugh Tinker later took up this theme in his book *A New System of Slavery*. Beaumont called Indian indentureship the new slavery because, he said, indentureship was not simply a matter of,

> *an occasional defect here or excuses there but it is that of a monstrous rotten system rooted upon slavery, grown in its stale soil, emulating its worst abuses and only the more dangerous because it presents itself under false guise, whereas slavery had a brand of infamy obviously displayed upon its forehead.*

He said that many Indians were brought to the Caribbean against their will, with some being kidnapped, just like the enslaved Africans. Indians were kept in depôts, were shipped in cramped quarters, female Indians were sexually abused by the crew and were subjected to harsh conditions of labour in the Caribbean. Indians were not housed, fed nor medically treated adequately, so that the death rate was high in some territories. They lacked proper sanitary facilities and had to follow a wide range of rules. If they broke these, then they were fined and imprisoned. They were not free to move without passes and were fixed to the estates by restrictive contracts.

The Indian family was also under constant threat. This was because Indian women were sexually abused by employers and managers and because of the gender inequalities in migration schemes. These caused competition for scarce Indian women and caused violence against women.

But, unlike slavery, there were no wars which resulted in death and disruption of family life to capture Indians. More care was taken on the voyages from India with better conditions on board and lower death rates. And no Indian was thrown overboard to lighten the overcrowded ships. There was also a major legal difference between indentureship and slavery: Indians were not owned as property. Under the law the labour of the worker was purchased, and the labourer himself/herself did not belong to the landholder.

Indians were paid a wage, no matter how small and did not have to work the kind of hours worked by the enslaved. The status of indentureship, unlike that of slavery, was not automatically passed on from female immigrants to their children. Indians were allowed to keep their culture. Where there were families, they were not separated but kept together on the same estates. Children

Fig 7.6 Indian women cooking

were not removed from their mothers and forced to move to another property.

The Commission appointed in colonial Guyana after the Leonora protests of 1869, concluded in 1871 that, unlike enslaved people, the Indians had civil rights. However, the differences between indentureship and slavery should not be used to underestimate the exploitation and humiliation that people suffered under the indentureship system.

13 Post-indentureship experiences

Repatriation

At first Indians were guaranteed a free return passage by their contract, unlike enslaved Africans and most other immigrants to the Caribbean. But this was not always honoured. It was not until 1853 that immigrants from colonial Guyana and Jamaica's first groups were returned to India, although they should have returned in 1850. By 1895 those immigrants who were not sick and disabled were asked to pay a part of the cost of their return passage. Men had to pay 25 per cent and women 17 per cent. This was doubled in 1898 to 50 per cent for men and 35 per cent for women.

In Jamaica and colonial Guyana the wives and children of returning immigrants would travel for free, but not in Trinidad. Many could not afford the money to subsidise their passage back to India. Whereas the passage from Mauritius cost £2 per head, that from the Caribbean cost £15. So while free repatriation from Mauritius was discontinued in 1851, free/assisted repatriation was kept on in the Caribbean. Indians were given the choice of accepting 10 acres of Crown land or £12 cash instead of a return passage. Up to 1879, most accepted the cash grant in Jamaica. Between 1845 and 1848, 1,467 immigrants accepted land or cash instead of return passages.

Up to 1877 Jamaica had spent £32,000 on cash or land grants. They removed the choice of a cash grant in 1879 and the land grants in 1906. This was because the cost of the land grant (£12 per head) was becoming just as expensive as the cost of the return passages (£15 per head). The price of a return passage was still higher than most Indians could afford, so the authorities did not have to offer them land to get them to stay in the Caribbean as they could not afford to go back to India anyway.

At first immigrants could go back to India after five years. But after a while, only those from the French-colonised territories could go back to their homeland after five years. Those from the British-colonised territories could only go back after 10 years.

Some territories allowed Indians to claim their return passages up to two years after they had become due. The planters preferred the Indians to stay and work in the Caribbean and so they tried everything in their power not to send them back. Some immigrants did not go back because they had found permanent partners and settled down. Some were afraid of a second voyage. Others feared ridicule in India because they had crossed the dark waters (*Kala pani*) and had become outcasts and had not become rich, as they had hoped.

Nevertheless, approximately 38 per cent of Indians returned from Jamaica, 32 per cent from colonial Guyana, 30.5 per cent from Suriname, 38 per cent from the British Windward Islands, 18 per cent from Guadeloupe, 22 per cent from Trinidad, and 20 per cent from Martinique. About 23.4 per cent of the Javanese returned to their homeland from Suriname. The French-colonised Caribbean had the lowest return figure. This was because those who chose to re-indenture could not also claim repatriation.

14 Emigration to third countries

Officials in India and the Caribbean were consistently opposed to the Indians emigrating from the Caribbean to third countries, and placed many obstacles in their way. These obstacles were in addition to the other obstacles that the immigrants had to face. For example, Gov. Musgrave showed his opposition to the presence of recruiting agents from Cuba who came to Jamaica to persuade Indians to re-emigrate there. A year earlier, Lieutenant Gov. Dundas of St Lucia forwarded a letter from Captain Havelock, Inspector of Immigrants, to the Secretary of States, Hicks Beach. In the letter Havelock made it clear that he opposed the unauthorised deportation of East Indians from St Lucia to Cuba.

The Indian population of St Lucia was far smaller than Jamaica's. In 1878, it was only about 400 and so there was great concern about labour shortages. The government in India ruled that Indians should not be allowed to leave the territory of their first location except to return to India. This was unless the Indians could prove that they could support themselves on their own in a third country.

Despite what the landowners wanted, the Immigration Law made provisions for those immigrants who wished to re-emigrate. Between 1913 and 1930, 2,011 immigrants left Jamaica – mainly for Cuba, Panama and other Central American destinations. Indians who wanted to emigrate had to get permission from the Governor as well as clearance from the Immigration Department before they could get a passport. Anyone who tried to leave without a passport was fined.

The Immigration Department in Trinidad reported that 47 passports were issued in 1914 for Indians to emigrate to Venezuela (36), colonial Guyana (7), Grenada, Jamaica and Suriname. Those found guilty of tricking Indians to leave the British Caribbean could be fined £20.

Before 1906, Indians in Jamaica were told that if they decided to emigrate to a third country, they would lose their right to land instead of repatriation to India. They were also told that they had to give up their right to the protection of the British Consul in the countries to which they emigrated.

Certain countries were considered prohibited destinations for Indians and it was illegal for them to sign contracts to work in these countries. Cuba, close to Jamaica and a long-standing destination for Jamaican workers, was one of the earliest prohibited places. However, everyone consistently ignored the ban. The prohibition was eventually lifted in 1905 as there was a need for workers in the sugar mills of the Guantanamo Valley.

Other prohibited places were Mexico, Ecuador and Guatemala. Despite the ban, agents from these countries tried to trick Indians to emigrate. The United Fruit Company, for example, tried to recruit Indians for their plantations in Guatemala. Agents from Mexico recruited Indians for work at Coatzocoalcos. This was one of the terminal harbours for the proposed Interoceanic railway. And, in the early 20th Century, J P McDonald, the contractor in charge of the Guayaquil to Quito railroad in Ecuador, tried to recruit labourers for this project.

After 1930 Indian re-emigration lessened because of restrictive immigration policies, war conditions and the unfavourable economic climate in Cuba, Panama and elsewhere during the post-war depression.

To sum up

Planters in the Caribbean imported additional labourers, mostly from India, to solve the labour crisis primarily in the sugar industry after the abolition of slavery. Colonial Guyana pioneered the scheme, and between 1838 and 1917 imported most of the Indians who came to the Caribbean. Indians served under indentureship contracts, but resisted when contract terms were flouted by employers. While there were no fresh importations after 1917, indentureship itself (the system of contract labour) ended in 1922; for those imported in 1917 had to complete their five year contract.

Revision questions

1. Read the passage and answer the questions that follow:

   Despite its usefulness to Caribbean planters, the system of indentured servitude imposed great hardships on the immigrants, especially on women whose numbers were not as large as the numbers of the male immigrants. Indentured servitude has often been referred to as a new system of slavery.

   a State two reasons why male Indians outnumbered female Indian immigrants on the Caribbean plantations.

   b Give three 'great hardships' which indentured servitude imposed on female immigrants specifically.

2. How true is it to say the passage of Indians from India was just like the Middle Passage?

Chapter 8

Chinese, Javanese and other arrivals

'One love, one heart, let's get together and feel alright.'
(Bob Marley)

Introduction

Two other major groups of Asian immigrants who were relocated to the Caribbean were the Chinese and Javanese. The main Caribbean countries that imported Chinese labourers were Cuba, colonial Guyana, Jamaica and Trinidad. Chinese contract labourers also went to the French and Dutch-colonised Caribbean and Puerto Rico. Cuba imported Chinese labourers even before it abolished slavery. There were also other groups who came to the Caribbean – the Javanese (from Indonesia), Japanese and Annamites (from Cochin China or Vietnam in South East Asia).

In this chapter we will concentrate on Chinese immigration to the Caribbean; and briefly look at the other immigrants. Finally we will bring together the theme of the past three chapters by summarising the effectiveness of immigration and its impact on the economy of the region – in particular the sugar industry.

In this chapter we will learn about:
1 Destinations and numbers of Chinese imported
2 Chinese women and emigration
3 The Chinese as contract labourers
4 The end of Chinese immigration
5 Javanese, Annamites, Japanese and Yucatecans
6 Indian immigration versus other scheme in retrospect
7 The impact of immigration

Chinese temple

1 Destinations and numbers of Chinese imported

In 1846 the Council for Economic Development in Cuba entered into an agreement with Zulueta and Company to import 600 Chinese, in the age group 15 to 40, for 8-year contracts. In 1847, 571 Chinese actually arrived in Cuba. Each person cost the Council 170 pesos of which the planters paid back 70 pesos.

International protests and local difficulties led to Chinese immigration to Cuba being stopped until 1853. Then more Chinese were imported at a cost of 125 pesos each. By 1861 Cuba had 34,834 Chinese. They made up 2 per cent of the total population. In 1877 the number increased to 53,811 or 3 per cent of the population. Between 1853 and 1874, 150,000 Chinese were imported into Cuba.

Puerto Rico was the other Spanish-colonised island to try to get support for Chinese immigrants. In 1875 the *Sociedad de Agricultura* of Poncé petitioned the government for the introduction of Chinese. The petition was ignored because of reports coming out of Cuba regarding planters' problems with Chinese labourers.

In the British-colonised Caribbean, Chinese immigration was proposed in Trinidad in 1806, even before the abolition of slavery. It was again proposed in 1843, but no Chinese were imported until the 1850s. The reason was that the British legislative had banned the importation of workers who signed contracts before they arrived in the Caribbean and the Chinese would not agree to leave their country without contracts. Chinese immigration into the British-colonised Caribbean only began in earnest in the 1850s, first to Trinidad in 1853/4, then to colonial Guyana and then to Jamaica.

Historian Walton Look Lai notes that 50 vessels with Chinese immigrants came to the British-colonised territories in the 19th Century; 39, sailing directly from China, went to colonial Guyana, eight to Trinidad, two to Jamaica (plus two from Panama), and one to British Honduras (Belize). These ships sailed from Amoy, Canton, Hong Kong and Swatow. The direct shipment from China to Jamaica in 1854 was from Namoa and Whampoa.

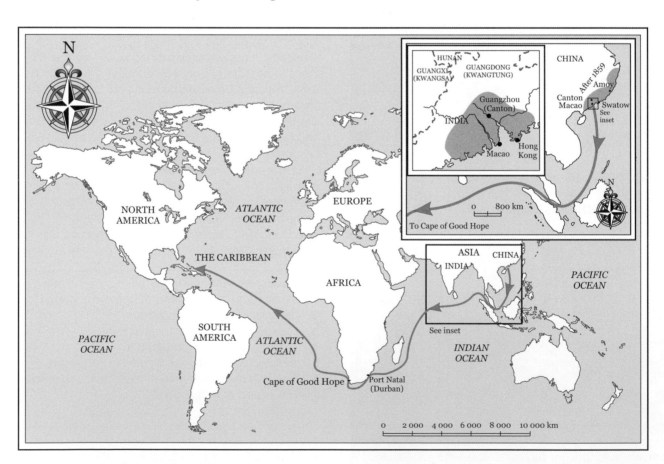

Fig 8.1 *The route from China to the Caribbean*

Chapter 8 | *Chinese, Javanese and other arrivals*

The scheme was abandoned in 1854 because of the high death rate and the expense of importing the Chinese. It was restarted in 1858 when two shipments reached colonial Guyana with 761 immigrants. By that time the British had occupied Canton and it was fairly easy to get Chinese from the ports of Canton and Hong Kong. Between 1859 and 1866, colonial Guyana received 11,282 Chinese and Trinidad 1,557.

The French-colonised Caribbean showed interest in Chinese immigration in the mid-1850s. The first shipload of Chinese reached Guadeloupe in 1855. About 1,000 Chinese went to Martinique and 500 to Guadeloupe. The Dutch-colonised Caribbean territory of Suriname also tried to see if Chinese immigration would solve their labour shortage and imported 2,502 of these workers. But as in the rest of the Caribbean, the Chinese in Suriname generally preferred the retail trade and commercial occupations.

Table 8.1	Number of Chinese immigrants: 1853 to 1884
Colonial Guyana	13,533
Trinidad	2,645
Jamaica	1,152
Suriname	2,502
Antigua	100
Cuba	150,000
Martinique	1,000
Guadeloupe	500

Source: Walton Look Lai, *Indentured Labor, Caribbean Sugar*, 42-49; K.O. Laurence, *Immigration into the West Indies*, 26-43.

2 Chinese women and emigration

After the 1860s most colonies tried to have 10 per cent of women on each shipment of Chinese immigrants. Spain insisted that 20 per cent of Chinese immigrants to Cuba should be female, but it was just about impossible to get Chinese women to leave China. Recruiters often resorted to bribes, deception and other fraudulent methods to get Chinese women – but usually without success. Many Chinese men hoped to do well in the colonies and return home so they did not take their wives with them. For many Chinese, the further they went, for example to Latin America, the less likely it was that they would return. So the women did not want to take the journey. These factors contributed to the low female emigration from China. In all, a mere 1 per cent of Chinese immigrants to the Caribbean were women.

Even though Chinese men were paid a bonus of 20 pounds sterling for wives taken to the British-colonised territories, still the percentage of Chinese women remained way below that of Indian women. Between 1859 and 1866, 2,000 Chinese women came to colonial Guyana. At the height of their immigration to colonial Guyana in 1863, there were only 13.64 women for every 100 men. In 1880, there were only 25.7 women for every 100 men; and in 1884 when the scheme ended, a little over 3,000 Chinese women had been imported.

From 1862 to 1866, about 309 Chinese women landed in Trinidad in five ships. The first Chinese women to arrive in Trinidad came on the *Wanata* in 1862. They came from the Cantonese Delta area. There were 124 women and one girl. Of this number 115 were formally located on the estates, not as contract workers, but officially as companions or wives of the males. Within a year, 104 had deserted. In 1866, 597 Chinese arrived alive on the *Riding Hood* and *Dudbrook* from Amoy to Trinidad. Only six females came on the *Riding Hood* and one on the *Dudbrook*. They were mainly urban dwellers, not used to agricultural labour. The female who came from Amoy on the *Dudbrook*, had travelled with 271 men.

In 1865 there was one shipment of Chinese who arrived in British Honduras from Amoy on the *Light of Age*. There were 474 immigrants, including 14 women and two girls.

3 The Chinese as contract labourers

In Cuba, the majority of Chinese were absorbed by plantations in Matanzas, Cárdenas and Colón, Flor de Cuba, San Martín and Santa Susana on eight-year contracts. African-Cubans did mainly the field and mill work. Male immigrants mostly did the more specialised, industrial tasks. The Chinese were paid four pesos a month for men and three pesos for women. This was much lower than the rate paid to non-contracted unskilled labourers in Cuba, which ranged between 17 and 25 pesos a month. According to the laws that governed their presence in Cuba, in addition to their wages, the immigrants were supposed to receive food, shelter, two sets of clothes each year and medical care. Wages were not to be suspended if they were ill for less than 15 days. The laws prohibited flogging, and made sure that workers had a right to marry, to family life and to property. But laws also made re-indenture or re-contracting compulsory and limited the movements of the immigrants.

Fig 8.2 *Chinese immigrants*

Many of the Chinese were poorly treated in Cuba and the death rate therefore was high. From 1844 to 1860, 75 per cent of them died. It was no surprise that some of them ran away from the estates and got involved in other resistance strategies.

In the British-colonised Caribbean, Chinese women were not legally required to enter into contracts, unlike Indian women and Chinese men. They signed only contracts of residence, which bound them to a particular estate for a fixed period of time. They were not required to do any plantation work at all, although researchers have found cases in which Chinese women chose to do field work.

A report from the Agent General of Immigrants (AGI) in Trinidad stated that 380 Cantonese men and 205 women arrived on the ships *Montrose* and *Paria* in 1865. One planter who employed some of those on the *Paria* noted that they were eager to work as soon as they arrived.

The AGI noted that, 'when Saturday night came around, and the women saw their husbands receiving payment of the wages they had earned, they too expressed a wish to be sent into the field, which was of course readily complied with'. According to Look Lai, the newspaper, the *Port of Spain Gazette*, reported that, 'this is the only instance, we believe, of Chinese female

immigrants here voluntarily offering themselves for fieldwork. In Demerara the Chinese women cannot be induced to perform any labor at all in the field'.

Chinese women were expected to work in Belize. Those who arrived on the ship *Light of Age* in 1865 were expected to do tree-felling, so not only the men were expected to work.

4 The end of Chinese immigration

Chinese immigration to the Caribbean did not last as long as Indian immigration. Among the reasons for the stoppage of Chinese immigration were the reports of their poor treatment in Cuba. It was reported that they were flogged and put in shackles, leg irons and the stocks. Other reasons included: the high cost of transporting them to the Caribbean (425 pesos each to Cuba by 1874); the shortage of women; the absence of return passages; French and Spanish competition with the British for Chinese immigrants; the greater importance of Indian immigrants in the British- and French-colonised Caribbean and Suriname; and the possibility for the

Chinese to find work nearer home or, later, in the United States of America.

There were additional reasons specific to Cuba. After the abolition of slavery, Cuba increasingly moved towards free European labourers instead of Asians. In the late 19th and early 20th Centuries ex-indentured Indians and African-Caribbean peoples increasingly emigrated to Cuba. For the British-colonised Caribbean, Chinese immigration was expensive and, in addition, the workers left the estates for other activities as soon as they could, thereby reducing the labour force. So, attempts to import Chinese labourers were abandoned by 1885, especially in the light of the more important Indian immigration, which continued until 1917.

Finally, there were anti-Chinese emigration protests in China in places like Shanghai, Hong Kong and Macao. In the colonies, too, the workers protested against their terrible conditions of servitude.

5   Javanese, Annamites, Japanese and Yucatecans

The other groups who came to the Caribbean were the Javanese, Japanese and the Annamites from Cochin China. The Javanese came specifically to Dutch Suriname as the Dutch-colonised Java. This meant that there were no political barriers to Javanese emigrating. Between 1874 and 1931, just over 32,000 Javanese emigrated to Suriname.

From 1890 to 1931, 37 per cent of the Javanese imported were female. Female immigrants from Java were often tricked into emigration by promises of marriage to Javanese men on the plantations. Some were kidnapped and many below the age of 16 years were recruited, although this was against the regulations. The Javanese women who came to the Caribbean consisted of women skilled in batik craft; and others were maids and nannies.

Javanese immigrants worked under indentured contracts like the Indians and Chinese. The immigration of the Javanese people was stopped in 1931. About 25 per cent returned to Java. So, fewer Javanese returned home than Indians (33 per cent returned to India). The greater tendency of the Javanese to remain in the Caribbean was one reason why planters liked them as workers. Two other groups of people came to the Caribbean: Annamites and Japanese. About 272 Annamites reached Guadeloupe and in 1894, 500 Japanese were imported to that territory.

The Cuban Carlos Tolm was the first to lead the immigration of 175 contract labourers from Yucatán to Cuba in 1849. After this 75 Yucatecan prisoners soon followed. The Governor of Yucatán sold them for 25 pesos each. Some of them came voluntarily, others were kidnapped. According to historian Lucia Lamounier, up to 1859 about 2,000 Yucatecans arrived in Cuba.

6   Indian immigration versus other schemes in retrospect

Why did Indian immigration prove to be the most significant and long-lasting scheme of them all? A number of factors help to explain it.

- India was under British rule and so there were fewer political obstacles in the way of emigration, compared to Chinese and African emigration.
- Indians were employed under longer contracts and remained in the Caribbean for ten years before they could legally claim a return passage to India. They could of course pay their own way and return earlier, but few could afford this.
- The owners did not have to pay for all the costs of Indian immigration. The colonial taxes contributed a percentage of the cost.
- Wages paid to the Indians, particularly to the women, were low, as planters could give better paying jobs to Black people whom most planters preferred for some tasks, such as factory tasks.
- The terms of contract included clauses limiting the movement of the Indians so they were virtually imprisoned on the estates and planters were assured of a resident force of labourers.

7   The impact of immigration

So far, we have established that after slavery workers emigrated to the Caribbean, generally because there was a demand for labour in the dominant sugar plantation economy. It is now left for us to summarise the effectiveness of immigration and its impact on the economy of the region – in particular the sugar industry. There were five main aims of immigration. We will revisit each of these to examine the extent to which they were met.

To change the African-European population ratio
Through the importation of European immigrants there was an attempt to change the African-European ratio in the Caribbean. However, Europeans were imported in too few numbers. Also they could not be imported at a fast enough rate to make up for the freed people withdrawing their labour. The famine in Madeira had made some people emigrate to the Caribbean, but once the famine was over very few people wanted to go to the Caribbean. The wages they were offered were too low to be attractive.

Also, there was inadequate provision for accommodation and health care for them in the colonies. So the few thousand European immigrants who were brought in had no dramatic effect on the numbers of White people. Not only was it difficult to recruit European and Portuguese from Madeira, but the death rate among those who came was also very high. In addition, many left the properties on which they were indentured. For example, in colonial Guyana and Trinidad the Portuguese immigrants saved their money and within three years of arrival usually left the estates. Despite this, the planters thought that the Portuguese from Madeira were good workers.

In the French territories, at first there were good reports on the Europeans. One Governor noted that,

> the intelligent and active work of these newcomers has been a happy example for the cultivators of several neighbouring plantations not wishing to remain behind in what the foreigners could do.

But not too long after this, Governor Fieron in Guadeloupe, was calling the Europeans 'weakly, overworked and beaten up'. Workers were asking to go home and their death rate was high. This made them unsuitable workers as far as the French landholders were concerned. The Governor-General finally admitted that, 'European immigration to which all the planters were so enthusiastically attached after emancipation, now encounters only doubt and apprehension'.

To alter the balance between land and population

Another aim of immigration was to alter the balance between land and population. Again, to achieve this, planters would have had to import immigrants in significant numbers. We have already seen that European immigrants could not be imported in large enough numbers. The same applied to immigrants from the other Caribbean Islands. Their governments put obstacles in the way of their emigration. Black people from Nassau and North America could not be tempted to go to the Caribbean because of low wages offered, and neither could Africans be tempted. By the mid-1860s the flow of 'liberated' Africans had dried up as the transatlantic trade in Africans ended. Free emigration from the Kroo Coast and Sierra Leone could not successfully attract the numbers required. The Chinese were far away and too expensive to import. And even though Indians were numerically the most important, they too had little effect on the balance between land and population in the period before 1876. In any case, Indian labourers had to remain within the boundaries of the sugar estates and could not move out.

To build up a pool of labourers and create competition for jobs and lower wage rates

The above aims were all related, and to achieve any of them depended on importing large numbers of labourers. None of these aims was achieved in Jamaica and the British Windwards. Although many freed people emigrated to these territories, the immigrants were still a small percentage of the total population up to the end of indentureship. However, there was some success in Trinidad and colonial Guyana after 1850. By 1865, Trinidad, for example, had already imported close to 30,000 Indians. Wages rose in Trinidad between 1860 and the 1880s, but unfortunately a sharp fall in the industry in the late 1880s caused wages to drop again.

In colonial Guyana, wage rates rose after 1870 because more labourers were needed to expand production. The European market needed sugar because the European beet crop had failed. By 1879 the number of labourers had again been built up and this drove wages down. The wages paid to British Caribbean immigrants in Puerto Rico and Santo Domingo were higher than in their home countries. In 1916, unskilled workers in Santo Domingo were paid between two shillings and six pence and four shillings a day.

Carpenters, blacksmiths, engine drivers and mill mechanics received even higher wages, 5s to 8s a day. However, these wages were still lower than the wages local workers were demanding. This was exactly what the landholding class wanted. The reaction of the local labourers was to accuse immigrants of weakening their bargaining power. The French territories also reported that at first immigration drove the local labourers back to the estates and kept their wages down.

To restore planter control over labour

Control of workers could be guaranteed by strict legislation, long contracts and forcing people to live on the estates. But up to 1847 the British government did not allow labour contracts to be signed once immigrants were inside the colonies. After 1847 they allowed one-year contracts to be signed in the colonies and in 1850 they introduced three-year contracts. Not all who signed these contracts honoured them. In addition planters wanted longer contracts of five to ten years in order to secure ongoing labour.

After 1845, estates who employed Indians were guaranteed that their labour force would live on the estates under long contracts. From 1862 there were five-year contracts so they had a steady group of continuous labour even out of crop season. This was the greatest advantage to Jamaican planters using Indian immigrants.

The immigrants imported to Puerto Rico and Santo Domingo all agreed to verbal or written contracts. The immigrants from the Leeward Islands were less likely to have signed written contracts while those from the British Virgin Islands almost always had signed contracts. Most of these workers agreed to seasonal labour and specific wages. In most cases the estates agreed to provide accommodation and limited medical care.

Immigrants were not necessarily 'controllable' or passive. They used various methods of resistance to show their disgust with contract labour and with their exploitation by employers.

To maintain existing estates and increase production through expansion of the sugar industry

In the period 1824 to 1833, the British Caribbean colonies together produced 204, 699 tons of sugar. After the end of Apprenticeship, sugar production fell to 184,060 tons. By 1846 it was 131,177 tons. However, by 1851 production levels increased largely because of immigration, especially in Trinidad and colonial Guyana. By 1876 sugar production reached 240,221 tons. This was more than before emancipation.

Before 1845 it was mainly African immigration that helped the sugar planters to survive but then many Africans deserted the estates and went to the existing Free Villages. Those who remained on the sugar estates were satisfactory workers, particularly the Kroo people.

However, it was Indian immigration that had the greatest impact on sugar production. Guadeloupe, Martinique, the British Windwards and Jamaica recorded only small success with contracted Indians.

Table 8.2 Exports before and after immigration schemes: Trinidad

Year	Tonnage of sugar exported
1831 (before immigration)	14,997
1841	13,103
1851 (6 years after immigration began)	12,899
1866	40,000
1871	93,506

Planters in Trinidad and colonial Guyana found Indians particularly valuable when sugar production began to increase directly because of immigration. Trinidad had exported 14,997 tons of sugar in 1831 to a value of £20,029. In 1841 the figure stood at 13,103 tons. Indian immigration to Trinidad began in 1845. By 1857 all the sugar plantations in that island, except one, had applied

for immigrants. In the 1850s planters could expand cultivation, replant abandoned land and clean new lands. By 1851 Trinidad was exporting 12,899 tons of sugar. Fluctuations in the sugar industry often resulted in the cessation of immigration and unemployment among the Indians.

By the 1860s sugar cultivation in Trinidad had increased. By 1866, the yearly production reached 40,000 tons, and by 1871, 93,506 tons. In the period 1845–1870 planters recognised that the sugar industry had survived because of the Indians.

Immigration countered the effects of emancipation in three ways – there was economic growth, sugar prices increased, and new technology was introduced.

In Cuba, the story was a little different. Here Chinese and European workers had the most impact. In Cuba, planters privately recruited the Canary Islanders and Catalonians as contract labourers. They were effective cane-cutters and general workers, but after a short initial success this collapsed. Catalonians, reportedly, did not want to work alongside the enslaved; they began to desert the estates and move to the cities or buy their own land. The European people who were brought in the 1850s under five-year contracts also proved unsuccessful: some mutinied, some complained of poor treatment and a dislike of the climate. Cuban wages also failed to attract large numbers of European people. The Europeans imported in the 19th Century after the abolition of slavery were more successful. They helped to increase the acreage planted in cane.

Rebecca Scott claims that Chinese labour was important to the survival and development of the Cuban sugar industry because they were imported before the abolition of slavery and the trade in Africans. So they delayed the crisis in the sugar industry which would have accompanied abolition. She does not believe that they were essential to mechanisation as many did not in fact work with machinery but as fieldworkers. Only a few Chinese, mainly free workers, were in technical operations. They, however, helped to keep labour and production costs down. Chinese contract labour was banned after 1898. By 1899, 70 per cent of Cuban agricultural workers were European.

The Chinese were productive workers in the other Caribbean territories in which they were used. But planters complained that they tended to leave the estates for the retail trade and were bad-tempered. This was probably because they were militant about their rights as labourers.

In Puerto Rico, the immigrants from the islands had a positive effect on the sugar economy. Some of the estates in Vieques, for example, Playa Grande and Campo Asilo, relied almost exclusively on British Caribbean contract workers. These labourers lived on the estates and provided regular, full-time labour. As far as the workers were concerned, it was in their interest to live on the estates as it was cheaper than paying rent elsewhere.

Immigration to Puerto Rico declined after 1878 because of the crisis in the sugar industry. There was less demand for workers as the number of haciendas decreased. The French Caribbean planters also said that the sugar industry recovered because of immigration. Apart from the sugar economy, immigrants also helped to expand other industries such as cocoa, banana and rice.

These economic benefits were not only because of the immigrants. African-Caribbean people continued to contribute to agriculture and added to the effect of immigrant labour. In fact, some landowners relied heavily on the Black people for non-field labour in the sugar industry, especially in Jamaica.

Social impact of immigration

The presence of immigrants often affected race relations in the importing countries. In Santo Domingo, the mulatto elite was hostile to African immigrants and demonstrated against their entry. These demonstrations were especially marked after 1911. In 1912, demonstrators threatened to torch cane fields if the immigration of British Caribbean workers did not stop. The troops had to be called in to stop the protests. Again in 1915, just before the harvest, a society was formed to press for the banning of immigrants on behalf of local workers.

The first contingent of Anguillans was greeted with a protest in that year. The efforts of the Society to encourage the use of local over foreign labour led to widespread protest and attempted strikes. They tried to influence the government to impose a tax on the importation of Haitians and other African immigrants or ban them entirely. The immigrants were also opposed because their African culture was deemed inferior. They did not speak Spanish and were not Catholics. But the landowners were highly influential and managed to retain government support for immigration.

A plural society was created in Trinidad, colonial Guyana and Suriname. Race tensions increased as Indians and African-Caribbean people developed stereotypes about each other, each viewing the other as inferior. There were anti-Indian, anti-Chinese and anti-Portuguese protests in the British-colonised Caribbean. In some cases Creoles resented the presence of Indians who competed with them for jobs; in other cases the peasantry benefited from a new group of consumers for their crops. Only gradually did relationships improve and race mixture occur.

In some territories tensions also developed within the Indian community because initially there was an imbalance in the numbers of men and women, leading to competition for spouses. This situation sometimes led to violence. Tensions eased as better gender balance was achieved. On the other hand, immigrants contributed much to the region's culture. They introduced new religions such as Hinduism and expanded existing ones like Islam. They introduced new musical instruments, festivals, dress styles, food and religious observances. Their positive impact on the sugar industry in territories like Trinidad and colonial Guyana enabled the planters there to maintain their social and political status. The increased population caused by immigration placed additional stresses on the social services in the colonies, especially health; but on the other hand the provisions which had to be made for the immigrants improved medical services in the colonies.

The immigrants themselves did not always benefit from immigration. Female immigrants faced sexual and physical abuse from men. Some were abused by estate managers and spent many years in prison for breaking immigration laws. There were male/female tensions among the immigrant communities, especially among Indians where there was a sexual disparity. They suffered from abuse as a result of racial tensions and were not provided with proper medical, housing and educational facilities. Many could not afford to move off the estates and seek a better life; neither could they afford the cost of repatriation to India and they did not in all cases get land or money in exchange for repatriation.

To sum up

In this chapter we have looked at how planters used immigration as a solution to their 'labour problem' and the effectiveness and impact of such solutions. It should have been evident that immigration could only solve a labour shortage. To have a positive impact on the economy in the post-slavery period, immigration had to be used along with other measures such as mechanisation, improved fertilisers and a general rationalisation of the sugar industry. It should also be noted that immigration placed a burden on the colonial revenue. In 1846 immigration took up 50 per cent of the budget of some colonies. Immigration continued the inefficient use of labour as indentured workers still had to be maintained out of crop season. Local labourers were also taxed to pay for passages of immigrants, who then eroded their bargaining power. All in all, imperial state policies, not the immigrants and African-Caribbean people themselves, must be assigned most of the blame for much of the race relations tensions that emerged in the 19th and 20th Century Caribbean over the issue of immigration.

Revision questions

1 a. On the blank map of the world provided by your teacher, write the names of two Asian countries, one continental European country and one Portuguese island, which supplied immigrant labourers to the Caribbean after 1838.

 b. Write the names of five Caribbean territories on the map which imported Asian indentured labourers after 1838.

2 State two reasons why male Chinese immigrants outnumbered female Chinese immigrants among the recruits for the Caribbean plantations.

3 Name three reasons why, despite the difficulties, recruiters kept on recruiting immigrant women for the Caribbean plantations.

4 Give three 'great hardships' which indenture imposed on the female immigrants specifically.

5 State four ways in which Chinese immigration was useful to the Cuban sugar planters.

6 Discuss the impact of intra Caribbean migration on the economy and society of the Spanish-colonised Caribbean.

Chapter 9

The new working classes: social and political experiences: 1834–1900

'Long time, we no have no nice time … think about that.'
(Bob Marley)

Introduction

We have seen that in all territories the abolition of slavery was long in coming and bitterly fought against by slaveowning elites and their allies. The elites resented the collapse of class rule at emancipation. So, they were slow to usher in economic and political change, including social democracy, that would improve the physical and social well-being of the working classes. This meant that inadequate attention was paid to education, constitutional reform, health facilities and general social welfare and that there was scant respect for non-elite cultural practices.

Immigrants, as well as the previously enslaved, designed their own strategies to help themselves and their communities within this unsupportive and occasionally hostile environment. They did have a few allies, such as charitable and benevolent organisations. This chapter will explore the social experiences of freed people after the abolition of slavery and the social experiences of indentured immigrants who arrived in the Caribbean.

In this chapter we will learn about:
1 The social domination and control of freed people
2 Education and health of freed people
3 Religion, missionaries and freed people
4 The social experiences of indentured immigrants

19th Century Jamaican police constable

1   Legislation and social control

When slavery ended together with some of the old laws used to control the enslaved, the colonial elites looked for new ways and means to dominate and control the working population. They did not want to see the rise of self-confident and independent communities. They wanted to keep as much of the old social order as possible to make sure that elite domination continued. Louis Rothe, who observed conditions in Antigua and the Danish-colonised Caribbean in the 19th Century lamented that:

> The politeness and friendliness with which a person of higher standing is treated by the lower orders in a slavery colony has become less and less frequent in the emancipated colonies. There are also frequent indications that emancipation and the manner of its introduction in the British West Indies have subverted not only respect for superiors and for White skin, but also regard for the higher station conferred by education and achievement.

Elites turned to anti-settler laws to control the workers' attitudes to them. For example, the Contract Law and the Masters and Servants Act in Antigua restricted the freedom of newly emancipated people so much, that at first the Imperial Government would not allow these laws to be used. Later these laws were modified. In September 1836 the Antiguan Assembly tried to make it almost impossible for workers to leave the island. They laid down over a dozen conditions under which they would allow emigration. Workers had to prove, for example, that they were not leaving behind needy parents or children under 14 years and they had to get clearance to leave from two Justices of the Peace as well as the island secretary.

Did you know?

Contract law set out the terms of labour. Many freed people refused to sign these contracts as they favoured the ex-enslavers.

Government officials added important new conditions to the criminal justice system. In the British-colonised territories after emancipation criminal laws, similar to those in England, were applied to the entire free population. In slavery, special laws and codes were used to govern relations between enslavers and those enslaved. These were called 'slave laws'. Now the system of punishment was no longer part of special laws and courts that were used to try the enslaved. They were part and parcel of the whole justice system.

In Jamaica between 1835 and 1838, there was such concern about property crimes that the Police Act was changed. It now allowed constables to arrest any persons found carrying agricultural goods without a note of permission from the owner of the land from where the produce came. In some British-colonised territories laws were passed to limit side walk trading of goods, just like in the slavery period. These laws were passed because the officials believed that trading in goods encouraged praedial theft. In Jamaica, throughout most of the 19th Century, the punishment for praedial theft (i.e. theft of agricultural crops) was flogging.

In all British-colonised territories prisons were called Houses of Correction. They were brutal places, intended to break rather than rehabilitate inmates. In prisons, for example, women's hair was cut as a form of punishment as the authorities thought that nothing shamed a woman more than to have her hair closely cut. There were laws to restrict trading in the market on a Sunday to encourage people to observe Sunday as a Christian day of worship. These attempts were also designed to limit the economic development of freed people, as at first they were prevented from selling certain goods that could be profitable, like sugar.

The colonial administrations tried to make the working poor pay taxes. During slavery there was a poll tax that the free community had to pay for enslaved workers and other personal property. This tax made up the bulk of the colonies' money. African people were no longer taxable as the property of others. So the government had to find other sources of money. Taxes were charged on Crown Lands, on spending and on trading; and licensing fees were charged for the right to buy and sell services.

Lord Grey of the British Colonial Office proposed taxing the crops and the produce of provision grounds and doing away with customs duties on foodstuffs coming into the colonies. This would reduce the demand for peasant produce as it would be too expensive and the freed people would be forced back to the plantations. There was quite a lot of colonial support for Grey's suggestions, but the Imperial Government did not accept them. The peasants were willing to resist these harsh taxes being imposed.

They saw tax laws as the way in which the elite would take the surplus they made from their productive efforts and they were determined to protect themselves.

The government also passed Vagrancy Laws. Under these laws, vagrants included 'anyone found wandering, staying temporarily in piazzas, outhouses, sheds, mills, etc', and people who did not have any visible means of supporting themselves. The Vagrancy Laws also included people who exposed obscene books, pictures or prints in public, or who exposed themselves, and people 'wandering abroad and endeavoring by the exposure of wounds or deformities to obtain aid'. So the law made the healthy unemployed, and the wounded and deformed who could not work and therefore begged for a living, all equally guilty of vagrancy.

Police force

In most territories it was considered necessary to have a police force to prevent protests, to enforce the new laws and to maintain 'law and order'. The prison system was also expanded to deal with offenders. The colonies wanted a police force because in the 1880s the West India Regiment had been disbanded in colonies such as the Bahamas, British Honduras, Barbados, colonial Guyana and Trinidad. This is how Rothe explained the need for a police force in Antigua:

> ... a strong and well-organised police force was indispensably necessary to protect [White] society against the dangers which threatened from the sudden transition to freedom, and the abolition of the control and discipline masters hitherto had exercised over their slaves.

The Bahamas recruited members for the force from outside, especially from Barbados. They believed that local recruits would protect the population they were supposed to control, especially in cases of racial conflict with the dominant Europeans. In fact, such an incident of racial conflict did take place in 1886 when an insane European man shot a local policeman. A police force was considered important for the Bahamas even though one official, Sir Charles Lees, said in 1882 that the population of The Bahamas is 'law-abiding'. But, he further said that 'it is almost entirely composed of a race easily excitable, and when under the control of passion, capable of but little self-control.'

Cultural power and control

There was also an attempt to control the cultural life of the poor. Government officials said that many of the African cultural practices and institutions that had survived slavery were socially undesirable and disrespectful to the Christian church. African-Cuban rural workers, for example, were very protective of the cultural practices and beliefs that had been passed down orally by African male and female elders. The Yoruba people, from what is now called western Nigeria, maintained the Lucumi tradition and values of their ancestors. The Angolans lived the religion, folk medicine, music, dance and food cultures of their traditions.

In Cuba, African cultural influence was very important in the *Cabildos de nación*. There were also all male Abakuá secret societies that were based in the cities and whose members were known as *ñañigos*. According to historian Aline Helg, these groups 'became icons of fear in the 1880s'. The government used the law to say that they were criminals and they tried to stop the *Cabildos de nación*.

Did you know?

Cabildo de nación was a town-based mutual association of enslaved or free people of African origin in Cuba. Their aim was to preserve aspects of African culture. The *Cabildos de nación* were organised around African ethnic groups and were a form of identity to Afro-Cubans.

Cabildos de nación were semi-religious organisations. Cuban planters did not encourage missionary activity among the enslaved. However, because the *Cabildos de nación* were technically Christian groups, but had some Africanisms, the planters allowed them to continue. The planters felt that they could be agents of social control.

During slavery the authorities allowed these associations to continue because they thought they would form an outlet for the energies of the enslaved and they would prevent resistance. After abolition the authorities made an effort to prevent Creole children from joining these associations and even tried to get rid of the associations entirely. They were now viewed as institutions to preserve African culture and therefore a threat to Spanish cultural supremacy, as they had the potential to separate African-Caribbean people from the dominant culture. The Imperial Government did not legally ban them, but hoped they would fade with increasing creolisation. In fact, by the 20th Century, *Cabildos de nación* had lost their strength and being replaced by Mutual Aid Societies.

In the British-colonised territories laws were passed that made the practice of some African cultural practices such as *obeah* and *myal,* a crime.

In Cuba, the elite made a huge apartheid-like effort to keep Spanish and African people from sharing social facilities such as restaurants, parks and entertainment houses. In the cities there were second and third class cafés for African and mixed-race people. In 1885 the Governor ruled that no one could be legally excluded from public parks and eating places on the basis of colour. Two years later the *Conséjo de Administración* ruled that no one could be legally excluded from first-class coaches of trains. However, there was no real enforcement of these regulations and racial segregation was a common feature of that society.

2 Education and health of freed people

a Education in the British-colonised Caribbean territories

Before emancipation, very few African children were given an education. In June 1833 the British House of Commons promised to help educate the freed people in the British-colonised Caribbean territories. In 1834 a sum of £25,000 was made available for education. It was called the Negro Education Grant. £20,000 of this grant was to be spent on the building of schools and the remaining £5,000 was to be used to build non-denominational teacher training colleges. In 1837 the Negro Education Grant was increased to £30,000 and it remained at that level until it was stopped in 1845.

Did you know?

Crown colonies were ruled directly from England. The Old Representative System gave mostly Europeans a measure of elected government and internal self-rule.

Grants to churches to run schools

When the grant was stopped, Caribbean governments were expected to provide local money to continue education. While few of them provided adequate sums for this purpose, the response was better in the Crown Colonies than in those governed under the Old Representative System. For example, colonial Guyana, made £2,500 available for education in 1836 and 1837 and Trinidad also provided funds. But Jamaica did not provide any money for education until 1844. Even then it only provided £3,000 each year for the next 10 years – that is, one and a half pence per student per year! The Barbados Assembly only began to give general educational funds in 1846 with a grant of £750 although it later made larger grants. These grants were given to various denominations – Anglican, Catholic, Wesleyan. In other colonies, grants were given to the Anglican Church – the Established Church – to avoid competition among missionary groups. In 1840, the parish vestry and colonial government in

Barbados gave £8,623 to support the efforts of the Established Church.

Mico Charity

An extra sum for education came from the Mico Charity – a private agency which Dame Jane Mico founded in the 17th Century for 'saving' enslaved Christians from the Barbary States of North Africa. The grant started at £2,000 and increased to £100,000. This money was eventually distributed to the colonies to be used to 'save' enslaved people in the British-colonised Caribbean. The funds did not go to religious denominations and were used for the freed people. It was particularly welcomed in territories like Trinidad and Tobago which were Roman Catholic and had fewer non-Roman Catholics, as Catholics did not get any of the Negro Education Grant. The Mico Charity operated schools in Jamaica, the Cayman Islands, The Bahamas, Barbados, colonial Guyana, St Vincent, Antigua, Montserrat, Tobago, Trinidad, Dominica, Grenada and St Lucia. By 1838 the Mico Charity had established 138 day-schools in the Caribbean, with 146 teachers reaching nearly 9,000 students. By 1841 the Mico Charity had established 196 schools with some 15,000 students throughout the British-colonised Caribbean.

The Mico Charity grant was for the building of 'normal schools' or teachers' colleges. Four of these (with boarding facilities) were set up in Jamaica, Antigua, Trinidad and colonial Guyana. By 1840 Mico normal schools had 241 candidates, 158 of which had teaching jobs in schools of every religious denomination, as well as in the day schools of the Mico Charity. The day schools supported by the Mico Charity closed in the Cayman Islands in 1841. By 1854, out of a total population of 2,000 in the Cayman

Fig 9.1 Mico College in Jamaica

Islands, only 358 could read and write and 414 could read but barely sign their names. At that time there were only two schools – at Georgetown and Prospect. From 1862 to 1888 several churches tried to establish schools and the vestry made small grants for these schools. In 1908 the government brought in compulsory education for children of 6 to 14 years.

Church schools

The dominant type of schools were schools run by the church. In Jamaica the Anglicans built and ran several elementary schools. In the early 20th Century they also built secondary institutions:

- St Hugh's, St Hilda's, St Helena's High School in Montego Bay. Ms B Jeffrey-Smith ran the Cathedral High School in St Catherine.
- York Castle School was opened in 1876, and was the work of the Wesleyans.
- In 1881 Wesley High School for girls and the Quaker-run Westwood High School for girls were opened, giving girls' education a boost.
- The Moravians built the Bethlehem Teacher's College for training women teachers.
- The Baptists opened schools like Calabar.
- The Roman Catholics in Jamaica founded St George's College for Boys in 1852.
- The Jesuit Order established several other schools.

In the Eastern Caribbean and colonial Guyana, the Anglican Church schools increased from 34 to 405. Baptists, Methodists, Presbyterians, the London Missionary Society, Wesleyans and Catholics all set up schools and competed with one another.

Tension in Trinidad between church and state

Tension and competition among the churches were particularly strong in the Crown Colony of Trinidad. Roman Catholicism was introduced when Trinidad was under Spanish and French rule, and it was still strong after years of English rule. Henry George McLeod, who became governor in Trinidad in 1840, was a staunch Protestant and wanted to reduce the Roman Catholic influence in the island. This was in contrast to Lord Harris's 1848 plan for education which was to establish secular or non-religious ward schools in each ward, to reduce the influence of the church schools. This plan was opposed by the Roman Catholic Church, but was implemented in 1851. By 1868 there were 31 of these ward schools in Trinidad.

Church schools were affected because government funding now went to the ward schools. But the churches still built and funded their own schools even in areas that already had ward schools. In 1868 there were 32 church schools. The Roman Catholics carried out secondary education until 1859. At that time the government built Queens Royal College. The Roman Catholics built St Mary's College in 1863 to facilitate a new college in Trinidad. As historian Carl Campbell states, ward schools were never completely non-religious or secular as governments still felt that religious education was what the masses needed.

The Keenan Report, drawn up by Patrick Keenan in 1869, assessed the state of education in Trinidad and recommended that a dual system of education be put in place – with both ward and church schools. So after 1870 ward and church schools both received funding from the colonial government.

Fig 9.2 Baptist school at Calabar

b Education in the French-, Danish- and Spanish-colonised Caribbean territories

In the French-colonised Caribbean on the whole, elementary education was available after the government took over the schools in 1886. The government also opened secondary schools called *lycées*. A law school was set up in Martinique in 1882, and the government also provided a small number of scholarships to French Universities. Island schools taught French under the supervision of officials from Bordeaux. Before 1886 only a few educational institutions had existed, and they had catered only for European and mixed-race people. These schools were maintained by religious institutions, like the Capuchins, the Jesuits, the Brothers of the Christian Schools (catering mostly for boys); and the Ursulines and Daughters of Providence (catering for girls, some in boarding schools).

In the Danish-colonised Caribbean an 1839 law called for free elementary education for both free people and enslaved. Shortly after this schools were opened in St Croix, in St Thomas in 1878 and later in St John. English was the dominant language used in public schools after 1850.

In the Spanish-colonised Caribbean, notably Cuba, Mutual Aid Societies pushed for the education of African-Cubans to help them become more upwardly mobile. After slavery ended there was inequality in educational opportunities for different groups in the society. There were few African-Cubans in primary and secondary schools; and there was almost none in private schools, which were dominated by Spanish children. In 1878, mixed-race people were allowed into secondary schools, professional schools and the university, and in 1879 they were allowed into local public schools but in Cienfuegos, mixed-race people petitioned for the setting up of separate schools. Instead, the government allowed them to enter the municipal schools. This ruling was not without conflict, as the conservative groups in society did not want racial integration and they continued to support segregated education.

c The content of education: examples from the British-colonised Caribbean

In 1835 Rev J Sterling compiled a report for the British government in which he said that their educational efforts had some success. The report also said that education was a system of control that seemed to have 'secured' or tempered the behaviour of the labouring population. In Rev Sterling's words:

> Five years hence, their performance of the functions of a labouring class in a civilized community will depend entirely on the power over their minds of the same prudential and moral motives which govern more or less the mass of people here [in England]. If they are not so disposed as to fulfill these functions, property will perish in the colonies for lack of human impulsion; the Whites will no longer reside there and the liberated Negroes will probably cease to be progressive; the law having already determined their civic rights.

But Sterling's view was in conflict with the view of parents and children. His report did not mention the tensions over several issues that had developed between the providers of education and the receivers of education. C J Latrobe was an Englishman who was originally a Governor of Australia, and was given a government commission in the Caribbean in 1837. He inspected schools in the Caribbean in 1837 and pointed out some of these tensions. He said

there was conflict over the aim of this education and over the purpose of the 'Negro Education Grant'.

Education in the Caribbean had a strong 'moral' content. Stipendiary Magistrates had in fact pushed religious education as a way of improving the 'morality' among the labouring class.

Tensions also existed over industrial education. Industrial schools were based on the English model. These schools were supposed to care for and educate destitute, 'vagrant' and orphaned children and had been opened in Jamaica since 1857. In 1890, for example, the Sisters of Mercy began their educational work at Alpha, an orphanage and industrial school. They also founded St Clavier's Orphanage in St Catherine. But the industrial schools and orphanages pushed a type of education that trained African-Jamaican people, especially girls, in domestic duties. The labourers also saw industrial education as a way of tying their children to plantation labour. So, where they had a choice, they resisted sending their children to these schools.

The education that was provided for children in the period after slavery was not very broad. It consisted mainly of reading, writing, arithmetic and some religious education, and it was based on reading material from Europe. The material, therefore, dealt with things that were unfamiliar to Caribbean children. The teachers were sometimes just 'monitors'; in other words, they were advanced students supervised by a schoolmaster. Except in some of the special immigrant schools, the language of instruction was English, in which many Caribbean children were not fluent.

In the British-colonised territories, peasants began to realise that the type of education their children were receiving was designed to limit them and make them more effective estate labourers and loyal colonial subjects.

Fig 9.3 Codrington College, Barbados

This caused some parents to eventually withdraw support of the missionaries and lose interest in schooling their children.

As was to be expected, school attendance fell off by 1850. This was especially because many parents could not afford the school fees. In Jamaica, for example, by 1865, there were fewer pupils enrolled in schools than in the final stages of Apprenticeship. In Trinidad, there were fewer pupils in school in 1870 than in 1846. In Barbados, however, greater progress was made. By 1860 every district in the island had a primary school. Codrington College offered degrees in divinity, and was one of the oldest educational institutions in Barbados and the British-colonised Caribbean. Even so, up until 1865, fewer than 30 per cent of children between five and fifteen-years-old received formal day school education.

d Health

Hospitals

Enslavers provided very basic health care for the enslaved population. After slavery ended freed people became responsible for their own medical care. Plantation hospitals were to be closed and so public hospitals were needed for the general population, and asylums were needed for the insane and lepers. The closing of plantation hospitals after Apprenticeship and the stopping of weekly and bi-weekly visits by doctors had a dramatic effect on medical service in rural areas in the British-colonised territories. Many doctors encouraged freed people to pay them a form of medical insurance. This means that they paid a fixed sum in return for regular treatment over twelve months. Few of the labourers agreed to this arrangement. They took their illnesses to indigenous practitioners and to other freed people who had served as hospital attendants. The local governments of course tried to stamp out this 'quackery', as they called it.

In some colonies public hospitals were built in the major towns and cities in response to the health needs of the population. In the early 1840s such hospitals were built in Barbados and Antigua. Separate hospitals were built in these territories for lepers and lunatics. Some islands in the Eastern Caribbean could not provide such facilities because of their limited resources. But there was also a certain lack of concern among the elite class in these colonies. For example, insane people wandered about on the streets and were put in jails if they showed signs of violence. However, in Jamaica, before emancipation a public hospital was built in Kingston, and next to it was a lunatic asylum (Bellevue).

Poor living conditions lead to bad health

Labourers' health problems increased because of their poor housing. Few estate owners bothered to improve sanitary conditions in the houses they rented to the tenants; and few tenants had the security of tenure or the resources to make their own improvements. Many lived in temporary structures (such as the chattel houses of Barbados) which could be taken apart and moved if conflict developed with their employers.

After the abolition of slavery, the overcrowding in towns and cities also caused health hazards. Many people from the rural areas moved to the towns, looking for better conditions of life, but they often ended up in overcrowded tenement yards. The poor quality of the water available to these yards combined with poor sewage disposal added to the health situation. Many of the urban and rural poor could not afford medical treatment for the many illnesses which resulted from poor living conditions. After 1846, the economic crisis that the landowning class experienced meant that giving money to improve health conditions was not a priority for them. However, even in good economic times this was not a priority for them!

These poor health conditions ended in the dreadful cholera epidemic of the 1850s which broke out in Jamaica in October 1850. The first epidemic started in Port Royal and the deaths there increased from 10 to 20 per day after the first case was noticed. The disease spread to Kingston. There were also outbreaks in other parts of the Caribbean. In June 1854 Bridgetown, Barbados was the scene of panic. Governor Colebrook estimated that between 14,000 and 15,000 people died in Barbados; and in Martinique, where the epidemic broke out in 1865, there were 1,200 reported deaths in Pointe-a-Pitre. Other epidemics (typhoid, yellow fever) broke out at various times in Martinique in the 19th Century. As in other colonies, leprosy and hookworm also affected mainly the Indian immigrant population. Leper hospitals were established on Desirade and Marie Galante, islands in the Guadeloupe archipelago.

Barbados attempted to control the outbreak of cholera by appointing local health inspectors and bringing in a system of free vaccinations. About 15,000 people were vaccinated. The Barbadian government also made improvements to the water systems. But in territories where there was little cash, improvements were slower.

3 Religion, missionaries and freed people

In the face of their declining influence among the industrial poor in Britain, missionaries stepped up their activities among the newly freed people in some territories in the Caribbean. Of course planters were quick to realise the disciplinary value of religious teaching and they saw the missionaries as agents of public order. The missionaries concentrated on education and the stamping out of traditional African customs. They saw these customs as a threat to the Christian religion and European culture, which they believed was superior. They also had the support of the colonial governments. The Jamaican government had even tried to outlaw myalism.

In Jamaica the House of Assembly also passed an Act to increase the penalty for persons found guilty of practising obeah. The authorities set up Free Villages in which missionaries kept in contact with freed people in the most out-of-the-way areas, in an attempt to stop the freed people from 'lapsing' into so-called 'barbarism' and to maintain the idea of European cultural supremacy. Missionary James Philippo, who helped to establish the first Free Village in Jamaica, was asked to establish a school and chapel on just about every plantation in his district.

By 1845, in some territories, the freed people were no longer so loyal to the missionaries. They resented the missionaries' low regard for their cultural habits and practices, and they ignored certain teachings of the church. For example, they ignored the churches' ban on 'common-law relationships', which increased in the post-slavery period. Methodists, for example, insisted on monogamy and sexual faithfulness and breaking these rules could lead to expulsion from the church. The missionaries liked to use this threat of expulsion to control the labouring population. The freed people called the missionaries 'macroon hunters' because the missionaries charged macroons for bibles and church dues. Nancy Prince Gardner reported that some missionaries in Kingston could only attract African-Caribbean membership if they used African-Caribbean people in certain key positions in the church.

Did you know?

A macroon was a Jamaican coin of small value.

Missionaries encouraged freed people to marry and live in small, nuclear families. In fact, marriages (illegal under slavery) did increase in most colonies as soon as freedom came. The table below shows an example from Antigua:

Table 9.1: Marriages in Antigua, 1833-1843

Year	Marriages
1833	188
1834	276
1835	474
1836	330
1837	243
1838	316
1839	468
1840	526
1841	519
1842	470
1843	511

Source: Louis Rothe, *A description of the island of Antigua, with particular reference to emancipation's results.*

However, by 1850 missionaries were losing their influence and following in the Caribbean. In any case, by then the missionaries were more interested in the so-called 'pagans' in Africa and Asia. Between 1846 and 1868, membership in the Methodist church fell by over 30 per cent. Among the contributing factors for this decline was the Revival Movement that swept Jamaica in the early 1860s. It was more a revival of African religious traditions rather than Christian ones. By 1862, there were very few African-Caribbeans congregations in churches.

Having looked at the experiences of the freed African people, we will now turn to the experiences of indentured immigrants.

Table 9.2: Chapels, Mission Houses and Reform School-rooms built after 1835, Jamaica

Location	Cost of Chapel (£)	Accommodation
Montego Bay	8500	3000
Shortwood	3500	1500
Mount Carey	1000	1000
Bethel Hill	1000	1000
Falmouth	6700	2500
Refuge	1400	1500
Waldensia	1200	1000
Salter's Hill	3500	2200
Bethetphil	1000	1000
Savanna-La -Mar	3500	2200
Fuller's Field	1000	800
Lucea	3400	1400
Green Island	1000	600
Stewart Town	1200	1000
Rio Bueno	1300	1000
New Birmingham	500	550

Location	Cost of Chapel (£)	Accommodation
Brown's Town	3300	2000
Bethany	2600	1500
St Ann's Bay	3500	2000
Jericho	2035	2000
Springfield	510	800
Smyrna	920	1400
Mount Herman	816	1400

Compiled from: Caldecott, A. *The church in the West Indies.* London: 1898.

4 The social experiences of indentured immigrants

The immigrant community in the 19th and 20th Centuries was made up of mainly indentured or ex-indentured agricultural workers. They were mainly Indian, but there were also Chinese, Portuguese and the 'liberated Africans' – enslaved people freed from slavery bound for Cuba, for example. In all cases their working and living conditions were degrading, especially for those who still worked or lived on the plantations. We have seen that the lack of proper housing and medical care often resulted in a high illness and death rate. In Chapter 8 we read that the immigrants' wages were inadequate and often paid late; and there were many conflicts between immigrant and employer over wages. Women and working children were paid a lower wage than the men and this increased their hardships. Also, it was not until the late 19th Century that provisions were made for the education of the children of the immigrants.

Housing

On the estates, immigrant workers lived separately from other ethnic groups. Couples, married and non-married, lived together. Landowners imported women to be potential spouses in an effort to try to keep indentured men on the plantations. Many Indians were housed in what had been slave barracks. When these deteriorated, estate owners built houses for the immigrants. The gang supervisors, sirdars and drivers had better accommodation than the other workers and were more likely to live in family groups.

5 Medical care of indentured immigrants

Despite the laws to control the health conditions of Indian immigrants, the conditions were still poor. Yet, the medical care of immigrants on the estates was crucial to the success of the indentureship system. There were public hospitals in some of the towns, for example, in Georgetown in colonial Guyana and Port of Spain in Trinidad. But there were no public hospitals in the rural areas. The governments knew that even though there were immigration laws, they could not rely on employers to make proper provisions for health care. So the government had to take on this responsibility.

The governments were concerned about the high death rate of the workers because the anti-immigrationists accused them of starting a new system of slavery. Those workers who were not well enough to undertake agricultural labour were sent to hospital: some recovered enough to go back to work; others died. The death rate among the first Indians who came to colonial Guyana under the Gladstone experiment was high: 67 of the 396 died (17 per cent). The major causes of death were malaria and ulcers; many also suffered from hookworm. Between 1853 and 1870, of the 20,352 Indians introduced into Guadeloupe, 8,680 (or 42 per cent) died. In Martinique, 5,084 (or 32 per cent) of the 15,741 introduced in the same period died. Death rates were higher during the rainy season when Indians were more likely to get diseases. In Cuba the death rate among the Chinese was high, with 75 per cent of them dying in the period 1844 to 1860.

Colonial Guyana

To help with the situation, estates at first kept their own hospitals. In colonial Guyana an Ordinance was passed in 1859. This law stated that each estate hospital had to have a nurse, a certain minimum standard of equipment, and a medical Inspector of Estates Hospitals, who had to visit each hospital every six months. Those patients with serious illnesses were moved to the public hospital. By 1861 the hospital system was working fairly well in colonial Guyana. Because of these estate hospitals the death rate of workers fell from 10 per cent in 1861 to 4.4 per cent in 1866.

Trinidad

However, the health system was not working well especially in Trinidad where people in remote areas could not get to the hospital. Until 1865 there were no estate hospitals in Trinidad like those in colonial Guyana. In 1850 Trinidad governor Lord Harris passed a regulation providing that immigrants should not be sent to estates that did not have adequate medical provisions. Each estate was supposed to have a doctor who visited regularly – once or twice a week, as compared to three times in colonial Guyana. But this medical arrangement was not adequate. In 1850 there were only doctors in Port of Spain, San Fernando, Couva, and St Joseph, and there were only two public hospitals.

In 1862 there were still no government medical posts in Trinidad to help to increase the number of doctors. In 1865 an Ordinance was passed in Trinidad that made it compulsory for employers to send sick immigrants to hospital. By 1866 the government made estate hospitals compulsory with the result that by 1867, 92 of the 155 estates had hospitals and 50 more were being built. The other 13 estates preferred to stop using immigrants rather than build hospitals. Under an 1870 regulation in Trinidad and a regulation in 1873 in colonial Guyana, government medical officers (MOs) were appointed to take over the care of sick immigrants in estate hospitals. Each district now had its own doctor, even the remote ones. By 1911 some estate doctors had been appointed MOs. In 1911 24,000 cases of illness were reported for the 10,000 registered immigrants on plantations in Trinidad.

Jamaica

In Jamaica, Governor J P Grant described the death rate among Indians in 1869 as 'lamentable'. Of the 1,625 who arrived in April to June 1867, 239 had died (15 per cent). On one estate, 51 per cent of those from the 1867 group of immigrants died by the end of 1868. Up to 1869, Jamaica also had the system of estate hospitals for immigrants, although this was not compulsory by law. The law also said that immigrants must be sent to the public hospitals. The hospitals, however, did not keep to the dietary regulations laid down and this too contributed to ill-health and a high death rate among workers. After 1879 when estate hospitals were done away with, sick Indians were treated in what were called 'union hospitals'.

Fig 9.4 Governor Sir John Peter Grant

However, each estate was given medical supplies to treat minor ailments.

Union hospitals were established in each parish so that all estates could be served. By 1870 the government had taken over the medical expenses of immigrants from employers. Medical officers were appointed and paid by the government. The death rate was lowered from a range of 6.20 per cent to 12.11 per cent before 1869 to 1.5 per cent to 2.5 per cent.

By the end of the 19th Century immigrants in Jamaica, the Leeward and Windward Islands had to go to public hospitals where the government paid for their treatment. Other workers who had to pay for their own treatment resented this. They also resented being taxed to help pay for the importation of immigrants and their care.

6 Education and schooling of indentured immigrants

When immigration first started, employers were only interested in agricultural workers and showed very little interest in educating immigrants or their children. Up to about 1870, very few Indian children received any education outside of the home. Indian children were not excluded from going to the schools that existed, but their parents initially did not want them to mix with children of a different culture and ethnic group. There were many Protestant teachers in schools, and Indian parents feared that their children might be converted to Christianity. However, the Canadian and Scottish Presbyterians and the Quakers made some efforts to educate the Indian children and set up schools late in the 19th and in the 20th Century. They had some support from a few planters and the government.

Colonial Guyana

In colonial Guyana the government encouraged estate schools to be set up. In 1868 the Canadian Presbyterians, under Rev J B Cropper, began to provide denominational schools for Indian and other children. They joined the Catholics and Anglicans, Moravians, Wesleyans, Lutherans and Congregationalists in the setting up of schools. By 1917 there were 28 Canadian mission schools. The attendance by Indians was low: of the total number of pupils in primary schools in colonial Guyana in 1920 only 24 per cent were Indian children; and in 1925 to 1929 only 29 per cent were Indian children compared to 83 per cent Chinese, 79 per cent Afro-Guyanese and mixed-race Guyanese people, 75 per cent Portuguese in 1911. However, in 1920 Indian children constituted 41 per cent of the school age population, and 45 per cent in 1930. As in other territories, more boys than girls were sent to school. In 1925, only 25 per cent of Indian children in primary schools were girls.

Trinidad

In the 1850s orphanages helped to meet the educational needs of Indian children in Trinidad. One example was the Catholic-run Tacarigua Orphanage and Training School opened in 1856. Up until 1869, hardly any Indian children in Trinidad attended the ward schools. Those who did go to school attended private schools. The Keenan Report encouraged separate schools for Indian children as parents did not initially want children to attend schools with other ethnic groups, especially Afro-Trinidanians. The Catholics established quite a few of these in the 1870s, for example the Pers Village, Rosehill, Phoenix Park, Cedras and Columbus Indian schools. The Roman Catholics built three more schools: two in Port-of-Spain and one in San Juan. By 1890 these schools had 250 students.

The Canadian Presbyterians also did much for the educational development of Indian children in Trinidad. Sarah Morton, wife of a Presbyterian missionary, described in her diary of 23 March 1868 how her husband 'began to teach Kunjah's three children on our doorstep. In the afternoon he went throughout the village inviting others to send their children'.

Early in 1869, her husband, the Rev John Morton, proposed to Governor Sir Arthur Gordon a scheme for the education of Indian children in Trinidad and said that the government should pay for this scheme. As a result, a special Indian school was opened by the Presbyterians in 1871 in San Fernando. By 1874 the number of schools in the south had increased to twelve. The planters supported ten of these financially while the Canadian mission itself supported one school and the government supported another. The Education Ordinance of 1896 offered all religious denominations government assistance to build schools for Indians. By 1899 there were sixteen of these schools under Morton's direction; fourteen of these received government aid. By 1917 the Canadian Presbyterians had opened 70 schools with 11,375 students. Ninety per cent of Indian children who received an education did so in the Presbyterian schools.

In Trinidad in 1899, of the total number of children in Canadian mission primary schools, only 28 per cent were Indian girls. In 1913 there were 661 girls (28 per cent) and 1,705 boys (72 per cent) in the 18 Canadian mission schools in the San Fernando District. Secondary education for Indian girls was very limited whereas secondary education for Indian boys started from 1883. The Naparima Girls High School was only founded in 1912.

Even when the Canadian Presbyterians started their mission to educate Indian girls, they were mainly interested in giving them 'feminine' education. In other words, they only taught domestic skills. The curriculum included the three 'Rs' both in Hindi and English, as well as bible study, food preparation, domestic duties and some history and geography. Up to 1946, only 30 per cent of Indian women in Trinidad were literate compared to 50 per cent of the Indian men. Among those over 45, only 10.6 per cent of women were literate.

Table 9.3 Progress of the Canadian Mission Schools in Trinidad, 1871–1915

Year	Schools	Enrolment	Attendance
1871	7	331	159
1881	29	1139	749
1891	52	2951	2018
1901	59	5032	2764
1911	61	8080	4542
1915	65	9340	5181

Source: K. O. Laurence, *A Question of labour*, p. 265.

Jamaica

A larger number of Indian children did not attend the government schools in Jamaica. This led to calls for the establishment of special Indian schools. These requests were largely ignored, except by the Quakers and Scottish Presbyterians. By 1898 these churches opened day schools for Indian children as part of their religious conversion activities. The Quakers operated schools at Seaside (Happy Grove), Amity Hall, Quaker Hill, Albany, Orange Bay, Spicy Grove and Cascade. The Scottish Presbyterians, with planter support, opened a school at Ewings Caymanas in St Catherine in 1891. The churches also established industrial schools and orphanages which helped to educate Indian children.

In 1916 the government heeded the call for special Indian schools funded by public funds. In that year they opened three schools – at Smith Village in Kingston (the present day Denham Town), Fellowship and Orange Hill in Portland. The Quakers and the Scottish Presbyterians ran these schools. The government established other schools at Alley in Vere, at Trinity in St Mary, and at Constant Spring in St Andrew (attached to the Wortley Home run by the Anglicans).

The special Indian schools all closed in 1930. This was partly because of financial difficulties and partly because the government said that the Indian population in Jamaica was too small to merit special attention. They said that if the Indians decided to settle on the island, they should become part of the population and mix with other children in the elementary schools. Up to 1943, 51 per cent of Jamaican Indians were still illiterate. The government educated those who were literate mainly up to the primary level. Only 3 per cent of the Indians were educated above the elementary school level.

7 Indian women's experiences

Emigration and indentureship may have given Indian women some financial independence; however, some writers, for example Jeremy Poynting, view their experience as one of multiple oppression. They were oppressed as indentured workers in a system of semi-slavery. They were oppressed as Indians whose culture was disrespected by other sections of the population. They were oppressed as women who suffered from the sexual abuse of the overseer class; and they suffered from the patriarchal domination of Indian men within the Indian family structure.

There were several murders of Indian women by angry and jealous men. Some Indian men accused the women of having so much choice that they practised 'polyandry'. This accusation was mostly unfounded. The men thought that the women were acting too independently, especially in their sexual lives and so they often challenged this independence in violent ways.

Cases of murder of Indian women by husbands occurred in colonial Guyana, Grenada, Jamaica, Suriname and Trinidad. From 1859 to 1863 there were 27 cases of 'wife murders' by Indian men in Trinidad. Between 1879 and 1898, out of 109 murders committed by Indians in Trinidad, 63 were murders of women by spouses. From 1872 to 1900, 87 Indian women were killed in Trinidad (65 by their husbands or lovers). In colonial Guyana between 1886 and 1890, there were 31 such murders of women; 25 of these were by Indian men. From 1894 to 1905, there were 29 'wife murders'. In Suriname, 40 Indian women were killed in crimes of passion from 1885 to 1890.

When the courts treated so-called wife murders as 'crimes of passion', the men were not hanged but imprisoned. If the woman did not die because of the attack, then the men could be transferred to another estate. But if the woman did die and there were no 'mitigating circumstances', the man was hanged. For example, Gopaul of Grenada was hanged, 'within the walls of the common gaol' for murdering his wife '... under circumstances of great cruelty'. The witnesses reported that Gopaul used a cutlass to chop his wife on the head, neck and hands. In fact, he completely chopped off three of her fingers. When the police constable who came upon the murder scene instructed another Indian, Joseph, to '... tell Gopaul in coolie that what he had done was not right', Gopaul is reported to have replied in French '...I do not care for what I have done.' He claimed that his wife was living with another man.

Similarly, in Jamaica in 1915, Chedda of Tremolesworth was hanged for killing Basharan, his wife, as well as a male immigrant called Chrooni. The motive was jealousy, just like the case of Gopaul.

Some Indian women refused to stay in abusive relationships because of the constant threat of violence. African-Caribbean men were sometimes the target of Indian men's hostility, for some Indian men did not like it when Indian women had sexual relationships with African-Caribbean men. Indian men also came into conflict with British estate overseers over Indian women, as some of the British overseers were sexually abusing the women. The government passed regulations to stop British estate personnel from sexually abusing female immigrants, but the practice never stopped. Some Indian women became pregnant because of these abusive sexual encounters. Managers often had to transfer the men whom they thought were sexually abusing other men's wives to restore peace on the estates.

8 Missionary activities among indentured immigrants

Immigrants that were not from Europe found themselves in a society where their culture was despised and where attempts were made to get rid of parts of their cultural practices. For decades in Jamaica, marriage according to Indian customs were not recognised; and when these marriages were recognised, the law required that the marriage had to be registered in ways uncharacteristic of the Hindu and Muslim culture. Cremation by the pyre system was banned in most places – with the exception of Trinidad and Guyana.

The Indian experience was different to the experiences of the so-called 'liberated' Africans in the Bahamas. Here most churches ignored the call by some elites to convert the Africans to Christianity. The Church of England was concentrated mostly in New Providence. It had little to do with the Africans who were settled in the 'Out Islands', but some Africans joined various non-conformists groups of their own free will.

Many Indians and Chinese resisted missionary efforts to christianise them. Evidence from Jamaica shows that those Indians who converted to Christianity and were sent out by the missionaries to convert other Indians, were chased away by their compatriots. In one case in Vere, Indians torched the Christian church as a way of resisting the conversion activities of the church. The churches in

Vere usually wanted Indians to stop certain of their cultural practices, such as the Muslim festival, the Hussay.

Christianity did not affect the larger Indian populations of colonial Guyana, Suriname and Trinidad, despite the activities of the schools and the Christian churches. By 1891 the Indian community in Trinidad had 2,258 Roman Catholics, 1,712 Anglicans, 1,622 Presbyterians and 122 'other Christians'; 55,180 Hindus, 8,619 Muslims and 436 other 'non-Christians'. There were more Hindus and Muslims among the Indians, even among those Indians born in Trinidad. And there were more Hindu and Muslim Indians who were born in Trinidad than those who converted to Christianity. The majority of Muslims in Suriname were Javanese rather than Indians.

9 Mutual Aid and Friendly Societies

Under slavery, the enslavers were supposed to be responsible for the welfare of the enslaved. As they did not always carry out their responsibilities, Friendly Societies and other initiatives for the enslaved provided some help. After the abolition of slavery, employers had very little concern for the material welfare of the freed people. They left this responsibility to the church, individuals or privately-funded charitable organisations. It is quite clear that after slavery the freed people tried to help themselves and improve their social conditions, but that some help also came from missionaries and charitable organisations. The help of the colonial and metropolitan governments was inadequate.

In colonial Guyana it was usual for the enslaved in a district to appoint a mature and respected male slave, as 'king'. Under the 'king' there were lesser officers or 'subaltern' officers of the same ethnic group. Together this group would take care of the sick, conduct burials and see that the customary rites and dances were observed at funerals. In the years just before emancipation various clergymen had established friendly societies. The earliest Friendly Societies were found in Barbados: an 1835 report noted that 'in the parish of St John there have been for some time two societies of this description, one White one Coloured'.

Cuba

In Cuba, the enslaved had established the *Cabildos de nación*. Some mixed-race members had fought for emancipation through these organisations. The *Cabildos de nación* were primarily established in the towns like Santa Clara. They were semi-religious and grouped their African-born members by their places of origin. The groups owned

property, engaged in rituals, festivities and activities of mutual aid. Many *Cabildos* received support from colonial officials. Leaders of the *Cabildos* acted as mediators between different groups and the colonial authorities and worked to raise political consciousness among their members.

By the 20th Century in Cuba, Mutual Aid societies had largely replaced the *Cabildos de nación*. This is partially because there was a large new membership for Mutual Aid organisations. In fact the main form of association in the 20th Century became the Mutual Aid society. These societies were organised along various lines, sometimes still tied to particular African origin; sometimes divided by work status such as artisan; sometimes established for a particular charitable purpose, such as helping children. They were to be found in Havana and other places. In Santa Clara province alone by 1889 there were 32. The names of some were 'El Trabajo', 'El Amparo', 'Socorros Mutuos', 'La Fraternidad'. The main focus of these societies was on education, recreation and social welfare. A few had political goals, such as the *Casinos Espanioles de Hombres de Color*. Some were made up of only Black people, some only of Coloured people, and others of both.

Colonial Guyana and Jamaica

In colonial Guyana, some of these Mutual Aid societies were formed during Apprenticeship. But the Freemasonry lodges were different from these societies. They were made up of elite men who offered assistance to their own members and not to the poor. In Jamaica and elsewhere in the Caribbean, churches established these Mutual Aid societies. Archbishop Enos Nuttal of the Anglican Church in Jamaica maintained right up to his death in 1916 that concern for the material welfare of his congregation was just as important as evangelical work.

The various denominations did not only build schools and churches, but also engaged in other types of charitable activities. The Anglican Church was very active in forming church-sponsored friendly societies and it also built orphanages. The Baptist churches, which had the largest group of African followers, had associations for their total membership. In fact in Jamaica, the Baptists had the largest single insurance and Mutual Aid organisation for the emancipated population.

The Salvation Army was a religious institution dedicated to voluntary and charitable work in Jamaica and elsewhere in the Caribbean. They came to Jamaica in 1887. Various charitable organisations such as the Kingston Charity Organisation Society also helped the needy. Women's organisations and associations/societies were also formed to help women. For instance, the Women's Self-Help Society was founded in 1897 under the patronage of Lady Musgrave. In Jamaica, the Moravian Upward and Onward Society and the Women's Social Service Association targeted poor women for help. These associations were concerned with the education, moral guidance and domestic roles of mostly poor women.

These societies were used to encourage the newly emancipated to save their earnings and they also helped with their material welfare.

Indian and Chinese settlers also established their own Associations and Societies, which were concerned with poor relief and mutual aid. The Quakers and Presbyterians also set up special facilities to help the Indians. The Indians established various communal associations, for example the East Indian Association of Jamaica, the East Indian National Union and the East Indian Progressive Society. These helped the Indian community in various ways. Indian associations also emerged in Trinidad and Colonial Guyana in the 19th and 20th Centuries. Examples were the East Indian National Association and the East Indian National Congress of Trinidad. These had wider objectives than mutual aid.

The Chinese Benevolent Society was registered in 1890. Its aim was to provide relief for wives and children affected by illnesses and accidents, to maintain the Chinese sanitorium, the Chinese public school, Chinese cemetery and Alms House. In addition, the Jews in Jamaica set up the Hebrew Benevolent Society, among others, to help their members. Patrick Bryan claims that 'since the Black population did not constitute a minority grouping as such, there were no Black ethnic groupings in the sense that there were Jewish, Indian and Chinese...'. But there were organisations and practices which served the needs of the African-Jamaican working class although they were not identified as 'Black' or 'African'. Garvey's UNIA had some features of a benevolent society, aimed at helping the fallen of the race.

Antigua

Antigua was also known for its Friendly Societies, which were mainly run by the churches to help the sick and needy. These societies often helped those who were formerly enslaved to meet medical bills, to bury their dead, and support the old. The Moravians directed eight Friendly Societies in Antigua in 1842 with 4,830 members. The Daily Meal Society in St Johns later developed into a poor relief agency. Other Benevolent and Friendly Societies in Antigua were the Spring Garden Benevolent Society, Gracetown Friendly Society, Newfield, Lebanon and Gracebay Friendly Societies.

Barbados

In Barbados, relatives who had migrated to Panama and other areas of Central America, sent money home and this allowed the newly freed people to develop island-wide financial institutions, which they designed and managed by themselves. The Friendly Society became the leading force in this working class financial culture. Societies allowed workers to insure for sick and death benefits. They paid these benefits off weekly, at a fixed rate. The treasurers managed the money and put the funds in the savings banks. Between 1907 and 1910, about 110 such societies were formed in Barbados. The traditional landholding class felt threatened by these societies and influenced the government to pass laws to limit landownership by these societies. By 1905 there was a law that said that no society could own land bigger than one acre. Societies later became even more attractive to workers because they paid Christmas bonuses, in other words, they paid a lump sum at Christmas for those who paid their weekly subscriptions.

Trinidad and St Vincent

By 1841 there were five Friendly Societies in Trinidad. They were all linked to the Anglican Church and had a membership of 656 people. At this time St Vincent had nine friendly societies with 1,128 members. Reports from Stipendiary Magistrates in Trinidad suggest that the friendly societies there had existed from during the period of slavery. Writing from St Joseph in 1841, one Stipendiary Magistrate noted:

> The benefit societies that exist now existed since the time of slavery; these consist of a certain number of persons who pay weekly, or monthly a certain sum for the maintenance and support of the sick, and for the burial of the dead.

10 Inter-ethnic relations

As we have seen, the working classes were culturally and politically divided. In some colonies, African-Caribbean people saw the immigrant workers as a threat to their social and economic status, and this caused conflicts between Asian and African-Caribbeans. In the French-colonised and British-colonised territories, both groups felt that they were racially superior to each other, and so both disliked each other. As Indians had been brought in to do the tasks that were thought to be 'unskilled' by society, Black-skinned people began to use negative terms to describe Indians: coolie slaves, liars, weak/fragile labourers. Some black skinned people regarded Indians as culturally inferior because their lifestyle was not European or African. The Indians, for their part (and despite the black skin of the southern Indians whom many regarded as 'Blacks'), regarded African-Caribbean people as inferior on cultural grounds. The whiter-skinned Indians from North India regarded black skin as inferior. They saw their own physical features as closer to those of Europeans.

These ideas and misconceptions created tensions which at times turned violent. Anti-Chinese and anti-Portuguese riots also took place. The racial conflicts which erupted in Caribbean society, especially among the working classes, worked to the advantage of the government and ruling classes as they did not want any working class unity amongst the various groups. In fact they promoted a 'divide and rule' policy by using immigrant workers as strikebreakers when there were disputes between African-Caribbean workers and the White employer class. However, in Jamaica, colonial Guyana, and Martinique this did not always happen, and there were cases of African-Caribbean-Indian unity in the class struggle against the largely White capitalist class. Overtime, greater knowledge and understanding removed some of the tensions.

11 The search for political representation and legal rights

Another way that the ruling classes made sure that they kept the social order linked to its slavery origins was to maintain the political system that existed at that time. There were similarities and differences across territories with regard to control of African-Caribbean people's political rights.

African-Cubans got the right to vote in gradual stages. Four years before full emancipation, the electoral law of 1882 provided that those who had been enslaved did not have the right to vote until they had been excused from patronato for three years. After 1888, as long as African-Cubans met the qualifications for the vote, political parties – mainly liberal ones – fought one another for their votes.

However, in the French-colonised territories after 1848, every adult male had the right to vote, while women only gained this right in 1946. Each French colony sent three deputies to the National Assembly in Paris. Mixed-race men, such as Francois Auguste Perrinin, Pierre Marie Pory-Papy and Louisy Mathieu, and some African-descended people were elected to positions of deputies, mayors, senators and councilmen.

In the immediate period after slavery in the British-colonised Caribbean, planters wanted the government to increase the qualifications for voters and those wanting to be elected to the House of Assembly. In Jamaica in 1858, for example, a voter had to have the following qualifications: he had to own land which had a clear annual value of £6, or pay a rent of £20 per year, or be paid a salary of £50 a year, or pay taxes to the amount of 20 per cent, or have £100 in the bank for the twelve months prior to voting. So the number of voters naturally was low – 2,500, made up of planters, attorneys, agents, clerks, and shopkeepers. The Colonial Office opposed these attempts to deny freed people the vote and they would not pass bills which would use the taxation system to achieve this. But the Colonial Office kept the Crown Colony government in Trinidad, St Lucia, and in colonial Guyana. And European planters continued to control the 'Court of Policy', which was left over from the Dutch system of local government. Among other things, this meant that only European people had the nominated positions in councils.

African-Caribbean men lost finally got the vote in most territories after the suppression of the Morant Bay Rebellion of 1865 in Jamaica. To keep political control and to continue to deny the newly freed a role in government, the Jamaican Assembly chose a Crown Colony government after 1865. Other territories, which were not already Crown Colonies followed, except for Barbados, Bermuda and the Bahamas. The result was a strong government, less local input and the strengthening of British rule.

Women were particularly disadvantaged politically. For European and black men who had some property got the vote up to 1865, but there was a backward gender ideology that said that women were unsuitable for the 'public' world of politics and so women were denied the vote until universal adult suffrage in the 20th century.

To sum up

This chapter has tried to show that the European elites used their political and cultural power to discourage community development amongst the African and certain Asian population. They refused to recognise or respect many aspects of their cultures; they used their control of the state to pass certain discriminatory laws, which were backed up by the newly established constabularies; and they secured their European social culture with the help of the Christian missionaries. However, immigrants and the formerly enslaved designed their own measures of community aid. They had some allies in the form of charitable and benevolent organisations.

Freed people would become increasingly dissatisfied with the existing political system, and protest against the denial of the right to participate in government in the years after 1900.

Revision questions

1 Read the extract and then answer the questions which follow:

'A characteristic feature of the post-slavery period was the attempt by colonial governments to bring about what they termed 'social order' among the labouring classes.'

   a What does the term 'social order' mean?
   b State two reasons why the colonial governments wanted to bring about 'social order' among the labouring classes.
   c State two ways in which colonial governments tried to bring about 'social order' among the labouring classes.
   d State two ways in which the labouring classes opposed the attempts by the colonial governments to control their social lives.

2 Select one Caribbean territory and write an essay about the state of the following conditions in the period 1838–1900:
   Education
   Social services
   Mass political representation

3 Read the extract below and answer the questions that follow:

'Health conditions in the British-colonised Caribbean were poor despite the existence of laws to regulate the health conditions of Indian immigrants. Some improvements were made towards the end of the 19th Century.'

   a Give two examples of the laws passed to regulate the health conditions of Indian immigrants.
   b State two reasons why health conditions remained poor despite the laws to regulate the health conditions of Indian immigrants.
   c State three improvements which were made in Trinidad to regulate the health conditions of Indian immigrants.
   d State two ways in which the social conditions of the Indian immigrants differed from those of the African-Caribbean people.

4 Write fully on the reasons that African customs have survived in the Caribbean.

Vacuum pan

Reorganised sugar economy: 1846 – circa 1985

'When things get bad, down in Trinidad, Jah, Jah never leave us alone.'
(General Grant)

Introduction

The way work, money and the economy were organised in the Caribbean after slavery was significantly different from how they were organised during slavery. One general trend was to broaden the economic base, and move away from excessive reliance on the sugar industry, which in most Caribbean slave systems had been considered 'king'. In the British-colonised territories, for example, the Sugar Duties Act was passed in 1846. This Act affected economic life within and outside the colonies; in negative and positive ways. One important effect of the Act was that it accelerated a real decline in the sugar industry. Some territories responded to this decline by reducing dependence on the sugar crop and developing their expertise in a wide range of agricultural activities. For years many colonies had grown and exported crops other than sugar cane so they now took the opportunity to deepen and strengthen these activities.

In this period the Caribbean also became more deeply incorporated into the international economy. Asia became more important as a major source of immigrant labour. The United States of America, and to a much lesser extent Canada, became important to the growth of new trade and investment opportunities.

Over the next three chapters we will discuss the various economic activities in the Caribbean from 1846 through to 1985. In this chapter we will focus on the sugar industry in various colonies. In Chapter 11 we will look at other economic activities and in Chapter 12 we will look at the integration of the Caribbean into the international economy through emigration.

In this chapter we will learn about:
1   The British-colonised Caribbean territories: producers' crises and adjustments
2   The sugar industry in the French-colonised Caribbean
3   The sugar industry in the Spanish-colonised Caribbean
4   The sugar industry in the Dutch-colonised and Danish-colonised Caribbean territories
5   The World Wars and the sugar industry

1   The British-colonised Caribbean territories: producers' crises and adjustments

Even before the Sugar Duties Act (SDA) was passed in 1846, the sugar industry was weakening in several British-colonised Caribbean territories. Some of the reasons for the weakening were:
■   the landholding elite could not bring together the needs of labour and capital
■   many planters owed money to their creditors
■   poor administration of the estates caused loss of profits
■   competition on the world market from low cost sugar cane producers in Brazil, Cuba and Puerto Rico who still used enslaved labour.

Other reasons for the weakening sugar industry and the move towards freer trade after 1846 were:
■   the rising cost of sugar production
■   a labour shortage in some territories
■   the lack of credit and therefore of money to buy machines, pay wages and import labour
■   the collapse of financial institutions
■   competition on the world market from beet sugar producers
■   world trade and investment shifted away from the Caribbean (except for Cuba, Puerto Rico and the Dominican Republic)
■   industrialisation in Europe.

Some of these reasons will be explored in more detail in this chapter.

The Sugar Duties Act and free trade

Historically sugar production had been profitable for two reasons: the trade in enslaved Africans (chattel slavery supplied unwaged labour) and the priority and special treatment given to sugar from the Caribbean in the British market. Even though the costs for producing sugar were high, sugar colonies in the British-colonised Caribbean were protected. They paid lower taxes in the British market than Spanish and French sugar producers and they had a guarantee that their sugar would be bought in Britain. This last advantage was gradually removed after slavery and Apprenticeship were abolished in 1838. The Sugar Duties Act of 1846 was an important sign of the decline to come.

Fig 10.1 British Prime Minister, Lord John Russell

In August 1846 the British Prime Minister, Lord John Russell, announced that everyone would pay the same sugar duties or taxes. This meant that no Caribbean territory had special treatment as sellers in the British market. The Sugar Duties Act said that taxes on all foreign sugar would be reduced to 21s, whether it was slave grown or free grown. The way this would happen was that the tax on foreign sugar would be reduced by 1s 6d per year until 1851. This date was later extended to 1854. By this time the taxes on all sugar entering the British market would be the same.

This development satisfied European customers who were calling for 'free trade', meaning they wanted the freedom to buy from any producer, at the best price. Free trade would allow the consumer to get cheaper sugar. However, this call for free trade went beyond the need to buy cheaper sugar. Britain was rapidly developing industries which needed plenty of cheap raw materials like cotton. It could not get all of these raw materials in enough quantities and at good prices from its own colonies, so it had to look elsewhere.

Beet sugar competition

In 1747, a Berlin scientist Andreas Marggraf demonstrated how sugar could be taken from the red and white beet. Others continued his experiments until beet sugar became a commercial crop in the 1880s. Beets gather sugar in their thickened roots and could be grown outside of the tropics, which was the usual environment for cane sugar. Eventually beet sugar took over a large share of the market for sweeteners. In fact, since the 1880s when beet sugar became a serious competitor in the sugar market, there has usually been too much sugar on the world market – except during war times.

The growing of commercial beet sugar crops started in France and then spread across Europe to Belgium, the German states, to Austria-Hungary, Russia and to England. Some reasons for the commercialisation of beet sugar were: the abolition of slavery in the British and French-colonised Caribbean and the decline in sugar production in these colonies; the removal of the high taxes charged on foreign sugar sold to Britain – a major market; the fact that some European countries helped to finance the export of beet sugar; the depressed state of European agriculture and the need for farmers to grow a profitable export crop; and the fact that if beet sugar were planted in rotation with other crops it increased the harvest of the other crops.

New producers of sugar

In the slavery period the British-colonised Caribbean sugar producers also faced competition from cheaper producers. First they had to compete against the French who produced more sugar at a cheaper rate, especially before the Haitian revolution. Then, after the collapse of the sugar sector in Haiti, the British-colonised Caribbean faced competition from sugar producers in Brazil, Cuba, Florida, Louisiana and European colonies in Asia.

Even in the post-slavery period, in addition to beet sugar competition, the British-colonised Caribbean had to compete with new producers of cane sugar. This was because sugar plantations developed in colonies in Asia, Africa and the Pacific. Cane sugar industries developed in Bengal, Mauritius, Reunion, Java, Fiji, Natal, Queensland and Hawaii.

Another competitor was the western states of the USA, which produced beet sugar. The US producers had some advantages over the British-colonised Caribbean: they still had enslaved labour and a lower cost of production. These factors attracted investments in new and more fertile land which was brought under sugarcane.

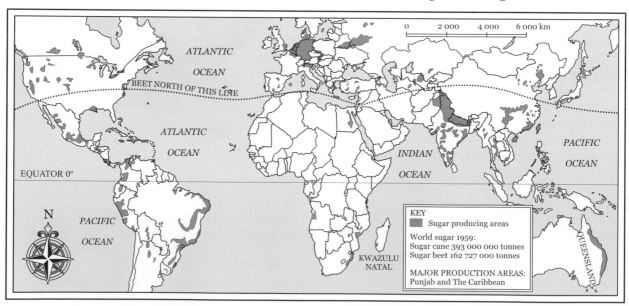

Fig 10.2 Sugar- and beet-producing countries

Industrialisation in Europe

As the Industrial Revolution progressed in Europe, large cities and towns developed into enormous market centres. The general pattern in the urban areas was for the prices of imported goods to fall to low levels. Cheaper sugar was now available and more and more working class people could afford it.

Urban areas developed and grew at a fast rate. As this happened, there was greater demand in the cities for other foodstuffs. For example, the growing population needed more wheat and beef, at cheaper prices. There was an equally demanding need for raw cotton for the increasing number of textile factories.

The Caribbean only produced a small quantity of cotton which was not enough to supply the factories in Europe. In addition, the sugar from the Caribbean was also not enough to supply the sugar refineries. British consumers wanted the government to stop giving their Caribbean colonies preferential treatment. The industrialists pressed the government to open the market and get more and cheaper foreign supplies.

The consequences of the beginning of free trade

At first when the Sugar Duties Act was passed, it did not seem that it would make any significant impact upon the Caribbean. In 1847 when the Act came into effect, the colonies had produced a large crop – 23 per cent above the average of what they had produced in the previous eight years. But the British market soon began to buy more and more sugar from other foreign sources. In the next five years (after 1847) there was a 30 per cent drop in the export of sugar from the British-colonised Caribbean and in addition, the price of sugar fell. In 1846 the price of sugar was 34s 5d per hundred weight (cwt). By 1855 Britain imported foreign sugar at the same price and under the same conditions as British Caribbean sugar. In this year, sugar cost less than 26s 10d per cwt.

Did you know?

Cwt – hundred weight – is a full weight measurement created by US merchants in the late 1800s. This unit is equal to exactly 100 pounds.

Price of sugar per cwt in the British-colonised Caribbean

Year	Price of sugar per cwt
1846	34s 5d
1852	35s 2d
1855	26s 10d
1914	12s 0d

Between 1855 and 1857 prices did rise a little to 35s 2d per cwt, but by 1860 they had declined again. They continued to fall during the next ten years, which were unstable due to the American Civil War and fluctuations in the world market. During the American Civil War, Cuban, Brazilian and other foreign sugar producers sold to the British market instead of the US market. This created a further oversupply of sugar and prices deteriorated.

In the 1870s the British Caribbean sugar producers suffered even more because Europe could buy sugar much cheaper from local beet sugar producers. From the 1870s the British-colonised Caribbean suffered a 25 per cent drop in the sale of their sugar to the British market. By 1914, sugar from the British-colonised Caribbean cost just 12s per cwt in Britain. By this time about 125,000 tons of the total of 1.6 million tons of sugar consumed in Britain came from cane sugar.

The main reason why prices did not fall even further was because the world population was growing at a rapid rate and this meant there was a higher demand for sugar. But not even small increases in sugar prices could make up for rising cost of sugar production and the rising shipping costs. The reduced sugar prices also added to governments' financial woes. Unemployment and emigration had increased because of financial problems in the British-colonised Caribbean countries. This meant that fewer taxes were collected to pay for public administration.

Under these changed circumstances Caribbean sugar producers found it difficult to make a profit. Only producers in Cuba, and to a lesser extent in Puerto Rico, seemed confident that they could make large profits from sugar. These colonies attracted large US and European investments in the sugar industry, but at the same time dozens of trading houses in the British-colonised Caribbean went bankrupt.

The trouble was not yet over. Caribbean planters found it difficult to get credit or loans because banks and other credit institutions were closing. This meant that planters could not pay their wage bills or their financial commitments in Britain. Both the West Indies Bank in Barbados and the Planters Bank in Jamaica closed. The value of estates fell sharply and estates changed hands.

For example, an estate called Bog Estate in Jamaica, which was valued at £80,000 during slavery, sold for only £500 in 1849.

There were other disastrous effects for capitalists of the beginning of free trade. There was general decline and economic ruin everywhere in the British-colonised Caribbean. Colonial governments found it more and more difficult to collect taxes because merchant shippers could not sell their full cargo and could not pay customs duties. This meant the government could not always pay the salaries of public officials or the wages of workers on time, as they had a shortage of money. Workers became increasingly agitated as planters tried to reduce their wages. The result was an industrial culture that had social and political conflict at its centre – which was not altogether different from the culture during slavery.

In the 1890s sugar still made up 97 per cent of the exports of Barbados and St Kitts-Nevis; 95 per cent of Antigua's exports, and 92 per cent of colonial Guyana's. But, by 1900 the sugar industry just about disappeared in some territories. Even in those territories in which the sugar industry remained important, planters abandoned a significant number of estates.

Antigua, for example, had 107 estates in 1865, but only 53 in 1900. In Jamaica the number of estates decreased from 513 in 1846 to 140 in 1896. In Trinidad there were only 56 by 1900. Altogether the sugar estates declined from a total of 2, 200 in the entire British-colonised Caribbean at Emancipation to about 800 by 1900.

By this date too the sugar industry had collapsed in Montserrat, Nevis, St Vincent, Grenada. Here former sugar lands were turned over to other crops. In Dominica the sugar sector was already handicapped by the mountainous terrain and labour shortages. Now it struggled to remain workable. By 1900 the only territories which still got most of their income from sugar exports and where this industry employed a significant percentage of the labour force were Antigua, Barbados, colonial Guyana, St Kitts, St Lucia, and Trinidad.

How the Caribbean producers reacted to all of this

Planters in the British-colonised Caribbean protested against the Sugar Duties Act, arguing that the movement towards freer trade would ruin them. For example, Barton Premium, a planter in colonial Guyana, complained that, 'In 1844 when [Prime Minister Peel] brought forth his free trade scheme, he declared that the British planter could bear a little more competition; ... We [the planters] have been like men bound hand and foot and thrown into a stream, while our countrymen stand quietly on the bank and allow us to sink ...'

The West India Committee in London, in its role as representative of Colonial Assemblies, supported these planters. Members called for the monopoly that these planters had in the British market, to be restored. They threatened not to pay salaries of government officials and to prevent the functioning of the government. However, free trade was developing and growing and it was evident that these protests would have limited, if any, effect. What the planters needed was to respond more positively to their changed circumstance. They could go out of business, as many did, invest in non-traditional activities, or try to find new and more efficient ways to run a profitable sugar industry.

We can group planters by how they responded to the 19th Century challenges facing the sugar industry:

- Those who could not or would not make initial adjustments to control the systematic decline of the sector. This included planters in Jamaica.
- Those planters who tried to reorganise the sector. They managed to increase their productivity, but not their production of sugar. Among this group were the planters of Barbados, St Kitts. Nevis and Antigua.
- Those planters who developed the plantation sector anew and managed to compete on the international market, either because they used new forms of forced labour or because of significant investments in their fertile land. The planters of colonial Guyana and Trinidad fell into this group. Along with planters in Barbados they showed an increase in sugar production in the post-slavery decades.

Adjustments that planters had to make

People inside and outside of the Caribbean who had invested in the colonial economy, realised that there were serious economic difficulties and that they had to find some solutions to overcome these difficulties. One of the main investors was the British government. It introduced the Encumbered Estates Court Act in 1854 to make the sale of estates that owed debts much easier. Under earlier laws, properties could not be sold unless their debts were paid. But it was more and more difficult for landholders to pay their debts in the post-slavery period, especially as the value of their estates fell drastically after 1846.

In most cases the market values placed on the estates was so low that the actual sale did not bring in enough cash to take care of the debts. These estates could not be sold easily as there was too much debt. Those to whom the debts were owed did not want to take the debtor planters to court, as they were scared that they would not even get back enough money to even pay their legal fees.

The Encumbered Estates Court Act allowed any owner of an estate that owed debts in the Caribbean to have the estate sold by a special court, which was set up in London as well as in the colonies. The courts decided how to divide up the proceeds of the sale between the estate creditors so that the new owner would receive the estate free of debts and burdens. St Vincent and Tobago made use of this Act in the 1850s; Jamaica and others followed in the 1860s; St Kitts adopted it in 1860. The first estate in St Kitts to be affected by the act was Hermitage. Antigua introduced the Act in 1864; Montserrat in 1865; and Nevis in 1867.

Barbados, Trinidad, colonial Guyana and St Lucia did not adopt the Act. The Barbadians were afraid that the effect of the Act would be to transfer ownership of their lands to 'foreign' investors. This would threaten their social order, which was based on plantation ownership. Instead, they adopted a local solution in the form of the Court of Chancery. In this way the elite of the country, through the Master of Chancery, had control over all estate sales, and this ensured that Barbadian planters remained in control and in ownership of the estates rather than give power to foreigners.

The Encumbered Estates courts went out of existence after 1893, but between 1854 and 1893 382 estates were sold under the authority of the Court. Of these estates 148 were in Jamaica. So new owners came into possession of estates in the British-colonised Caribbean which they then developed. Many of the new owners were merchants, sometimes based in England, who had money to make new improvements in the sugar industry.

The British government set up various Select Committees and Commissions to investigate the state of the economy in the British-colonised Caribbean. One was the Select Committee of Enquiry of 1847 to 1848, which was appointed to enquire into the condition of sugar and coffee planting in the British colonies. Lord Bentinck, chief spokesman of the sugar interests in the British Parliament, chaired the Committee which took evidence from many planters. Its report proposed that British colonial sugar be given a preference of 10 shillings per cwt over foreign sugar for six years. The government did not accept this but they did postpone the implementation date for the Sugar Duties Act to 1854. A Royal Commission of 1882 was sent to Jamaica, the Leeward and the Windward Islands. The aim of the Commission was to look into public finance and the methods of raising revenue as well as to see if the public service could be reduced without seriously affecting the public interest.

The report of the 1882 Royal Commission was published in three parts. Among the recommendations were: the reduction in the number of public servants in Jamaica; the coming together of various offices to reduce costs; a single government for the Leeward and Windward Islands; further reductions in offices and salaries of public officials in these islands; a standard tax system for all islands; a lowering in the rate of import duties especially on basic food items, such as flour, fish, rice and tea; higher import taxes on luxuries; doing away with export taxes; immigration of workers so that the plantations could continue; and encouraging small farmers to farm crops other than cane. So, the Commission wanted to see the large estates continuing. Hardly any of these recommendations were put in place.

Finally, the 19th Century came to a close with the Norman Commission of 1896, headed by Sir Henry Norman and appointed by Secretary of State, Joseph Chamberlain. The Caribbean in 1896 still showed no serious signs of significantly reducing its heavy dependence on the sugar plantation sector, despite the evidence of the full effects of beet sugar competition on the region, and the fact that lower cost producers of cane sugar had increased their share of the sugar market.

The Commission concluded in its 1897 report that the price of foreign beet sugar was the main cause of distress in the British-colonised Caribbean. It recommended certain measures to improve efficiency among cane sugar producers. These included: the setting up of central factories; the development of other alternative crops to sugar be developed; greater encouragement of banana cultivation and trade; the expansion of the peasantry so as to expand local food production and reduce dependence on imported food; the promotion of agricultural and industrial education; the establishment of a Department of Botany to help small farmers; and a financial grant of £20,000 for five years to the Leeward Islands and £30,000 to Dominica and St Vincent for road development and land settlement.

After the submission of the report, the government made significant financial grants. In March 1898 Joseph Chamberlain voted £120,000, and in August £41,500 was to be used by the various colonies to balance their budgets and to put in place the recommendations of the Norman Commission. The Imperial Department of Agriculture for the West Indies was founded in Barbados to help the economies in the region diversify away from the sugar economy. The government also granted a subsidy for improved shipping services to the Caribbean to assist the banana trade.

The sugar producers eventually found ways of putting into practice some of the ideas of the various Commissions, especially the Norman Commission. They took steps to increase their harvest by planting new varieties of cane, they changed their field operations, and they made technological improvements. They also tried to find new markets for their sugar and eventually to diversify their economic activities. Some of these solutions will be explored below.

New markets

Competition in the British market forced its colonial producers in the Caribbean to look for other markets for their sugar. They found some of these markets in the USA, and by 1884 they were selling close to 50 per cent of their total production to the USA. In 1895 the USA bought almost half of Trinidad's sugar crop but, after 1898, it was Cuban and Puerto Rican rather than Caribbean sugar which dominated the US market.

But the USA was developing its own sugar industry. It was also putting high taxes on foreign sugar to help its own companies who had invested in sugar in Cuba and Puerto Rico. The British-colonised Caribbean tried to increase sales to Canada to balance its declining sales to the USA and Britain. In fact Canada in 1897 agreed to give British-colonised Caribbean sugar lower custom taxes on their market. During the First World War sugar prices in Britain went up and war conditions made it difficult for the sugar to get to Britain. However, Canada provided an outlet for British-colonised Caribbean sugar.

Technological changes

In the post-slavery British-colonised Caribbean there were significant advances in the industrial technology associated with sugar production and manufacturing. Before 1800 the only significant technological change in the sugar industry was the introduction of the 3-roller mill and the Jamaican train. After 1800 new forms of knowledge in engineering and chemistry, associated with the industrial revolution, were used in the sugar industry in many countries.

Fig 10.3 Old sugar mill

The new technology created larger mills and factories and allowed new and more efficient equipment to be used in the sugar factories. In the Caribbean the extent to which this new technology was used, depended on how available money was, the spirit of entrepreneurship, and the planter's optimism about the future. So the pattern of implementation varied from one territory to another.

Steam power

As early as 1768 John Steward had used steam as an energy source in agriculture in Jamaica. Steam power became more widespread after 1846 in other parts of the Caribbean where the sugar industry survived. One English company exported 114 steam mills between 1802 and 1820; and another 80 from 1813 to 1817 to customers in the Caribbean and Latin America.

Steam-driven mills were expensive, especially for estates in the Leeward Islands as they did not each produce the 375 tons per annum necessary to make steam-driven mills economical. A high-pressure steam engine could cost £1,250 and a steam-heated clarifier could cost £400. The shipping, installation and maintenance of steam engines and steam-driven equipment would naturally push up the cost of producing sugar. By 1878, there were only 35 steam-driven mills in Antigua and 74 in St Kitts; but these were small mills. By 1820, only 20 per cent of mills in Cuba were steam-driven. This increased to 70 per cent by 1860. Out of 500 estates in Barbados in 1862, only 30 used steam mills.

By 1900 steam engines were used in many territories to drive the machinery in the factories. They replaced the old animal mills and water/wind mills and helped producers get more sugar from the canes crushed.

Central factories and estate amalgamation

Instead of every estate having its own factory, central factories were created to service several estates. The central factory was first established in the French-colonised Caribbean territories in the 1840s. The change to central factories was gradual as it needed large sums of money – more than individual landowners could raise. Between 1896 and 1917 the number of factories in Trinidad fell from 39 to 14. Of these only two corresponded to what formerly constituted a plantation.

The establishment of central factories and the closing of some individual estate factories had social implications for the traditional planter elite. In the past a sugar estate had been more than an economic unit. It represented social status for the planter elite, and consisted of both the land and the factory with its capital equipment. Central factories took some power away from the planter elite who now had less input into decisions like which buildings were erected where.

Many estates were combined or amalgamated, instead of operating as separate properties. Several British and North American companies were involved in this amalgamation process in a few different Spanish-colonised Caribbean countries. This process reduced the number of estates in the territories that still grew sugar on a fairly large scale. Amalgamation involved the combination of cane areas so that a larger supply of could be provided for one central factory. This amalgamation took place earliest in Cuba, colonial Guyana and Trinidad.

In Trinidad, a Scottish capitalist, Norman Lamont bought up many small and less profitable estates in the Naparima valley and amalgamated them. By 1895, 34 out of the 59 estates in Trinidad were owned by British corporations or individual capitalists. By 1897, most of Trinidad's sugar was produced by 11 units owned by British Corporations or individual investors. An example was the Colonial Company which in 1872 had completed the first central factory, called the Ursine St Madeline, in Trinidad. Besides the Colonial Company, there were Tennant & Co. which owned Malgretoret and La Fortune, Gregor Turnbull & Co.

By 1938, there were two major company operations in Trinidad: Caroni Ltd, which was a subsidiary of Tate & Lyle, and St Madeline Sugar Company, which was a subsidiary of Henckel du Buisson. These two firms accounted for two-thirds of the island's sugar production. Eight other firms shared the balance.

In colonial Guyana, the amalgamation of sugar plantations under large British firms occurred from 1840. The result was the pooling of machinery and the joining of irrigation systems. For example, Diamond Estate came into being when five estates were united. Vryheids Lust, a large estate on the east coast of Demerara, was an amalgamation of several estates.

By the 1870s the process of amalgamation had reached such a level in colonial Guyana that, of the 404 estates in operation in 1834, only 135 remained in 1870. Of the 135, people who did not live in colonial Guyana owned 85 estates. Owners with the largest land holdings, the Colonial Company, owned nine large estates. Other investors included Messrs. James Ewing, Sandback, Parker & Co., Messrs Bosanquet, Curtis & Co., and other well-established houses such as Booker Brothers, Barber & Co., and Winter and Preston. Amalgamation combined with modern machinery, resulted in increased output of sugar. Between 1886 and 1897 some 610,000 tonnes were produced.

In Cuba, by the end of the 19th Century, the *centrales* were the main sugar producers. The sugar mills could not produce the level of sugar of the *centrales* and disappeared rather quickly, especially after the Ten Year's War. In 1877 Cuba recorded 1,190 mills, but only 207 in 1899. Some of the large corporations included the Cuban American Sugar Company which had six mills; the Cuba Cane Sugar Company which owned twelve mills; the General Sugar Company and its subsidiaries which owned nine mills; and the United Fruit Co. with two mills. The giant *centrales* owned land and sugar factories. They were known as *latifundia*, or large corporations.

Jamaica and other territories only moved to this solution of amalgamation later. Records from 1884 show only six amalgamations. Later in 1909 to 1910, Amity Hall merged with Perrins, Pusey Hall, Sutton-Chesterfield and Low Ground estates in Clarendon while Morelands combined with Hillside-Raymond. Eventually in Jamaica, British sugar companies like Tate and Lyle worked through the West Indies Sugar Company to buy up several properties to grow sugar on a large scale and run central factories, for example at Frome in Westmoreland.

The process of amalgamation in Jamaica resulted in a decrease in the number of individual estates from 670 in 1836 to 39 in 1930.

It was only toward the second decade of the 20th Century that Barbados began to mechanise, when it was affected by the emigration of its agricultural workers. The planters in Barbados did away with inefficient mills for which they needed windmill repairmen and carpenters, many of whom had emigrated. So they brought in steam engines for the windmills and increased the area under cane. By late 1911, fourteen sugar mills in eight of the eleven parishes in Barbados had improved their production methods and by 1921 there were nineteen modern central sugar factories, which milled canes from surrounding estates.

By 1913 Antigua had two central factories at Gunthorpe's and Bedall's and one in St Kitts at Golden Rock.

New equipment

The establishment of central factories allowed the landowners to install new machinery in the boiling and curing houses and to close inefficient factories. The ideas for the introduction and design of new equipment came from refineries in Europe and research in the sugar beet industry.

Two significant types of equipment were the vacuum pan and the centrifugal dryer. Under artificial conditions of reduced pressure, the vacuum pan lowered the boiling point of the cane juice and greatly economised on fuel. It dated back to 1813 when Edward Charles Howard patented his invention.

In 1832 the first vacuum pan was installed in colonial Guyana on the estate Vreed-en-Hoop. By 1895 most of Trinidad's sugar was produced by the vacuum pan. They used the Multiple Effect Evaporation Units, which were first used in Louisiana in 1845. In this unit two or more pans were linked in a series so that vapour from one pan could be used to evaporate liquid in the one above. But these were expensive: even a small unit could set the producer back by £40,00 to £50,000. So these pans were really best suited for large enterprises, which had central factories and which had increased the acreage under cane so that the factories could get larger supplies for the mills.

Despite the expense some territories, including Barbados, introduced vacuum pans. Some of the Leeward Islands experimented, unsuccessfully, with substitutes for the vacuum pan. Some of these were the Gaddesden and Evans or Schroeder's disc pans, or Kneller's concentrating pan, and a vacuum chest for the curing of sugar by using air pressure to push the molasses away from the crystals. The vacuum pans allowed the sugar to be boiled at a lower temperature than the old method. This reduced the possibility of destroying the sugar crystals through too much heat.

Large estates using steam engines installed centrifugal driers, which were also used in Europe in the beet industry. These were more efficient at separating sugar crystals from the molasses and increased the amount of sugar produced. So they lost less through molasses leaking from the casks. The centrifugal driers gave a drier sugar and did away with the old dripping method of drying the sugar in the curing house.

Railways

Railways revolutionised transportation within the plantation sector. They connected the fields to the factories and connected the plantations to the towns. By the second half of the century, this was how the modern plantation sector functioned. In contrast, the traditional plantations depended upon oxen and mule carts, in addition to the use of humans as beasts of burden.

Railways allowed for the faster and greater transportation of canes to the mills. This was important for the new mills needed larger quantities of cane supplied at a faster rate. Operations in the field itself were not that affected by technological changes. Field operations continued to use manual labour in the period up to 1962, as so many labourers were dependent on the sugar industry for employment.

The railway also allowed workers to live away from the plantations. In fact they could now live in towns and travel to work, as many did in Cuba and Puerto Rico. This separation of work place and living quarters had a huge effect on workers' social life. In some areas it broke down the traditional tying of workers to estate villages and allowed them to have far greater social and cultural freedom.

There were also some improvements in field operations and agricultural methods. Cultivators ratooned less, used more fertiliser, used the plough where the land was level enough to allow it to be effective, and planted the rows thinner to give canes space to grow. By the 1960s farmers used mechanically-driven ploughs, tractor-drawn gyrotillers, disc ploughs and sub-soilers on a wide-scale.

Fig 10.4 Hauling cane with tractor, Cuba

New varieties of cane

The development of new varieties of cane was another way in which planters met the challenges that faced the Caribbean sugar industry. Planters were looking for new varieties of cane even before the abolition of slavery. By 1800 Otaheiti and Bourbon cane had replaced older types but the new types were still not resistant to disease. By 1890 Otaheiti was replaced by Cheribow cane and other types that were more resistant to diseases.

Caribbean producers also scientifically experimented with the cane plant itself. Towards the end of the 19th Century they discovered that sugar cane could produce fertile seeds. This fact, together with the new field of research in plant genetics, was an enormous advantage to the industry. Local research was helped when a Department of Agriculture was created in Trinidad in the 1890s and the Imperial College of Tropical Agriculture was created in the 1920s. Also, the Imperial Department of Agriculture had been opened in Barbados in 1898.

Other efforts to maintain the sugar industry

Some plantations survived by using seasonal labour to bring down the cost of wages and by importing indentured Indian workers on a large scale. The British government assisted colonies by lending them money to import indentured workers, and by removing restrictions on immigration. The positive effects of these efforts filtered down to the owners who made a profit. However, the workers did not benefit from this. So it is not surprising that as the planters increased their wealth, they experienced more and more labour protests.

The sugar culture in the region was so deep-rooted, that even small farmers continued to participate in the sugar industry into the 20th Century. Some of them did so by renting lands and supplying canes to the central factories. They were often exploited and they protested that they were not being paid for their canes at the same rate as the big planters.

By the 1920s the British government seemed more responsive to the argument that the sugar sector in the Caribbean could not re-organise to compete with other producers and become independent. So the government began to consider ways in which it could be more supportive of the sector, and of the whole colonial order or organisation of the colonial society and economy. It brought in policies that gave some protection for sugar exported from the region. In 1932 at a conference held in Ottawa, Canada, Britain also announced that it would take steps to import supplies from its colonies at lower taxes than from elsewhere.

These developments encouraged more producers to increase their efforts to export sugar. The production of sugar rose considerably in Trinidad and colonial Guyana. In the 1930s cane sugar prices showed some improvement from the steep drop of 1929, which was caused by competition from beet sugar farmers. Planters in colonial Guyana and Trinidad were at the top of the list of colonies that showed they had benefited substantially from the government's efforts.

The outbreak of World War II in 1939 created an enormous increase in the demand for sugar in Britain. One effect of this was that cane sugar from the colonies was bought at special prices. Jamaica and colonial Guyana responded by increasing their output of sugar through farming more land.

However, sugar production did not increase in Trinidad. The reason for this has to do with an alternative to the sugar industry – the income generated by the establishment of the American naval bases at Chaguaramas. Also by 1939 the indentureship system was abolished, and this led once more to a labour shortage in the sugar industry.

Did you know?

The International Sugar Agreement of 1953 was negotiated by the United Nations to introduce a degree of stability in the world sugar market. Its aim was to oblige the countries that were parties to the agreement to import only from those member countries whenever the prices of sugar fell below 4 cents per pound.

Belize developed late as a sugar-exporting country, producing only 1, 000 tonnes per year in 1935. Even when a sugar factory was built in Corozal in 1935, this still did not bring about any dramatic increase in their sugar output. But by 1955 when British and Jamaican investors took over the factory, production increased rapidly. By 1961 they were producing 28,000 tonnes. The company's estates and about 500 independent farmers supplied the factory with cane.

By 1962 the British-colonised and independent Caribbean was no longer the most important sugar supplier to the world. Before World War I, the Caribbean supplied 33 per cent of the world's cane and over 38 per cent in 1951 to 1955. But in 1968 to 1972, it only supplied 21 per cent. Some territories increased their output after 1962 as the following table shows.

Table 10.2: Sugar producers compared

Territory	1934–1939	1951–1955	1968–1972
	Output [thousand tons]		
Barbados	123	176	146
Cuba	2,741	5,512	5,809
Dom. Rep.	445	613	914
Guadeloupe	52	100	154
Guyana	192	242	358
Haiti	39	55	65
Jamaica	104	330	404
Lee/Wind	63	89	34
Martinique	57	61	33
Puerto Rico	839	1,118	399
T & T	140	162	235
USVI	4	10	0
Carib. Total	4,799	8,468	8,612
World cane	14,525	22,091	41,247
World beet	24,580	36,900	71,831

From: Internet Sugar Council (1963); 1956, United Nations (1949) FAO 1971.

The ending of World War II in 1945 created circumstances that worked against the profitable development of the sugar industry. Shipping facilities were scarce and this resulted in a setback for the Caribbean sugar industry. This was rather frustrating for producers as after the war there was once again a high demand for Caribbean sugar on the world market.

In 1951, the Commonwealth Sugar Agreement was signed which offered the British-colonised Caribbean a partly protected sugar market. Under this agreement sugar from the British-colonised Caribbean was given a fixed quota in the British market and any extra sugar could be sold in the Commonwealth and to other world markets. This helped the sugar industry in the region between 1951 and 1962 because efficient producers had some stability in prices and markets.

The Caribbean started benefiting a little from the provisions of the International Sugar Agreement adopted at the United Nations in 1953. This agreement was aimed at regulating the export of sugar from producing countries and at establishing set amounts or quotas for each country. By 1962 countries could not agree on quotas and so this system was stopped.

When the United States and Cuba broke off economic ties, the British colonial producers got a greater share of the USA sugar market. Part of the sugar quota that was previously given to Cuban producers was now given to other Caribbean territories. Efficient producers could now bring in further mechanisation and lower their cost of production.

Remember that the USA and Cuba broke off economic ties after Fidel Castro came to power. The US government does not support in any way Castro's communist regime.

Political changes within the Caribbean also affected the sugar industry. Sugar estate lands that were owned by foreign companies were seen as supportive of colonialism. But many countries were pushing for national independence and brought in policies to nationalise the sugar industry. For example, in Guyana, the Demerara Company was nationalised in 1975.

In most colonies the pattern was the same: the sugar yield declined and workers drifted away from the estates to urban areas, looking for better education and general life prospects. Cane workers wanted to work in the newer industries that offered higher wages. The result was that the quantity of land under cane decreased in most territories.

By 1962 when Jamaica and Trinidad and Tobago became independent, St Lucia and St Vincent had just about stopped sugar production although St Vincent did try to re-establish this industry later on. In the ten years between 1956 and 1966, total sugar production in Antigua, Grenada and St Kitts fell from 70,518 to 54,400 tons. By 1965, sugar production in Grenada was really for the local market only, while Montserrat with only 1,000 acres in sugarcane, was using its sugar in the syrup and rum industries. By contrast, up to the 1960s, sugarcane cultivation made up 44 per cent of the land of Barbados that could be cultivated. By 1950 there were 34 factories and production reached a peak of 212,000 tonnes in 1967.

The sugar industry in the former British-colonised Caribbean today

Today sugar is no longer the strong 'ruler' that it was in the economies of the former and present British-colonised Caribbean. It is still an important export crop in the economies of Barbados, Trinidad and Tobago and Guyana. But the industry survived up to the 1970s partly because of preferential trade agreements with major importers. For example, the Lome Convention which protection to former European colonies.

Did you know?

The Lome Convention is an international aid and trade agreement between the African, Caribbean and Pacific countries to promote economic development. The first convention (Lome1) was signed on 28 February 1975.

Sugar and rum were protected in the 1980s and 1990s by special trade 'protocols' or sets of rules. The European Union (EU) used to buy Caribbean sugar from territories such as Barbados, St Kitts, Trinidad and Tobago at the same above market prices which they paid European beet producers. This kind of protection gave the farmers price stability and guarded the industry from collapse. It is probable that the industry would have collapsed if it had had to compete with big producers, like Brazil.

However, most producers are down from their peak years. For example, while Barbados produced 204,500 tonnes in 1957, it produced only 69,000 tonnes in 1990 (see Table 10.2 below). In 1968/69 Jamaica produced 413,000 tonnes, and Trinidad and Tobago produced 203,000 tonnes. But in 1990 Jamaica only produced 216,000 and Trinidad and Tobago, 118,000 tonnes. Production in Trinidad in 1988 was 82,000 tonnes, 44 per cent of what it was in 1970. In fact, since 1984, Trinidad has had to import raw sugar each year to meet its export commitments and local demand. And, as production costs rise the government has had to subsidise the state-owned Caroni Company.

Table 10.3: Production levels in 1990

Barbados	69,000 tonnes
Belize	100,000
Guyana	130,000
Jamaica	216,000
St Kitts-Nevis	15,000
T&T	118,000

Source: Neal Sealy, *Caribbean world: a complete geography.* 1992, p. 125.

Chapter 10 | Reorganised sugar economy: 1846 – circa 1985

Table 10.4: Comparative production levels

Territory	Year	Production (tonnes)
Barbados	1957	204,500
	1990	69,000
Jamaica	1968/69	413,000
	1990	216,000
Trinidad	1968/69	203,000
	1990	118,000

By the end of the 1990s there was no longer any protection for the former British Caribbean sugar industry. The free-market emphasises competition, rather than price-fixing. The World Trade Organisation (WTO), which replaced the GATT (General Agreement on Tariffs and Trade), considers protectionism an obstacle to free trade. It rather tries to reduce import tax barriers globally. By 2003, for example, rum from Puerto Rico and the US Virgin Islands will enter Europe free of tax. So, it can compete with Lome beneficiaries, that is, former European colonies in the Caribbean.

2 The sugar industry in the French-colonised Caribbean

During slavery St Domingue (later Haiti) was France's largest producer of sugar in the Caribbean. But the successful rebellion of the enslaved people, which led to emancipation and eventually to national independence and the expansion of the peasantry, caused a drastic decline in sugar output. In 1983 Haiti produced a mere 71,000 tonnes of sugar.

Unlike most of the British-colonised colonies, up until the 1970s the French-Antillean territories of Martinique and Guadeloupe remained primarily sugar producers. For the period 1955 to 1968, Guadeloupe produced some 195,000 tons and Martinique 85,000 tons of sugar. In 1961 Guadeloupe produced 159,276 tons of sugar to the value of 9,353,000,000 francs and 40,837 tons of molasses. In 1969 sugar made up 115 million francs or almost half the value of exports from the French Islands. The main importer was France.

Guadeloupe and Martinique managed to remain in production because of several factors. Firstly, the railway revolutionised transportation on the plantations and replaced the old oxen-driven carts. These territories already had a private narrow-gauge railway in place by 1845. In fact, Martinique and Guadeloupe had two each by 1847. Secondly, these territories also modernised the industrial aspects of sugar manufacturing and they had two central factories as early as 1844 and four by 1845.

By 1883 80 per cent of Guadeloupe's sugar and 95 per cent of Martiniquan sugar cane production came from central factories. By 1900 Guadeloupe had 20 central factories and Martinique had 17. The *Société de Credit Agricole* helped to develop central factories and to merge the estates in the French territories. The *Société de Credit Agricole* was established in 1860 (later the *Credit Foncier Colonial*) and it focused specifically on improvements in the sugar industry.

The effect on the different social classes created by the establishment of central factories was greater in Guadeloupe than in Martinique. By the early 20th Century, the old sugar elite in Martinique (as in Barbados) was still in place. This was because they had more local capital. But by the 20th Century in Guadeloupe, the sugar industry was mainly in the hands of overseas French investors. The sugar industry has suffered decline because of the effects of hurricanes (between 1965 and 1969); high production costs; and rural to urban migration of workers and potential workers (young people).

In 1969 Guadeloupe and Martinique could not fill the EEC quota allocated to them. They reorganised and replanted in the 1970s and this helped to restore production. But even so, sugar exports from the French Overseas Departments have fallen permanently. This is despite generous EC quotas and prices. Guadeloupe's sugar exports fell from 56,000 tons in 1981 to 30,000 tons

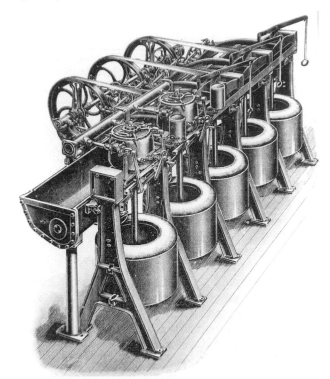

Fig 10.5 Combined water- and belt-driven centrifugals

in 1985. It revived to 59,000 tons in 1990. Martinique stopped exporting sugar altogether in 1979.

3 The Spanish-speaking Caribbean

The former Spanish colonies managed to expand their sugar cultivation in the 19th Century. Sugar exports in Cuba, for example, increased more than 3,000 per cent between 1800 and 1914. This was in contrast to the 400 per cent increase in production in Barbados. The revival of the sugar industry in the Dominican Republic was even more dramatic. In 1875 it was exporting merely 3,500 tons of sugar, as compared to 120,000 tons in 1916.

What advantages did these former Spanish colonies have? They had an abundance of natural resources for fuel and building timber; fertile soils and comparatively lower land prices than in the older sugar colonies of, for example, Barbados and St Kitts. These factors allowed estates to merge at a lower cost. Estates and factories were much larger than in other islands and there was more land in cane. They had mechanised early, installing machinery such as steam engines, and this gave them an added advantage. Indeed, steam power was first introduced to Cuba in 1797 and was generally used by the 1820s.

In addition, the sugar industry was helped by new sources of capital, high labour productivity and better techniques of rewarding and keeping labour. Cuba imported Chinese labourers even before the abolition of slavery. The Spanish islands also kept slavery up to the 1870s and 1880s. They also benefited from the British Free Trade Policy which gave them access to markets that had previously been dominated by British-colonised Caribbean producers.

The Cuban sugar industry was affected by the Civil War of 1868 to 1878 (the Ten Year's War); the abolition of slavery and *Patronato*; beet sugar competition on the Spanish market; and the 1895 to 1898 War of Independence. In the latter period, thousands of hectares of cane were destroyed by fire and some sugar mills were damaged or totally destroyed. The war caused the destruction of about 100 old sugar mills – especially in the eastern sections of Cuba. Also, seven large *centrale* (sugar factories) were destroyed and four damaged. But after this, there was a quick increase in foreign investment, mostly from the United States, and this enabled sugar producers to increase their output and consolidate the industry.

Many producers were forced to sell their estates in the 1880s due to economic hardship. Some US companies took advantage of this situation and bought up abandoned or indebted estates. This change in ownership was only really apparent by 1895. At this time only about 17 per cent of the owners of *centrales* came from the old plantation-owning families. The new owners re-organised the industry and centralised the factories. They reduced the number of *centrales* from 1,191 in 1877 to 470 in 1895.

In the period 1899 to 1927, 63 new mills were built in Cuba. In 1895 there were 250 sugar mills, a decrease from the 1,318 that existed during slavery in 1860. The decrease in the number of mills meant that there was a decline in sugar production for production almost doubled in the post-slavery period. In 1860 the output was 515,000 tons. In 1895, output climbed to 1,000,000 tons.

From 1903 Cuba had privileged access to the US market through a reciprocal agreement. In this agreement tariffs for sugar exports to the US were reduced by 20 per cent in return for the reduction of up to 40 per cent on various US imports into the island. Until 1920 the price of sugar held up well and the island enjoyed a period of growing prosperity. The *colonos* or smaller producer planted the cane and supplied the *centrales* with sugar. This meant that in the Cuban sugar industry the agricultural and industrial/manufacturing sectors were separate. In the 19th and 20th Centuries the railway and electrical power plant helped to expand the sugar industry. Some *centrales* also laid their own tracks to make sure that the movement of cane to the mills and the movement of sugar from the *centrales* to the ports was quicker and more efficient. Independent growers also supplied sugar for these central factories. Some of these independent growers rented land from the large estate owners.

So even after slavery was abolished, Cuba produced more sugar than the entire British-colonised Caribbean territories combined. But while the US investors profited, Cuban and foreign workers in the sugar industry gained little. The foreign companies forced even the rich Cuban planters to compete against each other. Like the British

Fig 10.6 *Loading cane*

Chapter 10 | *Reorganised sugar economy: 1846 – circa 1985*

during slavery, the US also did not encourage the importation of refined sugar so as to protect their own sugar refining industry. This stifled the refining industry in Cuba and deprived many people of potential jobs.

In 1871 sugar accounted for 68.5 per cent of exports from Puerto Rico. By 1897 this had declined to 21.6 per cent. In 1870 there were 550 old style mills in Puerto Rico, which together produced 96,000 tons of sugar. By 1880 there were 325 mills producing 50,000 tons. Puerto Rico was annexed to the US in 1898. This tied the sugar industry to the US market and the Puerto Rican sugar had duty free status in the US.

Foreigners dominated the sugar industry. After 1900 four large American corporations virtually controlled the Puerto Rican sugar industry. They owned nearly 25 per cent of all cane land and nearly 50 per cent of all the land

Fig 10.7 Sugar factory in Cuba

held in plantations. Central Aguirre owned nearly 25,000 acres and leased a further 18,000; Eastern Sugar Associates held a total of 51,000 acres and leased 20,000.

By 1910 these external financiers had put money into the industry to help it to recover from the slump. Also by 1910 certain improvements had taken place in the sugar industry. There were, for example, 41 central factories and more land was used to plant cane. Wage labourers included Puerto Ricans as well as cheap imported labourers. By 1920 yields had improved significantly and by 1987 the island produced 96,000 tons of cane. Operation Bootstrap encouraged all sectors of society to industrialise. But this caused a decline in agriculture in Puerto Rico, including a decline in the sugar industry. So, for example, in 1950 the share of Gross National Product (GNP) from agriculture had been more than 17 per cent; by 1980 it had fallen to just 3.6 per cent. By contrast, the share from manufacturing had increased from 16 per cent in 1950 to 48 per cent by 1980.

US citizens also invested heavily in the sugar industry in the Dominican Republic. By 1940, 90 per cent of US investments in the Dominican Republic were in sugar. By the early 20th Century, the West Indies Sugar Corporation and the South Puerto Rican company together owned six of fourteen mills. Together the production of these six mills represented 75 per cent of Dominican production in 1939/40. Sugar exports remained important to the Dominican Republic right into the 1970s. During the Balaguer regime, the sugar quota to the US market was a top priority, as it was the main source of foreign currency. Also, in the period 1974 to 1976 the average price paid in the US was higher than in the world market. The Dominican Republic's sugar industry continued to benefit from high sugar prices into the early 1980s. They produced 1,250,000 tons in 1982.

4 The sugar industry in the Dutch- and Danish-colonised Caribbean territories

The Dutch had long ago given up trying to grow sugar successfully in the islands in the Netherlands Antilles. Only their mainland colony of Suriname remained in sugar, helped largely by the use of immigrant labourers. By 1982 Suriname was producing only just over 7,000 tons of sugar each year.

In the Danish-colonised Caribbean territories (which became the US Virgin Islands in 1917), sugar cane cultivation was important on the islands of St John and St Croix. After the abolition of slavery, many former enslaved people migrated to St Thomas. Here wages were higher and there was a growing commercial sector. By 1870 only one sugar estate remained in operation in St John, even though planters had used their slave compensation money to mechanise and so reduce the cost of production. By 1930 there were only two mills in operation in the former Danish Islands. By 1936 sugar production had declined on large estates and the government was making efforts to keep the sugar industry going among small farmers through the 'homestead' programme.

According to the 'homestead' programme, large estates were sub-divided and rented to small farmers. In 1937 small farmers produced 16,117 tons of cane valued at $53,081. In 1930 there were only 329 small farms; by 1937 there were 828, each with an average size of 4.28 acres. During World War II, islands were used by the US naval bases and this took the emphasis away from agriculture. When the war ended labourers lost interest in agriculture. By 1946 there were only 500 small farmers in all the United States Virgin Islands. By 1966 sugar production had ended with workers being more interested in more 'modern' jobs in industry than in jobs in the agricultural sector, which was considered less lucrative..

5 The World Wars and the sugar industry

Between 1914 and 1918 (World War I) and again between 1939 and 1945 (World War II) many countries of the world were involved in global conflicts. These conflicts involved most of the European continent, but the Caribbean was also affected as it depended upon the European markets.

One effect of the wars was that the price of sugar rose because military action in Europe disrupted the beet sugar industry on the continent. The price of sugar in 1918 was twice what it had been in 1914. Eventually the allied powers that were fighting their former sugar suppliers Austria-Hungary became almost totally dependent on Cuba for their sugar needs. By 1916 Cuban sugar output stood at three million tons. As the demand for sugar increased, more and more land was cultivated, new *centrales* were built, and more labour was imported.

Did you know?

Allied powers was the term for countries that fought on Britain's side against Germany (and its supporters) in the World Wars.

From 1919 to 1920 about 50,000 Jamaicans went to work in Cuba. In the post-war years of 1919 to 1920 there was unmatched wealth in Cuba's sugar industry as prices soared because Eastern European suppliers of beet sugar were slow to recover from the ruins of war. In 1920 the Allied Committee deregulated sugar prices. This led to an incredible spiral called the 'Dance of the Millions'. From February to May 1920, world sugar prices rose from just over 9 cents a pound to 22.5 cents a pound.

Of course prices fell dramatically once European beet sugar producers recovered and with the post-war economic depression world wide, Cuba's largest bank, Banco Nacional, was forced to close in 1921, and others followed. Investors had taken out loans to expand the sugar industry, thinking that they could make large profits from sugar. They could not repay their loans and many investors went bankrupt. In the middle of this the USA raised sugar taxes by 1 per cent. In 1921 the First National Bank of New York took over nearly 60 bankrupt mills. This meant that the USA became even more heavily involved in Cuba's economy.

The 1920s was a period of decline for Cuba. The 1926 sugar harvest reached nearly five million tons, but it brought in an average price of only 2.2 cents per pound. By 1933 Cuba had only 25.3 per cent of the US sugar market – almost a 50 per cent loss from its position in 1930. Mills closed and workers lost their jobs. The World Sugar Council was formed with the specific task of dividing up the world market among producers. This restored Cuba's share of the USA sugar market to 29 per cent. But, the profits from Cuba's sugar went to the USA in any case. By 1930, 80 per cent of Cuba's sugar production was in foreign hands, 56 per cent being in US hands.

World War II brought about another boom in Cuba's sugar industry. In 1944 sugar output reached its highest level since the 1920s depression. But soon competitors like the Philippines expanded their sugar production to meet the increased demand and to benefit from the high prices. So once again prices fell as a result of too much sugar on the market. In 1955 sugar output had reached 4,396,603 tons and 161 mills were in operation in Cuba. They exported about 500,000 tons to Russia.

The sugar industry became increasingly more crucial to the Cuban economy after the Revolution of 1959 and the trade ban imposed by its main market, the USA. In 1970 President Castro's government targeted a 10 million ton sugar harvest. People from a cross-section of the population, including the military and office workers, were mobilised in this harvesting effort. They harvested 8.5 million tons, which was a major effort. The country benefited from the rise in world sugar prices from 1970 to 1974.

The Soviet Union continued into the 1980s to be the chief market for Cuban sugar. Cuba exchanged fixed-priced sugar exports to the Soviet Union for oil. Some of this oil it resold on the world market to get hard currency. In 1979 the Soviet Union was paying Cuba five times the average world price for sugar and selling oil to the island for one-third the Organisation of Petroleum Exporting Countries (OPEC) price. This was beneficial to Cuba, when sugar prices fell in the late 1970s but oil prices rose. The political changes in the former Soviet Union brought in by Mikhail Gorbachov in the 1980s have had a profound and negative impact on the oil-for-sugar deal and on the Cuban economy in general.

To sum up

For several centuries sugar and its by-products, e.g. rum, had been the most profitable export commodities from the colonised Caribbean. By the late 19th Century, however, the sugar industry was on the decline in most British- and Danish and Dutch-colonised territories. One reason for this decline was the loss of the protected British market and the coming of free trade. Immigrant labourers helped to bolster the work force in territories like Guyana, Jamaica, Trinidad and Tobago, leading to some recovery of profitability by 1900. Recovery was also aided by mechanisation and improved agricultural methods. The French and Hispanic Caribbean (especially Cuban) sugar industry fared better and remained profitable even into the mid-20th Century. Still, efforts were made to diversify the Caribbean economy away from the traditional dependence on the cultivation of the cane and the export of sugar. In the next chapter we will see how the expansion of crops other than sugar aided the Caribbean economy.

Revision questions

1 'The emancipation of enslaved peoples was not the major cause of the post-slavery decline in the sugar economies of the British Caribbean.'
  Discuss.

2 The Cuban sugar industry was said to have enjoyed a 'Dance of the Millions' around 1920.
  a Give the meaning of the term 'Dance of the Millions'.
  b State three reasons why the Cuban sugar industry enjoyed a 'Dance of the Millions'.
  c State two reasons why this 'Dance of the Millions' was only temporary.
3 Examine the reasons for sugar no longer being economic 'ruler' in the Caribbean.

Bay Rum

Chapter 11

Agricultural diversification and industrialisation

'Banana, banana, banana, is nice and sweet, Try de banana, banana is very good to eat.'
(Cari-Folk Singers, Jamaica)

'It's outrageous and insane, the crazy prices in Port of Spain, capitalism gone mad.'
(The Mighty Sparrow)

Introduction

After the abolition of slavery and the decline of the sugar industry in many territories, Caribbean people of different ethnic groups expanded the cultivation of many crops or introduced new crops. In other words, they diversified activities away from the sugar industry. Cotton, for example, was important in Barbados, but by 1907 the yields of cotton were so low that commercial cotton production was discontinued in that island. Cotton actually replaced sugar cane as the main crop in St Vincent. Nutmeg and mace were important in Grenada and Jamaica. Trinidad, Grenada, St Lucia and Dominica expanded the cocoa industry. Dominica and St Lucia grew limes, and Cuba and Jamaica produced tobacco. The Leeward Islands remained sugar producers into the 1880s, although Montserrat tried to diversify by growing arrowroot, limes, potato and tamarind, as well as producing charcoal in 1846. Trinidad and Tobago, Jamaica and Montserrat produced citrus for export. Haiti produced sisal, and Puerto Rico and Martinique, among others, produced pineapples.

As well as diversifying agriculture, the Caribbean also engaged in non-agricultural economic activities, most notably manufacturing and the tourist industries.

In this chapter we will learn about:

1 Alternatives to sugar in the British-colonised territories

The coffee industry

Jamaica, Haiti, the Dominican Republic, Puerto Rico and the Windward Islands had been coffee producers since the slavery period. The Spanish had grown coffee in Trinidad and when the English took over, they continued this crop.

After the abolition of slavery, coffee plantations went into decline. In Jamaica, for example, this decline was greatest between 1839 and 1849. In 1808, there had been 607 coffee plantations in Jamaica – by 1900 there were only 39. In 1808, the industry was second only to that of sugar. Between 1838 and 1847, planters abandoned 465 coffee plantations covering 188,400 acres. Between 1838 and 1900 coffee production changed greatly, ranging from a high of 110,000 cwt in 1838 to a low of 31,000 cwt in 1849. There was also a fall in coffee prices from 123 shillings per cwt in 1839 to 65 shillings per cwt in 1900. However, in the years between 1839 and 1900, there had been a slight recovery in prices. For example, in 1876 the price was 114 shillings per cwt.

After 1900 there was an increase in production, not so much by large planters but by peasant farmers. Until the present day, coffee production in Jamaica has been slowly increasing, with the area under cultivation in the Blue Mountains continuing to expand.

Expansion has also taken place in Puerto Rico. According to 1987 data Puerto Rico earns more from the export of coffee than does Jamaica.

Livestock farming

Before the abolition of slavery, livestock farming was an important economic activity in Jamaica, Barbuda and the Spanish-colonised islands. Most British-colonised Caribbean territories imported cattle from North America. The livestock industry serviced the needs of the sugar plantations and was very dependent on the survival of the sugar estates. When sugar went into decline, so did livestock production. The recovery of this industry only took place in Jamaica in the late 19th Century as farmers bought abandoned sugar estates and expanded the more profitable livestock industry. At times they combined this with banana cultivation. The new livestock industry served the growing population who needed meat and dairy products. In Jamaica there was an increase from 129,849 head of livestock in 1879 to 132,699 in 1884. Jamaica also began exporting cattle to Cuba for that island's expanding sugar industry.

Fig 11.1 Livestock farming

The introduction of Indian workers in the 19th Century positively affected the livestock industry, because trade with India increased. A variety of new breeds of cattle were introduced from India, such as the Zebu and Brahman. Breeds already in the region were crossed with new imported breeds. This gave rise in Jamaica, for example, to the Jamaica Hope and the Jamaica Red. Colonial Guyana and Belize also developed a local livestock industry, to meet part of the local demand for meat and dairy products. Belize had 60,000 head of cattle in 1983. This number has increased since then and Belize exports live cattle to Mexico and Martinique.

Fig 11.2 Banana farming

The banana industry

The history of the banana industry dates back to the Spanish period. The Spaniards had transplanted the fruit from Hispaniola to Jamaica, but the British introduced the Gros Michel variety from Martinique. Between 1866 and 1880, small farmers, not the large producers, grew and exported bananas.

Indeed only one large banana plantation existed in Jamaica in 1879. Large-scale banana cultivation started in earnest around the 1880s. More and more merchants and professionals bought up abandoned sugar estates and planted bananas, mainly using imported Indian labour. Bananas needed less capital than sugar and most of the expenses were for wages, not for equipment. By 1900 banana cultivation was the leading agricultural activity in Jamaica with 29, 163 acres under cultivation compared to 26, 121 under cane. Over 8 million stems of bananas were being exported at a value of over £600,000. This was an increase from 2, 000 stems in 1867 and 441, 000 stems in 1880.

By 1914 the banana industry accounted for 52 per cent of Jamaica's total exports. By contrast, sugar accounted for only 11 per cent of the value of exports in 1900. This growth in the banana industry had a negative impact on small farmers who could not compete with the large producers. In fact, many small farmers eventually sold out to the large farmers or leased land from them on which

they grew stems to supply the large exporters like the United Fruit Company.

Lorenzo Dow Baker was an American fruit merchant. He began buying and leasing thousands of acres in Jamaica for banana cultivation, especially in Portland and St Thomas. This led to the expansion of the industry. In 1880 he started the Boston Fruit Company. The United Fruit Company took over this company in 1899 and it dominated the Caribbean banana industry until 1930.

Did you know?

In 1899 the Boston Fruit Company became the United Fruit Company when the US railroad entrepreneur, Minor Keith, merged his holdings with those of the Boston Fruit Company, the Cuyamel Fruit company and Vacarro Brothers (later Standard Fruit Co.)

The other major banana producers in the Caribbean were the Windward Islands. By about 1925 bananas had taken over sugar as the major export crop of the English-speaking Windward Islands. By then, as in Jamaica, it was the large landholders who dominated the

Fig 11.3 Lorenzo Dow Baker, founder of the Boston Fruit Company

***Chapter 11** | Agricultural diversification and industrialisation*

banana industry. In 1925 the Swift Banana Company (a subsidiary of the United Fruit Company) acquired land for banana cultivation. They planted the Gros Michel variety in St Lucia. Banana was shipped to Liverpool from both St Lucia and Dominica, which had also become a producer. The Swift Banana Company was liquidated in 1927.

In 1933 the Canadian Buying Company made another attempt to expand the banana industry. Expansion continued after the 1939 report of the Moyne Commission, which encouraged landholders to stop being dependent on just one crop or one variety of banana. By 1937 the Lacatan variety of banana took over from the Gros Michel in the Windward Islands and Trinidad, where production had also increased. As sugar production continued to decline in the 1950s, bananas became more and more important in the Windward Islands with St Lucia the largest producer and exporter amongst these islands. More and more sugar estates in St Lucia, for example Roseau and Cul de sac, were bought up and turned over to banana.

In 1952 a British Company, Geest, signed a contract with Dominica, Grenada, St Lucia and St Vincent, which gave these territories a monopoly to export their bananas to the UK. Windward Island bananas were given guaranteed and tax free access to the UK market, while other exporters had to pay taxes and had quotas. Up to 1965 Jamaica remained Britain's main supplier of bananas, with the Windward Islands, Cameroon and Trinidad following in order of importance. But by 1989 Jamaica had only 10 per cent of the British banana market, compared to St Lucia's 25 per cent and Dominica's 18 per cent.

The US railroad entrepreneur, Minor Keith, bought land in Colombia, Panama and Costa Rica to plant bananas. Small farmers also originally grew bananas in Belize. In 1880 over 6, 000 acres were planted in banana. By the 1890s large companies' such as the Boston Fruit Company which also had properties in Cuba, Jamaica and Puerto Rico, dominated the industry.

Later the United Fruit Company (UFC) got 15, 000 acres in Honduras in exchange for building the Tela railroad. Instead of building a national railroad linking the capital to the coast, the UFC built 900 miles of railway to link banana plantations with the ports. By 1900, the UFC controlled 80 per cent of the US banana market. The Latin American countries produced over 6 million tonnes of banana in 1989 compared to 247, 300 tonnes from the British Windward islands; 35, 000 from Suriname; 43, 000 from Jamaica; 27, 000 from Belize; and 281, 000 from the French islands.

The logwood industry

The logwood industry has been important in the Caribbean for a long time. In Jamaica the trees were introduced in 1715 from British Honduras, originally for medicines. This use became less important after it was discovered that the bark of the trees gives off a red dye. St Elizabeth developed as one of the main logwood-producing areas. Mainly small White and Coloured farmers grew logwood during slavery and enslaved people cut the trees. There was some decline in the industry immediately after the slavery period. By 1850 only 4, 300 tonnes of logwood were being exported. However, peasants became heavily involved in this industry, as did large landholders who used private land to grow logwood. So the tonnage increased to 15, 000 in 1869. In the 1870s too much cutting caused a decline in exports, although prices remained stable. There was some recovery by the late 1880s with 115, 500 tonnes being exported in 1889. By the 1890s the peasantry was heavily involved in this industry.

By 1908 exports from Jamaica and other producers declined because of competition from Haiti and Campeche and the development of synthetic dyes. In 1908 only 21, 000 tonnes were exported from Jamaica. The trade recovered temporarily during the World War I, but fell off again by the 1920s when it averaged 25, 000 tonnes per year. Some of the attractions of logwood were that it was usually self-sown; it could exist alongside other crops as it did not compete for land with them; it did not need much processing before sale; and it did not need a large capital outlay or heavy investment in equipment.

The logwood industry expanded in Belize. Ever since the British settled in Belize in the 17th century they began exporting the limited natural resource – timber. Even after the abolition of slavery, logwood, chicle and mahogany were the main exports. In the first 75 years of the 19th Century, the mahogany trade increased and began to

Fig 11.4 Logwood factory

dominate the economy of Belize. Mahogany exports in 1846 totalled 13 million broad feet. By 1856 the Blue Books containing import and export statistics for Belize stated officially that, 'no cultivation has hitherto been attempted... nor is it likely to become so while the great staples of mahogany and logwood demand the service of all available labour of the country'. This situation changed when some Mestizo and Maya people from neighbouring Latin American countries came to Belize and moved into the interior. In 1857 these settlers focused on agriculture and even produced exportable quantities of sugar and rum. In 1930 in Belize the logwood industry and its products accounted for 85 per cent of exports and employed most labour. This remained the case up to 1958. By the 1940s there had been too much cutting down of the forests and this led to a decline in timber.

Did you know?

That chicle is a latex substance from the gum of the sapodilla tree?

Up to the 1930s the timber industry relied heavily on manual labour. After this it became increasingly mechanised. The use of caterpillar tractors and log wagons meant that logging operations could proceed in remote areas. In the 1930s there was less dependence on animal and water transport. By then roads had been built and this allowed for the use of trucks for hauling wood. There was also mechanisation in the felling and hauling of trees.

The rice industry

Rice became very important to colonial Guyana, Jamaica, Trinidad and Suriname. The freed Africans from the American South resettled in Trinidad in 1815 after fighting on Britain's side in the war of 1812. They introduced the art of cultivating dry rice in Trinidad. In Jamaica, it was introduced by ex-slaves from Haiti, but the industry expanded after Indians and Chinese immigrants arrived in Jamaica. In colonial Guyana, the period of rapid expansion of the sugar industry had come to an end by the 1880s. The country tried to grow other agricultural products and of all those they tried, rice proved to be one of the most profitable.

By 1895 the Guyana Rice Company had already been formed. The company folded in 1897 but rice cultivation continued to increase every year. The majority of cultivators were Indian small farmers. They tripled their rice output in the periods between 1898 to 1902 and 1903 to 1907. It tripled again in the following five year period. Soon colonial Guyana was self-sufficient and was also exporting rice to other Caribbean countries. The

expansion of the industry took place despite certain difficulties of rice farmers, the most crucial difficulty related to drainage and irrigation facilities. From 6, 778 acres of rice in 1898, colonial Guyana exported 58, 046 acres in rice by 1922. These were mainly located along the country's coastal strip from the mouth of the Corentyne River to Essequibo.

Rice remains a major export crop in Guyana, grown on 100, 000 ha. (250, 000 acres) of land. This is about twice the area that cane is grown on. In 1978 there were 29, 000 rice farmers, many of these were small farmers with 15 acres each. Guyana exports rice to other Caribbean countries as well as to the UK, Canada and Eastern Europe.

Rice cultivation also developed in other Caribbean territories, influenced by the expanding Indian and Chinese immigrant communities. While Guyana remained the largest producer, Trinidad, Suriname and Jamaica were also significant producers. By 1911 there were 138 rice farmers in Jamaica. Wet rice cultivation was the main form of rice farming done mainly by Indian male cultivators in Westmoreland and Clarendon and to a lesser extent in St Catherine.

Until 1959 western Jamaica had large tracts of swamp lands suitable for rice cultivation. In 1959 the West Indies Sugar Company drained this land thereby decreasing the rice lands. Sugar companies only helped Indian rice farmers when the sugar industry was in decline. This was because landowners did not wish to have their labour used by peasant farmers when it was needed on the sugar estates. Still, rice cultivation in Jamaica increased from 315 acres in 1926 to 530 acres in 1942, and to 5, 400 acres by 1950. But after the 1950s it became cheaper to import rice and this affected local rice production.

Although Africans were the first to cultivate rice in Trinidad, this industry was developed on a large scale by ex-indentured Indians. Many of them cultivated small plots of swamp or lagoon lands. Rice was cultivated for local use, and the output never became as large as in colonial Guyana. In 1897, 6, 000 acres were under rice. This increased to 10, 000 by 1907 and 12, 000 by 1911. By the late 1980s Trinidad was producing around 4, 500 tonnes of rice for local use.

Indians also cultivated rice in Suriname. Up to the 1920s yields per hectare were low. However in the 1920s, the Government Agricultural Experiment Station began paying increasing attention to rice cultivation. With government help, farmers expanded the acreage under rice, for example in the Nickerie area, as well as rice yields. By the 1930s rice farming grew into a large commercial business, with improved machinery and farming techniques. Suriname became self-sufficient in rice in the period 1926 to 1930. Exports fell during World War II, but recovered

Chapter 11 | *Agricultural diversification and industrialisation*

after the war. By the 1990s Suriname was producing around 200, 000 tonnes mainly for export to Europe.

Small quantities of rice were grown in Honduras and Puerto Rico. In Puerto Rico rice is grown in the tobacco areas and harvested after the tobacco crop. Production of milled rice in Puerto Rico increased from 2, 112 metric tonnes in 1939 to 5, 989 metric tonnes in 1945. But it declined after the end of World War II to 1, 102 metric tonnes. Up to 1914 in the Honduras, rice production was enough to meet the needs of the small population. By 1939 it had become unprofitable to grow paddy rice it was cheaper to import this from Asia. Local rice production was re-activated during the Second World War.

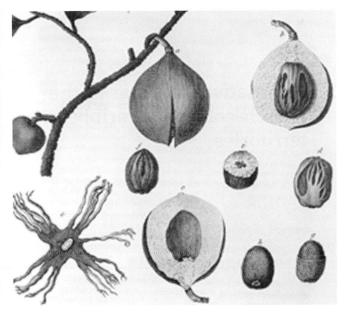

Fig 11.5 Nutmeg

The cocoa industry

As we have seen, the cocoa industry was an important one in the Caribbean. For example, cocoa had been grown from the time Trinidad was under Spanish rule and even after the British took over in 1797, Trinidad continued to ship cocoa to Spain. Production of cocoa took second place to sugar during slavery but expanded after slavery.

By 1870 cocoa was an important industry in Trinidad. From 8 million pounds in the 1870s, the island was exporting 56 million pounds in 1919. The value of exports in this period rose from £241,876 to £1,553,000. By 1900 cocoa had taken over from sugar as the main export crop in Trinidad. By 1920 cocoa made up 43 per cent of Trinidad's exports. In that year nearly 17 per cent of all agricultural land in the island was planted in cocoa trees. Prices increased during the war years but labour shortages affected production levels. So by 1946 cocoa exports stood

only at 6 million pounds, down from 42.5 million pounds in 1938.

Other crops

Around 1865 the Bahamian merchant class expanded the production of pineapples because of the growing demand for canned fruits in the US. Pineapples were grown mostly by peasant farmers and sold by large merchants. Many small farms became dependent on the merchant class for loans until their crops were reaped.

Severe winters in the US affected citrus production in that country, especially in Florida which produces oranges. Several major growers leased land in the Bahamas and Belize to grow citrus. Papaya cultivation was also encouraged. The Harmon Fruit Co of Florida leased 20,000 acres on Abaco in the Bahamas. Belize continues to be a major citrus producer of oranges and grapefruit.

In 1985 Coca-cola bought a large area of land in northern Belize to grow citrus; however, they cancelled this project as winters became milder in Florida.

2 Alternatives to sugar in some Spanish-speaking territories

Cuba

The Spanish-colonised Caribbean had a European farming community not involved in the cultivation of sugar. European farmers operated farms in the east of Cuba and in Puerto Rico and grew coffee, maize, rice, cotton and tobacco. The crises in the sugar industry in the 1950s forced the government to pay more attention to growing other crops. As the aim was to reduce Cuba's dependence on the export of sugar by diversifying their exports, commercial banks gave more loans to the non-sugar sectors. By 1956 agricultural produce apart from sugar had increased by 36.3 per cent. Some examples of these exports are tobacco, coffee, citrus, cocoa, rice and livestock.

Tobacco has remained important to the Cuban economy. It was estimated that in 1955 tobacco production was at 590, 360 bales compared to 656, 572 in 1954.

Did you know?

A bale is a large amount of material, such as hay or cloth, that has been tied tightly together.

Coffee was also important to Cuba and small farmers in the mountains of Northern Oriente Province grew 80 to 90 per cent of Cuba's coffee. Cuba produces a large quantity of citrus: 800, 000 tonnes in 1987, of which 500, 000 was sold to the former USSR and Eastern European communist countries.

Fig 11.6 Tobacco plantation

Cuba's livestock industry expanded as former sugar lands were turned over to pasture. In 1952 4.1 million head of cattle grazed on 4 million hectares of land. At this time there were 89,934 'cattle farms' on the island, whereas in 1946 there were only 28,836. In 1952 there were 75,000 farms of less than 50 acres each which controlled roughly 25 per cent of Cuba's stock of cattle. The big farms or ranches controlled 43 per cent of the island's cattle. In 1960 there were 5.1 million head of cattle and 4.5 million hectares of pasture land.

Rice-growing in Cuba also showed steady growth with the result that imports of rice slowly declined. From 1950 to 1954 areas under rice doubled and output rose by over 150 per cent. In 1955 over 60 per cent of the land under rice had been mechanised. In 1954 exports of copper, nickel and manganese amounted to $29,913,458.

Puerto Rico

By the end of the 19th Century the Puerto Rican economy included a large variety of agricultural crops. Coffee took up just over 40 per cent of the land, edible foods 32 per cent, sugar 15 per cent and tobacco 1 per cent. Puerto Ricans owned most of the farms. The US occupation of Puerto Rico in 1898 changed all this. By 1962 the US had broken up the large sugar estates in Puerto Rico although some effort was still made to help sugar survive in some areas. But in 1961 the Department of Agriculture launched a programme to stimulate the fruit (especially citrus) and vegetable industries. The government offered tax benefits to firms that processed more 50 per cent of local fruit and vegetable products.

The US invested heavily in Puerto Rican agriculture and this helped it continue to diversify up to the 1960s. Rice was planted in the tobacco-growing areas and harvested after the tobacco crop. Production of milled rice increased from 2,112 metric tonnes in 1939 to 5,989 metric tonnes in 1945. But rice production declined after the end of World War II to 1,102 metric tonnes. Since the 1850s, coffee cultivation was important to Puerto Rico's economy. The rise in world prices of coffee by the 1880s caused this crop to expand and emerge as the island's main export by the 1890s. The value of exports doubled from 9.5 to 18 million pesos between 1886 and 1896.

By 1920 Puerto Rico produced 53,299,362 pounds of coffee and today it earns more from the export of coffee than Jamaica does. In 1989 the Dominican Republic produced 32,400 tonnes of coffee and 40,600 tonnes of cocoa, and has a growing citrus industry. Cuba has achieved self-sufficiency in food and it has banned imports and rationed food to the population. Puerto Rico and the Dominican Republic import a large amount of their food.

3 Alternatives to sugar in the French-colonised Caribbean territories

By 1961 bananas had taken second place to sugar in Guadeloupe. It produced 122,363 tonnes of bananas valued at 6,545,000,000 francs. The island also produced coffee, cocoa, wheat, wine, grapes and tobacco for export. Cattle were also raised for sale and export. In Martinique in 1961 bananas were the most valuable export crop even though sugar took up more land space. Bananas earned over 16 million francs compared to over 5 million francs from sugar. In fact sugar had fallen to third place behind pineapples, which earned about 12 million francs. Other crops grown in Martinique were coffee, fruits and vegetables. Banana exports continued to be significant in the 1980s.

4 Alternatives to sugar in the Dutch- and Danish-colonised Caribbean territories

In the whole region the most limited choice of agricultural crops was in the Dutch Antilles. In the islands of Aruba and Bonaire it was not possible to develop a viable agricultural sector during the slavery period due to small size and unsuitable soil. This meant that Emancipation did not bring about the same kinds of concerns as it did in other islands like St Kitts and St Thomas which were also small in size but rich in sugar lands. Aruba and Bonaire grew aloes for export while Curaçao produced Seville oranges for the juice industry. The mainland colony of Suriname produced bananas, cocoa, coffee, rice and tobacco for exports, in addition to sugar.

The former Danish-colonised territories in the Caribbean had all but stopped sugar production by the early 20th Century. They had expanded cotton cultivation during the American Civil War with exports reaching a high of 71, 000 pounds in 1865 to 1866. When the Southern States started cultivation after the Civil War, the sugar industry went into decline. Other commercial agricultural activities were cattle rearing, and the production of food, bay oil, bay rum and lime. The expansion of the tourist industry, the start of oil refining, and the expansion of commerce eventually attracted labourers away from agriculture. The United States Virgin Islands became fully dependent upon imported food.

5 Crises affecting crops

Diseases

Caribbean agriculture was plagued with diseases and pests, natural disasters, problems with marketing and production, foreign invasion, wars and competition. In 1892 scale insects destroyed Montserrat's limes and root wither tip disease also affected those limes replanted after the 1899 hurricane.

The tobacco industry in Puerto Rico suffered from insect plagues. Pink bollworms/weavil affected cotton fields in the region. In 1928 in Trinidad, cocoa suffered from witch broom disease. This frustrated some planters who stopped production. As a result of the disease, cocoa exports fell from 75, 000, 000 pounds in 1921 to just over 6, 000, 000 pounds in 1946. The fungal disease called 'Panama disease' affected the banana industry in Jamaica. This disease hit the Gros Michel variety in particular. By 1931, according to some reports, at least 15, 000 acres and more of banana were destroyed.

Along with the Panama disease, the Sigatoka Leaf Spot disease affected banana trees in Belize. The disease affected output and by 1950 production levels were still low, with 28, 302 bunches valued at $21,607. A plague of locusts and a hurricane in Belize in 1941 caused widespread crop damage. The Coffee Borer disease affected coffee.

Markets

Montserrat and other lime producers found a market for their produce in Britain. They shipped lime juice to factories in Liverpool and Birmingham to be used as the citric acid component in sauces and cordials. The impact of diseases on the lime industry in Montserrat led Europeans to find an artificial alternative to citric acid. They imported limes from a closer source – the Mediterranean. So Caribbean producers were at a disadvantage when they lost their market for limes.

Caribbean fruit exporters faced stiff competition from South America, South Africa, Israel and Palestine on the European markets. In Trinidad and the Windward Islands, which were the main cocoa producers, the industry was hit by falling prices on the international market in the 1920s and 1930s because of increased supplies from West Africa.

Although the prices for Caribbean crops remained reasonable for a while, farmers soon faced severe competition from other producers. The cotton market weakened as the market preference for other material grew. This affected the demand for high-cost Caribbean cotton. Grenada experienced considerable competition for spices from the East Indies and Zanzibar.

The coffee industry was affected by the fall in world coffee prices from 123 shillings per cwt in 1839 to 65 shillings per cwt in 1900. The US occupation of Puerto Rico so severely affected that island's coffee production – because the USA did not offer a protected market for the crop – that Puerto Rico became an importer of coffee.

Competition from Campeche, Mexico, and the introduction of synthetic dyes affected the logwood industry in the Caribbean, especially in Haiti and Jamaica. By 1908 Jamaica was exporting just 21, 000 tonnes of logwood. The trade recovered for a while during World War 1, but fell off again by the 1920s when exports averaged 25, 000 tonnes a year.

War conditions

Cocoa, sugar, rice, and industries like oil in Trinidad benefited from war conditions, but the price of bananas fell. As bananas had largely taken over from sugar as Jamaica's lead export crop, this development was disastrous for many banana producers. The price of cotton also fell. The factories in Europe that relied upon sea island cotton from the Caribbean, especially from Montserrat, were mostly in Belgium and Northern France and the German army now occupied these areas.

However, during some relief came as the Admiralty and War Office began buying the entire British-colonised Caribbean crop for use in the war effort. When war broke out, the price of cocoa shot up, but it fell again in 1918 to a level of 10 per cent above the 1914 price. In Dominica, as a result of World War 1, the lime industry thrived until the US entered the war and banned the importation of such products, with the result that prices dropped.

By 1910 there was too much sugar, rum and bananas on the USA's local market. This affected the French islands of Martinique and Guadeloupe as they had increasingly sold their products to the US market. However, in 1914, the US authorities allowed the French-colonised territories to export rum, sugar and bananas to Morocco. They helped this trade by supplying extra fuel. This helped the French-colonised islands to effectively sell their surplus.

The terms and conditions of the Treaty of Versailles in 1918 ended the First World War. However, this Treaty could not prevent the outbreak of war again in 1939. The Second World War (1939–1945) had a considerable impact upon the Caribbean economy. Again, some crops were affected negatively and others positively.

The war years brought a global shortage in cocoa. So as long as cocoa from Trinidad could reach the world market, prices were fairly high.

In Jamaica during the war years the government embarked on a War Food Programme to meet the shortfall in food importation. Jamaican landowners realised that they could make large profits from rice cultivation. So they tried to monopolise potential rice lands, and rented them to commercial rice farmers at very high prices. The possibilities raised by food shortages because of the difficulties of shipping encouraged other Caribbean governments, like Trinidad and Tobago, to embark on a War Food Programme, encouraging the local production of food crops.

The war affected the agricultural industry in other ways. The building of naval bases in territories like Trinidad encouraged labourers to move from rural to urban areas. Wages on the bases were higher than wages paid by cocoa and sugar plantation owners. Between 1942 and 1944, perhaps as much as 15 to 20 per cent of the entire Trinidad and Tobago labour force worked on bases. Apart from building these bases, many labourers also found work in the provision of food, housing, transport and recreation. Some women earned money from selling their sexual services.

Natural disasters and production problems

A hurricane in 1899 destroyed the lime orchards in Montserrat. Drought affected the cocoa industry in Trinidad in the early 20th Century.

In addition to diseases and the interruptions in trade caused by war and social protest, the banana industry suffered from the effects of hurricanes. Hurricane Frederick in 1979 and Allen in 1980 severely damaged Jamaica's banana industry. As a result the island produced only 10, 000 tonnes in 1984. In 1988 the crop was totally destroyed by Hurricane Gilbert.

These factors caused the rise and fall of various companies that had come to invest in banana in the Windward islands, such as the Swift Banana Company.

Over-use and exploitation of forest resources also resulted in the decline in mahogany and logwood reserves in places like Belize.

In 1929 a severe hurricane destroyed the coffee trees in Puerto Rico, forcing former growers to join the ranks of the unemployed. Production in the Trinidad cocoa industry (1,400 tonnes in 1989), was affected because planters could not attract labour during depressed times in the industry.

Not only the large producers faced problems. For example, the expansion in banana cultivation had a negative impact on small farmers as they could not compete with large producers. Many small farmers eventually sold out to large farmers or leased land from them on which they grew stems to supply the large exporter.

There was no deep-water port in Belize and so there were basic problems of how to ferry large animals out to ships. Other factors that affected the livestock industry in the Caribbean were how to expand pasture land, how to raise money to afford feed, and how to compete with more efficient overseas producers who could sell cheaper meat and dairy products to the region.

The lessening interest in rural agriculture and the access to cheaper markets for food have had a severe impact on food production in the region. Farmers complain that they do not get a high enough price for their foods, vegetables and fruits to make a profit. Consumers who can buy imported vegetables and other foods more cheaply from large supermarkets complain that locally produced foods are too expensive. Barbados spends about US$100 million a year on imported food. The Bahamas imports about 80 per cent of its food needs.

6   Help with problems

In Trinidad and Tobago the government increased its help to cocoa farmers who were plagued by many problems in the 20th Century, including debt. They were given grants and loans to finance operations that would make production more profitable. Another way in which the government assisted the industry was with the planting of disease-free seedlings. But most of the help went to the large growers and not to the small peasant farmers. The British government also tried to help by agreeing to buy up to 4, 000 tonnes of cocoa a year at a fixed price during World War II. The cocoa industry survived up to 1945, although it formed a less important part of export earnings than in the 1920s. By 1989 the output was 1, 400 tonnes.

Farmers also received help and encouragement from the West Indian Department of Agriculture in Barbados, the botanical stations set up in the various territories, and the Imperial College of Tropical Agriculture in Trinidad. These institutions helped farmers with improved farming techniques, the distribution of seeds at fairly reasonable prices, and in the fight against plant diseases such as the Panama disease that affected the bananas, and the Coffee Borer.

Preferential trade agreements into the late 20th Century also assisted the producers of banana. In 1952 a British Company, GEEST, signed a contract with Dominica, Grenada, St Lucia and St Vincent giving GEEST an export monopoly of their bananas. Under a British government scheme, the bananas brought into the UK from the Windward Island producers were given guaranteed and tax free market access. Other fruit producers had to pay import tariffs and had quotas.

Currently, the preferential market for Windward Island bananas is increasingly under threat. In 1997 the World Trade Organisation ruled that the EU's special treatment of Caribbean banana exports discriminated against Latin American competitors and was illegal under international trade law. By the year 2006 it is expected that the EU will change its banana import policy. The EU has decided to create a new system called a tariff-only system that is scheduled to take effect on 1 January, 2006. Until then, bananas imported to Europe will do so through import licences that will be distributed on the basis of past trade. Quotas will be adjusted to ensure greater access for Latin Americans while securing specific quantities for bananas from the African, Caribbean and Pacific producers. This will severely hamper the production of bananas in the Commonwealth Caribbean.

The Dominican Republic benefited from a US$40 million project for both cocoa and coffee which was announced in 1981. The object of the project is to repair the damage done by several hurricanes. In Belize, the American Hershey Corporation has planted a large cocoa estate in Cayo and local farmers are growing the crop.

7 Cattle-rearing and fishing in the 1980s

Many of these non-sugar activities have survived setbacks and have even expanded as a result of aid and other improvements and developments.

Belize, Jamaica and Cuba continue to be cattle raising areas, even though the Caribbean in general is a major importer of meat and dairy products. In Jamaica domestic meat production increased by about 25 per cent up to

1978. However, as the actual consumption of meat has increased by about 100 per cent, there still was a shortfall that had to be made up by imports. Jamaica still produces more cattle than any other Commonwealth Caribbean territory.

It was only when large dairies were developed in the region that wide scale dairy farming developed. Dairies were developed in 1941 in Jamaica and in 1966 in Barbados, the year the Pine Hill Dairy was built. In Guyana livestock, poultry and pig production all expanded.

Fishing and the utilisation of marine resources have always been important to the Caribbean, especially to The Bahamas and the Cayman Islands where turtle-rearing for export is important. However, the resources have not been fully utilised in all regions, and so some territories still import large quantities of salted cod and tinned tuna .

The Bahamas has no sugar plantations and the cotton industry did not last long. The islanders have effectively exploited their plentiful marine resources and today they have one of the most thriving fishing industries in the region. The most important part of the Bahamian fishing industry is the lobster fishery. Lobster is also exploited in other territories.

Guyana and Suriname are also self-sufficient in fish. The fishing industry has developed more recently in Belize where 90 per cent of exports are lobsters for the US and European markets. The industry is based on five co-operatives which were established by the government in the 1960s. Raising fish in inland, artificial lakes has increased fish production in places like Jamaica, Belize, The Bahamas and Trinidad.

There is also a thriving shrimp fishing industry in the Caribbean, including territories like Barbados, Cuba, Suriname, French Guyana and Guyana. The Barbados government had a shrimp fleet that operated until 1978. The socialist government in Guyana tried to control the shrimp industry so that more of the profits could stay in the country but the industry declined in the 1970s as some foreign companies, fearing nationalisation, removed their bases from Guyana. There has been a revival of the industry in the 1980s, partly helped by US multinational corporations. By 1988 Guyana, Suriname and French Guyane were producing 6 000 tonnes of shrimp, mainly for the US market. But competition from other Latin American countries and Asia (through aquaculture) has meant a loss of part of the US market.

Did you know?

Aquaculture is the husbandry of aquatic organisms including fish, shellfish, crustaceans and algae.

Cuba has the largest fishing industry in the Caribbean. A major deep-fishing industry using fish-factory ships was started which handles more than 200, 000 tonnes of fish every year. Many Cubans were trained in Russian fleets. The fish is processed and consumed locally as well as exported to Eastern European countries.

8 Manufacturing and mining

Manufacturing is an important part of the Caribbean economy but did not take place in any planned and structured way until the late 1930s and 1940s. The traditional emphasis upon the plantation economy and the export of agricultural goods worked against any meaningful search for other ways to attain development. In fact those who controlled production in the colonies did not want any real development that might have led to socio-economic change.

There were few industries in the colonial Caribbean during slavery. But industries developed in several Caribbean territories in the late 19th and early 20th Century. Colonial Guyana, Jamaica and Suriname, for example, developed a bauxite industry and the Virgin Islands processed alumina. The US Virgin Islands processed alumina in the 1960s through the Harvey Alumina Virgin Islands Inc.

The Dutch Antilles and the US Virgin Islands processed crude oil from Venezuela and developed a petroleum industry. As early as 1595 the Europeans recognised the tar or pitch lake at La Brea in Trinidad as an important industrial resource. Throughout the colonial period it was exploited for commercial reasons. It was the main source of raw materials for the asphalting of road surfaces. Trinidad also exploited its oil reserves. The first well was drilled in 1857.

Phosphate was exploited in the Dutch Caribbean. Mineral deposits like diamond, gold and manganese were important in Guyana. In Puerto Rico, Trinidad and Jamaica, the manufacturing and industrial sectors almost tripled their output after World War II up to the early 1960s. Belize, Guyana, Jamaica and Suriname continued to also exploit their forest industries.

Fishing and the exploitation of marine resources grew as important industries. Most territories began canning fruits, fruit juices and vegetables and bottling soft drinks. In 1980, Jamaica alone had 40 factories devoted to agro-industry. Today most territories also have a craft industry, using local wood and straw. Some manufacture furniture, garments and produce cement. But cheaper imports have affected the garment, furniture, craft and agro-industries, leading to the closure of some factories and increased unemployment.

Fig 11.7 Pitch lake, Trinidad

9 Operation Bootstrap in Puerto Rico

Puerto Rico was the first Caribbean territory to industrialise on a large scale and to pursue a direct policy of industrialisation.

This strategy was launched by President Luiz Muñoz during World War II as a national economic scheme to change the country. The core of the economy was to be the manufacturing industries. Between 1942 and 1952, Puerto Rico was changed from a rural agricultural economy to an industrial economy.

There were many reasons why Puerto Rico needed to transform its economic structure: the decline of sugar in Puerto Rico, the disadvantages of a monocultural export economy, and the competition from beet and sugar cane in Hawaii, the United States and the Philippines. By the 1940s these factors motivated the state to experiment with the new strategy of planned large-scale industrialisation. There was not enough local investment capital to fuel the process so the object was to attract massive foreign investment to the island by promising tax concessions, factory space support, and cheap labour.

Supporters of the policy expected that if large sums of foreign capital, mostly American, poured into the island, employment opportunities for Puerto Ricans would increase, new local industries would develop and the social conditions of the people would radically improve. They also expected that, once there was economic development and social transformation, the nationalist, anti-colonial, independence movement which opposed US political control of the island, would be ineffective.

Industrialisation in Puerto Rico developed in two stages. The first stage was from 1942 to 1947. In this stage firms were attracted to the island by the promise of low-cost, disciplined labour and tax exemptions. The firms that arrived in this period were labour intensive operations. They needed a lot of people to help manufacture their goods. They manufactured, for example, textiles, footwear, sports equipment, glass and cement. In 1947 more than 50 per cent of all investments came from overseas including the US Federal government, external investors and foreign banks. By 1953 over 300 manufacturing plants had been established in Puerto Rico. A total of 25,000 new jobs had been created and the average annual income per person increased from $122 in 1940 to $426 in 1953. By the 1970s, 75 per cent of investment funds came from abroad.

Did you know?

Labour intensive refers to a situation where an industry requires a lot of labourers to produce its goods. Capital intensive refers to a situation where a business or industry uses a lot of capital to invest in machines to do a lot of work that people would do, thereby reducing the number of labourers needed in that business or industry.

The second stage of industrialisation started around 1947. In this stage, the government gradually began to remove full tax exemptions. As a result some firms withdrew from the island. Also in this period, an effort was made to attract capital-intensive firms rather than labour intensive ones. These industries included the petro-chemical firms of Caribe Nitrogen, Gulf Caribbean and the Commonwealth Oil Refining Company. They needed skilled and semi-skilled labour and created an increase in the wages of Puerto Ricans.

Between 1952 and 1958 new firms in the petro-chemical industry pumped $78.4 million into Puerto Rico. This amounted to 27 per cent of total investment in manufacturing. Other firms that were established were in the area of machinery, chemicals and metal industries. Within the chemical sector, drugs and pharmaceuticals took the lead. By 1957 industry had replaced agriculture in Puerto Rico as the major income earning activity. The total number of factories established had increased to 500 by

1958 and to 600 by 1960. By 1960 the annual average income was $677.

To what extent did Operation Bootstrap benefit Puerto Ricans? First, one has to realise that there are different opinions about what is meant by development. For some people, development means rising living standards. For others, development includes political freedom and sovereignty. And for others, the critical matter is social and cultural development in terms of national identity.

It is true that nearly 2,000 firms came to the island and there was growth in the areas of clothing and textile manufacturing. By the 1960s Puerto Rico was the largest supplier of clothing to the United States. The Gross Domestic Product (GDP) more than doubled between 1950 and 1960, the rate of annual growth averaged 8.3 per cent and nearly tripled between 1960 and 1970. By 1970 agriculture accounted for a mere 3 per cent of the GNP, with manufacturing industries accounting for the larger share. There was also growth in services, finance, insurance and real estate.

Did you know?

GDP is the total value of all goods and services produced by a country during a calendar year.

But many had to admit that there were also negative effects: ruinous economic dependence on the United States, indebtedness, balance of payment deficits, unemployment, social tensions and a loss of local control of certain factors of production such as labour and capital. Other negative effects were the increased foreign ownership of the Puerto Rican resources, lack of growth in the local business sector, and massive emigration to the United States. Operation Bootstrap did not stimulate the growth of local industries. This was especially true in the first stage when most industries were 'screw driver' industries with hardly any spin-off industries developing in the island. In other words, no industries developed locally to supply raw material to the US firms and so the firms imported all their material and supplies from the USA. Puerto Ricans simply assembled the machinery and goods. Capital accumulated in Puerto Rico was sent to the US and was not reinvested locally. The wages of local Puerto Ricans remained lower than wages in the USA. In fact, the concept of 'cheap labour' was one of the reasons why the firms were attracted to the island in the first place, so they ignored workers' demands for higher wages.

By the 1960s, only about 16 per cent of the income from foreign industries was paid as employee wages. The greater portion of income was sent back to the US. Whatever benefits there were remained in the urban areas. There was no growth in the rural areas. Despite the government's efforts to attract some firms to rural areas rural-urban migration continued to increase. Importantly, in a region of mostly sovereign or self-governing states, Puerto Rico is in fact a politically 'dependent' nation. For some people in the nationalist movement this means that it is a US 'colony'.

Some changes in industrialisation came in the 1970s when there was a greater emphasis on capital-intensive rather than labour-intensive manufacturing. Over time, the low wage 'sweat shops' were replaced with assembly plants which needed a skilled and higher-paid workforce. So wages increased, though most still were behind wage levels in the mainland USA.

Today the important industries are textile, electronic components, chemicals and pharmaceuticals. These industries are capital-intensive and have had good benefits on wages. However, they have created high unemployment and high levels of poverty, especially among the unskilled labour force who cannot find alternative employment in the declining agricultural sector. Most of the profits from present industries are still sent back to the USA by investors who do business in the island, precisely because of the tax incentives.

10 Industrialisation in Cuba

The leadership of Cuba's revolution believed that an expansive industrial sector was the way to achieve development. By 1962, the industrial sector had expanded. After the revolution, part of Che Guevara's responsibility as Minister of Industries was to move Cuba towards rapid industrialisation and to reduce its dependence on sugar. This focus was not as immediately successful as had been

anticipated and sugar remained a major income earner. Nevertheless, by the end of the 1960s progress did take place in the area of manufacturing.

There were three leading manufacturing industries, excluding sugar and its by-products: clothing and footwear, tobacco products, wood and wood products. Cuba produced nickel, synthetic fibres, sugar, beer and malt, yarn and plain fabrics, rubber, cigars and cigarettes, cement, metal containers and refinied petroleum. Cuba also produced paper, minerals, artificial wood, matches, ferrous metals, glass, gas, natural fibers, paper products, leather products, machinery, ceramics, soap and perfume knit and fabric goods, paint, basic chemicals, ready-made textile goods, plastics, soft drinks and so on.

In 1954 at least 45 per cent of more than 1,800 manufacturing plants employed five workers or less; 18.2 per cent of them employed between 6 to 10 workers each; and 17 per cent employed from 11 to 25 workers. In 1962 only four factories had 1,000 or more workers. (These figures do not include the sugar sector.) Two of these factories were the nickel processing plants of Moa Bay, which had 1,002 workers, and Nicaro, which had 2,094 workers. Cuba's largest electrical plant employed over 12,000 employees and the largest textile firm had 3,567 workers.

There was expansion in the textile industry. Although one large firm dominated, there were small firms too. 24.4 per cent of all workers were employed in spinning and 54.7 per cent of all workers were employed in weaving. There was a lack of low cost raw material and this prevented the textile industry from growing. Also competition from better quality imports limited the domestic market. Since the late 1970s Cuba has benefited from the relaxation of constraints on foreign investment. The US imposed an economic boycott on Cuba in the 1960s, but despite this countries like Canada, Britain, Germany and Spain have entered into joint ventures with the Cuban state in areas such as nickel extraction, oil exploration and telecommunications. Foreign investors are also looking at the declining sugar industry for possible investment.

11 Industrialisation in the Commonwealth Caribbean territories

The newly independent countries of the former British-colonised Caribbean also used the economic development of 'industrialisation by invitation', as the St Lucian economist Arthur Lewis's idea was called. This meant that the host nation enabled guests to manufacture in its space, just like in the Puerto Rican 'Operation Bootstrap' model. In other words, foreign investors were invited to invest in the region and were given incentives to do so.

Governments pushed for industrialisation for various reasons. It was argued that it would provide capital which could not be raised locally, it would contribute to economic growth, it would produce jobs for surplus labourers, and it would provide an alternative to the heavy dependence on income from agriculture. It would not only increase the revenue of the country and provide money for infrastructural development, but it would also improve the social and economic conditions of the working class.

Trinidad and Tobago

An article in the *Port of Spain Gazette* in 1896 said that the asphalt industry in Trinidad brought in £30,000 to £40,000 in revenue. By 1890 the Trinidad Asphalt Company was mining as much as 70,800 tonnes. Other individuals mined an additional 12,000 tonnes. Trinidad's main markets for asphalt were the USA and Europe. Oil was discovered in Trinidad in 1866 and by 1868 a few oil wells were in operation around the Pitch Lake, with crude oil being extracted and exported to Britain and the USA. In 1902 the first rotary drilling rig was introduced.

After 1909 the British began to invest heavily in the Trinidad Oil Company. In 1910 a British factory, Trinidad Gilfields Ltd., was established. Between 1911 and 1913 the La Brea-Guapo Point Fortin area began exporting oil on a small scale. A small refinery also went up at Brighton. Six wells were drilled at Barrackpore in 1913–14 and thirteen at Tabaquite. The United British Oilfields of Trinidad (UBOT), a subsidiary of Shell, and the Trinidad Leasehold Company (TLC) also began operating. There were five refineries by 1919, producing 1.9 million barrels every year, while 60 per cent of crude oil was also produced locally.

Fig 11.8 Oil refinery in Trinidad and Tobago

The oil industry was modernised in the 1930s. The introduction of new technology helped to increase production. By 1944, the oil industry was employing 15,000 persons. By the early 1960s, the oil industry accounted for 80 per cent of exports from Trinidad and Tobago. The oil industry experienced a boom in the 1970s when OPEC increased oil prices fourfold. 'Petrodollars' (money earned from the petroleum or oil industry) flowed into T & T from revenues from oil companies, such as TEXACO. 'Petrodollars' were used by the People's National Movement's administration (1974-1983) to further industrialise and diversify the economy. Many T & T nationals became wealthy from the oil boom.

However, there were also negative effects such as high inflation, a further neglect of agriculture, increased import bills and high prices of goods. According to the Calypsonian 'The Mighty Sparrow', it was 'capitalism' gone mad. By the 1980s, Trinidad and Tobago's per capita income was far higher than any other British West Indian territory. Despite this, poverty remained. The economic recession of 1982 – 89, coincided with the post-Eric Williams years (the Prime Minister who died in 1981).

The oil industry has facilitated the production of petrochemicals: detergent, sulphur, and lubricating oils. From natural gas (used at the industrial port at Point Lisas) ammonia, urea and methanol are produced for export. Other industries sprang up as the economy was diversified: for example, the production of Angostura bitters, fertilisers, iron and steel, textile, clothes, match and soap-making, tanning, brewing and electric printing. The Iron and Steel Company of T&T (ISCOT) located at Point Lisas opened in 1980. It was designed to provide material for the local building industry, which was booming and was meant to reduce dependence on imported building products. Today, the plant also exports to Puerto Rico and the Dominican Republic. Factories processing food and food products also sprang up in Trinidad. The government exempted many new industries from taxes for a period of 5 to 10 years to assist them to develop.

Jamaica

Although Jamaica identified its extensive bauxite deposits in 1869, these were not exploited until 1942 and soon Jamaica was recognised as the world's largest producer of bauxite. Unlike in Guyana where bauxite is found under thick layers of soil, Jamaica's bauxite deposits lie not very far below the surface and can be mined by open-cast methods. Bauxite deposits were found in the parishes of St Catherine, St Ann, Clarendon, Manchester, St Elizabeth, St James and Trelawny.

Fig 11.9 Mining of bauxite

By the mid-1950s three bauxite companies were extracting more than five million tonnes of bauxite annually; and by 1973 Jamaica was exporting 7,390,000 tonnes of bauxite and 2,312,000 tonnes of alumina. Alumina is a white powder that looks like table salt and is extracted from bauxite. It takes about three tonnes of bauxite to produce one tonne of alumina. Alumina is manufactured into aluminium, which is important in the making of many products like aeroplanes. Jamaica does not manufacture aluminium as it is too expensive to do so. Rather aluminium is manufactured abroad in countries like the USA and Canada.

By 1974, six foreign-owned companies, including Alcoa, Alcan and Reynolds were mining bauxite quite profitably in Jamaica, while paying the government only a small royalty. In 1974 the government imposed a Production Levy on all bauxite mined in the country. In this way it got a greater return from the companies. Before the country collected J$25 million annually in royalties but after 1974, Jamaica earned about J$150 million annually in royalties. The Michael Manley regime, which renegotiated the revenue paid by Bauxite companies to the country, also proposed a cartel of bauxite-producing nations. They could then negotiate better terms with North American aluminium producers.

Did you know?

Michael Manley was the leader of the People's National Party and was the Jamaican Prime Minister from 1972 to 1980 and from 1989 to 1992. His ideology was one of democratic socialism.

In addition to bauxite and alumina, Jamaica produces limestone, gypsum, cement, marble, glass from silica sand, pottery, bricks, crockery and tiles from local clays. The manufacturing and processing industry is also important in Jamaica and brought in $110 million dollars in foreign exchange in 1974. Agricultural products are processed as follows: sugar-cane, processed into sugar; molasses into rum and industrial alcohol; citrus into canned juice and segments; coffee beans into coffee (with the Blue Mountain beans being world famous); cocoa is made into powder and chocolate; and many fruits and vegetables are processed in various ways.

Other economic activities include the craft industry and a wide range of products made from imported raw materials. These include textiles, garments, paper products, electronic equipment and oil refining from imported crude oil from Venezuela. Oil companies like Esso, Shell and Texaco operate in Jamaica. Such products facilitate the island's trade and commerce.

Barbados and Guyana

In 1966 Barbados had three industrial parks; by 1982 it had ten containing 161 factories, many of them import-export operations owned by foreign companies. The greatest expansion has been in the area of high technology with the island assembling parts for large computer firms like INTEL in the US.

Guyana's bauxite deposits were discovered in 1898 and exploited in 1916 during World War 1. The Alumina Company of Canada [ALCAN] established its subsidiary, the Demerara Bauxite Company, in Guyana. After the discovery of bauxite in Berbice, Reynolds Co. Ltd became active. The search for and exploitation of bauxite became more intense during the Second World War, as the need for material to build airplanes and other equipment increased.

12 Industrialisation in the Netherlands and French Antilles

As in the British-colonised Caribbean, Puerto Rico and Cuba, industrialisation was a 20th Century phenomenon in the territories controlled by France and the Netherlands. Traditionally, the economy of the Netherlands Antilles relied on trade, limited agriculture, livestock farming, the craft industry and the export of phosphate. In the 20th Century the oil industry, combined with tourism, had a positive impact on the economies of Aruba and Curaçao. These islands did not themselves produce oil, but imported crude oil from Venezuela for processing.

Under the control of the Royal Dutch Petroleum Company, a refinery was built in Curaçao during the First World War. Refining began in 1917. In 1924 another refinery was opened in Aruba. The decision to build an oil

Chapter 11 | Agricultural diversification and industrialisation

refinery in Curaçao, says historian CC Goslinga, was made because of political stability, cheap labour, safety and the spaciousness of the port. Oil companies were reluctant to invest in refining facilities in politically volatile Venezuela. By 1924 oil imports from Venezuela to Curaçao had reached 7,624,000 tonnes, or 38 per cent of Venezuela's total production.

Curaçao in turn exported fuel oil and other oil products to other parts of the Caribbean. The oil industry attracted employment from the islands themselves but also from Suriname, Bonaire, St Eustatius and elsewhere. It also increased income and purchasing power, developed the ports further and increased trade. By 1929, 80 per cent of the ships that called at Willemstad were involved in the oil industry. This was a 50 per cent increase from 1922. In 1918, traditional exports from Curaçao fetched £1,716,500 and oil and oil products £180,000. By 1933 these fetched £566, 000 and £42,372, 000 respectively.

Direct and indirect revenues from oil caused the colonial budgets of Aruba and Curaçao to be balanced (or not to be in debt) by 1924. The colonial governments could now undertake public works programmes, including the building of roads and the extension of port facilities. Colonial governments also improved health, education and social legislation. The booming oil industry helped local banks to establish themselves and brought wealth to many merchants and top-level employees in the oil industry.

Up to the 1970s industrial development had not reached its potential in Martinique and Guadeloupe. Scholars Guy Laserre and Albert Malibeau record that despite considerable amounts of investment in the 1960s, industrial production of goods – excluding those that are agriculture-based – accounted for only 4 per cent of GDP in Guadeloupe in 1965 and 6 per cent in 1968. The figures for Martinique were 5 per cent for 1965 and 6 per cent in 1968. The reasons for these figures include colonial history, shortage of raw material, a limited local market and Departmental status. The Department has imposed on the islands a high level of salaries and social costs that do not encourage private investment. (See chapter 18 for more on Departmental status.)

In 1968 three factories in Martinique produced tinned pineapple for export. Since the islands have had to comply with European Economic Community (EEC) regulations for fruits and vegetables, they have experienced a fall-off in demand for the product. Still, the Ivory Coast and the French overseas Departments supply half of the French market. The production and export of rum are still important.

13 Analysis of the expected results of industrialisation

Many have noted that local raw material was hardly used in the new industries that developed in the Caribbean, with most of this being imported. Other criticisms were that expatriates, and not nationals, were used in many areas of the industries, no local technological research was stimulated, employment opportunities did not increase very much for unskilled labourers, and the purchasing power of the people remained low. So only a small local market for manufactured goods existed.

Additionally, the masses hardly improved their social life. Many of the manufactured products were simply assembled in the territories, so that no significant new primary or secondary industries developed in the region. Products such as radios, television sets, refrigerators and automobiles all were assembled and not manufactured in the region. Most of the benefits went to the manufacturers who had lower labour costs in the Caribbean, could send their profits home, had a good infrastructure laid out for them, and received tax exemptions.

Industrialisation caused a decline in agriculture, livestock farming and the craft industry in places like the Netherlands Antilles. By 1932, Curaçao no longer exported aloe and dividivi.

Did you know?

'Dividivi' is the name of a plant with pods that are flattened and cured for leather manufacture, among other things.

Goatskins exports amounted to only £8,000, and there was also a decline in export earnings from orange peels, phosphate, salt and straw hats. In times of depression in the oil industry, some people were forced to return to agriculture.

The outflow of profits to overseas countries merely continued the process of under-development of the region. Since the 1970s more and more overseas manufacturing companies have established themselves in the region because it is close to the USA, wages are relatively low, and the cost of producing manufactured goods is low compared to within the USA.

A US policy initiative of the 1980s known as 'The Caribbean Basin Initiative', has indicated that there was economic growth in the region. This measure advances US economic interests by strengthening relations with the Caribbean economies. It is essentially a trade act between the two groups. It has encouraged more and more US companies and service industries to invest in the Caribbean. But these offshore industries are little more than assembly plants for US goods. Clothes, for example, are merely stitched together rather than made in places like Jamaica, where clothing companies exist.

The Caribbean continues to import more from countries like the USA than they export. The creation of North American Free Trade Area (NAFTA) has further affected the manufacturing and service industry in the Caribbean. Under NAFTA, tariff barriers between the USA and Mexico were lowered and the US market is opening up to goods from just across its borders. Many US companies have left the Caribbean to relocate to Mexico. Caribbean countries will have to join NAFTA to benefit from some of the favourable tariff agreements.

14 The tourism industry

Tourism is a large foreign exchange earner for Caribbean countries. In addition it provides employment for many people, especially in the high season. Caribbean people find employment in the tourist industry as hotel workers, guides, bus and taxi drivers, while construction workers benefit when new hotels are built. Craft vendors, owners of food establishments and craft shops also benefit.

Early in the 20th Century, territories such as Puerto Rico, Cuba and the US Virgin Islands developed a thriving tourist industry. Tourism also became important to the Dominican Republic and the Commonwealth Caribbean territories. It is a crucial income earner in places like Antigua, The Bahamas, Barbados and Jamaica, attracting visitors mainly from Europe, the USA and Latin America. Currently the Caribbean receives over 20 million tourists annually. This number shows us the increase in the number of people who can afford vacations. Many take cheaper charter flights and choose all-inclusive hotel package deals.

There are two types of tourists: those who stop over in the Caribbean for at least two nights and those who are cruise ship passengers, spending only a few hours on the land. Some visit the Caribbean during the winter months (December to April) and the younger ones come for Spring Break and during the summer when school is out. The low season, when hotel rates are cheaper, is in the fall or autumn.

Trinidad and Tobago
Some writers such as C R Ottley record that the Pitch Lake was responsible for the early development of the tourist industry in Trinidad. Around the 1890s ocean liners started bringing visitors to the island to see this 'wonder of the world'. Thomas Cook and Sons became the main promoters of this excursion, attracting tourists from England and New York. Visitors stopped in Port of Spain to view the Botanical Gardens and then were taken on to La Brea. Many boatmen got jobs ferrying passengers from the ocean liners to shore. So did taxidrivers who lined the docks to take visitors driving into the countryside.

Soon hotels were built with the Queens Park Hotel opening in 1895. From 1946 tax incentives were offered to those investing in hotel construction. A Hotel Development Corporation was established in 1957 to lend money for the construction and expansion of small hotels. In Tobago, Crown Point Hotel was completed in 1958. In the same year, a Tourist Board took responsibility for promoting tourism. Tourism eventually became more important to the economy of Tobago than that of Trinidad. However, the annual carnival in Trinidad attracts numerous visitors.

Fig 11.10 Mariano Beach, Havana, Cuba

Cuba, Puerto Rico and the USVI
The tourist industry really began to seriously take off in the 1950s, with the rich and leisured classes from the USA and Europe being attracted by the hot climate, sunny white sand beaches, and gambling in Cuba. Cuba remained a playground for North Americans up to the revolution of 1959. After this, other Caribbean territories benefited from the decline in Cuba's tourist trade. The US Virgin Islands and Puerto Rico were two obvious beneficiaries because of the close proximity of these islands. In fact, the USVI tourist industry, which started in the 1950s with the creation of the Tourist Development Board and the production of an annual carnival, recorded substantial growth in its tourist sector by the 1960s.

The number of tourist arrivals was 16,000 in 1949, 164,000 in 1959 and 1,122,317 in 1969. In the 1960s tourism was given much attention in Puerto Rico and several large hotels were built. Income from the tourist sector in Puerto Rico increased from $58 million in 1960 to $84 million in 1966. The Cuban revolution turned tourists to Puerto Rico. The gradual opening up of Cuba since the 1980s has caused a revival in that country's tourist industry. Companies from Caribbean neighbours like Jamaica and from Canada, Mexico, Spain, Britain and Germany are investing in new tourist complexes.

Cuba now attracts over 1 million tourists every year. US tourists also go to Cuba although US companies are forbidden from investing there on account of the 1960s embargo. Tourists enjoy Cuba's beaches at Varadero, nightspots such as the Tropicana, as well as its culture and heritage tourism sites.

Fig 11.11 Myrtle Bank Hotel, Kingston, after 1907 earthquake

Jamaica

In Jamaica tourism had become the third largest industry, by the 1970s. Contributing factors were the improved communication with North America through the banana trade and publicity of the island's attractions. The number of hotels and boarding houses more than doubled from 54 in 1910 to 114 in 1930. In 1964, 227,417 visitors came to the island and spent $32 million dollars. By 1975, 553,000 visitors arrived in the island and spent $116.8 million.

Kingston (with the Myrtle Bank Hotel), Montego Bay and Port Antonio were the first to set up hotels and attract tourists. Montego Bay and Port Antonio continue to be popular resorts, though Ochos Rios and Negril, with its seven miles of white sand beaches, are now major destinations. The tourist industry has continued to expand since the 1980s with a major player in the industry being Butch Stewart who owns many hotel chains in Jamaica and other Caribbean territories including St Lucia. The larger hotels, especially the popular all-inclusives, do better business than the smaller hotels and self-catering guesthouses.

Dutch and French Antillles and the Dominican Republic

Other territories that rely heavily on tourism are the Dutch and French Antilles and the Dominican Republic, the latter being a leading tourist destination in the Caribbean. The Dominican Republic earns twice as much from tourism as it does from all its exports. Most tourists to Guadeloupe and Martinique are from France. St Martin/Sint Maarten, an island shared by both France and the Netherlands, is a popular tourist destinations for people of all ethnicities. Even Saba, an island near St Martin, with a population of 1,000, welcomes about 50,000 visitors annually. The French territories lagged behind in the tourist industry up to the 1960s. The number of tourists nevertheless increased from 9,000 in 1961 to 50,000 in 1969; but then a total number of 3 million people united the entire Caribbean.

Problems and challenges

In some countries, fear of tourist harassment, in the form of theft and vendors preying on tourists, has caused hotel owners to imprison the visitors within the walls of the all-inclusive fortresses rather than allow them to enjoy local cuisine and shops and spend money with the locals.

While climate and physical characteristics – sea, white sand and sun – remain great selling points, Caribbean territories are now trying to diversify their tourist product to include heritage and eco-tourism. Many tourists, especially of the educated class, are no longer satisfied with visiting the Caribbean and lying on the beach. Burning in the hot sun is especially unappealing to African-Americans and others conscious of the threat of skin cancer. Eco-tourism is important in places like Belize, Guyana, Dominica, Jamaica and Suriname. All territories have the potential to exploit heritage tourism as the Caribbean has a rich history and is full of historic sites and buildings. Jamaica plans to develop the old city of Port Royal into a major heritage tourism site.

The Caribbean tourist industry is also vulnerable because of several factors. Among these are natural disasters like hurricanes, which often close airports and damage hotels and beaches. The political instability and high crime rates in certain territories also creates problems. The US, for example, issued a 'travel advisory' which warned potential visitors not to visit Jamaica during the turbulent and violence-riddled 1970s. Sporadic protests such as the April 1999 protests over the hike in petrol prices in Jamaica also affected visitor arrivals. European visitors also tend to travel to the Caribbean during their winter season. This means that the hotels in the Caribbean are often poorly occupied in the summer. Since the 1980s local Caribbean people have been choosing to vacation in the region and this has helped the tourist industry during the slow summer months. But many African Caribbeans complain of discrimination in the hotels where some workers tend to to give good service only to overseas visitors, who are usually European.

Reported high levels of crime in certain parts of the region also deter visitors. Part of the reason for crime is poverty, and so Caribbean governments need to solve the region's economic problems and improve the lives of ordinary citizens. This would have a positive impact on the tourist industry. There are also complaints of low wages paid to the workers in the tourist industry, and the failure of employers to give workers a greater part of the profits that their labour helped to create. These factors, in turn, affect the delivery of service.

Table 11.3
Cruise ship arrivals, 1978 to 1989

Year	Bermuda	Bahamas	Jamaica	Barbados
1978	132	450	149	156
1981	105	597	140	136
1984	111	908	231	99
1989	131	1,645	444	337

Source: Neil Sealy, *Caribbean world*, p 187.

Table: 11.4
Percentage increase in tourist arrivals, 1979 to 1989

Country	per cent change	
	1979-84	1984-89
Barbados	-0.9	+25
Bahamas	+11.7	+23
Aruba	+11.9	+64
Jamaica	+29.3	+19
Cayman Is.	+32.3	+42
All Caribbean	+11.8	+38

Source: Neil Sealy, *Caribbean world*, p. 18

15 Industrialisation and Caribbean women

Women, like men, were caught up in the economic changes that took place in the post-enslavement period but at times their experiences were different because of their gender. One immediate difference was that women's participation in the wage labour force as plantation labourers declined. It remained significant in places like Barbados where in 1911, 77 per cent of women were in the plantation labour force. However, by 1960 this had declined to 37 per cent.

In some cases this decline in women's participation in the plantation labour force was because of new gender ideologies which favoured men as workers in the 'public domain' because women wanted to be full-time housewives, and because of immigration. In other cases, women chose to withdraw from plantation labour to explore other occupations. Most of these women remained in agriculture but as peasant farmers and small farmers who participated in the local and export markets.

Many of those women who remained as wage labourers shifted from sugar estates to properties cultivating other crops: coffee, cocoa, banana, rice, etc. Some left rural areas for urban centres where they were involved in domestic service and petty trading, or they found jobs as, wharf/port workers, coal carriers, laundresses and seamstresses. Women dominated the domestic service sector because employers preferred them in an occupation which was seen as 'women's work'.

Fig 11.12 Women working in a garment factory

According to Rhoda Reddock, women made up 89 per cent of a total of 24, 274 domestic workers in Trinidad and Tobago in 1931. As educational opportunities expanded for women, some qualified themselves to enter the professions and the civil service. However, the number in the professions always lagged behind the number of men in such areas.

In World Wars I and II women broke out of gender confines and worked in jobs traditionally seen as being for men who went off to fight. The new thrust towards industrialisation and manufacturing after World War II gave women yet another outlet for their work skills. Indeed, during the latter decades of the 19th Century and the start of the 20th, the industrial and manufacturing sectors were the second largest employers of women. They employed some 80 per cent of the female working population. In 1946 in Barbados, 7,400 or 18 per cent of the

    Chapter 11 | *Agricultural diversification and industrialisation*

total female working population were employed in the manufacturing sector, though by 1960 this had declined to 11 per cent.

Women were important in the textile and garment manufacturing industries. In the late 19th and early 20th Centuries, garment production was totally controlled by small producers. In Trinidad dressmaking engaged 95 per cent of women, and in 1911 there were 13,000 seamstresses who worked in their homes. Girls in the early 20th Century Caribbean were trained at home and school in needlecraft. So a pool of skilled and semi-skilled labour was available for these industries. The majority of seamstresses were of African – not Indian – descent. By 1931, though, this number had fallen to 9,000 as garment manufacturing shifted to factories and as women increasingly preferred ready-made imported garments. By 1985, women formed the majority of workers in the garment factories in the free zones.

Women found work as domestic workers and waitresses in the expanding regional tourist industry. They found work in steam laundries, the metal and glass trades, in companies that produced paper boxes, Angostura bitters, cigars, furniture, matches, soaps and drink. They worked in brewing, tanning, canning, electrical printing and a whole host of other industries including food-processing and other agro-industries.

Industrialisation and manufacturing had an impact on the number of women employed. The opening up of commercial steam laundries affected the number of women who had made a living as private laundresses/washerwomen. In Trinidad and Tobago between 1946 and 1960, the number of private laundresses fell by 3,300. The shift towards dependence on the petroleum industry in countries like Trinidad and the Dutch Antilles affected agriculture, and this had an impact on women's employment. Industry also employed more men than women. While women found jobs in the ever-growing number of factories and industrial estates, they had to work long hours for low pay. Those who worked in assembly type factories did not receive training that enhanced their skills; for example, in some of the garment factories in the free zones some women only stitched/attached collars or sleeves and never learned to make a whole garment.

16 Ethnicity, commerce and industry

After the abolition of slavery, the local merchant class expanded throughout the Caribbean. Merchants were important in distributing manufactured goods. They grew in influence, especially with growing industrialisation which increased the importance of the merchant manufacturer within the Caribbean economies. The merchant class was dominated by Jewish families in Jamaica, St Lucia and Dominica; French Creoles in Trinidad and Grenada; Portuguese in Guyana; and later Asians (Indians and Chinese primarily but also some Koreans) in Trinidad, Guyana and Jamaica. The Lebanese were active in Jamaica and the Greeks, Chinese and Lebanese in the Bahamas.

The Bahamas had a European merchant class that lived mostly in Nassau. This class controlled the import-export trade and retailing. They were also major investors in the pineapple and sponge industries on which the colony's economy depended. Immigrant groups such as the Greeks, Chinese and Lebanese competed with these traditional classes for economic dominance with the result that local Bahamian merchants resented them. The Greeks like Theophilous Mangos, Theophanese Tiliacos and George Miaoulis got involved in the sponge industry in the 1880s. They bought, packed and exported sponges and provided jobs for Bahamians. By the 1920s they had branched out into other areas of business such as baking, the sale of perfumes and ladies wear, fruit stores, restaurants and the tourist industry. The Lebanese such as the Amourys and the Bakers went to the Bahamas in the 1890s to escape from Turkish rule in Syria, which was then a part of the Ottoman Empire. They concentrated on the selling and peddling of dry goods and later became involved in the retail trade. They operated in Nassau as well as on other islands where they sold pins, buttons and cheap cloth. In this way they saved enough money to open stores. They also became involved in distributing imported goods for overseas firms. Both the Lebanese and Chinese used family members in their businesses. This meant they paid no wages and could keep their stores open longer.

The Chinese began to settle in the Bahamas from 1879. Their immigration continued into the 20th Century. Some came from Cuba where there was a large Chinese population. Some like Luis Chea who arrived with money, opened restaurants and established laundries. Some worked as carpenters, contractors, painters, furniture wood polishers, cooks and footmen.

In Jamaica, the Chinese and Lebanese were also quite prominent in the commercial sector by the end of the 19th Century. Many of them became shopkeepers, displacing the Indians and Afro-Jamaicans who had up till this time dominated the retail trade. In 1908 they made up 13.2 per cent of the total number of people engaged in shop keeping and the retail trade, compared to the Lebanese who comprised 1.4 per cent. In that same year Indian shopkeepers made up 7.1 per cent and African and other people were still a dominant 78.4 per cent. The Chinese later went into other aspects of the economy, such as opening restaurants. The majority of the Chinese in Jamaica are part of the merchant class even today. We know the ethnicity of the retail traders as it was often written beside their names on the list of persons (recorded, for example, in the *Jamaica Gazette*) who had been granted spirit licences in the 19th Century. In the case of the Chinese, 'Chinaman' was written beside their names on these lists.

The Lebanese and Syrians sold cloth and other items, mostly in the rural areas. They specialised in the retail trade of cloth and other goods. By the 1920s the Lebanese and Syrians had a monopoly over the retail dry goods trade and had opened small shops all over the island of Jamaica.

Towards the late 19th and early 20th Century large numbers of Jewish families, who were natives of Syria and Egypt, emigrated to Jamaica and entered the area of business. In the 1660s, Jews had come to the Caribbean from Brazil and England, others emigrated from Germany in the 1830s. So the Jews have been in the region since the early days of colonisation and settlement, although it was not until the 19th Century that they gained their civil rights. In addition to Brazil, England and Germany, Jews came to Jamaica from Curaçao, Demerara and Suriname. In 1838, their only relationship with Europeans was around commercial transactions. The American Consul in Kingston, Robert M. Harrison, had this to say in 1838:

> the Jews in this island have been admitted to all the rights and privileges of freemen, however, not the least intercourse exists between them and the white Christian inhabitants further than in mercantile transactions.

Some Jews were expelled from the island as a result of differences with European people. During slavery, some became rich from their occupation as commission agents, traders and merchants. In this time, commerce rather than manufacture was a route to wealth for the Jews because of the British policy of discouraging manufacturing in overseas colonies. Their economic position improved dramatically after the abolition of slavery. In the post-slavery period the Jews made up an increasingly wealthy and influential urban-based merchant class.

The Jewish community consisted of an upper class of wealthy merchants and a middle class of less successful commercial business people. Some were traders, peddlers and shop keepers. Between 1907 and 1960 there were fourteen merchants, six solicitors, four business

managers/company executives, two merchant/manufacturers (producers and sellers of rum), and two insurance agents among this minority group in Jamaica. By 1962, members of the merchant class who were from the Middle East were heavily involved in the match, cement, clothing and textile, and other industries.

Unlike the Jews in Jamaica, the Jews in Barbados were mostly Sephardic Jews, the decendants of Jews from Portugal, Spain and Italy. They had fled from religious persecution in Brazil, Holland and Martinique and many came via Pernambuco in about 1654. Under the English constitution they were given the right to settle as Englishmen with all civil rights. So they did not have to struggle for legal equality. This did not mean that there were no hostilities between Barbadian Jews and the White planter class. There had always been racial tension between the two groups. In Barbados, Jewish families like the Abrahams were among the leading auctioneers; the Cavans were agents for Lloyds of London; the Azuedos and Montifiores owned several stores. Some of them owned plantations.

In Guyana, the Portuguese formed a significant part of the commercial sector. They operated a variety of businesses: retail trading (even on Sundays, which was largely prohibited in the early centuries), banking, pawn-broking and the sale of spirits. At times they were accused of fraudulent business practices such as putting lead in the scales to cheat those buying flour rice.

In Guyana, in the 19th Century, many plantations had shops run by either Indians or Chinese who increasingly challenged the Portuguese dominance of the retail trade. Indians introduced a rival spirit trade in coconut toddy (an alcoholic beverage). The spirit trade of the Chinese was often illegal. The Chinese families like the Kwong-san Lung started a direct import trade with China. By 1891, Indians and Chinese in Guyana together held 300 licenses for provision shops. The Chinese introduced a sort of credit and truck system as they had done in The Bahamas and often exploited their creditors. Under this system goods could be taken away from the shops and paid for at a later stage. By the end of the 19th Century the Chinese had successfully challenged the Portuguese dominance in commercial activities and had established commercial outlets in the Lombard Street area of Georgetown and along the Main Street in New Amsterdam. They were partly responsible for the introduction of the chain shop enterprises such as Ho-A-Shoo Ltd.

By 1915, one Evan Wong owned a vast chain of shops and stores as well as several rubber, coconut, cocoa and coffee plantations. Some families, in addition to chain stores and shops, expanded into gold-mining and plantations (rubber, cocoa, coconuts, coffee). Some became involved in the jewellery business, though this was later dominated by Indians. By 1900 the Chinese owned property in Georgetown valued at $93,150 and in New Amsterdam valued at $71,375.

In Suriname, the Lebanese were involved in the textile trade. By the 1940s they dominated the drapery and textile trade in the capital city, Paramaribo. Jews there who earlier had been involved in the urban trade moved into the colonial civil service. Portuguese from Madeira had been part of the urban trade in the 1870s, but Portuguese emigration caused a decline in their participation in this area.

In many territories, like Puerto Rico and the USVI, the expansion of the tourist and oil industries led to the growth of the local commercial sector. Businesses thrived on the demands created by these two industries. The occupation of Haiti by US marines also led to the growth of a largely European and mixed-race/Creole merchant class. They benefited from having 2,000 marines spend part of their salaries in the country.

To sum up

Non-sugar economic activities, both agricultural and non-agricultural, contributed greatly to the development of the Caribbean economy in the post-slavery and modern periods. Some of these activities represented new enterprises, but others represented a continuation from the pre-emancipation trend. Coffee cultivation, for example, was started even before 1834, while the bauxite industry was a new, 20th Century development. These economic activities did not develop without some difficulty, among them natural disasters and international market competition.

All ethnic groups participated in the development in Caribbean economy, including the 19th Century immigrants.

Revision questions

1   'In the 1860s the sugar industry (in Trinidad) had been aided to recovery because of increased production. Cocoa production boomed and French Creole and peasant 'contractors joined in its production'. (Adapted from Kevin Yelvington, *Producing power: ethnicity, gender and class in a Caribbean workplace*. Temple University Press, Philadelphia, 1912, 1995, p.51.)

a   State three reasons why the Trinidad sugar industry experienced increased production in the 1860s.

b   Name two ethnic groups, apart from French Creoles, who were cocoa producers in Trinidad.

c   State three reasons why sections of the population in Trinidad became engaged in cocoa farming.

d   Name four crops apart from cocoa which Caribbean producers cultivated as alternatives to sugar in the late 19th Century.

e   State three problems faced by cocoa cultivators in Trinidad by the end of the 19th Century.

2   Read the extract and answer the questions that follow:

By the mid-20th Century, most Caribbean territories had embarked on a process of industralization. The British Caribbean-colonised territories were encouraged by a leading economist to adopt the Puerto Rican model of 'Operation Bootstrap'.

a   Define the term 'Operation Bootstrap'.

b   State the main aim of 'Operation Bootstrap'.

c   State two positive and two negative effects of 'Operation Bootstrap' on Puerto Rico.

d   Which 'leading economist' encouraged the British-colonised Caribbean territories to adopt 'Operation Bootstrap'?

e   To what extent did the British-colonised Caribbean territories benefit from their experiment with 'Operation Bootstrap'?

Chapter 12

Emigration and the economy

'Exodus ... movement of Jah people.'
(Bob Marley)

'Man ah felt so bad, so very sad, everybody leaving, imagine how ah feeling, who going Canada, also America.'
(The Mighty Scraper, 1970 Grenadian Calypsonian)

Introduction

After the abolition of slavery, the Caribbean became increasingly affected by emigration – both intra- and inter-territorial. Important factors that attracted workers to move to new countries were:
- higher wages in receiving countries, especially for men
- better working conditions
- the possibilities of using the wages to improve emigrants' families' lives back home
- the desire to be educated
- to join relatives who had already emigrated.

Factors that caused freed people to leave their home countries included:
- poor economic conditions
- the dramatic increase in population and the growth in the labouring population
- the decline in the sugar industry (the major employer of labour)
- the failure of diversification to solve the need for alternative jobs
- limited opportunities for work outside agriculture in industry and manufacturing or crafts.

Malcolm X, US Black Power leader

Favourable press reports of life in the receiving countries, reports from returning migrants and recruiting agents about the opportunities for improved wages, and conditions in other countries were other push factors.

In this chapter we will learn about:
- countries affected by emigration
- economic effects of emigration
- gender and emigration.

1 Countries affected by emigration

The uprooting of slavery affected every Caribbean territory regardless of size, and started emigration almost immediately after Emancipation. As early as 1835, for example, Nevisians left for colonial Guyana. By 1846, they were also migrating to Trinidad and by the 1880s to Central and South America and even further afield.

Ships and boats that carried goods and mail to and from the Caribbean territories also transported passengers. Transportation was not as easy from the Caribbean to non-Caribbean countries, and was expensive. Passages ranged from 3/- to -11/- for children and 22/- to £2.10/- for adults to Panama. These high transportation costs did not stop emigrants; neither did the restrictive emigration policies Caribbean governments implemented to stop the outflow of people. Governments justified the restrictive legislation by arguing that the Caribbean still needed a large number of agricultural labourers.

Movement within the region

Jamaica was among the first to experience emigration to a non-Caribbean country. Between 1850 and 1852 a number of people left for California gold mines. Some may even have gone to the goldfields of Australia. Most of these emigrants returned without the expected fortune. About 2,000 people left to work for US companies on the building of the Panamanian railroad from 1850 to 1855. Others went to build the canal when a French company, De Lesseps, began to dig across the Isthmus of Panama in 1881. The company went bankrupt in 1888 and this threatened to stop migration. The US took over from the French in 1905 and completed the canal.

Table 12.1 Caribbean emigration to Panama in Central America

Caribbean Territory	Year(s)	Numbers leaving
Jamaica	1850–1890	28,000
	1891–1915	91,000
Barbados	1881–1914	45,000
Other BC	1881–1914	24,000

In the 1890s Windward Island migrants went to Guatemala, Colombia, Ecuador, Costa Rica, Nicaragua, Cuba, Santo Domingo and Venezuela – mainly for railroad construction. When the railways were completed they stayed on and worked in the agricultural sector. Barbadians and Leeward Islanders went to Cuba and the Dominican Republic to cut cane during the season.

Barbadians also emigrated to St Croix, Jamaica, Suriname and Honduras. Jamaicans went to Honduras, Mexico and Costa Rica. Leeward islanders went to the US Virgin Islands, Santo Domingo and Costa Rica. Haitians went to the Dominican Republic to cut cane during the season. The world economic depression in the 1930s caused many workers to be sent back to their own territories. The depression created competition for jobs and this resulted in the resentment of 'foreign' (albeit fellow Caribbean) workers. The so-called 'Trujillo Massacre' in the 1930s, in which 15,000 to 20,000 Haitians were killed, was said to have been carried out under the direction of the Dominican dictator and carried out by those who resented the presence of Haitian migrants.

Table 12.2 Sample of destinations of Caribbean migrants: 1850 to 1950

Windward Islanders	went to	Guatemala, Colombia, Ecuador, Costa Rica, Cuba, Nicaragua, Dominican Republic, Venezuela, USA, UK and other BC territories
Barbadians	went to	Other BC territories, mainly, Trinidad and Guyana; but also to St Croix, Suriname, Honduras, Panama, Cuba, USA, UK

Emigration to Britain and the USA

The era of massive emigration ended shortly after World War I. During World War II, intra-Caribbean migration again increased to places where there were US military bases, but these new job openings disappeared at the end

Fig 12.1 *Workers building the Panama Canal*

of the war. After World War II another wave of emigration began, this time to the United Kingdom, reaching its peak in the 1950s. The ship *Windrush* is credited for taking the first set of Caribbean emigrants, all with British passports, to the UK in 1948. Migrants from all Caribbean territories also headed for the United States. Intra-Caribbean migration also continued with many heading for Aruba and Curaçao where there were job opportunities because of the construction of petroleum refineries, the building of factories, roads, piers, warehouses and barracks.

Britain

From 1948 to 1961, according to Karen Fog Olwig, approximately 270,916 British Caribbean people left for Britain. Table 12.3 and Table 12.4 show the percentage that left for Britain indicated by the 1960 West Indian census. The increase may have been due to post-war economic problems in the Caribbean and new post-war opportunities in the UK.

Table 12.3 Emigration to Britain, 1960

Territory	per cent of total that emigrated from the Commonwealth Caribbean to Britain	year
Leeward Islands	1.3	1960
Barbados	8.2	1960
Guyana	1.3	1960
Jamaica	9.2	1960
Windward Islands	8.6	1960

Table 12.4 Emigration to Britain, 1960, by Caribbean Territory (further breakdown of the Leeward and Windward Islands)

Territory	per cent of total that emigrated
Antigua	8
Dominica	13.3
Grenada	8.6
Montserrat	31.5
Anguilla/Nevis/St Kitts	13.2
St Lucia	8.5
St Vincent	5.3

A census in Britain in 1966 showed that emigrants from the Commonwealth Caribbean consisted of 273,700 Jamaicans and 180,300 from the Eastern and Southern Caribbean. The 1950s wave of emigration to the UK was to help rebuild a country affected by war, as the war had depleted the British labour force.

The new immigrants concentrated in cities where there were the most jobs: London and the industrial cities of Leeds and Bradford. In London some found jobs in the transportation industry (buses, trains). Jamaican poet and folklorist, Louise Bennett, captured Jamaican emigration to England in the following poem:

> *What a joyful news, Miss Mattie*
> *Ah feel like me heart gwine burs*
> *Jamaica people colonizing England in revers*

Fig 12.2 Emigrants on their way to Britain, 1948

The USA

Emigration from the British Caribbean to the USA numbered 150,000 people between 1962 and 1972. These did not include contract labourers. About 55 per cent of these people came from Jamaica and about 14,000 were skilled and professional workers. In 1971, 54 per cent of the emigrants from the Commonwealth Caribbean to the USA who were skilled or professional people came from Jamaica. The rest included farmers and farm managers, clerical workers, crafts people, private household workers, farm labourers and other labourers. Asian Indians from the Caribbean initially had a hard time getting into the USA.

Where Britain attracted mainly professional workers with skills, labourers went to the USA to pick cotton and reap tobacco. Some built railways in the west; some went to the industrial north to work in factories. From the late 19th Century Bahamians left for Florida to work on tomato and other farms and in the construction industry in Miami.

The southern US was the main destination of the Bahamians. Caribbean people settled in many US cities but New York City and Boston were popular destinations. Emigrants from Puerto Rico went mainly to the US. This was true of both males and females. They came mainly from large, poor families. More male than female migrants were educated above the elementary school level. Women moved because there were fewer and fewer opportunities for them in agriculture and because of the tendency of factories to employ women at low wages. The educated ones wanted to earn college degrees.

Currently, inhabitants of Puerto Rico and the US Virgin Islands are free to move to the US but visa requirements are strictly enforced for the nationals of other Caribbean countries.

The USA is also a mecca for Haitians, people from the Dominican Republic, and Cubans who are anti-Castro or who are simply seeking a better economic life. By the 1980s, overloaded boats with Haitian and Cuban people coming ashore in the US were a familiar sight. While Cubans have been welcomed as political refugees, Haitians (especially since the Jimmy Carter administration) are regarded as 'economic migrants' and are usually deported.

In 1980 Fidel Castro allegedly took advantage of this discriminatory policy, allowing US coastguards to pick up thousands of Cubans at the port of Mariel. Among them were (allegedly) criminals and mentally challenged people, released from Cuban gaols and psychiatric hospitals. The majority of Cubans in the US live in Miami, Florida. US immigration officials in Puerto Rico are constantly on the look-out for illegal immigrants arriving from the nearby Dominican Republic. According to some estimates, over five million Caribbean people live in the USA.

Fig 12.3 Cuban boy, Elian González (right)

The incident in early 2000 which involved the Cuban boy, Elian González, placed the issue of Cuban immigration to the US at the centre of the national and international political agenda. Elian's mother had drowned as she tried to escape Cuba on a shaky boat with others and Elian, who survived, was refused permanent settlement in the US.

Canada

Canada has also received British Commonwealth immigrants.

Table 12.5 British Commonwealth emigration to Canada

1966	3,935
1970	12,456
1974–6	26,779 from Jamaica alone
1953–74	132,412 from the BC

Source: Passaris, *Immigration to Canada in the post-war period*, 1983.

Between 1968 and 1976 Quebec recorded an arrival average of 510 immigrants, mostly professionals, from Jamaica and 595 from Trinidad and Tobago. Between 1974 and 1976 it was estimated that 26,779 people emigrated from Jamaica to Canada. The emigration of seasonal contract workers was put at 8,755 for the period 1975 to 1977. The 1981 Canadian census showed 172,245 people in the country originally from the Commonwealth Caribbean. Thousands of Haitians currently live in the greater Montreal area.

Other emigration

Emigration also took place to the gold mines in Venezuela and to the oilfields of Aruba and Curaçao. By 1940 the refineries in the Dutch Antilles employed around 15,000 workers. Many additional workers were recruited from the Windward and Leeward Islands. It was tourism that attracted workers from the Virgin Islands, especially St John, and Dutch St Maarten, to the domestic and industrial sectors on the east coast of the US and the industries and public services in Britain. Migration to the US Virgin Islands started in the 1950s, but increased in the 1960s after the passing of a special labour certification programme that made it possible to hire aliens on a temporary basis.

The slowing down of emigration

The early migration wave was temporary, but after 1950 the movement, especially to the US and Britain, has been more permanent. Up to 1961, people from the British-colonised Caribbean freely emigrated to Britain, regardless of their skill level, because they were British citizens. The 1961 Commonwealth Immigrants Bill passed in Britain, however, stopped this open-door policy that had pertained to Commonwealth citizens as Britain reacted to the ever-growing numbers of African-descended choosing to settle there.

According to this Act, Caribbeans who had already settled in the UK could send for their dependents (wives, husbands, children). This was the end of open emigration to Britain and the beginning of the impositioning of strict regulations on those who still wished to emigrate or even visit that country. Non-immigrant visas are still optional for those visiting the UK from some of the Commonwealth Caribbean. Visa requirements are now in effect for Jamaicans. However, many Caribbean people complain about the hostile reception and the searches they often have to undergo at UK and other ports of entry. It has been shown by some un-scientific surveys that customs officers in England, as in other countries including Canada, are more likely to stop and search African-descended visitors – especially young females branded as 'drug mules' from Jamaica and other places.

France and Netherlands

The major destinations of emigrants from the French and Dutch Antilles as well as from Aruba and Suriname are metropolitan France and the Netherlands respectively. By 1954, according to migration historian Bonham Richardson, there were already 15,620 emigrants from Guadeloupe and Martinique living in France. This had increased to 38,740 by 1962. Unemployment, especially among younger people, was a primary push factor.

Since 1963 a Bureau for the development of migration interests, the BUMIDOM, has handled emigration to France from the Caribbean. In 1969 some 2,500 persons from each island in the French Antilles migrated to France. By the 1970s this figure had reached 8,000 a year. The 1982 census showed that 190,000 citizens from the Caribbean lived in metropolitan France, mostly from Martinique.

It is argued that the massive emigration of people from Suriname to the Netherlands was a major factor for the granting of independence in 1974. Still, it is believed that as many Surinamese live overseas as live in the country. Many go to Holland though other European destinations are pursued, and many go to work in the thriving oil-based economy of the Dutch Antilles and to the USA.

At present, the people of the Netherlands Antilles and Aruba have Dutch passports and are entitled to unrestrained settlement and social benefits in the Netherlands. In January 1988 it was recorded that 61,000 Antilleans and Arubans, out of a total population of 280,000, lived in the Netherlands.

Immigration to the Caribbean

We should not lose sight of the fact that the Caribbean itself is the destination of people from other countries who wish to settle there. Admittedly many use the Caribbean as a point from which to enter the USA, but the recent influx of Asian business people into the region and the emergence of a new trend of granting 'economic citizenship' by some Commonwealth Caribbean territories, cannot be ignored.

2 Economic effects of emigration

The Caribbean

Returning migrants brought new skills to their country of origin and their own countries did not have to contribute to the cost of their training. In some cases those left behind had better chances of employment. Emigration resulted in an expansion in less labour intensive agricultural activities, for example citrus and bananas, as the number of workers available for the sugar industry decreased. There was also an increase in cattle rearing as the number of small farms declined in the Leeward Islands as this demanded less labour.

Much of the money for investment in the cattle farming came from returning migrants. Emigration also forced improvement in the sugar industry: it was only when emigration began to affect the availability of labour in the sugar industry in Barbados that planters began to seriously think about mechanisation.

Did you know?

The Caribbean benefits from the money sent back by those who emigrate. This money is called 'remittances'.

In islands such as Nevis, St Kitts and Montserrat, remittances from Caribbean nationals in other countries accounted for disposable income more than any other source. In Barbados between 1911 and 1920, money orders sent back to relatives, savings of returning emigrants and other remittances to relatives in the island came to a total of £1,122,000. In Jamaica in 1962, US$1,486 was remitted and in 1972, $2,202.

Remittances were used to help with weddings, funerals, children's education and general care, and with cultural events such as carnivals. Many relatives also depended on those abroad to send them a variety of material goods, such as beds, tables, chairs, radios, television sets. When migrants in nearby Caribbean Islands sent these goods home, this increased the number of ships/boats calling at island ports. In Nevis, for example, ships transporting goods from nearby Caribbean islands increased from 61 calls in 1969 to 163 in 1979.

Remittances also helped to improve living conditions: installing running water, electricity, building on additional rooms to the house, and building small shops. Remittances allowed some people to acquire land and this in turn increased the number of peasants and small farmers. Finally, remittances allowed for increased savings and increased spending power of the recipients. This benefited retailers and businesses.

There were some negative economic effects of emigration on the Caribbean. For example, small farming, which had replaced plantation agriculture in smaller territories, declined because of the loss of active members of the work force. Provision farms in St Kitts and Nevis, which were formerly cultivated by men, were left abandoned. These men's dependants now used more money to buy imported food. The abandoning of plots caused an increase in the uncontrolled grazing of animals because the previously cultivated plots were now overrun with weeds and grass.

The population of territories like Barbados, Montserrat, St Kitts, Nevis, Anguilla, Antigua and the British Virgin Islands decreased in the short term. In Barbados the population decreased from 182,000 in 1891 to 172,000 in 1911 and to 156,000 in 1921. There was a particular reduction in the size and natural growth of the agricultural labour force.

In the Bahamas, the rural agricultural economy declined as more and more labourers emigrated to Florida. In fact, by the second half of the 20th Century, Bahamas was more important as an exporter of labour than as an exporter of commodities. Emigration also altered the gender composition of the population. Populations in Jamaica, Barbados and the Leeward and Windward Islands had more females than males. Emigration also changed the age structure of the remaining population, lowering the average age of adults, and lowering birth and fertility rates in places like Barbados and the Leeward Islands.

Caribbean governments complained of an increase in public expenditure on services such as police and customs. The state claimed that it had to find more funds for repatriation of distressed emigrants and destitute returnees and to help destitute dependents that were left behind until remittances flowed back. There was a noticeable 'brain drain' as educated, middle-class professionals left the region. In 1981 a United Nations study done in Trinidad and Tobago found that emigration generally resulted in a serious 'brain drain' on the actual and potential higher level human resources. The study found that emigration from Trinidad and Tobago was highest among medical doctors, engineers and nurses.

The receiving countries

We usually focus on the impact of emigration on the source countries, but often forget to record that emigration helped the economic and social development of the places to which people emigrated. Emigrants helped to transform the Virgin Islands and the Bahamas into successful tourist resorts. In both places they assisted in the building of hotels such as the Colonial Hotel in the Bahamas, and women served as maids in these hotels. Local Bahamians on their own could not fill the job needs of the contractors for the hotel.

Immigrants made a tremendous contribution to industry. Immigrants developed the sugar industry in Cuba, colonial Guyana, Trinidad and the Dominican Republic, and the banana industry in Central America. They helped to facilitate world sea transport through work on the Panama Canal. They put up with terrible working conditions and racial discrimination in Britain and the USA in order to develop agriculture and industry in those places.

Bahamians were essential workers in the building of the city of Miami and they helped to develop agrarian capitalism in south Florida. They developed the

Fig 12.4 Colin Powell, Secretary of State in the first George W Bush Administration.

wrecking industry in Key West. They provided domestic servants for hotels and skilled workers for other industries.

Commonwealth Caribbean nationals also helped Britain in the war effort during World War II. Not only did young men serve in the Royal Air Force, but many West Indian men and women filled vacancies in the British work force.

Many emigrants and descendants of early Caribbean migrants have contributed to the cultural and political life of the USA, Canada and the UK. Between 1900 and 1930 some of the Caribbean people who settled in Harlem and Brooklyn in the USA quickly came to dominate neighbourhood politics. Many of New York's elected officials, judges and civil servants are of Caribbean background. Former Congresswoman, Shirley Chisholm, for example, is of Barbadian and Guyanese parentage. Colin Powell's parents are Jamaican. He rose to a position of power in the USA as Head of the Joint Chiefs of Staff and was US Secretary of State in the George Bush Administration for four years. Louis Farrakhan's father was Jamaican and his mother was from St Kitts. Malcolm X's mother was Grenadian.

Others of Caribbean ancestry who became influential in the USA were Marcus Garvey, Amy Ashwood Garvey (who established UNIA branches in the US), Louise Little (Malcolm X's Grenadian mother) and Claudia Jones from Trinidad (freedom fighter, communist, writer, public speaker and convenor of Afro-Asian and Caribbean Organisations). Garvey had first settled in Harlem when he arrived in the US in 1916 but later moved to New York City to the UNIA headquarters.

Did you know?

UNIA (Universal Negro Improvement Association) was the self-empowerment organization headed by Marcus Garvey during the 1920s. Through this body, Garvey preached African pride and unity for the African diaspora.

In the UK people of Caribbean ancestry, such as Diane Abbot (Jamaican) and the late Bernie Grant (Guyanese), also entered the House of Commons.

Caribbean nationals have influenced the culture of many US cities in many ways, most notably New York City and Miami. They have influenced people's dress, language (it is considered 'cool' to be able to speak Jamaican – even by actors and actresses in sitcoms and films), food, music (reggae, soca, calypso), carnivals (held annually in Brooklyn and Notting Hill).

3 Gender and emigration

Scholars are paying more attention to the gender differences in migration patterns from the Caribbean. More men than women left the region in the period up to the 1970s. For many men emigration was a natural extension of their role as 'provider'. More men than women may have been able to afford the cost of emigration as in that period male employment was higher than female employment. Women were more reluctant to leave the Caribbean as they had more domestic ties and responsibilities. There were more literate men than women and this was important as in some countries you had to be literate to qualify for emigration.

Still, more and more women formed part of the emigrating population; for example, 44 per cent per cent of all those who left Nevis for Trinidad in the post-slavery period were women. By the 1970s more women than men were emigrating from some territories; for example, in the 1970s, 55.6 per cent of emigrants from Trinidad and Tobago, 54 per cent from Jamaica and 51 per cent from Grenada were female. Female participation rose and fell, depending on the opportunities for their employment.

Up to the 1920s, for example, males dominated migration to Panama. After the completion of the canal, male migration dropped and female migration rose. This was because there was a need for female workers in the growing tourist industry in the Caribbean. According to Fog Olwig, younger women and women over 45 dominated the wave of female migrants. Emigrating women from the 1960s included both professional and working class women. They worked as nurses, teachers and domestic workers.

One effect of migration was that not all absent men and women with dependents sent money back home – at least not in the short term. The lack of financial support from their male partners meant that more women back home were forced into the agricultural labour force. Male migration also increased the parenting responsibility of women. However, when their partners did send the remittances faithfully and regularly, this often helped to cushion the responsibility of single parenting. In some territories the emigration of more men than women altered the gender composition of the population. By the 1970s, for example, emigration of males meant that there were too many women in territories like Nevis, Barbados and Jamaica.

Fig 12.5 Marcus Garvey's UNIA headquarters

Of course, these significant contributions were not accomplished easily. Many of the migrants who settled in the USA and Europe became disillusioned because of the racism and discrimination they experienced in those countries. Interviews conducted with those who went to the UK in the 1950s and 1960s reveal that they were not welcomed into the 'Mother Country'. They had to face racial slurs and had to settle for the worst houses in South London, in for example, Brixton. Some could not get rooms to rent once landladies realised that they were of African descent. They told of signs that said, 'no dogs, no blacks'. In August 1958, riots broke out between Caribbean immigrants and British residents in Notting Hill, London. In the USA, as Caribbean migrants abroad experienced racism or as children saw their parents grapple with it, many became activists in the 1960s Civil Rights Movement.

To sum up

By the time of independence Caribbean territories had largely moved away from the pre-emancipation economic system and were even more integrated into the global capitalist economy. The sugar industry was modernised, alternatives to sugar were sought, and industrialisation embarked upon. International warfare and growing social tensions affected the economy and the lives of the working classes who increasingly emigrated as a way to ease their economic problems. Caribbean settlers in the USA, Canada and the UK contributed, by their remittances, to the economic development of the region. Today these 'returning migrants' are re-settling in the region in ever-increasing numbers, though some become disillusioned with the Caribbean and return to their adopted countries.

Revision questions

Read the extract from Paule Marshall's novel that describes the experiences of Barbados migrants in the USA and answer the questions that follow:

> Each morning they (the women) took the train to Flatbush and Sheepshead Bay (in Brooklyn, New York) to scrub floors. The lucky ones had their steady madams while the others wandered those neat blocks or waited on corners – each with her apron and working shoes in a bag under her arm until someone offered her a day's work.

(adapted from Paule Marshall, *Brown Girl, Brownstones*. The Feminist Press, CUNY, New York, 1981, p. 11)

a   Why did women like those described in the passage leave Barbados for the USA in the 20th Century?

b   What occupations, apart from domestic service, did Caribbean women in the United States pursue?

c   Name three countries, apart from the United States, to which Caribbean men and women emigrated in the 20th Century.

d   State four benefits that the Caribbean gained from having some of its population living overseas.

e   State four problems created for the Caribbean by the emigration of some of its people.

2   Write an essay either on, 'The reasons why I like living in the Caribbean' or on, 'The reasons why I would leave the Caribbean and settle in a foreign country'.

Chapter 13

US political influence and military intervention since the 19th Century

'Left, right, left right, the government boots. Is it necessary, to have so much soldiers in this small country? No, no, no. Was it necessary, to hire those soldiers to out a fire? No,no,no.'
(The Mighty Gabby, Barbados)

Introduction

The arrival of the Columbus mission in 1492 was the beginning of European imperial interference in the Caribbean. For the next 500 years almost all major European imperial powers, and, after the 1890s, the United States of America (USA), launched military and political invasions in the Caribbean. With its strategic mid-Atlantic geographical setting and natural beauty, the Caribbean has captured and held the attention of European and US colonial powers and commercial interests.

This chapter will focus on the latest military power – the USA. Since the 19th Century, the USA has attempted to influence or dominate politics and commerce in the Caribbean. Its political and commercial expansion into the Caribbean has been driven by its own nationalist ideals, such as security and strategic concerns, global status, anti-communism, and human rights and democracy.

Whatever the justification, US interference in the economic and political affairs of the Caribbean and its growing cultural influence have not been welcomed by all.

US President James Monroe

Opposition to US attempts at attaining a dominant influence or military power has been reflected in the activities of Caribbean nationalists like the Haitians Jean Price-Mars, Jacques Romain and Jean Bertrand Aristide; Fabjo Fiallo from the Dominican Republic; and Alejo Carpentier, Fidel Castro and Nicolás Guillén of Cuba. Other Caribbean cultural opposition movements have supported the ideologies of *noirisme, négritude* and *creolité*, embracing African-Caribbean and Creole independence as a way of expressing their anti-US/anti-European sentiments.

In this chapter we will learn about:

1 Important terms and treaties
2 US involvement in the Caribbean up to 1898
3 US involvement in Nicaragua, Colombia and Panama over the canal issue
4 The USA and regional policing policy
5 Dollar Diplomacy, Big Stick Policy and Good Neighbour Policy
6 The USA in Cuba in the 20th Century
7 The USA and Puerto Rico
8 The USA in Haiti
9 The USA in the Dominican Republic
10 The USA and the Danish Caribbean Territories
11 The USA in the Commonwealth Caribbean

1 Terms and treaties: definitions

Before detailing US involvement in the Caribbean, there are terms and treaties which need to be familiar, as they will occur several times in this chapter. They are:

Monroe Doctrine: a statement issued by US President James Monroe in December 1823 in which he warned that European and other imperial powers should no longer view the Caribbean as a place for future colonisation. He further warned that if the European nations did not observe this 'doctrine', it would be considered 'the manifestation of an unfriendly disposition towards the United States', and would attract US action.

Manifest Destiny: a belief that the United States was destined to 'conquer' the whole of the Americas, and even beyond. It would then incorporate territories into the United States based on democratic and federal principles.

Platt Amendment (1903): an 'agreement' exacted from the Cuban people by the United States government in 1902. According to this 'agreement' Cuba could not sign any treaties without US permission, the US would moderate the Cuban debt, US jurisdiction would extend to Cuba,

Cubans lost their sovereignty, and the US would approve the acts of a military government; and would provide sites for naval bases on the island.

Teller Amendment (1898): A document stating that the US would not take over Cuban sovereignty but would allow Cubans to control the country after peace was restored.

The Roosevelt Corollary to the Monroe Doctrine (1904): A document saying that it was necessary for the USA to intervene in the internal affairs of countries under its sphere of influence (the Caribbean and Latin America) so as to maintain democracy and ward off European powers.

Dollar Diplomacy (1909–1913): An expansion of the Roosevelt Corollary. It said that diplomacy would be used to promote American business interests and dollars would be provided to promote foreign policy goals. It represented the effort of American bankers to obtain adequate safeguards from the US government for loans made to Caribbean republics. This policy was interpreted as an attempt by the US government to control Caribbean countries via investment.

Gunboat Diplomacy: the interventionist method of controlling the Caribbean region. Simply put, the territories either had to comply with the dictates of the US government or face US 'bullyism' via military intervention or other forms of pressure, e.g. economic pressure. This policy might be viewed as the exact opposite of Dollar Diplomacy.

The Treaty of Cession: signed 16 August 1916 by President Woodrow Wilson regarding the sale of Danish islands to the USA.

Big Stick Policy: a policy by which the US government used diplomacy or direct military force to coerce Latin American and Caribbean nations. The policy had under its umbrella the Roosevelt Corollary to the Monroe Doctrine as well as Gunboat and Dollar Diplomacy.

Good Neighbour Policy: the name given to F D Roosevelt's 1933 policy. When applied to the Caribbean and to Latin America, it was taken to mean the end of armed intervention. From a US ideological standpoint, the policy was supposed to promote respect and goodwill and hemispheric solidarity.

Spanish-American-Cuban War: sometimes this is called only the 'Spanish-American War' as if Cuba and the Caribbean had no part in it. It was a 110-day war between Spain, Cuba and the US which brought an end to the Spanish-American Empire. At the end of it the USA became an imperial power with respect to Cuba and Puerto Rico.

The following is a list of treaties, which are important to the study of the US influence in the Caribbean:

Clayton-Bulwer Treaty (1850): an agreement between the US and Britain which said that there would be a neutral canal which would not be used to enhance the colonisation of Central America.

Treaty of Paris (1898): a treaty signed between the USA and Spain after Spain's defeat in the Spanish-American-Cuban War. In this agreement Spain gave up colonial ownership of Cuba and the US annexed Puerto Rico, the Philippines, and Guam. This treaty committed the US to imperialism, not only in the Caribbean, but in the Orient (Asia) as well.

Hay Pauncefort Treaty (1901): a treaty signed between the USA and Britain by which the USA was given the right to build and operate a Central American canal, which the US would also defend. This canal would be open to military and commercial vessels of all countries.

Hay Herran Treaty (1903): an attempt by the USA to exact a strip of land from Colombia (the present site of the Panama canal) for the purposes of building the canal. This treaty was not approved by Colombia, and so the US encouraged a Panamanian uprising against Colombia, which controlled Panama at the time.

Hay-Bunau-Varilla Treaty (1903): this treaty gave the USA total control over a 16 km strip of land (the isthmus). Under this agreement, the canal zone was tax-free and the US could take extra land for canal construction. The US also had the sole right to defend the canal zone. In return, Panama received US$10 million and an annual payment of US$250,000 beginning nine years after the confirmation of the treaty.

Hull Alford Treaty (1936): a treaty signed between the US and Panama ending US protectorate status over Panama. Panama now jointly defended the canal zone with the US.

2　US involvement in the Caribbean up to 1898

The USA did not, with the Monroe Doctrine, suddenly develop an interest in the Caribbean. The USA had a prior history of economic and political relations with and involvement in the region. It had a particularly close relationship with the British-colonised Caribbean (especially before 1776 and independence) in the area of trade. In general, English trading regulations banned trading between England's colonies and those of other imperial nations. But for a long time there was a thriving trade between the British American colonies and the French-colonised Caribbean. They traded timber, flour and other foodstuffs for sugar, rum and molasses.

War between Britain and her North American colonies (1776)

The British-colonised Caribbean territories, especially the territories of the Eastern Caribbean, depended heavily on the North American colonies for various plantation supplies: livestock, foodstuffs from the Middle Colonies, barrel staves, shingles, etc.

Did you know?

New York, Pennsylvania, New Jersey and Delaware were called the Middle Colonies.

When war broke out between Britain and her mainland colonies in 1776, there was much sympathy for the rebels in the British-colonised Caribbean, despite the hardships created by the shortage of supplies caused by the war. Jamaica thought about breaking away from Britain and joining the American rebels. Bermuda sent delegates to the second Continental Congress; and the Assemblies in the Bahamas and in Barbados declared support for George Washington. Troops from St Domingue, both Mulatto and African-Caribbean, fought against the British, while other islands, such as the Dutch entrepôt of St Eustatius, acted as bases for weapons and supplies intended for rebel forces.

As historian James Ferguson reminds us, in retaliation for Bermuda's support of the Continental Congress, the British invaded and captured the island port of Oranjestad in 1781. They confiscated the cargoes of 150 merchant ships. This was a terrible blow to an island whose lifeblood was trade through its strategic location and free port status. After the declaration of US independence from Britain in 1783, pro-British colonists or loyalists fled to various places in the Caribbean, including the Bahamas, Jamaica and St Vincent. The cotton industry in the Bahamas grew, because these loyalists expanded their investment (financial capital and enslaved labour) in this crop.

USA declares independence

After the US colonies declared their independence, trade between the newly independent nation and the Caribbean was disrupted. Under English mercantilist regulations, the USA as a foreign power could not legally trade with the British territories and US ships were banned from British-colonised Caribbean ports. So the Caribbean had to look for other sources for plantation supplies. The increase in the prices of goods from other markets caused much agitation on the part of the Caribbean. It wanted to normalise trading relations with the USA once again.

The French colonies did not take the same approach towards the US as the British colonies. They freely opened their ports in St Domingue, Guadeloupe and Martinique to US ships. This led to British naval efforts to prevent any illegal trade between her colonies and the USA. The Caribbean and Latin America were well placed as obvious outlets for US goods. This, together with the USA's support of free trade, meant that the USA continued to be interested in the region. In fact, the USA developed an almost 'ownership' interest in the Caribbean and Latin America and tried to discourage the traditional imperial powers of Western and Southern Europe from extending their control in the Americas.

The 'scramble for the Caribbean'

Just as the Europeans had tried to carve up Africa among themselves and move into that continent after the 1880s, so the USA tried to move into the Caribbean. From as early as the announcement of the Monroe Doctrine in 1823, the Caribbean became the arena in which the USA sought to establish its political rule. President Monroe was anxious about possible European influence in the emerging independent Latin American Nations in the 1820s. So, in 1823, in a unilateral policy initiative, he warned European powers from seeing the Caribbean (in fact the whole of the hemisphere) as subject for future colonisation. He threatened that if they did not comply with this US policy, it would be seen, in the words of Monroe, as 'the manifestation of an unfriendly disposition towards the United States'. Previously, at England's request, the US administration had considered entering into a US/British cooperation to prevent European states led by France, from helping Spain get back its lost colonies in the Americas.

In 1845 President James Polk, in what came to be called the 'Polk Corollary', expanded the Monroe Doctrine by which European powers were prohibited from interfering diplomatically in relations between American hemisphere countries. Polk stated that Latin American nations should not accept European domination over them, and that they could not transfer or cede any of their territory to an external power.

A few years after the Monroe Doctrine and the 'Polk Corollary' came the notion of 'Manifest Destiny'. This proposed that the USA was destined for dominance and that she would eventually expand and incorporate the entire North American continent. In fact, 'Manifest Destiny' has also been taken to mean eventual global control by the US. One could view the US purchase of Alaska in 1867 for US$7,200,000 (less than 2c an acre!) and its interest in purchasing and controlling Cuba, as part of the expansion which went with 'Manifest Destiny'.

In 1848 President James Polk expressed the willingness of the United States to purchase Cuba by offering the Spanish government $100 million for the island. This offer was rejected by Spain and the US proceeded to encourage military forces to seize the island. As Cuba, in 1848, still had a slave system, more than anything else, the USA's politics involved the issue of slavery. Anti-slavery groups opposed the purchasing of Cuba as they perceived this as a slave owner's plot to create a stronger slave lobby in Congress. Cuba would have entered the Union as a 'slave state' and the delicate balance of slave-based to free states in Congress would have been upset.

Again in 1854, the USA tried to purchase Cuba for $130 million. This bid too was unsuccessful, but it led to the Ostend Manifesto – a declaration by the ministers (ambassadors) to Spain, Britain and France, meeting in Ostend, Belgium. It stated that if Spain refused to hand over Cuba to the US by diplomatic means (i.e. a negotiated sale), the US would use forceful measures to acquire the island. By 1855 Cuban-US trade already accounted for one-quarter of the total US world trade. This made Cuba perhaps the US's single most important trading partner, and the US wanted to increase its influence even more.

Between 1861 and 1865 US interest in Cuba remained strong even though the US government was trying to deal with restoring the Union after some eleven states had broken away from what was the United States of America. The issue of slavery was dividing the nation. This was the period of the US Civil War, which broke out because the slaveholders and planters in the Southern states wished to maintain slavery even though many countries in the hemisphere had already abolished it. The economy in the Northern states was not heavily based on slavery as was the economy of the Southern states and so these states were pro-abolition. A view was that slavery was an obstacle to industrialisation in the South and that, therefore it should be abolished (some economic historians oppose this view). During the fighting, in September 1862, President Abraham Lincoln proclaimed the freedom of the four million enslaved peoples.

From 1868 to 1878 there was a Ten Years' War between Cuba and Spain about ending Spanish domination of the island. In this time the relationship between the US and Spain was severely strained. After the war, as far as the Cubans were concerned, Spanish trade was basically unfavourable if not intolerable. The United States became increasingly important in terms of Cuban trade and investment.

The Spanish-American-Cuban War of 1898

The US made another attempt to control Cuba in 1898 during the war with Spain and Cuba. The Spanish-American-Cuban War of 1898 was fought between the US and Spain, but also involved Cubans. It began with the sinking of the USS Maine in Havana Harbour on 15 February 1898. The war which followed, supposedly over this event, was one of the shortest of the modern wars. By mid-1898 the war was over and this brought an end to the Spanish-American Empire.

After the war Spain had lost the last of her colonial possessions. On 10 December 1898 the Treaty of Paris was signed between the US and Spain. Under this treaty, Spain recognised the independence of Cuba and gave Guam, Puerto Rico and the Philippines to the US. As compensation for the Philippines, the US gave Spain $120 million. As a result of the Spanish-American Cuban War, the United States expanded its role as an imperial power. It gained its objective of being the dominant power in the Caribbean/Americas. Cuba had gained independence from one power, but soon became controlled by another.

3 US involvement in Nicaragua, Colombia and Panama over the canal issue

By 1870 the US had started to respond to the challenges of being an imperial nation by expanding trade and investment and by creating a strong navy. Having expanded its territory westwards and southwards, the US now had a need to extend its trading links in order to market the products of an increasing industrial age, as well as to speedily deploy naval vessels from the Atlantic to the Pacific shores and vice versa. For the US the need for a canal through Central America was now both a military and technological necessity. The US interest in commercial dominance in the Caribbean and Latin America provided the kickstart for later US interventions in the region. These began with where the proposed canal would be geographically located. In 1850 the Clayton-Bulwer Treaty was signed between the US and Britain. Under this treaty, the US and Britain agreed not to exercise exclusive control over an isthmian canal or railroad, and that they would not see Central American as subject to colonisation. Later the US opted out of this agreement in favour of total control over any canal constructed.

The initial site for the canal was Nicaragua, from the San Juan River Realejo, but it was soon discovered that the best site for a Central American canal was the Isthmus of Panama.

Once the US decided to build a canal across the Isthmus of Panama, it secured permission from Colombia which had provincial control over Panama. The US offered to pay the Colombian government US$10 million for the 16 km strip of land from Colón to Panama City and an annual rental of $250,000. The Colombian government did not approve the Hay-Herran Treaty (1903) for the transfer of this land. This so annoyed the US government that

President Roosevelt initiated a move in Panama to remove Colombian sovereignty, which was speedily done. After Panama's declaration of independence the Hay-Bunau-Varilla Treaty was signed between the US and Panama. This gave the US sovereign status over the 16 km canal zone and also gave tax exemption to all property and personnel. The US made the same offer to Panama as it had made to Colombia (i.e. $10m US and $250,000 annually for 9 years after ratification). The US now had the canal zone and remained in control of it. The completion of the canal in 1914 strengthened US political influence in the hemisphere.

4 The US and regional policing policy

The effective control of Cuba, Puerto Rico and the canal zone led to further US actions in the region. The US adopted a military role which became obvious in its army's involvement in the various Caribbean countries in the 20th Century:

Table 13.1 US Marine intervention in the Caribbean Basin between 1899 and 1983

Colombia	1902, 1904, 1912, 1903-14
Cuba	1906-1909, 1912, 1917-1933
Dominican Republic	1903, 1904, 1914, 1916-24
Grenada	1983
Guatemala	1920
Haiti	1914, 1915-34
Honduras	1903, 1907, 1911, 1912, 1919, 1924, 1925
Mexico	1913, 1914-17, 1918-19
Nicaragua	1910, 1912-1925, 1926-1933
Panama	1921, 1925

The first wave of regional policing by the US began in 1902 when Venezuela failed to repay a debt to French, German, and British bankers. Britain and Germany sent vessels (gunboats) and blockaded Venezuelan ports. Although President Theodore Roosevelt was disturbed by the actions of the Europeans, he held short of intervening militarily when Venezuela agreed to go to arbitration and the European powers withdrew their blockade in February 1903. It was as a result of the Venezuelan debt crisis that Roosevelt decided to extend the Monroe Doctrine to what has come known as the Roosevelt Corollary to the Monroe doctrine.

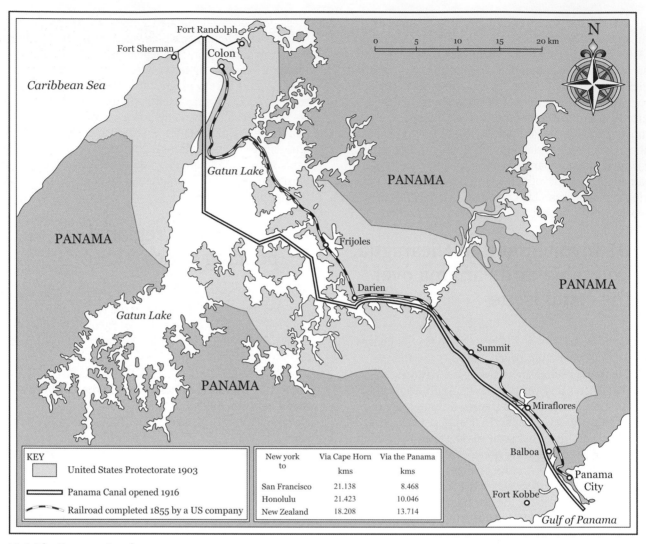

Fig 13.1 *The Panama Canal*

The Roosevelt Corollary stated,

> *If a nation shows that it knows how to act with reasonable efficiency and decency in social and political matters, if it keeps order and pays its obligations, it need fear no interference from the United States. Chronic wrongdoing, or an impotence which results in a general loosening of the ties of civilized society may, in America as in elsewhere, ultimately require intervention by some civilized nation, and in the western hemisphere, the adherence of the United States to the Monroe Doctrine may free the US, however reluctantly, in flagrant cases of such wrongdoing or impotence, to the exercise of an international police power.*

The Roosevelt Corollary to the Monroe Doctrine, along with the 1904 Platt Amendment, governed 'Teddy' Roosevelt's Big Stick policy. They became the instruments that were used to justify US military intervention in the Caribbean states. As far as President Roosevelt was concerned, his corollary was a 'logical extension of the Monroe Doctrine'. In his view, if any form of instability led to European intervention, the US should act to prevent such intervention. It was that this corollary called for 'preventable intervention', which led to US interference in the internal affairs of its neighbours.

5 From Dollar Diplomacy to Good Neighbour

William Howard Taft succeeded Theodore Roosevelt to the presidency in 1909. His policy was known as 'Dollar Diplomacy'. This was the use of diplomacy to advance US business interests as well as the use of money (usually in the form of investments) to achieve the foreign policy goals of the US government.

Under the programme, Taft pressured Caribbean and Latin American nations to take loans from US banks rather than from European banks. The US could then dictate to the countries what economic path to undertake to ensure economic growth and, more importantly, could ensure the repayment of the loans to the US banks.

Following on the heels of Taft's 'Dollar Diplomacy' was President Woodrow Wilson's 'missionary policy'. This was designed to cultivate the friendship and confidence of Caribbean and Latin American countries. Accordingly, it was Wilson's intention to prevent instability in Latin America and to promote the idea of political stability and

Fig 13.3 Big stick policy

electoral government. It is important to note, however, that more than Taft and Roosevelt, Wilson used the interventionist method to enforce dollar diplomacy in the Caribbean and Latin America.

When Franklin Delano Roosevelt assumed the presidency in 1933, he outlined yet another policy – the Good Neighbour Policy, which determined the relationship between the US and the Caribbean and Latin America. President Herbert Hoover had already laid the groundwork for this policy when he tried to stop the US's interventionist role and even began pulling US troops out of Haiti and Nicaragua. However, it was Roosevelt who gave the policy its name. When it was applied to the Americas, it meant the end of armed intervention. Roosevelt referred to this policy in his first speech after he became President, 'I will dedicate this nation to the policy of the good neighbour'. So serious was Roosevelt about this policy that the US signed a treaty with Cuba in 1934 doing away with the provisions of the Platt Amendment and allowing the US to end her protectorate over Panama. In 1941 the US also gave up the right to intervene in the Dominican Republic.

Fig 13.2 President Teddy Roosevelt

Fig 13.4 President Howard Taft

6   The USA in Cuba in the 20th Century

The Treaty of Paris signed in 1898 did not specify the future of Cuba. After the Spanish-American-Cuban War, Cuba came under the control of a US military governor, General Leonard Wood. But the Cubans wanted full independence. The Platt Amendment of 1901 specified the relationship that was to exist between the US and Cuba. This amendment to the Cuban constitution gave Washington a virtual veto power over Cuba's diplomatic and financial dealings with foreign governments.

Under the provisions of the Platt Amendment, Cuba was forbidden to negotiate any treaty that would impair its independence or to borrow any money from a foreign power if it could not repay the debt. The US had the right to intervene in Cuba to preserve law and order and uphold electoral government. Cuba had to accept all aspects of the US military government and to sell or lease lands necessary for naval or coaling stations. It is important to note that the Platt Amendment was demanded from the Cuban government, limiting the independence of Cubans.

Did you know?

Coaling stations are points along a railroad where fuel is kept for supplying locomotives.

In 1902 US military forces were withdrawn from Cuba and a new Cuban government was established. The US troops, however, returned in 1906 at the request of the president of Cuba, Estrada Palma. At this time civil protest threatened to turn into open revolt. The 1906 US intervention was part of the ideology of Theodore Roosevelt, which was outlined in the Roosevelt Corollary to the Monroe Doctrine (see p.149/8).

There were other causes of US military intervention in Cuba such as:

1917   Election irregularities surrounding the re-election of General Mario Garcia Menocal.

1933   Political crisis along with an army revolt; President Machado lost power to Carlos Manuel de Céspedes.

Gradually US business interests dominated the Cuban economy. By 1927, for example, 42.7 per cent of the Cuban sugar industry was US-controlled. Of this percentage, nearly two-thirds of Cuba's total sugar output came from US-owned factories.

Cuban tourism also developed in the 1920s during the Prohibition era when alcohol was banned in the US. In this period many tourists flocked to Havana to escape

Fig 13.5 Woodrow Wilson

Prohibition. To accommodate this influx of tourists, US investors built many resorts and other tourist-related facilities and earned millions of dollars from tourism.

Did you know?

The Prohibition era was the period from 1920 to 1933 when the sale of alcoholic beverages was banned by a constitutional amendment.

The US, Fulgencio Batista and Fidel Castro

Fulgencio Batista came to prominence in Cuba in 1933 when he led the Sergeants' Revolt, which ousted President Carlos Manuel de Céspedes. Batista forged an early alliance with the US. Under the Batista-US alliance, urban Cuba developed and showed signs of prosperity but rural Cuba was very underdeveloped.

Batista later lost power and went into exile in the US in 1944. After he regained power in 1952, his regime became a brutal dictatorship. Some Cubans invited US intervention to get rid of the Batista regime, but as US interests were protected, 'Uncle Sam' did not agree to intervene militarily in Cuba. Also, this would have gone against the non-interventionist Good Neighbour Policy.

On 26 July 1953 a young revolutionary, Fidel Castro, launched the 26 of July Movement by attacking the Moncada Army barracks in Santiago in eastern Cuba. His attempt at revolution failed and he was taken prisoner by the Batista government. In 1956 Castro was released in an attempt by the Batista government to present a new image of tolerance. Castro left for Mexico to prepare for the 1959 revolution. Fidel, his brother Raul Castro, Che Guevara and nine other revolutionaries fled to the Sierra Maestra Mountains. From there they launched a guerilla war against the Batista regime. With the assistance of the peasantry, the initial group of twelve revolutionaries (or disciples as they were sometimes called) grew from strength to strength.

On 1 January 1959, Fidel Castro and the Fidelistas marched triumphantly into Havana. In the eyes of the Cubans, Cuba had obtained its freedom at last.

In the eyes of the USA, however, revolution was proof of 'chronic wrongdoing in Cuba'. It sent three destroyers and two submarines to Havana. This was a direct military intervention. Many followers of Batista fled to the US and were used to testify against the Castro government.

Land reform in Cuba was carried out via the National Institute of Agrarian Reform (INRA). The Cuban revolutionaries believed that one reason for the hardships they experienced was that land was in the hands of the large estate owners or *latifundistas* – the small group of rich corporations and individuals. In 1959 INRA aimed to

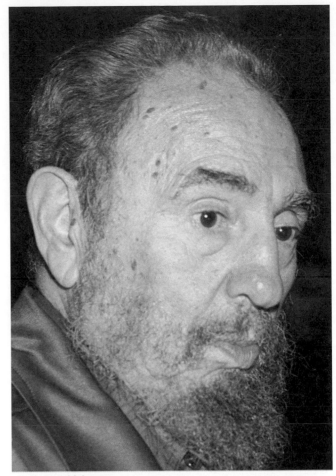

Fig 13.6 *Fidel Castro*

Fig 13.7 *Che Guevara*

Fig 13.8 Fulgencio Batista

let the state take over part of this land, provide some compensation to the previous owners and make land available for the landless, at the rate of 27 hectares per family. By 1960 extensive land was given back to Cubans. This, then, was the end of foreign-owned *latifundia* or large plantations in Cuba. US investors owned about 75,000 acres of Cuban land at this time and the loss of property enraged the US government.

Fig 13.9 Moncada barracks

By 1960 Cuba had a 'limited' trade agreement with the Soviet Union, trading its sugar for Soviet oil and manufactured goods. When US oil refineries in Cuba refused to refine Soviet crude oil, this led to the nationalisation of oil refineries by Castro, which further enraged the US government. The US retaliated by cutting the Cuban sugar quota, which led Castro to nationalise the remaining US possessions in Cuba.

The US government began training anti-Castro Cuban exiles to invade Cuba and overthrow Castro. In 1961 the USA invaded in what is known as the Bay of Pigs fiasco. The US, apart from the humiliation associated with the defeat, realised that Castro was the people's choice.

Did you know?

The Bay of Pigs incident (1961) was an invasion of Cuba authorised by President Kennedy. US forces trained 1,500 Cuban exiles and they landed at the Playa Giron (Bay of Pigs). The hope was that those who opposed Castro would revolt against him in Cuba, but this did not happen and the USA was humiliated.

The US refused to sell Cuba weapons and cut off loans to the new republic. From as early as October 1960, President Eisenhower announced a ban on all exports to Cuba, except essential foodstuffs and medicine. This was followed by Castro nationalising US investments in Cuba. In January 1961, Castro ordered the USA to reduce its embassy staff to eighteen, which led to President Eisenhower severing diplomatic relations with Cuba.

As the US and Cuba drifted apart, the Soviet Union came closer, forging economic and diplomatic ties with Cuba. The Soviet Union had wanted to establish itself in the US sphere of influence and Cuba provided the opportunity.

The missile crisis

In May 1961 Castro declared Cuba a socialist state, adopting the Communist model of government. This was the era of the Cold War. In its self-declared role as regional policeman, the US wanted to prevent the spread of communism in the region and therefore was enraged by close links between Cuba and the Soviet Union. In the spring and summer of 1962 intelligence sources in Washington reported that the Soviet government was supplying arms to Cuba, (though Russia later denied that the weapons were intended for offensive purposes). President Kennedy announced that the US Navy would impose a blockade on Cuba. On 16 October 1962 President Kennedy was convinced by his military advisors that Cuba was installing ballistic missiles with atomic warheads. It was calculated that 42 missiles capable of reaching any city in the US were either in Cuba or on their way to Cuba. On 22 October 1962 Kennedy requested Premier Kruschev of the Soviet Union to remove the missiles from Cuba.

On 26 October 1962 the Soviets agreed to withdraw the missiles if NATO missiles were removed from Turkey. This was rejected by the USA. But by 28 October Kruschev agreed to withdraw the missiles under United Nations supervision, providing that the USA lifted the naval blockade of Cuba and gave the USSR the assurance that it would not invade Cuba. The naval blockade ended on 20 November 1962.

In 1962, the USA forced the Organisation of American States (OAS) to expel Cuba from that body, and to have a policy of hemispheric exclusion towards Cuba from then.

7   The USA and Puerto Rico

From 1506 to 1898 Puerto Rico was a Spanish-colonised territory and was of great strategic and economic importance to Spain. This was because it guarded the approaches to the centres of mineral wealth in Latin America; and it was fortified against North West European attack on Spanish-colonised territory. It was Puerto Rico's strategic position that attracted the attention of the USA. Of course, there had also been long-standing commercial ties between the USA and Puerto Rico, and trade actually expanded during the Napoleonic wars of 1802–1815.

Puerto Rico came under the political control of the USA on 25 July 1898. After a treaty with Spain, US troops entered the island and gradually occupied its chief towns. In September 1898 Governor Macias officially ordered that the constitutional powers of the Spanish judges be ended in favour of US sovereignty. The US forced this treaty as they were afraid that Spain would grant internal self-government to Puerto Rico which would make it more difficult for them to gain a foothold in that island. Indeed, during the Spanish-American-Cuban War of 1895 to 1898, Spain had promised the island internal self-rule to win Puerto Rico's support and to appease the radical Puerto Ricans who wanted independence.

Spain actually granted Puerto Rico a constitution in 1897. But before it could come into effect, a US military force was sent to the island in July 1898. By August the US had taken the island and the Treaty of Paris in 1898 ceded Puerto Rico to the US. A US military government, lasting two years, was installed. In 1902 the US Congress passed the Foraker Act which set up a civilian government controlled by US appointed officials. Though Puerto Rico was made an overseas territory of the USA, the US constitution did not apply to Puerto Ricans so they lacked similar civil rights as mainland citizens. There was no free trade between the countries for the first two years. The USA that stood for self-determination and civil rights for its

Fig 13.10 *President John F Kennedy*

Fig 13.11 *Nikita Kruschev (left) with Che Guevara*

citizens now imposed imperial domination and exploitation on Puerto Ricans.

The Foraker Act also limited the size of sugar plantations to 200 hectares each. This was not enforced, so large estates emerged and up to 1920, the island was still described as a monocrop export economy, dependent on sugar cane and its by-products. In fact, 75 per cent of the population depended on the sugarcane industry for jobs.

The Jones Act of 1907 made Puerto Rico a territory of the USA after which there was a period of organised colonial domination. Limited political reform took place in 1917 which meant that the USA still appointed the governor of the island, but the people could now vote for their senate representatives. Still, the island remained an 'unincorporated territory of the United States'.

After the military invasion, US control was executed through legal and governance control, economic exploitation and a process of deculturation of Puerto Ricans which some historians refer to as 'ethnocide'.

Did you know?

Ethnocide is the destruction of aspects of a culture without destroying the people who have that culture. Usually, a new culture – dress, language, religion and cutoms – is imposed on those people who are victims of ethnocide.

Most areas of government were controlled by the US Congress, which also controlled various policies. These policies related to immigration (Puerto Ricans have no control over who settles there), transportation, tariffs, trade, financial laws, communications, environment, citizenship, judicial appeals, wages and other labour matters, planning, navigable water, transfer of federal lands and the military use of the island. Puerto Ricans, while subject to all these forms of constitutional domination, cannot vote directly for a US president, but they can be drafted into the US army. So Puerto Rico remains a province, subordinate to the United States.

8   The USA in Haiti

In 1915 the US undertook two invasions that resulted in the establishment of military government in the Dominican Republic and a civilian regime closely supervised by US Naval Officers in neighbouring Haiti. The particular incident, which led to the invasion of Haiti, was the overthrow of Haitian President Guillame Sam in July 1915 when he was killed by a mob. The USA wanted to prevent President Arias from taking power – they saw him as an anti-American nationalist, as he refused to bow to pressure from President Wilson. Wilson said that Haiti needed internal reforms in government and because presidents rose and fell so quickly in Haiti, such 'political instability' had to end. US Marine detachments moved against Arias's supporters in the north of the country. The military force of 1915 consisted of 300 US sailors and marines who landed at Port-au-Prince on 28 July. They were quickly reinforced by troops dispatched from Guantanamo Bay, Cuba. In spite of courageous guerilla warfare, the Haitians lost out to the invading forces. The resulting US occupation lasted 19 years. When the US entered World War I in 1917, the entire island of Hispaniola became a US base. The US gave political and strategic interests as the reasons for intervention; but they also had economic interests. The US had significant investments in Haiti in banking, railway and agriculture, and had lent money to the country. By 1910, US interests in Haitian finances had increased. The USA had enjoyed a half-century of regular diplomatic interchange in Haiti, but the relationship had produced little friendliness and even less understanding.

After intervening the US claimed certain 'victories', including the restoration of the Haitian Treasury Service to the Banque Nationale – these services had been earlier suspended. The US set up a ruler in Haiti to whom they could dictate. Their first choice, Leger, refused, but they found a governor in Phillipe Dartiguenaue, who ruled from 1915 to 1922. He was followed by other governors: Borno (1922 to 1930), Roy (1930), and Vincent (1930 to 1941).

There had been a long-standing conflict between African and mixed-race people for dominance in Haiti after the end of slavery and colonialism. The US occupation resulted in the decrease of Afro-Haitian political influence in the island and saw the re-establishment of mixed-race elite control in government as well as in business. These businessmen benefited from the presence of 2,000 marines with salaries to be spent in Haiti. The US occupation also saw the return of European and North American elitism in the form of US officials and marines. US nationals filled many top positions and although they promised to train Haitians to fill these positions, they failed to do so.

The US occupation resulted in the decrease in the size of the Haitian army. The marines trained about 2,000 men as a constabulary force who combined military and police duties. Extra men were drawn from the army and put to labour in agriculture and other areas. Of course, by restructuring the army, the US also removed the constant fear they had of armed revolution. The new elite felt more secure, for traditionally it was the Afro-Haitian-dominated army that had supported Afro-Haitian presidents in power or helped them to rise to power.

While they were in Haiti, the marines made attempts to improve the health and educational services. They built schools, health clinics and hospitals. They improved the water supply and sewage system, contributed to the eradication of diseases, built miles of paved road, undertook electrification and railroad construction, improved banking services and budgetary control.

The USA claimed that it had many 'successes' in Haiti – it was involved in improving the physical and material conditions of some of the people most of these improvements were made in the urban centres. However, many Haitians opposed US presence. Haitians saw the US presence as a backward political move, after they had won their independence since 1804. With the US occupation, for example, came a reversal of a policy excluding White people from landownership. The marines had reimposed forced labour and taxes on the peasants. Social and class tensions surfaced and the majority of Haitian peasants saw no significant improvements in their lives. The people who lived in the areas in which marine barracks were located, had rising expectations about acquiring American goods – radios, automobiles, clothes, etc.

By 1930, President Stenio Vincent had started negotiations with the US to withdraw and there was an active Haitian movement demanding the withdrawal of the occupation forces. Of course the *caco* guerrillas had long fought for freedom and many had died at the hands of the marines. The 1930s were favourable times for withdrawal, because it was in the period of the Good Neighbour Policy and Roosevelt was anxious to win support in the region. The marines left in 1934, although the US controlled the Haitian national budget until 1941 and their cultural influences remain in the way of language, music and clothes.

The US also continued to invest in Haiti and to keep a close watch on political events for any signs of communist tendencies and influences. For example, they became concerned in 1938 when President Vincent announced his intention to abolish presidential elections and also when Daniel Fignole organised supporters and encouraged working-class militancy against the Lescot regime. (Vincent had left in 1941 because of ill-health when he was replaced by the more pro-US mulatto politician, Elie Lescot.) By 1946 Lescot lost his popularity, and the US was fearful of the leftist threat. But Lescot was removed by a military coup and replaced by a moderate Afro-Haitian politician, Dumarsais Estime. He, in turn, was replaced by General Panul Magloire who established friendly relations with the USA. His dictatorial style and unacceptable actions soon made him unpopular and fuelled strikes and demonstrations. He fled to the USA.

In the elections of 1957, Francois Duvalier ('Papa Doc') came to power, helped by the army. Duvalier was an Afro-Haitian nationalist who opposed the US occupation of Haiti. Aided by his loyal paramilitary police force called the 'Tonton Macoutes', Duvalier began a period of dictatorship and terrorism. While the USA opposed this, they did not intervene militarily. Duvalier used the 'communist bogey' to his own advantage – he forced the US to give Haiti financial aid to guarantee Haiti's vote in the Organisation of American States in support of sanctions against Cuba. When 'Papa Doc' died in 1971, he was succeeded by his son, Jean Claude Duvalier, 'Baby Doc'. In fact, Francois Duvalier had named his son as his successor before he died.

Did you know?

'Tonton macoutes' are called 'bogeymen' in Haitian creole. They were the personal police force of François Duvalier of Haiti. These unpaid volunteers were licenced to torture, kill and extort when deemed necessary. They murdered Duvalier's opponents; under his son, Jean-Claude Duvalier, the name was changed to 'National Security Volunteers'.

Fig 13.12 *Francois 'Papa Doc' Duvalier*

This transition to power was watched keenly by the USA. They had a warship between Haiti and Miami, and they had troops and tanks guarding crossing points on the Haitian-Dominican border to prevent any exiles from trying to leave Haiti. The Nixon administration offered cautious encouragement to Jean-Claude along with improved cooperation in aid and military training. Nevertheless, the US was not comfortable with 'Baby Doc'. There were conflicts between his regime and the US over the increasing arrival in Florida of Haitian 'boat people' or refugees, fleeing his regime. The USA felt that 'Baby Doc' did not do enough to discourage this flight. The Jimmy Carter government of the 1970s also insisted that Haiti improve its human rights as a condition for US aid. In spite of the terrorism of the political regime in Haiti, US investment increased in the 1970s as companies were attracted by the low labour costs in the country.

Duvalier developed better relations with the Reagan administration in the 1980s, although the 'boat people' crisis escalated and created conflict in the relations between the USA and Haiti. By 1985 anti-Duvalier sentiments had become so strong inside and outside of Haiti that it was clear that his reign was coming to an end. The USA voiced open criticism of Duvalier, and George Shultz (the Secretary of State under President Ronald Reagan) called for a return to democracy in Haiti. Meanwhile, radicals such as the priest Jean-Bertrand Aristide were preaching radical action to end Duvalier's repressive regime. A US military aeroplane eventually flew Duvalier into exile in France in February 1986. The USA had moved to stop any escalation in popular protests.

Fig 13.14 *Jean-Bertrand Aristide*

9 The USA in the Dominican Republic

In 1821, Santo Domingo claimed its independence from Spain. From 1822 to 1844, it was controlled by Haiti after that country's war for independence. In 1844 Santo Domingo broke away from Haiti, declared its independence and called itself the Dominican Republic. It still feared Haitian annexation though. From then on, many people called on the US for annexation/protection.

The chance for US intervention came in 1905 during the Roosevelt Corollary to the Monroe Doctrine. The rationale the US gave for intervening was the 1899 assassination of Governor Ulises Heureaux, who had ruled since 1882. His regime had been supported by the US who feared political instability and a governor hostile to its interests. At the time, the Dominican Republic had accumulated a large foreign debt with the US as well as with Germany and other European powers. The US was concerned by possible European action to collect such debts. It invaded with the excuse that it was administering the customs to collect revenue in the Dominican Republic and pay off foreigners.

This was not the end of US intervention in the Dominican Republic. The establishment of the General Customs Receivership had solved some of the economic problems, but political infighting continued. According to historian Frank Moya Pons, the government of President Ramón Cáceres in the Dominican Republic at first received popular support especially as it brought a period of wealth

Fig 13.13 *Jean Claude Duvalier*

Chapter 13 | US political influence and military intervention since the 19th Century

and stability. In 1911 the assassination of Cáceres ended a brief period of political stability and created a political vacuum that Dominican *caudillos* (military leaders) and politicians tried to fill immediately. Long repressed hostilities erupted into violent confrontations and dragged the country into a period of civil wars that eventually allowed the Jiminista Party to resurface. In the meantime, Congress made frantic attempts to choose Cáceres' successor. The US installed Eladio Victoria in 1912, but there was stiff opposition to his regime. President William Taft sent a pacification (or appeasement) commission, accompanied by 750 US marines, to Santo Domingo to try to negotiate the end of the Civil War. The pacification commission threatened military invasion if their demands were not met. This threat became a reality in 1916 after the escalation of opposition, for example Desiderio Arias's opposition to the regime of Archbishop Adolfo Nouel who took over after Victoria's resignation at the end of 1912. Stability did not return even after José Bordas Valdez was installed as interim president until elections could be held. Valdez indicated his intention to stay in the post, and indeed organised the municipal and congressional elections so that he could stay in power. This led once more to civil war.

President Wilson's plan to solve the crisis failed and there was continuing instability under the presidency of the US supported Juan Isidro Jimenes.

Did you know?

The Jiminista Party of the 1900s was named after the politician Jimines. The supporters of this party were suppressed when the opponent Vasquez came to power, but resurfaced when they were led to rebellion by Carlos Morales in 1903.

He later fell out of favour with the US and resigned on 7 May 1916. The failure of Haitian presidents to solve the political crisis caused US military intervention on 16 May 1916. The US marines occupied the capital and began sending troops to other parts of the country. Despite resistance by Arias and his followers in Puerto Plata and Mao in the northwest, the US continued to occupy the rest of the country throughout the summer of 1916. The US justified their invasion by saying that the Dominican government had broken the 1907 treaty by incurring unauthorised debts. They also said they wanted to prevent a perceived German threat during World War I. The US installed a regime in which the real power lay with the US military governor. Nationalist resistance escalated in the period after the US occupation. The occupation was also criticised in Latin America and among sections of the US population, who saw it as neo-colonial.

After the election of US President Warren Harding in 1921, the need for rapid withdrawal from the Dominican Republic became more urgent, especially as Harding had opposed Wilson's interventionist policy. A provisional government was created in 1922 and the marines oversaw general elections in March 1924. They withdrew in July 1924, having left a pro-US governor, Horacio Vásquez, in power as president.

10 The USA and the Danish-colonised Caribbean territories

Denmark was in possession of St John, St Thomas and St Croix for varying lengths of time extending over a period of 245 years. These islands were sold to the US and in 1917 for $25 million and became known as the United States Virgin Islands. The sale was agreed by a national referendum in Denmark where 283,694 people voted in favour and 157,596 voted against it. It received the Danish king's signature on 22 December 1916. The Treaty of Cession was signed on 16 August 1916 by President Woodrow Wilson, and the transfer took place on 31 March 1917. Formal transfer ceremonies were held all over the islands.

But the 1917 sale was simply the end of several attempts to sell these islands to the US. The sale was first discussed in 1846 and then raised again several times. For example, negotiations were restarted in 1865 by US Secretary of State, William Seward. Other negotiations took place in 1867, when a price of $7.5m was agreed by popular vote of the people of the islands and the government of Denmark. However, the US did not agree to this because among other things, the strategic importance as military base was not appreciated at that time. Negotiations were held again in 1892, 1896, and 1902, but all came to nothing. Why did Denmark part with her Caribbean colonies? Why was the US so interested in the former Danish-colonised islands? What impact did the US presence have in these islands?

Denmark was willing to get rid of its Caribbean colonies because of the declining state of the economy of the islands by 1865. Denmark increasingly came to view the territories as liabilities. Their combined internal revenue was not enough to meet the expenses of maintenance, and Denmark was unwilling to meet the shortfall. Denmark claimed increased financial strain after the war with Prussia in 1864. In fact it saw the sale of unprofitable overseas territories like Greenland and the Danish-colonised Caribbean as sources of revenue to meet expenses of war. The islands were also not really a market for goods from Denmark. By 1901 sugar exports to Denmark from her Caribbean states totalled only 300,000 lbs.

The abolition of slavery and the withdrawal of most labourers to other occupations in commercial St Thomas or to non-agricultural labour in the towns of St Croix and St John just made the situation worse for employers and the Danish government. Finally, there were few firm social and cultural links between Denmark and its Caribbean possessions. The English language was the one most widely used in the islands; there was no widespread use of the Danish currency; and the educational system was heavily influenced by the British system. In the islands themselves, the majority of the population believed that they would get more economic and social benefits if they ended their Danish status.

There is some difference in opinion as to whether the US purchase of the Danish Caribbean territories was motivated by economic or military considerations. Even though the islands may not have been economically viable at the time of the purchase, they certainly had economic potential and would help the US to safeguard the approaches to other more profitable territories like the Panama Canal. Therefore, it could be said that both economic and strategic or military considerations were important.

The US had a long commercial association with the Danish-colonised Caribbean. By the 19th Century, trade with the US accounted for one-third of the imports of the islands. They would also help the trading partners of the US as a place for recreation and transport refuelling. The US itself could use the islands as lookout points during wars with other nations as the islands were well located for that purpose. Finally, there was a growing expansionist stance in the US in the early 20th Century. Under the purchase agreement the US would not take private property. Those who wished to remain as Danish citizens could do so. Others were to become US citizens (although this was not effected until years later). Civil rights and political status were to be decided by the US Congress.

The US embarked on a programme of road construction, construction of schools, improvement of social services, water supply, sewage, police and fire services. Not much was done to expand agriculture, though, and by the 1950s tourism had become the main economic activity.

11 The USA in the Commonwealth Caribbean

The US did not confine its military activities to the former Danish and Spanish colonies. In 1940, during World War II, it leased and established military bases in British-colonised territories. Before this date the USA had been a neutral power in the war. Now it said that Germany wanted to occupy British-colonised territories and that if the US remained a neutral power, it could not do anything to stop Germany. Germany was in fact interrupting British and Allied shipping in the region. The USA abandoned its neutral position in 1940 when Franklin Roosevelt negotiated the erection of these bases with Britain. The agreement was that the US would supply Britain with 50 destroyers in exchange for the right to establish bases in Trinidad (built at Chaguaramas), Jamaica, Bermuda, Antigua, colonial Guyana and St Lucia on a 99-year rent-free lease. The US reserved the right to build immediately or later. Bases or marine garrisons already existed in Cuba (Guantanamo Bay) Puerto Rico, Honduras, Haiti, the Dominican Republic and the USVI. In 1942 German submarines sank ships in the Caribbean, including one near Barbados and St Lucia.

Military bases (e.g. in Trinidad)

The USA had long had economic interests in the British-colonised Caribbean, but now it also had military interests. The establishment of US bases had social and economic consequences for the islands. In Trinidad, people complained that the development of Port-of-Spain was limited because so much land was released for the base and its environs. Port of Spain lost some popular beach spots. Still, many local people got jobs on the bases, especially in construction. The entertainment industry, especially calypso, grew tremendously. Some people married US nationals working at the base. The economy benefited from the inflow of US dollars. Prostitution increased around the areas near the base.

After the war, the USA gave back many of these bases to Britain. In the case of Trinidad, the people demanded the base back, as it was seen as the site of the Federal capital. The closure of the bases also caused social disruption as they had created economic opportunities for the country as a whole. But many people felt that it was more important for the country to have back control of its own land.

Post-World War II economic influence

After the war there was still evidence of US cultural and economic influences in these territories. Indeed, in the post-war years the British-colonised Caribbean territories were even more linked economically to the US than to the United Kingdom. Major US cities, rather than London, became the preferred destination of many emigrants. More and more the US became involved in the economic affairs of the independent and British-colonised Caribbean through the International Monetary Fund (IMF) and the World Bank. Jamaica and other Commonwealth Caribbean territories imported most of their supplies from the US.

Multinational corporations were established in these territories, and they sent back large sums of money to the US. Examples of these corporations are the Bauxite companies of ALCOA and REYNOLDS in Jamaica, the oil company TEXACO in Trinidad and Tobago as well as in Jamaica, and the KAISER bauxite company in Guyana. The United Fruit Company and Chase Manhattan were also present. The US has also invested in the tourist industry, with US-owned hotels and casinos in many islands, but especially in The Bahamas.

Cold War actions in Commonwealth Caribbean politics

The US also continues to play a vigilant role in Commonwealth Caribbean politics. During the Cold War it claimed to be concerned about the spread of Cuban and Soviet style communism in its 'backyard', especially in light of the political turmoil in colonial Guyana and the suspension of the constitution there in 1953. The US used economic aid (for example through the 1961 Alliance for Progress) and the Central Intelligence Agency (CIA) formed in 1947, to combat communism overseas.

The USA supported Britain's Prime Minister Winston Churchill's removal of Cheddi Jagan from office in colonial Guyana, and they supported the expansion of the International Confederation of Free Trade Unions (ICFTU) in the region to counter the influence of the Moscow-aligned World Federation of Trade Unions. Major Jamaican trade unions, the Bustamante Industrial Trade Union (BITU) and the National Workers Union (NWU) became members of the ICFTU. This showed their anti-communist stance. Norman Manley's People's National Party even expelled prominent left-wing members (e.g. Richard Hart and Ken Hill) from the Party. US Senator Joe McCarthy personified this outright anti-communist attitude. He was known for seeking out those suspected of communist and 'unAmerican' activities. Anti-communism anxieties affected the Commonwealth Caribbean as it did Latin America.

The US sponsored the formation of, and has since dominated, the Organisation of American States (OAS) to which independent Caribbean states have membership. The OAS replaced the old Pan-American Union and was intended to strengthen inter-American cooperation. The OAS issued the Caracas Declaration in 1954, which was little more than a modification of the Monroe Doctrine. The US prodded the OAS to adopt resolutions declaring that the presence of Marxism-Leninism and alien ideology in the Americas was tantamount to 'foreign aggression'. They reserved the right to act by themselves, if necessary, to protect the hemisphere from such aggression. This meant suppressing any radical left-wing challenges.

In the post-war years, the normal US intervention strategy was not to send in marines, but to use counter-insurgency and other security assistance programmes to ensure that local security bodies had the capacity to handle any situation. The exception was the case of Grenada in 1983 (see below). According to one analyst the CIA was used as the instrument of intervention, where stronger and more direct action was not needed.

Jamaica

The US often acted unilaterally in situations that demanded collective action by the region. This approach encouraged anti-US feelings in the Commonwealth Caribbean, especially among nationalist politicians and intellectuals. Some of these people, like Michael Manley, tried to take their countries along alternative paths to the capitalist model of free-market development. Not surprisingly, it was widely suspected that the CIA sought to destabilise the Manley regime. Manley's anti-imperial attitude and economic and social reforms made him popular among the masses and radical intellectuals. But these attitudes alienated the USA and fuelled the anti-communism of the opposition Jamaica Labour Party (JLP) under Edward Seaga. The 1970s was a politically volatile and violent period in Jamaica. The USA issued a travel advisory, warning US tourists not to visit Jamaica. They also tried to impose economic sanctions on the island. Manley sought aid from the IMF in 1977. In the traditional model of 'aid as imperialism', the IMF imposed a series of conditions in exchange for aid. The Manley regime could not meet these conditions and this led to further economic crises and social tension in the island. The JLP took full advantage of this atmosphere and won the 1980 general elections. The USA was clearly relieved and openly supported the Seaga regime. Seaga and Reagan visited each other's countries in 1981 and 1983 respectively.

Grenada

In March 1979, the socialist Maurice Bishop, the popular charismatic leader of the New Jewel Movement (NJM), staged a revolutionary coup against the increasingly unpopular Eric Gairy (see Chapter 17). International institutions like the World Bank and the IMF had given hesitant support to Bishop's economic reforms, in particular his mixed economy model, but Ronald Reagan's regime was suspicious about Bishop's close relations with Cuba. In this period of the Cold War the US continued to be concerned about the communist influence in the region and the leftist leanings of some regimes. It therefore viewed Grenada as a potential security threat, especially after Cuban construction workers and engineers arrived there to help build an international airport. The view of the

Americans was that these were more than construction workers. So relations between Bishop's People's Revolutionary Government and the Reagan administration became increasingly tense, with Bishop accusing the US of bullying and destabilising tactics.

The specific moment of the US military action in Grenada was created by the NJM itself. A fierce power struggle broke out between the NJM members over the direction and leadership of the revolution. An extremist Marxist faction led by Bernard Coard demanded a system of joint leadership. When Prime Minister Bishop refused to accept this alternative model he was put under house arrest by a faction of the island's armed forces which supported Coard. Popular protest resulted as Bishop's supporters demonstrated and successfully freed him. However, his refuge at Fort Rupert was attacked by the pro-Coard military and Bishop and several of his NJM leaders were killed.

US warships soon arrived in Grenada with 6,000 troops, allegedly to 'protect US citizens' and restore order. Several Caribbean leaders, including Dominican Prime Minister

Fig 13.15 Maurice Bishop

Eugenia Charles and Tom Adams of Barbados, supported the US action. Even within Grenada some pro-Bishop supporters also welcomed the US presence and condemned the Coard group. In the fighting that followed, many US and Grenadian lives were lost. The Cuban construction workers were also fired on and fought back.

The US was determined to weaken Cuban/communist influences in the region and to promote regimes based on free-market and export-led development. During the rest of the 1980s, the US used its economic power, via financial aid to the Eastern Caribbean, to assert its influence in the region. By the end of 1983, for example, Grenada had become one of the highest per capita recipients of US funding despite the fact that high wages made it a less attractive place for US investment when compared to Haiti, Mexico and the Dominican Republic.

What is the situation now?

With the collapse of the Soviet Union, the US is no longer on military alert in the Commonwealth Caribbean, but maintains diplomatic relations and embassies in several territories. The low-key interest in the region was clearly expressed by Madeline Albright (the US Secretary of State in the Bill Clinton administration) in a lecture at the Johns Hopkins University on 18 January 2000. While the lecture was titled 'US foreign policy in 2000', hardly any attention was paid to the former British colonies; but there was a significant focus on Colombia because of the US preoccupation with the production of and illegal trade in drugs.

The closeness of the Caribbean to the US mainland raises a number of security and strategic issues which remain highly important. US fears are no longer linked to communist infiltration, European super power rivalry and imperial interest. The new concerns are about illegal migration, terrorism and drug-related crimes. The US continues to provide financial aid to the region to help fight drug trafficking, with a specific focus on Colombia. It is a worrying factor that the US government does not have the ability to curb the demand for drugs at home – it is partly this demand which fuels the supply from Central America and the Caribbean.

The Caribbean Basin Initiative of 1983 and other US-sponsored finance and trade programmes are aimed at getting the US private sector to invest in the region as a way of creating jobs and stemming the tide of emigration. However, these schemes have had little effect on emigration. Although they intended to create jobs, they have also created cheap labour, especially of female workers who work long hours for low pay. The US still remains the preferred destination for thousands of Caribbean migrants. However, in the aftermath of the terrorist attacks in the US on 11 September 2001, immigration to the US has become more difficult for Caribbean people.

The continuing US cultural influence

The US cultural influence in the Commonwealth Caribbean is strong and widespread. This cultural influence has had a long history. By the early 1900s the mass media had penetrated the region, spreading American culture through radio, cinema and newspapers. Later the television became a powerful means of transmitting US culture. By the 1960s, the media had succeeded in transmitting many aspects of US culture to the region, especially in the areas of sports, technology, language, dress, music, film, news, food and education. Since the 1980s, the widespread availability of Cable TV has brought US culture even closer to millions of people in the Caribbean. Local TV stations transmit more US than local programmes and many now speak of the 'CNNisation' of the region.

The presence of Caribbeans in the US has also contributed to the expansion of the US cultural influence, with relatives sending/taking back US products (clothes, electronic items, etc.) in the now familiar barrels. In the area of sports, the popularity of the US influenced basketball (along with the sports stars like Michael Jordan), is now quite marked. Many in the region say this is why young people are less interested in cricket, considered the cornerstone of Caribbean sports. Americanisms have crept into the languages of the region, and the American influence is evident in jazz, disco, funk, rock and roll, and the blues. The US currency is commonly used in all Caribbean territories, and US fast food chains are familiar sites: McDonalds, Burger King, Popeye, Pizza Hut.

While the method of delivering primary and secondary education is still very much grounded in the British culture, tertiary education has shown greater signs of US influence, for example, in the adoption of the two-semester system. Many students choose to study in US colleges and universities qualifying themselves locally for the vital SAT, GRE and GMAT.

We will see in the next chapter that US cultural influence has not meant the loss of Caribbean tradition. Indeed, the Caribbean has also exported its culture to the US. Sections of the US population have embraced soca, reggae, DJ and dancehall music, calypso, steelband, carnival, Jamaican nation language and Caribbean dishes. While the attraction for many North American tourists continues to be sun, sea and sand, for others, the pull of Caribbean culture is unmistakable. Finally, there are those in the region who, in response to the 'cultural penetration' from the US and Europe, have made a more serious effort to promote Caribbean culture, especially African-Caribbean and Indo-Caribbean culture. Cultural nationalists from all classes are in the forefront of this movement to reclaim Caribbean culture, and include poets, singers and musicians, artists, academics and writers.

To sum up

US military intervention in the affairs of the Caribbean region has produced changes in governance, either through its support of governments or through economic policies which, in some cases, impoverished regimes that see their interests and those of the USA as not one and the same. The results of these policies are seen in the heightened awareness among some sectors of Caribbean society in relation to cultural emphasis, strong nationalistic tendencies and anti-US feelings. In other cases, the injection of US capital investments has brought social and economic improvements which allow the US to have favourable ratings in some areas of Caribbean society. The US (and French) invasion of Haiti in 2004 – ironically the bicentennial year of Haitian independence – and their alleged role in the exiling of Jean Bertrand Aristide, have once more heightened Caribbean sensitivity towards US imperial tendencies.

Revision questions

1 Read the extract and answer the questions that follow:
   Between the end of the Spanish-American-Cuban War, which broke out in 1898, and 1934, the United States of America tried to turn the Caribbean into a US Lake.

   a State two reasons for the outbreak of the war mentioned in the extract.
   b Use examples to explain how the US tried to 'turn the Caribbean into a US Lake' after 1898.
   c State three ways in which people in the former Spanish-colonised Caribbean territories reacted to the attempt by the US to 'turn the Caribbean into a US Lake'.

2 a What was the nature of US activities in the British-colonised Caribbean territories during World War II?
   b How accurate is the claim that the British-colonised Caribbean benefited from the US presence in the region in World War II?

c What evidence is there to suggest that US cultural imperialism has been quite pervasive in the Caribbean in the 20th Century?

3 a Explain fully why the US has refused to lift its trade embargo imposed on Cuba since 1960.

b Explain fully how Cuba has managed to survive the impact of the trade embargo imposed by the US.

Chapter 14

The labour movement and development

'... pot a boil but wi hungry; a hungry man is an angry man.'
(Bob Marley)

Introduction

In the 20th Century, many Caribbean people in the British-colonised territories lived and worked under extremely harsh conditions. It was against this background that there were mass protests during the period 1900 to 1939 by workers in all sectors of the economy. The unemployed and the under-employed were also involved. It was another stage in the history of the radical politics of the working classes – rural as well as urban, men as well as women.

From the post-slavery period many middle class professionals and a few well-off skilled workers who had the vote had been pushing for changes in the constitution as they wanted greater participation in governance. The working classes, however, wanted more drastic, extensive changes which the elite considered revolutionary. The working classes engaged in violent protest from 1934 to 1939, starting in Belize and ending in colonial Guyana and Jamaica. Later the middle class leaders used working-class support to take political power from the traditional colonial elites.

In this chapter we will learn about:
1　The causes of protest
2　Responses to poor socio-economic conditions
3　The role of women in the protests of the 1930s
4　Male activists
5　Gains/results of popular protests
6　Legalisation of trade unions
7　The workers' movement in Haiti, the Spanish-speaking Caribbean and the French Antilles

Uriah 'Buzz' Butler

1 The causes of protest

Poverty, despair and disenfranchisement were the overriding problems facing the working classes in the early 20th Century in all Caribbean territories. Their general misery was made worse by unemployment; poor wages paid by employers even if they could pay more; poor working conditions and labour relations; lack of adequate health services; lack of relevant and adequate educational services; lack of access to affordable land by more people; political exclusion and the failure of governments to adopt policies to improve the conditions of the mass of the people.

British colonialism was mainly concerned with economic exploitation; in other words, colonisers were principally concerned with taking as much wealth from the colonies as possible. They were not concerned with providing efficient social services, such as health and education, or granting political and civil rights. They were even less concerned with the wages and the living conditions of the masses.

Fig 14.1 Una Marson

While poverty was one cause of the protests that erupted, another cause was that people were not unionised. There was also the rise of nationalism and Black consciousness spurred on by Marcus Garvey. There were external factors such as the World Wars, which led to declining colonial revenues because of poor international economic conditions, and the return of radicalised soldiers and emigrants. Let us look more closely at some of these problems.

Population, health and education

In Chapter 9 we saw that the system of education in the British-colonised Caribbean in the 20th Century was poor. The illiteracy rate was high and had not improved much since the 19th Century.

Table 14.1   Illiteracy rates in the British-colonised Caribbean 1946 (expressed as a percentage of the population over 10)

Barbados	7.3
Virgin Islands	12.6
Antigua	13.3
St Kitts	14.6
Br Honduras	16.1
Grenada	18.2
Montserrat	18.8
St Vincent	18.9
Br Guiana/colonial Guyana	21.4
Trinidad	22.6
Jamaica	23.9
Dominica	35.0
St Lucia	44.8
Total average.	22.0 per cent

Source: K. Brathwaite and A. Phillips, *The people who came* Bk. 3
Many people, including women like Una Marson, Amy Bailey and Aggie Bernard in Jamaica, called for reform in education, especially as illiteracy rates were often higher among women than among men. This meant that women were denied access to higher paying jobs which required them to be literate.

Health services were also still poor, leading to high death rates. In Barbados, 217 out of every 1,000 babies died before they reached the age of one. Still the population was growing and there were not enough hospitals to take in the many who got sick. No wonder several epidemics broke out throughout the region. Tuberculosis, yaws, venereal disease and hookworm were the most prevalent of these diseases. Since 1919 there had been a campaign against hookworm. The Jamaican Nutrition Committee reported that 70 per cent of the population were affected by the parasite.

Also, one in eleven people died of yaws and tuberculosis. The number of people who could not afford a private doctor and had to use the so-called 'ticket' system rose from 37,500 to 200,000. Malnutrition caused by poor diets was also a cause of ill health. The schools' medical officer from Kingston, Jamaica, reported that an examination of 1,200 children in 1936 showed that 28.7 per cent were of sub-normal nutrition and 9.3 per cent were malnourished. Another source placed the proportion of malnourished children as high as 60 per cent in some rural schools.

Wages, agriculture and agricultural labourers

The majority of Caribbean people were employed in agriculture in the rural areas. Most depended on wage labour – even those who were peasant farmers. But wages were low, especially on sugar estates. In most territories, wages for those characterised as 'unskilled', ranged from 10 pence to 1 shilling per day. In St Croix, wages even fell below the rate stipulated in the labour ordinance.

The Blue Books of the various British-colonised Caribbean territories paint a general picture of low wages for agricultural, domestic and industrial workers. For example, in 1930, male agricultural workers earned between 10 pence in St Vincent and 1shilling 6 pence in Grenada and St Lucia; and women earned between 6 – 8 pence in St Vincent and 10 pence – 1shilling in Grenada. In Trinidad & Tobago in 1930, skilled agricultural workers earned between $1.20 and $3.00 a day and unskilled 40 cents to $1.20 a day. The same level of wages was paid to workers in manufacturing and mining industries. Domestic workers, who worked long hours averaging about 54 hours in Trinidad & Tobago (compared to 87 hours in Grenada), earned between $4.00 and $12.00 a month. In Barbados, the daily wage of most workers remained below the one shilling mark and had hardly improved since the mid-19th Century. This means that by the mid-1930s, living standards in Barbados were no higher than at the end of the 19th Century.

In rural Jamaica, it was estimated that some 160,000 of the 240,000 adult males involved in agriculture needed to supplement their income through wage labour. On a typical sugar estate, workers were paid a rate of one shilling for each ton of cane cut in the first gang; and three pence in the second gang. The average weekly earnings of members of the gang ranged from 18 shillings 4 pence to 6 shillings in the first gang; and 9 pence to 10 shillings 7 pence in the second. Women earned less than men. Twenty-three-year-old Sarah Agal worked for ten weeks earning an average of 6 shillings 1 pence a week. On Jamaican banana plantations, a gang of 14 loaders and a boss were paid 22 shillings for a thousand bunches.

Some territories attempted to lower wages even further when the return of soldiers and economic migrants in the early to mid-20th Century created a surplus labouring population that resulted in a competitive labour environment. For example, the 1930 Report of the West Indian Sugar Commission singled out Barbados as one colony where planters used wage reduction to increase their profitability instead of devising ways to increase yield and productivity. Between 1925 and 1935, wage rates for sugar factory and building workers in Jamaica dropped by a quarter. In 1935, official estimates indicated that 70 per cent of those employed received an average income of 14 shillings a week, and this left many in dire poverty.

Other causes of economic hardships on the peasant working class who depended on agriculture were: restriction on emigration which used to help alleviate unemployment at home; and a series of diseases which affected all the major crops sugar, cocoa, limes and bananas.

Not surprisingly, these worsening economic conditions in rural areas caused many people to drift to urban sections in search of jobs: to Bridgetown in Barbados, Kingstown in St Vincent, Port-of-Spain in Trinidad and so on. Wages were low for urban workers also. Earnings in Kingston were between 2 shillings and 2 shillings and 3 pence for men. Casual workers, who were generally employed for less than one week, earned an average of 6 shillings a week. There was also an increase in those applying for poor relief. In 1936, for example, 11 of Jamaica's 14 parishes spent one third of their estimated revenue on poor relief.

World War I

The social and economic conditions of the working classes worsened in the period up to 1938. This was because of specific happenings such as the outbreak of World War I. The shortage of sugar on the world market during the war caused the price of Caribbean sugar to rise..

After the end of the war, however, sugar production fell off in the US and England, who were the main market and source of imports for the region. Prices dropped after the war and there were very few imports from these countries. The world demand for sugar and banana dropped, leading to unemployment for workers in these industries. In countries which were heavily dependent on imported food, such as Barbados, the working class found it difficult to afford the rising cost of such food and people grew more and more dissatisfied in rural and urban centres.

The World Depression

From 1929 the industrial world faced an economic crisis called the 'Great Depression'. This crisis shook the finance, industry and commerce of the world in the 1930s and caused widespread distress in Britain and the United States. This depression had very serious consequences for the people of the Caribbean. It caused Cuba, Santo Domingo, Puerto Rico and Central American countries to send migrant labourers back to their homes. These people now swelled the ranks of the unemployed and increased competition for jobs. The price of sugar dropped to five shillings a hundredweight, the lowest it had been since the 1880s. Many territories still had no viable alternative to sugar. So when the cane sugar market fell in the 1930s, the colonies were left distressed. In Belize, the big landowners had always discouraged agriculture for fear of losing labour needed for their forestry operations. Merchants had also discouraged agriculture to maintain a high level of imports. Between 1928 and 1933 the prices of the main Caribbean exports were halved, on average. Workers had to accept drastic wage cuts, increased taxation and unemployment.

The most severe impact of the depression was that the money that relatives overseas sent home was substantially reduced. This money had begun to make up the greater portion of the working class income. For example, the total value of remittances from the United States, the main source, fell from £5,667 in 1981 to £1,635 in 1933. This sharp decline in remittances was accompanied by labourers being forced to return home.

Even workers who were fortunate enough to keep their jobs felt the cost of the economic depression. In St Kitts, the Basseterre sugar factory instructed the local management to reduce wages by one penny in every shilling. The leading sugar planters also all decided to reduce all wage rates for estate workers by 25 per cent.

In Belize the majority of workers depended on work in the forest sector which made up 85 per cent of the country's exports. But employment in that sector kept falling as the demand for chicle gum (derived from the sap) and mahogany fell during the depression. By June 1931, relief work was being organised for those who had no work in the forest sector. The 1931 hurricane caused further distress among the working class, many of whom lost their homes. By 1933 the value of exports had declined and this caused the conditions of the working class to continue to decline up to 1937, with many cases of malnutrition, poor nutrition and ill-health being observed.

Fewer rations were given to those in wood camps. The average diet of a mahogany worker in one of these camps per week was: 7 qts of inferior flour; 1 pkt of baking powder; 2 qts of beans; 1 pkt of tea; 1 lb of salt; 4 lbs of pork; 2 lbs of sugar with a few fresh vegetables.

The conditions in Belize can be summarised as: dependency upon reduced rations; poor wages; inferior food; absence of medical attention; increase in health problems associated with malnutrition; and poor and unsanitary accommodation.

The socialist initiative

Some 15,000 men had served in the West India Regiment of the British army during the World War II. They experienced racism even within the ranks of the army. They were placed in the West Indies Regiment – a separate African wing of the British army. They were paid less than the British soldiers and could not rise to the rank of officers. Many of them did not fight during the war but were in labour service in Egypt or they were the ones to dig the trenches and carry ammunition to the British soldiers who were facing the Germans in France. After the war, many were stationed in Italy, doing work like digging latrine pits and doing laundry. They were not allowed to use the same facilities as the British soldiers. These men returned home with an even greater awareness of the plight of African people and a determination to change things.

When they returned home, they faced the same racism and reduced pay they had left. Many of these disgruntled members of the West India Regiment vowed to force change in the Caribbean. One such person was the Trinidadian Captain Arthur Cipriani, an activist for changes in colonial government.

Fig 14.2 Captain Arthur Cipriani

In the meantime, African-descended people from the Commonwealth Caribbean territories who had gone to Britain were also facing racial hostility. In 1919 British mobs went around attacking African-descended people in London and other large British towns. This also happened in US cities. Returning soldiers and radicals were frustrated with these situations and tried to encourage local opposition. They got support from their fellow Caribbean people – many of whom not only had their own experience of racism at home, but also knew about all the racism abroad which had been reported about in the press. So the Caribbean migrants came back to a climate of unrest. Along with many other migrants who were sent back by receiving countries because of the poor economic situation, they became a part of the labour movement.

Observers on Caribbean conditions

There were quite a number of observers who complained about the conditions under which the working class lived. For example, Lord Sydney Olivier, Governor of Jamaica, in his book *Jamaica the blessed island*, wrote about the conditions of the people of Jamaica:

> *Ragged figures, girls and women, such dirt, their dresses were just bundles of rags that once had been decent cotton Sunday gowns. They were spotted and streaked from shoulder to hem with dark stains of banana juice.*

Marcus Garvey drew attention to the conditions of urban sections of the working class in Jamaica in 1938. He observed that:

> *a new social phenomenon has come into existence in Jamaica. On the edge of the city of Kingston is a city of poor people whom nobody sees except something unusual happens. In what is called the Spanish Town area of Jamaica, there are more people living in the most primitive unfortunate state than can be found in a recognised city of the world. The people who live there outnumber the rest of those who live in other sections of the city, yet the Governor never goes there nor legislators nor anybody of importance. Whenever anything unusual happens there people break away from their shacks and invade the other part of the city. To see them in this part of the city is to wonder if it is the same Kingston that everybody knows under its peaceful guise of business.*

The lack of unionisation; repressive labour laws

Workers could not appeal to the law about their poor social and economic conditions. Repressive labour laws and practices ensured that workers remained controlled. These laws created a form of life-long debt which kept workers in the same employment. Trade unions were not legal and so workers had nobody to press for benefits such as minimum wages and sickness insurance. In Belize, the old Masters and Servants Act, which was still in force since 1846 (though revised in 1883), said that if a worker was in breach of his labour contract, this was a criminal offence. He could be imprisoned for up to 28 days and do hard labour. It is unclear if women could also be imprisoned.

One of the most important reasons why the working classes in St Kitts were not more militant was the Masters and Servants Act of 1849. This Act said that those workers who were absent from work could be prosecuted under criminal law and could be punished by a fine of £50 – almost two months wages for the average worker. Or they could be sentenced to one month's imprisonment with hard labour. Picketing was illegal and employers could sue strikers for damage or simply call out the troops.

Strict control

Governments maintained tight security in the region. Any breaking of any of these repressive laws often brought out the police and military forces. This was called enforcing 'law and order'. 'Law and order' were of vital importance to the property-owning classes as they needed to protect their investments. They feared social upheaval which would jeopardise their wealth and production.

The most common law-enforcing body in the colonies was the police force, which was formed after abolition in most regions. The military character of the constabulary force reflected the experience of British imperialism. The military forces and outposts saw it as their responsibility to protect any system of oppression such as colonialism. The character of the constabulary force in the British Caribbean was modelled on that of Sierra Leone.

Garveyism: the role of Black organisation

Marcus Garvey's Black Nationalist Movement did much to inspire workers' actions, particularly after the end of World War I. In fact, from 1919 to the 1930s, the Black Nationalist Movement and the workers' movement were almost one.

Marcus Mosiah Garvey was born in St Ann, Jamaica on 17 August 1887, of peasant origins. He left school at 14 and went to work with his godfather who was a printer in St Ann's Bay. A few years later he went to Kingston and

Fig 14.3 Marcus Garvey

found work in the printing trade. He was involved in the Printers' Union Strike, which was caused by the disrupting effects of the 1907 earthquake and fire in Kingston. Garvey lost his job after that strike and went to work at the Government Printing Office. He soon began editing his own newspaper, *The Watchman*. When financial problems caused that to collapse, he founded a political organisation, called the National Club, which had a fortnightly publication called *Our Own*. He was influenced by Robert Love, editor of the *Jamaican Advocate* who had lived in Haiti and had become conscious of the importance of Africa and Black Nationalism in the lives of Caribbean peoples.

In 1909 Garvey left Jamaica for the first time to travel to Central America – he got a job as a timekeeper on a banana plantation in Costa Rica. While there he saw for himself the exploitation of African-descended workers on the railroads and banana plantations. He soon gave up his job and began lecturing workers to have pride in their race and to improve conditions. He further protested to the British Consul in Port Limón, Costa Rica, about the treatment of African-descended workers.

When Garvey travelled to other parts of Central America and saw similar poor conditions of African-descended workers, he became convinced that something had to be done for them. He went to London in 1912. Here his experiences and the influence of people like Duse Mohammed Ali, the publisher of *African Times* and *Orient Review* with whom he had many discussions about Africa and the plight of Africans outside of Africa, caused him to ask, 'Where is the Black man's government?', 'Where is his King and his Kingdom?', 'Where is his ...country...?' He vowed to return to Jamaica to devote himself to the cause of African people who seemed to be in bondage everywhere. When he returned to Jamaica in 1914, he formed the Universal Negro Improvement Association (UNIA) with the motto, 'One God, One Aim, One Destiny' with Amy Ashwood as the associate secretary. This association aimed at raising African consciousness and inspiring the people to struggle for more economic, political and social rights. The UNIA was the world's largest Pan-African Movement. By the 1920s there were 1,120 branches in 40 countries. Its headquarters was established at 'Liberty Hall' in Harlem in the USA. Other Liberty Halls were established in places with UNIA branches.

Garvey's newspaper, *The Negro World*, was widely distributed and fostered feelings of nationalism, anti-colonialism and African consciousness. Its Spanish and French versions allowed it to reach many non-English-speaking peoples. He established a steamship company, the Black Star Line, with the aim of facilitating the Back to Africa movement. Garvey's activities gained him enemies and he was arrested in the USA and later deported to Jamaica. The UNIA was kept going by his wife, Amy Jacques Garvey, while he was in prison and before he was deported. He arrived in Jamaica in 1927 in the midst of the post-war turmoil. He founded the People's Political Party with a fourteen-plan manifesto which set out all the improvements he sought for African-Jamaicans in the island. He failed in his efforts to become a member of the Jamaican Legislature but became a member of the Kingston and St Andrew Corporation (KSAC).

Garvey formed the Workers' and Labourers' Association and continued to petition for the improvement in the conditions of the poor. He eventually left Jamaica in 1935 for London, some years before the labour protests in the region, because he was frustrated at the lack of support from influencing sections of the African-Jamaican community for his activities. Still, Garvey gave the concepts of African consciousness, African pride and dignity to the 1930s movement. This inspired other activists to lead the 1930s struggle. Garvey died in 1940 in England. In 1964, after 24 years, his body was returned to Jamaica for reburial in what is now National Heroes' Park. He was the first to be declared a Jamaican National hero.

Chapter 14 | *The labour movement and development*

2 Responses to poor socio-economic conditions

The Caribbean people took both non-violent and violent measures to bring about an improvement in their conditions.

Non-violent means: the professional middle classes

In the century after emancipation, the middle classes in the region demanded changes in the direction that their countries were taking. For example, professional men like Conrad Reeves, Edward Jordan, Samuel Prescod Jackman, Charles Duncan O'Neale, and the French Creole Dr Louis de Verteuil, all took steps to press for political and social reforms in their various territories. Jordan, a mixed-race Jamaican who published newspapers like the *Watchman, Jamaica Free Press*, and the *Morning Journal*, had agitated for political representation in government for mixed-race people. Jackman was the first mixed-race man in Barbados to become a member of the House of Assembly. Like Jordan, his main means of expression was a newspaper. He was editor of the *New Times* and he founded a paper called *The Liberal*.

Conrad Reeves was a mixed-race Barbadian who became Solicitor-General in 1874, Attorney-General in 1884 and Chief Justice from 1886 to 1902. He advocated for the people to have a share in political power and opposed the Crown Colony government.

Fig 14.4 Edward Jordan

In Trinidad, Dr Louis de Verteuil who was chairman of the Port-of-Spain Town Council in 1853, spoke out against Crown Colony government. In 1893 he said that 'the system of Government at present existing in the colony is not only injurious to the best interests of the country and its inhabitants, but it is a great public grievance and cause of public dissatisfaction'.

In Jamaica, after the UNIA Convention of 1934, a wide range of Jamaicans assembled in Kingston to discuss plans for the economic development of the island. They passed resolutions that called upon the government to raise £10 million to be used in various projects including, housing, land settlement and road construction. They also demanded greater control of Jamaican businesses by Jamaicans. On the social level, they demanded that there should be higher education in all territories, especially for children from the lower stratum of the social classes. The demand for education was urgent since this was the passport into the prosperous and 'white-collar' positions. Illiteracy only served to tie people to lower paying jobs.

There were other levels of the struggle. Both Amy Bailey and Una Marson took action to establish the Jamaica Save the Children Fund, an organisation that began operation in 1938 to help alleviate the needs among the less fortunate. They encouraged other women to give material support.

The professional middle class hardly ever encouraged violent means of protest to bring about political changes. As a result, the authorities could eventually co-opt the middle classes to prevent radical changes from 'below'. The mixed-race and African-Caribbean middle classes had made early demands for constitutional changes and later demanded independence. But they actually preferred gradual constitutional changes as the route to greater political participation by Caribbean peoples. Garvey himself formed the Peoples' Political Party in 1929 to seek office as a route to bring about radical changes.

Rhoda Reddock has interpreted the 'Water Riots' in Trinidad in 1903 as a middle class struggle for greater political power. This is because it was mainly middle class people who would have been affected by the new rates levied on the use of water in Port-of-Spain. The majority of people, even washers and laundresses, used 'free water' from springs or communal 'standpipes'. The government, under Sir Alfred Maloney, had introduced a new Waterworks Ordinance to conserve the water supply of Port of Spain. Public metres in municipal residences and people were charged for the use of water.

The Ratepayer's Association was formed in 1901 to monitor government's use of taxpayer's money after the abolition of the Port-of-Spain Borough Council. They mobilised people to protest against the water rates and organised a march on the Red House, the house of parliament in Trinidad and Tobago. Violence erupted when the people entered the Legislative Chambers. In the suppression of the 'Water Riots', sixteen people (five women and eleven men) were killed and 51 wounded. A commission was set up to investigate the matter. The larger issue was that the colonial authorities realised that they had to have the support of the middle classes, who were mostly affected by paying rates, to control the rest of the population. The commission reprimanded the Maloney government for not taking into consideration middle class opinion on matters of legislation and finance. Maloney himself was replaced as governor. The Ratepayer's Association was discredited and its political activities decreased.

Attempts to form trade unions

Some middle class and worker leaders believed that collective bargaining might persuade the government and employers to improve the conditions of the people. But trade unions were illegal in the Caribbean prior to 1918, unlike in Britain and the USA where they were legal and thriving. In the colonies it was a criminal offence to form unions so what was legal for workers in the 'mother country' was illegal for workers in the colony.

By the end of World War I the time was right to form unions. There was an increase in the non-agricultural labour force because opportunities for artisans and craftspeople had increased during war conditions. These workers were more likely to join unions, especially as their conditions again worsened after the war when there was an economic depression. Also, the return of thousands of Caribbean men and women who had participated in the war gave a boost to union formation. The returning soldiers and others saw the need to form organisations to press for the needs of the workers and rural and urban poor. They pressed for trade unions.

After the second wave of social protest in Jamaica in 1919, the government passed a trade union law allowing unions to exist. This law was also applied to colonial Guyana in 1921. But these kinds of laws were not extended elsewhere. When Marryshow tried to form a union in Grenada in 1933, it was not recognised. Strikes remained illegal, picketing was still banned and there was no immunity for workers for breach of contract during strikes.

Trinidad, Tobago, St Kitts, St Vincent and British Honduras

In 1897 Alfred Richards formed the Trinidad Workingmen's Association (TWA). It collapsed in 1903 after the 'Water Riots', but was revived in 1906. It faded as membership fell off during the post war crises, but was restarted in 1919. In the 1920s Captain Cipriani led it and by the 1930s it had a membership of 120,000 out of a population of 450,000. It was never registered as a trade union and in 1932 it changed its name to the Trinidad Labour Party. There was also the 1929 Trinidad and Tobago Trade Union Centre.

Other unions formed before the 1930s protests were the Workers' League and the Universal Benevolent Association, two working class societies in St Kitts, and the Workingman's Association which became the focus of radical opinion in St Vincent. In 1922, the Civil Service Association of British Honduras was officially registered as a union.

The early unions had too many difficulties to thrive. They were weak and short-lived; they were met with hostility from employers (who usually had the support of the Colonial Office) and suspicion from the salaried middle classes. Also there were no laws to make it legal for them to operate. Outside of the Caribbean unions thrived among miners, construction and railway workers. In the Caribbean, though, most workers worked in agriculture and many of them had no regular wage or could not afford the union fees and so it was hard to organise them. In Jamaica, colonial Guyana and Trinidad, Indian agricultural workers at first remained outside the union efforts, looking instead to the Protector of Immigrants for the redress of their grievances. In addition, strikes were brutally suppressed.

Jamaica

The first trade unions in the British-colonised territories began among skilled craftspeople and were called 'craft unions'. In 1889 the carpenters, bricklayers and cigar makers organised the first craft unions in Jamaica. Many others were started in the next two decades. In 1909, SAG Cox, an elected member of Jamaica's Legislature, pushed for trade unions. Governor Sydney Olivier referred the matter to the Colonial Office, but he attached his own comments which advised the Colonial Office against trade unions because he said that the trade union movement in Jamaica was being encouraged by the American Federation of Labour and that Britain should not encourage such Americanisation.

In Jamaica in 1907 the Bricklayers and Painters Union was founded. In 1907 as well, the Jamaica Traders and Labour Union and an organisation of printers and cigar makers came into being. An early attempt to form a trade union in 1916 was disrupted by the colonial government with the introduction of the Trade and Labour Unions (Prohibition) Ordinance. This ordinance imposed a fine of £50 or six months imprisonment on any person involved in the formation of a trade or labour union, or who received or solicited subscriptions on behalf of such a body, or who printed or distributed any communication

Fig 14.5 *Trade unionist Alexander Bustamante*

concerning trade or labour unions. Union activity was banned during World War I as it was said to be disruptive. Most unions were short lived, and the strikes they called usually failed. Marcus Garvey led a failed strike of the Printers' Union in 1907, for example. In 1918, the Jamaica Trade and Labour Union was reformed, and Bain Alves formed the Jamaica Longshoremen's Union No. 1 of the Jamaica Federation of Labour.

Marcus Garvey – who returned to a hero's welcome in Jamaica in 1929 – formed the Jamaica 'Workers and Labourers' Association. Like others he pressed for a minimum wage, and an eight hour work day, land reform, rural housing, and the reform of the legal system. In 1935 Father Coombs and Alexander Bustamante started the Jamaica Workers and Tradesmen Union.

A survey in June 1938 showed twelve craft unions in Jamaica. The most notable in terms of size of membership were the Jamaica Workers and Tradesmen Union, which represented agricultural and waterfront workers, and the Jamaica United Clerks Association.

Colonial Guyana

In 1919 the British Guiana Labour Union, with Hubert Critchlow as secretary, was registered as a trade union. It gradually drew most of its members from urban areas. In 1936 the Manpower and Citizen's Association was formed and it was registered as a trade union in 1937. By 1939 it had 10,000 members from all ethnic groups. It published the *Guyana Review*.

Dominican Republic and Cuba

In the Dominican Republic and Cuba the trade unions were severely attacked by political dictators. The assassination of prominent labour leaders took place and as a result, unions in both these countries went into decline.

In Cuba in 1912 there was a protest by rural workers. This was put down by armed forces and several thousand people lost their lives.

Fig 14.6 *Rafael Trujillo, dictator and president of the Dominican Republic*

Demonstrations and strikes: non-violent methods of the working classes

While the middle classes and some labour leaders formed organisations to press for political, economic and social change, the mass of Afro-Caribbean and Indo-Caribbean workers chose strikes and demonstrations as their method of protest. The majority did not have the vote and could not use constitutional means to win changes so the street became their political platform. They believed that this was a faster way to get the authorities to attend to their demands for wage increases and a better standard of living. Striking as a method of protest had been used from the days of slavery and continued in the post-slavery period by all categories and ethnic groups of workers, such as the indentured Indians in Jamaica, Trinidad and colonial Guyana.

So, when all other measures failed workers resorted to strikes, demonstrations and violent protest. We have already discussed the Morant Bay Rebellion, but we should also note that protest over wages and general working conditions erupted all over the region. In St Vincent, a labour strike in 1862 over wage disputes and the withdrawal of customary allowances of rum and sugar turned into a protest as Vincentians attacked plantation property and personnel. The authorities killed four people and wounded at least seven in response. Others were flogged and/or sentenced to prison terms. In Tobago at the end of April 1876, there was the 'Belmanna riot', named after one of the policemen, Corporal Belmanna, who fired on the crowd of protestors, killing a woman and injuring one man and causing violent protests as a result. There had been cases of arson on Roxborough estate in Tobago as workers protested low wages, irregular payment, arbitrary stoppages of pay and the forced indebtedness to estate shops through the 'truck system; and the police had been called in to arrest the alleged arsonists. In October 1879, an agricultural labourers' revolt broke out in St Croix, the day that yearly contracts for the workers began. Under these contracts, workers could be forced to work for an estate against their will. Protest over this policy erupted in Frederiksted in which shops were ransacked and homes and plantations attacked. The loss of life was high, with estimates ranging from 84–250 African-descended and three European-descended people. These labour protests were a feature of the modern Caribbean. They marked the transition from colonialism to national consciousness and self-determination. Strikes, demonstrations and other forms of protest occurred in three stages.

Stage 1: the late 19th Century

Before the 1930 protests, workers resisted forced labour and expressed their dissatisfaction in many ways. In Belize, for example, the magistrates' records list several convictions for absenteeism, assaults on bookkeepers, and breaking of contracts and strikes. There were occasional demonstrations and protests. For example, in 1894 mahogany workers returned to town to find that currency devaluation had severely reduced the value of their wages. John Alexander Tom had led a peaceful group of workers to the governor to present the workers' case, but without success. They went on strike because they could find no other redress for their complaints. British troops were called in to stop the protests that broke out when news reached the people that the employers and the governor had said that they could do nothing. Workers broke store windows and looted shops. The governor reluctantly

raised wages to prevent further protests. Most of the leaders of the protests fled to Mexico as they felt that they would not get a fair trial in Belize.

Stage 2: the early 20th Century

After 1919 the return of migrants and ex-servicemen facilitated an increase in strikes and demonstrations. In July 1919 a race protest erupted in Belize City. This protest was sparked off by soldiers who, as part of the BWI Regiment that supported Britain in World War I, had been subjected to racism and pay cuts on their return. The soldiers were joined by urban African-descended people in Belize City who took out their resentment against their employers by looting and through violence.

It seemed that the rebellions were also fuelled by the 1919 banning of the *Negro World* – the official organ of Garvey's UNIA. The protests caused even more support for Marcus Garvey and led to the formation of a local branch of the UNIA in 1920. The governor called in an imperial warship and the marines reasserted the Crown's authority. A Commission of Enquiry into the incident found that the newspaper *Belize Independent* edited by Herbert Hill Cain, had encouraged African solidarity, just as the *Negro World* had done in Jamaica.

In Trinidad the TWA had reorganised itself more effectively since 1906 and had new leaders such as Alfred Richards, William Bishop, James Brathwaite and John Brathwaite. The TWA called a strike of all waterfront workers in November 1919. Eventually dockers, railwaymen, city council workers and asphalt workers all responded. Port workers in Port-of-Spain and workers in other towns joined them. Estate workers in Trinidad as well as in Tobago also went on strike. From Cedros to San Fernando to Carapichima to Couva to Chaguaranas, then east to Sangre Grande and Toco – workers all struck. They

Fig 14.7 *Workers on strike*

demanded increased wages and they supported the cause of the waterfront workers.

The strike ended in December 1919 and the dockworkers got a slight wage increase. The governor called out the British servicemen to put a stop to the protest. Many workers were imprisoned and a few were deported. The government stressed that strikes were not legal and that peaceful means of settling disputes should be tried first, otherwise the strike leaders would get into trouble. The government took repressive measures against leaders and supporters, clamping down on newspapers or any literature which seemed to encourage protest against it. Nevertheless, the TWA claimed some success and its membership increased.

There was also protest in colonial Guyana where the post-war years saw the cost of living rise tremendously. The price of imported goods increased mainly because they were in short supply. Wages did not keep pace with the cost of living. In January 1917 the dockworkers, led by Hubert Critchlow, went on strike to protest against these conditions. They took strike action because the government refused to force employers to increase their wages and reduce their working hours.

Critchlow continued to press for these improvements for the workers. When they eventually got a small increase, he still was not satisfied. When he stepped up his agitation, his employers, Bookers, fired him. Still, he was not deterred. In 1919 he organised the British Guiana Labour Union, which was open to all labourers – dockworkers, plantation workers, craftspeople, etc. But the dockworkers still formed the majority of members. With support from British trade unions, the government legalised the BGLU in 1921.

The post-war conditions led to protest in Antigua too. As an Antiguan workman, Samuel Smith observed:

> *During and after the war people nearly eat one another. There seem to be no end to the hunger and starvation... Every week, small as our village was, somebody died. Following the war life in Antigua come much harder. Especially in the 1930s when we get hit by more hard times.*

In these conditions, said Samuel Smith, 'for the first time in my lifetime, the ... people was standing up.' Estate factory workers demanded more pay; cane farmers demanded higher returns from the mill owners; cane cutters at Delaps, Sanderson and North Sound refused to cut cane for the price being offered and for the usual hours. 'The *bakkra* (white overseers and owners) was surprised for they never accustom to that kind of thing.'

There was a demonstration at All Saints crossroad near the Nelson's Dockyard where one Charlie Martin addressed the crowd. The meeting broke up after the governor sent a horse guard to take Martin's name and address, but he was not arrested.

At Palmer Jelly protest broke out because cane cutters said they would only cut the cane after it was burnt. A week later the planters decided to make an example of the ringleaders and ordered them to be taken before the magistrate. But almost immediately fires broke out on that estate, followed by fires at Villa Estate and Gambles. The police claimed that it was George Weston who had set the fire at Palmer Jelly, but when they tried to arrest him the crowd got involved and threw bottles at the police. The police sent for reinforcement but even the extra police could not control the protests. The militia was called out. The protests developed into a race riot with the Afro-Antiguan people pitched against the all-white security forces. An emergency meeting was called at government house and the people gathered outside to await the results. After the meeting ended, the Riot Act was read and the police fired shots. All ran except the wounded. Thinking there would be no further protest, the police arrested Weston and others. Charlie Marin fled the island. Weston was imprisoned for seven years. Others got four to six years in prison. Governor Mereweather and the security forces effectively silenced protest by these harsh and repressive measures; and 'not a single soul – worker or farmer – got a farthing more on the pay'.

The new governor, Fiennes, who arrived in 1921 did much to improve conditions in Antigua. Still, wages were not increased until 1924. In 1924 the workers again got restless, but before a protest could break out, the governor ordered the planters to raise workers' pay. Fiennes's replacement in 1928, Governor Johnson, did not do much to improve conditions.

Stage 3: the violent mid-20th Century

From 1934 to 1938, a third wave of mostly violent protests erupted across the Caribbean. Workers went on strike in Belize (February 1934), St Kitts (January 1935), Trinidad (July 1934 and June 1937), St Vincent (October 1935), St Lucia (end of 1935 and again in August 1937), colonial Guyana (1935, June 1938 and 1939), Barbados (March 1937) and Jamaica (May 1938 to 1940). In many cases the government imposed strict censorship on the press, and for some territories no official report was ever published. So we only have a few details about these strikes.

In the Caribbean Basin: Belize

The 1930s again saw Belizean workers expressing their discontent in a more organised form. The effects of the 'Great Depression' and the 1931 hurricane worsened the economic struggles of the Belizean people. Those in the urban centre were worse off as they had no agriculture to fall back on. The poor lived alongside the rich local elite and the colonial administrators. In February 1934 the people showed their discontent by forming the 'Unemployed Brigade' which marched through Belize Town. This started a broad movement that was to end in the birth of the nationalist movement and the formation of the country's first political party. Antonio Soberanis took up the struggle in March 1934 and formed the Labourers and Unemployed Association (LUA), which organised mass meetings, strikes and protests. Even before the legislation of trade unions, he formed a trade union and held mass meetings, strikes and protests.

Fig 14.8 Belizian trade unionist Antonio Soberanis

In the Leeward Islands

Among the Leeward Islands, the protest was most widespread in St Kitts. There was widespread protest also in Montserrat, Nevis and Antigua in this period.

St Kitts

St Kitts, like most other British-colonised Caribbean territories, was severely affected by the 1930s with sugar prices falling to record low levels. The economic problems facing the islands were increased by a severe drought which led to a decline in the sugar crop: from 150,937 tons in 1930 to 98,288 tons in 1931. In response to the economic hardships, sugar planters substantially reduced workers' wages. In July 1930 1,130 estate workers were recorded as unemployed. At Basseterre Sugar Factory, the island's central sugar factory which processed the entire sugar crop, the labour force was cut by 140 workers and Saturday operations were suspended. Since 1930, sugar factory workers had seen their wages reduced from 1/- to 10d.

The labour rebellion in St Kitts started on 28 January 1935 – just over 100 years after the passing of the Abolition Act. The estate workers in St Kitts who started the general strike and protest marches had well-defined objectives. They wanted a return to the standard wage rates which were established before the general reduction in agricultural wages in 1932.

Sugar workers in Basseterre approached the estate manager demanding a restoration of cane cutting rates to the 1932 level of 11s per ton. These workers were from Shadwell Estate on the outskirts of Basseterre. They had been offered 8 pence (16c) per ton of cane cut and had refused this offer. The estate manager, EDB Dorbridge, refused the workers' demand. Dorbridge was well known for the poor treatment of his employees. The cane cutters reacted immediately by holding a meeting with other workers from Buckley's Estate in an open field and deciding that they were going to strike. They returned their cutlasses to the estate and convinced the estate workers to join in the spontaneous strike.

On Shadwell cane cutters refused to allow the reaping of the crop. They decided to go, 'spreading the word', as they themselves expressed it, marching round the eastern side of the island from estate to estate armed with sticks and stones and calling on their fellow estate workers to strike. Workers from Lodge Estate joined in. On that estate the manager brandished a gun at the strikers. They disarmed him and found out that the gun was not loaded. Workers from Estbridge Estate also joined in, and the police were called in.

Almost the entire estate labour force was drawn into the general strike. As the strikers approached many workers simply abandoned their posts and returned home. Others were persuaded to join in the march around the countryside. The striking workers marched in an easterly direction along the island's main road as far as the village of Dieppe Bay on the northeastern side of the island. On 29 January there were two different marches by estate workers. The workers of Basseterre who had started the general strike on the 28th also resumed their protest.

The police, a military British warship and marines were called out. In the violence that ensued, several people died. Among these were labourers John Allen, James Archibald and Joseph Samuel, a factory watchman. Eight workers were wounded, 39 were arrested, and six received jail terms ranging from two to five years.

Trinidad and Tobago

In Trinidad there was much violence and people were killed. These incidents happened in the oil belt of Fyzabad and in other villages on the outskirts of the oil fields. Here poverty and low wages caused workers to strike. We must remember that oil was very important to the economy of Trinidad and Tobago. Oil exploitation had started in 1908 and the oil companies were doing well. In 1936 five oil companies produced 88 per cent of the total output and four of these companies declared in 1936 to 1937 that their profits totalled £1,540,000. The oil companies were powerful and exercised much influence on the government.

Although the oil industry employed fewer labourers than either the sugar or cocoa industry, these workers seemed more insistent on using radical methods to get their labour demands met. In 1933 oilfield workers in Trinidad organised a hunger march to protest starvation level wages, but Cipriani called off the march when the government promised to pass a Minimum Wage Bill. The bill was passed but never put into effect. In February 1935 Tubal Uriah Butler, a Grenadian by birth, led a band of about 120 poor people on a hunger march from the southern oilfields to the capital, Port-of-Spain. By 1937 the oilfield workers' strike spread and the sugar workers and urban workers also joined in.

In 1937 the specific grievances of workers had to do with the rise in the cost of living, which was estimated at 17 per cent. Another grievance had to do with the 'Red Book System' used to identify workers in the oil industry and which the workers said could be used to victimise them. It may have remained a peaceful strike if the police had not arrested 'Buzz' Butler, but they interrupted a meeting at which Butler was speaking in the evening of the day of the strike. At first the crowd ran from the police, but when the government arrested Butler, the people got even angrier and violence broke out. The government called out the navy from Bermuda, the British marines and a British destroyer to put down the protest. Forces from the naval vessels, the *Ajax* and the *Fieter* were quickly landed, and the protest was suppressed.

At the end of the strike, fourteen workers had been killed; 59 wounded and hundreds arrested. By 5 July most of the workers had returned to work. A committee had been set up to look into workers demands. The 'Red Book System' was abolished, wages were increased slightly and the unions pressed for other improvements in workers' conditions. The government also gave in to a few of the demands of agricultural and rural workers who had joined the strike.

St Vincent

In St Vincent, a newly formed Workingmen's Association pressed for land settlement and political reform. Protests in St Vincent were about the government's attempt to raise taxes on imported food. This put an additional burden on people who were getting low wages, were unemployed or were already in depressed social conditions.

In October 1935, the governor even made additional taxation proposals. Before the bill could be passed, protests broke out. On 21 October 1935 an angry crowd gathered at chemist George McIntosh's shop. They asked him to present their grievances to the governor as the chemist was a member of the legislature. He wrote to the governor asking for a meeting; he wanted the people to try peaceful negotiation. He sat in the public gallery of the council to await the governor's reply. The crowd had meanwhile gathered outside, armed with cutlasses, sticks and stones.

McIntosh was not granted a meeting as soon as the people wanted so they forced their way into the council shouting, 'We can't stand any more duties on food or clothing; we have to work we are hungry'. The governor had to call a halt to the meeting of the legislature. On his way out, a man attacked the Attorney General who had drafted the new taxation measures. Other protestors pushed and hit the governor who received several cuts. The crowd damaged the courthouse, stampeded the prison, released ten prisoners and stormed and ransacked the merchant FA Corea's business. The Riot Act was read and the police called out. One person was killed and several injured.

From Kingstown, the protest spread to Georgetown and Chateaubelair. The crowd cut telephone wires and destroyed bridges. If the police had not taken action the crowd would have attacked the electrical plant and the wireless station. A state of emergency was declared on 22 October, the same day that the British warship arrived. While the protests in the capital were quickly suppressed, those in rural areas (Byera's Hill, Campden Park, Stubbs, etc.) lasted three weeks.

The protest resulted in the formation of the Workingman's Association which had a radical programme, with urgent demands for land settlement and constitutional reform. The Association was not at first registered as a trade union, although it represented the workers in all negotiations.

St Lucia

There were some 60,000 people in this island and although the main occupation was wage labour on plantations, there was also an important trade in supplying ships with coal. This trade was at its best in the pre-World War years when it provided employment for large numbers in the neighbourhood of Port Castries and contributed a large amount to the country's revenue.

It appears that the most militant workers were those working in the coaling industry. There had been sporadic strikes among them before, one such strike occurring at the end of 1935 but this had been non-violent as the governor had quickly called out the troops and promised to set up a committee to investigate the conditions in the coal industry. The workers then returned to work. The quick settlement of this strike made the governor confident and he dismissed the workers' demand for increased pay. In August 1937, the agricultural labourers on sugar plantations struck for higher wages. This followed on the news of similar strikes in Trinidad, Barbados, Jamaica and colonial Guyana. The governor again called out the troops and again set up a committee to investigate the level of wages in the sugar industry. He granted only a slight wage increase and gave a minimum wage order. A trade union was formed in 1939 to represent the demands of agricultural and urban workers.

Barbados

The workers rebellion in Barbados followed on protests in the Leeward and Windward islands. The young man who brought dynamic leadership to the workers was Clement Payne, born in Trinidad to Barbadian parents. He was taken to Barbados at the age of four, but returned to Trinidad later on. There he became involved in the workers' movement; and he was a supporter of 'Buzz' Butler. He arrived in Barbados from Trinidad on March 26, 1937, and with the assistance of Israel Lovell, a Garveyite, he rapidly established a large following in the Bridgetown area. A major part of Payne's activities was organising workers into a strong trade union force to counter the power of the merchant-planter elite and to deal with depressed wages, price inflation and victimization of workers in the workplace. In his speeches, he kept workers informed about the labour movement in other parts of the Caribbean so that they understood that they were part of a regional movement. Trade unionism was still illegal, but Payne sought to impress upon his followers the critical importance of confronting capitalism with strong trade unions. Government officials and police authorities considered Payne dangerous to the social order and someone to be removed. They decided to charge him with falsely declaring to immigration officials on his arrival from Trinidad that he was born in Barbados. They wanted to deport him.

Payne's trial, in which he was defended by Grantley Adams, was a major public event; and thousands of

workers came out to keep informed about the proceedings. He was convicted, but granted bail. He led a group of about 5 000 to appeal his conviction before the governor; but the police prevented him from seeing the governor. When he persisted in his efforts, he and some of his followers were arrested. A deportation order was then issued; and with the collaboration of the police in Trinidad, secretly spirited out of Barbados back to Trinidad. Some of his supporters, not knowing about the execution of the deportation order, planned to rescue him from police custody.

When they realized that he had already left Barbados, they became angry and turned Bridgetown into a riot zone. One account of the protest stated:

> … *shop windows were smashed, cars were pushed into the seas, passers-by were attacked; police patrols caught unarmed and unawares fled beneath a hail of bottles and stones … During the next 2 days the trouble spread to rural parishes where a few lawless souls stoned cars on the highways while bolder spirits among the hungry took advantage of the general fear and confusion to break into shops and to raid the sweet potato fields in isolated incidents of spontaneous opportunism. Shops remained closed, work came to a standstill in town and country alike.*

Fig 14.9 Lewis demonstration, 1949

Strikes also intensified at the Central Foundry and among lightermen, the people who worked on the small boats, called lighters. They returned to work on 4 August after their demands were met.

The governor responded to the protest by calling out the security forces, who fired on the crowd several times. In the end fourteen people died, 47 were injured and 500 were arrested. The leaders who stayed with the struggle after Payne was deported were arrested for inciting protests. Ulric Grant and Mortimer Skeete got ten years in prison, Israel Lovell and Darnley Alleyne, five years, and Fitz Archibald Chase (who on 27 July had reportedly said, 'tonight will be a funny day') got nine months for saying words which allegedly incited protests. The Deane Commission was charged with the responsibility of investigating the cause of the rebellion. Back in Trinidad, Payne became active in Trinidad's Trade Union Movement and was a founding member of the Federated Workers' Trade Union. He also became a member of the radical political group, the Negro Welfare and Cultural Association. He died in Trinidad on 7 April 1947.

Colonial Guyana

Colonial Guyana experienced several strikes and demonstrations in 1935 on various sugar plantations. Many of the demonstrators were former Indian indentured workers. At first a Protector of the Immigrants had seen to their grievances, but that post was discontinued in 1932. But even while the Protector was functioning, there were protests by Indians on the plantations where conditions were very bad. The 1935 outbreak was non-violent. The main demand in 1935 was for increased wages, as there had been a bumper sugar crop in that year. The strikes were spontaneous, widespread and determined and lasted on and off through September and October. A Commission of Enquiry suggested that the workers needed an organisation to represent their demands. In 1936 the Manpower and Citizens' Association was formed and registered as a trade union in 1937 with the main leaders being Indians. They were in favour of collective bargaining rather than strikes and riots.

Still, despite the union, there were further protest actions in 1938 and again in 1939. In the outbreaks of 1938 the union negotiated with management and urged workers to return to the plantations on the assurance that their demands would be met. They did, in fact, secure wage increases.

Jamaica

Unemployed and ex-servicemen demonstrated in Kingston in August 1937, but the police dispersed the crowd with batons. Banana workers also struck for more wages in 1937. As they got some increase there was little 'disorder'. In 1938, though, things became violent. On 5 January there was a strike which we can see as a forerunner to the 1938 events. This strike took place on Serge Island Estate in St Thomas. The reserves were dispatched from Kingston and a number of arrests were made. The protest was settled by the granting of small wage increases. The governor, to prevent further protest, extended the Public Works Department programme so that more people could get

jobs. He also set up a committee to look into the whole matter of wages in the island.

On 2 May 1938, though, a protest broke out at Frome in Westmoreland. A strike, which mainly affected workers building a new factory for Messrs Tate and Lyle (the West Indian sugar company), resulted in a clash between strikers and police. The large new factory was part of the £500,000 development programme of the New British Company that was hiring construction workers and general labourers. However, workers were hired and laid off in quick succession. This caused feelings of insecurity among workers. Rumours of a daily wage of four or five shillings brought desperate men and women from all parts of the island. The wages actually paid were two shillings a day for ordinary male labourers, and a little over three shillings and six pence for skilled men.

The clash between strikers and police led to the police opening fire and killing four people – two of them women, one of whom was pregnant. Police detachments from Kingston were immediately sent to Westmoreland to boost the forces there and 85 people were arrested. On 2 May a protest meeting attended by 3,000 people was held. After the meeting St William Grant led a march to the Jamaica Standard Office, where he and IW Rose led a delegation to draw attention to the conditions of estate labourers and the Kingston poor. A series of quickly settled strikes occurred from 11 to 20 May, for example among construction workers in Trench Pen.

On 21 May a general strike of waterfront workers broke out. It was followed on the 23 May by a strike of the street cleaners employed by the KSAC and afterwards by an island-wide upheaval. On that morning, at about 8 a.m., the strikers began to march through the centre of Kingston, closing shops and factories as they went. Workers from the government establishments all joined the strike, like the workers from Sewage Pumping Station, the gas workers, and the tram workers. A crowd of 500 marched up from West Kingston to the office of the *Jamaican Standard*. The streets and roads of Kingston were blocked, street lamps were broken to hamper the work of patrolling police and troops at night, and rubbish bins were overturned in the streets. The demonstrators soon controlled the streets of central Kingston. Some of them gathered to hear Bustamante and Grant. They attacked Chinese shops and bakeries and many shopkeepers had to close their shops as the crowds grew larger and as the police seemed unable to cope. Tramcars were attacked and streets blocked. There continued to be sporadic flare-ups and it was not until about 10 June that anything like normality was restored. In the end, seven people were killed, 171 wounded – the largest number of wounded in the Caribbean – and over 700 arrested.

Alexander Bustamante and St William Grant spoke to the strikers, urging them to hold out their demands for a shilling an hour. The government dispatched troops to break up the meeting. The government took back key points but the struggle continued on the streets.

In Spanish Town in St Catherine on 8 June, labour protests began. On 6 June there were shootings with two deaths in Hanover, St James, St Ann and Trelawny. Crowds at one sugar factory were dispersed by the sea plane from the *Ajax*.

During these events, Bustamante was arrested – on 24 May to be exact. He was released on 28 May and tried to restore order. Norman Manley also became involved, negotiating as a lawyer on behalf of the people. Even when he was released, Bustamante continued to call for strikes all over the island, and unrest continued until 1940.

Antigua

When news of the labour rebellions elsewhere reached Antigua, the planters met and agreed to prevent similar outbreaks in the island. They requested a visit from the Moyne Commission to look at conditions and make recommendations. A team led by Sir Walter Citrine arrived in 1939. He urged unionisation and this seemed to have prevented any protests happening in Antigua.

3 The role of women in the protests of the 1930s

Women played an active supportive and a leadership role in the labour movement, even though their efforts have largely gone unrecorded. These protests brought changes for the good of the community; they contributed to democracy, and enabled women to consolidate their reputations as leaders and members of the anti-colonial front. The evidence of women's political activism in labour organisation before the birth of the trade unions shows this.

Women's participation helped to ensure that struggles for better wages, for better working conditions, and for ultimate political independence were successful. Women of all ethnicities and classes were involved in the protests of the 1930s, though their participation varied along class and colour lines. Many could be defined as early feminists, speaking out where there was discrimination based solely on gender. Like men, many supported the ideologies of anti-imperialism and pan-Africanism.

Why did women become involved?

From the days of slavery and in the immediate post-slavery period, working class women had always been political activists. In this particular period, women had specific grievances. They formed a considerable part of the work force yet their economic life was threatened because they were part of the declining group that was called by the census 'gainfully occupied'. Unlike during slavery, the agricultural workforce was increasingly male. The census did not include all women who worked, leaving out full-time housewives and those who worked part-time on the estates. But it provided a general guide to the percentage of women in the labour force. It shows, for example, that in Trinidad the proportion of women in the labour force fell from 63 per cent in 1921 to 44 per cent in 1934.

In Jamaica, as in Trinidad, there had been a dramatic decline in women's participation in the wage labour force. The census indicates that between 1921 and 1943, the entire Jamaican female labour force declined from 219,000 to 163,000.

Between 1911 and 1943 women's participation in the labour force had declined from 60 per cent to 34 per cent. The Jamaican female agricultural labour force declined from 125,000 in 1921 to 45,000 in 1943. Denied access to the vote and the formal political process, the street became the women's only platform to press for changes. They were also highly politicised by the events of the period and by Garveyism. It was no wonder that women were so militant in the unrest of the 1930s. In fact, some newspaper reports give the impression that the female participants in the protests were more militant than the men. They dared to throw stones at the police.

Women in Belize

Women in Belize were among the earliest to become involved in the third wave of 20th Century protests. They joined the men in the struggle against large companies and the colonial government. Many were members of the LUA. Individuals like Cleopatra White organised women to speak up for themselves against oppression. In October 1934 Belizean women led a shutdown strike against the Belize Estate and Produce and Sawmill Company on North Front Street. They demonstrated at the Town Board Office and were quite loud at the courthouse where Antonio Soberanis was being arraigned for organising the LUA to demand social and economic change from the colonial government.

Women in Jamaica

Middle class women supported the efforts of working class women. Agnes ('Aggie') Bernard, one of the heroines of the 1938 Kingston waterfront strike, converted her Princess Street home into a soup kitchen to feed hungry Longshore strikers. During the early years she worked alongside Norman Manley and Bustamante in the struggle for political independence. Support for working class women also came from Edna Manley and Gladys Longbridge (Lady Bustamante). The latter travelled extensively with Alexander Bustamante across Jamaica in the 1930s to gain first-hand information and eyewitness accounts of the conditions under which the poor and disenfranchised lived. She marched with the crowds during the labour rebellions in Kingston in 1938.

Amy Bailey and Una Marson were two middle class activists in Jamaica with a special interest in the affairs of women. Marson wrote for *The Jamaica Standard* and Bailey also contributed articles from time to time. In one article written at the height of the 1930s protests in Jamaica, they stressed the extent of female participation:

> *The tragic events of the last few weeks must have revealed to those who have eyes to see and ears to hear that young girls and women played a prominent part, and are still doing so. We have seen the women as advance guards, flanking the sides and bringing up the rear of the strikers and unfortunately, the hooligan crew. They were among the principal stone throwers. I saw young girls dragging coconut, brought old tins and parts of motorcars to barricade several thoroughfares, and the language of many of the women and young girls was rich in expletives.*

Women in Kingston as well as in rural parishes were active in the 1938 events. On 23 May 1938 *The Jamaica Standard* wrote, 'Women and children assisted the able bodied men strikers in smashing the doors and windows of the laboratory of the Kingston Public Hospital after assistants there had rescued the doctor by putting him in the laboratory buildings.'

On 18 June 1938 an article entitled 'We must save our girls' appeared in *The Jamaica Standard*. The article drew attention to the strike at the Jamaica Biscuit factory owned by Lascelles de Mercado and Company:

> *The factory hands were not all willing at first, but afterwards left the factory, the majority joining them in the demonstration, particularly the women, as the wave of strikers struck in Trench Pen. Over 300 men and women laid down tools demanding 6/- a day for men and 4s for women.*

At the Kings of Cap Manufacturing Company at 254 Tower Street, it was reported that:

> *More than 30 women refused to work under conditions which they described as very hard ... They made caps at a rate of 3, 6d, 9d and 10d per dozen and shirts were made at 1/3 and 1/9 per dozen. Employees refused to go back to work until rates were increased.*

In Trench Pen in Kingston, hundreds of men and women put down their tools and demanded increased wages, 6/- a day for men and 4/- for women. It is interesting that they did not request the same rates for men and women. The dressmakers of Kingston called on Bustamante and asked him to help alleviate their hardships. They did not have any work because store operators had imported ready-made garments. These dressmakers even proposed to call a demonstration.

In St Elizabeth workers deserted one estate near Aberdeen. About 3,000 men and women with sticks and cutlasses marched and sang. On 4 June 1938 *The Jamaican Standard* told about the involvement of women in St Thomas. It noted that, 'Seaforth, St Thomas, Serge Island Estate, men, women and children marched to the wharf of the Hon K Ehreh Stein asking that as a member of the Legislative Council for the parish, he should see that property owners dealt more satisfactorily with their employees.'

Women were at the centre of the struggles in Westmoreland, taking part in strikes, demonstrations and riots. Some women faced police bullets, some were wounded, some died at Frome, Westmoreland. Kathleen from Burnt Savannah in Westmoreland was among the first four fatalities in the 1938 riots in Frome. Although she was seven months pregnant and was unemployed, this did not prevent her from being an activist in the political struggles of the time. Others among the list of casualties were: Beatrice Powell who was shot in the hip, Ann Hutchinson who received a bayonet wound in her side, Medora Williams who suffered a fractured knee, and Irene Campbell who received a gunshot wound.

The men and women of Runaway Bay went on a hunger march. The men armed with large sticks sang 'Onward Christian Soldiers'. Women followed singing and shouting. Both Chinese shops in the village community were forced to close. On Thursday 24 May, *The Jamaican Standard* wrote about the activities of women in Portland, 'Demonstrators in Portland gave the authorities some concern yesterday at Bull Bay, a crowd of 300 men and *women* marched through the town compelling Chinese shops to close'.

Twelve-year-old Joyce Gooden, a schoolgirl, was one of the main speakers at the mass meeting of the Social Reconstruction League at North Parade, Kingston. She spoke bitterly of the lack of education in Jamaica and urged men and women to see to it that the government provided for the children, who would one day be the mass of the country. She is reported to have said, 'My school brethren need a leader and I am determined as one of them to lead to acquire that which is for their future benefit.'

Women in Trinidad and Tobago

Trinidadian women were also active in the early labour movement and organised workers for the struggle. As far back as 1919 women coal carriers of Archer Coaling Station went on strike. They then formed the Trinidadian Workers' Association (TWA). Albertina Husbands had plans to organise a strike. She wanted women to use poison in their employers' households as a mark of the seriousness of the cause they fought for. The Colonial Office learned of this plot, and recommended that Albertina be one of the foreign-based leaders who should be deported.

Women could become members of the Trinidad Workers Association as it organised workers along occupational and regional lines. The women who joined the Association included domestics, seamstresses, clerks, and casual or general workers. At the peak of its organisation around 1929 to 1930, the TWA had at least three sections, or divisions, including one for domestics. This section was led by Albertina Husbands and is usually referred to as the 'women's section'. Eldica Atkins, a Barbadian milliner, led numbers 1 and 2 'women's sections'. Theresa Ogoe (hat maker) led the third section. In 1929, another 'women's section' was formed in California in South Trinidad.

Other women leaders included Helena Manuel who formed the Trade Union Centre and Daisy Crick, who figured prominently as an early member of the Oilfield Workers Trade Union. Daisy Crick became president of the 'women's section' of the La Brea branch of the TWA. She was a leading platform speaker, especially during 1937-1938, when the association was organising and mobilising members. She urged women to leave the kitchen and join men in the struggle for social justice.

A noted female activist was Elma François, who was a member of both the UNIA and the TWA. She was originally from St Vincent and founded the Negro Welfare, Cultural and Social Association (NWCSA). She was a member of the Trinidad Working Men's Association and laid the foundation for The Seamen and Waterfront Workers' Union, the National Union of Government, and the Federated Workers and Trade Union.

Women in Trinidad were also active in highlighting the plight of women in the country in the late 1930s. Some, like Beatrice Greig, Audrey Jeffers and R M Scott, wrote letters to the editors of various newspapers like the *Labour Leader*. For example, in 1937 Estelle Antoine Duncan wrote that domestics worked under poor conditions from 6 a.m. to 6 p.m., Mondays to Sundays, and that there was no official control over their working conditions. Butlerite Mary Patrick wrote that wives had to make tremendous sacrifices to make ends meet on their husbands' low

Fig 14.10 Elma François, trade unionist in Trinidad and Tobago

wages. For this reason, they were willing to support their husbands in the struggle.

Did you know?

Butlerites were supporters of Uriah 'Buzz' Butler, trade union leader and political activist in Trinidad and Tobago.

As in Jamaica, the women in Trinidad – including self-employed women – were directly involved in the protest actions in 1937. On 25 June, the *Trinidad Guardian* reported that many of the strikers on the strike docks were women. In an article, *Strikers Move Fast*, it reported that, 'Men, young and old, women and children brandishing sticks, cutlasses and other weapons, walked from factory to factory in the district infecting workers with the strike fever.' Women travelled to the south of Trinidad to San Fernando, moving through the streets, closing stores, interrupting traffic and threatening individuals. Women were among those arrested and charged after the government suppressed the protests and some women even faced prison terms. Women like Albertina Grant, Edith Beckford, Hilda Cunningham and Angella Smalling were among the women who were charged with riotous assembling during these struggles.

On Wednesday 30 June 1937, five men and six women appeared before Magistrate Jules Mahabir in the Siparia

Magistrate Court. They were charged with carrying weapons and taking part in an unlawful assembly-related strike. The women were Mary James, Doris Alexandria, Adrina Brizan, Louissa Lewis, Jestina Douglas and Albertina Solomon. On the same Wednesday, seven more women were arrested in Siparia in connection with strike actions. They were refused bail. On 2 July Nazim Williams, Ivy Chase, Cordella Williams, Norma Fraser, Netty Rennie, Narissa Church and Verna Renrit were all given bail of $50 each.

On 2 July 1937 the Trinidad police arrested and charged five women for the murder of police Charlie King. They were Maud Charles, Bantin Rodney, Nora Cooper, Henrietta Joseph and Hilda Maitland.

4 Male activists

Popular male activists were usually labour leaders who for a long time had been speaking out about the concerns of the people – from Paul Bogle, Alexander Bedward and Robert Ramble, to Marcus Garvey in Jamaica. Bogle was the acknowledged leader of the Morant Bay rebellion; Bedward had led a small Pentecostal sect in August Town, Jamaica, in the 1890s; and Robert Ramble organised a peasant political movement in the 1920s.

Most of the leaders who have been written about and recognised as heroes in the 1930s labour movement are more middle class male leaders like Norman Manley, Captain Cipriani, Grantley Adams, Alexander Bustamante and others. Why is this so? Firstly, the British government preferred to negotiate with the educated class of doctors, lawyers and newspaper editors to bring about a solution to the 1930s problems. The popular leaders were often arrested and imprisoned or deported. So the mixed-race middle class people took over the leadership of the workers' movements and tried to get a following that would vote for them when they formed political parties and pressed for independence. Secondly, even though women were active, their political role was kept in the background in the written accounts due to the gender ideology at that time.

Barbados

In Barbados, the following people had important roles to play in the labour movement: Clement Payne, Fitz Archibald Chase, Ulric Grant, Herbert Seale, Clennell Wickham, Charles Duncan O'Neale, Wynter Crawford, Mortimer Skeete, Israel Lovell, Darnley Alleyne and Grantley Adams. We have already looked at Clement Payne and will now learn more about Grantley Adams regarded by some as the 'hero' of the period following Payne's deportation.

Grantley Adams was born in 1898. He was from a African middle class family and was educated at Oxford University in England. His education and class position allowed him to move in social circles that embraced him initially as a 'liberal' rather than a 'radical' like O'Neale, Wickham and Payne. He moved for gradual constitutional change from above and not through mass action from below. However, the events during and after the rebellion of 1937 made him reconsider his approach. Gradually, he shifted towards the radical front and demanded reforms that would enfranchise the working class majority. At this stage he became a keen advocate of trade union activity.

While he was still a young lawyer, he defended Payne as well as other leaders who were arrested. In this way he became the 'champion of the people'. In 1938, with 'Chrissie' Brathwaite, he founded the Barbados Progressive League. Out of this movement, emerged the Barbados Workers Union (1941) and the Barbados Labour Party. Throughout the 1940s, Adams contributed to the struggle for the franchise, for liberal reforms to restore a healthier socio-economic climate, for a greater personal role in representational politics and for political reform. Of course, radicals like the anti-colonial activist Wynter Crawford of the Congress Party, on the Left of Adams, considered Adams too liberal in his politics.

Grenada

Albert Marryshow was the acknowledged Grenadian hero. He was born on 7 November 1887, the child of Eugenia DeSouza of Lucas Street in the parish of St George's. He attended the Roman Catholic St Louis Primary School and later the Methodist School. William Galaway Donovan took him on as a newspaper delivery boy at the *Federalist and Grenada People*. In this time he learned to write articles and eventually became a sub-editor. In 1909 he became editor of the St George's *Chronicle and Grenada Gazette*. In 1915 he reached his full potential and took over as managing editor of the *West Indian*.

Between 1915 and 1925 Marryshow established himself as a journalist and political agitator who was an uncomfortable 'thorn in the flesh' of the governors and administrators. In the 1930s he was part of the fight for racial equality. One of Marryshow's main aims was to introduce a representative government in Grenada. He was interested in and concerned with the various organisations that were fighting to improve the status of the masses. Marryshow was also involved in the British Caribbean Federal Labour Party, later renamed the British Indies Federal Labour Party. In 1937 Marryshow organised a non-violent demonstration in Grenada to show solidarity with the workers in other islands.

Jamaica

Alexander Bustamante, the 6' 4" Jamaican who was so vital to the labour and independence movements, had an Irish father from the planter class (Robert Clarke) and a mixed-race Jamaican mother named Mary Wilson-Clarke. He was born in Blenheim, Hanover, on 24 February 1884 and died in 1977. From 1905 he travelled widely to places in Central America, the United States and elsewhere. He claimed to have served in the Spanish Army in the campaigns against political leader Abdel Kym. He is reported to have also worked as a soldier in Spanish Morocco and Casablanca. On his return to Jamaica he set himself up as a moneylender with an office in Kingston. His main clientele was the less affluent members of the middle class.

Bustamante, like Norman Manley, was an important labour leader in Jamaican history and founder of the union that bore his name. He had a deep sympathy for the poor. He also had political aspirations, seeing politics as away to further represent the concerns of the poor. He articulated quite early in his career his intention of winning a seat in the Legislative Council in the elections scheduled for early 1940. In 1934 he was involved with the Jamaica Agricultural Society. In 1936 he was involved in issues around getting government to support local industry, improving the position of Jamaicans in Cuba, and campaigning for better pay and working conditions for police. By 1936 he was active in the Citizens Associations Movement, speaking at their public meetings. Between 1934 and 1938 he used the *Gleaner* to express his concern for the plight of the poor.

By 1936 Jamaicans were organising under the union leader A G S Coombs, and the popular leader Hugh Buchanan, who was an ex-Garveyite and later a Marxist. Bustamante had helped both men with loans in his capacity as a petty moneylender. 'Busta', as he was popularly called, and another leading Garveyite, St William Grant, joined Coombs and Buchanan and supported their activities. But it was 'Busta' who became the acknowledged leader. From 1935 to 1936 he conducted an 'anti-water metre protest. In January 1937 he intervened in a strike at Serge Island Estate and offered his services as a mediator.

Later that year Bustamante became treasurer of the Jamaica Workers and Tradesmen Union, which he had founded with A G S Coombs in 1936. He expressed his support for the labour movement in St Kitts and Barbados where protest had taken place earlier than it had in Jamaica. He and Coombs travelled around the island promoting their union. By January 1938 he was speaking on platforms in Kingston with St William Grant.

In May 1938 news reached him of the protest at Frome. He closed his business and went by car to Frome, along with Gladys Longbridge, his secretary (whom he later married). He became intimately involved in the labour rebellion of 1938, giving speech after speech condemning the government for the plight of the people. He encouraged a strike of waterfront workers on 23 May and the following day continued public meetings.

At one meeting the police threatened to fire at the crowd. It has been reported that Bustamante unbuttoned his shirt, thrust his chest forward and invited the soldiers to leave the people alone and shoot him. Later he and St William Grant were arrested and charged with sedition (treason) and put in jail for eighteen months. No bail was granted. On 27 May Norman Manley went to the waterfront to find out what the workers wanted so that he could continue the struggle. They said, 'We want Bustamante'. They would not return to work until he was released. Manley joined a team of lawyers to represent Grant and Busta, who were released on 28 May.

Once out of jail, Bustamante continued to join the workers in their protest. In January 1939 strikes broke out at Constant Spring Hotel and there were other strikes at the Canadian National Steamship Company. Bustamante said, 'I have made up my mind to fight for the workers of this country. No longer are the workers afraid of bayonets. They are prepared to fight for their rights'. In February 1939 strikes broke out in the banana industry and among the longshoremen on the wharves. The governor, Sir Arthur Richards, declared a State of Emergency and called out the military.

Though he was threatened with imprisonment, Bustamante continued to encourage strikes until 1940. In this year he was imprisoned at Up Park Camp for violating the Defence of the Realm Act and went to jail for eighteen months.

Did you know?

Defense of the Realm Act: on the outbreak of World War I in August 1914, Herbert Asquith's government passed this Act. It gave the government emergency powers to requisition property, apply censorship and control labour.

The Colonial Office and the Jamaican governor saw him as a threat to peace and stability. After the labour rebellion he was released. In addition to being the leader of the BITU, he became leader of the Jamaica Labour Party and eventually prime minister in 1962.

Norman Washington Manley was himself an important labour leader. He was born in Hanover, Jamaica. As a teenager he went to Jamaica College and excelled in sports. In 1914, as a student at Jamaica College, he won a Rhodes Scholarship to Oxford and later became an

Fig 14.11 Jamaican leader Norman Manley

Trinidad

The outstanding male labour leaders and activists in Trinidad were Clement Payne, Captain Arthur Cipriani, Victor Bryant (who represented small farmers in eastern counties), Uriah 'Buzz' Butler, John Royas (active in the oil belt), Roy Joseph and Cola Rienzi.

Captain Arthur Cipriani was a Creole of Corsican descent. He had served abroad during World War I as part of the West India regiment. On his return he threw himself into Trinidad's labour movement. He was an unofficial member of the Legislative Council and a member of the Port-of-Spain city council. He was mayor of Port-of-Spain eight times. He reorganised the Trinidad Working Men's Association in 1919, renamed the Trinidad Labour Party in 1932. In 1935 he started a newspaper called *The Socialist*. He pressed for changes in the government, for better conditions for the people through a minimum wage and old age pensions, and for local control over key companies, (electricity and telephone). By 1938 the TLP had 120,000 members, both Afro-Trinidadians and Indians. During the labour protests Cipriani asked the British Labour Party to help bring about reforms. He had a cautious approach to change, which was overtaken by more radical leaders like Uriah 'Buzz' Butler.

Butler, born in Grenada in 1891, organised and represented workers who broke away from Cipriani's less radical Trinidad Labour Party. Unlike Cipriani, Butler was a labourer and unlike Cipriani, believed in radical struggle to bring about change. He was active in the hunger marches of the oil workers in 1935 and was later expelled from the Trinidad Labour Party. In 1936 he formed his own organisation, the British Empire Workers' and Citizens' Home Rule Party. He had an active religious background as a Pentecostal and his experience as a public speaker in church added to his effectiveness at public meetings. In fact, he called himself 'God's appointed' and 'Chief Servant of the Lord'. He referred to his supporters as working class warriors. He got a lot of support from the workers because he pressed for higher wages. He would have preferred not to call a strike of the workers to press for these demands, but had no choice. The strike was called on 19 June 1937 and was well supported. But as usual the governor called out the troops and events became violent. Butler slipped away into hiding when the troops tried to arrest him. Eventually he gave himself up to the authorities.

Adrienne Cola Rienzi, first named Krishna Deonarine, was born in 1908 in the village of Victoria, near San Fernando. He studied at Trinity College, Dublin, and the Middle Temple in London. While in the UK he became a founding father of the New India Political Group, which was formed to assist Indian nationals in their independence struggle against British rule. When he

honorary member and fellow of Jesus College. In 1914 he participated in World War I and became a sergeant in the Royal Horse Artillery, earning a military medal for bravery. In 1922 he studied law at Oxford and Gray's Inn. On his return to Jamaica he became an outstanding barrister and an international advocate. In Jamaica, he was the main advocate of self-government for more than 25 years. He had an active plan to release Jamaica from the yoke of colonial bondage into the world of freedom.

Although he helped to build up the BITU, he stated that he had no ambition to take charge of the labour movement. However, the events of 1938 propelled him into the labour movement and he promised to support the progressive forces of the country and to raise the standard of living of the common people. He acted as Bustamante's lawyer, helping to get him released from jail. From September 1940 until 1942, he and members of the leadership of the People's Political Party acted as a caretaker of the BITU while Bustamante was in prison. As Chapter 18 will show, he was active in Jamaica's independence struggles.

returned to Trinidad he became involved in the labour movement and other political activities. For example, he formed the Trinidad Citizen's League and was president of the San Fernando Branch of the Workingmen's Association. In 1937 he emerged as a key figure in the working class struggles in Trinidad, using his training as a lawyer to defend those arrested for their role in the rebellions.

Fig 14.12 A.C. Rienzi

Guyana

Guyana has a long history of outstanding mass leaders. During slavery there was Coffy, Akara, Jack Gladstone, Quamina and Damon. Their message was unconditional freedom. After slavery other leaders arose such as James Orr who was called 'Angel Gabriel'. He led a protest against Portuguese merchant exploitation of the Afro-Guyanese. Other leaders were James Jupiter, Blucher Dorset, Webster Ogle and Hector John, who all opposed the government's excessive imposition of rates on the villagers. Patrick Dargan, A B Brown and A A Thorne did much to get White planters and officials to listen to the local leaders who were representing the needs of the local people. Thorne was active during the protests of the 1930s. He held a meeting in the Town Hall and managed to get the crowd to press the British government to send a Royal Commission to investigate the unrest.

Hubert Critchlow was also an outstanding personality in Guyana's labour movement. He was a stevedore (wharf worker) and a brilliant athlete, footballer and cricketer. In 1905, at the age of 21, he organised and led the first strike of dockworkers and sugar estate workers into Georgetown. The police were called out, as the march was illegal, and opened fire on men and women. In the suppression they cut off the women's hair as punishment and many men were flogged with the cat-o-nine tail whip. Critchlow was also flogged but this did not stop him from continuing with the protest; in fact he organised another strike in 1906. He lost his job in further activities after World War I when protest action increased. In 1919 he formed the British Guiana Labour Union, which was officially registered in 1922.

Belize

There were several pro-working class members of the middle class in Belize: Herbert Hill Caid, I D Kemps, Robert Haynes (who later went with Garvey to work in the USA) and Benjamin Adderly. Antonio Soberanis Gomez, however, was the most noted labour leader of Belize. He was a barber by occupation and came to be called the 'Moses of British Honduras'. He was called 'Moses' after the biblical Moses who led the oppressed Israelites out of Egypt. in a similar manner, Soberanis was seen as a liberator of Belizian masses. In March 1934 he formed the Labour and Unemployed Association (LUA) at a time when trade unions were illegal.

The month before some 2,000 unemployed people had formed the Unemployed Brigade and had marched around the city petitioning the governor for assistance. Soberanis criticised the leaders of the Brigade for being too passive and turned the workers in a more militant direction. He used strikes, picketing and demonstrations to protest against the conditions of the working class. Before the end of 1934 he had organised a strike in Stann Creek, and was arrested in connection with a major protest in Belize City. The LUA challenged the colonial system and carried the struggle beyond Belize Town to the rest of the country.

Long meetings were held twice a week, by workers to voice their support for Soberanis and his attacks on the government, big business and the Belize Estate and Produce Company. He managed to involve Blacks, Maya, Mestizo and Garifuna peoples in the struggle. He formed an organisation in 1939 and after the amendment of the Labour Law in 1943, this organisation registered as a union, called the General Workers Union. Its membership grew from 350 in 1943 to over 3,000 in the late 1940s. Branches were established all over the country. It later gave rise to the political party Peoples United Party (PUP).

Soberanis was secretary of the Workers and Tradesmen Union in 1940.

St Vincent

In St Vincent the people who emerged as the labour leaders in the protests of 1935 were Sheriff Lewis, Bertha Mott and George McIntosh (who was a popular member of the town council). Sheriff Lewis was the main working class leader in the capital Kingstown. He was previously known as 'Pablo' but later nicknamed Selassie because he promoted the cause of Ethiopia when the Italians were invading that country. Bertha Mott, called 'Mother Selassie', also played a leading role in the 1935 rebellion. It was George McIntosh however who became the acknowledged popular leader, despite the fact that he urged the people to seek peaceful means to settle their grievances and he took their petition to the governor. He was arrested and charged with treason on 23 November 1935. He had a five-day preliminary hearing before a Stipendiary Magistrate and because of the unfairness of the charge and his prosecution, the people soon hailed him as a sort of 'victim'.

5 Gains/results of popular protests

What did the Caribbean people gain as a result of the 1930s labour protests? Once the Colonial Office realised that victimising or persecuting labour leaders and their supporters would not stop the protest, they sent out various commissions to look into the causes of the labour protest in the Caribbean. These officials suggested ways of improving and preventing further outbreaks. Based on their suggestions, new labour legislation was passed, trade unions were legalised, and some programmes were put in place to improve the social and economic conditions of the people. However, the commissioners also made some negative suggestions, which affected women more than men.

Commissions of Enquiry

The Deane Commission stated that the rebellion in Barbados were caused by extreme poverty.

In August 1938, the Colonial Office sent out another Royal Commission, this time under the chairmanship of Lord Moyne. The Commission had ten members and spent fifteen months going from territory to territory to collect evidence. Among the team were Sir Walter Citrine (who headed the team to Antigua) and J D Tyson who was specially placed in the Caribbean on behalf of the government of India. His job was to find out about the conditions of Indians who had settled in the region

Fig 14.13 *Lord Moyne, whose commission recommended important changes*

especially in Guyana, Trinidad and Jamaica and had formed the bulk of the plantation labour force in those territories.

In 1939 Major Orde-Brown and Governor Burns looked into the situation in Belize. They admitted that the workers had real grievances and proposed legal solutions. They suggested a minimum wage, reforms in the labour laws to make them less harsh for the workers, and a compensation package for injured workers. Orde-Browne's report, *Labour Conditions in the West Indies*, gave details of the poverty of the masses in the region. He said that it was a mistake not to allow unionisation to give the workers a voice other than using riots. He pointed out that social services were poor. Some of these laws were not passed and put into effect until the 1950s.

The commissioners conducted interviews with people from all classes and ethnic groups and from different ethnic groups. The Moyne commission published its report in 1944 near the end of World War II. The major findings were that the working class lacked adequate health and educational facilities and that their economic state was poor. It said that wages for all categories of workers were too low to allow them to afford goods and services to improve their lives. Their housing was deplorable. The report said that Britain should assist the territories to the tune of £20,000,000 to improve conditions and stem another tide of unrest. More local industries should be established to provide more jobs. They suggested that the Crown Colony government be dismantled and that universal adult suffrage be granted, with a gradual move to self-government. They recommended the passing of laws to legalise trade unions and to protect workers rights – especially in the oil industry, which needed to be stable during the war because of its essential supply of oil.

The Moyne Commission further recommended that a Colonial Development and Welfare Act be passed to set up a fund to help in economic and social schemes in the territories. Subsequently the British government allocated one million dollars to the British-colonised Caribbean territories. Also, the Colonial Development and Welfare Office was born out of the recommendations of the Moyne Commission. It administered the money from its headquarters in Barbados. One criticism of it was that most of the staff were non-Caribbeans. Another criticism was that the money was not used in major schemes but on minor projects. The money was spent on construction work on roads and bridges, new schools and medical centres, training for nurses, and agricultural research.

Plans were put in place for a government land settlement scheme so that more people could have access to the land. Many poor people could still not qualify for the land as they had to pay a 10 per cent deposit on the total price of the land and had to take at least five acres. Many poor Indians in Jamaica asked the government to let them not pay the deposit, but the government refused saying that it could not treat them any differently from the rest of the population. The government also refused their application for smaller pieces of land from 1/4 acre to 1 acre.

Tyson's report on the conditions of the Indian-Caribbean people

J D Tyson was an officer on the West Indies Royal Commission headed by Lord Moyne. He was supposed to investigate the conditions of Indians in Guyana, Trinidad and Jamaica. After visiting the three territories and speaking with many Indians, he remarked:

The Indians in Jamaica struck me as the most backward, depressed and helpless of the Indian communities I saw in the West Indies. They have no real organisation and little solidarity and cohesion except in so far as the differentiation against them forces them to stand together as a race apart.

He said that in Jamaica, Indians (from Asia) were targets of racism, they were generally unemployed and received insufficient poor relief, their housing was deplorable and their educational standard poor. He found that there were fewer Indians in commerce, industry and non-agricultural labour in Jamaica than in the other territories, and they owned less land. He said that Indians who worked on banana and coconut plantations were living in a condition bordering on destitution:

Their poverty is illustrated by the almost complete absence of property of any kind in their barracks and … their children are undernourished and kept away from school for lack of suitable clothing to wear there.

He felt that the post of Protector of Indians should be maintained, and encouraged the Indian Associations to lobby on behalf of the Indians. He also encouraged the government to do more to alleviate their plight.

Women and the Moyne Commission

Women stood to gain from some of the suggestions of the Moyne Commission – if they were implemented. Two positive suggestions were the right to organise and the right to vote regardless of gender as up to 1943 only men and wealthy women – usually White – had the vote. Woman were now allowed to join unions and even held lower level positions in unions, but in other respects women gained little.

As part of its programme, the Colonial Development and Welfare Office was to promote and create an organisation for women. In Jamaica this was the Jamaica Federation of Women (JFW). The JFW helped to spread the old-fashioned view that women's place was in the home as most of its members were middle class women who did not work inside or outside of the home. On the other hand, other classes of women had always worked outside of the home. When the Moyne Commission called on the JFW to get involved in social work the middle class women began to train working class women in domestic skills. The Moyne Commission had blamed some of the problems in the Caribbean on the breakdown of family life and put the blame for this on women. The Commission promoted the male as breadwinner and encouraged women to get involved in housewife duties, like childbearing.

New Industrial Legislation

On the recommendations of the various commissions, new industrial and labour laws came into force. By industrial legislation we mean that government passed laws to improve working conditions with respect to wages, hours of work, compensation for injury sustained while on the job, health insurance, the ending of child labour, safer factory conditions the implementation of an old age pension scheme, and the legalisation of collective bargaining through trade unions. In Belize, a new Masters and Servants Act replaced the 1883 one and trade unions were legalised in 1941.

It was believed that collective bargaining would be the correct process for getting reforms. The existence of labour advisers and labour departments helped to get some of these improvements implemented. Their staff set standards so that machinery was made safe and there were plans for sanitation and first aid. Tribunals were put in place to decide how much workers should be paid if they were injured on the job.

6 Legalisation of trade unions

One of the recommendations of the Moyne Commission was for workers to be unionised so that collective bargaining could begin and so that workers could channel their struggles through institutional means.

Did you know?

Trade unions are organisations in which workers of a particular trade or employment – e.g. carpenters, dockworkers – come together into a group or union. This union is then recognised by their employers as the group to represent these workers in any disputes. A union ensures that it secures and protects the rights of its clients, whether it is in the form of wages, or economic and social fringe benefits. Workers pay a fee to be a part of the union and they get a union card.

Industrial peace is one of the basic and overriding objectives of the trade union movement. Industrial peace does not mean the complete non-existence of conflicts or disputes, but rather peaceful resolution of these disputes and conflicts.

In 1939 there were 28 unions in the Caribbean, most of which were unregistered that means they were not officially recognised as representing the workers. By 1945 there were around 40 unions representing over 100,000 workers.

In 1937 the Jamaica Workers and Tradesmen Union was registered. It was an umbrella union with a central executive and represented all categories of workers. In 1939, the first St Lucian Trade Union was formed. The Trade Union Act of 1939 facilitated the formation of the St Kitts-Nevis Trade Union Congress (TUC). It was registered in May 1940 with Edgar Challenger as the first president. Robert Bradshaw was elected to serve as a member of the first Executive committee of the Union and by 1946, he had become the elected president of the TUC.

The table below shows some of these unions and the dates they were formed:

Table 14.2
Trade Unions in the Commonwealth Caribbean, 1919–46

	registered
British Guiana Labour Union (1919)	21 July 1922
Longshoremen's Union No. 1 of the Jamaican Federation of Labour	14 Feb. 1922
Civil Service Association of British Honduras	1922
Longshoremen's Union No. 2 of the Jamaican Federation of Labour	19 Oct. 1926
St Vincent Working Men's Association	1935
Amalgamated Building Woodworkers' Union of British Honduras	30 March 1936
Jamaican Workers' and Tradesmen's Union (1935)	29 June 1937
Trinidad Federated Workers' Trade Union	27 August 1937
Trinidad Oilfield Workers' Trade Union	15 Sept. 1937
British Guiana Manpower Citizen's Association (1936)	5 Nov. 1937
Trinidad Seamen and Waterfront Workingmen's Union	19 Nov. 1937
All-Trinidad Sugar Estates and Factories Trade Union	24 Nov. 1937
Trinidad Public Works and Public Service Trade Union	26 Nov. 1937
Jamaica Hotel Employees' Association	1 Dec. 1937
Bustamante Industrial Trade Union	23 Jan. 1939
Antigua Trades' and Labour Union	2 March 1940
St Lucia Workers' Co-operative Union	9 March 1940
St Kitts-Nevis Trade and Labour Union	15 May 1940
St John's Workers' Union (Grenada)	24 July 1941
Barbados Workers Union	4 Oct. 1941
St Vincent Civil Service Association	3 May 1943
British Honduras Workers Union	1943
Dominica Trade Union	31 Dec. 1945
Montserrat Trade and Labour Union	28 may 1946
National Workers' Union	1952

Source: K Braithwaite and A Phillips, *The people who came*, Bk. 3

Both men and women contributed to the formation of trade unions and participated in their activities. We have already pointed out that Elma François was instrumental in the formation of at least three unions in Trinidad and Tobago. Other female unionists in the twin island were Ursula Gittens and Daisy Crick. Crick, a supporter of 'Buzz' Butler, was a founding member of the Oilfield Workers' Trade Union (OWTU). In fact, she headed the powerful women's auxilliary of the OWTU and was president of the La Brea branch. Lucy Stroude of Grenada was a founding member of the Grenada Manual and Metal Workers' Union controlled by Eric Gairy. By 1980 she was the second vice-president of the Union. Trade union activists in Antigua included Ruth Ambrose of the Antigua Workers' Union (AWU), Hyacinth Walters (AWU), Hilda Huggins of the Antigua Trade and Labour Union, and Sylvia Locker of the AWU. Women founded the Pares Village section of the AWU and were the majority on its executive committee.

In Montserrat, Ellen Peters was a member of the Montserrat Trade and Labour Union and Vereen Thomas-Woolcock was a member of the Montserrat Allied Workers Union. Women members of unions played strong roles: they canvassed members, led unionisation drives, negotiated, walked picket lines, defied back-to-work orders, organised and served on committees and branch executives, and worked in union offices. However, men typically held top positions in trade unions.

There were few trade unions formed exclusively around gender issues. Exceptions were the Women Workers Trade Union (1947) and the Domestic Workers Trade Union of Trinidad and Tobago. But there were gender-specific issues which unions were called upon to address, such as discrimination in the wages paid to men and women, the long hours of female shop workers, and the lack of legislation to protect pregnant women.

Some of these unions, as well as those formed later, became linked to political parties and provided the mass base for the election of union leaders to political office, e.g. the National Workers Union formed by Norman Manley in 1952.

Trade unions did not exist without problems. These included the difficulty of getting domestic and agricultural workers to join, low wages of workers which meant that some members could not pay dues, and the fact that many workers had only seasonal or part-time jobs, especially during the difficult period of World War II. In addition, certain obstacles remained despite the willingness of the Secretary of State for the colonies to encourage trade unions and collective bargaining, and the appointment of labour advisers in each colony to encourage unionisation. For example, there was no legal

right to peaceful picketing and governments could refuse to register unions they did not like.

Apart from the legal obstacles, there were also the negative attitudes of employers and governments who saw trade unions as treasonable. The police constantly followed union leaders, they prohibited street processions, and stopped trade union leaders from meeting abroad with other leaders. Many employers harassed trade union leaders and withheld recognition of the union for as long as possible. They victimised union members and many employers discharged these workers. At times union members could not find other jobs because employers banded together to prevent 'trouble makers' from working in other businesses.

Currently the Caribbean has a high level of unionisation. Between one-quarter and one-third of most CARICOM labour forces are unionised, while countries like the Dominican Republic have 15 per cent or less unionisation. Figures from 1979 show that Trinidad and Tobago, Barbados, Dominica and Jamaica account for a range of 31 per cent to 43 per cent unionisation among wage labourers, compared to 5 per cent for the Dominican Republic. Women comprise a high percentage of union members. In Antigua in 1972, women accounted for 58 per cent of the AWUs membership, and 62 per cent by 1991. In fact George Weeks, President General of the OWTU of Trinidad and Tobago, referred to the AWU as a 'women's union'.

7 The Workers' Movement in Haiti, the Spanish-speaking Caribbean and the French Antilles

The 20th Century workers' protests in the French- and Spanish-colonised Caribbean were closely associated with their anti-imperial and anti-US struggles. In the case of the Spanish-speaking Caribbean, the economic and social impact of the 1929 Great Depression was severe. The Depression exposed the islands' chronic dependence on the USA. In Cuba, for example, the hardships created by economic crisis contributed to a growing mood of radicalism, anti-Americanism, patriotism and unrest in the island, which contributed to growing support for the Communist Party, founded in 1925. Supporters came from several sectors of Cuban society but especially from among the intellectuals, students and the nascent labour movements. It was within this climate that Machada had come to power, but he was unable to solve Cuba's economic woes. Between 1930 and 1933 Cuba's share of the US sugar market fell from 50 per cent to a quarter, while production fell by 60 per cent. Wages were cut by as much as 75 per cent for agricultural workers, some receiving food and lodging in lieu of wages. About 250 000 people out of a population of 3.9 million were unemployed. Public-sector wage cuts and redundancies hit the urban middle classes. Anti-immigrant sentiments grew and many Jamaicans and Haitians were deported. Workers' unrest grew and was met by heavy repression. The banned Cuban National Workers' Federation (CNOC) organised strikes, which closed down key economic sectors. In the midst of the workers' protests, Machada was forced to step down and was replaced by Manuel de Céspedes. The Depression still continued, however, despite this change in ruler, and strikes and political protests still continued. Indeed, even the military joined the protests, forcing out Céspedes and installing a provisional revolutionary government. This provisional government gave way, through coercion, to a regime headed by Carlos Mendieta, but Mendieta's regime soon collapsed in the face of continued strikes. It was within this context that Batista came to power, later to be brought down by Fidel Castro.

The Depression also hit Puerto Rico hard, affecting sugar production levels, prices and the wages of plantation workers (to about 75 cents a day). The tobacco and needlework industries also suffered, with women in the latter industry being paid just 4 cents an hour. Many US-run companies cut wages and laid off workers. It should be noted that in the 1930s, almost 92 per cent of Puerto Rico's imports came from the USA. Not surprisingly, poverty and unemployment became endemic in the 1930s. Emigration to the US became an outlet for some. In the island itself, declining economic conditions were met by political unrest, with some people calling for independence and an end to US control of the island. The US control, though modified, continues. Operation Bootstrap was the 1940s panacea for the economic ills of Puerto Rico.

Haiti was less changed by the Great Depression than more developed economies. Most Haitian workers lived and worked in isolated villages, most far from roads or electricity supplies, engaged in subsistence farming; so most peasants were less affected by the Depression. However, the forced repatriation of workers from Cuba and the falling off of remittances affected the ordinary Haitians. Haitians, deported from Cuba because of the Great Depression, sought alternative emigration routes, particularly to nearby Dominican Republic, as a solution to the economic crises of the 1930s. Of course, the Dominican Republic itself was also affected by the Depression, manifested in widespread unemployment and low wages. Predictably, efforts were made to reduce or prevent immigration of Haitians and workers from British-colonised territories such as St Kitts. The Trujillo regime has been said to have been so anti-Haitian that it allowed the killing of close to 20 000 in 1937. It is believed that the monetary compensation to the families that the Dominicans were forced to pay later never reached the pockets of the Haitian families. Successive rulers in Haiti also did not seem able to solve the economic crisis, with the result that by 1946 a wave of strikes and riots broke out in that country. The voices of the discontented workers and peasants found support in Daniel Fignolé, who organised the militant working classes into what was called the *rouleau compresseur* (the steamroller). Neither the Haitian military nor the US government liked what seemed like a communist-influenced movement. A coup removed Lescot, the unpopular leader whose regime had given rise to the protests, in what seemed like an attempt to diffuse the workers' movement. Dumarsais Estimé, a president who it was expected would protect the interests of the working class, replaced Lescot. But as post-1946 developments demonstrated, the working classes in Haiti continued to suffer grave social and economic problems in the years after Estimé.

Martinique and Guadeloupe also experienced some social unrest in the economic depression of the first half of the 20th Century. In 1946, elections swept left-wing candidates such as Aimé Césaire, into positions of power. Such candidates argued for a redistribution of resources from Paris to the islands and a reduction in the power of those from France in the islands. The early years of 'departmentalization', however, did not see the gains expected or promised. Many who had supported departmental status in 1946 now began to press for greater autonomy in the islands. After strikes and protests a series of measures were enacted to speed up reform. Césaire broke with the Communist party in 1956 and founded his own left-wing party, which has since argued for greater autonomy within the departmental relationship.

To sum up

In the 20th Century Caribbean people were faced with many social, economic and political problems. When regional governments failed to address these problems satisfactorily, the masses and their leaders took protest actions to seek solutions. The Caribbean people were successful in getting some of their problems attended to; for example, by 1941 some had the right to vote and to form trade unions.

Revision questions

1. Elma François was an important figure in the labour protests of the 1930s.
   a. In which country was Elma François born?
   b. Give one reason why Elma François left the country of her birth to settle in Trinidad and Tobago.
   c. Give the name of the important association which Elma François formed in Trinidad and Tobago.
   d. State four ways in which women like Elma François helped the labour movement in the Caribbean.

2. *Most of the acknowledged labour leaders who emerged in the 1930s were men. Two acknowledged male labour leaders were Antonio Soberanis of Belize and 'Buzz' Butler of Trinidad.*

   Write an essay **either** on the role that Antonio Soberanis played in the history of Belize in the 1930s and 1940s, **or** on the role of 'Buzz' Butler in the labour protests in Trinidad and Tobago.

3. Identify a senior citizen in your community who was an adult in the 1940s. (You will need a tape recorder and a prepared list of questions.)
   a. Interview him/her about the social conditions in your territory in the 1940s.
   b. Ask him/her if he/she believes that the 1930s labour rebellions helped to improve the social conditions in the territory.
   c. If you live in a territory with a large population of Indian-Caribbean people, find out the extent to which Indian-Caribbean people were involved in the labour movement of the 1930s.

Chapter 15

Caribbean civilisation 1: social life and culture: 1888–1962

*'Remember the songs ... used to mek we rock
Away/those were the days.'*
(Beres Hammond)

Introduction

The Caribbean has always been an ethnically diverse region. During the period 1888–1962, its population comprised people descended from the indigenous Maya, Taino and Kalinago as well as from Africans, Asians, Europeans, Latin and North Americans. Africans, Americans, Asians and Europeans did not represent homogenous groups. For example, Africans included ethnic groups like the Ga, Fanti and Ashanti from Ghana; the Igbo, Yoruba, Hausa and Fulani from Nigeria; and the Mandingo and Wolof from present-day Senegal. Asians included Chinese and Indians; and Indians included several high and low castes. North West Europeans included people from England, Wales, Scotland, France, the Netherlands, Spain and other countries. Inter-ethnic marriages/unions gave rise to the mixed race groups (mestizos and mulattoes, for example). Ethnic diversity resulted in a multi-cultural society, where, even though cultural mixing took place, several ethnic groups practised cultural traditions unique to their community.

Wedding ceremony

In this chapter we will look at a sample of the social life, culture and customs of the different ethnic groups in the Caribbean.

We will also learn about:
1 Class, ethnicity, hierarchy and lifestyle
2 Inter-ethnic and gender relations
3 Religions and different religious beliefs and customs
4 Festivals, celebrations and observances
5 Birth, death and work traditions and practices

1 Class, ethnicity, hierarchy and lifestyle

Where modern societies are made up of different ethnic groups, these groups inevitably develop methods of ranking or positioning themselves on the social ladder. Caribbean post-slavery society was no different. European settlers and colonialists were the political elite within the imperial system. They needed to rationalise and maintain the enslavement of Africans and indentureship of Asians, and so assigned them a place at the base of the social order. The Europeans developed and implemented the ideology of European supremacy that called for racial hierarchising; so European people believed that they were culturally superior to Africans and Asians. The laws and systems that went with this ideology were racist and Eurocentric. This racist view was central to the colonial worldview of Europeans. They believed that, if they enforced such a view, African and mixed-race people would be kept in a subordinate position and facilitate European dominance.

Mixed race groups in which European ancestry was evident were divided about their cultural identity. Even though they knew that the dominant European group enjoyed greater social benefits, there was a vocal group among them that publicly identified with and supported the European supremacy system. This system offered them considerable benefits. As a result this group of so-called 'Coloured' people played an important role in the post-slavery social order. They saw themselves as inheritors to European people in terms of achieving political and economic power. However, an equal number of them threw their support behind the radical movement as they had done during slavery.

African- and Asian-Caribbean people did not accept the political and social order. Indeed, the end of slavery had partly come about because African-descended people refused to accept the legitimacy of the colonial system. As the memory and history of slavery and indentureship were strong in the late 19th Century,

democratic opposition to European minority rule intensified. The Asian community that developed during this period contributed to this radical opposition. They built a new political culture based upon racial inclusion rather than racial exclusion. In effect the modern political culture of the region, with its democratic institutions, was created out of this Afro-Asian anti-racist struggle. African nationalists like Marcus Garvey and Aimé Césaire urged African-Caribbean people not to let Europeans shape their views of themselves. Rather they should embrace the ideology of négritude – African consciousness/pride – and, 'emancipate (themselves) from mental slavery'.

In addition to ethnic ranking, a class system evolved in the colonial Caribbean. Initially professional European people and mixed-race people formed the middle class while rich, Europeans and later 'Americans' formed the upper class.

By 1962 the middle classes had expanded and included professionals within groups like the Asians and Portuguese, and mixed-race people. Some African-Caribbeans had also, by then, achieved upward mobility through education and economic activities. Some rich Middle-Eastern people, mostly Lebanese, as well as wealthy French Creoles and Portuguese, were also amongst the elite by 1962. Poorer groups of African, Asian and Europeans formed what was called a 'working class'.

The labour migration process in the post-slavery period brought in new ethnic groups. This reorganised the ethnic ranking to some degree. The relationship between Asians and Africans, owing to a common opposition to colonial elitism, was co-operative and also often conflictual because there were limited opportunities for social advancement. Together they had a major impact on the political process.

The newly arrived Asian indentured worker was assigned the lowest place within colonial society. This was because, on the one hand, the European elite wanted to maintain the plantation system, as well as European supremacy as a social system, and, on the other hand, Africans who were free from bondage pitied the bonded Indians and felt superior to them. But, Asians, on the basis of ethnicity and cultural awareness, did not accept this ordering, and projected their own independent social attitudes. Many consolidated this sense of freedom and cultural independence by gaining economic strength while the system of indentured servitude was still in place.

In general, each group had an independent and culturally competitive opinion of the other. This opinion was usually based on ideas of ethnic nationalism, as well as a fair amount of prejudice and a willingness to emulate European cultural outlooks and attitudes.

In Guadeloupe and Martinique, the old class system of the slavery period prevailed in the post-slavery period. The economic upper class was European or mixed-race, while the lower economic class was the mainly African-Caribbean group. These social divisions were even maintained in some of the churches. According to some writers, in the French-colonised Caribbean territories, there was a clear demarcation within the church building which separated African-Caribbean people from European people. Just after emancipation, and continuing even into the 1950s, some Anglican churches in the British-colonised Caribbean kept separate pews for European people, mixed-race people and African people.

Ethnic group affiliation dictated culture and lifestyle to some degree, but economic class differences were also relevant. The working classes – assuming they wanted to – often did not have the money to enable them to live in the way the middle and upper classes lived.

Many of the upper classes had professional and commercial jobs or lived off inherited wealth. The elite enjoyed a comfortable – even luxurious – lifestyle. They had large houses, plenty of leisure time, and lived apart from the masses. Most upper class residential areas were in the towns or the suburbs and were set in more 'exclusive' environments than those of the African- and Asian-Caribbean working classes. In Georgetown, Guyana, for example, the main middle class areas were the wards of Cummingsburg and Staebrock, with Main and Camp streets and Brickdam as the favoured locations. In Jamaica, the hills of Upper St Andrew became the exclusive residential area for the elite. They also had many servants whom they paid cheaply. Generally speaking, an upper class person never carried out any task that a servant could possibly do.

The way the elite dressed was markedly different from the working classes in cost, material and style; and they dressed to suit each occasion. Glory Robertson noted in her study of dress in Jamaica that dress mirrored class and ethnicity. But, as Caribbean seamstresses were very skilled, they could copy the style of the elite, so that a working class woman could very well dress in a style that resembled that of an elite woman.

Dress was also a way of showing that people had kept their culture. By the 1960s, although Indians in Jamaica rarely used their traditional dresses (except for the priests), those in Trinidad, Guyana and Suriname had kept them to a larger degree. Brian Moore, who wrote about colonial Guyana, noted that, 'the dress of the Indian revealed a strong identification with their parent heritage,

and only slowly did they adopt the dress code of the host society'.

The African consciousness movement of the 1960s caused African-Caribbean people to project African styles. Whatever the class, there was general agreement in the region that the dress should suit the occasion, work clothes being differentiated from 'going out' clothes, especially clothes worn to weddings, church, and sporting events.

Fig 15.1 A Hindu woman in traditional dress

2 Inter-ethnic and gender relations

Ethnicity, culture, class, colour and gender were among the factors that determined, and even dictated, how the various groups in Caribbean society related to one another. Some writers claim that there was minimal cultural mixing among the different ethnic groups in societies where there were large ethnic minorities. Rather, people lived their separate lives and practised separate cultural forms. They mostly came into intimate social contact when they carried out economic activities. These societies were called 'plural' and the main 'plural' societies are usually said to be Trinidad, Suriname and

Guyana. This model is not supported by some scholars who deny that people exist in such limited ways.

Jamaica is a society where African-Jamaicans are overwhelmingly in the majority. Up to 1962 most of the social tensions were around the traditional African/ European issues, even though there also were other ethnic groups. The late Jamaican sociologist, M G Smith, describes Jamaica as a 'bi-racial' society, meaning it has two races. Whether plural, bi-racial or multi-racial/ethnic, at times there were racial tensions and conflicts in all racially-mixed territories as members competed with each other for economic resources and political power.

One reason for bringing people of different races into the Caribbean after the abolition of slavery was to create competition for labour – this would lower wages and force the freed people back to the plantations. It was therefore inevitable that tensions between immigrants and African-Caribbeans would develop. The planters and European people in general, as well as the government in Britain, wanted to divide the society so that immigrant workers would not side with the African population. They hoped that dividing people according to race, religion, language and culture would prevent them from ever effectively uniting against European control. For example, in 1848, the manager of an estate in Berbice, colonial Guyana, said that he believed that the safety of the European people depended on 'want of union' among their labourers, arguing that the Indian, Chinese, and Portuguese workers would always 'stand by the White people'.

In 1897, a wealthy Guyanese planter said of the Indians, 'They were totally different people; they do not inter-mix. That is, of course, one of our greatest safeties in the colonies where there has been any rioting.'

Tensions between African-descended people and Indians

Guyana

On the Guyanese estates resident workers of both races shared similar experiences and conditions, although a tendency developed for African-Guyanese and Indians to do different, specialised tasks. African-Guyanese would normally work in the factory and cut canes while Indians, especially the females, did the routine agricultural tasks. But there was conflict on the plantations, and later also in the villages where Indians settled after about 1870. For instance, on the plantations the Indians often resented African-Guyanese drivers (headmen) of Indian gangs. After 1880, it became less common to have African-Guyanese drivers in charge of indentured Indian gangs. Tensions also developed over the different wage rates for African-Guyanese and Indians. After 1880 the African-

Guyanese increasingly got the better-paid skilled jobs on the estates, or worked as artisans.

There were also charges that African-Guyanese policemen tended to abuse their authority with respect to indentured Indians. They would stop them and demand to see their contract papers without adequate reasons. In 1875, for example, there was trouble between Black Barbadian and Indian labourers on Plantation Blankenberg. But these types of events were not common away from the estates when Indians began to settle in villages along colonial Guyana's coastal plains and along the riverbanks where they came into contact with Black people. Although Indians had a tendency to settle in places where few Black people lived, forming villages which were almost entirely Indian, villagers of both races often lived close together. Tensions sometimes did arise when Indians competed for jobs that were previously done by African-Guyanese (such as those on the roads or in maintaining the defence against the sea) or when Indians bought land that African-Guyanese had owned. After 1880, when the government set up special settlement schemes for Indians, Black people resented this, feeling that it proved that Indians received unfair advantages.

When the Indians moved into well-established villages, there sometimes was friction. In Buxton, East Coast Demerara, a crowd of Black people refused to help put out a fire destroying an Indian family's house. It is said that they shouted, 'We don't want Coolies in Buxton'. But despite the conflicts that erupted periodically between Creoles and Indians in Guyana and the desire of the ruling class to divide and rule as a way of keeping power, working class solidarity did develop. As historian Walter Rodney has shown for colonial Guyana (and as Rosamund Renard found for Martinique), there were cases of African-Caribbean-Indian solidarity in the class struggle against the largely European employer class.

Jamaica

At the working class level the relationship between Black people and Indians was sometimes harmonious and co-operative. In Jamaica, from the 1840s, the two groups worked together on the estates, sharing much of the same conditions, and they hardly clashed in outright fights. In the early 1840s a fight broke out between Indians and Black people in Jamaica on an estate in Clarendon. An Indian worker claimed that an African-Jamaican worker in the millyard deliberately allowed the horse to step on his foot. The police were called in to stop the fight. In St Thomas parish in Jamaica, Indians took part in the religious practices of the free African immigrants. The Africans in the same district used a myth to explain their relationship with the Indians, 'We are the same people ... is two sisters give birth to Africans and Coolies'.

African Jamaicans on the whole greeted the Indians in a friendly way. The peasants in the hills who grew produce to sell would say, 'Make them come now, massa; they will buy our provisions fro' we'. In the period 1850 to the end of indenture in Jamaica in 1921, there were very few cases of African-Jamaican-Indian conflict. There were some overt tensions after the labour rebellions of 1938, but these were unusual. However, because there was no overt conflict, this did not mean that each group did not feel superior to the other; and many African-Jamaicans blamed the Indians because they could not negotiate higher wages for estate labour.

Trinidad

On the whole Trinidadians of other ethnic groups were not sympathetic to the new arrivals and freely expressed their opposition to the Indians religions, culture, methods of dress and family life. For their part, some Indians looked on the African-Trinidadians as a culturally defeated people with cultural and family practices without tradition. Yet actual conflict between the races was rare, and on the whole, African-Trinidadian people and Indians did not do much social mixing until Indian immigration ended in 1917. But the pattern of race relations set up during the period of immigration (1845 to 1917) persisted for long afterwards, in much the same way as in colonial Guyana.

Tensions between Chinese and African-Caribbean people

Tensions also developed between Chinese and African-Caribbean people. In colonial Guyana and Trinidad, the Chinese worked as market gardeners, pedlars and shopkeepers and soon became rivals to the Portuguese. They built stores and shops in the villages and on the plantations as well as commercial establishments on Lombard Street in Georgetown and Main Street in New Amsterdam. These shops laid the foundations for the development of chain stores such as Ho-A Shoo Ltd. It is said that in comparison to the Portuguese, the Chinese offered more reasonable terms on which African-Guyanese people could purchase their goods, and that these goods were generally cheaper. Like the Portuguese, many Chinese men married African-Guyanese women.

Still the African-Guyanese population tended to see the Chinese as 'outsiders' who spoke bad English, socialised mainly with those of their own ethnic group or practised unfamiliar customs. In Jamaica in July 1918, there were serious anti-Chinese riots during which Chinese shops in several parts of rural Jamaica were looted. The cause of the riot was a domestic dispute. It involved a man called Fong Sue and a African-Jamaican policeman whom Fong

Sue accused of having a relationship with his African-Jamaican girlfriend. Rumours went around that Fong Sue had killed the policeman so large crowds gathered in several parishes to loot Chinese shops.

In the widespread rebellions of 1938, Chinese properties were again attacked. So relations between rural African-Guyanese and the Chinese were mixed: the Creoles needed the Chinese shops, yet tended to resent the Chinese people's economic success and racial and cultural separateness.

Tension between Portuguese and African-Caribbean people

As with the Chinese, the Portuguese success as traders made them a target for resentment. Anti-Portuguese attitudes in colonial Guyana and Trinidad often led to outright violence perpetrated by African-descended people against the Portuguese. Many reasons have been put forward for the opposition of African-descended peoples to the Portuguese. Among these reasons are that African-descended people resented the Portuguese for displacing them in the retail trade; the tendency of the Portuguese to undersell Creole shopkeepers, allegedly, at times through devious means; and the better terms of credit that the Portuguese could get. The merchants of Georgetown allegedly helped many Portuguese to set up as shopkeepers by lending them money and giving them goods to sell on easy credit terms. This was help they had refused to give struggling African-descended and mixed-race shopkeepers.

Resentment turned into protest in colonial Guyana as early as 1846 when a mob looted the shop of Manuel Pereira in Albert Town. In May 1847, a mob of some 2,000 to 4,000 African-Guyanese 'breathing fury against the foreign invaders' attacked various Portuguese shops. Again in 1848, Portuguese shops in East Bank, Berbice, were vandalised. The 'Angel Gabriel' riots of 1856 one of the most significant anti-Portuguese outbreaks in colonial Guyana. James Sayers Orr, known as 'Angel Gabriel', allegedly incited African-Guyanese to oppose the Portuguese presence. When he was arrested, protests erupted in Georgetown on the east coast, Demerara in Essequibo and in Berbice on the west coast. Numerous Portuguese shops were destroyed. The damage was estimated at $267,204. Historian Sister Menezes argues that African-Guyanese may have used the Portuguese as a scapegoat for the ruling class.

Elsewhere in the Caribbean, where the Portuguese were far less numerous than in colonial Guyana, relations between them and the African-Caribbean people were free of organised conflict. Some of the Portuguese men married Creole women and their children fitted into the Creole population.

African-European conflict

Traditional African-European conflicts remained even up to 1962. For example, mixed-race and European people clashed in Martinique. In 1870 a fight broke out when supporters and opponents joined in the dispute between Augier de Maintenon (a European) and Lubin (of mixed-race). Crops and buildings were set on fire and many involved were arrested, tried, convicted and imprisoned.

Social interaction

The attitude of different races and classes to each other can be seen in their social interaction. At first, there was little social interaction among the various ethnic groups. Gradually, cultural interaction occurred. More intimate social relationships, like marriage, took longer to be formed, but were quite noticeable by 1962 as prejudices and ethnic stereotypes gradually became less intense. Consequently, mixed marriages between Indians, Africans, Chinese and Portuguese became more frequent. The imbalance in the female-male ratio among the immigrant populations also encouraged immigrant-Creole social relationships.

The gender imbalance was particularly evident among Asian immigrants. Brian Moore shows, for example, that in 1863, at the height of Chinese immigration to colonial Guyana, there were fourteen Chinese women to every 100 Chinese men; by 1880 the ratio was 26:100. The situation was slightly better among the Indians. By the 1880s and 1890s the ratio was 30 females to every 100 males. It was 40:100 on ships to Guyana. Chinese men in colonial Guyana were still reluctant to marry outside of their ethnic group, but some in Jamaica and Trinidad formed sexual unions with African-Caribbean women.

There was also a tendency for European and mixed-race people not to marry partners of a darker skin colour. In Puerto Rico, for example, one observer said that, 'It is not immoral for a European man of any class to marry a Mulatto woman, providing she is not too dark'. It was stated that although such marriages did not threaten a man's status, they were nevertheless not encouraged. There were also gender differences in the area of mixed marriages. Marriages between European men and mixed-race women occurred three times as frequently as marriages between European-descended women and mixed-race men.

In the French-colonised Caribbean territories it was recorded that European people opposed marriages with mixed-race or African people. European people and mixed-race people maintained social relations, but a 'line' was drawn. In pre-revolutionary Cuba the situation was similar. According to Lowry Nelson, the 'upper class', which consisted mainly of Spanish people, in a subtle way remained closed to the African-Cubans. While there were probably the same number of mixed-race and Spanish landowners in Cuba, African Cubans were among the small tenants.

Gender inequalities

Another feature of social relations in the Caribbean up to 1962 was that men of all ethnicities, cultures and classes believed that women were and should be subordinate to men. Although enslaved women were the backbone of the plantation economy, in the post-slavery period the tendency was to encourage women to operate in the 'private' or domestic sphere of labour, which was unpaid. Many women opposed this culture and worked in the wage economy, but they were paid less. Elite and middle class men thought it was a bad reflection on them if their wives worked outside of the home. So these elite and middle class women tended to stay at home or to get involved in voluntary social work. Women who were educated were steered towards female professions: nursing and teaching, for example. In the home, where there was no domestic help, women did the bulk of the domestic chores, and the majority of women were excluded from the vote until after 1919 in the case of propertied women and 1943 in the case of other women.

Traditional Hindu custom said that the wife should subordinate herself to her husband. Some Hindu men acted in a dominant, patriarchal and authoritarian manner, especially in cases where the wife was a young adult. Child marriage was prevalent in India as well as in some parts of the Caribbean. This was despite the attempt of governments in some territories to outlaw it. However, many Indian women like African-Caribbean women, opposed patriarchal domination, despite the personal risks.

3 Religions and different religious beliefs and customs

As the Caribbean is home to a diverse mix of cultures there are muliple religious beliefs. Rastafarians, Confucians, Christians (of different denominations), Hindus, Moslems, Jews – all have their own religious beliefs and practices.

Christianity

Among the Christians, religious practices often varied according to denomination. Denominations like Anglicans and Catholics had different religious customs from Baptist, Methodist, Moravian, Presbyterian or Congregationalist. It should also be pointed out that up to 1962, the Anglican and Catholic churches had a primarily upper and middle class congregation, while the others had a larger working class population. This was true of Antigua, the Bahamas, Guyana, Jamaica and Tobago. In 1861, half of the church-going population of Kingston was

Native Baptist. By 1881, the census showed that approximately 25 per cent of the inhabitants of Kingston were Anglicans, 25 per cent Methodists, 12 per cent Catholics and 8 per cent Baptists. Jews were an important minority while Hindus and Moslems were present only in small numbers.

Roman Catholics were in the majority in territories such as Belize, Trinidad and Tobago, St Lucia, Grenada and Dominica, which were once under French and Spanish control. This is in comparison with Jamaica, Barbados and St Kitts, which had a strong Anglican presence among the elite and middle classes. By 1962 there were more ethnically mixed congregations in the Anglican churches than was the case in the 19th Century.

Islam and Hinduism

Muslim and Hindu practices are quite different from Christian practices. Indian immigrants brought their two main religions to the Caribbean – Hinduism and Islam. In the 1850s, Hindu temples and Muslim mosques were erected in colonial Guyana and Trinidad. Muslim mosques were erected in Suriname. Jamaica's Hindu temple was built after 1962. Hindus worshipped their gods and goddesses and celebrated the Hindu festivals of Divali and Holi and Phagwah, and the Moslem festival of Hussay became important to both Hindus and Moslems.

Euro-Christian missionaries believed that Hinduism and Islam were 'pagan' and so made great efforts to convert the Indian population in the Caribbean to Christianity. They had more success in areas were there were small Indian populations than in territories like

Trinidad and colonial Guyana. By 1891, for example, the Indian community in Trinidad consisted of 2,258 Roman Catholics, 1,712 Anglicans, 1,622 Presbyterians and 122 'other Christians', 55,180 Hindus, 8,619 Muslims and 436 other 'non-Christians'. Hindus of varying castes and Muslims (Shiites and Sunnis) were dominant, even among Indians born in Trinidad. In 1936, for example, a survey in colonial Guyana revealed that out of an Indian population of 130,540, there were 96,342 Hindus and 21,789 Muslims, compared to 9,045 Christians. However, in Trinidad and Tobago, in the same year, there were 94,125 Hindus and 20,747 Muslims, and 23,183 Indians had converted to Christianity. In Suriname, out of a total Indian population of 39,393 in 1936, 29,841 were Hindus, 6,412 were Muslims and 3,140 were Christians. The majority of Muslims in Suriname were Javanese rather than Indians.

Table 15.1 Denomination of Indians

Denomination of Indians in various territories 1936:

Territory	Indian population	Christian	Hindu	Muslim
Colonial Guyana	130,540	9,045	96,342	21,789
Trinidad	138,055	23,183	94,125	20,747
Suriname	39,393	3,140	29,841	6,412

By 1962 the majority of the smaller Indian community in Jamaica had converted to Christianity, outwardly at least. This did not mean that they abandoned all of their cultural customs.

Chinese beliefs

The Chinese also brought their religious beliefs that featured a mixture of Confucianism and tradition. In China people practised ancestor worship, which meant that much reverence was given to their ancestors and their parents. Part of the teaching of Confucianism is the idea of thrift and hard work, and this was seen in Chinese people's aptitude for business. The Chinese also adopted the Christian faith. Today many Chinese in Jamaica and in Trinidad and Tobago are Roman Catholics and fewer of them are Anglicans.

African-based religious beliefs and practices

The African element in Caribbean religious groups remained strong. This was especially so among the new arrivals from Africa in the 19th Century, the so-called 'Liberated Africans', and among African-Caribbean people who lived in remote areas away from Christian influences. Africans believed in the spirit world. This together with the idea of a person having several spirits with different functions, the concept of death and life hereafter, along

Fig 15.2 A Hindu temple

with other rites and practices brought over from Africa, persisted. The 'Liberated African' immigrants in Guyana worshipped their traditional gods, for example, the Kongos worshipped the Bantu gods *Gorgonzambe* and *Jammypoongo*. Brian Moore believes that their religious rites, which persisted in undiluted forms until at least the end of the 19th Century, were similar to the *Kumina* practised by the 'Bantu' in Jamaica. Some of the African-Caribbean people originating in West Africa who were Muslims continued the Islamic rituals.

Among the African Guyanese people, the most popular religious rituals of West African origin were those known as *Cumfo*. *Cumfo* worship involved elements of spirit mediumship and spirit possession. These practices came from the Dahomean *Komfo*. In Guyana this religious practice was also referred to as *Watermamma* and in Suriname it was called *Watra-mama*, in honour of the river gods. *Cumfo* sessions were typically held when misfortune befell a family or district.

Some of these rites included *obeah* (from the Akan word *Obayifo*), which was done in secret as the state deemed it illegal. Moore explains that the medicine men among the Ga in West Africa use the Twi word *Obeye* to describe the won-like entity that is within the witch. Those people who practised *obeah* could be fined, imprisoned, or in the case of Guyana, flogged publicly. *Obeah*, like other African rituals, was supported and practised even by those who had converted to other religions, although it was not practised by the elites. By 1962, *obeah* had spread to other ethnic groups in Jamaica and there were many Indian believers and practitioners.

Followers of the belief placed much confidence in the power of the *obeah* (wo)man to do good as well as evil on their behalf. *Obeah* practitioners were called upon to use their powers to cure diseases and illnesses, cast off spells, discover theft/thieves, tell fortunes, predict winning horses, seek revenge on enemies, etc. Some people also visited the *obeah* practitioner if they wanted to increase their children's chances of passing examinations or to ensure success in love. The *obeah* (wo)man used various charms to carry out his/her jobs. The belief in and practice of *obeah* is still prevalent in the modern Caribbean.

Myal was another rite practised by African descendants in the Caribbean, particularly in Jamaica. This rite was used to counter the *obeah* (wo)man's activities. The *myal* (wo)men were said to be the spiritual descendants of the Ashanti *okomfies* or priests. Unlike the *obeah* (wo)men, they worked publicly to destroy obeah's spells and release the shadows.

The *myal* (wo)men's rites were revived in 1841 to 1842, and their work included demonstrations in front of crowds of followers, including those who were said to be victims of *obeah*. The *myal* practitioners, unlike the *obeah*

practitioners, included elements of Christianity in their rites. Many of their songs, used to release the spirits from the *obeah* victims, had the names 'Christ' and 'God' in them, to assist in the task.

Orisha

This is an African-rooted religion practised by people in Trinidad and Tobago and Cuba by people who are descended from the Yoruba of West Africa. Some refer to this religion as 'Shango'. Shango was King of the Oyo people, a prominent group among enslaved Yoruba. In African theology, Shango is one of the gods who originally walked the earth. In a recent article, David Tindall explained that Orisha spirits, many of them equated with Christian saints, are regarded as messengers between humankind and His Divine Kingdom. Oya, Shango's wife, for example, who is associated with speed and wind, is paired with St Catherine. Oshun, goddess of water and beauty, is paired with St Philomena. Osain, Yoruba god of herbal medicine, healing and prophecy is paired with St Francis and Ogun, the warrior god of iron and steel, is paired with St Michael. The saints or gods are there to help the faithful to cope with the stresses of life, and to protect the water, food and soil. These practices are passed down from one generation to the next by oral tradition as there is no sacred book like the Christian Bible.

Orisha worshippers seem to include aspects of the Catholic faith. This may have originated during slavery when enslaved Yoruba, who were baptised into the Catholic Church, used the trappings of Catholicism to disguise their African cultural practices. Singing, dancing, the burning of candles and drumming are essential aspects of Orisha worship. Today, people of other religious faiths in Trinidad and Tobago (e.g. Hindus) also visit Orisha ceremonies, and vice versa.

The Revival Movement

The Revival Movement also has its origin in African-based religion. In 1860 to 1861, Jamaica was swept by the 'Great Revival'. At first the traditional churches, for example the Baptists and Moravians, encouraged this. Later followers were overtaken by African and Myalist practices and became Afro-Christian. Their practice involved 'getting in the spirit', going into trances, speaking in 'tongues' (unknown languages), and healing one another by touch. Their bodies gyrated during worship and they used musical instruments such as tambourines, drums and cymbals. These were typical of worship rites carried out in Africa.

Trinidad also had revivalist-type groups such as Shouter and Shaker Baptists. Healing was important as was water baptism. In water baptism, candidates were immersed fully into the water, usually in a river. This group also 'got in the spirit'. They were also called the 'Holy rollers' because when the spirit possessed them, they shouted and rolled on the ground.

Rastafarian movement

Rastafarians are members of a social movement established in Jamaica around 1930. It combines elements of religious prophecy, specifically the idea of an African God or Messiah, the Pan-Africanist philosophy of Marcus Garvey, and the ideas of the 'Black Power Movement'. The word Rastafari is taken from 'Ras' meaning 'Chief' in the Amharic language, and 'Tafari' ('creator'), the title of the Emperor of Ethiopia.

According to social scientist Barry Chevannes, as a spiritual philosophy Rastafarianism is similar to the beliefs of the Maroon societies and comes from both the African Myal and the Revivalist Zion Churches. Essentially, then, Rastafari was born out of people's resistance to colonialism and oppression. Chevannes and other scholars who have studied this social movement reveal that the earliest preachers of the Rastafarian worldview were the Jamaican workers Leonard Howell, Archibald Dunkley, Joseph Hibbert and Robert Hinds. They asserted the idea of an African god who physically lived on earth and preached about the returning of African-Caribbean people to Africa. The Rastafarian leaders preached that all Africans who were taken or migrated from Africa were exiles in 'Babylon'. They further claimed that Rastafarians in this 'Babylon' can only be delivered out of captivity by a return to Zion or Africa, land of their ancestors and Jah Rastafari, their Messiah Haile Selassie 1, former Emperor of Ethiopia described as 'the first King of Creation, the Conquering Lion of the Tribe of Judah, God of the Black Race'. After provision of land in Ethiopia in the 1950s at Shashamanie by the Ethiopian emperor for Africans worldwide, several attempts at repatriation were made.

Members of the Rastafarian movement also use cannabis/marijuana (ganja – a herb brought over from India) in their worship and on a daily basis as their sacranebt of choice. Rastafarians sport the symbolic colours red, green and black, taken from the Garvey Movement, and represent the Ethiopian tricolour. They drum and chant as part of their rituals and embrace reggae music. Many 'Rastas' will not drink alcohol or eat salt, pork or shellfish and many are vegetarians. They prefer 'ital food' – food that has no chemicals or preservatives. In the Caribbean, most of the working class male 'Rastas' are craftsmen, carpenters, tailors, wood carvers, artists, fishermen, and a few till the land. The movement attracted many middle class members in the 1960s and it was this group that formed a sect called the Twelve Tribes of Israel. Rasta demonstrations against

Fig 15.3 *Rastafarian preacher Leonard Howell*

injustice, oppression and colonialism intensified in the 1960s. However, after the visit of Haile Selassie 1 to Jamaica in 1966 the movement has more and more embraced peace.

By the 1970s Rastafarianism had spread from Jamaica to other parts of the Caribbean. Today Rastafarians wearing 'dreadlocks' can be found in practically every country, as far away from Jamaica as New Zealand, where the Maoris gave Bob Marley a hero's welcome when he visited in the 1970s. The late Jamaican reggae super star, Bob Marley, is still, arguably, the most famous Rastafarian internationally.

Despite the global spread of Rastafarianism, not all who claim to be followers obey all its tenets. They may wear dreadlocks and sport the 'Rasta' colours, but they do not have an interest in the religious beliefs and practices. Indeed, since the 1980s the Rastafarian movement and its symbols have become commonplace in the Caribbean landscape. Many of the symbols have lost their traditional religious and ideological significance.

Fig 15.4 A Jamaican 'Rasta'

There are several contemporary autonomous groups in Jamaica that together make up the Rastafari Movement. The Bobo, who currently live in Bull Bay, nine miles east of Kingston, adopted many of the revival traditions. Prince Emmanuel emerged as Rastafari leader of the Bobo during the 1950s. They wear dreadlocks, but unlike most other sects, they live together in a commune and practise certain rituals. They wear tightly wrapped turbans, sometimes long flowing black or white robes and handmade sandals. The main rituals of this group include 'reasoning' and 'binghi', both sometimes referred to as 'groundings'.

Asian religious rituals

Indentured immigrants tried to practise their religious beliefs and practices despite the interference of the plantation regime. Ajai and Laxmi Mansingh, in their latest book *Home away from home*, noted that some Hindus offered prayers to the sun by chanting mantras and pouring water on a plant. Others thanked God in common words, gave reverence to elders and ancestors, watered a plant and fed an animal as the prescribed daily offering.

Muslims offered *namaz* and thanked Allah for everything. Their work schedule did not allow them to perform their five prayers a day; neither could they meet on a Friday for their religious observances. They could only occasionally perform their community prayer. It is called *milad* and is a session of Koran readings followed by dinner without music or dancing.

Plantation life did not allow the performing of the various *sanskars* or purificatory rites normally done in Indian villages. Each community had a full-time or part-time Hindu priest or pandit; and community religious activities took place on Sundays, mainly in the form of *Sat sangh* meaning 'Meeting of the Truth'. On these occasions, people told stories about the true God and also read of *Suraj* and *Bhagwat purani* (mythological stories and parables). Rural Jamaican Hindus did not have elaborate temples but had their meetings in the community shed that they built and decorated. At these meetings they chanted mantras from the Vedas and the devotees carried out rituals as instructed by the priest. On some occasions the *Kali puja* was performed.

In Guyana and Trinidad, sacrifice and prayer were essential parts of the Hindu worship. Much of Hindu worship took place in the home and each home displayed a particular deity. But there was also community worship in the temples. Muslims worshipped in their mosques. Up to 1870 in Guyana, there were no permanent structures that could be identified as Muslim mosques, although there were two Hindu temples. In Trinidad early temporary structures called *kutiyas*, and *medeis* in Guyana, served as temples. As the immigrants became permanent settlers, they built more elaborate structures. Unlike in India, these temples were hardly ever dedicated to just one god, but to several gods and goddesses. Some of these gods were Ganesh, Hanuman, Kali, Ram, Durga and Krishna. Priests conducted the prayers (mantras) in the temple. In the mosques, the Imam, Khuteb and Muezzin participated in leading different aspects of worship. Fasting was an important part of the Indian religious custom.

4 Festivals, celebrations and observances

Caribbean people observed and celebrated several religious and secular events in the period 1838 to 1962. People of all ethnic groups, classes and genders celebrated some of these events; others were specific to one ethnic group or the other. We will discuss just some of these festivals below.

Christmas

The majority of people in the Caribbean have long observed or celebrated Christmas, even if they did not support its religious significance or agreed on the date of Jesus' birth. Caribbean people observed (and still observe) Christmas's religious significance by going to church, but they also celebrated with much feasting, dancing and music. Traditional Christmas dinner was important, as it is today, with increased consumption of food and drink. People of all classes, but mostly of the elite and middle classes, put up Christmas trees in their homes and handed out presents on Christmas morning. They entertained themselves with 'Chinese crackers' and 'star-lights'.

In some territories, a major Christmas event was the John Canoe or Jonkonnu. Jonkonnu (spelt 'Junkanoo' in the Bahamas) was also a noted part of Christmas festivities in Belize, and in Nassau, Bahamas, where it was observed from around 1810. In Nassau, people paraded on the main street (Bay Street) in their costumes. Unlike the Jamaican Jonkonnu, this parade in the Bahamas featured no animal characters, nor any specific characters within special roles. Stilt dancers in African costumes (called 'moko jumbies') were popular in the early 1900s. So were costumes made from sponge. In the 1930s, Bahamian officials tried to revive the festival and organise it as a tourist attraction.

In Belize, the festivity was celebrated with street parades involving flagmen, drumming, and dancing. The mixed-race and Kalinago people, called the Garifuna, also put on a 'John Canoe' dance on 25 December, and 1 January, along with some of their own traditional masks. Masquerade bands which sang, danced and played music on drums and other instruments, were also popular in Guyana. The masqueraders of both sexes, were costumed and masked, as they were in the Junkanoo or 'John Canoe' in Jamaica and elsewhere. In Bourda, Albert Town, Packwood Dam and other suburban quarters masquerading and rope dancing were the main amusements. In Guyana, as elsewhere in the region, fireworks and the firing of squibs completed the Christmas festivities.

'John Canoe' was also celebrated in Tortola, British Virgin Islands for many years after emancipation but by 1930, it had died out. Instead, Christmas festivities featured house-to-house visiting by Long Tom. This was a masked figure standing ten feet high on stilts. He terrified the children as he paraded along, accompanied by dancers, players and minstrels. Drums were no longer used and the music was provided by guitars, kettle drums,

triangles, and instruments made from gourds. The Long Tom mass or worship service, was combined with all-night prayer meetings and carol singing, which went on until 1 January.

In Antigua in the 1920s the Christmas masquerading involved bands that went from house to house performing skits. As in Tortola, the music was made using gourds, which were home-made from gas pipes. In 1935 European instruments replaced these home-made ones. Antigua and St Kitts too, had a traditional Christmas masquerade. Colourful street festivals of dance, music and song marked Christmas. Each village had its own celebrations, but the centre of attraction was Scott's Row or Market Street as it is now called. Here was the main hive of activity with Revellers, Masqueraders, John Bulls, Highlanders, Moko Jumbies and groups in a variety of colourful costumes which showed historical figures, like Lord Nelson and Sir Francis Drake.

Fig 15.4 Jonkunnu festival

Perhaps the most ancient figure of Christmas was John Bull. It had both cultural and religious significance. 'Sammy Pero' was a character who came out at Christmas time in his costume of crocus, swab cloth and other decorations. He chanted the chorus, 'children, children' to which the children would answer, 'yes papa'. This conversation-in-song culminated with John Bull chasing the youngsters.

Christmas began to lose its cultural popularity in Antigua and Barbuda when the carnival was introduced in the 1950s. After this the emphasis was on an August festival. Now, the John Bulls, the clowns and Moko Jumbies are all gone. But Christmas is still a time for family reunions, gaily decorated shops with extended hours, an increase in visitor arrivals and increased shopping which gives a boost to commercial activity.

Jamaica's Jonkonnu featured costumed characters such as 'cowhead', 'oxhead', devils, warriors and 'pitchy patchy'. Some Jonkonnu bands featured 'Babu', an Indian character. The performers mimed, danced, and created their music from banjo and grater. The animal head characters and head-dresses that looked like houses or ships were definitely African. 'Pitchy Patchy' reflected both African and European influences. He/she was dressed in strips of brightly coloured cloth, probably replacing an older costume made of straw or palm leaves. Jonkonnu was especially important to the Jamaican folk culture in the post-slavery period. The masquerade bands danced through the streets, stopping at people's gates and also visiting rum shops. Though Jonkonnu disappeared from the towns, it never died out in the rural areas.

Parang has been famous in Trinidad for 200 years. It is the country's traditional Christmas music, introduced in the period when Spain occupied the island. Parang is sung to the accompaniment of acoustic guitars, cuatros (miniature guitars) and mandolins. No electric instruments are used. The Latin rhythms of Parang are often mixed with African-style call-and-response arrangements. The Parang season runs during November and December each year.

The day after Christmas, Boxing Day, was also a public holiday. But Caribbean people hardly observe it in its original meaning – putting left-overs from Christmas in boxes and handing these out to the less fortunate. Many used this day for picnics and other outings. On Boxing Day in Guyana, people congregate along the seawall in Georgetown and participate in various amusements.

Carnival

Carnival can be traced to African and European pre-colonial cultures. It was celebrated in several territories in the two days before Ash Wednesday, which marks the start of the Christian Lent season. Trinidad and Tobago had (and still has) the most spectacular and developed Carnival. After the abolition of slavery the Black Creoles were free to take part in Carnival. The festival gradually grew into a much more lively celebration centred on Port-of-Spain and other towns.

Carnival developed three important features. The first feature was that special songs were composed and performed about people and events that had been in the news in the past year. These developed into the modern calypso. The second feature was the rivalry between bands or gangs, which divided up Port-of-Spain and other towns. Each band had its own territory and at carnival they had fights between their champion stick fighters. These often led to full-scale street battles. The third feature was the colourful street parade, and the song and costume competition on the last day, with different sponsored revellers playing 'mas'.

Carnival began on a Sunday night with a torchlight procession of stick men and their followers. This was known as *canboulay*. Tobago also had its own carnival with all the traditional characters such as devils, clowns, 'Carib Indians', soldiers, dragons with keepers, as well as donkey or horse costumes. Since 1962, the costumes worn by those who 'play mas' have become more and more elaborate.

In Dominica, like Trinidad, Carnival had a strong French influence. In Roseau and Portsmouth bands of participants were organised into 'regiments' for stick fighting on the streets. There were many African costumes including the *sensay* (cowhead mask) character and the *bois bois* (stilman or *moko jumbier*). At first mainly the working classes supported the carnival. But after about 1900 it attracted middle class people. Carnival has now spread to many other territories including Jamaica, which was the last to come on board, officially in the 1990s. Before that Jamaicans travelled to Trinidad for the annual carnival and some still do.

Trinidadian students at the Mona campus of the University of the West Indies were responsible for exposing Jamaicans to the taste of this spectacular event.

Emancipation Day

The first of August was (and still is) a very important anniversary and public holiday in the Caribbean. It was also observed among groups of Caribbean people in the United States. In fact, even before their own emancipation, Africans and African-Americans in the US observed the first of August and used it as an occasion to press for the end of slavery. The first of August was the date finally agreed on for the legal ending of the condition of slavery in the British Empire in 1834. In later years it was associated with the granting of full freedom ('full free') on the first of August 1838 when Apprenticeship ended.

From the start the churches, especially the Baptists, staked out their claim to manage the celebrations and church services were the major focus of activity (as they are in Jamaica today). There were other church-sponsored functions such as processions, church bazaars and tea parties. This type of celebration continued into the 1840s. Then it faded away as the church had less and less influence on the emancipated. Also, the sober type of celebrations favoured by the church soon gave way to more 'secular' and lively celebrations by the people. In Jamaica, for example, the first of August 1847 was celebrated in Trelawney parish by gangs of people 'going about from one estate to another drumming, fifing, dancing and John Conooing'. The elite complained that these celebrations often led to violent confrontations. As a result the celebration was suppressed by the colonial government. By the 1860s the first of August was largely abandoned in that island because it was seen as an occasion for lively, often 'riotous' entertainment.

However, the first of August was revitalised and celebrated in Jamaica until the early 20th Century. For example, in 1888 the 50th anniversary of 'full-free' was observed. The African-Bahamian, Robert Love, pressed for the celebration of the 60th anniversary of emancipation in 1898. There were other observances up to the early 20th Century, for example those organised by one Rev. Wilson from 1914 onwards. Garvey's UNIA celebrated the first of August in the 1930s. After the granting of independence in 1962, Jamaica abandoned Emancipation Day in favour of Independence Day, but later re-introduced it. However, many people still see the first of August as just another holiday for going to the beach or engaging in fun not associated with the historical significance of the day.

The first of August was also observed in Guyana, Grenada, The Bahamas, Trinidad and Barbados. In Grenada in the very early 1900s, dances and picnics were held on 1 August. The estate people organised a 'nation dance' (a traditional African dance) at night and put up special African flags and banners.

Crop Over in Barbados

Crop Over is a five-week summer festival in Barbados. It dates back to the 1780s and was linked to the celebration by the enslaved workers of the end of the sugar-cane reaping season. When the harvest was over, there was a large celebration to mark the culmination of crop. The festival declined in the 1940s but was revived in 1974. Crop Over begins with a parade in mid-July with the ceremonial delivery of the canes and the crowning of the king and queen of the festival – the most productive man and woman cane cutter of the season. The celebration provides the occasion for people (many beautifully costumed during the carnival-like show) to display their artistic and cultural talents and their products (art & crafts, food, etc). Calypso is one of the main features of the Crop Over festival, with calypsonians organized into 'tents' and competing for several titles (e.g. the Road March Monarch and the Pic-O-De-Crop Monarch) and prizes. Crop Over ends in August with Grand Kadooment, a carnival parade featuring large, costumed bands.

Ethnic-specific festivals, celebrations and observances

Some ethnic groups had their own celebrations and festivities which were specific to themselves and in which 'outsiders' did not always share. The Asian Indians provide a good example. There is a strong move to maintain cultural identity among the Hindu and Moslem groups in the Caribbean, especially among those in Trinidad, Guyana and Suriname. However, some of the customs and traditions of the rural, indentured immigrants which were strong up to the 1920s eventually disappeared under the pressure from Creole society to merge. While Indian cuisine has survived, certain traditional customs associated with death and burial/cremation, birth, weddings, etc. have been changed. The traditional languages are not familiar to the majority of Indo-Jamaicans. The work by Brian Moore on Guyana, in which he also makes comparisons with other territories, and the work of J C Jha and the Mansinghs on Jamaica, are invaluable for revealing aspects of Indian culture.

Fig 15.5 Chinese girls dancing

Hindu festivals

The Indian immigrants brought their special festivals to the Caribbean. The Hindu section of the Indian community, whether in Trinidad, Guyana or Jamaica, celebrated many important occasions. For example, the birthday of Lord Rama (Ram Naumi/Ram Navami). Lord Krishna's birthday and Dasshera Lord Ram's victory over the demon king, Ravana. They participated in Ramleela, a play taken from the epic Ramayana, and they celebrated Holi/Phagwah, and Divali/Diwali. Divali/Diwali (also spelt Deepavali), the festival of lights, was celebrated in honour both of the goddess Lakshmi and of Lord Rama's return from the forest. The celebration of this festival included the illumination of homes and businesses with little earthenware bowls (*deyas*) filled with coconut oil and lighted wicks. In Guyana and Trinidad, Divali is celebrated on the 13th day in the month of Katik/Katrick, around October/November.

Holi or Phagwah was celebrated from the early plantation days and was an annual holiday in both colonial Guyana and Trinidad. The plantation owners encouraged it and there was much festivity, singing and dancing. It became a true folk celebration, especially important for the poor Hindu labourers and villagers. The elite Indians often frowned on it, considering it 'rowdy'. Holi was a spring festival and one of the features of its celebration was the throwing of liquid or dry coloured powder on participants.

In Guyana, Dasserah or Durga Puja was another major Hindu festival that was religious in nature. It was held in honour of Durga's (wife of Siva) victory over Maghisan, the giant and seemed similar to the Dasshera in Jamaica. It was celebrated over nine days and involved the building and decoration of a shrine, at one end of which a small temple was placed. An elaborately dressed image of the goddess Durga was placed in this temple. A large feast, with lots of meat, was prepared and consumed.

Hindu festivals were supposed to be celebrated according to the lunar calendar and almanac brought by the priests from India to the Caribbean territories. In Jamaica there were few priests to guide the Indian population about the auspicious month and day for certain events. In any case, the dictates of the plantation routine altered the traditional schedule of these rites, rituals and festivals.

Weddings

Weddings provided Caribbean people of all classes and ethnic groups with a great occasion for festivities and rituals. While the church service is fairly similar among Christians, traditional Indian weddings are quite different. There are different practices among classes and castes as well as among urban and rural people – particularly in how elaborate the bride's wedding dress and the reception was. In the 19th Century and early 20th Century, rural weddings were often preceded by many nights of 'set-up', during which ring games were played. Special food and cakes were served at these weddings. Once prepared, the food and cakes were carried to the place of the reception by a procession of young girls, all wearing white veils. After the marriage was performed there was a feast which might include roast pig, curried goat, boiled green bananas, wine and rum. This was followed by dancing such as the quadrille. Weddings, like Christmas, Easter and church attendance were occasions for people to dress in their best and most expensive clothes. At some rural weddings money was collected to help the couple begin their married life. By 1962, while some people gave money, other presents consisting of household and other necessities were more usual.

The pandit (*velan andi* among the Tamils) performed Hindu marriages, with all the attendant rituals, including gifts to the priest and to the couple. Weddings were occasions for festivities with much music and feasting. The Bevha or marriage was a sacred affair, and was carried out with much pomp and ceremony and with pre-wedding celebrations at the homes of the bride and the groom. In the Indian villages of Guyana and Trinidad, Hindus would give *pujas* and *katha* (the recital of sacred Hindu texts to an audience). Among the richer families the celebrations could last several days. In Guyana, among the Tamil

Fig 15.6 *African-Caribbean wedding*

Hindus, an essential part of the ceremony was the tying of the 'marriage knot' (*tali*) around the bride's neck, followed by the playing of several musical instruments. This varied slightly among non-Tamils where instead of tying the tali around, the groom impressed upon the bride's forehead a straight line with vermillion or red ochre.

In 19th Century Guyana, the people from the Bhojpuri culture of northeastern India began the wedding ceremony with the worship of Ganesha, the elephant headed god whom they believed could ward off evil that might befall the couple. Gifts were then presented. The couple followed the pandit around the sacred fire, the groom made an offering of *loma* (burnt oblation: the act of offering something, such as worship or thanks to a deity) and vows were exchanged. Then there was the ritual binding together of the couple by putting on a gold or silver necklace and the pandit made a speech. After this, the groom's sash was knotted to the end of the bride's sari, and the couple circled the sacred fire, throwing in parched rice each time. After the ceremony (if child marriage was not involved) the bride was taken to the groom's house and put under the care of her mother-in-law.

In Jamaica marriages arranged by parents, the community or individuals, were performed with all the ceremonies common to the villages of Uttar Pradesh and Bihar where some of the Indian immigrants originated. The *vivah/biyah* (wedding ceremony) and *guana* (after which the bride moved to the husband's home) were merged into one among the early immigrants and settlers in Jamaica. In territories where child marriage was the practice, days or even years would have separated these two ceremonies. In Jamaica, the marriage was performed under a *mandap/madua* (canopy) made of bamboo posts and covered with mango or banana leaves for shade. All the wedding rituals were conducted under this canopy. In Guyana that such a 'nuptial shed' (*maro/manro*) was constructed at Tamil weddings.

Among high caste Hindus, a dowry from the bride's family was presented to the groom's family at the *tilak* or betrothal ceremony, which was held a week before the wedding. The Muslims and lower caste Hindus gave a dowry from the groom's family to the bride's family. The shortage of women in the Caribbean made this a more common practice among all castes in all territories. Because women were so scarce, the dowry became almost a 'bride price'.

At first some territories like Jamaica and Guyana did not recognise the legality of marriages performed according to Indian rites and required them to be registered. If this was not done, the children of such unions were not recognised as legal heirs. This caused some Indians to conform, at least outwardly, to the dictates of the host societies.

Moslem festivals

The Moslems celebrated *Eid-ul-fitr* (the end of Ramadan), *Eid-ul-zuha* (the sacrificing of a goat) and the *Hussay/Hossay* or *Moharram* (commemorating the anniversary of the killing of Hosain, a grandson of the prophet Mohammed). The Shia Muslims traditionally relived the killing of Hosain each year during the first 10 days of Moharram, the first month of the Islamic calendar. This festival eventually became a festival celebrated by Hindus and Creoles as well as Moslems. The Hussay became quite secularised, losing its special religious character to some extent and becoming an annual demonstration of Indian national feeling. In Trinidad, the harshness of the past has disappeared from this festival and the procession more and more assume a carnival character.

This also holds true for Jamaica where the Indo-Jamaicans in Clarendon currently are among the few who still celebrate the Hussay. They celebrate in August, however, and not during the traditional month. This comes from the plantation influence, which allowed holidays during times when the estate routine would be least disrupted. The main features of the festival are: building a *tazia/tadjah* (an imaginary tomb of the two sons of Ali, Hosain and Hasan); burning of incense; reading of the Koran; singing of mourning songs; and marching of flag bearers accompanied by drummers. On the last day, the 'burial' of the *tazia* takes place in a procession which includes drummers, flag bearers, sword and stick fighters and mourners. The structure itself is disposed of in a sea or river. In Jamaica, there are fewer and fewer *tadjahs/tazias* and those that exist are not so elaborate as before. Years of missionary efforts in Jamaica contributed to the almost total elimination of this Muslim festival.

Muslims also had their own marriage customs. After exchanging gifts, the marriage was celebrated by the reading of the first chapter of the Koran. The groom repeated the five creeds, the articles of belief, and the prayer of praise. The real bride was not present at Muslim weddings, but a proxy or 'stand in' bride took her place, according to Muslim traditions. It was with this 'stand in' bride that the groom linked hands and pledged faith. The priest then said prayers. The priest also sent candy and sugar to the real bride with a message that she was married. Her friends then took the bride to her future home.

5 Birth, death, and work traditions and practices

Certain customs that were brought to the Caribbean by enslaved Africans continued throughout the century after Emancipation and even up to 1962 and beyond. Some customs and beliefs were religious, some were secular; and most were practised and held sacred by the rural working class rather than the middle class. Among the more secular customs and beliefs of the African-Caribbean people were those associated with the life cycle: pregnancy, birth, death. Other ethnic groups also had their peculiar beliefs and practices though by the 20th Century, some cross-cultural fertilisation had taken place.

Pregnancy

According to Madeline Kerr, in her book, *Personality and Conflict,* an almost universal belief in Jamaica (and also in other parts of the Caribbean) is that each woman is destined to have a certain number of children and that she should 'have out her lot'. Fertility was highly valued and women who could not conceive were branded 'mules'.

It was customary too that certain precautions were taken during pregnancy for the safety and well-being of the child. Expectant mothers were advised as follows, according to Kerr:

> Mothers must work so the baby won't be lazy, they must be careful what to look at in case it is deformed, they must not sleep on their backs or baby's face will be broad, and no one must pass behind her or baby's eyes will be cast ...

Customs during pregnancy also related to determining the sex of the baby. The midwife, or nana as she was called, felt that she could determine the sex of the unborn child and often predicted that 'if her abdomen is round, it's a girl; if it is elongated, it's a boy'. There were also a vast number of foods that were discouraged during pregnancy to ensure easy labour and health of mother and child.

Birth

Moore notes that in Guyana there were some beliefs about the relationship between the day on which the child was born and his/her personality. For example, elite people who were influenced by British culture felt that a child born on a Sunday would want for nothing, while those born on a Saturday would have to work hard for a living. Christenings and baptisms were more elaborate affairs, with a party following the formal church ceremony.

Kamau Brathwaite described some customs associated with birth in Jamaica. He wrote, 'When a child was born, the placenta and navel string were carefully disposed of.' Navel strings were to be carefully buried under a tree which then became that child's special tree. This custom continued into the 20th Century among some rural people.

In the first nine days of its life, the baby would stay indoors with its mother. But the bringing out of the baby on the ninth day was treated as an occasion. All the immediate family and a few selected relatives were present. Although the mother came out of the house on the ninth day, she would not leave the yard for three months. The formal naming of the baby was done at the christening or baptism among the elite, and the names they chose were European. Those who were not elite did not always engage in formal christening ceremonies. Many African-Caribbean people also adopted European names, with some also giving their children African names. The widespread use of African names was more a phenomenon of the post-1960s period.

Asians also had their own customs and rituals associated with birth. In Guyana, as in India, (and not so much in Trinidad and Jamaica), the birth of boys was valued higher than the birth of girls. This was surprising, as there was a shortage of females. But apparently girls were considered expensive to raise. Soon after the birth of a child, Hindu and Muslim parents in Guyana gave the newly-born a drop of honey, syrup or sugar as dictated by the religious books. Priests were consulted to give advice on the name, in accordance with astrological indications. As with other ethnic groups, the day on which the child was born was considered to have special significance. Among Muslims and Hindus the naming ceremony itself took place on the 10th or 12th day after birth. Both mother and child were purified after coming out of their isolation. Muslim women were purified after six days and again at the end of 40 days seclusion. In Jamaica, the ceremony of shaving the child's head by a barber, while the priest chanted mantras, was common among many Hindus. In both Trinidad and Guyana the baby's head was shaven at the first purification ceremony in keeping with Muslim beliefs. The Muslim naming ceremony differed slightly among the upper castes. In Jamaica, the higher caste Hindus practised the initiation or sacred thread ceremony.

In Jamaica, babies were given both traditional and Christian names, the latter more so in the 20th Century. Among the early immigrants, however, Hindu boys were named after mythological gods, heroes and divine virtues. Girls were named after goddesses and their virtues, the seasons and flowers. Normally the Hindu priest would prepare a horoscope and give the most appropriate letter for the name. But as priests were in short supply in Jamaica, many parents simply called their children after the day on which they were born, for example, Manga (Sunday). In Jamaica, among the indentured Indians, a special prayer area (chowk) was prepared by decorating the eastern wall of the maternity room with yantirc signs and writing with flour paste, says the Mansinghs.

Not all of these traditional customs and rituals that were performed by the immigrants in 19th Century survived in their 'pure' form up to the present.

Death, funeral and burial

In writing about Indian culture in the late 19th and early 20th Century Guyana, Brian Moore notes that Indians had their own fears and beliefs which some people regard as superstitions. They believed in lucky and unlucky days and in ghosts. They feared the 'evil eye' or the malice of enemies bad magic, or *maljo* as it was called in Trinidad. They used various charms and signs to ward off evil. Muslims, as in Brazil, wore amulets for protection. To ward off evil, they used cow dung in various ways. They would place a black spot on their children's cheeks or foreheads before allowing them to go on visits or play with other children in order to ward off evil. Government officials in the Caribbean equated some of the witchcraft and sorcery of the Indians with the African *obeah* and deemed these illegal.

Most religions have come to terms with death by their acceptance of a superior world to which they transcend after death. So it is not unusual that African-Caribbeans kept their African customs relating to the dead and to their burial. According to Martha Beckwith in *Black Roadways*:

> All the acts connected with the burial of the dead (are related to the belief in) power to return and disturb the living, unless precautions are taken to inter him properly.

Cultural historians indicate that African customs that survived in the Caribbean prescribed the exact way in which the body should be washed. They indicated also that the body of either a male or female must be clothed in white. Those practising African burial customs believed that no knots should be made in the thread used to sew the shroud, as the ghost would then return. Several people believed that once the deceased had been removed from the room in which he/she died, the position of the bed should be changed to stop the spirit returning to try to take ownership of the bed.

African-Caribbeans believed that for nine nights after the death the ghost rose out of the grave and returned to familiar haunts. It was also believed that it was not until the last of the nine nights that the dead departed completely. This belief gave rise to the custom of the wake of nine nights or 'set up'. The nine nights is an organised custom to say a final farewell to the person. The way it is organised in each territory is slightly different. There may be singing of hymns, followed by a feast. Most rural folk in Jamaica serve fried fish (sprats), bread, rum and coffee. The 'setting/sitting up' or wake was also practised by the British in the Caribbean as a social mark of respect for the departed and his/her relatives. These wakes were not as 'joyful' as those of the African-Caribbeans.

Indians and Indo-Caribbeans also had rituals associated with death and burial. Hindus had no traditional cremation facilities in Jamaica and the government never allowed the disposal of the dead by the pyre system. In this system the bodies were either buried or immersed in the sea within 24 hours of death. But during indentureship Hindus did not use coffins, rather they placed the body on a bamboo stretcher lined with banana leaves. This stretcher was carried on the mourners' shoulders to the burial site. In Guyana burial also seems to have been the more usual way of disposing of the dead among Indians. Just like in Jamaica, estate managers discouraged cremation and the pyre system.

When a man was dying among the Tamil Hindus of Guyana, a goat was taken to his bedside. The man would place his hand on the goat's head and his sins were told to the pujari. The animal was then let loose and was never touched or killed by relatives. This goat became the 'scapegoat' or 'goat of dismissal'. Among some of the Indians, special purifactory rites were performed on the third day of the person's death. This day signified the return to earth of the dead, and the assumption of a new form. To mark this, the house was cleansed, linen and clothes were washed and all earthenware used for cooking and storing water were thrown away. Some Indian groups held a wake on this night. On the eighth and tenth days, flowers and jewels were removed from the bereaved and the widow's jacket was deliberately torn at the back. Married Tamil women wore a *tali* around the neck, which was severed at the death of a husband.

In Jamaica, Hindu mourning lasted for thirteen days. In this time the priest read scriptures and conducted prayers every morning and evening. On the tenth day relatives of the dead person shaved their heads and faces. The widow's bangles were broken in a ritual. A dinner on the thirteenth day marked the end of the mourning period. But the Hindu family which suffered the loss would not participate in any festivals or hold any weddings for one year after. In Guyana, after the burial, mourners returned to their dwellings and performed the necessary purifactory rites.

Muslims had always buried their dead. They used a *Kathia* as the coffin. Muslims mourned their dead for 40 days. Like the Hindus, they held a dinner to mark the end of the period of mourning; and during those 40 days they read from the Koran in the evenings.

Indians who became creolised and who converted to the Christian religion observed Christian death and funeral practices. For example, by the end of the 19th Century some had adopted the African-Caribbean practice of holding a wake on the day on which a person died. Like African-Caribbean people, Indians visited the tombs of their dead relatives and friends. Some of these visits were more like pilgrimages with rites and feasts at the graveside. Both Indians and African-Caribbeans of the working class sprinkled rum around the grave. Finally, Indians showed ancestor reverence by sending, large quantities of food to their friends and neighbours and giving presents to the poor, in the name of the dead person.

Work habits and traditions

Specific habits and traditions have always been associated with work among rural folks in the Caribbean and many of these rituals have survived. For example, rural women who did not have access to piped water washed their clothes in the rivers and spread them over the banks of the rivers to dry. The women went to the rivers in groups to wash their clothes or to fetch water for domestic purposes. On washing days, the women sang songs while they worked. Those with babies would leave them on the riverbanks, in clear view. Singing was also popular among the men and songs like 'Woman a heavy load' and 'Day da light and mi waan go home' were favourites in some territories.

To sum up

The multi-ethnic nature of British-colonised Caribbean society has created a rich, culturally diverse heritage in the region. Caribbean culture reflects the input of the indigenous peoples, Africans, Chinese, Indians and Europeans. The beauty about the Caribbean is that people are free to participate in all cultural forms, even if those cultural forms are not specific to their ethnic group. That is why it is not unusual to see African-Caribbean people participating in the Indian Hussay festival. Unfortunately there are still people who engage in cultural and social hierarchising. The legacy of slavery ideology with regard to ranking people according to their gender and skin shade has not disappeared totally.

Revision questions

1   When Jamaican DJ, Buju Banton, came up with the lyrics for his song 'Mi luv mi browning', many people in Jamaican society were upset.
    a   Why do you think that many Jamaicans were upset with Buju Banton over his lyrics?
    b   Write two paragraphs on how negative attitudes towards colour are manifested in the Caribbean.

2   As a class project, compile a scrap book of magazine/newspaper clippings and pictures of one of the following in your territory or community:
    a   African cultural practices
    b   Indian festivals
    c   Chinese customs and festivals.

3   As an individual oral history project, interview a woman in your community who is over 70 years old. Ask her to compare women's status now with women's status at the time she was a young woman. Share your findings with the class.

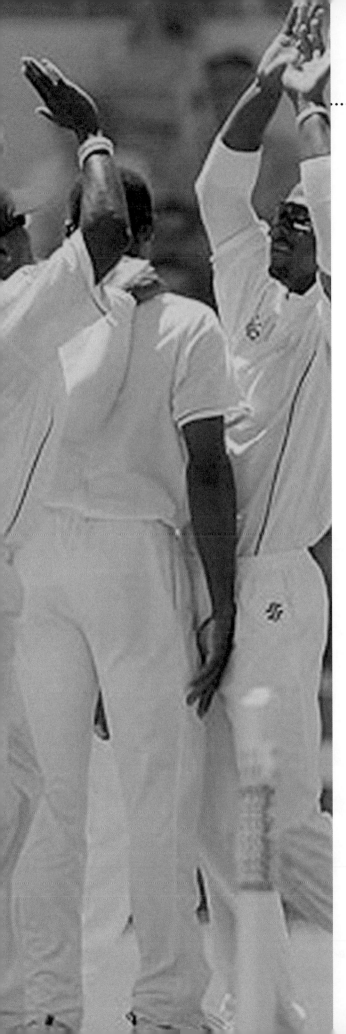

Chapter 16

Caribbean civilisation 2: work, leisure and artistic culture

'Rally, rally 'round de West Indies.'
(David Rudder)

Introduction

In Chapter 15 we looked at the issue of ethnic diversity in the Caribbean and its manifestations in the beliefs, customs and general cultural activities of different ethnic groups. In this chapter we continue to look at the social and cultural life of the people of the Caribbean by focusing on their occupations, modes of transportation, leisure activities and the use of their creative talents to produce art, architecture, dance, music, drama and literary works.

In this chapter we will learn about:
1 The occupations of different classes in the Caribbean
2 Family life and gender relations in the Caribbean
3 Sports and recreational life of Caribbean people
4 Transportation and communication
5 The artistic life of Caribbean people

West Indies celebrate the wickets of Brad Hodge

1 The occupation of different classes

The working classes

Up to 1962 agricultural work was still important to Caribbean people. Despite industrialisation the region still relied on the export of major crops to earn income. Many African-Caribbeans and Asians worked as full-time or part-time agricultural labourers or cultivated their own farms or peasant holdings. In fact, as described in previous chapters, nearly a century after emancipation, many Portuguese, Indians, Africans, Chinese and Creoles from within the region were contract labourers on sugar, banana and other plantations.

As chapter 14 has shown, up to the 1930s, the wages paid to agricultural labourers were quite low, resulting in a low standard of living and even widespread malnutrition

The 1938 Moyne Commission that investigated the causes of the 1930s labour protests, had noted that the daily wage for fieldwork in the first half of the 20th Century still averaged just over one shilling for men in St Kitts, Grenada, St Lucia and St Vincent. As in the post-slavery period, women earned less than men.

Agricultural wage rates moved only marginally higher in the period between 1938 and 1962. More significant increases were noted in the post-1962 years. For example, the average daily wage for female citrus workers in Trinidad & Tobago in 1976 was TT$4, while males earned TT$5.10. Women and men working in the copra industry earned TT$5.34 and TT$6.98 per day respectively. In Jamaica in 1980, 34 per cent of female agricultural workers earned between JA$20 and JA$50 weekly. In St Lucia, the guaranteed minimum daily wage for the category of 'general agricultural labourers' in 1982 was EC$9.36 for females and EC$10.41 for males. In the same year in St Vincent, female workers earned EC$10.00 and males EC$13.00

People who kept animals, cultivated crops for the local markets, or participated in the export of bananas and sugar earned a better income and enjoyed a better standard of living. By 1900 Tobago was almost exclusively a small farmer, peasant island, and so was Dominica. By the 1930s in Dominica, the great majority of the population depended solely on their own food crops for a

Fig 16.1 Canefield workers in Jamaica, circa early 20th Century

living. There had been a thriving peasantry in Jamaica since the 1840s, and by the 1880s this was true also of colonial Guyana where there were several communities of farmers who depended entirely on their own crops. These communities lived mainly along the riverbanks and in the more isolated parts of the colony. Both in Trinidad and in colonial Guyana, Indians were an important section of the peasantry after about 1870. They cultivated rice, provisions and other food crops.

The peasants enjoyed some independence and had a higher standard of living than the plantation labourers and town workers. However, only the minority who owned between four and 20 hectares could be described as prosperous. They made enough income from the land to enable their families to eat well, to support their children in school, and to take an active part in local religious and social affairs. For other people, independent farming provided, at best, a minimum living standard. It made starvation unlikely, but it could not provide a decent living for the rapidly-growing rural population. (See chapters 4, 5 and 9.)

Artisans, commercial and industrial occupations

Caribbean people found many ways to make a living outside of agriculture. Not all these other activities gave them the means of upward social mobility. Non-professional and 'unskilled' women, for example, lagged behind men in the wages they earned. Women worked as laundresses (washerwomen), seamstresses, domestic servants and higglers. Some women also worked in the industrial and manufacturing sectors. Those who were formally educated, entered professions such as teaching, nursing, surveying, architecture, the civil service, banking and the military. Others were potters, rope makers, furniture makers, jewellers, carpenters, etc. Men, however, held most of these occupations. In 1946 in Barbados only 18 per cent of women were in the manufacturing sector. This percentage declined to 11 per cent by 1960. In 1946, according to the West Indies census, men outnumbered women in the professions, particularly in Barbados, colonial Guyana and Trinidad and Tobago. Men also dominated in all territories until the 1950s when the gender balance shifted.

Fishing was an important occupation of the African-Caribbean and Asian-Caribbean people. The African-Caribbean people kept alive the ancient occupation of making boats by hollowing out a cottonwood tree by axing the relatively soft and spongy wood. With these boats fishermen and women would catch fish at various points off the coasts of the various territories. People fished in nearly every coastal village in the region and then sold the fish in the markets. In St

Kitts, owning boats was very prestigious and a person could invest his or her life savings in one of these boats.

In islands such as Carriacou and Anguilla, quite a large number of the men worked as seamen on the inter-island sailing boats and later on the steamers. In the Bahamas, between 1838 and 1900, wrecking was a major occupation for Black men. In 1856 nearly one half of the able-bodied men of the colony held wrecking licences. This licence allowed them to board ships wrecked off the reefs and coasts of the islands and remove and sell their cargoes. Of course this occupation was dangerous. It was also a highly irregular source of income since months might pass without a shipwreck. Bahamians also dived for sponges and between the 1890s and 1930s, sponging was the colony's chief industry.

Just as the sea offered a living to many Caribbean people, so did the forests. In islands such as Dominica men could earn a living as woodcutters and as 'carriers' for the estates in the interior, carrying supplies on their heads. In colonial Guyana there was a special group of woodmen living in isolated settlements up the great rivers. These were the Bovianders, people of mixed Dutch-Amerindian-African descent. They lived by cutting timber, making charcoal and trading with the indigenous peoples. But it was in Belize that the forests dominated the economy of the whole colony. The main export was timber (mahogany and logwood) and most African-Belizean men were seasonally employed as woodcutters. Wages were very low and most loggers were in debt to their employees. But logging was the traditional work of African-Belizean men and, in any case, there were few alternatives.

Marketing and domestic service

Some men and women found employment as domestic workers and as higglers although these occupations were traditionally female-dominated. Higglers typically bought goods from others and resold them but some sold produce from their own plots. Some sold in established markets, others peddled their goods from door-to-door, and some sold from roadside markets. Although markets were held on different days in different territories, Saturday was a major market day in all territories. In addition, Trinidad continued the Sunday market tradition established during slavery. Foreign visitors to Jamaica or other British Caribbean territories in the late 19th Century and early 20th Century frequently commented on the role of women in bearing goods to the market. In *Traveller in the West Indies*, Owen Ruller commented:

And one meets so many negresses on the roads all carrying loads upon their heads – heavy loads like bundles of sugarcane, sacks full of fruit, baskets of fish.

Fig 16.2 *On the way to the market*

Lord Oliver, in his book *Jamaica the Blessed Island*, stated that the women would carry the produce to the market, do the housekeeping and travel with head loads on donkeys or mules.

After the abolition of slavery there was an ongoing decline in the importance of domestic service. However, after 1880 the Caribbean servant workforce began to grow again at a rapid rate. By the 1970s the service industry had taken over from agriculture as the major employer. In Barbados, for example, 15,200 women worked in this industry.

Up to the 1960s most domestics worked in private homes. By the 1970s many were choosing to work in the service industry in the tourist industry. In Jamaica in 1844 there were 20,571 domestic workers; by 1943 there were 62,792 female domestic workers. The majority of these domestic workers were African-Jamaican. By 1970 the number had declined significantly as the table below shows. In 1891 there were 2,653 male and 14,849 female domestic servants in Trinidad and Tobago, some from other Caribbean territories. In 1931 women formed 89 per cent of the total of 24,274 domestics in Trinidad and Tobago. Women dominated because this occupation was regarded as 'women's work'. Where men were hired as domestics, their tasks were different from those of women. Most were employed as gardeners, butlers, valets, grooms, and chauffeurs. A few were cooks. Women made up the majority of cooks and were the nannies, house cleaners, waiting maids and laundresses. Male domestics were paid a higher wage than females, even though females often worked longer hours.

In addition to gender, ethnicity and colour were crucial factors determining who did domestic work. During slavery, mixed-race and a few working class European women were the main domestic servants. But in the post-slavery period, African- and Asian-Caribbean women performed this occupation. By the 1960s some of the employers were middle class mixed-race people.

Table 16.1 Numbers employed as private domestics, workers, washerwomen and seamstresses (not in factories) in Jamaica 1834-1970

Period	Domestics	Washerwomen	Seamstresses
1834	38,865	-	-
1844	20,571	-	-
1861	16,253	-	-
1871	16,287	5,631	14,565
1881	14,907	8,104	14,773
1891	26,503	10,400	18,966
1911	35,701	11,715	20,340
1921	49,965	9,380	23,237
1943	70,568	3,873	17,038
1960	63,180	1,948	-
1970	43,690	-	-

Fig 16.3 *Domestics at work*

The occupations described above involved mainly adults. Children of working class parents also did domestic work in their own homes; and they also worked on the family peasant holdings. Children of the elite generally had servants to attend to domestic work. Many rural children stayed at home to help with washing on Mondays and with reaping provisions for markets on Fridays. Children of parents who owned businesses, such as Chinese retail establishments, worked in these establishments after school. By 1962 ethnic mixing in the schools was the norm even though there were schools specifically established to serve particular ethnic groups. Many children spent the greater part of their time at school or at play.

2 Family life and gender relations

The family unit has always been important in the Caribbean, although under slavery and indentureship there were obstacles to the way it was formed and maintained. One of these obstacles was the gender imbalance at the time. The structures, relationships, and conventions of the Caribbean family did not always conform to the elite European ideal of the nuclear family, with a married couple and their children living as a unit without extended family members. So in the post-slavery period, Christian missionaries fought for the establishment of 'Christian' marriages, that is, legally sanctioned, male-headed, monogamous unions with one household base. Edith Clarke's book *My Mother Who Fathered Me*, reveals that three quarters of the households studied in Jamaica were headed by single females.

For many women there had to be economic security before they considered marriage. Money was also vital so that they could organise a lavish marriage ceremony, buy the ring or rings, and have a honeymoon. The elite and middle classes had established precedents by wearing expensive clothing and entertaining lavishly to celebrate occasions so now the working class felt that they could do no less. So, it was really the older rural people with better economic resources who celebrated marriages. Many of these people had lived together in what elites called 'common-law' relationships for years prior to marriage. The children born in such common-law unions were called 'bastards' or 'illegitimate' and could not legally inherit property. In 1885, 60 per cent per cent of all births in Jamaica were 'illegitimate' according to Alfred Caldecott who wrote, *The Church in the West Indies*. This discrimination against children born to unwed couples is no longer allowed in most Caribbean territories.

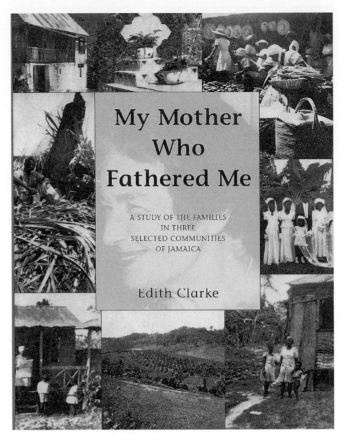

Fig 16.4 *Cover page of Edith Clarke's book*

Discrimination against the common-law wife is also no longer allowed.

It was not only the working classes that lived in family settings where commonly the mother and father were not married. The shortage of women among the immigrant population for most of the 19th Century caused instability in the marital unit, and militated against formal marriage. This increased the occurrence of common-law relationships or 'concubinage'.

There were other forms of family structures apart from the nuclear and common-law. The extended family was, and still is, prevalent among African- and Indian-Caribbean people. Here, the husband, wife and their children lived together with their own parents and/or other relatives. While Indians worked on the estates as indentured servants, the nuclear family and the 'common-law' relationships were prevalent. When they moved off the estates to establish their own homes, some continued these kinds of family arrangements. They also maintained the patrifocal or male-headed joint family structure (at times in a modified form from that which existed in India). Such family structures were noted in colonial Guyana by the end of the 19th Century and later in

Trinidad where the nuclear family remained the dominant unit for a longer time.

Caribbean people also lived in other household units, with people not necessarily related to each other. Gender roles were quite well laid out and understood in Caribbean families. Until the 1960s when the effects of the feminist movement were being felt, the man was recognised as the head of the household in nuclear families. Older women were influential in the extended families, though their sphere of influence was primarily within the house. Men were the acknowledged breadwinners, though many women also worked, defying the main gender ideology in the post-slavery Caribbean. In female-headed households, the situation was different, although even in these households there could be a man in a 'visiting relationship' capacity.

Caribbean societies were patriarchal and this affected the family. However, many sociologists argue that African-Caribbean women in working-class families tended not to believe totally that the man was the head of household as the women also had considerable decision-making powers. Religion contributed a lot to the ideas about women's role in the family. All the major religions supported the subordination of women. Christianity, in particular, preached that men were the acknowledged head of the household.

3 Sports and recreational life

Sports and recreation were essential aspects of Caribbean people's culture and social life. Some types of sports and recreational activities cut across class, colour, gender and ethnicity while others were confined to a particular class, colour, ethnic group or gender. The extent to which North American and European culture affected the region also dictated the games and recreational activities. For example, baseball and basketball developed late in the English-speaking territories in comparison to the Dominican Republic and Puerto Rico. Cricket and soccer, on the other hand, were never major sports outside of the British-colonised territories.

In addition to cricket, soccer, basketball and baseball, other sports that were popular with Caribbean people were golf, lawn tennis, horse racing, netball, volleyball and boxing. Heavyweight boxer Peter Jackson, who was born in 1861 on the island of St. Croix, travelled to Sydney, Australia where he won the Australian heavyweight title. In San Francisco he was persuaded by the Earl of Lonsdale to settle in England.

Some of these sports were differentiated by gender with netball, for example, seen only as a 'women's game'.

Initially only men participated in sports like cricket, soccer and golf, but women gradually entered these games. Some of these sports were also class-based. Golf and tennis, and indeed any sport which required expensive equipment, were 'middle class' sports. Golf clubs such as the St Andrew Golf Club, Moneague Golf Club and the Constant Spring Golf Club were formed in Jamaica. The Jamaica Lawn Tennis Association was only formed in 1903, although competitive tennis was introduced in the 1890s.

Track and field athletics tend to be more competitive than purely recreational. The Caribbean region has produced many outstanding track and field stars. Arthur Wharton, who was born in Jamaica, in 1886, became the first man to run 100 yards in ten seconds during championship conditions at Stamford Bridge in the UK. In the 1920 Olympics, Guyanese Harry Edwards collected two bronze medals for the 100 and 200 meters. The 1948 Olympics saw Trinidad participating for the first time where Trinidadian weightlifter Rodney Wiles won Trinidad and Tobago's first ever medal, a silver. McDonald Bailey another Trinidadian, who was running for Great Britain at that time, went on in 1951, to become the only Trinidad-born athlete to hold a world record in an individual athletic discipline. Both Bailey and the accomplished Jamaican sprinter Arthur Wint served in the British Royal Air Force during World War Two.

Caribbean athletes have built on the achievements of the pioneers and have brought much pride to the region through their participation in international and regional events. Among the outstanding stars (including recent ones) are: Alleyne Francique, (Grenada); Haseley Crawford and Atto Bolden (Trinidad and Tobago); Obadele Thompson (Barbados); Kim Collins (St. Kitts); Herb McKinley, Lennox Miller, Donald Quarrie and Merlene Ottey (Jamaica), Asafa Powell, Veronica Campbell and Usain Bolt, and rising star from Antigua, Daniel Bailey.

Horse-racing

Horse-racing, a sport encouraged by large penkeepers, emerged as a sport during slavery. Although jockeys were usually young working-class males, at first only the elite and middle classes went 'to the races'. The crowd became more 'democratic' by 1962, but the owners of the horses continued to be fairly wealthy people. Race day was a gala event in Georgetown, Guyana. Some went to the races while others went out early to place their bets at a betting establishment. Those who attended the races were clothed in their fineries.

Cricket

Cricket was, and still is, the most popular sports in the British-colonised Caribbean. It was introduced to the region by the British colonisers in the early 19th Century during slavery and was initially a British male sport. 'Members only' clubs supported its elite nature. It seems that St Ann's Garrison Cricket Club in Barbados was a pioneering Caribbean social institution. Cricket was also played in other British-colonised territories; for example, Jamaica established the Kingston Cricket Club in 1863. By the end of the 19th Century there were several cricket clubs in colonial Guyana. There were the two elite clubs, the BG Churchmen's Unions CC and the Demerara CC. But most villages also had their own clubs. By 1900 there were 19 major cricket clubs in Barbados and Jamaica alone. White women in the Caribbean saw the game as their husbands', sons' and fathers', unlike women in England who had played the game since the 1830s. But women in the Caribbean participated as spectators at cricket matches. By the 19th Century, mixed-race and African men challenged the view that cricket was for the elitist British planter-merchant class and by the 1940s the era of British domination of the game had ended. By the late 19th Century African and mixed-race people had started to participate in the game other than as enthusiastic supporters at matches. By the end of the century some were either playing for British clubs or had formed their own. African men became the main force in the inter-colonial contests (started in 1865 when teams from Demerara and Barbados competed) and the West Indies team. They were perhaps first formally recognised in this collective way in 1886 with the tour of North America. Young boys also played the sport at school, and this expanded their past-times from playing tops (gigs) and marbles. Just about every open space could become a cricket pitch for young boys, even a town street, if necessary. A tin would be used as a wicket and a palm/coconut leaf rib for a bat.

Fig 16.5 Maypole dancing

The West Indies made their first tour of England in 1900, the first of many to come. By 1980 the West Indies team of mainly West Indian men under West Indian leadership (the first established West Indian captain being Worrell in 1960) had reached a position of dominance in world cricket. Cricket has become a widely supported game in the Caribbean and people of all social classes listen to matches on the radio, attend them or watch them on TV. Caribbean people love their early cricket heroes such as Garfield Sobers (Barbados), George Headley (Jamaica), Clyde Walcott (Barbados), Learie Constantine (Trinidad), Everton Weekes (Barbados), Frank Worrell (Barbados), Rohan Kanhai (Guyana), Wes Hall (Barbados), Conrad Hunte (Barbados), Lance Gibbs (Guyana) and Jackie Hendricks (Jamaica). They also embraced the new heroes of the 1980s and 1990s such as Lawrence Rowe (Jamaica), Viv Richards (Antigua), Gordon Greenidge and Desmond Haynes (Barbados), Clive Lloyd (Guyana), Courtney Walsh (Jamaica), a female player, Vivalyn Latty-Scott (Jamaica), Curtley Ambrose (Antigua), Jeffrey Dujon

and James Adams (Jamaica), Malcolm Marshall (Barbados), Shivnarine Chanderpaul, Carl Hooper (Guyana) and the highest test scorer, Brian Lara (Trinidad and Tobago).

For a long time cricket remained a male sport at the organised, competitive level. Women played cricket as a leisurely past-time in rural villages and urban slums, but they did not attain a level of professionalism and organisation until the 1960s.

In 1966 Jamaica became the first in the region to establish a women's cricket association. This came about because there were about 30 to 40 women who were interested in the game as a profession and who arranged a series of friendly matches on a fairly regular basis. These matches were so popular that John Wong-Sam, the cricketer-coach-umpire was urged to facilitate the formation of the association. Among the first women in the JWCA were Vivalyn Latty (later Latty-Scott) and its first president, Monica Taylor, who in 1967 arranged a series of test matches in Trinidad. After the Jamaica initiative women in Barbados, Grenada, St Vincent, Guyana and St Lucia took steps to professionalise women's cricket. In 1975 the Caribbean Women's Cricket Foundation (CWCF) was formed. This was the vehicle on which women's cricket would progress in the future.

Fig 16.6 Garfield Sobers

Fig 16.7 Brian Lara

Chapter 16 | *Caribbean civilisation 2: work, leisure and artistic culture*

Outings

There were many opportunities for recreation and for playing popular sports, weekends and major holidays being the most obvious. People organised trips or 'outings' to parks, gardens and the beach. Church outings were also popular among the rural people. African-Caribbean people even used communal workdays as occasions for having fun, with much food served and songs sung. Kite-flying was popular throughout the region and in Guyana, Easter Monday (a public holiday) was the great kite-flying day. Village cricket was also a favourite on holidays or even Sunday afternoons in some British territories.

The tea meeting

The tea meeting was an important social event in rural Jamaica and Guyana. At first in Guyana these meetings were religious in nature, but in Jamaica they always tended to be secular. In Jamaica they were also a fund-raising event. Hand-printed notices were often stuck at shops around the village like this one below, reading:

> There will be a Tea Meeting at the house of Mr. and Mrs. Mullings at Liberty Vale on the night of Tuesday, the day after Christmas. Come one, come all, but please contact Miss Eliza Mullings for an invitation.
>
> Prices: Gentlemen, one shilling. Ladies, six pence. Children, three pence.
>
> Eliza Mullings
> Manager.

Not all invitations or announcements of tea meetings were this formal, however. Some writers claim that the tea meeting was a fairly late social activity, which was influenced in respect to dress by the style and dress of the masters and the growing elegance in the attire of the free coloured (people).

Tea meetings were held in a coconut or bamboo booth, with seating of chairs and planks as well as hurricane lanterns for lighting. Musicians would play and there would also be long speeches. The prime concern, however, was the auctioning of the cake. The cake was veiled, and was called the queen. The real queen of the evening was a young girl who was veiled and led in by a king (a young man of the village). Members of the audience were required to bid for the queen to be unveiled or for the veil to remain. Stories, riddles and dances were also a feature. During refreshment time, coffee and bread or crackers were served.

Gambling

Although gambling was a past-time activity of some Caribbean people, others did not consider the practice socially acceptable. Nevertheless, Caribbean people continued to bet on horses at the races and to participate in Chinese number games such as 'whe-whe (Trinidad) and 'peaka pow' (Jamaica). These number games were deemed illegal by the state but continued underground; and the profits generated made their organisers rich. Cock-fighting was also practised and provided yet another activity for gambling, as participants placed bets on which bird would win. Some gambling also took place in bars, popular venues for socialising and playing games like domino.

Cinema in the Caribbean

In the early 1900s, the cinema became a leading form of popular entertainment, especially those cinemas showing US films. At the turn of the twentieth century, among the wealthier European population of Port-of-Spain in Trinidad, there was an interest in 'moving pictures'. These animated pictures were shown in regular exhibitions given by Ireland Brothers in Prince's Building. The entrance fee was high and only a few people could afford the 2 shillings for front seats with seats in the 'gallery' costing 1shilling. Similarly, a contemporary writer recorded that in Barbados in the 1920s, African-Barbadian people sat in the cheaper section, the 'pit' while the elite sat in the more expensive 'gallery'.

In the 1930s in Trinidad & Tobago, the British Colonial film exchange allowed exhibitors to rent films instead of having to buy them outright as they did in earlier times. This allowed exhibitors to show more films at prices that more people could afford. The presence in Trinidad and Tobago of the United States armed forces played a major part in the growth of cinemas and by 1943 the United States army and navy had erected sixteen outlets on the island. By 1976 there were 74 cinemas.

The major earthquake in Jamaica in January 1907 hindered the development of the cinema. Prior to the earthquake the Theatre Royal in Kingston had shown a few 'animatograph' entertainments. From 1909 moving picture shows could be seen at the Rockfort Gardens Theatre. The price was sixpence, still a lot of money in those days and out of reach of most local people but much cheaper than in Trinidad. In 1913 the Fisher Amusement Company visited Port Antonio, Spanish Town, Annotto Bay, Port Maria and Montego Bay. By 1920 there was a dramatic expansion of cinemas as well as audiences. It is likely that the audiences of the era were almost exclusively European. The onset of the World War II seems to have brought the rapid expansion of cinemas in Jamaica to a halt, but there was a growth spurt in the 1960s.

Fig 16.8 A storyteller

The films that were shown in Jamaica from the 1930s were almost exclusively US in origin. From the 1920s right up to the 1970s and early 80s Jamaicans were fed a steady diet of Hollywood westerns that were eventually superseded by Kung Fu and Martial Arts films.

The Chinese community in Jamaica had been able to enjoy Cantonese and Mandarin films from the1950s, and in Trinidad the Hindi film was a major force. During World War II the Astor cinema in Guyana, run by Cyril Young, gave public news updates on the war. In the 1920s, silent films featuring Charlie Chaplin were shown at the Gaiety cinema, which may have been Guyana's first cinema. The Gaiety was destroyed by fire in 1926. Many of the early cinemas still stand today and one worthy of mention is the Olympic on Lombard Street that had four walls and no roof – a forerunner of the open-air movie theatre. Perhaps due to prolonged colonial involvement or a decline in interest, the former Dutch colony of Suriname had only one cinema in 1997, and in 2002 there were two internet service providers with a total of 14,500 users.

Dancing

Dancing was always a popular past-time. African-Caribbean people danced to the rhythm of musical instruments like drums, shak-shaks, banjos, flutes, guitars, trumpets, saxophones and clarinets. While traditional African dances survived in many places, there were also European and Asian influences on dances. Dancing was done at Christmas time as well as to celebrate emancipation, and independence. Some of the dances were religious and were done as part of 'nine night observances'; others were purely secular and were done at functions such as the 'tea meeting' in Jamaica and Guyana and at a ball (e.g. the African-Guyanese working class 'dignity balls') and parties.

Chapter 16 | *Caribbean civilisation 2: work, leisure and artistic culture*

The African-Guyanese also held fancy dress balls. Those who attended came out in their fineries and danced the quadrille and other country dances. These 'fancy balls' seemed to attract a different crowd from the 'dignity balls', which were attended mainly by the urban working class and where people had to pay an entrance fee at the door. The Maypole dance was European in origin and was performed at ceremonies associated with birth and marriage. We will explore this subject in more detail later.

Story-telling and other recreational activities

Story-telling was a favourite past-time among the rural folks. In Guyana, for example this was a feature at death wakes. Anansi stories, which can be traced to West Africa, were by far the most popular. The Anansi figure was half-spider, half-human in appearance and was agile, crafty, cunning and intelligent. The stories always had an important moral. Story-telling has not disappeared, as is indicated by the popular Amina Blackwood Meeks and Paul Keans-Douglas, from Jamaica and Trinidad respectively.

Among the Jamaican upper classes, recreation included such activities as card playing, hunting, grand balls on special occasions, vaudeville and visiting theatrical groups.

In Trinidad, according to Anthony de Verteuil, there were similar activities – hunting and shooting birds, swimming (at the beaches or private pools), vaudeville, operatic and dramatic theatre, walking, reading, playing cards and whaling. In Guyana elite past-times included participation (by young men mostly) in sports like cricket, soccer, rugby, rowing, cycling, tennis, golf and horseback riding. They indulged in gambling, hunting, rifle-shooting, archery and drinking. They attended the races, and went to the theatre. They participated in reading, writing and debating. Elite women also participated in some of these activities, which were seen as 'unladylike' and more suitable for men. Elite women, though, attended public balls, private dinner parties and went on 'river cruises'.

Theatre in the Caribbean

According to Richardson Wright in his book *Revels in Jamaica 1682-1838*, the theatre was not a post-slavery phenomenon. What was new was the movement towards local theatre, a development that has been better documented since 1948. A continuation from the slavery period, however, was that up to 1962 it was mainly the elite class that went to the theatre. Trinidad & Tobago has one of the world's largest street theatres – Carnival – that displays all aspects of the creative and performing arts and is accessible to classes that would not have gone to 'the theatre' in the formal sense.

Important years for the development of Caribbean drama were from 1947 to 1966 when the Trinidad Theatre Workshop began performing regularly as a company. In 1947 Errol Hill, the recipient of a British Council scholarship, formed the Whitehall Players. The University of the West Indies (UWI), founded in 1948, played an important role in creating a strong foundation for Caribbean Theatre. Between 1950 and 1957, a group of dramatists, actors and directors came together at the UWI and talented people from the region performed plays by Derek Walcott, Roderick Walcott, Errol Hill, Slade Hopkinson and others. The tireless work of Beryl McBurnie and Helen Camps, who took Trinidad theatre to an international audience, should also be acknowledged.

Errol Hill has mentioned that the few theatre groups that were active before 1948 were amateur. These groups consisted of mostly European or mixed-race people who performed plays from the USA or Europe. After World War II, the British Council began to promote the English language through drama, an easily accessible form of community education and entertainment.

In Jamaica, between 1866 and 1901, the urban population was entertained by theatre groups from overseas like the George Benson Shakespearean Company and the Glessop Harris Company. Colonel Charles Ward, who was the Custos of Kingston and a wealthy rum magnate, presented the Ward Theatre as a gift to the city of Kingston and to the Jamaican people in 1912. This beautiful theatre, with exceptionally good acoustics, was built on a site that had been used for theatres since the 1770s and has been associated with the development of an indigenous theatre movement. It was at the Ward Theatre that The Right Honourable Marcus Garvey held his first public meeting after returning to Jamaica following his deportation from the USA in 1927. The Ward Theatre was also the venue for the first in a series of live stage shows produced by the Twelve Tribes of Israel that took place across the island in the 1970s.

For a short time the island of Grenada also had a dramatic movement, but when dramatist Wilfred Redhead left for Barbados, dramatic activity became intermittent. Barbados and Guyana also had expatriate theatre groups. Guyana had an interracial Theatre Guild and New West Indian drama was to be found in Trinidad & Tobago, St Lucia and Jamaica. Actor, writer, poet, playwright, director and Nobel Prize winner Derek Walcott has played a major role in the development of Caribbean Theatre.

Leisure and ethnicity

The concept of 'leisure time', as well as what constituted leisure-time activities, at times varied according to ethnic groups. For example, much of the free time of the Portuguese in Guyana was taken up with family and ethnic community activities in association with the Roman Catholic Church. The Portuguese observed Christmas, Boxing Day, Good Friday and Easter and what was called 'Pentecost'. They also celebrated various 'Saint's days'. Elaborate feasting, band music, fireworks and gunfire marked Portuguese celebrations. They organised picnics and also did charitable work. As they became more and more settled in Guyana, they took on the trappings of the European elite society in terms of the sports they played, the social clubs they formed, and the houses in which they lived.

Smoking and the staging of acrobatic, dramatic and musical performances were noted among the Chinese. Their lunar New Year festival, which some people call 'Chinese Christmas', was very important to them and required elaborate preparations, with much feasting. Denied access to European elite clubs, they formed their own. The Chinese community also practised Tai Chi and carried elements of Peking (Beijing) Opera and Kung Fu with them.

Like the Chinese and Portuguese, Indians did not initially have much spare time. Religion and community (caste) determined much of what they did in whatever leisure time they allowed themselves or were allowed by the plantation regime during the indentureship period. As soon as immigrant groups made the transition from transients to settlers and adopted Creole culture, they began to practise the culture (e.g. playing cricket) of the African-Caribbean. However, Indians spent some of their spare time practising Yoga and traditional athletic exercises, as well as participating in traditional Indian dance, songs and chants and playing traditional musical instruments. They also participated in religious and caste-based ceremonies, gathering around, and listening to, the tales or sacred books read by the pandit or mullah.

4 Transportation and communication

How did Caribbean people travel around so that they could socialise and carry out their various activities within their own territory as well as with their Caribbean neighbours and relatives further afield? There were three levels of transportation and communication: territorial, regional and international. For a very long time communication and transportation in the Caribbean territories was very bad, and in some territories these conditions persisted into modern times.

Road transport

During slavery, European colonisers only saw fit to construct dirt roads where they could fulfil the function of moving goods from the plantation to the ports for exportation. The means of transportation then were horse-drawn coaches or ox/donkey carts. The colonisers did not create a viable infrastructure that would serve to aid the development of each Caribbean country. They began to construct really durable roads in the Caribbean region only in the early 20th Century, but such roads were at first only constructed in the urban areas. The West India Royal Commission stressed this fact when they visited territories like St Vincent in 1939, pointing out that for decades, whole populations had been kept virtually imprisoned in their villages because of the lack of proper roads - a situation that created difficulties for peasant farmers trying to get their produce to markets. Heavy rains often eroded these tracks/roads. For example, in September 1911 a portion of the Cameron road in the Cumberland valley area of St Vincent was washed away by rainstorms when the river burst its banks. The Indo-Trinidadian novelist, Samuel Selvon, wrote about the young South Asian women in rural Trinidad, who had no need for shoes because there were no roads on which they could walk.

According to Bridget Brereton, movement and communication in 19th Century Trinidad were rather difficult and people wrote of the journey to Mayaro or to Blanchisseuse as if they were trying to discover the source of the river Nile. Farmers' produce would be rendered unfit for consumption by the time it reached the market. In the late 1890s there was a push to build and maintain roads and bridges. However, as was the case in other islands, many of the peasantry remained isolated in their remote villages well into the 20th Century. The exploration and discovery of oil in Trinidad was a dangerous and difficult process. In 1910 the lack of road or rail transport made the whole venture into a terrible battle with the forces of nature. All the heavy equipment required had to be hauled into place by human muscle power. Men and women dug and moved tons of dirt using the most primitive of tools, with the women carrying away the dirt on trays, which they balanced on top of their heads.

With the coming of the United States Armed Forces during World War II, many new roads were constructed in Trinidad and Tobago. The pitch lake at La Brea in Trinidad provided high quality pitch for the road surfacing, and is not only used in Trinidad &Tobago but also exported across the globe.

The tramcar was introduced into Jamaica in 1876 and for over 70 years people in Kingston Jamaica were transported around the city in tramcars. The trams were eventually phased out in 1948 and other roads were built over the tracks. When motor vehicles were introduced in the 20th Century, and more extensively after 1948, oil-surfaced or 'pitch' roads were introduced.

Although roads, even highways, have been built in several urban areas of the Caribbean, in Guyana and other parts of the Caribbean today, the condition of the roads leading to many farming communities are extremely poor. In Guyana many farms are located in the remote depths of lands that are actually below sea level. These lands are called polderlands. Roads are especially difficult to construct in this area of Guyana as the ground is watery and there are many rivers and canals that require bridges and culverts. There is a trail through the rainforest that leads to the Brazilian border that will eventually be developed into an all-weather road. Although the costal strip is well served with a road network there are many road improvement projects yet to be completed.

Fig 16.9 Tramcar

Water transport
Caribbean territories have existed more or less in isolation from one another. This bred insularity among the region's communities some of which are separated by a wide expanse of sea. During slavery, there was more sea communication between each territory and its respective 'Mother Country', and trade among Caribbean territories discouraged. But, inter-territorial trade existed, especially among Eastern Caribbean territories. Until the late 19th Century, sailing ships dominated transportation and communication between the Caribbean and European countries. By the middle of the 19th Century, steamships replaced ships that used sails. Metropolitan and colonial markets were drawn closer together and larger amounts of goods could be transported as steamships became larger. Steamships allowed international trade and transportation to develop. Refrigerated cargo ships enabled perishable goods to travel long distances without spoiling. Cable and wireless brought producers in almost instant touch with market conditions.

Economic diversification during the late 19th and early 20th Centuries made more trade possible among Caribbean territories. The formation of Caribbean Free Trade Association (CARIFTA) required and encouraged better means of inter-territorial transportation.

The degree to which water transport within each territory was used depended on the local geography of the territory. Canals in Guyana are used to carry produce and the rivers are used to transport people and goods. In Jamaica rivers are used mainly for washing, for supplying water and for recreation (for example, Dunn's River and Rio Grande). Coastal services also exist in Belize, Guyana and Jamaica. Boats operate to transport people and produce between islands in the northern, southern and eastern Caribbean, e.g. between Trinidad and Tobago; Nevis and St Kitts; Antigua and Barbuda; Grenada and the Grenadines; Guadeloupe and Marie Galante, etc. This is cheaper than air. Inter-island shipping is important in Belize (to her offshore cays) as well as in the Bahamas where the mail boat service between the Family Islands is indispensable.

Railway transport
In the early post-slavery period, railways were constructed in the colonies of Barbados, Jamaica, Guyana and Trinidad. These linked the centre of production, usually the plantations, with seaside ports. As railways were usually built along public roadways, they competed with road transport. This often meant that, both the railway and road transport operated at a loss and had to be subsidised by government. Recent increases in the speed and number

of motor vehicles have resulted in trains being phased out as a means of transporting goods and passengers.

In explaining the poor transportation and system of communication which existed in the Caribbean in 1922, Major Wood reported that his mission was made possible only because a British warship had been detailed for his use. He said that a letter from Trinidad to Jamaica had taken five and a half months to arrive, and that Jamaican letters to Barbados, Trinidad and Guyana were usually sent via New York, Halifax and England.

Air transport

In the 20th Century air transport (after World War II) became available and national and international airlines were organised. These have a major value in catering for the growing Caribbean Tourist trade. The major regional carriers are currently CUBANA, BWIA, LIAT, Air Caribbean and Air Jamaica. American Airlines serves Puerto Rico, the US Virgin Islands, the Dominican Republic and elsewhere. Guyana still relies heavily on light air transport owing to the difficulties encountered with road construction.

Radio and television communication

The introduction of radio and television communication brought entertainment and information from other societies into Caribbean homes. These media instilled new values as well as high expectations of a higher standard of living, which had a great impact on the social, economic and political aspirations of people during the 20th Century. People, who in the past were content with a typical 'Caribbean lifestyle', were now exposed to First World ideas.

5 Artistic life

Art-forms represent important aspects of a society's culture as they arise out of the creative expressions of a people. The people of the Caribbean are blessed with a great deal of creative talent. Their creative energies find expression in architecture, painting, sculpture, and the performing arts of music, theatre, dance and drama. There are also many Caribbean literary artists who have enriched mime, theatre, dance and drama with their narrative and poetry. In some territories, formal institutions and government ministries were created in order to facilitate research and encourage the development of the arts. In the 1960s formal arts institutions became concerned with the creation and development of national identities. For example, the Institute of Jamaica was established in 1879, although it initially focused more on the management of the arts,

literature and sciences of the colonial rulers. This role changed in the post-independence era.

These various art forms reflect the influence of the many cultures which have shaped Caribbean society. The indigenous people – with their rock art and objects made of gold, silver, jade, stone, bone, clay and wood – have influenced Caribbean art. Caribbean art forms have also been influenced by the religious-based drawings and paintings of the early African artists and craftspeople and European master painters to whom local artists were often apprenticed. Often, art forms in the Caribbean represent resistance against European cultural imperialism – that is, the attempts by the colonial powers to impose their own cultures on the Caribbean people even where those people were Indian, Chinese or African. Caribbean art also represents an attempt by different ethnic groups to express their own identity.

Caribbean artists can be intuitive, formally trained or learn directly from the practitioner. For example, some art forms are passed down from parents to children who learn by watching and practising. Apprenticeship is also practiced in jewellery, graphics and textiles. Formal art training started earlier in the Spanish Caribbean than in the British-colonised Caribbean; and even then, some territories were ahead of others. For example, while formal art training only began in Jamaica in the 20th Century, it was available at St Mary's College and at Queen's College in Trinidad during the 19th Century and was well represented by the great Trinidadian landscape painter Jean Michel Cazabon, who died in poverty in 1888.

Painting began to develop in Cuba in the second half of the 18th Century in the form of religious art. Cuban artists gained insight into the creation of landscapes that would evoke an emotional national identity through the Hudson River School of landscape painting. Esteban Chartrand (1840-1883) was the first artist to capture on canvas the characteristics of the Cuban landscape. In the 1940s the pioneers of formal art training in Suriname received their qualifications as art educators in the Netherlands. The next generation was directly influenced by Nola Hatterman from Amsterdam. In 1981 the Government of Suriname opened the first officially backed university, the Academy of Higher Education in Art and Culture. At this time there was a need to affirm political independence especially within the field of the creative arts.

Many of the artists who trained abroad, or who had European or American tutors, show traces of European and US influences, ranging from romantic and pastoral to figurative, architectural, abstract, expressionist and surreal. In sum, Caribbean art is a dynamic and organic mix of the creative energies of several different ethnic groups and ancestral influences.

Architecture

We can define architecture as the designing and building of structures in which people live or work or use for some other purpose. Architecture is a valuable cultural resource as all buildings carry a message from the past to the future.

Three factors influence the architecture of any region: tradition, availability of material, and climate. In Guyana, because there were floods during the rainy season, many houses were built on stilts. Access to them was gained through a stairway leading to the 'gallery' or veranda. Houses are also elevated in some parts of Trinidad and Suriname. While many Caribbean buildings do not always suit the climate – as they were built in the style of temperate climates without proper consideration to the climate and daily weather conditions of the tropics – others have taken into consideration the need for shade from the tropical sun, as well as a way to make use of it for maximum lighting. The indigenous peoples were more sensible and used materials that suited their lifestyle and environment.

Fig 16.10 Building in the Dutch style, Suriname

Materials used consist of indigenous hardwoods, like spruce, fir and pine (some of which are no longer available and roofing shingles are imported from North America); plant materials like reeds, palm, thatch and bamboo; stone (granite and marble are imported) bricks, mud daub, tapia, wattle and daub walling. Concrete, steel and slab structures came later in the 20th Century.

In terms of tradition, there is no single architectural history of the Caribbean – no unified Caribbean architecture. Rather, the architecture of the Caribbean consists of many influences: indigenous, African, Spanish colonial, French Creole, English, Danish, Dutch and Eastern styles. European styles were themselves influenced by the architecture of Greece, Rome and the East. The various influences are seen in the variety of

structures that are built: domestic buildings, (houses, large and small), commercial buildings, factories (especially on the plantations), military establishments (such as barracks and forts), churches, temples, mosques and public buildings (such as government/administrative buildings). Some influences have lasted longer than others, with indigenous architecture among the earliest to disappear. European, and later US, influences were the strongest, and to these were added African and Asian influences. It is important to note that the all pervasive terror and torture that were part of everyday life on the plantation, had an influence on the European buildings of the time. As late as 1730 the sugar planters surrounded themselves with defensive architecture. Many of the 18th Century plantation houses had gun-ports on the upper stories. In a society that was based on the violence of slavery, the European forms of architecture reverted to almost mediaeval level. The fortified farmhouse is an example of this.

African Influences

Africans not only provided the labour to build European houses and influenced the ways in which Europeans had to incorporate defensive mechanisms into the architecture of their houses, but also stamped their own influence on the houses they built for themselves. The Shotgun style home is one example. This house type is one room wide, one story tall and several rooms deep (usually three or more) and has its primary entrance in the gable end. Its perpendicular alignment breaks with the usual Euro-American pattern, in which the gables are on the sides and the entrance is on the façade or long side. Although gable-entry houses occur in some parts of central Africa, the shotgun house is a New World hybrid that developed in the Caribbean and entered the United States via New Orleans in the early 19th Century.

The Chattel house, found throughout the Eastern Caribbean and which had become commonplace by the early to mid 1800s, is another example of African architecture. The name is derived from the old feudal term for movable property. The chattel houses were easily moved because after 1838, in the Caribbean, the workers were free and could own the house but not own the land. They took their houses to where work was available.

African styles blended with European to form what is sometimes called a Creole style. The houses are raised off the ground and are set on stone or concrete pillars. They usually have two rooms and a veranda or porch at the front of the house.

The Cunucu houses found in Aruba represent yet another example. 'Cunucu' is a Papiamento word for countryside. This style reflects a blending of traditional

European and African building styles and techniques. The cunucu house has a central section with one or two side rooms and a kitchen extension. The walls of the houses are made of thick plaster and may originally have been made from wattle and daub.

In Cuba, the School of the Plastic Arts took the form of an African village that evoked the country's African heritage. Construction continued until 1965 when workers had to be diverted to other projects after the Cuban Missile crisis. The school was never completed. However, it eventually opened with only one or two buildings completed. After nearly thirty-five years there are plans now underway for the completion of this World Heritage Monument.

SPANISH ARCHITECTURE

There were four infusions of Spanish style architecture in the Caribbean: Gothic in the early period of settlement, Plateresque in the 16th Century, the late Renaissance and Baroque of the late 17th and 18th Centuries, and the Neo-classic in the late 18th and 19th Centuries. The Spanish used mahogany, which was native to Cuba and Hispaniola, to build houses, furniture and carvings. The woodwork in the Cathedral of Santo Domingo is still in excellent condition. Spanish houses were known for their wooden grills and railings on balconies and stairs. The Gothic style emerged in Santo Domingo in 1510 when a shipload of stone carvers and bricklayers arrived in the city.

In Cuba, the Baroque style can be seen in the house of Don Matio Pedroso, built in 1780 in what was referred to as the Plaza Nueva. Door frames with groupings of pilasters and engaged columns characterise this style. In houses influenced by Spanish architecture, artwork was used to add a decorative dimension. Old San Juan in Puerto Rico is an excellent example of a building influenced by Spanish architectural styles. Outstanding examples can also be seen in forts like El Morro and La Forteleza (where the present Governor lives), and in the façades of the houses. The old town hall in Trinidad reflects Spanish influence.

ENGLISH ARCHITECTURE

The English built in the Georgian style, seen in many great houses in the region. In the 19th Century the English popularised the sash window flanked on either side by jalousies. Other English contributions were the 'fretsaw' and decorative fretwork and cast iron (by the early 20th Century). The large plantation houses had the least cost constraints and were more elaborate than the houses of the working-class British people and the workers of the Caribbean. Noted ones in Jamaica are Rose Hall, Marlborough and Bellevue. English architectural styles are also evident in the commercial buildings of Bridgetown,

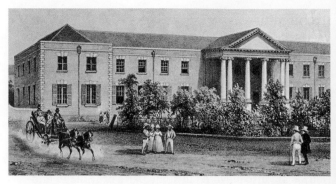

Fig 16.11 *The English Regency style*

Barbados, downtown Kingston, Jamaica, and Nassau in The Bahamas. Military establishments were built in stone.

Drax Hall and St Georges are thought to be two of the oldest homes in Barbados. They may have been built around 1650 to 1660. According to authors Fraser and Hughs, St Georges gives the impression of an English manor house with its formal garden and four corner fireplaces. Drax Hall has a steep carved hall archway of master wood.

When the English began to build in Trinidad and Tobago, Georgian architecture was in its heyday. Building materials included bricks imported from England and local stone. The Town House destroyed by fire in 1940 was a good example of this type of architecture. There were seven buildings around Woodford Square which displayed the different types of colonial architecture in Trinidad, among them:

- the old colonial fire brigade of Italianate influence
- the Red House of Renaissance influence
- the Ministerial building of Victorian influence
- the old Town Hall of Spanish influence
- Gretias Church of Gothic influence
- the Deanery of Georgian influence.

FRENCH ARCHITECTURE

Initially the French used classical forms derived from Italy. Later in the French Caribbean concrete and cement plaster became popular and clay blocks and hand-made blocks were used in place of timber frames. The use of concrete blocks led to the use of a flattened pitch roof and the doing away with the gable. A lower roof became dominant instead of the high gable.

DUTCH ARCHITECTURE

The Dutch produced their characteristic parapet and gabled façades in Curaçao and the other Dutch territories. The Brievengat 'land house', for example, has a tiled roof, dormer windows and massive shutters. Paramaribo, the capital city of Suriname, is rich in examples of Dutch architecture.

US ARCHITECTURE

We can see the US influence in what came to be called the 'balloon frame' technique (the buildings go up as quickly), which was popularised by George Washington Snow around the middle of the 19th Century. This style is used in the building of wooden houses with the 4 x 2 timber and nails. The American architectural influence intensified after World War II and can be seen in the somewhat bizarre hotels in tourist resorts. Trinidad has suffered the least from such influence.

The US settlers in Nassau established their own variations of Georgian architecture. Bahamian historian Gail Saunders tells us that Americans built elegant and luxurious mansions, churches and civic buildings on the eastern seaboard. The East Hill Club on East Hill is an example of this Georgian-colonial style. In 1783 houses in Nassau were built mainly of wood. Early in the 1800s Daniel McKinner introduced durable stone buildings.

Newly emancipated people in the 19th Century and early 20th Century were housed in structures built from mass produced timber from North America. Concrete 'box' houses with a low-hipped shed-roof replaced these in the later 20th Century.

ASIAN ARCHITECTURE

The arrival of Asians in the mid-19th Century further diversified Caribbean architectural styles with mosques and temples built in the Eastern architectural tradition.

ARCHITECTURE AND CLASS

When it comes to the construction of homes, there is a relationship between architecture and class. The houses of the people in the Caribbean reflect different architectural styles, the most elaborate being the houses of the elite and middle classes. The plantation workers usually lived in barrack style and chattel houses. As they moved into their own villages, they used other material and styles, but as Moore notes for Guyana, most of the houses were built for functional purposes rather than for style. Their houses were made out of local hardwoods, such as wallaba, greenheart or mora. Roofs were of ordinary pitch the sides were boarded around with white pine or American timber. Windows were wooden shutters and were not made of glass until much later. In rural Jamaica, the wattle and daub house persisted into the early 20th Century, though other material were used by some peasants.

The visual arts

INFLUENCES

The earliest painting and sculpture belonged to the era of the indigenous peoples who painted their bodies and decorated domestic articles with motifs. Their 'art tools' were flint, shell and stone. The enslaved Africans also had their distinctive art forms. They decorated masks, weapons, tools and costumes with impressive and original motifs and designs. The Haitians were noted for their paintings done in local dyes and paints from earth, clay and vegetables. They used these to decorate drums and other musical instruments. They were noted for their wood carving and modelling in clay. Religious art became an important aspect of Caribbean culture and was noted among African-Caribbean communities.

During slavery Caribbean planters mostly looked to Europe for their artistic commissions. The most important portraits of Jamaican landowners, for example, were done by people outside of the region. English neo-classical sculpture that decorated churches and statues were all done abroad and imported. John Bacon was responsible for the Rodney Memorial in Spanish Town, Jamaica. The enslaved were exposed to mission schools art and handicraft were compulsory subjects.

Immigration introduced Asians who also influenced Caribbean art. Hindus use the folk art of painting decorative patterns on portions of walls and floors for ritualistic and ceremonial purposes. These paintings which depict, among other things, animals and mythological figures, are called *Chowk* (or *Kohbar*) and *Alpana*. They are done with natural dyes and paste of powder or lime, flour and rice.

PAINTING AND SCULPTURE: A SAMPLE OF ARTISTS

Painting and sculpture were, and remain, important artistic expressions and the region has produced a number of painters and sculptures. The painting tradition that developed in the British-colonised Caribbean began with travelling artists who came to the region to paint landscapes and portraits of planters. These included

Fig 16.12 An example of the art of 'Kapo' Reynolds

George Robertson who came to Jamaica (1773), James Hakewell (1825), Isaac Belisario (1835), Fredric Church (1860), and A S Forrest (1902).

The early 19th Century saw talented local artists being influenced by the European school. Among these were Michael Cazabon (1813–1888) of Trinidad, James Cockburn of Barbados, and Percy Justyne of Grenada. The early 20th Century saw the rise of the self-taught artists like Jamaican John Dunkley, David Miller Sr and David Miller Jr, and Mallica 'Kapo' Reynolds. 'Kapo' was inspired to take up sculpting in the 1940s, and formed his own church. Before he died, he was considered one of the top six living self-taught painters in the world. His art, like that of Dunkley and the Millers, is called 'intuitive' because he did not have formal training. His work was featured in the 1983 Smithsonian travelling exhibition of Jamaican art. John Dunkley produced some 45 canvasses and is considered by some to have been Jamaica's greatest painter. It is elitist to divide painters in this way.

Art in Jamaica

Edna Manley (wife of Norman Manley and mother of Michael Manley) became an essential part of the artistic movement in Jamaica in the 1930s. The Jamaican artistic tradition, specifically the field of sculpture, benefited from her arrival. Among her best-known pieces are 'Negro Aroused' (1935), 'The Prophet', 'Young Negroes', 'The Diggers' and 'Horses of the Morning'. 'Kapo' Reynolds and Alvin Marriot were also well-known Jamaican sculptors.

After 1940 institutes for formal art classes were established. This, together with Edna Manley's mentorship, caused a new generation of artists to evolve in Jamaica, among them Albert Huie, Henry Daley and David Pottinger. They laid the foundation for an indigenous iconography by focusing on Jamaican landscapes and themes. In the 1950s groups of independent artists emerged in Jamaica, some self-taught, but uninfluenced by Manley and the Institute of Jamaica group. They included Gloria Escoffey and Carl Abrahams who painted the classic 'Last Supper' in 1955. The post-independence era saw the dominance of painters like Barrington Watson, Karl Parboosingh (born in Jamaica and educated in New York, Paris and Mexico City) and Eugene Hyde.

Art in Barbados

Karl Broodhagen, a contemporary of Edna Manley as well as of Carlisle Chang and Sybil Atteck of Trinidad, is Barbados' best-known sculptor. He was born in colonial Guyana in 1909 and, along with his mother, emigrated to Barbados in his teens in 1924. He worked as a tailor for years before focusing on painting and sculpture. Some of his early works include a bust of the Barbadian writer

George Lamming (1945) and Grantley Adams. More recent figures include those of Bussa, leader of the 1816 revolt of the enslaved in Barbados, and the late Dame Nita Barrow. Golde White (1890–1977) and Aileen Hamilton (1907–1987) are important to the establishment of art in Barbados. The Barbados Museum and Historical society has over a thousand items from Hamilton in every technique, but mostly works on paper. White preferred watercolour and depicted the inner life of people as it is reflected in their outward features. Apart from 'Kapo', all these other sculptors had formal training. For example, Broodhagen studied at Goldsmith's College in London. There are many ordinary people in Barbados, as in the rest of the Caribbean, who sculpt and sell their art but who are not recognised by the artistic world. The tourist industry has helped these ordinary people who display their works along well-traveled roadways in an effort to attract business.

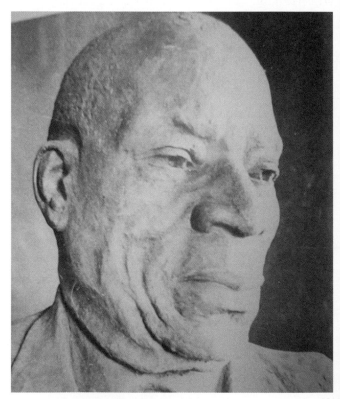

Fig 16.13 Karl Broodhagen

St Lucia

An important local St Lucian painter was Harold Simmons. His art was influenced by local folk tradition, which he studied. He was also responsible for encouraging Derek Walcott as a painter, lending him his studio. Dunstan St Omer, a contemporary of both Simmons and Walcott became the first eminent St Lucian modernist painter. He was famous for his church murals.

HAITI

Haitian art, like that of the Dominican Republic and Puerto Rico, is internationally recognised. Haitian intuitive paintings are highly valued. There are a number of factors that distinguish Haitian art from other art. One important factor was the country's early independence which allowed Haitians to maintain their West African beliefs and traditions free from outside interference. Another factor was that the visual arts, along with oral tradition, were the main forms of cultural expression and the main way people passed on their culture. These factors have influenced the themes used in Haitian art, especially in the art of the intuitive. Those artists who were trained in France expressed little of the indigenous spirit of the country. In contrast, the establishment in 1944 in Port-au-Prince of Le Centre d'Art helped Haitian visual arts to flourish. Haitian artists explore Africa-Caribbean themes and many use the expressions of voodoo in their paintings and sculpture. The sculptor Georges Liautaud, for example, transformed the Christian cross so that it became also a *veve*, a spiritual symbol of voodoo. Among the best known Haitian artists are Hector Hypolite, Philome Obin, Jasmin Joseph, Rigaud Benoit, Wilson Bigaud and Paul Claude Gardere.

CUBA

Cuba has an impressive artistic tradition. Some of the artists, especially after the 1959 revolution, focused their work on their own country even though some have been trained outside of Cuba. There is also a great deal of freedom of expression in the art produced in Cuba. Religious influences are also evident in Cuban art. Santeria and Palo Monte (also known as Conga Rule) are the two main Afro-Cuban ritual systems that influenced the arts.

Did you know?

People originally from the Congo followed Conga Rule Palomante religious ceremonies dealing with natural forces.

Among Cuban artists are Wilfredo Lam, Manuel Mendive (1944-), Jose Bedia, Juan Francisco Elso Padilla, Jose Manuel Fors and Leandro Soto. Wilfredo Lam (1902-1982), son of a Chinese father and Mulatto mother, was considered Cuba's leading painter. He studied at the San Alejandro Academy from 1918-22 and in 1942 was heavily influenced by African themes, for example, santeria. This was no surprise as he grew up in an environment where santeria was a part of everyday life. One of his best-known works is 'The Jungle' (1943). Mendive also used this tradition of

santeria in his work, which is described by some as an actual extension of the santeria ceremony.

Did you know?

Santeria, also known as Ocha Rule, came from Yoruba culture in Nigeria. The worship is focused on a group of gods connected to different myths. Some of these gods include Olofin and Olodduware.

Fig 16.14 *Painting by Cuban artist Wilfredo Lam*

ART IN TRINIDAD AND TOBAGO

It would be impossible to include in this text all the important artists in Trinidad & Tobago, for the list of Abstract artists, Realists, Intuitives, watercolourists, muralists and sculptors is long. We will highlight a few. Cazabon is an important figure in the history of art in Trinidad & Tobago. Son of a mulatto migrant from Martinique, Jean Michel Cazabon was born in Naparima on the outskirts of San Fernando. His parents sent him to school at St. Edmund's College in Ware, England in 1826. He then went to Paris with the intention of studying medicine. However, he switched to art, and studied with Paul De La Rouce. Jean Michel returned to Trinidad in 1850 with his French wife and two daughters. In 1860 he migrated to Saint-Pierre in Martinique. He moved back to Trinidad in 1870, where he taught art at Queen's Royal

College and St. Mary's College. He lived his last days in relative poverty and died in 1888 of heart disease while working on a painting.

Boscoe Holder, who by the 1960s had established himself as one of the leading artists not only in Trinidad but also throughout the Caribbean region, was born in Port of Spain in the 1920s. He began painting at age five. He was also interested in music and dancing and as a teenager he formed his own dance company. Dances such as shango, bongo and bélé influenced his paintings, and his dancers (including his wife, Sheila Clarke) were often models for his paintings. His black consciousness, developed out of travels to New York, Martinique and London, also influenced his paintings.

Fig. 16.15 Painting by Boscoe Holder

Geoffrey Holder, Boscoe's younger brother, is also an artist. As a child he used to borrow his older brother's paints. He did ten paintings that were shown in the Trinidad Public Library. Geoffrey continued painting and by 1954 had his first successful one-man show in New York at the Barone Gallery. In 1957 he was awarded a Guggenheim Fellowship in art and this gave him the time and resources to paint. He has done two large murals, both in Trinidad – one at the Trinidad-Hilton Hotel and one at the UWI. His style is 'impressionistic', drawing from the influence of French settlers from the island of Martinique.

Sybil Atteck commenced her career as an artist making botanical drawings. She studied with the German Expressionist, Max Beckman, and was influenced by the birth of the new nation and the hopes and aspirations of her people. In 1955 she was the first artist from the Caribbean region to have her work shown at the Royal Academy.

CERAMICS AND OTHER CRAFTS

In the pre-colonial period, the production of crafts across the region drew from the natural resources that were available and the items produced were both artistic and functional. There is much archaeological evidence of the crafts of the early people. For example, the remains of pottery in Trinidad & Tobago that date back more than 2,000 years, have been found. However as the European system of domination emerged, the artisans and craftspeople that managed to survive remained on the edges of the emerging colonial society. By the 18th Century, the major craftspeople were African and European; but it is possible that in the early stages of plantation life the indigenous people shared their knowledge, skills and craft techniques with other groups, who then incorporated them in their own crafts. Some of the early craft items were utilitarian articles for life on the plantation. For example, baskets were used on the plantation for everything from carrying manure and dirt, to germinating crops and carrying produce. Pottery was used to store water and food as well as for cooking.

The post-slavery period was a prolific one for craft production in all territories, with territories like the British Windwards, Haiti and Santo Domingo – where there were descendants of the Taino, Kalinago and African Maroons – projecting these influences in their products. Kalinago influences are evident in craft items in Dominica, St Lucia, and St Vincent; and Garifuna and Maya influences were obvious in Belizean crafts. African themes heavily influenced Haitian craft. The influx of other ethnic groups to the post-slavery Caribbean diversified the types of craft items produced. For example, Hindu and Muslim influences are obvious in Trinidad & Tobago, Guyana and Suriname.

There were certain noted craftsmen and women in the Caribbean in the period up to 1962. Cecil Baugh (who got his early training from potters along Mountain View avenue) and Ma Lou and her daughter, were noted Jamaican potters. To a certain extent the craft producers of the Caribbean satisfy the quaint and picturesque requirements of the tourist trade; but they also produce decorative and functional items for the Caribbean market: pottery, calabash utensils, dinner ware, drinking vessels, vases, masks, busts, tiles, ashtrays and other ceramic objects. Clay 'yabba' pots and flower pots are popular items.

The performing arts

MUSICAL FORMS AND INSTRUMENTS: INFLUENCES

The Caribbean musical heritage is the result of the mixing of rhythms from Africa and Europe, the Caribbean itself, Asia and modern America. Caribbean music ranges from traditional folk music like Puerto Rican aguinaldo and

Jamaican mento to more modern salsa and reggae. The West African contrapuntal music, with its cross rhythms and its heavy down beat is also present in European musical forms whether they are from Spain (the pasillo), from Scotland (the jig and reel), or the quadrille from France. It is impossible to make sense of the study of these European musical forms in the Caribbean without carefully studying the African music from which they are derived. Most of the African-derived music is religious or semi-religious/semi-ritualistic. The music of the Nigerian Yorubas dominates the ceremonies of the santeria of Cuba, the shango of Trinidad, the saraca of Grenada and the vodoun of Haiti. This music has kept its African character over centuries. In these ceremonies the leader chants a line and the rest of the congregation – the chorus – responds. Some types of music in Trinidad, like the parang, reflect the Hispanic influence, although some songs are sung in English.

TYPES OF MUSIC

The styles and cultural origins of Caribbean music are as diverse as the people. Music in the Caribbean can be divided into three very broad categories: folk, classical and popular.

Folk Music: The folk forms of the Caribbean tell us about daily life and significant events of the past as well as reflect the attitudes and values of the people. The folk forms that originate from Africa tend to consist of call and response vocals and harmonies combined with the use of percussion instruments. This category includes the Cuban traditional rumba, Puerto Rican bomba, and music associated with African Caribbean religions such as Haitian Vodoun, Cuban Santeria , Trinidadian Shango, Jamaican Kumina and Surinamese Winti. Other folk music reflects a more European ancestry; for example, Puerto Rican jíbaro music and Cuban punto are both influenced by classical Spanish music, featuring the guitar and other plucked instruments such the quatro.

Some ring-games rhythms and ring-play songs demonstrate a mix of both African and European origins. The leading folk singer from modern day Barbados, the Mighty Gabby, has written hundreds of songs since the age of 15. Much of his work has its foundation in distinctive Caribbean Folk rhythms, with lyrics that enable the listener to visualise the colourful sights of the Caribbean islands. His music demonstrates his wide range of talents as an actor, a writer, calypsonian and folk singer. Not only has the Mighty Gabby been a consistent and prolific creator of folk songs and hit calypsos, but he has also commanded his piece of calypso history with the title of

the youngest calypsonian when he won the Calypso Monarch title in Barbados.

The mento is the original folk music created by Jamaicans. It is all encompassing in its use of instruments. It is a form in which everyday life, community concerns, and political directions are presented with touches of humour. The musicians use a combination of instruments ranging from saxophones, flutes, bamboo fifes, violins, banjos and bamboo fiddles rather like the berimbao, a Brazilian instrument originally from Angola. Rumba boxes, double basses, shac-shac and drums are played both with sticks and the hands. Most Caribbean territories have their own folk choirs such as the Grenada National

Fig 16.16 Calypsonian Adonijah

Folk Group and the award-winning Guyana Police Male Voice Choir that was established in 1944.

Folk music is kept alive by cultural agencies, schools' participation in festivals and events, as well many rural folk who still create their own entertainment in spite of advances in technology.

In the post 1938 period Caribbean folk music also began to reflect elements of South Asian folk music. Folk songs are sung all over the Caribbean and are a way that people remember and record special events, especially funerals.

Classical Music: in the 19th Century formally trained composers in Cuba and Puerto Rico began to create distinctively local forms of light classical music such as the contradanza or habanera, as well as the danzon and Puerto Rican danza. In the early 20th Century Cuba produced several distinguished classical composers like Ernesto Lecouna and Amadeo Roldán. In Jamaica Samuel Felsted, who was possibly taught to play the organ by Samuel Patch from Kingston, and John Raymond from Port Royal became the organist at the St Andrew Parish Church in his twenties. He held the post until 1783. He died in 1802, and nothing further seems to be recorded of his personal life or career. In keeping with the desire of the colonisers to preserve their culture, James Thomas Dunhill visited Jamaica in 1910 with his chamber music orchestra.

Trinidadian born Hazel Scott (b. 1920) began playing the piano aged three and by the age of seven was performing in New York City where she received a scholarship to study at the Juilliard School of Music. Hazel went on to become one of the foremost pianists in the USA.

Carrying on the varied Caribbean 'classical' musical tradition is Theodore and his group The Sunshine Violin Band. Theodore was born in Choiseul, St Lucia, in 1934. As a child, an accident forced him to stay at home for weeks and his uncle's eldest son lent him his own violin to play to help pass the time. This started his musical career. Theodore and The Sunshine Band now play and reside in Europe and keep strong the Caribbean musical traditions that fuse classical with folk.

In Trinidad, Prime Minister Eric Williams wanted to bring steel pan to a wider audience by arranging for adjudicators to come from England for the festivals. One such judge was Professor John Russell. The judges were amazed when they realised that the musicians were performing intricate classical music on steel drums, combined with the fact that the majority of the musicians had never seen a musical score, especially not one written for pan. The pan men and women gained access to the classical music by listening to the radio and hoping that a particular piece would be played often enough to learn all

of it. At that time no tape recorders were available. The musical director would listen to the radio then teach the band each section, translating the conventional instruments of the orchestra into the various voices of the different pans. Classical music was said to give pan a degree of respectability and to this day you can still hear classical pan live and on the road, especially during the Jouvert celebrations.

Pop Music: the best known forms of Caribbean music are the modern popular genres which by the 1930s and 1940s were already more widely listened to than the folk forms. The gramophone record and the radio helped to bring music from Europe, the USA and South America to the Caribbean region. Bebop, Jazz, Blues and later rock and roll from the USA as well as the African influenced tango and samba from South America all had a significant

Fig 16.17 Bob Marley

Chapter 16 | *Caribbean civilisation 2: work, leisure and artistic culture*

impact on the popular music of the region. A popular music force to be reckoned with in the Caribbean was Perez Prado, one of the founders of mambo. Prado grew up in Cuba and worked with the casino orchestras in Havana for most of the 1940s. In 1948 he moved to Mexico to form his own band and to record for RCA. After 1963 RCA stopped releasing his music in the USA. Popular Caribbean music styles continued to evolve with the global movement of musicians. The son, mambo, cha cha cha, bolero, salsa and meringue are now popular world wide. Cadence – Lypso, popularly referred to as 'cadence', has been defined as a mixture of African musical patterns that has its roots firmly in the Caribbean and can be found in Martinique and Guadeloupe along with zouk music that combines elements of jazz funk. Cross-over rhythms continue and in the Commonwealth Caribbean, Jamaican reggae and Trinidadian calypso were the most popular in the 1960s.

Reggae music evolved from mento, ska and rock steady. Reggae is sometimes used as a term to refer to all Jamaica popular music since 1960; however, it refers to a particular style of music that has different types of beat and phrasing. Some of the great pioneers of reggae music in Jamaica include Bunny Wailer, Toots Hibbert (who is credited with the first use of the word 'reggae' in 1968 in 'Do the Reggay'), Robert Nesta Marley, Peter Tosh, Dennis Brown, Jacob Miller, Burning Spear, Bob Andy, John Holt and Jimmy Cliff. The lyrics of reggae often reflect the historical past, the artist's philosophy and protest against social ills.

Calypso: although Calypso music is mostly associated with Trinidad and Tobago, it is played in almost all Caribbean territories. It has a West African origin, although there is some debate about the first Caribbean island on which it evolved. The most popular belief is that the word 'calypso' comes from the Hausa word 'kaiso', which means 'bravo' or 'well done'. On hearing a good calypso, people still shout, 'Kaiso! Kaiso!' Other people, however, say calypso came from the Carib 'cariso' (the war song of the Caribs). (The chanteulle – the leader of the song or chant – was the first calypsonian and he enriched other musical forms called the belair and kalinda, which were music used to accompany the stick fights, with men drumming and women chanting.) Earlier calypsos were used to ridicule enslavers. When slavery was abolished, the calypsonian was still seen as someone who championed the cause of the masses in song as he often mocked and 'chastised' those in authority for social ills. The European people looked down on calypsonians and classed them as the lower orders of society. They also disapproved of the activities surrounding the calypso performances at carnivals. Some calypsonians became masqueraders, leaders and participants in the carnival. Calypsos were first sung in Creole and only from around 1898 in English. Early calypsonians in Trinidad were called Attila the Hun and Philip Garcia (the Executer). Trinidad and Tobago has boasted a long list of internationally acclaimed calypsonians, including Lord Kitchener (born Aldwyn Roberts in East Trinidad in 1922), the Mighty Sparrow (the Grenadian born Slinger Francisco who later moved to Trinidad and who is famous for songs such as 'Jean and Dinah'), Hollis Liverpool ('The Mighty Chalkdust', so named because he was a school teacher) and David Rudder.

Fig 16.18 The Mighty Sparrow

Kitchener first started singing aged 14 in 1936 and by age 16 he was a full-time calypsonian. In the 1930s and 40s the singers had to follow the rule of being a gentleman in the calypso tent and wear a jacket and tie. Lord Kitchener kept up this tradition throughout his whole career. In 1947 he left Trinidad to tour the Caribbean and the UK. He landed in Tilbury in 1948 onboard the legendary *Empire Windrush* and was filmed singing a tune that he had just written on the boat – 'London Is The Place For Me'.

Influenced by Jazz and the African Shango, David Michael Rudder from Belmont, Trinidad, is a legendary artist and entertainer. He began singing at age 10 and later joined a group called The Solutions. His first ever song was

Fig 16.19 David Rudder

basic ... musical form using only the human voice into a sophisticated total experience that combines voice, orchestration and to one degree or another, elements of costuming, dance'. Calypso is created, sung and performed in many territories including Barbados, Jamaica and the Leeward and Windward Islands.

Women in calypso

Women have always been the subject of calypsos. According to Elma Reyes they are portrayed as money-crazy, promiscuous, and evil schemers. These negative images changed when women became calypsonians, and in 1980 a male calypsonian, Scrunter, deplored rape in his 'Take the number' – 'Lady Jane ... send those rapemen to gaol'. Up to 1962 it was rare to have female performers. Women were involved in calypso but information about them before the 1960s is scarce. Still, it is known that in the 1880s in Trinidad, 'Cariso Jane' and 'Petite Belle Lily' were known to be names of female calypsonians. This neglect or absence of female calypsonians inspired this song by Marvelous Marva in 1991:

> where is the woman
> where is the woman... I want to know
> where is the woman of calypso
> is she neglected
> is she neglected in Trinbago.
> (Rudolph Ottley, *Women in Calypso*, 1992)

In Trinidad in 1952 there was a group called Girl Pat Steel Orchestra. The members were Hazel Henley, Irma Waldron, Celia Didier, Elie Robertson, Joyce Forde, Norma Brathwaite and Eugene Gowan. Gemma Worrell played for Desperados and Savoys in the 1960s. Even earlier, Daisey James began to play pan in 1944 when at the age of six she

Mother Earth in the late sixties. Some of his big hits include, 'This is Madness', 'The Hammer', 'Rally Round The West Indies' and the biggest selling 'High Mas'. In 1986 he created history by being the first and only person to win the Trinidad and Tobago Calypso Monarch, Young Kings and Road March all in the same year.

Calypso is not unique to Trinidad and Tobago, and each territory has its famous calypsonian. For example, calypso in St Lucia seems to have started in the late 1940s. Some older calypso fans say they recall a man called Battle Axe, a sailor, who sang about the 1948 fire. Other early calypsonians included Ezekiel from Conway, and Piti Quart (a Vincentian) who used to sing calypso on the streets. There are also the Mighty Cobra, Mighty Blake, Lord Rock and Roll and the Mighty Session. The pioneer of steel bands in St Lucia is said to have been one 'Scrubb'.

By the 1950s calypso gradually became integrated into carnival. The Mighty Terror (Theodore McGriffiths) became famous for winning the calypso song competition five times between 1957 and 1961. Kendal Hippolyte says that, 'in the last 40 years calypso has grown in St Lucia from a

Fig 16.20 Tobagonian Calypso Rose

Chapter 16 | *Caribbean civilisation 2: work, leisure and artistic culture*

saw her brother Fitzroy with a pan. She did this without her mother's knowledge or approval. In 1951 Hazel Henley got together with Pat Maurice to start Girl Pat – the first female steel band in Trinidad, consisting of middle class women, all of whom had some piano lessons. This group played at the US base in Chaguaramas, in the Little Carib and at parties. They even visited Guyana in 1951 and Jamaica in 1952. Their travel was stopped because the Education Department would not give them leave to 'play pan'. Girl Pat was short-lived and broke up in 1958.

Since then, women like the Tobagonian Calypso Rose (Linda McArthur Sandy Lewis) have become famous. She is regarded as the mother of calypso and has been singing calypso since 1968. Others joining this early group were Lady Jane, Singing Francine and Singing Diane. Not all of these women use female-centred lyrics.

Steel bands

The steel band is also a distinctive musical art form. Steel bands are said to have originated in the bobolee bands, which came into being in the 1860s and 1870s. These were made up of people of all ages and ethnic groups who beat images of Judas Iscariot on Good Fridays and participated in other celebrations. These bands supplied music for revellers on carnival day in Trinidad. Their instruments were pans – dustbins, paint tins, etc. – and so they were called 'pan bands'. This term was used up to the 1930s, but it was renamed the steel band in the 1940s. There were also the bamboo stick bands and the tamboo bamboo. They used the bomb, the cutter, the foules (all made out of bamboo), the gin bottle and table spoon which preceded the steel bands. The police later banned revelry in which sticks were used.

Like their predecessors, steel bands provided music for revellers at carnival time. From paint and garbage pans, zinc sheets and motorcar brake hubs, biscuit drums, steel bands now use oil drums.

Fig 16.21 Steelpan

The Indian influence in Caribbean music

The Indians brought with them instruments such as the mridangam and dholak (a double-ended drum played by hand), nagara (drum played with sticks); tasa (portable drum tied around the player's waist and played with sticks); and majeera (cymbals). The harmonium and tabla were introduced in the 1950s (at least in Jamaica). Some of these instruments are no longer available, but the dholak and tasa are still popular Indian drums.

Indian music consists of classical, light, modern, and folk. In Jamaica, until the 1950s, classical music like bhairavi, thumri, dadra, todi, rag malhar and rag basant were sung. Not many Indo-Jamaicans can still sing classical Indian music, but new arrivals have revived this musical form. Mercia singing (mourning songs) was the major activity during hosay, but has gradually been replaced by other songs among the Indo-Jamaicans. New types of classical songs have emerged in Trinidad: the dhrupad, tilana, thumri, gazal, marfat, behag, kafi, piloo, dadra and bhairavi. Some famous pioneers of Indian music in Trinidad are Phiramat, Imami, Ramcharan, and Dharam.

Folk music has always been popular among Indo-Jamaicans, mostly in Oudhi and Bhojpuri dialects with songs that are suitable for rainy days and weddings, etc. Some are love songs or devotional songs. Folk songs, like the kajri or work songs, were popular among the indentured workers and workers in the rice fields. Other folk music were pisoni (songs of women grinding grains on the jata or handmill), the panihari songs of the water carriers, and kohar songs of the potters.

The Raga system is the backbone of all Indian music. This is a melodic order or scale in which a series of notes are employed in a particular formation and upon which a musical composition is based. Indian music is melodic – that is, a singer or musician does not have to depend on aids like harmony or counterpoint as in western music. Another essential element is improvisation. Indian music is not easily notated so that keyboard instruments like the piano are unsuited to play Indian music.

The music now enjoyed by most Indians and lovers of Indian music is the modern contemporary music which has developed out of classical and folk music. This has been influenced by the Indian film industry. The first Indian film to be shown in Trinidad was *Bala Joban* in 1935. The movie songs and dances have had a great influence on Indo-Trinidadians.

There are similarities in the musical forms in Trinidad, Guyana and Suriname, although these may have deviated somewhat from pure Indian, sub-continental musical forms. Indian music and songs have not survived to the same extent in places like Jamaica, which have smaller Indian communities. In the 1950s well-known singers were

Lachman Suragh, Ramlal Malgai and Dukhi Ramsamooj who sang classical songs. Young Indo-Jamaican singers are now influenced by the classical music of Trinidad and Guyana and Indian film music.

INDIAN CHUTNEY MUSIC

It was the 1930s that saw the first signs of an Indian presence in the calypso. But Indians initially appeared in calypsos as exotic figures. For example, the Duke of Normandy sang:

> *after she gave me paratha / she had me coorjai.*

In *Dookani* (1939), in the second verse, Attila boasts that:

> *She was exotic, kind and loving too. All her charms I could never describe to you. When she smiled her face lit up rapturously. Radiating joy, life and vitality.*

By the 1980s, Indians themselves were singing calypsos; and it was the Indians that evolved the Chutney musical style. The village of Penal was the origin of Trinidad's very first South Asian, female calypsonian Drupatee. She migrated to Port of Spain in 1987 with the melodic cross-over rhythms of Chutney Soca. Drupatee was a Chutney singer of some reputation and Chutney Soca became the beat of the late 1980s and early '90s moving also into the area of Chutney Soca Parang. It is said that Chutney music originated from the female musical ritual of the Mathkor ceremony in Indian weddings.

Drupatee Ramgoonai received acclaim locally and in Port of Spain with her smash hit single 'Pepper Pepper'

Fig 16.22 Drupatee Ramgoonai

where she describes the life of an Indian housewife. Her acclaim, however, was not without its critics who thought that Drupatee was throwing away her high upbringing and culture by entertaining in the Carnival tents.

DANCE: INFLUENCES

Dance has always been an integral part of the lives of Caribbean people, from indigenous times to the present. Caribbean dance and dance theatre are distinctive in content, style, and technical potential and demonstrate a variety of ethnic influences.

During slavery, Africans brought their dances to the Americas and used them to keep their cultural tradition and the memory of Africa alive. Among their dances in the 18th Century were the ring shout or ring dance, the caldena, the chica and the juba. The juba was a jig-like competitive dance in which dancers challenged one another to demonstrate their agility and rhythmic abilities. The caldena and chica were sensual dances which horrified the conservative European elites. Another dance was the bele – a dance in which the enslaved mocked the European people and sexually teased them for misusing their bodies. This dance had a French influence and continued after emancipation.

The Spanish influence is seen in the castillian and the sebucan or maypole. Trinidad, which was nearby, was also influenced by Venezuelan dances, such as the galleron, the joroppo and manzenaries. The English influence is seen in the minuet, waltz, the lancers, the quadrille, the polka, maypole (English style as distinct from the Spanish style) and other courtly dances. Both adults and children perform the maypole dance. In Haiti the French influence can be seen in dances such as Le Bal des Afframetis, Le Bal Champêtre, Le Minuet, La Contradanse while the Bele and Pique in Trinidad also show French influence.

The Scots have left their influence in the jig and the reel as well as in the heel and toe. The 'Bouquet Ball', which is partly dance, partly theatre, is common in some parts of the Caribbean. Couples dance a round dance (roundel) passing under a bouquet of cut flowers suspended from the roof. When the music suddenly stops, the couple exactly under the bouquet must take responsibility for hosting the next ball.

Classical ballet is an art form that shows Russian and English influences and is considered 'high art'. Many middle class people still encourage their daughters (hardly their boys) to take ballet classes. Those in Trinidad who influenced ballet were Helena Dunn and Pamela Chizzola.

In the modern period several individuals have contributed to the development of Caribbean dance, putting it on the local and international stage. These people include Beryl McBurnie, Percy Horde, Helena Dunn,

Fig 16.23 Beryl McBurnie

Pamela Chizzola, Pearl Primus, Boscoe and Geoffrey Holder of Trinidad, Ivy Baxter (Jamaica), Rex Nettleford (Jamaica), Lavinia Williams, Katherine Dunham, Jean Leon Destine (Haiti) and Alicia Alonso (Cuba). Pearl Primus, who trained as an anthropologist, contributed much to African-American dance research. She began presenting her choreography of African and African-American themes in the 1940s. Indian classical dances have been revitalised by Rajkumar Krishna Persad, Satnarine and Mondira Balkaran and the Pawas of Trinidad.

African influence

Traditional dances that developed in the Caribbean received a boost with the Black Power movement of the 1960s. These dances are part of religious ritual, ring games and action songs, and have a strong African influence. In Jamaica, the National Dance Theatre Company (NDTC), directed by Rex Nettleford, was formed in 1962. It has done much to develop an appreciation for traditional dance in the island and to take it to the international stage. Certain traditional dance forms are associated with specific territories. Many of these reflect African influences, such as kumina, pocomania, etu, tambu,

gerrah, dinki-minnie, zion, revival, and rastafarian dances in Jamaica. In Haiti the voudoun, congo and juba are famous, with the vodoun dance being the most popular. The drums and dances and the animal sacrificial rituals are part of vodoun ceremonies.

The santería is associated with Cuba, in Trinidad the shango, and in Guyana the cumfah all demonstrate African influence. In the French speaking islands the main traditional dances were the calender and the belair. In Grenada in the 1880s, 'Old Congo Negroes' performed a solemn ring dance. This involved stamping of feet, clapping of hands, bowing of heads and chanting. This was not as lively as the calender and belair and was perhaps religious in nature.

Did you know?

The word *belair* was also used to mean the calypso-like satirical song that was sung as part of the *belair* dance.

The que que dance in Berbice, Guyana, was Igbo in origin and involved drumming songs and dancing in a circle. The Raccoon was a traditional dance in Guyana. It was accompanied by drumming to provide the rhythm for the chants of dancers and audience. Another African-Guyanese dance was the S'iku of the Yoruba. People of Coromantee and Congo descent held their own dances with different steps and drum beats. National dances of this kind were also evident in Grenada and Carriacou. In St Lucia, after the abolition of slavery, the Creoles were organised into two societies for dancing: the Roses and the Marguerites. Each had kings and queens and a chantrelle who clapped and sang belairs at public dances. The leading dance was the bamboula, held outdoors and accompanied by drums.

Jamaican traditional dances include the dinki-mini (now confined to the parish of St Mary), Brag and Queen party, Brukins party, Etu, Pocomania, Gere/gerreh, Hosay, Mento, Shay shay, Tambu, Kumina, John Canoe (Jonkanu) or Burru, and Revival. Dinki-mini is usually performed to cheer the bereaved on the second and eighth night of the traditional 'nine night observances'. It takes the form of singing to lively mento music.

In the Brag and Queen party, the Brag is the processional dance done on the way to the Queen party. It is associated with Tea Meetings and it serves the function of introducing the queen at the Brukins party. In Portland only the Brukins party was associated with the celebration of the anniversary of Emancipation in the British Caribbean on 1 August. It is a dipping, gliding dance typified by the thrust and recovery action of the hip and leg. Time dancers were couples dressed in either red or blue, from the red and blue sets of the enslaved of the plantation era. A feature of the brukins dance is the king and queen who wear crowns of gold or silver paper. Different parts of the body are engaged in different movements (a clear African influence) and the dancers perform in a contest between Kings and Queens of both sets. Famous Brukins songs are 'Recreation around the Booth' and 'Queen Victoria Set Me Free, this is the year of jubalee'. The dance step of the Mento is a series of sideways, backways and turning two steps. Mento is often part of the Maypole and Quadrille dances. Kumina is associated with wakes and funerals but can also be performed at births and anniversaries. Dance and music are two strong features of Kumina and the drum playing is essential. White rum and special incantations are often used to anoint the players and instruments before the start of the Kumina ceremony.

The Jonkanu or Burru is another Jamaican dance of African origin that survived into the post-slavery period. It is a feature of the Christmas celebrations. It has dancers who wear masks and costumes and who dance steps that at times match what they represent. It emerged around 1700. When it started it involved men and women, but after Emancipation only men were involved, though they impersonated female characters. The Pocomania dance is also very popular and is used by the NDTC performances.

It is associated with obeah and takes its steps, rhythm and styles from the pocomania religion, which is peculiar to Jamaica.

Indian and Chinese dance

The indentured Indians probably had no knowledge of classical Indian dance. Rather, folk dance was their way of expressing moods, feelings and happy occasions. In Muslim culture dancing was not popular except among elite classes of women. In Jamaica, up to 1921, only men did the dancing. Women became involved later on, especially with new migration from India. By 1974 there were trained female Indian dancers in Jamaica.

One of the popular folk dances performed by the Indians was called Naach. This involved a male dancer in a long red gown who displayed footwork and various gestures. There was also Paturia, which was performed by women in sari. And there was Phirki or Nat – a courting dance. Two men in colourful shirts, caps and shorts and with bells attached to them would perform a dance called Janghia. Other dances are called Kathghora and Gutka. Various drums accompany the dances – dholak, majeera, tasa and nagara. Hindu film dances and more classical styles are now performed on recorded music. Jaipal Chamar, Muneshwar Shankar and Ram Baran are

Fig 16.24 Gere/gerreh traditional Jamaican dance performed by the NDTC

associated with the development of Indian dance in Jamaica.

Ram Lila and Krishna Lila are two popular dances in the major centres of the Caribbean culture (Trinidad, Guyana and Suriname). They were performed on a few plantations until the 1930s.

DRAMA

Drama is an art form that involves literature and action. The literature is translated into the acting of a play on a stage. The dramatic arts are important in the Caribbean even though many works have not survived in a written form.

Caribbean drama developed in four stages: the pre-Columbian stage up to the 17th Century (little is known about this stage), from the 17th Century to the abolition of slavery, from the abolition of slavery to the 1940s, and from the 1940s to the present.

Some popular forms of drama are Drag-you-bow, Kele, Crop-over and Simadag. 'Speechifying' at weddings, tea parties, etc. and story-telling (especially of Anansi stories, perfected by Jamaican Louise Bennett) are perhaps among the oldest forms of dramatisation. In Trinidad, the 'robber speech' was developed at the close of the 19th Century. According to this custom, a 'midnight robber' dressed in cowboy attire would stop random victims on the street (usually during carnival) and launch into a long speech. The victim often pays off the 'robber' and spares himself/herself his attention. Speechifying also occurred at tea party in Antigua and Jamaica – this is a Sunday social where participants are expected to give sermons on various themes from the Bible. A similar tradition exists in St Croix and Barbados. The Barbadian version is called 'Service O Song' and may include extempo, or improvising, songs about incidents and people of the village. Women mainly practise this drama form.

Men are often found in the 'debate' – an informal grouping of men at which they debate politics, crime, etc. A few from the group would 'lead' the debate, while those on the outer circle interject their comments at any time. This form is often used in Caribbean skits and plays. These men use much of the skills of the storyteller and actor – voice control, gestures, expressive language and timing. In this 'informal theatre' the outcome is never certain.

Caribbean people have also sought to 'indigenise' theatre in the region, moving away from purely Shakespearean type theatre. With the establishment of the University of the West Indies in the 1940s came a department of extra-mural studies which appointed staff tutors. In Jamaica they produced West Indian drama, which included plays written about Jamaica by Jamaicans

and English residents in Jamaica. The Federal Theatre Company under Errol Hill led a campaign against the dominance of imported scripts on the Jamaican stage.

Hill started the Whitehall Players in Port-of-Spain, the first predominantly non-European, inter-racial theatre group on the island. He left to study in the UK but returned, along with the Jamaican Noel Vaz, to tutor in the Extramural Department at the UCWI. They worked with the University Drama Society and staged workshops in other islands. The very first Secondary Schools Drama Festival held in Jamaica in 1950 was a festival of Shakespearean plays coached and judged by an English actor-director lent by the British Council. The object was to transmit British culture. But the later 1950s saw the emergence of Sam Hillary (who wrote Jamaican comedy) and influential poet-playwright Derek Walcott (1992 Nobel Prize Winner and poet laureate) at this festival.

In the1930s Marcus Garvey wrote and mounted theatrical events with titles such as, *The coronation of an*

Fig 16.25 *Nobel laureate Derek Walcott of St Lucia*

African king, *Roaming Jamaicans* (dealing with migration to Central America, Cuba and Haiti), and *Slavery – From hut to mansion*. In 1929, he established an open-air stage and auditorium at the UNIA headquarters in Kingston.

Greta Fowler, helped by her husband Henry Fowler founded The Little Theatre Movement (LTM), which opened in 1961. It introduced the national pantomime. At first they produced English Christmas musicals but later produced Jamaican folk-muaicals. Popular performers in these pantomimes were Louise Bennet and Ranny Williams. Many of the pantomimes were based on Anansi

Fig 16.26 Louise Bennett

stories. Every year, since 1941, what is now known as 'the pantomime' has been opened on Boxing Day. Noel Vaz also was an important director of Jamaican and Caribbean theatre arts in the 1950s and 1960s (working also in the Eastern Caribbean).

Some of the early dramas had a religious theme. The Spanish had a religious play called *Los Pastores* (drama of the Shepherds) and Trinitarians still put this on at Christmas. The peasantry of French origin had Le Rois (play of the three kings). Indo-Caribbean peoples introduced the LILAS (folk plays) in which they act out the lives and adventures of their folk heroes, Ram and Krishna. Theatricals accompany the festivals and dances at Hold.

THEATRE FOR THE ELITE

Early theatre was for the elite and plays were performed by touring companies. As early as 1682 there was a public theatre in Jamaica's capital city – Spanish Town. Antigua had a theatre in 1788, Barbados by 1812 and St Lucia in 1832. Barbados organised dramatics from as early as 1729. When George Washington visited Barbados in 1751, he expressed the hope to attend a performance at the Arrison Theatre. The American Company of Comedians, a troupe of mainly English actors, fled to Jamaica in 1781 after the outbreak of the American War of Independence where they wrote and performed plays. In 1832, E L Joseph, a Scotsman living in Trinidad, produced *Martial Law*. A West Indian play was performed in 1847 and dealt with the revival of carnival. By the end of the 19th Century, Trinidad had a small theatre, which provided a venue for touring companies. By 1920, there were three. In Jamaica, the Ward Theatre, renovated in 1897, was the venue for dramatic presentations. In 1893 Guyana also had a building in which a theatre was housed. Ethnic-specific dramatic clubs were then established, for example, the Georgetown Dramatic Club formed in 1891 for mixed-race people only, and the colonial Guyana Dramatic Society, which existed between 1936 and 1948, promoted the Indian plays of Tagore and Kalidasa. By 1956 Guyana had an inter-racial Theatre Guild with good actors.

Historical dramas were produced in Trinidad at the end of the 19th Century (*Carmeleta, Bele of San Jose*, among others). The Trinidad Dramatic Club survived until the 1960s. There was a flurry of dramatic activity in the 1920s and 1930s. In 1921, a Jamaican playwright, MacGregor James, wrote *A Soul's Sacrifice* which was produced at the Ward in 1926. In 1937 the BG Dramatic Society was formed to perform the drama, music and dance of the East.

Two Trinidadian primary school headmasters, Arthur Roberts and De Wilton Rogers, wrote plays, and large expatriate companies performed these with the establishment of the Imperial College of Tropical Agriculture which facilitated them. There was also the Point a Pitre Players, based at the British-owned oil company. Wilfred Redhead started an early dramatic movement in Grenada but this collapsed when he left for Barbados.

The post-World War II years saw another upswing in dramatic productions in the Caribbean. Many of these began to reflect social themes, influenced by the labour movement of the 1930s and 1940s. A Jamaican woman, Una Marson, wrote *Pocomania* – a play dealing with the effect on a middle class family of a religious cult. The journalist Frank Hill wrote about the 1938 labour rebellion in Jamaica in *Upheaval*. Theatre companies were established in Jamaica in 1941, in Barbados in 1942 and in Trinidad in 1943 and 1946. In 1946 the Whitehall Players was founded in Trinidad and this became the training ground for actors and playwrights. The companies influenced the writing of plays and in this period we saw writers like Roger Mais with *George William Gordon*, in 1958. In 1957 Freddie Kissoon started the Strolling Players, a company dedicated to theatre for the masses (i.e. popular theatre) in Trinidad.

Out of St Lucia came the Walcott brothers, Derek and Roderick, who together wrote some 20 plays. The St Lucia Arts Guild under Roderick's leadership (until 1968) became one of the leading new drama companies in the Caribbean in the 1950s and 1960s. Roderick's play, *Harrowing of Benjy* won the best West Indian Comedy Award at the Adults Drama Festival in Jamaica in 1957. Derek Walcott founded a performing company, the Trinidad Theatre Workshop (TTW) in 1959 and led this until 1976. Among Walcott's plays were *Ti-Jean and his brothers* and *Dream on Monkey Mountain*. After Walcott resigned as artistic director, Errol Jones, who had first acted in a Walcott play in 1954, along with Stanley Marshall, Claude Reid, Albert Laveau (who became artistic director), and Nigel Scott kept the TTW going.

CARIBBEAN LITERARY TRADITION
The Caribbean has had a long literary tradition dating back to the 16th Century. Between the 16th and mid -19th Century, the most prevalent literary works contained themes that would later become common in Caribbean literature: exile, migration, displacement and identity. One of the earliest examples is the 1831 narrative of the enslaved woman Mary Prince. There were also writings in Spanish including the poetry and autobiography of the runaway slave, Esteban Montejo. José Maria Hereto (1820) is recognised as the earliest Cuban writer. The enslaved man, Placido also wrote *Poesías* (poetry) in 1838 and *Poesías escogidad* (selected poetry) in 1842. The Dominican

Republic and Haiti also produced 19 literary works by people such as Max Henrique Urena (DR), Emeric Bergaud (Haiti) and Demescar Delorm. *Francesca, les jeux du sort* (Francesca, the game of fate) was written in 1873.

The 20th Century produced more literary works. In the period 1900 to 1939, the Caribbean produced a spate of writers who wrote about African identity and what was to be called *négritude*. These writers included René Maran, who was a prominent writer from Martinique (author of *Batoula*, 1921); and Aimé Césaire, who published *Return to My Native Land* in 1939. They both called for identification with African culture. *Négritude* in the French Antilles found an echo in *négrismo* in the Spanish-speaking Caribbean, with Luis Pales of Puerto Rico and Emilio Ballagar of Cuba taking their inspiration from African identity. The works of Cuba's most famous poet, Nicolas Guillén, from the 1930s shared some of the politics of *négritude*. Another Cuban, the novelist Alejo Carpentier, won critical acclaim for his book *El Reino de este mundo* (The kingdom of his world) in 1949.

The Commonwealth Caribbean produced important literary works in the early 20th Century by well-known writers such as Tom Redcam, Herbert DeLisser (author of *The White witch of Rosehall*), and Claude McKay (1890-1948) who became associated with the Harlem renaissance in New York City in the 1920s and 1930s. Trinidadian C L R James's *Minty Alley* (1936) and *The Black Jacobins* (1938) were works protesting colonialism. James founded two literary magazines, *Trinidad* and *The Beacon,* to which writers like Ralph Boissiere and Alfred Mendes contributed articles. Jean Rhys's novel *After leaving Mr McKenzie* was published in this period (1930). She went on to win international acclaim for other books like *Wide Saragasso Sea*.

The period leading up to independence and starting roughly from 1940 gave birth to a new generation of writers whose works voiced the desire for liberation. This was epitomised in Jamaica, in Vic Reid's *New Day*. Along with Reid, there was the writer and poet, Roger Mais (Jamaica), Una Marson (Jamaica), Edgar Mittleholzer and Martin Carter of Guyana, Phyllis Shand Allfrey (Dominica) and George Lamming (Barbados) whose novel *In the Castle of My Skin* (1935) portrayed the coming of age under colonialism.

The 1960s, the decade of intense struggle for political independence, produced novels by Guyanese Wilson Harris and Jamaican, Sylvia Wynter (*The Hills of Hebron*, 1966). It was also in this period that South African novelist Peter Abrahams, who had settled in Jamaica in 1955, wrote his first novel with a Caribbean setting, *This Island* (1966).

In the post-1960s the Caribbean literary tradition continued to flourish. This was the post-independence era for territories like Barbados, Jamaica and Trinidad &

Tobago and . In this period there emerged the works of poets Derek Walcott (winner of the Nobel Prize for Literature in 1992), Kamau Brathwaite (who, like Louise Bennett of Jamaica, challenged the structures, reference, language and rhythms of European poetry by adopting those of Africa and the Caribbean), Indo-Trinidadian V S Naipaul (winner of the 2001 Nobel Prize for Literature), Earl Lovelace and Sam Selvon (Trinidad), Daniel Maximin and Maryse Conde (Guadeloupe), Patrick Chamoiseau and Edourd Glissant (Martinique), the Cuban poets, Nancy Mojerón, Jamaicans Olive Senior, Lorna Goodison, Erna Brodber and a host of others. Many others lived abroad although they were born in the Caribbean, for example, Jamaica Kincaid of Antigua, Joan Riley of Jamaica, Janice Shinebourne of Guyana, Caryl Philips of St Kitts and Astrid Roemer of Suriname.

The next chapter will show the ways in which the struggle for decolonisation was taken up by political activists. This struggle was reflected in the works of these Caribbean writers.

Fig 16.27 Kamau Brathwaite

To sum up

The lives of Caribbean people were not all defined by work. When Caribbean people of all classes and ethnic groups were not working, they found time to participate in various types of sports and other recreational activities. Some of these social activities eventually took on a competitive character, allowing some Caribbean people to excel as individuals and as team members in such sports as cricket and athletics. In addition to outstanding sportsmen and sportswomen, the Caribbean has produced accomplished architects, artists, choreographers, dancers, musicians, actors and actresses, novelists and poets. Some literary artists like Derek Walcott and V S Naipaul have won the Nobel Prize for Literature.

Revision questions

1 Select any two of the following and discuss their contributions to the artistic life of the Caribbean:
   a Rex Nettleford
   b Beryl McBurnie
   c Derek Walcott
   d Edna Manley

2 Discuss the ways in which any one of the following groups influenced art forms in the Caribbean: Europeans, Asian Indians, Chinese.

3 Read the passage and answer the questions that follow:

   The motions of the dancers are lascivious to such a degree that the calinda (a dance practised by Africans in Martinique and Guadeloupe), has been officially prohibited. (Adapted from Jean Labat, 1722.)

   a State two reasons why the motion of the calinda dancers was described as 'lascivious'.
   b Name two territories outside of the French Caribbean in which people danced the calinda.
   c Name four other types of dances performed by people in the Caribbean.
   d Name three reasons, apart from its alleged 'lasciviousness', why Europeans tried to prohibit dances like the calinda in the Caribbean.

Chapter 17

Nationalism, decolonisation, independence

'Every man has a right to determine his own destiny.'
(Bob Marley)

Introduction

For three centuries after the 1492 Columbus 'colonising' project, Spain was politically dominant in the Caribbean. By 1898, however, Spain had lost its political power in Cuba, the Dominican Republic and Puerto Rico. Today, direct Spanish imperial authority in the Caribbean no longer exists. But other European colonisers still exercise constitutional power in the region in the form of colonial-style relationships with the so-called 'dependent' territories.

From the outset, starting with the indigenous peoples, Caribbean people resisted colonial rule. In time, Africans (including Maroons) and Creoles (including some of European descent) created their own versions of the anti-colonial movement, seeking greater independence from European rule. This struggle resulted in the winning of territory for Maroon communities, that existed as proto-independent nations, as well as matured into the rise of a nationalist movement that ultimately conceived and pressed for complete independence from European political domination.

Today most Caribbean territories have won their political independence and become nations. A few, however, are still under colonial rule. This chapter focuses on why and how colonial rule was resisted and why some territories have become independent while others have not.

In this chapter we will learn about:
1 Reasons for disaffection among people in the British-colonised territories
2 The changing of the Crown Colony system after the Morant Bay Rebellion

T Albert Marryshow

1 Reasons for disaffection

The type of government which typically existed in the British-colonised Caribbean, even after the abolition of slavery, was the 'Old Representative System'. The exceptions to this were Trinidad and St Lucia, which had Crown Colony government from the early 19th Century. Colonial Guyana also had a form of Crown Colony government. Tobago, unlike Trinidad, kept its Assembly-type government, like other Old Representative Systems, when the British took the island back from France in 1814.

Under the Old Representative System, the governor was sent out from Britain and governed with the assistance of a nominated Legislative Council (the Upper House) and an elected (on a limited franchise) Assembly (Lower House).

Crown Colony government meant that the territories were governed directly through the British Government in London and the people had little or no say in the government of their land. Crown Colonies had no elected Assembly but a nominated Council that assisted the Governor. They were governed by Orders-in-Council or laws approved by London. The social protest in places like colonial Guyana showed that the people were not happy with this foreign, centralised and undemocratic system of government in which they had no elected rights.

More on the Old Representative System
The Old Representative System represented only part of the population. A few wealthy planters and merchants or their agents elected the Assembly. The Assembly had the power to pass laws, but these laws could be vetoed or set aside by the British Parliament. The Assembly often attempted to dominate the governors through their law-making and financial powers.

What was common to all territories was that freed men could not vote unless they owned land or paid taxes. So, even though slavery had ended and European people were a tiny minority in comparison with the African-Caribbean and Asian populations, it was the European people who held political control. There were only a few freed people in the Assembly in some colonies. The members of the Legislative Council and the Assembly mainly represented the minority of European landowners whose livelihood depended on sugar. This minority did not wish to share political power in any way. They wanted the vote and election to the Assembly to continue to be based on high property qualifications.

This state of affairs led to bitterness and created grievances among the inhabitants – the workers as well as the educated middle classes. Emancipation and improved education in the schools in the British-colonised Caribbean territories were producing a multi-ethnic professional class including lawyers, doctors, civil servants, and teachers who were increasingly dissatisfied with the system. As early as 1830 some mixed-race people were eligible to vote, sit in the Legislature and serve on juries or as magistrates. After the abolition of slavery a few mixed-race people like George William Gordon and Edward Jordan of Jamaica, Samuel Jackman Prescod and Sir Conrad Reeves of Barbados, used these new political privileges open to qualified mixed-race and African-Caribbean people. They pressed for a larger voice in government.

The British government was undecided as to what to do. Henry Taylor, an imperial official, had long believed that a society emerging out of slavery needed education and experience before it could operate democratic political institutions. He believed that in the meantime the British government should run the administration. In a memorandum in 1839 he recommended abolishing the Old Representative System and establishing Crown Colony government. This was not done immediately though, but the British government strengthened its position by gradual constitutional changes. For example, they introduced the Executive Committee to achieve greater control of government in the colonies governed under the Old Representative System and to lessen the power of the Assembly.

The Jamaican Constitution Act of 1854 established a four-member Executive Committee chosen by the Governor – three members from the Assembly and one from the Council. Ultimate responsibility continued to be with the Governor. The Act also maintained a Legislative Council, nominated for life by the Crown. The Council served without decision-making functions. This system was tried in Antigua, Tobago, Grenada and St Lucia during the 1850s but each proved unsatisfactory and was soon discontinued.

The Morant Bay Rebellion
When the Morant Bay Rebellion broke out in Jamaica in 1865, less than one in every 200 Jamaicans had the right to vote, and most of those who could vote were British. The rebellion was caused by several factors but among them was the lack of access to land and the right to vote, and this was made worse by the economic impact of the American Civil War. Rural economic hardship was made

worse because there was no broad-based democracy and those in political power did not need to be accountable to the masses. The planter class did not wish to help freed people access commercial land.

As squatting became more commonplace (since many African-Jamaicans could not buy land), so did evictions. In 1865, a group of Jamaican labourers from the parish of St Ann petitioned Queen Victoria requesting the right to rent unused Crown lands. The reply attributed to her urged the petitioners to work harder on the planters' estates. This 'Queen's Advice' only served to make the rural poor more angry and protests increased in the depression years of the mid-1860s. A major rebellion erupted in St Thomas in the East in 1865. This was called the Morant Bay Rebellion; some writers still insist on referring to it as a 'rising' or a 'disturbance'.

Many workers, male and female, participated in the planning and execution of the armed rebellion. Some women, for example, stoned the constables and raided police stations for guns and ammunition. The recognised leader was Paul Bogle of Stony Gut. He was one of George William Gordon's deacons in the Baptist church. Gordon was a mixed-race member of the Assembly and a businessman who championed the cause of the masses. After unsuccessful attempts to get redress for the suffering of the people, on 11 October 1865, Bogle led his followers into the town, seized weapons, and marched on the Morant Bay courthouse. The militia responded and shot several demonstrators; the courthouse was torched and a handful of British people were killed.

Armed protest spread to other parts of the parish and several plantations were attacked. The rebellion was severely put down under orders from Governor Edward Eyre, a former Lieutenant-Governor of New Zealand and a former governor of St Vincent. He had previous experience in dealing with indigenous peoples in Australia and New Zealand and with Indian indentured workers in St Vincent. He developed a harsh and intolerant policy of dealing with people in Jamaica. He was clearly hostile to the African-Jamaican and mixed-race people and represented the unyielding stance of the ruling elite.

It is alleged that at Governor Eyre's direction Paul Bogle was caught by Maroons in a cane-piece, and was hanged from the roof of the Morant Bay courthouse. George William Gordon, who had long been critical of the government's policies and attitudes towards the poor, was accused of being intimately involved in the rebellion. He too was put to death. Almost 600 people were killed and as many flogged. Political scientist Clinton Hutton tells us that as part of the punishment, many women who were suspected of hiding male rebels, were raped or had their heads shaved. Over 1,000 houses were burned. The British

Fig17.1 *Paul Bogle*

Fig17.2 *George William Gordon*

government sent out a Commission of Enquiry which concluded that the system of government in Jamaica was unworkable. Eyre was recalled and the legislature was given a choice: give more people the right to vote or surrender the government to the Crown.

The Jamaican Assembly was thoroughly alarmed by the rebellion and so decided to vote for its own abolition. In 1866, a British Order-in-Council replaced the 200-year-old Representative System, with a Crown Colony government in Jamaica. Crown Colony government was rapidly extended to other colonies – it had a Legislative Council without any elected members. Barbados, like Bermuda and the Bahamas, kept an elected Assembly and rejected Crown Colony rule. But Crown Colony government was introduced to Montserrat in 1866, the British Virgin Islands in 1867, Nevis, Grenada, St Vincent and Tobago in 1877, St Kitts in 1878, Antigua and Dominica in 1898.

Crown Colonies

The most fundamental change brought about by Crown Colony government was that the Crown had the power to override all domestic political opposition. The Crown ruled the colonial legislature through its representative – the Governor. Crown Colony government meant the abolition of both the elective members and of bicameralism (two houses, the lower and upper). The Governor ruled the colony with the help of a Legislative Council, which was made up of ex-officio, or automatic, and nominated members. The Council alone had the right to introduce legislation and the colonial office kept ultimate power.

Critics of Crown Colony rule wanted to secure for the African-Jamaican majority a better and fairer government than the small administration of wealthy British men had provided in the Old Representative System. The imperial government was just as afraid that 'order' would not be maintained if Whites and Browns lost power to a African-Jamaican majority.

Opposition to Crown Colony government

In the beginning, planters in many territories including Jamaica, St Lucia and Trinidad, resented Crown Colony rule. The early 19th Century British governors were faced with petitions from British planters demanding trial by jury and free representation in a House of Assembly, like they had in Barbados. Two noted petitions were those of 1820 and 1823, which the planters presented to Governor Woodford of Trinidad. The 1820 petition was signed by 280 British people, and the 1823 petition by 344 British people. The 1823 petition was led by St Hiliare Begorrat, a French landowner of long residence in Trinidad. From the 1840s, there were more petitions, like the one signed by 207 Coloured people in Trinidad in 1843.

A problem with Crown Colony government was that those who managed it were responsible to a distant imperial government, not to the communities in which they served. Also, because most major administrative posts were reserved for British men, the system gave Caribbean people little experience of political responsibility. Another reason for opposition was that there was little effort by the government to know what the public thought or felt; and even if this was known, there was no way of knowing if the public's opinion would be taken into consideration. One way to redress grievances was to petition the Colonial Office, and this was generally unsuccessful. The role of the majority of the people was confined to paying taxes and performing servile labour. Many people were also dissatisfied that sugar interests, and the absentee-planters especially, continued to be politically and economically dominant.

Large sections of society were dissatisfied with the administration. They said that officials were corrupt and inefficient and that public spending was extravagant. There was a deep-seated grievance about the appointment of expatriates to most top posts in the Civil Service and the exclusion of Creoles. So the people's desire for more self-government came from a well-founded conviction that without self-government, social progress was impossible. There were no effective constitutional channels for the expression of such grievances.

There was also dissatisfaction with the way the Crown Colony system of government was organised. Firstly, the executive, consisting mostly of elite council men chosen by the governor, ruled the legislative system and could stamp out opposition. Secondly, government responsibilities were in the hands of the executive, and through the governor in the hands of the Colonial Office thousands of miles away. This made the system less representative of the people and open to intense criticism.

2 The changing of the Crown Colony system after the Morant Bay Rebellion

There were, however, some changes made to the system. Crown Colony government began to change when some unofficial members, those who were not elected to Council, were nominated to the Legislative Councils. Later provision was made for a number of elective seats. Eventually there were more elected members than nominated members in both the Executive and the Legislative Councils. Governors became increasingly obligated to accept advice from elected legislatures and so the Crown Colony system gradually evolved into a more responsible form of government.

Attempts to throw off the imperial yoke

Even though there were some early changes to the autocratic Crown Colony government, the pressure from the people for more constitutional rights continued. These small changes did not satisfy the desire of Caribbean people to govern themselves without external control. In the twin-island colony of Trinidad & Tobago (formed with the annexation of Tobago in 1889), the question of constitutional reform demanded urgent answers. During the 'Water Riots' in 1903, the main government offices in Trinidad were burned to the ground, 16 people were shot or bayoneted to death by the police, and 40 others were injured.

One of the most distinguished leaders of the movement for self-government was T Albert Marryshow of Grenada. He was strongly critical of Crown Colony rule and he mobilised a group of middle-class professional Grenadians. In 1914 they formed a Representative Government Association. In some Eastern Caribbean territories other middle-class professionals such as Ebenezer Duncan and George McIntosh of St Vincent, and Cecil Rawle of Dominica, founded Representative Government Associations during the first two decades of the twentieth century. They promoted a united West Indies with democratic political institutions. In St Kitts-Nevis-Anguilla, where members of the Legislative Council were appointed for life, there was also a movement for representative government. St Vincent and St Lucia demanded similar reforms in 1920–1921. Other colonies formed associations which demanded a wider franchise, constitutional reform, and in some cases, political federation.

The fight for reforms was successful in some territories where there was a shift from Crown Colony government to modified elective government, then to responsible government, back to internal self-government or representative government, and finally to federation and independence.

Did you know?

Responsible government is one in which there is a minority of elected members. Representative government is government where there is a majority of elected officials.

The Wood Commission

It was partly in response to these struggles for political freedom that the British government sent the Honourable E F C Wood (Lord Halifax) to the Caribbean in 1921 to review governance. He recommended that elections should be restored so that there were elected members in government, and that official members should be in the minority. So elected members were introduced to the Legislative Councils of Trinidad and the Crown Colonies of the Windward Islands as well as Dominica. The governor still had power except in Guyana where elected members had effective control over government's revenue and expenses. However, the British government took away this limited authority in 1928.

Fig 17.4 Lord Halifax, head of the Wood Commission of 1921

These modifications to Crown Colony government did not end the discussion on the best form of political structure for the Caribbean. Critics wanted outright and full independence, others wanted the Caribbean to form itself into a close and unified political structure through federation.

The federal interlude

For almost three centuries inhabitants and colonial officials had proposed some form of closer association as a solution to some British Caribbean problems. The Leewards were divided in 1816 into two parts – one composed of Antigua, Barbuda, and Montserrat; and the other of St Kitts, Nevis, Anguilla, and the British Virgin Islands. In 1833 they were again united under one governor, and Dominica was added to the group. Almost 40 years later, in 1871, the local Legislatures agreed to a loose form of federation. However, there was little enthusiasm, as each colony feared losing its limited sovereignty. Under this agreement,

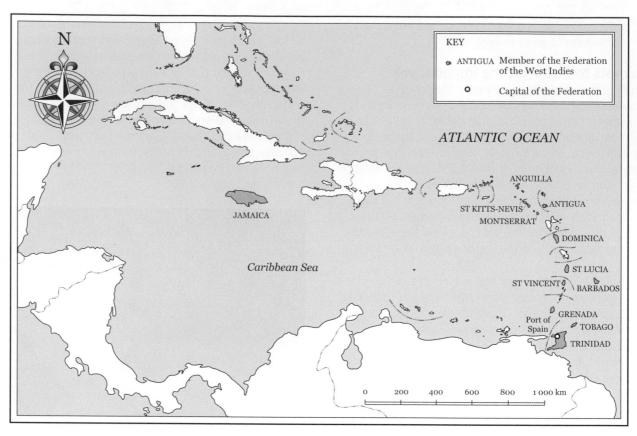

Fig 17.5 Constituent members of the Federation of the West Indies

however, the Leewards formed one colony with six presidencies – Antigua (with Barbuda), Nevis, St Kitts (with Anguilla), Dominica, Montserrat, and the British Virgin Islands. Twelve years later when St Kitts-Nevis-Anguilla were joined into one tripartite colony, the total of presidencies was reduced to five. The seat of government was at St Kitts, which remained the dominant partner. Thirteen years later, the Leewards Federation was a weak union with only member financially secure namely St Kitts.

After previous attempts had failed, in 1876 Britain tried to bring about Confederation or union involving Barbados and the Windward Islands, with Barbados as the central unit. Governor Hennessy of Barbados had the responsibility of implementing this union.

The six essential provisions of the Confederation were:

- The Auditor-General of Barbados should be appointed Auditor-General of the Windward Islands.
- The Governor-in-Chief could authorise the transport of prisoners from Barbados to the Windwards and vice-versa.
- Lunatics from the Windwards could be sent to the lunatic asylum in Barbados.

- There should be a common lazaretto (a hospital that treats leprosy and other contagious diseases) for lepers from Barbados and the Windwards.
- The judicial system should be centralised in Barbados.
- There should be a common police force.

There was deep opposition to Confederation among the British and mixed-race elite in Barbados. Confederation protests broke out in April 1876 as the masses demonstrated their support for the government and against planter opposition.

After this there were a number of proposals for West Indian Federation. To most people in the British-colonised Caribbean territories, the main argument for closer union was that it would facilitate self-governance. An unofficial conference early in 1932 in Roseau, Dominica, was attended by representatives from Antigua, Dominica, Grenada, Montserrat, St Kitts, and Trinidad & Tobago. The delegates attacked Crown Colony rule as a wasteful, inefficient, and discriminatory system, which denied opportunities to the governed, stifled popular initiatives and did not care about local public opinion.

The first conference on British West Indian Federation was held in Montego Bay in 1947. By a majority vote it accepted the principle of political federation and set up a Standing Closer Association Committee to study the possibility of federation and to draft a federal constitution. This report was submitted to a conference in London. After two conferences held in London in 1953 and 1956, a decision was taken to implement federation in the British Caribbean territories. On 2 August 1956, the Parliament at Westminster passed the British Caribbean Act to establish a federal union among the ten territories making up the British West Indies. Individual Caribbean governments, however, had to agree to the recommendation of a federation made by the London Conferences.

The federal constitution was semi-colonial in that it did not provide full internal self-government. Executive authority remained with the Crown, represented by the Governor-General who had the power to disallow and set aside bills. The Council of State that advised the Governor-General, was composed of the Prime Minister and ten other ministers, who were appointed by the Governor-General on the advice of the Prime Minister. At least three were senators and the remainder were members of the House of Representatives.

The Senate was the Upper House of the Federal Legislature. It was made up of 19 members who were nominated by the governor of the particular territory. The governor normally acted on the advice of his ministers. Senators served for five years, regardless of whether or not parliament was dissolved. Two of these senators were appointed from each of the nine largest units and one from Montserrat. This was to give roughly equal representation to the islands, whose wide variations in population meant that the smaller islands would be outvoted in the Lower House.

The House of Representatives was allotted 45 members elected by universal adult suffrage – 17 from Jamaica, ten from Trinidad & Tobago, five from Barbados, one from Montserrat, and two from each of the other territories. Procedure in both Houses was modelled on that at Westminster. The Federation of the West Indies Act came into being on 3 January 1958. It included ten British colonies with a land area of over 8,000 square miles, and a population of some three million people. The constituent units/members were Antigua (with its dependencies of Redonda and Barbuda), Barbados, Dominica, Grenada, Jamaica (with the Cayman Islands), Montserrat, St Kitts-Nevis-Anguilla, St Lucia, St Vincent, and Trinidad & Tobago. The Grenadines as dependencies of St Vincent were also included.

Problems with federation

All agreed that federation was the best system and the only path to independence. But this does not mean that federation was without any problems. Each territory objected to contributing more than the barest minimum to federal revenues. Federation also suffered from an imbalance of power among the members as there were differences in size and population, as well as in natural resources. Together Jamaica and Trinidad & Tobago accounted for seven-eighths of the population. The smaller and poorer territories were therefore fearful of domination by the twin giants – Jamaica, Trinidad & Tobago. In addition, political and economic developments in the islands reduced an earlier enthusiasm and increased doubts about the merits of the union. The more autonomy the territories had, the less willing they were to surrender any portion of it and the less convinced they were that the union offered the only road to independence. The economies of the members were generally competitive rather than complementary.

The less populated territories welcomed the prospect of a customs union, free migration and the extension of cooperation, which had been encouraged since 1952 by the Regional Economic Committee. They did not believe that they could attain their own independence and feared that in a federation dominated by the large territories, their interests might receive less consideration than was currently shown by the United Kingdom. The leaders of Jamaica and Trinidad & Tobago believed that their own critical economic problems demanded early consideration. They were alarmed that they needed to replace the UK as subsidisers of the small islands. Trinidad & Tobago feared that free migration would encourage an influx from the neighbouring islands. In general Indian organisations that represented at least one-third of Trinidad's population were opposed to a federal union. They feared that in such a federation they would be only a tiny racial minority. Jamaica, on the other hand, suspected that federalism would delay the territory's own progress towards self-government, hamper the development of new industries, and force a reduction in its profitable tariff. It also did not welcome being absorbed into a national state that at the outset was less independent than Jamaica itself.

The fact is that most people in the British-colonised Caribbean territories had little real understanding of how a federation works. The result was that when Norman Manley called for a referendum on Jamaica's position, the people of Jamaica voted against federation. Manley then resigned as leader of the West Indies Federal Labour Party, and Jamaica subsequently withdrew its membership from the federation. Eric Williams responded to this by arguing that Jamaica's withdrawal was illegal and that the federation had consequently ceased to exist. All that was left was a caretaker government, 'one from ten left zero', not nine was his view of it.

3 Movements towards independence

With the break-up of the federation in 1961, each British-colonised territory began to move towards independence on its own. There had already been a new preoccupation with people's rights since the radical 1930s. It was out of this radicalism that the trade union movement had been formed. Now Caribbean people took this radicalism to a new level, agitating for independence and constitutional change.

Political parties emerge
Several political parties were formed to spearhead the popular struggle for non-violent constitutional reforms, which would eventually lead to self-government. Among these were: the Jamaican Political Reform Association (1921), and the Peoples Political Party (1929 under Marcus Garvey). Quasi-political parties were: the Elected Members' Association (1935), the Federation of Citizens Association (1935), and the Jamaica Progressive League (1937). W Adolphe Roberts formed the latter in New York and a branch was established in Jamaica. There was also the Jamaica Democratic Party. All these political parties pressed for internal self-government.

In Trinidad & Tobago, an early party formed by Cipriani in 1932 was the Trinidad Labour Party. This was formed out of the Trinidad Working Men's Association by Alfred Richards in 1894. At that time, there was no elective principle and so its political activities were limited. The 'Butler Party' (Uriah Butler's British Empire Workers and Citizens Home Rule Party) had its aim clearly stated in the name. But it was the labour-based parties formed during or after the worker struggles of the 1930s that were really successful in terms of radical constitutional reforms leading to independence. The expansion of the franchise and the fact that the labour movement led the major parties increased the effectiveness of parties in the mid-20th Century.

Universal adult suffrage was achieved in 1943. After this the Jamaica Liberal Party, the United Rent Payers' Party, the Jamaica Radical Workers' Union and the J A G Smith party were formed. These were little more than party labels for independent candidates. In fact, in more recent times third or even fourth parties such as the National Democratic Movement first led by Bruce Golding

and, after he resigned, by Hyacinth Bennett, and the United People's Party (UPP) led by Antoinette Haughton have generally failed to thrive in the Caribbean. Major mid-20th Century parties were: The Jamaica Labour Party and People's National Party (Jamaica), the Barbados Labour Party and the Democratic Labour Party (Barbados), the People's National Movement (Trinidad & Tobago), the People's Progressive Party and the People's National Congress (Guyana). These parties largely took the various territories into independence.

Jamaica
In Jamaica, the struggle for nationhood had its beginnings in civil rights demands, which developed out of the political implications of Emancipation. The early 20th Century saw two major political parties in Jamaica – the People's National Party (PNP) (formed in 1938) led by Norman Manley, and the Jamaica Labour Party (JLP) (formed in 1943) led by Alexander Bustamante. These were both linked to trade unions, first to the Trade Union Congress and later to the National Workers Union in the case of the PNP, and to the Bustamante Industrial Trade Union, BITU, in the case of the JLP. So they emerged out of working class militancy in the 1930s. The PNP under Manley's leadership struggled against the conservative planter class and against the colonial power as it advocated full self-government. The Jamaica Progressive League became a co-operative affiliate of the PNP. The struggles of the JLP and the PNP over constitutional changes for Jamaica eventually helped to foster the general idea of a Jamaican national consciousness. The end result of this struggle was the achievement of universal adult suffrage in 1944 and independence on 6 August 1962. In the first national elections after the achievement of adult suffrage, the JLP won 22 seats and the PNP five; independents also won five seats.

In summary, independence came after a series of constitutional changes in Jamaica. In 1884, the elective principle, which had been lost in 1866, was restored. By 1944, there was a majority of elected as opposed to nominated members in the Legislative Council. Further changes were the granting of universal adult suffrage and the start of party politics, as well as ministerial government, in 1953. Under ministerial government, the leader of the majority party – the Chief Minister – formed the government and chose elected members of the party in the Legislative Council. These elected members headed particular ministries or areas of responsibility, such as agriculture, education, etc. Cabinet government was introduced in 1958 and full internal government in 1959. By 1960 government policy was decided upon and carried out by a committee selected by the Chief Minister/Prime

Chapter 17 | *Nationalism, decolonisation, independence*

Minister (without any input from unofficial members). Except for foreign affairs and defence, which remained under the governor, the Prime Minister and the cabinet were in control of the island's government.

The JLP came to office in 1962 and remained in power until 1972, although after 1967 this was not under Bustamante who led Jamaica to Independence. Donald Sangster was Prime Minister in 1967. Hugh Shearer took over after Sangster died and was Prime Minister from 1967-1972. The JLP lost the 1972 elections to the PNP under the leadership of Michael Manley (1924-1997), son of Norman and Edna Manley. The PNP remained in power until 1980 at which time the JLP, in opposition to socialism, again came to power under Edward Seaga. The JLP was defeated by the PNP once again in 1989 and has since been in power. By 1989, the government of the JLP had exhausted its popularity after nine years of free market reforms that brought no lasting economic benefits to the masses. Percival Patterson succeeded Michael Manley in 1992 after ill health forced Manley to give up the reigns of power. The PNP of the 1980s, however, adopted a less radical political ideology, moving away from the socialist policies and rhetoric of the 1970s.

Fig 17.6 *Michael Manley, Jamaican politician*

Trinidad & Tobago

In Trinidad & Tobago rapid constitutional change followed the introduction of the elective principle in 1924, which effectively ended Crown Colony government. By 1941 there was a majority of elected members in the Legislative Council. The granting of universal adult suffrage in 1945 and the beginning of party politics in the elections of 1946 brought in further constitutional changes. The 1946 elections were hotly contested by several political parties: the Butler Party, the Caribbean Socialist Party, the Political Progress Group, the Trinidad Labour Party, the Trade Union Council, and 91 independents. The achievement of ministerial government in 1950 was a further step on the road to independence.

Eric Williams and C L R James gave political energy to the national spirit of Trinidad & Tobago. In 1956 Williams emerged as the leader of the newly formed Peoples' National Movement (PNM). Chief among the opposition to the PNM were the Party of Political Progress led by Albert Gomes, Cipriani's old party the Trinidad Labour Party led by Victor Bryan, the Caribbean National Labour Party, the Butler Party, and the PDP established in 1953 under Bhadasee Maraj. The PNM won 39 of the votes and 13 out of 24 seats in the elections of 1956. The PDP won five seats and 20.3 per cent of the votes. Two constituencies went to independents and the TLP and the Butler Party each won two seats.

By 1959, Trinidad & Tobago had a system by which the leader of the majority party formed the government and chose certain colleagues in his party to head ministries. Cabinet government in 1959 and full internal self-government in 1961 paved the way for independence which was achieved on 31 August 1962. The PNM remained in power for 30 years. When Williams died in 1981, George Chambers became Prime Minister, remaining in power until 1986 at which time the PNM lost its long hold on power to a coalition of parties under the leadership of A N R Robinson who became Prime Minister (1986-1991).

Patrick Manning succeeded Robinson (1991-1995) after the PNM narrowly won the 1991 elections when there was a split in the coalition. Since independence all Prime Ministers of the twin-island republic have been African-Trinidadians until Indian-Trinidadian Basdeo Panday became Prime Minister in 1995. Panday's United National Congress (UNC), supported overwhelmingly by Indian-Trinidadians but with some African votes, won the 1995 elections after Prime Minister Patrick Manning lost the snap elections he had called in an effort to extend his majority.

Barbados

Barbados developed an elected planter-assembly in 1639. However, a race- and class-restricted franchise before 1950 meant that it was a government primarily of the European elite. The first political party was Charles Duncan O'Neale's Democratic League formed in 1924. It went out of existence when O'Neale, an elected assemblyman, died in 1936. Other groupings of politicians described either as 'conservatives' or 'liberals' represented commercial interests or workers respectively. The Barbados Labour Party (BLP) was formed in October 1938 with the aim of directing and mobilising the growth in political enthusiasm evident in the labour struggles of the 1930s. This was an essentially middle class party, representing people who wanted political changes through non-violent means.

The League changed its name to the Barbados Labour Party. Among its members were the liberal Grantley Adams, radical activists like C A Brathwaite (an African-Barbadian businessman), J A Martineau (a beverage producer), and Wynter Crawford (an anti-colonialist and a publisher). E Talma and the radical Garveyite, Herbert Seale, were other members. A split eventually developed within the ranks of the BLP between the liberal element led by Adams and the left-wing led by Seale who was less interested in appeasing the planter-merchant elite and more interested in radical worker empowerment.

Despite the limited franchise (there was yet no universal adult suffrage), the BLP won seats in the Assembly in 1940. In 1941, Adams, Hugh Springer and Dr H G Cummins were sitting in the Legislative Council on behalf of the BLP, and J T C Ramsey, a known grassroots politician, had won a by-election and was sitting in the Assembly, or Lower house. In 1943 there were discussions over the extension of the vote. The traditional elite opposed giving the vote to a larger section of the population, especially to the working class. Both Adams and Crawford (in a way his political opponent) pressed for universal adult suffrage instead of the government's proposal to lower the property qualification for the vote to £30. The motion for adult suffrage was defeated, but by the Representation of the People Act of 4 May 1943, the qualification for the vote was lowered to £25. The number of people who got the vote increased by 510 per cent. Women also got the vote for the first time. The first election after the extension of the franchise was held in 1944. Contesting the election were Adam's BLP, the newly formed West Indian National Congress Party of Crawford, and the planters political party, the Elector's Association. The Congress Party won eight seats, the BLP seven, and the Elector's Association seven.

There continued to be calls for greater democracy in Barbados. For even with a larger electorate sending representatives to the Assembly, the governor still had full responsibility for political administration. People felt that the Assembly should have more power. In 1946, there were some changes called the 'Bushe reform', after Governor Bushe.

According to these changes, membership of the Executive Committee would include members of all parties that had won seats. The governor, therefore, no longer selected the members of the executive as he pleased. This was the start of 'semi-ministerial government'. Still, Adams and more liberal members of the BLP were preferred over the more radical Crawford. Another aspect of the reform was that the majority leader became the Attorney-General. This system of government eventually led to the establishment of cabinet government in 1954.

In the elections of 1946, the first after the Bushe reforms, the BLP won most seats. However, they had to join with the Congress Party to push legislation through as the BLP did not have the necessary majority. The BLP coalition broke down, but Adams managed to get some Congress members to join the BLP, eventually giving him the majority needed.

The next political change came in 1950 when universal adult suffrage was finally attained and property qualifications were abolished. The electorate increased from around 30,000 in 1948 to nearly 100,000. Three main parties contested the subsequent elections of 1951: the Electors' Association (EA), the BLP, and Crawford's Congress Party. The BLP had the support of the Barbados Workers' Union, while the EA had the support of the Caribbean Workers' Union under Ernest Mottley (which was formed only to get votes and collapsed shortly after). The BLP won 16 seats and got 60 per cent of the votes. The EA won four seats with 30 per cent of the vote and the Congress Party won two seats. Ermie Bourne became the first female parliamentary representative, winning the St Andrew seat for the BLP.

The BLP, however, was growing in caution and this caused young radicals to break away from it. Errol Barrow and Lorenzo Williams were two of these young radicals, and they soon emerged as the parliamentary opposition to Adams. Still, Adams was in power when Barbados got a semi-cabinet system that became the main source of parliamentary power. So under Adams the island had achieved a significant degree of internal self-government. Internal dissent and subsequent opposition to Adams's rule gave rise to the formation of the Democratic Labour Party (DLP) in April 1955. This party embraced young radicals (like Crawford of the defunct Congress Party), trade unionists and working class agitators. However, the 1956 election was still won by the BLP, with the DLP and

Fig17.7 Errol Barrow

the Progressive Conservative Party (the old Electors' Association) winning only a few seats.

In the 1960s there was increased agitation for further political changes that would eventually result in independence for Barbados. The federal interlude of the late 1950s and early 1960s distracted the 'independistas' (i.e. those in favour of independence). But the failure of the Federation once more placed independence on the front burner. An indication of the changing political climate was when the DLP under Barrow (the 41-year-old lawyer-economist) won the 1961 elections. Barrow wanted more independence for Barbados as he did not see the British-conceived federal structure as a workable future political arrangement for Barbados. He was particularly concerned that British funding for the structure was inadequate. There was an attempt to federate the Eastern Caribbean islands. By 1965, after several countries had withdrawn from this planned Federation of the Leeward and Windward Islands, Barrow publicly declared his intention to press for independence for Barbados.

When the independence plan was presented to England, Barrow already had large popular support for Barbados's independence. Since 1962 the country had a 21-member Senate, with the traditional Legislative Council already abolished. On 30 November 1966 Barbados gained its full sovereignty. Errol Barrow became the country's first Prime Minister and the then imperial governor, Sir John Stow, became the first Governor General. The colonial status started in 1627 had finally come to an end. But the Westminster-style government became part and parcel of the post-independence era.

Independence was within the Commonwealth system and republicanism was not proposed as the alternative political model.

Fig17.8 Nita Barrow

The DLP also won the 1971 elections with a handsome majority. In the 1970s oil prices were rising and this adversely affected economies of islands without an oil industry. This created a favourable political climate for the opposition BLP, which under Tom Adams (son of Sir Grantley Adams), won the 1976 elections. Adams's election restored the decreasing confidence of the corporate elite within the country. In the period 1976 to 1986, the BLP increasingly swung to the right, especially under the leadership of Tom Adams. In 1986, however, the DLP again came to power under Barrow. The people saw Barrow as more attuned to the nationalist agenda. Barrow's death in 1987, however, meant that many of the expected changes were not fulfilled.

Colonial Guyana

Colonial Guyana had a long history of agitating for constitutional changes which would lead to self-government. Early parties were the Reform Association of 1891 and the Popular Party which was active in the 1920s. Just like in other territories, the mass-based parties were slow to develop because of the limited franchise. In 1950 though, the dynamic Indo-Guyanese Cheddi Jagan formed the People's Progressive Party (PPP) along with Forbes Burnham, an African-Guyanese lawyer and president of the British Guiana Labour Union. The people in colonial Guyana first went to the polls under Universal Adult Suffrage in 1953. In this election, the PPP – which had campaigned on a socialist platform – won 18 out of the 24 elected seats in the legislature. The National Democratic Party also contested the elections. After Jagan had been in office for 133 days, British troops (urged on by the United States) landed and suspended the constitution. They believed that Jagan was a communist revolutionary and did not wish a communist leader to be in power. In 1955 Forbes Burnham, promoting his differences with Jagan, broke away from the PPP and formed his own political party – The People's National Congress (PNC). The PNC was seen as a party for the African-Guyanese and the PPP of the Indo-Guyanese.

Despite the British subversive actions against Jagan and the PPP, the PPP won the elections of 1957 and 1961. The Kennedy administration in the USA was initially willing to establish relations with Jagan. However, the anti-communist stance and the fears that Jagan's government was becoming an ally of the Soviet Union, gave the Kennedy administration reasons to take a decision that colonial Guyana should not achieve independence under a Jagan regime – freely elected or not.

In 1963, the Central Intelligence Agency (CIA) and the American Institute for Free Labour, fostered a general strike that stirred up popular discontent. A wave of racial violence broke out with conflicts among the supporters of the PPP, PNC and a smaller party, the United Force. These actions weakened the Jagan government and frustrated his fight for independence.

The British government, urged on by the US, refused to give colonial Guyana political independence until a new (anti-communist) government was installed. Through a system of proportional representation introduced by the British in 1964, the Burnham-led PNC won the elections of that year; and together with Peter D'Aguiar's United Force, they formed the government. Colonial Guyana achieved its independence two years later in May 1966.

The PNC won the elections of 1968 and 1973 without this coalition. The PNC eventually adopted socialist policies but remained unopposed by the United States and Britain! It was not until 1992 that Cheddi Jagan finally regained power after 28 years in opposition.

The Bahamas and the Eastern Caribbean
Independence in Jamaica, Trinidad & Tobago, Barbados and Guyana ushered in a period of legal decolonisation of the British Caribbean territories. Since independence, these territories have been joined on the constitutional independence trail by Eastern Caribbean islands. In the 1960s and early 1970s, these islands had had a political status called Associated Statehood which means that they had full internal self-government but with defence and external responsibilities still in Britain's hands. The

Bahamas got its independence in 1973, Grenada in 1974, Dominica in 1978, St Lucia in 1979, St Vincent and the Grenadines in 1979, Belize, Antigua and Barbuda in 1981, and St Kitts-Nevis in 1983.

The Bahamas was the last of the major British territories to secure Universal Adult Suffrage and the vote by secret ballot. The secret ballot was first applied to the Bahamian island of New Providence in 1939 and universally applied to the other islands of the Bahamas in 1949. Political activity increased after the end of World War II. Interest in party politics also increased and in 1956 the Progressive Liberal Party (PLP) was formed. This was followed by a rival party, the United Bahamian Party (UBP) in 1958. By 1961 this party had the majority of seats in the Assembly.

The PLP sought to identify with the interests of the Afro-Bahamian majority, the UBP was linked to the interests of the elite. Randol Fawkes, a Afro-Bahamian labour leader, broke with the PLP to form the Bahamas Federation of Labour, a left-wing group. Fawkes and his BFL led several labour strikes and actions in the late 1950s. The Colonial Office took these labour actions seriously and began considering greater people participation in the political process of the Bahamas. In April 1958 Alan Lennox-Boyd, the Secretary of State for the colonies, arrived in Nassau to have constitutional talks. At the end, it was clear that the British government would make important electoral changes to ensure a majority opinion in government. So property qualifications for the vote were abolished and as a result the PLP almost doubled its representation in the Assembly in the 1960 elections.

Women secured the franchise in 1960 and voted in the 1962 elections. As many new enfranchised women voted BFL, the 'women's vote' is said to have caused the defeat of the PLP, which was expected to win. However, the economic downturn contributed to the defeat of the PLP. The traditional propertied classes were clearly disturbed by the possibility of a Afro-Bahamian majority in the government and preferred to vote in the BFL.

Further constitutional changes took place in The Bahamas in 1963 as pressure was increased for a greater degree of self-government. To this end, a delegation, led by Sir Robert Stapleton, went to London in 1963 to hold talks with the British government. The end result was that, from 1 January 1964, the Bahamas got full internal self-government. The country in 1964 was run by a Governor, a Prime Minister, a senate of 15 members (eight to be appointed by the governor, five by the Prime Minister and two by the leader of the opposition) and a House of Assembly with 33 elected members (to be increased to 38 in 1967). Independence eventually came in 1973 during the regime of Lynden Pindling. Pindling remained in power as Prime Minister until 1992.

Fig 17.9 Lynden Pindling

Did you know?

An Associated State is a territory that effectively has independence but maintains constitutional links with another country that handles its external affairs.

Associated Statehood had held out the promise of independence to Eastern Caribbean British-colonised territories.

By the early 1970s the idea that there was some firm association between size and sovereignty was exposed as a myth. So the less populated territories quickly moved towards seeking constitutional independence. According to the agreement with Britain when Associated Statehood was granted to these territories, all that was needed for the transition to independence was a two-thirds majority in a referendum. In other words, the majority of people, as opposed to only their leaders, had to agree to independence. In 1970 Eric Gairy, a once militant union leader who had been active in politics since the 1950s and who was then Premier of Grenada, began to examine the possibility of independence for Grenada. But he pointed out the difficulty of achieving a two-thirds majority of consensus in islands that were divided into partisan political parties, with supporters divided on the matter of independence. So, Britain changed its position, promising to agree to independence if Gairy won an election in which independence was a campaign issue. In 1972, Gairy won the elections and constitutional talks were announced.

Internal opposition to the prospect of independence under Gairy resulted in social unrest in the island. Despite this the British government held to its promise and introduced the legislation necessary for Grenada to achieve its independence. Gairy's government became increasingly politically repressive and was unpopular in the late 1970s. There were demonstrations against him and the radical Maurice Bishop ousted him from power in 1979.

Bishop was leader of a group of young, mostly middle class activists who organised against Gairy's regime. Along with others like Bernard Coard, a Marxist, Bishop formed (and led) the New Jewel Movement (NJM). This was a left-wing party which was determined to rid the island of Gairy. The NJM realised that because of Gairy's alleged dishonest election practices, they could not hope to win power through the ballots. So they decided to seize power by armed insurrection, executing their plans while Gairy was out of the country. Bishop then led the People's Revolutionary Government (PRG). Under the PRG, Bishop introduced reforms designed to improve the conditions of the poor. Health, education and housing were improved. He encouraged wider participation in the island's political affairs by women and the community and he tried to encourage economic diversification away from dependence on primary export products. Like Michael Manley, he established close relations with socialist and communist countries which did not endear him to the USA. But by 1983 a power struggle had developed within the party.

Bernard Coard led a faction that opposed Bishop and tried to force him to introduce changes within the PRG – changes which Bishop did not support. A faction of the island's armed forces under Coard's leadership subsequently placed Bishop under house arrest. Bishop was freed by supporters and he, along with some of his ministers and supporters, took refuge in Fort Rupert. The pro-Coard military faction fired on the Fort, killing some of those within. Bishop and about six of his ministers were killed by a firing-squad. Coard and the military took over for a short while, forming the Revolutionary Military Council. With the support of Jamaica, Barbados and Dominica, the US invaded to restore order to Grenada. After this Hudson Austin (1983), Nicholas Brathwaite (1983-1984) and Herbert Blaize (1984-1989) came to power.

Independence in the Eastern Caribbean

The Edward Heath government in Britain supported the speeding up of decolonisation for the territories that were still semi-dependent. In the post-war years, the maintenance of Caribbean colonies was seen as an economic burden. The policy of decolonisation without referendum that had been applied to Grenada was also carried out in other Associated states. The Labour government in Dominica that assumed office in 1974 requested that the same policy be applied to them. The independence of Dominica was led by Patrick John who remained in power until Eugenia Charles won in 1980. St Lucia's independence, led by John Compton, also did not require the referendum. Compton was in power between 1964 and 1979, and again from 1982 to 1996.

Since 1979 other Eastern Caribbean territories have achieved constitutional independence through collaboration between the British government and local premiers: Vere Bird in Antigua/Barbuda (1976-1994), Milton Cato in St Vincent and the Grenadines (who lost power in 1984 to James Mitchell); and Kennedy Simmonds in St Kitts-Nevis in 1983. Simmonds remained in power until he lost an election to Denzil Douglas in 1995.

Belize also experienced increased nationalist political activity after World War II. The labour movements of the early 1930s produced militancy that resulted in a new constitution in 1935. A major aspect of this new constitution was the re-introduction of the elective principle for the first time since 1871. In 1922, the Honourable EFL Wood of the Wood Commission had suggested that the official majority who could vote should be reduced and that elected members should be included in the Legislative Council. This was done in 1932. The property qualification for the vote and for election of unofficial members still remained high and did not encourage popular voting.

Male voters had to be 21 years old and over and female voters had to be 30 years old and over (until a change in 1950). They had to have a minimum income of $300 per year or property worth $500 or more, or be a householder paying rent of at least $97 per year. Candidates who stood for elections had to have real property valued at at least $500 or an annual income of $1,000. These high qualifications for voting meant that the number of registered voters was low – only 822 in 1945. Even those who could not vote still turned out at the polling stations at election time to support the candidates who were 'anti-establishment' and 'nationalists' – the people's men, like Arthur Balderamos, a lawyer, Robert S Turton, a millionaire who made his fortune from the chicle (gum) industry, and L P Ayuso, also a local businessman. All of them were elected to the Legislative Council, defeating two Englishmen and a lawyer from Guyana. These 'peoples' candidates were supported by the Labourers' and Unemployed Association (LUA) and the middle-class Citizens' Political Party, and were the chief parliamentary opposition after 1936.

Such limited constitutional reforms did not satisfy the social majority. They continued to be organised under Antonio Soberanis to demand more attention to working-class needs. In 1941, several meetings were held in various parts of the country to demand universal adult suffrage. Among those who took part in these mass meetings were elected middle-class politicians, radicals and trade unionists like L D Kemp and R T Meighan. The response of the government was that Belize was too 'backward for the masses to be given the vote'. So Soberanis and others stepped up their agitation for political independence. They did not support Belize joining the West Indies Federation. They rather saw any political union as being with Central America. The devaluation of the dollar at the end of 1949 and its negative impact on the working classes spurred on the campaign for self-government and independence.

Several political and quasi-political groups were formed, such as the Open Forum and the People's Committee, and the Natives First Independent Group. At the mass meetings, George Price and John Smith were speakers. The main political party of the 1950s was the PUP (People's United Party). The aim of the leaders such as George Price, Leigh Richards and Phillip Goldson was to gain political and economic independence for the country. The PUP had a strong alliance with the working class and launched a campaign against colonial oppression by such companies as the Belize Estate Company and the United Fruit Company. They pressed for, and won, universal adult suffrage in 1954. Full internal self-government came in 1964 and full political independence on 21 September 1981. Although Belize gained independence, up to 1992 it maintained troops on the Belize/Guatemala border.

A Governor-General served as Head of State in each of these independent nations. Since 1970 and 1976, Guyana and Trinidad & Tobago respectively have become republics and have abolished the Queen's representative. Instead they created the post of President as titular head of state.

4 Persistent imperialism and dependency in the Commonwealth Caribbean

Not all of the Commonwealth Caribbean territories took the path to independence before 1985, although by this date all of them had achieved significant steps towards full self-government. Bermuda, Montserrat, the British Virgin Islands, the Cayman Islands, the Turks and Caicos Islands and Anguilla are not independent and remain Britain's dependencies up to the present time.

Anguilla

Ever since the arrival of English settlers in Anguilla in the mid-17th Century, the island has been under British domination. From the beginning of its colonial history, Anguilla was an appendage of St Kitts. It entered a political union with St Kitts in 1883 because it was more convenient for British administration of the island. Britain made constitutional changes in Anguilla in 1953 when it decided that the Council in St Kitts (to which Anguilla had sent one representative) should now consist of three nominated unofficial and five elected unofficial members including the administrator. Later Britain interfered in the colony's affairs by creating the West Indies Federation in 1958 with St Kitts, Nevis and Anguilla becoming one unit. This political arrangement ended in 1962. In 1966 Anguilla became part of a Tri-island Associated Statehood with Nevis and St Kitts. According to the 1967 constitution it had one seat in the House of Assembly in contrast to St Kitts's seven and Nevis's two. The islands still had their locally elected councils which had limited powers, for example, managing their constituents' and internal affairs. This, together with the fact that the central government based in St Kitts had such wide powers over their lives and the 'neglect' of the colony by Britain, led once more to agitation in Anguilla to break with St Kitts.

Many Anguillans believed that they would be economically and socially better off if they made this break as the welfare of their population was regarded secondary to that of the people of St Kitts. They protested against what they referred to as 'St Kitts colonialism', choosing instead direct British rule. The British troops were called in to stop this protest in Anguilla and invaded the island on 19 March 1969. Although Anguillans voted in a referendum in 1967 to break away from the Associated Statehood with Nevis and St Kitts but this did not officially come into being until 1980. In 1971 the Anguilla Act was passed, permitting 'Her Majesty's Government in Council' to make provisions for the administration of Anguilla

Ministerial government was introduced to Anguilla in 1976. This meant that the island was administered by an Executive Council consisting of a Chief Minister, two other ministers, two ex-officio members and a Legislative Assembly of elected and non-elected members. The Speaker of the Assembly was called the Commissioner. Since 1976 there have been further constitutional changes. While Anguilla is no longer in Associated Statehood with Nevis and St Kitts, it is still not independent. The 1980 constitution changed the Commissioner's title to Governor and that of the Legislative Assembly to House of Assembly, which was to be dissolved every five years. But the powers of the Governor remained strong and the island is still very much a Crown Colony.

Nevis has also indicated its desire to become independent from St Kitts, but has not yet achieved that goal.

The Cayman Islands

In 1898 Britain took the decision to make the Cayman Islands a dependency of Jamaica. This gave the governor of Jamaica, who was himself an appointee of the British Crown, the right to enact, amend or repeal any Caymanian laws. The people of the Cayman Islands resented this as they felt that their affairs were not properly attended to from Jamaica. Although this dependency status with Jamaica was changed, Britain went back to having imperial power status over the Cayman Islands. A governor, who is appointed by the Crown and reports to Britain, rules the Cayman Islands. Politics and political organisation are based on the principles of authority and control laid down by Britain on how government should be organised. Until 1955 Britain controlled the right of entry to the Cayman Islands. Britain also decided on the type of taxes to be imposed on the islands and had the right to maintain established channels of trade and employment. The governor had veto powers over the local Assembly of Justices and Vestries.

After gaining independence in 1962, Jamaica transferred powers over the Cayman Islands to the administrator of the Cayman Islands. In 1971 the title of administrator was changed to governor and a new constitution came into effect in 1972.

Montserrat

England established imperial control over Montserrat from the earliest days of colonisation. From the 1630s its interest had always conflicted with local interests. This worsened under the Old Representative System when the colony was ruled by a council of twelve local landowners who were appointed by the King on the recommendation of the governor. Montserrat became a Crown Colony in 1866. Under this form of government Britain assumed direct rule over the island and interfered in its political and economic affairs. Support for independence exists in Montserrat, but this movement has had a setback in the aftermath of recent volcanic activity. This has disrupted all aspects of life on the island and forced thousands to flee, many to Britain.

Fig 17.10 Volcanic activity on Montserrat

The British Virgin Islands

In 1810 the administration of the Leeward Islands, of which the BVI formed a part, was divided into two parts. One part was to be governed from Antigua – the seat of the existing government. The other, which included the BVI, was to be governed from St Christopher (St Kitts). Further changes were made in 1833 when the Leeward Islands were reunited under one governor. This governor visited the Virgin Islands at least once a year and remained there for a short time so as to get local information and handle governmental matters which could not be handled from a distance. The governor visited individual islands also in cases of emergency. Otherwise he ran the affairs of all the Leeward Islands from a central base. In the Virgin Islands itself, a President carried out local administrative duties. After 1837 the British government made several attempts to limit or to do away with the local legislature. They joined the Virgin Islands with a neighbouring Leeward Island, making one legislature which contained representatives from the Leeward Islands. The British government also tried to include the Virgin Islands in a general legislature of the entire Leeward Islands. In 1853 there were riots in the Virgin Islands and Britain took this opportunity to bring about more constitutional changes in the Leeward Islands, with Britain assuming more political control. In 1867 Crown Colony government was introduced after the abolition of the elective franchise. This brought in a period of direct British rule.

Why have some territories not taken the path to independence?

One reason is the unwillingness of their leaders to promote independence. Britain has certainly hoped that independence would gradually be achieved and has even tried to build up public support for it. But while support is strong in Montserrat among a large section of the population and among opposition leaders and activists, in the other territories the local political directorate does not seem to want to go that route. In such a case Britain has no alternative but to continue colonial administration. This does not mean that such administration has been satisfactory. The territories have managed to survive because of their roles as tourist centres and tax shelters. They in fact enjoy higher per capita incomes than the small independent states in the Eastern Caribbean.

British policy towards her dependencies changed and became a little more efficient after the 1985 political crisis in the Turks and Caicos, when government officials were arrested and charged with drug smuggling to Miami. A British Commission of Enquiry was set up. The Marshall Report produced by the Constitutional Commission became the blueprint for the administration of the British dependencies. Britain no longer encouraged independence and in fact tightened colonial administration. Each territory has a ministerial government organised by political parties. They also appointed an Ombudsman and increased magisterial powers and the use of multi-party committees in the Legislative Council.

5 Implications of political independence

Independence gave the new Caribbean nations legal control over their foreign affairs for the first time. While they kept traditional ties in trading relations, they also made new ties. Independent nations entered the Commonwealth of Nations, an international organisation made up of independent British territories. The independent nations also joined the United Nations and the Organisation of American States. This gave them new access to sources of technical and financial assistance and the means to improve social services.

Independent nations also made attempts to forge regional unity with other independent and non-independent territories in order to resolve problems of a regional nature. The result was the formation in 1967 of the Caribbean Free Trade Association (CARIFTA) at the Georgetown Conference. This later gave way, through the Treaty of Chaguaramas, to Caribbean Common Market and Community (CARICOM) in 1973. At first, CARICOM's members were made up of the English-speaking territories. Later on, territories like Suriname and Haiti became members. The regional Caribbean Development Bank (CDB) was formed in 1970. Through these organisations the Caribbean nations have tried to forge regional integration and cooperation on a number of social, economic and political matters.

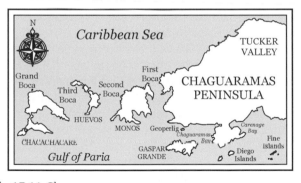

Fig 17.11 Chaguaramas

The aim was for CARIFTA to remove tariffs on trade between territories in the region, for the CDB to help fund developmental projects, and for CARICOM to improve on CARIFTA and solve regional problems and present a united front on international issues. One reason for co-operation was that the small size and limited resources of individual member states posed practical limits on development. However, barriers to full regional integration still exist, and the Caribbean territories have still not resolved issues such as freedom of travel, work permits

and competitive international relations. Nevertheless, CARICOM has survived into the 1990s with new members from the non-English-speaking territories being admitted.

The spread of globalisation and the creation of economic blocs around the world have changed attitudes in the Caribbean towards regional integration. The creation of the European Economic Community (EEC) in Europe and the Mercado Comundel Cono Sur (MERCOSUR) free-trade area in South America have shown the weaknesses of isolated, small states in an age of regional markets. While many are eager to join North American Free Trade Agreement (NAFTA), there is also the realisation that the economic future of the Caribbean depends upon a much greater level of integration than currently exists. There have been some recent initiatives in this direction, for example, the formation of the Organisation of Eastern Caribbean States (OECS) in 1981. This brought together seven territories who now share a common currency (the EC$), and manage shared initiatives on economic affairs, defence and the judiciary.

In 1994 The Association of Caribbean States was established as a body to bring together every Caribbean country and Central America, Mexico, Colombia and Venezuela. It has also been a positive move in the area of regional cooperation. CARICOM has started to move more positively towards creating a genuine free-trade area by abolishing restrictions on the movement of capital, human resources, and businesses in the region.

In 2006 the Caribbean single market came into effect. As independence did not tackle economic power and social justice for the masses, intellectuals have tended to side with the poor, marginalised youth and the unemployed. Members of a radical group called The New World Group which had branches in Guyana, Trinidad & Tobago, Barbados and Jamaica, criticised the continuation of colonial structures and activities after independence.

The New World Group was influenced by Garveyism, Rastafarianism, the writings of Franz Fanon (a Martinican revolutionary and psychiatrist who emphasised the destructive effects of racism on the minds of colonised peoples) and the concept of pan-Africanism. They were also part of the Black Power movement of the 1960s and 1970s, which promoted rebellion in Trinidad & Tobago and Jamaica and raised the political consciousness of the Black community. The various governments of the region were not all sympathetic and many radicals were persecuted. Indeed, the 1960s and 1970s were periods of instability in the Caribbean. Protest was caused only by high unemployment, social deprivation, the frustration of nationalism, persecution of African-Caribbean intellectuals and increasing US interest in what came to be called the 'Caribbean Basin'. Civil wars in Central

America, communism in Cuba and political crises in many Caribbean territories caused the US to develop policies about instability in its 'backyard'.

Social and political protest was evident in many Caribbean territories, including Barbados, Jamaica and Trinidad & Tobago. Jamaica experienced unrest in October 1968 over the immigration exclusion of the Guyanese historian and Black power activist Walter Rodney, by the JLP-led government. Rodney had been hired in that year to teach African history at the UWI, Mona campus. But, in addition to teaching his regular classes, Rodney offered open lectures on African history to the community. He also addressed youth groups outside of the university. The Jamaican political elite came to regard these activities, as well as Rodney's association with Rastafarians, as 'dangerous' and the state denied him re-entry rights. The riots which followed showed up the deep class, race and colour divisions in Jamaican society.

Under Barrow's DLP, in Barbados an alliance developed between European corporate power and African-Barbadian political administrators. Although the DLP was supportive of liberation struggles in Asia and Africa, in 1970 they banned Trinidadian Black Power Activist Stokely Carmichael from addressing public audiences in Barbados. A May 1970 Public Order Act sought to suppress the Black Power Movement and to increase police surveillance of radicals. The BLP, who came to power in 1976 and remained till 1986, was also critical and suspicious of African-Barbadian radicalism. The Public Order Act remained in force under Tom Adams.

In February 1970 a group of intellectuals, mostly Afro-Trinidadian nationalists, organised protests against Prime Minister Eric Williams because they regarded his PNM policies as neo-colonial. Radical activists led a series of demonstrations that escalated into full-scale confrontation with security forces. Williams declared a State of Emergency. When part of the twin-island's 750-strong national Defence Force mutinied and raised fears of a coup, Williams called in warships from Venezuela and the USA. He was also fearful of the Cuban influence. Williams, helped by a strong economy because of the oil boom in the mid-1970s, survived the threat to his regime. He died in office in 1981 and was succeeded by George Chambers who remained Prime Minister until 1986, when A N R Robinson succeeded him.

Jamaica also experienced political problems in the 1970s. The election of the PNP in 1972 brought Michael Manley, son of Norman Manley, to power. Michael Manley promoted democratic socialism. The PNP nationalised parts of the sugar industry, some banks, a handful of businesses and introduced a land reform programme.

The PNP significantly increased a tax levy on foreign companies operating in the island's bauxite industry and tried to bring different investors into the sector. Manley also fostered close ties with socialist and communist countries like Cuba and the then USSR, defying the USA and fuelling the anti-communism of the opposition JLP. The two parties became more defined by Cold War attitudes. Many of their supporters used violence in the name of their party. Political polarisation led to the creation of militarised constituencies in certain areas of Kingston. These areas were dominated by one party or the other and off limits to the opposing party. Elections in the 1970s and 1980s became increasingly violent. The 1976 elections that returned the PNP to power saw the loss of many lives.

Continued internal and external opposition to Michael Manley's policies gave the JLP political mileage and JLP leader Edward Seaga won the elections of 1980. Seaga endorsed the free-market economy and endeared himself to the Reagan regime in the USA and the business classes in Jamaica. He remained one of the USA's staunchest allies in the 1980s. Seaga, who remained in power until 1989, reversed most of Manley's social-democratic reforms.

To sum up

The people of the Caribbean have waged a consistent struggle against colonialism. They used various strategies to show how discontented they were with colonial rule. Their struggles resulted in many constitutional changes, changes that led to the abolition of the Old Representative System and Crown Colony government and eventually led to independence for some territories.

In the next chapter we will read about some of the individuals who helped to bring about independence. We will also see that, despite the struggles of individual nationalists, independence has not become a reality, for example, for some French- and Dutch-colonised territories.

Revision questions

1. Read the passage and then answer the questions that follow:

   By the late 19th Century, many people in the British-colonised Caribbean territories, especially in territories like Jamaica, Trinidad & Tobago, and St Lucia, were becoming increasingly dissatisfied with Crown Colony Government. Many struggled to get rid of it.

a   Explain what is meant by 'Crown Colony government.'
b   What system of government had been in place in Jamaica before the introduction of Crown Colony government?
c   State three reasons why the people in the British-colonised Caribbean territories were 'becoming increasingly dissatisfied with Crown Colony government' by the late 19th Century.
d   State four ways in which the British Government reacted to the people's struggle to get changes in the system of government in their colonies in the Caribbean between 1866 and 1922.

2. Esmie Bourne was the first woman to win a seat in the Barbados House of Assembly as the Barbados Labour Party's representative.

a   In which year did Esmie Bourne win her seat in the Barbados elections?
b   Suggest one reason why Bourne would not have run in an election before the year mentioned at a.
c   Name three other Caribbean women who won seats in general elections between 1944 and 1980.
d   State five reasons why more men than women enter electoral politics in the Caribbean.

3   Write an essay entitled, 'The benefits and negative aspects of independence in my country.'

Chapter 18

Political leaders, national freedom and regional integration

'We forward in this generation, triumphantly...'
(Bob Marley)

Introduction

Many individuals from all classes and ethnic groups are associated with the fight for independence in the different territories. Even in territories that do not have political independence, there are outstanding pro-independence agitators. We will look at a sample of some of the independence movements and their prominent individuals for Trinidad & Tobago, Jamaica, Barbados, Guyana, and the French-, Dutch- and Spanish-speaking territories.

In this chapter we will learn about:
1 Individuals and movements in Trinidad & Tobago
2 Individuals and movements in Barbados
3 Individuals and movements in Jamaica
4 Individuals and movements in Guyana
5 Individuals and movements in Belize
6 The role of women in political movements in the post-slavery period
7 Nationalism and colonialism in the French territories
8 Nationalism and decolonisation in the Spanish Caribbean
9 Some 19th Century Spanish Caribbean freedom fighters
10 Political conditions in the Dutch colonies

Advocate for Cuban independence, José Marti

1 Individuals and movements in Trinidad & Tobago

Arthur Cipriani (1875–1945)

The history of the Trinidadian independence movement and national affirmation involved several people representing different ethnic groups. One such person was Cipriani, who had Corsican ancestry. His social background was that of the old set of estate proprietors of early 20th Century Trinidad. His political awakening happened because of his experiences during World War I as a member of the British West Indies Regiment. His prolonged disagreement with the colonial government sharpened his powers of leadership and brought him back, even before he had gone to war, to Trinidad after demobilisation (the disbanding of troups at the end of World War I) to become the leading spirit in the rehabilitation of the Trinidad Workingman's Association.

Cipriani's platforms were the mayoral office of the capital, and after 1925, an elected seat in the Legislative Council. His real strength, however, lay in the Workingmen's Association which was later renamed the Trinidad Labour Party. In return for the support of the working classes, Cipriani gave them their first real lessons in courageous opposition to colonialism, in the growth of national pride, and in the art of directing social discontent into non-violent political activity. As a self-proclaimed socialist, he supported all sorts of social reform measures. As a Catholic, he defended the religious character of Trinidad against a Protestant-minded Colonial Office. Finally, he completely supported the ideas of compulsory education for all and universal suffrage.

After 1938 the more militant leadership of Uriah Butler and his supporters took over from Cipriani. The Butlerite agitators operated on the belief that the way to advance things was to challenge colonial governors. Their basic achievement was twofold: first they began the rise of trade unions, and then directed the entry of the working class into organised politics.

Eric Williams (1911–1981)

After 1956 politics in Trinidad & Tobago became associated with Eric Williams and the People's National Movement. Indeed, the political history of the Republic is tied to the PNM's effort. They were the first government under the modified Crown Colony regime. Later they were the first government of the independent nation (1962) to fulfil its promise to build up a 'democratic' party of men and women with a sensible programme of economic, social and political reform. This was largely because of the remarkable intellect and personality of Eric Williams.

Fig 18.1 *Eric Williams, scholar and statesman*

Eric Williams, born in 1911, was a brilliant Island scholar who studied at Oxford University in England. His path-breaking historical work, *Capitalism and Slavery* published in 1944, remains an influential book. He became a faculty member at Howard University and later, research secretary of the Caribbean Commission. Williams returned to Trinidad in 1948 as deputy chairman of the Caribbean Research Council, a body of the Caribbean Commission, after his short academic career in the UK and the USA. By 1950 he had become well-known as a scholar and orator and had built up a wide circle of admirers by public lectures, often on aspects of Caribbean history and governance.

His long scholarly training and rigorous intellectual discipline, combined with his strategic position in the Commission, gave him the opportunity to study the Caribbean economy at close hand. This helped him after 1955 to guide the Trinidadian society towards a new nationalism. He built up a mass following through his association with the People's Educational Movement (PEM) under whose umbrella he gave public political speeches. He also rallied people to his political ideas through public lectures in Woodford Square in Port-of-Spain, Trinidad. He campaigned for constitutional changes and, in consultation with George Padmore, C LR James and Arthur Lewis, formally launched a political party – The People's National Movement (PNM) – in 1956. He became Chief Minister of Trinidad & Tobago in 1956 under the changed constitution which ushered in the ministerial system. He was a leading supporter of the ill-fated West Indies Federation. He led Trinidad & Tobago to independence in August 1962.

2 Individuals and movements in Barbados

Grantley Adams (1898–1971)

The foundations of the Barbados independence movement were laid in the years after 1918 and gathered momentum in the years after the 1937–1938 workers' rebellion. Its leader was Clement Payne. Grantley Adams and his colleagues, including Chrissie Braithwaite, CA Brathwaite, JA Martineau, to name a few, defended the Payne movement. Clement Payne is traditionally associated with the rebellion, but he must be seen as one of those important pioneer political figures (as were General Bussa and General Green in 1816 and 1876 respectively) who

Fig 18.2 Grantley Adams, 'Father of the Federation'

helped to pull the fragmented political elements together in order to energise the early national movement.

It was not until the mid-1930s that Adams identified himself with the radical forces. Adams was first and foremost a liberal constitutionalist, convinced of the dominance of politics. He placed major emphasis upon constitutional reform in willing cooperation with liberal governors.

Errol Barrow (1920–1987)

While Adams is known as the 'Father of the Federation', Errol Barrow is regarded as the 'Father of Independence' in Barbados even though the Congress Party under Crawford had carried independence as a major issue in the 1940s. In 1961, the Democratic Labour Party led by Errol Barrow took over the fight for independence. Barrow tried to create a new infrastructure necessary for economic growth. Along with that he campaigned to modernise the machinery of government. At the local level there was the inefficiency and excessive administrative costs of the council system. At island level the Barrow leadership faced the task of revamping a public administration structure designed for colonial ends. Errol Barrow was also known as, 'the education Prime Minister' on account of his policy of compulsory free secondary education for all.

3 Individuals and movements in Jamaica

Alexander Bustamante (1884–1977)

A previous chapter gave some insights on Bustamente's early life and association with the labour movement. He was also associated with the coming of independence in Jamaica in August 1962. It is said that he initially opposed self-government; but later could see clearly the inevitability of independence. After Jamaica withdrew from the Federation in September 1961, Bustamante was a member of the joint parliamentary committee led by Premier Norman Manley. This Committee drafted the independence constitution. He also signed the independence agreement when it was concluded in London. After the general elections of April 1962, which the JLP won, Bustamante was appointed Premier. On independence in August 1962, he became the island's first Prime Minister. He died at the age of 93 on 6 August 1977 – the fifteenth anniversary of Jamaica's independence.

Norman Washington Manley (1893–1969)

Norman Washington Manley, Rhodes scholar and lawyer, is regarded as one of the chief advocates of the cause of self-government for Jamaica. He was also very important in the development of party politics in Jamaica, having formed the PNP in 1938. Through his party he campaigned for self-government and democracy for Jamaica. He supervised several constitutional changes from 1938 and actually helped to pave the way for the coming of independence.

Manley had long opposed Crown Colony government and until 1949 pressed for a total end to the system in Jamaica. He criticised the constitutional changes of 1953, which ushered in ministerial government. The 1953 constitution still left defence, justice and foreign affairs in the hands of the Crown. Manley said that nothing short of self-government would satisfy him and continued to campaign for more changes in the structure of government. He did not want any power to be left in the hands of the Crown through the governor.

Manley and the PNP came to power in 1955. In October 1956 a motion was put in the House of Representatives for a committee to make proposals for full internal self-government. Cabinet government soon followed. Manley temporarily put independence for Jamaica lower on the list of priorities in 1956 in preference for West Indian Federation and independence for the region through federation. So he tied federation to self-government. But it soon seemed that federation was a stumbling block to independence.

When Jamaica withdrew from the Federation, Manley once more took up the struggle for Jamaican independence. He called a referendum in 1961 so that the people could decide whether or not Jamaica should stay in the Federation. He made it clear to the people that Jamaica would seek its own independence if their answer was 'no' to Federation. The resounding 'no' by Jamaicans played right into Manley's plans. Now he could go all out and press for independence. He called an election only a few months after the referendum – in 1962 – and lost to the JLP. In 1962, as chairman, he presided over the joint parliamentary committee (consisting of JLP and PNP members) that framed Jamaica's constitution. The committee solicited contributions from the public and then put the document together. It was not a radical document and was still in the pattern of the Westminster model of government.

4   Individuals and movements in colonial Guyana

Cheddi Jagan (1918–1997)

Cheddi Jagan, a descendant of indentured immigrants, was Chief Minister-Premier of Guyana between 1957 and 1961, and Premier from 1961 to 1964. He studied dentistry in the USA, returning to set up a practice in Guyana in 1943. He soon became involved in politics in Guyana, getting elected to the legislature as an independent candidate in 1947. Shortly after, he joined the British Guiana Labour Party. When that party broke up, he and others formed the PPP. Forbes Burnham became the chairman of the PPP and Cheddi Jagan the leader, with Janet Jagan the secretary. The PPP went on to win the 1953 elections; but Burnham soon left the party on account of disagreements with Cheddi Jagan. Fearing that Jagan might declare Guyana independent and not go through the usual process of constitutional decolonisation, Britain landed troops in Guyana to prevent this. Jagan did indeed wish an independent Guyana; but not just constitutional independence. He wanted independence, economic transformation, social justice and a break with British colonialism in all its manifestations. These 'communist'

Fig 18.3 Forbes Burnham

tendencies were opposed by Britain as well as by the USA, which pressured Britain not to grant Guyana independence even though Britain had promised that whoever won the 1961 elections would take Guyana to independence. Jagan's party won, but the USA announced that Guyana might become a second Cuba under Jagan. Britain was concerned that Jagan would hand over the country to communist Russia. Guyana pressed along instead with internal self-government and the Ministerial system, with Jagan as Chief Minister. As Britain was opposed to independence under Jagan, it was under Forbes Burnham and the UNC that Guyana became independent on 26 May 1966. Jagan must be given credit for his anti-colonial struggle and his efforts to win independence for Guyana.

5   George Price and independence in Belize

George Price (1919–)

George Price was mayor of Belize City in 1958, Chief Minister of Belize from 1961 to 1963, Premier from 1964 to 1981 and Prime Minister from 1981 to 1984, and again in 1989. His political career began in earnest when he ran for election to the Belize City Council in 1944. He lost in 1944 but won at his second try three years later. It was during his time on the City Council that he realised the great need for political change in Belize. He saw that the existing political structures could not change the country for the better, and he was displeased with the fact that the majority of the people had little political power. In 1950, spurred on by the demonstrations against the devaluation of the dollar, he along with about 19 other people formed a People's Committee and agitated in vain, locally and internationally, for the restoration of the dollar. Frustrated and realising that real political change could only come through greater political organisation by the people, he, Philip Goldson, Leigh Richardson and others founded the People's United party (PUP). The PUP struggles for universal adult suffrage, and the first election under Universal Adult Suffrage was held in 1954.Until 1954, as Nigel Bolland has shown, electoral politics was restricted to less than 2 per cent of the population. The PUP won 8 of the 9 seats and continued to defeat the opposition parties in all elections up to 1984. Price was still not satisfied with the political system in Belize even when, under Britain's policy of constitutional decolonisation, the Ministerial and Member's System were introduced. He opposed Federation, and by the 1970s had adopted a pro-independence stance. Under Price's leadership, Belize achieved independence on 21 September 1981.

6   The role of women in political movements in the post-slavery period

The traditional view was that politics meant electoral or representational politics. This gave rise to the perception that Caribbean women were not a part of the political movement as politics at the formal, governmental level has traditionally been exercised by men. But politics must be more broadly defined to take in any activist action to bring about change in people's conditions. In this regard, Caribbean women have always been involved in political activities – from the resistance of indigenous women and female African captives through to the protests of the enslaved and post-slavery struggles.

The political activism of women like Ruth Ambrose, Edris James (Antigua), Nanny Grigg, Eldica Atkins (Barbados), Elma Francois (Trinidad & Tobago), Nanny of the Maroons, Aggie Bernard, Amy Ashwood and Amy Jacques Garvey, Amy Bailey and Una Marson (Jamaica) – to name some – is well-known. But even in the area of electoral and representational politics, a few women have played their part. Before the granting of the vote for women, a few upper and middle class women were appointed – not elected – to some government positions. This meant that from 1949 some women were in the Barbados Legislative Council. However, most upper-and middle-class women preferred to work in social work and voluntary organizations.

Initially, in Barbados, not only could women not vote, but they could not offer themselves as candidates in local or central government elections.

This changed in 1951 when women got elected in local government elections. The denial of the franchise was a factor causing the low participation of women in electoral politics, for most women could not vote until 1951 when the franchise law was implemented.

Even though Universal Adult Suffrage was only granted to Barbadians in 1951, women participated in the political life of the island before that date. The political careers of some women, such as the late Ermie Bourne, Muriel Odessa 'Nellie' Weeks and Muriel Greaves attest to this participation. Greaves was the first woman in Barbados to serve on the Legislative Council (1949–1954) and Florence Daysh the second (1954–1959).

Daysh was later elected to the Federal House of Representatives in 1958. Bourne ran for the BLP in 1951 and won; she won again in 1956 but lost in 1961. Between 1951 and 1961 there were never more than two female candidates in the Barbados general elections.

In Jamaica, women were involved in electoral campaigns before they could vote. The unpopular results of a mayoral election in Kingston in 1853 provoked a protest by opponents, which involved women as well as men. Four of the seven persons sentenced for protest and assault were women. For these women elections were no mere social outing. They had no vote but had clear perceptions of whose victory in the elections would benefit them.

After 1944, there were no longer any formal restrictions on women's participation in elections in Jamaica. In the first elections held in that island after the granting of Universal Adult Suffrage, four women ran as candidates – Mary Morris-Knibb in St Andrew eastern, Frances Brissett in southern Trelawny (both ran as independent candidates), Edith Dalton-James in western St Andrew (representing the PNP) and Iris Collins who represented the JLP in north-west St James. In the 1949 central government elections, Rose Leon was elected on the JLP ticket.

Gradually all women in the Caribbean won the right to vote as Universal Adult Suffrage spread – to Trinidad & Tobago in 1946, Dominica (as to Barbados) in 1951, Belize in 1954, and the Bahamas in 1962. Interestingly, despite the late acquisition of the franchise, by 1981 female voters outnumbered male voters. For example, in all elections in Barbados from 1951-1981, the majority of voters have been women. As the majority of registered voters, women possess the potential to influence the outcome of elections. In addition to voting, some women have helped to form political parties or have been members of women's arms of political parties.

The Barbados Labour Party [BLP] and the Democratic Labour Party (DLP) have autonomous woman's organisations within the party structures. These are the Women's League, which dates from the 1940s and 1950s, and the Democratic League of Women, which dates from 1966. As in other countries, women make up a significant part of the party membership. In 1979 and 1980 in Barbados, 30 per cent of the new members of the BLP and 35 per cent of the DLP were women. In the 1970s, approximately 13.4 per cent of the full membership of the National Executive Council of the BLP were female. The DLP had a similar proportion of females in key decision-making areas of its party. Elsie Burrowes was instrumental in the formation of the DLP. Ten women have held positions in the Barbados Senate and House of Assembly from 1951-1981. Only a few of these women rose to ministerial or cabinet ranks. Since the 1980s women have made great strides in politics in Barbados. Barbados, like Jamaica and Trinidad & Tobago, currently has several women in top political positions.

Other women who were active in the formation of political parties in the British Caribbean territories were Phyllis Allfrey (the DLP in Dominica), Eugenia Charles of the Dominica Freedom Party, who became Dominica's first female Prime Minister, Ivy Johnson and Janet Jagan (the PPP in Guyana), and Vilna Cox (St Vincent Labour Party). As in Barbados, many other Caribbean political parties developed women's arms. In Guyana, there was a women's arm of the PPP called the Women's Progressive Organisation which largely replaced the Guyana Women's Political and Economic Organisation founded in 1946. The Women's Revolutionary Socialist Movement was the women's section of the PNC.

Fig 18.4 Eugenia Charles of the Dominica Freedom Party

When the PPP won the elections after the granting of Universal Adult Suffrage, three women became members of government – Janet Jagan, Jesse Burnham and Jane Philips-Gay. Janet Jagan, co-founder of the PPP, trade union activist and early participant in local and central government politics, was Guyana's President until 1999. She took over when her husband died in 1997 and later won the (disputed) 15 December 1997 general elections.

Fig 18.5 Janet Jagan

In Belize in 1959, women formed the United Women's Group, led by Gwendolyn Lizarraga, as part of the People's United Party. Belizean women also founded the Women's League of Belize in 1935 as an arm of the Labourers' and Unemployed Association. Leading members were Virginia Sanford and Olive Blades.

Women got the vote only in 1962 in The Bahamas and in November of that year women voted for the first time. One historian, Michael Craton, attributed the outcome of the elections to the Cuban crisis and the alleged 'fickleness' of the female vote. The ruling United Bahamian Party (UPB) won the elections even though it was expected that the Black-dominated Progressive Liberal Party (PLP) would win. Dame Doris Johnson (1921-1983) was one Bahamian woman who participated in electoral politics and was an early advocate for giving women the vote. She was the first woman to be nominated to contest a seat in the 1962 general election (running for the Eleuthera district though she later withdrew from the race). She was also appointed to the senate, made a government leader, President of the Senate and a minister of government. She joined the Progressive Liberal Party in 1956.

Other women who have been active in the region's representational political life include diplomats like Lucille Mathurin-Mair of Jamaica; Florence Rapier of Grenada; and the late Dame Nita Barrow, Barbados' first female Governor-General. Not to be forgotten are: Floss Cassasola of Belize's National Independence Party who won a seat in 1952 in the Belize City Council; Vivian Seay, also of Belize, who was a nominated member of the Belize City Council in 1951; Gertrude Protain and Eva Sylvester, early members of the Legislative Council of Grenada; Mary Rose Tuitt of the Austin Bramble-led Progressive Democratic Party in Montserrat who won a seat in the

1970 elections; Margaret Dyer-Howe of Montserrat's People's Liberation Movement who had ministerial responsibility for education, health, women's affairs, community services, culture and sports in the John Osborne government of 1983. There was also Ives Heraldine Rock of St Lucia who in 1974 became the first elected female political representative in St Lucia and second vice-president of the United Workers' Party. Audrey Jeffers and Beatrice Greig of Trinidad & Tobago both participated in City Council elections, Jeffers being elected to the Port-of-Spain City Council in 1936.

7 Nationalism and colonialism in the French territories

The former French-colonised territory of St Domingue achieved its independence by revolutionary means in 1804, renaming itself Haiti. However, the other French-speaking territories have remained dependencies. The government of France did not recognise independence as a legitimate goal for its colonial possessions in the Caribbean. In fact it tightened its hold over its colonies after World War II. A 1946 law made the French colonies 'Overseas Departments of France' and promoted a policy of integration or assimilation of the French Caribbean people into the general French culture. The 1946 constitution put the legislative regime of the overseas Departments on the same basis as that of France. The post of Minister of Colonies was abolished. The Antilles sent representatives to the French Parliament and from this a system of centralised metropolitan rule resulted. A decree of 1947 gave each Department a prefect who had the same powers as those in France. Prefects were responsible for external defence and internal security; they regulated prices and imports/exports. Prefects are the agents of the Minister of the Interior supposed to ensure the loyalty of the departments. The 1946 decree mentioned earlier also abolished the financial powers of the General Council, which lost its former authoritative role in local politics. The government and parliament of France ensured that people from the French Caribbean would be regarded as French citizens just like people in France were.

Political changes to prevent the success of opposition forces

Spurred on by the Algerian revolution in 1954, there has been increasing dissatisfaction with the status of the French Antilles and with the policy of 'assimilation' or absorption into French society. To prevent a recurrence of the Algerian situation in the Caribbean, France made certain changes. In 1958 the constitution of the Fifth Republic transformed Overseas Departments of France into the Community. This was France's one last effort to stop or stall the movement for independence that was sweeping away the overseas possessions of the other European powers.

France appointed a Secretary-General for the French Antilles in 1958 and since 1960 the prefect has been the 'co-ordinator of activities' presiding over all the heads of local services. Since the decree of April 1960 France also increased the power of local authorities. The General Councils gained back some of their former powers. Also as French citizens, the inhabitants of the Overseas Departments have some control over law-making. They vote for deputies to the National Assembly and for members of their own Council-General in the departments. Guadeloupe and Martinique each has three deputies and two senators. Citizens have a judicial system up to and including a Court of Appeal.

Disaffection in the French Départments

Despite these reforms, support for decolonisation has increased, because some see French rule as not solving the problems of the départments. While the state props up the economy, the social structure has remained the same. The European people of French origin, many of whom have lived for generations in these islands, still look to France for protection. As a result, in 1960 thirteen mainly European-French-owned mills controlled about half of the agricultural land in Guadeloupe, and even the land reform of the 1960s has not weakened their control over the best lands. The economy is still dominated by the European-French population, who comprise 2 per cent of the population.

Social inequalities are worsened by economic changes. In fact the condition of the wage earning class has become worse with industrialisation. Social inequalities inevitably express themselves in terms of political protest and foster the rise of communist and socialist parties. Since 1960 there has been an increase in strikes and protests, for example, the arrest and trial of students accused of conspiracy in 1963, at Fort-de-France in 1959, new protests at Fort-de-France in 1965 and explosions of violence at Basse-terre and Point-a-Pitre in 1967. In Guadeloupe, pro-independence groups have burnt shops owned by White people. But then, protest and resistance have always defined the political culture of the Caribbean, and these 20th Century incidents have not meant that ties with France have been severed.

Opposition to independence

Local politics is split over the political status of the French Caribbean. Most of the political parties support only a modification of the existing arrangements. For example, the Union Nationale Radicale, which has a majority in the General Council and represents the majority of the population and the local elites that only modified assimilation will promote nationalism and give the islands and Guyane (French Guyana and formerly 'Cayenne') a social standard that is the same as that of France. *Match*, published in Guadeloupe, is the mouthpiece of the defenders of modified Departmental status. The local elites form a powerful barrier to independence. They fear that any change in the status quo will see a decrease in their power. There are also branches of these parties in France (the RPR and the UDF) which support the local branches.

The local communist party criticises certain aspects of the Departmental status but has not advocated independence. On the contrary, it supports assimilation. The Socialist parties advocate more decentralisation of power but not an abandonment of existing policies.

A change came in 1956 when Aímé Césaire, deputy mayor of Fort-de-France broke with the communist party and adopted a position against Department status. He created the *Parti Progressiste Martiniquais* (PPM) and chose a federal-type solution. To avoid being taken over by the PPM, the local communists also broke with the French Communist Party in 1958. From 1958 on, local communist parties in Martinique and Guadeloupe have criticised Departmental status and have projected an independent stance. They demanded the setting up of a territorial Assembly with its own legislative powers and of an executive responsible to this Assembly. They condemned the policy of integration/assimilation and called for an increase in the powers of the General Council.

The indigenous peoples in Guyane and a section of the African-descended population in Martinique and Guadeloupe believe that under French rule they are more protected from the power of the local elite, particularly the local European-French called *bekes* in Martinique. There is the feeling that they are better off than their independent neighbours. In fact, the per capita income of the inhabitants of Guadeloupe and Martinique is three times that of their neighbours in the British Islands.

Local political support for independence

On the other side are the supporters of local autonomy, e.g. the intellectuals, the PPM, the local communist parties, the *Parti Socialiste Unifie*, and the 'leftist' groups who draw their support from intellectuals – teachers, doctors, journalists [the Association of Antillian Students in France, Catholic students of the *Jeunesse Étudiante Chretienne*, (GONG) *Le Groupe d'Organisation National de la Guadeloupe*, (MIM) *Le Mouvement Independentiste*

Martiniquais, (GRS, banned in1984) *Le Groupe Revolution Socialiste*, the more radical (ARC) *Alliance Revolutionaire Caraibe* and *Groupe De Revolution Armée* (GRA). The latter two have strong trade union and radical student support.

In Guyane, in 1956, Justin Catayee founded the Socialist Party of Guyane. There is also the Communist Party of Guadeloupe, which was founded in 1959. Both these parties want to maintain some link with France but want legislative and executive power, which would ensure the running of Antillian affairs by the Antillians themselves. These calls remained, despite the French granting more local powers by the reforms of the 1960s. In fact, the events in Cuba and Algeria and China have all increased the resolve of the Socialist Party of Guyana and the Communist Party of Guadeloupe to fight for more local self-rule.

Some of these parties believe in a violent solution to the independence struggle and participate in strikes and riots. Members are consistently arrested and deported. Apart from violent activities, signs of unrest are:
- low voter turnout in elections (even when pro-independence parties are contesting the elections, they do not have majority support)
- the formation of cultural associations
- trade union strike activity.

On the whole, distrust of the local European elite and the lack of more attractive alternatives, means that support for independence is only found among the more radical elements. In fact, among those who have an opinion on it, there seems to be more support for decolonisation in metropolitan France than among the territories themselves. Some French-speaking Caribbean peoples also remember the political instability that characterised Haitian independence.

In Haiti the struggle for dominance between the traditionally antagonistic French and mixed-race elements meant that the immediate post-independence leaders – Dessalines, Christophe, Petión and Boyer – did not have complete popular support. There were many short-lived governments and many attempts by external powers to destabilise the country. The imperial powers had never really come to terms with Haitian independence and the clearly articulated intention of Afro-Haitians to rule themselves. The political situation became worse with the US invasions and interference after 1914.

Pro-independence nationalists in the French Caribbean territories

AIMÉ CÉSAIRE

Although there were several individuals in the forefront of the struggle for political changes in the French Caribbean

territories one outstanding personality was Aimé Césaire. He was born in Martinique in 1913 and spent the first 19 years of his life on the island, moving to Paris, France, to study in 1932. He was educated at the École Normale Supériéure in Paris. It was here that his nationalist spirit really grew as he became increasingly aware of the attitude of Europeans to people of African descent. He became a poet, writer and literary critic. He wrote many volumes of poetry and drama and a full-length study of Toussaint L'Ouverture. He also became a political activist. In 1945 he was elected mayor of Fort-de-France and Deputy to the *Assemblée Nationale* as a member of the *Parti Communiste Français*. This political participation contradicted what he said he wanted. According to him, 'It was an adventure... I was not at all predisposed to a political career'. Césaire, nevertheless, was the standard bearer of the Communist Party of Martinique for many years.

By 1956, Césaire had practically rejected communism and had emerged as one of the most outspoken critics of the departmental status of the French Caribbean. He opposed the policy of assimilation, for as he said,

'...in France people spoke of a civilized world and a barbarian world. The barbarian world was Africa, and the civilized world was Europe. Therefore the best thing one could do with an African was to assimilate him: the ideal was to turn him into a Frenchman with Black skin'.

Fig 18.6 *Aimé Césaire*

Chapter 18 | *Political leaders, national freedom and regional integration*

As a writer, the main theme of his literary works was decolonisation, African identity and independence in the Third World. He is most closely associated with the idea of 'négritude' – the assertion of the rights of African people and African pride.

8 Nationalism and decolonisation in the Spanish Caribbean

Independence was achieved in the Spanish Caribbean later than in mainland Latin America. In Latin America between 1814 and 1821 the Creole people through their juntas (military dictatorships), struggled for self-government and freedom from Spanish rule. Among the freedom fighters for Latin American independence were Simón Bolívar (Venezuela, Colombia, Ecuador, Peru), San Martín (Argentina, Paraguay, Uruguay), Manuel Hidalgo, José María (New Spain), and Augustin de Itúrbide (on behalf of Mexico and small Central American states).

Spain, on the other hand, tried to make several concessions to the Creoles in the three Caribbean territories of Cuba, Puerto Rico and Santo Domingo to keep them from breaking away. These concessions helped the enslavers who wanted to keep slavery going for as long as possible. So the Creoles in Puerto Rico and Cuba, for example, stayed away from any movement for independence and remained loyal to Spain. Despite this, nationalism and pro-independence movements still developed.

Dominican Republic

In the Dominican Republic the growth of national consciousness can be dated from around the early 19th Century. An influx of Spanish settlers into this section of Hispaniola led to the emergence of a nationalist middle class from 1815. This middle class pushed for independence from Spain. When in 1822 Haitian forces seized Santo Domingo from Spain, the Dominicans fought to free themselves from Haiti. They finally achieved this in 1844 when they declared the Dominican Republic independent. The emerging middle class formalised independence in 1865. However, independence was limited and weak and they were therefore anxious to consolidate and strengthen it. So it turned over Samaná Bay to the US as an economic base and finally attempted (unsuccessfully) to annex the whole country to the US in 1877. But the door had already been opened for US interests in the country and from 1916 to 1924 the country was occupied by US marines. In the end, the US installed an anti-communist dictator, General Rafael Trujillo who, it is said, killed, imprisoned, tortured or exiled opponents. He was executed in May 1961 (allegedly with CIA help). Trujillo's family and his puppet president, Joaquin Balaguer, tried to hold on to power. The military eventually intervened, set up an interim Council of State and set elections for December 1962. The Juan Bosch-led Dominican Revolutionary Party won the elections. Bosch was not a socialist but he did not persecute the leftists in the way the US wanted. He was more a liberal who permitted freedom of speech and introduced a system of land reform and land allocation to the landless peasants. He was eventually overthrown in 1963 by more conservative, right-wing elements after only seven months in office. An interim administration, led by the businessman Donald Cabral, was installed. In 1965 two coups occurred at the same time: one led by the right wing General Elias Wessin y Wessin, the other by pro-Bosch constitutionalists, consisting of young military officers who wanted to return the PRD, and the exiled Bosch, to power.

Civil war followed when the PRD militants headed by Colonel Francisco Caamaño Deñó seemed to have gotten the upper hand of the other faction it did not please the USA who suspected Deñó of communist links and tendencies. The US invaded in April 1965 to 'restore order'. Elections were held in June 1966. Much political violence accompanied the campaign and the June elections. Hundreds of Bosch supporters were killed, his bodyguard was murdered and his son was shot and wounded. The declared winner was Balaguer, who had been President under Trujillo and who had returned from exile in the USA to contest the elections, forming his own right-wing party. He remained in power until 1978, supported financially by the USA. He presided over a regime in which the PRD was demoralised and terrorised by paramilitary violence.

However, by 1978 the negative economic impact of rising oil prices weakened Balaguer's support base. Even though the PRD had not contested the 1970 and 1974 elections, in 1978 they felt more confident to enter the race. They chose as their candidate Antonio Guzman, who won the elections. Balaguer's supporters, however, kept a majority in the Senate, and Balaguer himself, returned to power in 1986 despite his opponent's charge of electoral fraud in the elections of that year. He again beat Bosch in 1990 when both were 83 and 80 years old respectively.

Cuba

In the case of Cuba and Puerto Rico, the coming of independence was more dramatic. The Cuban-Spanish-American War of 1898 liberated both islands from Spanish rule, but placed them firmly under the influence of the

United States. Cuba did not break out of this mould until 1959 when Fidel Castro took over.

The Cuban War of Independence (or the Ten Years' War, 1868-1878) and the Haitian Revolution were two of the several main revolutionary activities that were aimed at winning independence from colonial rule. Political protest in Cuba was supported by workers who were discontented with plantation society and with the conditions of the un-free and semi-free labouring classes. Creoles whose political aspirations came from the pressure of metropolis and colony also supported political protests. In the 19th Century, Cuba was trying to build a nation undergoing the struggle for national independence. In the 1830s opposition to Spanish rule intensified in Cuba and many young 'liberals' – students, lawyers, journalists – became 'independistas'. These were divided into those who wanted complete independence and those who wanted full internal self-government within the Spanish empire. Some of these liberals were forced into exile and planned Cuban liberation from places of exile in the United States and Latin America.

The search for national independence passed through four phases. The first phase ran from about 1820 to 1844. In this time Cuban Creoles and some *peninsulares* (Spanish-born residents on the island) wanted changes to the tax laws, and some modest changes in the political system. The second phase was from 1844 to 1854. In this phase people wanted a US takeover and the end of Spanish colonial rule. The third phase lasted until the outbreak of the Ten Years' War in 1868. It included the revolutionary wars for complete independence from Spain. The fourth phase started with the War of Independence in 1895.

When the revolution erupted in 1868, it started in the east among small to middling farmers of all colours. They had all along been resentful of the Spanish government. This revolution coincided with the Glorious Revolution in Spain, in September 1868. Most of the Caribbean leaders were respectable upper-class men. Francisco Vincente Aguilera, Pedro Figueredo, and Bartolomé Massó were planters of substantial means, as was Carlos Manuel de Céspedes, whose ancestors were among the early colonists of the 16th Century. Antonio Maceo, who later distinguished himself in the fighting, was a member of the Masonic Lodge of Santiago de Cuba. The war actually started after Céspedes freed his enslaved people and opened the war for independence with the declaration of *Yara* or *grito de Yara* – which called for freedom from Spain, a republican government and the abolition of slavery. Within a month of the outbreak of the revolution, the entire eastern part was up in arms and the revolutionary army had grown into thousands. The revolution later gained the support of the western leaders such as Miguel Adama, José Morales Lemus, and José Manuel Maestre.

The counter-revolutionary activities of the majority of the planters enabled them to successfully attack the rebels. Planters and merchants who wanted to preserve Spanish dominance on the island led these counter-revolutionary attacks. They succeeded in doing this by stalemating, or bringing to a deadlock or standstill, the military conflict. So, although some rebel leaders like Antonio Maceo and Máximo Gómez freed some enslaved people, the number of estates which fell to them was small and as soon as the fighting was over, some enslaved people returned to work on their estates. The rebels had failed to win the war. They signed the Treaty of Zanzon in 1878, which gave amnesty to the rebels if they ceased hostilities. Spain promised emancipation of the enslaved and a greater share in the government for the Creoles.

The final act in the struggle to free the islands from Spanish rule opened with the *Grito de Baire,* or 'Shout of Baire', in Oriente on 24 February 1895. This was the proclamation of the independence of Cuba on 23 February 1895 which took place in the town of Baire. By then, slavery no longer existed and the entire sugar industry had undergone tremendous technological changes, there was increasing restlessness with the inadequacy of the Spanish administration. Small farmers and labourers still suffered from the low prices for their cane, wealthier Cubans complained of high taxes, and all Cubans resented continued Spanish imperialism.

Cuban exiles played an important role in the 1895 War of Independence. José Martí, one of the leaders, made nationalist appeals to the vast majority of the working class. His views were the same as those shared by the veterans of the Ten Years' War who were exiled abroad in Spain. When these exiles returned to Cuba, the Spanish faced a nationalist revolution that they could never defeat. The fighting lasted until 1898 and crippled the entire economic structure in a very short time. By the time the United States formally declared war on Spain, the Spanish power in the Caribbean had been dissolved. The US entered the war because of the fear of continued Spanish influence in the region and its own economic interests in Cuba (see Chapter 13).

There was growing disaffection with the US influence and the policies of pro-US presidents and with military dictators like Batista who seized power in 1952. This disaffection eventually led to increasing protests in Cuba and paved the way for the 1959 revolution led by Fidel Castro. By 1959 Cuba had become a society split by wide income differences, in which rich and poor lived in separate worlds and in which public institutions and political parties were corrupt. Castro has remained in power since 1959, holding firm to his communist ideology and consistently defying US and Western embargoes.

Puerto Rico

Independence was a goal for many in Puerto Rico under Spanish rule. In the 19th Century, the main political division was between the wealthiest classes who often owned businesses, and the small group of educated middle-class liberals who wanted independence from Spain.

There were several conspiracies of these liberals to win independence. One was in 1865 and was led by a Venezuelan, M Rojas, and an exile in New York, Matias Bregman. The war started, as in Cuba, with a *grito de Lares* or declaration of Lares, which called for independence and the emancipation of the enslaved.

Did you know?

Lares is a small mountain town in the central-western area of Puerto Rico. On 23 September 1868 Lares was the scene of the events that gave birth to a social revolution against Spain for Puerto Rican independence.

Although this attempt was defeated, the liberal movement continued growing. As in Cuba there was a split between those 'autonomists' who wanted self-government and the 'unconditionalists' who wanted unconditional freedom from Spain. The autonomists feared that full independence from Spain would bring them under US control. Their leader, Manoz Riviera, got a promise from Spain of self-government in 1897. However, this limited political victory for the liberals was short-lived, as Spain practically surrendered Puerto Rico to the US as part of the settlement of the 1898 war over Cuba.

In the Spanish-Cuban-American war of 1895 to 1898, to win Puerto Rican support, Spain had promised the island internal self-rule. This was in an attempt to stem the tide of independence sentiments by Puerto Rican radicals. Spain also wanted to stop abolitionist sentiments. Spain actually granted Puerto Rico a constitution in 1897. But before it could come into effect, a US expeditionary force was sent to the island in July 1898. By August the island had been taken and the Treaty of Paris in 1898 ceded it to the US. In September 1898, Governor Macias officially ordered the Spanish judges to give up their constitutional powers in favour of US sovereignty. The US forced this treaty as they feared that Spain would grant internal self-government to Puerto Rico and this would make it more difficult for them to gain a foothold in that island.

Limited political reform took place in 1917. For example, the Jones Act of that year gave US citizenship to Puerto Ricans. The US still appointed the governor of the island, but the people could now vote for their senate representatives. Still, the island remained an 'unincorporated territory of the United States'. The wish for independence escalated in the aftermath of the 1930s depression which hit the island as hard as it did places like Cuba. Although high levels of unrest were prevented by direct US control, in 1937 there was a protest led by pro-independence activist Pedro Albizu Campus which ended in a massacre in the town of Ponce. In this 'Palm Sunday' incident, the police opened fire on Campus supporters and some 200 civilians and police were killed or wounded.

In 1940 Luis Muñoz Mann's (1898-1980) Popular Democratic Party came to power. He presented an economic solution to the political tension in Puerto Rico. He rejected the struggle between statehood and independence and stressed the need for economic reform and greater local government control over Puerto Rico's affairs. (See the discussion of Operation Bootstrap in Chapter 11). He pushed for a dominion structure or commonwealth.

Muñoz Mann became governor of Puerto Rico in 1947 when the governorship of the island was transferred from US direct nomination to an elected system. After this Puerto Rico became a Free Associated State. This meant that it had self-government in all local affairs but remained dependent on the US for defence and foreign relations. In 1950 Puerto Rico adopted a new constitution approved by the US Congress and by a majority of Puerto Ricans. This constitution was adopted as Public Law 600 under Harry S Truman's regime. It confirmed Puerto Ricans as US citizens although they were not allowed to send voting representatives to Congress. They had all the obligations of citizens, including military service, but were exempt from federal taxation. But the US government is still obliged to provide grants and other financial support to the island as if it were a state. Puerto Ricans travel freely to live and work in the US, but many still feel like second-class citizens there. Both in the island and on the mainland, many Puerto Ricans remain nationalist and attach great significance to their Hispanic culture. The dream of independence is still present among many on the island.

It was this strong anti-US and pro-independence sentiment that explains the actions of Luis Rosa and other radical nationalists in the 1970s and 1980s. According to a *New York Times* report of 27 January 2000, Rosa was linked to a militant group, Armed Forces for National Liberation (FALN). This group sought independence for Puerto Rico in an armed struggle. Rosa and ten others received sentences of between 35 and 90 years after they were convicted in the early 1980s for treasonable conspiracy and other charges. They served these sentences in US jails until 1999. At that time they were granted clemency by President Bill Clinton. Nine of them have since decided to live in Puerto Rico, among them Rosa himself, Carmen Valentin, Elizam Escobar, Edwin Cortés and Ida Luz Rodriquez.

Puerto Rico is currently governed through a Federal Relations Act and by US congressional government. But this does not mean that all Puerto Ricans are satisfied with their status. While some want to join the union as part of the USA, others prefer the present arrangement but wish to have greater local participation in government. Still others are nationalist and anti-American and wish complete independence. Opinion in the US is also divided and many Americans are ideologicaly opposed to the notion of the US having a colony. This is basically what Puerto Rico is, even though this is not the official designation.

9 Some 19th Century Spanish Caribbean freedom fighters

There were many freedom fighters in Cuba, the Dominican Republic and Puerto Rico. Among them were M Rojas (Puerto Rico), José Martí, Máximo Gómez, Antonio Maceo, Flor Crombet, Guillermo Moncada, Pedro Diaz and later Fidel Castro (Cuba). All of them served in the various revolutionary armies from the period of the Ten Years' War in 1868–1878 to the 1959 revolution. We will discuss three of these heroes and heroines.

José Martí (1853–1895)

José Marti was the son of a policeman. This revolutionary leader and writer was a poet of distinction, an essayist and an art critic. He was a firm believer in independence for Cuba and also believed that the masses had to be educated and mobilised to take part in the struggles for independence. He inspired Cubans to participate in the Ten Years' War (1868–1878) to gain independence. At the age of 16 he was sentenced to work in a chain gang for his role in the Ten Years' War. He was later exiled to Spain where he studied law. He also served periods of exile in Guatemala, Venezuela, Mexico and the US. For a time he was a professor at the University of Guatemala. He was a tireless advocate of Cuban independence and helped to build up support for Cuban independence among elements in the US and the other places of his exile. In 1894 he actually tried to launch an invasion of Cuba from the US but this attempt failed. He participated in the 1895 revolt, landing on the Cuban coast with an expeditionary force of Cuban exiles to join the mixed-race leader, Antonio Maceo, who was already fighting in the island. But he was among the first to die in battle soon after landing. He was afterwards regarded as a martyr for the cause of Cuban independence and became a national hero.

José Antonio Maceo (1845–1896)

José de la Caridad Maceo y Grajales was born on 14 June 1845 in the province of Oriente in Cuba. He was the son of Marcos Maceo, a Afro-Caribbean man, and a mixed-race woman, Maria Grajales y Cuello, both freed people. At an early age Antonio showed an interest in political issues. He was free at a time when slavery was still in force in Cuba and he developed a deep hatred for slavery. He viewed Spanish imperialism as the cause of Cuba's economic and social conditions and vowed to liberate his island. He was part of the army, first as a simple soldier, and rose rapidly in the ranks to become next in command to Maximo Gomez. Both he and Gomez fought in the Ten Years' War and in the 1895 War of Independence. Both symbolised the hopes of the Afro-Cuban people. In every statement that Maceo uttered he stressed independence for the nation and freedom and equality for African-descended people. The emancipation of the enslaved in 1886 did not stop Maceos' criticism of the social system. He continued to fight for Cuban independence from Spanish colonialism as well as freedom from US control. José Antonio Maceo's mother had 13 children, nine of whom lost their lives in Cuba's independence struggles. His mother was very supportive of his political activities and in recognition of her patriotism, the mayor of Havana declared her 'the mother of Cuba' in 1957. Antonio Maceo died in December 1896.

Máximo Gómez (1826–1905)

Gomez was a Dominican by birth, but was involved in the revolutionary struggles in Cuba where he participated in the Ten Years' War as a rebel leader. He returned to the Dominican Republic after the failure to win independence but was asked to return by José Martí. He returned to Cuba to organise rebels for the 1895 war. He was asked to be the president in 1901, but refused the honour.

Vilma Espin

The sister-in-law of Cuban president Fidel Castro, she was also a legendary combatant of the Cuban revolution. She is also the wife of Commander Raul Castro. She writes and speaks on health, political and economic matters. She led the 26 July 1957 movement in Santiago de Cuba Oriente Province. Today she is the national president of the Federation of Cuban Women.

10 Political conditions in the Dutch territories

The Dutch-colonised Caribbean was also affected by the decolonisation movement, though, until 1985, only Suriname had become independent.

Suriname

Suriname became a Dutch colony in 1667 and, except for two short periods of British rule, was part of the Kingdom of the Netherlands until independence in 1975. The question of independence did not surface until 1969 when protest by the people brought down the cabinet. Until then decrease in 1942 and then in 1954 had given more and more autonomy to the country. However, after 1969, support for independence grew in the Netherlands itself where there was opposition to the increased immigration of Surinamese. In 1970 there were 29,000 Surinamese in the Netherlands and by 1975 this figure reached 100,000.

Support for independence also increased in Suriname where in 1972 a new pro-independence government came into power in 1972. In 1974 the Surinamese Premier Henck Arron, leader of a coalition of African- and Javanese-Surinamese parties announced that Suriname was to become independent before 31 December 1975. His Dutch colleague, Joop den Uyl, also in charge of a pro-independence Christian Democratic Party, was only too happy to co-operate as the Dutch had come under international criticism for wanting to hold onto colonies in an age of decolonisation. At the same time there was internal opposition to independence, especially as part of the independence settlement was the phasing out of free emigration to the Netherlands. The major Hindustani Party, headed by Jagernath Lachmon, opposed the cabinet plan. In 1975, it seemed that 80 per cent of the Javanese and 99.9 per cent of the Hindustani population were opposed to independence whereas 50 per cent of Afro-Surinamese were in favour and 50 per cent against. Nevertheless, in 1975 independence came about with the Dutch government giving 2.3 billion guilders to Suriname.

The Antillian group

The Antillian group was part of the Dutch Caribbean since 1634 and consisted of Aruba, Curaçao, Bonaire, Saba, St Eustatius and St Maarten. Unlike Suriname it has not yet achieved full independence. Nevertheless, there have been outbreaks of unrest over the administration of Dutch political control by movements for separate status and independence.

By 1865 the government of the Netherlands Antilles was fully in the hands of the Netherlands. In the same year a constitution was decreed in The Hague for the colony of Curaçao. This did not grant the island independence, instead, it stipulated that a governor appointed by the Crown would have executive power. It also stipulated that Legislative power was to be exercised by the governor in collaboration with a colonial council appointed by the Crown.

This denial of a democratic form of government to the inhabitants of the colony of Curaçao led to protest. From 1895 to 1923 constant conflict existed between the Colonial Council and the government (i.e. the governor and the official staff) and the elite in Curaçao became more and more dissatisfied with the attitude of the colonisers. If a proposal somehow won the appeal of the governor at the local level, the government in The Hague could still reject it. The result was a strong influence by the Netherlands in matters concerning the allocation of government spending in the Antilles, especially in the case of the Dutch government correcting the budget deficits through subsidisation and loans.

In 1936, as a result of continued dissatisfaction on the part of the citizens of Curaçao, a new constitution was proposed for the territory. The representative body, now referred to as 'the Staten', would be made up of ten members chosen by a combination of elections and appointments (five appointed, five elected). The governor continued to have the most political power, and the Netherlands could still intervene in Curaçao's internal affairs. Nevertheless, the 1936 constitution represented a first step in the direction of a more democratic form of government, especially as it introduced limited voting rights, not universal suffrage. The first election under this partial suffrage was held in 1937 and was contested by two political parties: the Catholic Party and the Curaçao Political Unit.

The Dutch Antillian islands got greater autonomy in 1942 during World War II. This did not prevent the Dutch East Indies from declaring their independence in 1949 but Suriname and the Netherlands Antilles did not follow suit. Universal adult suffrage was granted to Curaçao in 1948 however, social unrest remained as the majority of people felt socially and economically insignificant. Their relations with the Netherlands was reformulated by the 1954 *Statuut* or Charter of the Kingdom of the Netherlands, Suriname and the Netherlands Antilles. At the time this was seen as marking the end of the colonial era and a first step towards further constitutional change that would result in full independence for the territories. The Netherlands, Suriname and the Netherlands Antilles would now be regarded as three equal partners, together making up the Kingdom of the Netherlands. Only defence and foreign affairs remained in the hands of the imperial partner in The Hague. All three had to agree on any constitutional changes in the Caribbean territories. Until 1969 the independence question remained at the bottom of the pile of important issues in the Kingdom of the Netherlands. This changed after a major riot broke out in Curaçao in May 1969. Although independence talks increased after this, so far only Suriname has achieved political independence.

Aruba wanted to break away from Curaçao and the separation movement grew in the 1940s. But the Dutch government and Curaçao did not want to break up the unity of the Antillian possessions and refused separation for Aruba. The outbreak of protest in Curaçao in 1969, however, scared the Aruban elite who feared unrest by hostile Afro-Aruban people. In the 1970s agitation grew in Aruba for separate status, through the *Movimiento electoral di Pueblo* (MEP), led by Betico Croes, a former schoolteacher. Their opposition to the new governor, B M Leito, spurred on their agitation. About 57 per cent of Arubans supported separation. Separation was granted in 1986 with a promise of full independence in 1996 because of mounting pressure for *status aparte* and the outbreak of violence in 1977 over the exclusion of the MEP from the federal government.

St Maarten, an island that the Dutch share with the French, half of which is still a colony of the Netherlands, has autonomy in its internal affairs, but the Netherlands controls security and Foreign Affairs. Proposals are currently being discussed to merge the central government with the island government of Curaçao. In 1975, the Prime Minister Juancho Evertsz still did not believe that the Dutch Islands were economically and socially ready to take such a step.

Alternatives to independence are still being debated in the other parts of the Dutch Antilles. Currently though, the inhabitants of the Netherlands, Antilles and Aruba, hold Dutch passports and are entitled to unrestrained settlement and social benefits in the Netherlands, unlike independent Suriname.

To sum up

While independence could not have been achieved without the radicalism of the Caribbean masses, who in many cases participated in anti-colonial protests, it is also recognised that certain individuals came to the fore to lead the various political movements. The list of such persons dealt with in this chapter is by no means exhaustive, but represents a sample. The leadership of Owen Arthur, Prime Minister of Barbados, in forging the

Caribbean Single Market Economy (CSME) in 2006, is an example of nationalist leadership with a regional integration context – the Caribbean as one nation. Men dominated the independence struggle as leaders, though women were not absent. Some of these individuals have now been elevated to the status of National Heroes and Heroines in their respective countries. Many more activists and leaders will emerge as Caribbean peoples continue their struggle for true independence and self-determination in the current age of globalisation.

Revision questions

1   Read the extract and answer the questions that follow:

While territories such as Barbados, Jamaica, Suriname and Trinidad & Tobago achieved independence by the end of 1975, some territories in the French, Dutch and British-colonised Caribbean have remained under the imperial yoke.

a   State the years in which the territories mentioned in the passage gained their independence.
b   Name four figures who were closely associated with the independence movement in the territories mentioned in the passage.
c   Select any one territory mentioned in the passage and outline the steps which that territory took to achieve independence.
d   Name two British, two French and two Dutch Caribbean territories which had not gained independence by 1985.

2   As a class project, research the lives of the following and construct biographical profiles on each. Indicate the role that each played in the political life of his/her country. Be sure to secure photographs of each of these personalities.
Joaquim Balaguer (Domincan Republic)
Vere Bird (Antigua)
Robert Bradshaw (St Kitts/Nevis)
Forbes Burnham (Guyana)
Milton Cato (St Vincent and the Grenadines)
Aimé Césaire (Martinique)
Eugenia Charles (Dominica)
John Compton (St Lucia)
Florence Daysh (Barbados)
Eric Gairy (Grenada)
Patrick John (Dominica)

Mary Morris Knibb (Jamaica)
Rose Leon (Jamaica)
Gwendolyn Lizarraga (Belize)
Janet Jagan (Guyana)
Audrey Jeffers (Trinidad)
Doris Johnson (The Bahamas)
Lynden Pindling (The Bahamas)
Florence Rapier (Grenada)
Heraldine Rock (St Lucia)
Kennedy Simmonds (St Kitts-Nevis)

References and sources for further research

Chapter 1

Beckles, H & Shepherd, V (eds.), *Caribbean slave society and economy: a reader* (Kingston, 1991). See articles by David Geggus, NAT Hall and Andre Midas.

Blackburn, R, *The overthrow of colonial slavery, 1776–1848* (London, 1988)

Bryan, P, *The Haitian revolution and its effects* (Kingston, 1984)

Leyburn, J, *The Haitian people* (New Haven, 1966)

Chapter 2

Beckles, H, *A history of Barbados* (Cambridge,1990)

Beckles, H and Shepherd, V (eds.), *Caribbean slave society and economy: a student reader* (Kingston, 1991) See articles by David Geggus, NAT Hall and Andre Midas

_____, (eds.), *Caribbean freedom: society and economy from emancipation to the present* (Kingston, 1993)

Bennett, J H, *Bondsmen to bishops: slavery and apprenticeship on the Codrington plantation of Barbados* (Berkeley, 1985)

Blackburn, R, *The overthrow of colonial slavery, 1776–1848* (London, 1988)

Bolland, O N, *The formation of a colonial society: Belize from conquest to Crown Colony* (Baltimore, 1977)

Brathwaite, E K & Phillips, A, *The people who came, Book 3* (Trinidad and Jamaica, 1972)

Bryan, P, *The Haitian revolution and its effects* (Kingston, 1984)

Burn, W L, *Emancipation and apprenticeship in the British West Indies* (London, 1937)

Green, W, *British slave emancipation: the sugar colonies and the great experiment* (Oxford, 1976)

Hall, D, *Five of the Leewards* (Barbados, 1971)

Johnson, H, *The Bahamas in slavery and freedom* (Kingston, 1991)

Leyburn, J, *The Haitian people* (New Haven, 1966)

Marshall, W K, *The Colthurst journal* (New York, 1977)

Mathieson, W L, *British slave emancipation and its abolition, 1823–1838* (New York, 1967)

Nicholson, D V, *Excerpts from contemporary sources concerning emancipation in Antigua and Barbuda* (Antigua, 1984)

Richardson, D (ed.), *Abolition and its aftermath: the historical context, 1790–1916* (London, 1985)

Rothe, L, *A description of the island of Antigua* (1846) Trans. Neville Hall (Social History Project, UWI, Mona, 1996)

Saunders, G, *Bahamian society after emancipation (Kingston, 1994)*

Shepherd, V, 'The effects of the abolition of slavery on Jamaican livestock farms', *Slavery and Abolition*, 10: 2 (1989), 188–211

Thompson, A (ed.), *Emancipation 1, a series of lectures to commemorate the 150th anniversary of emancipation* (Barbados, 1984)

Williams, N, *A history of the Cayman Islands* (Grand Cayman, 1970)

Wilmot, S, 'Not "Full Free": The ex-slaves and the Apprenticeship System in Jamaica, 1834–1838', *Jamaica Journal*, 17,3 (1984), 2–10

_____, 'Emancipation in action: workers and wage conflict in Jamaica, 1838–1840', *Jamaica Journal*, 19,3 (1986), 55–62

Chapter 3
Primary

MS 765, 1840. National Library of Jamaica

Parliamentary Papers: Report of the Select Committee, 1842

Secondary

Adamson, A, *Sugar without slaves: the political economy of British Guiana 1838–1904* (New Haven & London, 1972)

Beckles, H, *A history of Barbados* (Cambridge, 1990)

Beckles, H & Shepherd, V (eds.), *Caribbean slave society and economy* (Kingston, 1991) See articles by CLR James and Eric Williams

Beckles H & Shepherd, V (eds.), *Caribbean freedom* (Kingston, 1993) Articles by Bolland, Johnson, Lundhal, LaCerte, Renard, Marshall, Mintz, Scott, Wilmot

Bennett, G W, *An illlustrative history of British Guiana* (Georgetown, 1866)

Bolland, O N, *The formation of a colonial society: Belize from conquest to Crown Colony* (Baltimore and London, 1977)

_____, 'Systems of domination after slavery', *Comparative Studies in Society and History*, 23 (1981), 591–619

_____, *Colonialism and resistance in Belize* (Belize, Kingston, 1988)

Brereton, B, *A history of modern Trinidad, 1783–1962* (Kingston, Port of Spain and London, 1981)

Burn, W, *Emancipation and apprenticeship in the British West Indies* (London, 1937)

Carlyle, T, 'Occasional discourse on the nigger question', *Fraser's Magazine* (London, Dec. 1849)

Carmichael, G, *The history of the West Indian Islands of Trinidad & Tobago, 1498–1900* (London, 1833)

Claypole, W & Robottom, J, *Caribbean Story: Book 2: the inheritors* (London, 1989)

Curtin, P D, *Two Jamaicas: the role of ideas in a tropical country* (Cambridge, Mass., 1955)

Dookhan, I, *A history of the Virgin Islands of the United States* (Kingston, 1994)

Evans, L H, *The Virgin Islands: from naval base to New Deal* (Ann Arbor, 1945)

Fraginals, M M et al. (eds.), *Between slavery and free labour: the Spanish-speaking Caribbean in the 19th century* (Baltimore, 1985) Articles by Bryan & Scott

Green, W, *British slave emancipation* (Oxford, 1976)

Hall, D, 'The Flight from the estates reconsidered: the British West Indies 1838–42', *Journal of Caribbean History*, 10 & 11 (1978), 7–24

_____, *Five of the Leewards* (Barbados, 1971)

_____, *Free Jamaica: an economic history* (London, 1969)

Hiss, P H, *Netherlands America: the Dutch territories in the West* (London, 1943)

Haraksingh, K, 'Sugar estates and labour in Trinidad, 1838–1845', 11th Conference of Caribbean Historians, Curaçao, 1979

McLewin, P, *Power and economic change: the response to emancipation in Jamaica and Guyana 1840–1865* (New York, 1987)

Mintz, S & Price, S (eds.), *Caribbean contours* (Baltimore & London, 1985)

Moore, B, *Race, power and social segmentation in colonial society: Guyana after slavery* (New York, 1987)

Prince, N G, *A Black woman's odyssey through Russia and Jamaica* First pub. 1850 (reprint: New York, 1990)

Riviere, W E, 'Labour shortage in the British West Indies. after emancipation', *Journal of Caribbean History*, 4 (1972), 1–130

Sewell, W G, *The ordeal of free labour in the British West Indies* (London, 1968)

Shepherd, V, 'The Apprenticeship experience on Jamaican livestock farms [pens]', *Jamaica Journal*, 22:1 (1989)

Thompson, A (ed.), *Emancipation 1, a series of lectures to commemorate the 150th anniversary of emancipation* (Cave Hill: Barbados, 1984)

Williams, N, *A history of the Cayman Islands* (Government of the Cayman Islands: Grand Cayman, 1970)

Wilmot, S, 'Not "Full Free": the ex-slaves and the Apprenticeship System in Jamaica, 1834–1838', *Jamaica Journal*, 17,3 (Aug.-Oct, 1984), 2–10

_____, 'Emancipation in action: workers and wage conflict in Jamaica, 1838–1848, *Jamaica Journal*, 19:3 (1986), 55–61

Wood, D, *Trinidad in transition* (Oxford, 1968)

Chapter 4

Adamson, A, 'The impact of indentured immigration on the political economy of British Guiana', in Saunders, K (ed.), *Indentured labour* (London, 1984)

Beckles, H, *A history of Barbados* (Cambridge, 1990)

Beckles, H & Shepherd, V (eds.), *Caribbean freedom* (Kngston, 1993) Articles by Bolland, Johnson, Lundhal, LaCerte, Renard, Marshall, Mintz, Scott and Wilmot

Bennett, G W, *An illustrative history of British Guiana* (Georgetown, 1866)

Boa, S, 'Free villages in St Vincent', unpublished paper, 1998

Bolland, O N, 'Systems of domination after slavery', *Comparative Studies in Society and History*, 23 (1981),591–619

_____, *The formation of a colonial society: Belize from conquest to Crown Colony* (Baltimore and London, 1997)

Brereton, B, *A history of modern Trinidad, 1783–1962* (Kingston, Port-of-Spain, London, 1981)

Carmichael, G, *The history of the West Indian Islands of Trinidad & Tobago, 1498–1900* (London, 1833)

Curtin, P D, *Two Jamaicas: the role of ideas in a tropical society* (Cambridge, Mass., 1955)

Dookhan, I, *A history of the Virgin Islands of the United States* (Kingston, 1994)

Evans, L H, *The Virgin Islands: from naval base to New Deal* (Ann Arbor, 1945)

Farley, R, 'The rise of the peasantry in British Guiana', *Social and Economic Studies*, 2 (1954), 87–103

Fraginals, M M et al. (eds.), *Between slavery and free labor: the Spanish-Speaking Caribbean in the nineteenth Century* (Baltimore, 1985) Articles by Patrick Bryan and A Ramos Mattei

Green, W, *British slave emancipation* (Oxford, 1976)

Hall, D, 'The flight from the estates reconsidered: the British West Indies 1838-42', *Journal of Caribbean History* 10 & 11 (1978),7–24

————, *Five of the Leewards* (Barbados, 1971)

————, *Free Jamaica: an economic history* (London, 1969)

Hiss, P H, *Netherlands America: the Dutch territories in the West* (London, 1943)

Haraksingh, K, 'Sugar estates and labour in Trinidad, 1838–1945' 11th conference of the Association of Caribbean Historians (Curaçao, 1979)

Lewis, A, 'The evolution of the peasantry in the British West Indies', Colonial Office pamphlet, 1936

McLewin, P, *Power and economic change: the response to emancipation in Jamaica and Guyana* (New York, 1987)

Mintz, S & Price, S (eds.), *Caribbean contours* (Baltimore & London, 1985)

Paget, H, 'The free village system in Jamaica', *Caribbean Quarterly*, 1 (1949), 1–19

Prince, N G, *A Black woman's odyssey through Russia and Jamaica: the narrative of Nancy Prince* First Pub. 1850 (New York, 1990)

Riviere, W, 'Labour shortage in the British West Indies after emancipation', *Journal of Caribbean History* 4 (1972), 1–130

Satchell, V, *From plots to plantations* (Kingston, 1990)

Sewell, W G, *The ordeal of free labour in the British West Indies* (London, 1968)

Shepherd, V, 'The apprenticeship experience on Jamaican livestock farms', *Jamaica Journal*, 22.1 (1989)

Williams, N, *A history of the Cayman Islands* (Grand Cayman, 1970)

Wood, D, *Trinidad in transition* (Oxford, 1968)

Chapter 5

Adamson, A, *Sugar without slaves: the economy of British Guiana, 1838–1904* (New Haven & London, 1972)

Beckles, H, *A history of Barbados* (Cambridge, 1990)

Beckles, H & Shepherd, V (eds.), *Caribbean freedom* (Kingston, 1993)

Bennett, G W *An illustrative history of British Guiana* (Georgetown, 1866)

Boa, S, 'Free villages in St Vincent', unpublished paper (1998)

Bolland, O N, 'Systems of domination after slavery', *Comparative Studies in Society and History*, 23 (1981), 591–619

Brereton, B, *A history of modern Trinidad, 1783–1962* (London, 1981)

Curtin, P D, *Two Jamaicas: the role of ideas in a tropical colony* (Cambridge, Mass.,1955)

Dookhan, I, *A post-emancipation history of the West Indies* (London, 1975)

Farley, R, 'The rise of the peasantry in British Guiana', *Social and Economic Studies*, 2 (1954), 87–103

Fraginals, M M et al. (eds.), *Between slavery and free labour: the Spanish speaking Caribbean in the 19th century* (Baltimore, 1985)

Green, W, *British slave emancipation: the sugar colonies and the great experiment, 1830–1865* (Oxford, 1976)

Hall, D, *Five of the Leewards* (Barbados, 1971)

————, *Free Jamaica: an economic history* (London, 1969)

Hiss, P H, *Netherlands America: the Dutch territories in the West* (London, 1943)

Lewis, A, 'The evolution of the peasantry in the British West Indies', Colonial Office pamphlet, 1936

McLewin, P, *Power and economic change: the response to emancipation in Jamaica and Guyana 1840–1865* (New York, 1987)

Mintz, S & Price, S (eds.), *Caribbean contours* (Baltimore & London, 1985)

Paget, H, 'The free village system in Jamaica', *Caribbean Quarterly*, 1 (1949), 1–19

Satchell, V, *From plots to plantations* (Kingston, 1990)

Sewell, W G, *The ordeal of free labour in the British West Indies* (London, 1968)

Williams, N, *A history of the Cayman Islands* (Grand Cayman, 1970)

Wood, D, *Trinidad in transition* (Oxford, 1968)

Chapter 6

Primary

Stephen Harmer to Henry Harmer, 11 Feb. 1840, MS 765, National Library of Jamaica

Select Committee, 1842, Resolution 11

Secondary

Beckles, H & Shepherd, V (eds.), *Caribbean freedom* (Kingston, 1993) See articles on immigrant groups by Moore and Laurence

Bolland, O N, 'Systems of domination after slavery', *Comparative Studies in Society and History*, 23 (1981), 591–619

Carlyle, T, 'Occasional discourse on the nigger question', *Fraser's Magazine* (London, 1849)

Curtin, P D, *Two Jamaicas: the role of ideas in a tropical colony* (Cambridge, Mass., 1955)

Eisner, G, *Jamaica 1830–1930* (Westport, Conn.,1974)

Farley, R, 'The rise of the peasantry in British Guiana', *Social and Economic Studies*, 2 (1954), 87-103

Fraginals, M et al. (eds.), *Between slavery and free labor: the Spanish-speaking Caribbean in the 19th century* (Baltimore, 1985) See articles by Patrick Bryan and Andres Ramos Mattei

Green, W, 'The West Indies and indentured labour migration: the Jamaican experience', in Saunders, K (ed.), *Indentured labour in the British Empire 1834–1920* (London, 1984)

————, *British slave emancipation* (Oxford, 1976)

Hall, D, 'The flight from the estates reconsidered: the BWI 1838-42', *Journal of Caribbean History*, 10 & 11,(1978) 7–24

Johnson, H, *The Bahamas in slavery and freedom* (Kingston, 1991)

Laurence, K O, *Immigration into the West Indies in the nineteenth century* (Barbados, 1971)

Moore, B, *Race, class and social segmentation in colonial society* (New York, 1987)

Riviere, W, 'Labour shortage in the British West Indies after emancipation, *Journal of Caribbean History*, 4, (1972). 1–130

Satchell,V, *From plots to plantations* (Kingston, 1990)

Schuler, M, *Alas, alas, Kongo: a social history of indentured African immigration into Jamaica 1841–1865* (Baltimore & London, 1980)

Sewell, W G, *The ordeal of free labour in the West Indies* (London, 1968)

Vieira, A, 'Emigration from the Portuguese islands in the second half of the 19th century: the case of Madeira', in Higgs, D (ed.), *Portuguese migration in global perspective* Ontario, 1990)

Chapter 7

Green, W, 'The West Indies and indentured labour migration: the Jamaican experience', in Saunders, K (ed.), *Indentured labour in the British Empire 1834–1920* (London, 1984)

Hoefte, R, 'Female indentured labour in Suriname: for better or worse?', *Boletin de Estudios Latinoamericanos y del Caribe*, 42 (1987), 55–70

Laurence, K O, 'The development of medical services in British Guiana and Trinidad', Depts. of History, UWI, pamphlet, n.d.

————, *A question of labour* (Kingston, 1994)

Look Lai, W, *Indentured labour, Caribbean sugar: Chinese and Indian migrants to the British West Indies., 1838–1918* (Baltimore, 1993)

Mangru, B, *Benevolent neutrality: Indian government policy and labour migration to British Guiana 1854–1884* (London, 1987)

Ramesar, M, 'Indentured labour in Trinidad 1880–1917', in Saunders, K (ed.), *Indentured labour in the British Empire 1834–1920* (London, 1984)

————, *Survivors of another crossing: a history of East Indians in Trinidad, 1880–1929* (Trinidad, 1994)

Seecharan, C, *Tiger in the stars: the anatomy of Indian achievement in British Guiana, 1919–1929* (London, 1998)

Shepherd, V, *Transients to settlers: the experience of Indians in Jamaica, 1845–1950* (Leeds/Warwick, 1994)

————, *Maharani's misery: narratives of a passage from India to the Caribbean* (Kingston, 2002)

Tinker, H, *A new system of slavery: the export of Indian labour overseas* (New York, 1974)

Chapter 8

Hoefte, R, *In place of slavery: a social history of British, Indian and Javanese labourers in Suriname* (Gainesville, 1998)

Lamounier, L, 'Between slavery and free labour: early experiments with free labour and patterns of slave emancipation in Brazil and Cuba', in Turner, M (ed.), *From chattel slaves to wage slaves: the dynamics of labour bargaining in the Americas* (London, 1995)

Laurence, K O, *Immigration into the West Indies in the nineteenth century* (Barbados, 1971)

Look Lai, W, *Indentured labour, Caribbean sugar: Chinese and Indian migrants to the British West Indies, 1838–1918* (Baltimore, 1993)

Moore, B, 'The settlement of the Chinese in Guyana in the late 19th century', *Immigrants and minorities*, 7:1 (1988), 48–56

Scott, R, *Slave emancipation in Cuba: the transition to free labour, 1860–1899* (New Jersey, 1985)

Shepherd, V, *Emancipation and immigration: a pan-Caribbean overview* (Kingston, 1999)

Chapter 9

Anderson, B, 'The decline of Friendly Societies of Jamaica: a traditional voluntary association in a developing society', unpublished thesis, Boston College, 1988

Beckles, H, & Shepherd, V (eds.), *Caribbean freedom* (Kingston, 1993) See articles on immigrant groups by Renard, Moore, Turner, Reddock, Trotman, Shepherd, Laurence and Haraksingh

Beckles, H, *A history of Barbados* (Cambridge, 1990)

Bennett, G W, *An illustrative history of British Guiana* (Georgetown, 1866)

Bryan, P, *Philanthropy and social welfare in Jamaica: a historical survey* (Kingston, 1990)

Caldecott, A, *The church in the West Indies* (London, 1898)

Campbell, C, *Colony and nation: a short history of education in Trinidada and Tobago* (Kingston, 1992)

Craton, M, *Empire, enslavement and freedom in the Caribbean* (Kingston, 1997)

Curtin, P D, *Two Jamaicas: the role of ideas in a tropical colony* (Cambridge, Mass., 1955)

De Verteuil, A, *Sir Louis de Verteuil, his life and times: Trinidad 1800-1900* (Trinidad, 1973)

Dookhan, I, *A post-emancipation history of the West Indies* (London, 1975)

Eisner, G, *Jamaica 1830-1930* (Westport, Conn., 1961)

Gordon, S, *A century of West Indian education* (London, 1963)

Green, W, *British slave emancipation: the sugar colonies and the great experiment, 1830–1865* (Oxford, 1976)

Harrichan, Rev R T, ' The work of the Christian churches among the East Indians in Trinidad during the period of indentureship, 1845–1917', pamphlet (Port-of-Spain, 1981)

Helg, A, *Our rightful share: the Afro-Cuban struggle for equality, 1886–1912* (Chapel Hill, 1995)

Holt, T, *The problem of freedom: race, labor and politics in Jamaica and Britain, 1832–1938* (Baltimore, 1992)

Howard, P, 'Culture, nationalism and liberation: the Afro-Cuban Mutual Aid Societies in the 19th century', unpublished Ph.D. thesis, Indiana Univ., 1988

Johnson, H, *The Bahamas in slavery and freedom* (Kingston, 1991)

Laurence, K O, ' The development of medical services in British Guiana and Trinidad', Dept. of History, UWI, n.d.

Moore, B, *Race, power, and social segmentation in colonial society: Guyana after slavery* (New York, 1987)

Prince, N G, *A black woman's odyssey through Russia and Jamaica: the narrative of Nancy Prince* (New York, 1990)

Ramesar, M, *Survivors of another crossing: a history of East Indians in Trinidad, 1880–1946* (Trinidad, 1994)

Reddock, R, *Women , labour and politics in Trinidad and Tobago: a history* (London, 1994)

Rothe, L, *A description of the island of Antigua* (1846) Trans. Neville Hall (Social History Project, UWI, Mona, 1996)

Scott, R, *Slave emancipation in Cuba: the transition to free labour, 1860–1899* (New Jersey, 1985)

Seecharan, C, *Tiger in the stars: the anatomy of Indian achievement in British Guiana, 1919-1929* (New Jersey, 1985)

Shepherd, V, *Transients to settlers: the experience of Indians in Jamaica, 1845–1950* (Leeds/Warwick, 1994)

Tinker, H, *A new system of slavery: the export of Indian labour overseas* (New York, 1974)

Underhill, E B, *The West Indies: the social and religious conditions* (Connecticut, 1970)

Wrong, H, *Government of the West Indies* (New York, 1969)

Chapter 10

Baptiste, F, *War, co-operation and conflcit: the European possessions in the Caribbean, 1939–1945* (New York, 1988)

Beachy, R W, *The British West Indies sugar industry in the late 19th century* (Westport, Conn., 1978)

Beckles, H & Shepherd, V (eds.), *Caribbean freedom* (Kingston, 1993) See articles by Brewster and Thomas, Curtin, Dietz, Fraginals, Goslinga, Lasserre and Mabileau, Levitt and Best, and Lobdell

Brereton, B, *A history of modern Trinidad, 1783–1962* (Kingston, 1981)

Chalmin, P, *The making of a sugar giant: Tate and Lyle 1859–1889* Translated by E Long-Michalke (London, 1990)

Dookhan, I, *A post-emancipation history of the West Indies* (London, 1975)

Eisner, G, *Jamaica 1830–1930* (Westport, Conn., 1974)

Ferguson, J, *The story of the Caribbean people* (Kingston, 1999)

Fraginals, M M et al. (eds.), *Between slavery and free labour: the Spanish speaking Caribbean in the 19th century* (Baltimore, 1985) See articles by Bryan, Fraginals, Garcia, Segrera, Mattei

Fraser, P, ' Some effects of the First World War on the BWI', *Caribbean Societies*, Vol. 1, collected seminar papers, 29 (London, 1982)

Galloway, J, *The sugar cane industry* (Cambridge, 1989)

Guerra, R Y, 'An economic history of Cuban agriculture', in *Sugar and society*, trans. M Urquida (New Haven & London, 1964)

Hagelberg, G B, *The Caribbean sugar industries: constraints and opportunities* (New Haven, 1974)

Hall, D, *Free Jamaica* (London, 1976)

———, *Five of the Leewards* (London, 1971)

Hill, R, *Clear de road: a Virgin Islands history textbook* (US Virgin Islands, 1983)

Johnson, H, *The Bahamas in slavery and freedom* (Kingston, 1991)

Ottey, C R, *The Trinidad callaloo: life in Trinidad from 1851–1900* (Trinidad, 1978)

Premium, B, *Eight years in British Guiana, 1840–1848* Orig. pub. 1850 (London, 1986)

Sealy, N, *Caribbean world: a complete geography* (Cambridge, 1992)

Shepherd, V (ed.), *Women in Caribbean history* (Kingston, 1999)

Chapter 11

Anderson, A H, *Brief sketches of British Honduras* (British Honduras, 1958)

Ashcraft, N, *Colonialism and underdevelopment: process of political change in British Honduras* (New York, 1973)

Beckles, H & Shepherd, V (eds.), *Caribbean freedom* (Kingston, 1993) See articles by Brewster and Thomas, Curtin, Dietz, Fraginals, Goslinga, Lasserre and Mabileau, Levitt and Best, and Lobdell

Bent, R & Golding, E, *A human geography of Jamaica* (Kingston, 1978)

Bergad, L W, *Coffee and the growth of agrarian capitalism in 19th century Puerto Rico* (New Jersey, 1983)

Brereton, B, *A history of modern Trinidad, 1783–1962* (Kingston, 1981)

Campbell, C, 'The dual mandate of the Imperial College of Tropical Agriculture, 1922–1960', *The Jamiacan Historical Review*, Vol XVI (1988)

Dookhan, I, *A post-emancipation history of the West Indies* (London, 1975)

Eisner, G, *Jamaica, 1830–1930* (Westport, Conn., 1974)

Ferguson, J, *The story of the Caribbean people* (Kingston, 1999)

Fraginals, M M et al. (eds.), *Between slavery and free labour: the Spanish-speaking Caribbean in the 19th century* (Baltimore, 1985) See articles by Bryan, Fraginals, Garcia, Segrera, Mattei

Guerra, R Y Sanchez, 'An economic history of Cuban agriculture', in *Sugar and society*, translated by M Urquida (New Haven & London, 1964)

Hall, D, *Free Jamaica* (London, 1976)

———, *Five of the Leewards* (London, 1971)

Hill, R, *Clear de road: a Virgin Islands history textbook* (US Virgin Islands, 1983)

Johnson, H, *The Bahamas in slavery and freedom* (Kingston, 1991)

Knight, F, *The West Indies: genesis of a fragmented nationalism* (New York, 1978)

Luning, H A, 'The economic transformation of family rice in Suriname', (The Netherlands, 1969)

Newton, V, *The silver men: West Indian labour migration to Panama, 1850–1914* (Kingston, 1984)

Report on the economics committee (Trinidad and Tobago, 1949)

Sealy, N, *Caribbean world: a complete geography* (Cambridge, 1992)

Shepherd, V (ed.), *Women in Caribbean history* (Kingston, 1999)

———————, *Slavery without sugar: diversification in Caribbean economy and society since the 17th century* (Gainesville, 2002)

Yelvington, K, *Producing power: ethnicity, gender and class in a Caribbean workplace* (Philadelphia, 1995)

Chapter 12

Beckles, H & Shepherd, V (eds.), *Caribbean freedom* (Kingston, 1993) See articles by Brewster and Thomas, Curtin, Dietz, Fraginals, Goslinga, Lasserre and Mabileau, Levitt and Best, and Lobdell

Brereton, B, *A history of modern Trinidad, 1783–1962* (Kingston, 1981)

Ferguson, J, *The story of the Caribbean people* (Kingston, 1999)

Fog Olwig, F, 'The migration experience: Nevisian women at home and abroad', in Momsen, J (ed.), *Women and change in the Caribbean* (London, 1993)

Gordon, C, 'The effects of underdevelopment on migration from Trinidad and Tobago to the US', unpublished Ph.D. thesis, Howard University, 1984

Johnson, H, *The Bahamas in slavery and freedom* (Kingston, 1991)

Knight, F, *The West Indies: genesis of a fragmented nationalism* (New York, 1978)

Newton, V, *The silver men: West Indian labour migration to Panama, 1850–1914* (Kingston, 1984)

Passaris, C, 'Immigration to Canada in the post-war period', (The Netherlands: Dept. of Caribbean Studies, Royal Institute of Linguistics and Anthropology, 1983)

Richardson, B, *Caribbean migrants* (Knoxville, 1983)

———————, *Panama money in Barbados* (Knoxville, 1985)

———————, *The Caribbean in the wider world, 1492–1992* (Cambridge, 1992)

Sealy, N, *Caribbean world: a complete geography* (Cambridge, 1992)

Shepherd, V, *Transients to settlers: the experiences of Indians in Jamaica, 1845–1945* (Leeds/Warwick, 1994)

———————(ed.), *Women in Caribbean history* (Kingston, 1999)

Chapter 13

Beckles, H & Shepherd, V (eds.), *Caribbean freedom* (Kingston, 1993)

Brisk, W J, *The dilemma of the mini-state Anguilla* (New York, 1969)

Dookhan, I, *The United States in the Caribbean* (London, 1985)

Ferguson, J, *The story of the Caribbean people* (Kingston, 1999)

Jones, C L, *Caribbean interests of the United States* (New York, 1916)

Munroe, D, *Intervention and dollar diplomacy in the Caribbean, 1900–1921* (Princeton, 1964)

Petty, C, *Anguilla: where there's a wiill there's a way* (England, 1984)

Pons, F M, *The Dominican Republic: a national history* (New York, 1995)

Ramirez, E, 'The United States, the European powers and the status quo in the Caribbean, 1810–30', Ph.D. thesis, Oklahoma State Univ., 1979

Sunshine, C, *The Caribbean: survival, struggle and sovereignty* (Washington D.C., 1985)

Sutton, P, *Europe and the Caribbean* (Warwick, 1991)

Thomas, H, *Cuba: the pursuit of freedom* (New York & London, 1971)

Chapter 14

Beckles, H & Shepherd, V (eds.), *Caribbean freedom* (Kingston, 1993) See articles by Hart, Lewis and Martin

Bolland, O N, *Colonialism and resistance in Belize* (Belize, 1988)

———————, *On the march: labour rebellions in the British Caribbean, 1934–1939* (Kingston, 1995)

Brathwaite, K & Phillips, A, *The people who came Bk 3* (Trinidad and Jamaica, 1972)

Claypole, W & Robottom, J *Caribbean story. Bk 2: the inheritors* (London, 1989)

Daley, V T, *The making of Guyana* (London, 1974)

Duncker, S, *A visual history of the West Indies* (London, 1965)

Edwards, A, *Marcus Garvey, 1887–1940* (London, 1967)

French, J, ' Colonial policy towards women in Jamaica after the 1938 rebellion', in *Caribbean Quaterly*, Vol.34 (1988)

appendix | *References and sources for further research*

Hart, R, *From occupation to independence: a short history of the English-speaking Caribbean region* (London, 1998)

Innis, Sir P, *Whither bound St Kitts-Nevis?* (St Johns, Antigua, 1983)

'In memory of the late Ms Aggie Bernard', *NWU News*, (December 1980)

James, C L R, *A history of Negro revolt* (London, 1985)

Johnson, H, *The Bahamas in slavery and freedom* (Kingston, 1991)

Knowles, W, *Trade union development and relations in the British West Indies* (Berkely & Los Angeles, 1959)

Leslie, R, *A history of Belize* (Belize, 1996)

McFarlane, 'Women in protest', *Caribbean Studies* (Mona, 1992)

Nettleford, R, *Norman Washington Manley and the new Jamaica: selected speeches and writings 1936–1968* (1971)

Post, K, *Strike the iron* (Boston, 1991)

Reddock, R, *Elma François, the NWSCA and the workers' struggle for change in the Caribbean in the 1930s* (London, 1998)

_____, *Women, labour and politics in Trinidad and Tobago* (Kingston, 1994)

Richards, G, 'The 1935 labour disturbances in St Kitts: form and objectives', Dept. of History seminar paper, UWI, Mona, 1989

Samaroo, B, 'Politics and Afro-Indian realtions in Trinidad', in LaGuerre, J (ed.), *Calcutta to Caroni: the East Indians in Trinidad* (Trinidad, 1974)

Shepherd, V, *Transients to settlers: the experience of Indians in Jamaica* (Leeds/Warwick, 1994)

_____, (ed.), *Women in Caribbean History* (Kingston, 1999)

Sheppard, J, *Marryshow of Grenada* (Barbados, 1987)

Shoman, A, *Party politics in Belize, 1950–1986* (Belize, 1987)

Singh, K, *Race and class struggles in a colonial state: Trinidad, 1917–1945* (Kingston, 1994)

Smith, K B & F C, *To shoot hard labour: the life and times of Samuel Smith, an Antiguan workingman, 1877–1982* (Canada, 1986)

Stone, C & Brown, A (eds.), *Essays on power and change in Jamaica* (Kingston, 1977)

Tyson, J D, *Report on the conditions of Indians in Trinidad, British Guiana and Jamaica* (Simla, 1939)

Chapter 15

Antiguan woman (*Antiguan woman*, Vol 2:14, Dec. 1993, p.3)

Barrow, C (ed.), *Caribbean portraits: essays on gender ideologies and identities* (Kingston, 1998)

Beckwith, M, *Black roadways: a study of Jamaican folklore* (New York, 1969)

Brereton, B, *Social life in the Caribbean, 1838–1938* (London, 1986)

Caldecott, A, *The church in the West Indies* (London, 1970)

Clarke, C, Kingston, *Jamaica: urban development and social change, 1692–1962* (Los Angeles & London, 1975)

Dookhan, I, *A post-emancipation history of the West Indies* (London, 1975)

Doodnath, S, *A short history of the East India progress and lives of famous Indians, 1845–1984* (La Romain, n.d.)

Ford-Smith Honor, *Two experiments in popular theatre and women's history* (Jamaica, 1987)

Hall, D, *Free Jamaica, 1838–1865* (London, 1976)

Higman, B W, *Slave population and economy in Jamaica, 1801–1834* (Cambridge, 1976)

_____, 'Slavery remembered: the celebration of emancipation in Jamaica', *Journal of Caribbean History*, 12 (1979)

Horowitz, M (ed.), *Peoples and cultures of the Caribbean: an anthropological reader.* American Museum of Natural History (New York, 1971)

Hoetinck, H, *The two variants in Caribbean race relations* (London, 1967)

Jha, J C, 'The Indian heritage in Trinidad', in La Guerre, J, *Calcutta to Caroni: the East Indians of Trinidad* (Trinidad, 1974)

Look Lai, W, *Indentured labour, Caribbean sugar* (Baltimore, 1994)

Lumsden, J, 'The People's Convention: celebrating the Diamond Jubilee of full freedom in Jamaica', paper presented at the Emancipation symposium, 8 Oct. 1994, Dept. of History, UWI, Mona

Mansingh, L, 'Cultural heritage among East Indians', unpublished paper

Mansingh, A and L, 'East Indians in Jamaica', unpublished paper

_____, *Home away from home* (Kingston, 1999)

Mohammed, P & Perkins, A, *Caribbean women at the crossroads* (Kingston, 1999)

Moore, B, *Cultural power, resistance and pluralism: colonial Guyana, 1838–1900* (Kingston, 1995)

Nettleford, R, *Caribbean cultural identity: the case of Jamaica* (Kingston, 1978)

Olivier, S, *Jamaica: the blessed island* (New York, 1971)

Plummer, J, *Movement of Jah people: the growth of Rastafarians* (Birmingham, 1978)

Rogler, 'Role of semantics in the study of race distance in Puerto Rico', *Social Faces*, Vol XXII, (October 1943–May 1944)

Sewell, W, *The ordeal of free labour in the British West Indies* (London, 1968)

Smith, H F, 'Caribbean women in social change: some aspects of our history' (FES, 1986)

Smith, M G, *The plural society of the British West Indies* (Berkeley, Los Angeles & London, 1965)

Trollope, A A, *The West Indies and the Spanish Main* (London, 1860)

Wood, D, *Trinidad in transition: the years after slavery* (London & New York, 1986)

Yin, Lee Tom, *The Chinese in America* (Kingston, 1963)

Chapter 16

Ahye, M, *Golden heritage: the dance in Trinidad and Tobago* (Trinidad and Tobago, 1978)

Anthony, M, *The making of Port of Spain, Vol. 1* (Trinidad and Tobago, 1978)

Barrett, L, *The sun and the drum: African roots in Jamaican folk tradition* (Kingston, 1979)

Beckles, H, *The development of West Indies cricket: the age of nationalism* (Kingston & London, 1998)

————, *The development of West Indies cricket: the age of globalisation* (Kingston & London, 1998)

Bettleheim, J (ed.), *Cuban festivals: a century of Afro-Cuban culture* (Kingston, 2001)

Boxer, D & Poupeye, V, *Modern Jamaican art* (Kingston, 1998)

Boyce-Davies, C, *Caribbean literature* (Encarta website)

Brereton, B & Yelvington, K A (eds.), *The colonial Caribbean in transition: essays on post-emancipation social and cultural history* (Kingston, 1999)

Brereton, B, *Social life in the Caribbean, 1838–1938* (London, 1986)

Broodhagen, K, 'Tribute: an exhibition of Karl Broodhagen', National Culture Foundation, 1985 (See also feature in *Caribbean Beat*, BWIA in-flight magazine, 34, 1998, 33–39)

Buisseret, D, *Historic architecture of the Caribbean* (London, 1980)

Burnett, M, *Music of the Caribbean* (London, 1981)

Bute, E L, *The Black handbook: the people, history and politics of Africa and the African diaspora* (Kingston, 1997)

Bynse, P, *The architecture of Trinidad and Tobago, 1562–1962* (Port-of-Spain, 1962)

Caldecott, A, *The church in the West Indies* (London, 1970)

Camnitzer, L, *New art of Cuba* (Austin, 1994)

Caribbean Beat (November–December 1997)

Cashmore, E, *Black sportsmen* (London and Boston, 1982)

Chang, K O & Chen, W, *Reggae routes: the story of Jamaica music* (Kingston, 1998)

Chevannes, B, *Rastafari: roots and ideology* (Syracuse, 1994)

Clarke, A, 'The music and musical instruments of Jamaica', in *Caribbean Quarterly*, Vol.9: 2 & 3 (1975)

Clarke, C, *Kingston, Jamaica: urban development and social change, 1692–1962* (Los Angeles, 1975)

Cobley, A and Thompson, A (eds.), *The African Caribbean connection* (Barbados, 1990)

Constance, O Z, *Tassa, chutney and soca: the East Indian contribution* (Trinidad and Tobago, 1991)

Corsbie, K, *Theatre in the Caribbean* (London, 1984)

Dookhan, I, *A post-emancipation history of the West Indies* (London, 1975)

Doodnath, S, *A short history of the East India Progress and lives of famous Indians, 1845–1984* (La Romain, n.d.)

Dunham, K, *Dance in Haiti* (Los Angeles, 1983)

Dunn, H S (ed.), *Globalization, communications and Caribbean identity* (New York 1995)

Elder, J, *From steelband to Congo drum* (Trinidad, 1969)

Ford-Smith, Honor, *Two experiments in popular theatre and women's history* (Jamaica, 1987)

Edna Manley School for Visual Arts (Kingston, 1991)

Fraser, H, & Hughes, R, *Historic houses of Barbados* (Barbados, 1982)

Gift, E, Special issue of the Trinidad and Tobago Teachers' Association Journal, *Art forms in the Caribbean*

Gosner, P, *Caribbean baroque: historical architecture of the Spanish Antilles* (Colorado, 1996)

Higman, B W, *Domestic service in Jamaica since 1750* (London, 1983)

Hill, E, *The Jamaican stage 1655–1900: profile of a colonial theatre* (Amherst, 1992)

appendix | *References and sources for further research*

_____ , 'The emergence of a national drama in the West Indies', in _Caribbean Quarterly_, 18:4 (1972), pp 9–40

Hippolyte, K, 'Lucian Kaiso' (Folk Research Unit, 1990)

Jamaica Cultural Development Commission, Mento Yard Programme, 1994

Jamaica Memory Bank, 'Com mek me hol yu han: the imapct of tourism on traditional music' (Kingston, 1998)

Jha, J C ' The Indian heritage in Trinidad', in LaGuerre, J, _Calcutta to Caroni: the East Indians of Trinidad_ (Trinidad, 1974)

Kennedy, R G, _Architecture, men, women and money: America 1600-1860_ (New York, 1985)

King, B & Walcott, D, _West Indian drama_ (Oxford, 1995)

Lekie. L, _The origin and development of ethnic dance and music_ (Ann Arbor, 1956)

Macedo, L, _Fiction and film: the influence of cinema on writers from Trinidad and Jamaica_ (London, 2003)

Mbye, C B (ed.), _Ex-iles: essays on Caribbean cinema_ (New Jersey, 1992)

Manuel, P L, _Caribbean music_ (Encarta. MSN.com: Microsoft/Encyclopaedia/Encarta, 1993–1999)

Mansingh, L, 'Cultural heritage among East Indians', unpublished paper

Mansingh, A & L, 'East Indians in Jamaica', unpublished paper

_____ , _Home away from home_ (Kingston, 1999)

McCarthy-Brown, K, _Tracing the spirit: ethnographic essays on Haitian art_ (Seattle, 1995)

Moore, B, _Cultural power, resistance and pluralism: colonial Guyana, 1838–1900_ (Kingston, 1995)

Nelson, L, _Rural Cuba_ (Minneapolis, 1950)

Nettleford, R, _Caribbean cultural identity: the case of Jamaica_ (Kingston, 1978)

Nunley, J W and Bettleheim, J, _Caribbean Festival Arts: each and every bit of difference_ (London, 1988)

Ottley, R, _Women in calypso_ (Trinidad, 1992)

Rodriguez, L E, 'The architectural avant garde: from art deco to modern regionalism', trans. by John Beusterien and Narciso Menocal, in _The Journal of Decorative and Propoganda Arts_, no. 22 (1996)

Saunders, G & Cartwright, D, _Historic Nassau_ (London, 1997)

Social history workshop, 'Music, dance and society', Session 4, UWI, Mona, 1985

Stebich, U, _A Haitian celebration: arts and culture_ (Milwaukee Art Museum, 1992)

St Omer, D, _Popularised printing as 'communication'_ (St Lucia, 1976)

Walmsley, A, _The Caribbean Artists' Movement 1966–1972_ (London, 1992)

Yin, L T, _The Chinese in Jamaica_ (Kingston, 1963)

Chapter 17

Beckles, H & Shepherd, V (eds.), _Caribbean freedom_ (Kingston, 1993) See articles by Beckles, Belle, Hart, Lasserre and Mabileau, Lewis, Nettleford, Ruiz, Stubbs, Suchlicki and Wallace

Brereton, B, 'The reform movement in Trinidad in the later 19th century', in _Political protest and political organisation in the Caribbean from the late 19th century_, Vol 1, papers presented at the 5th Annual Conference of the Association of Caribbean Historians, UWI, St Augustine, 9–13 April, 1973

Bolland, N, _Colonialism and resistance in Belize_ (Belize, 1988)

Campbell, C, 'The opposition to Crown Colony government in Trinidad before and after emancipation, 1813–1846', in Higman, B (ed.), _Trade, government and society_ (Kingston, 1983)

Carter, E H et al., _History of the West Indian people: 18th century to modern times_ (Trinidad, 1976)

Craton, M, _Empire, enslavement and freedom in the Caribbean_ (Kingston, 1997)

Dookhan, I, _A post-emancipation history of the West Indies_ (London, 1975)

Lewis, G K, _The growth of the modern West Indies_ (New York, 1968)

McLaughlin, S J, _Development of parliamentary government in the Cayman Islands_ (Cayman Islands, 1992)

Pons, F M, _The Dominican republic: a national history_ (New York, 1995)

Reddock, R, _Women, labour and polilitcs in Trinidad and Tobago: a history_ (London & New Jersey, 1994)

Sutton, P (ed.), _Europe and the Caribbean_ (Warwick, 1991)

Wallace, E, _The British Caribbean: from the decline of colonialism to the end of Federation_ (Toronto, 1977)

Williams, E, _History of the people of Trinidad and Tobago_ (London, 1962)

Williams, N, _A history of the Cayman Islands_ (Grand Cayman, 1970)

Shepherd, V (ed.), _Women in Caribbean history_ (Kingston, 1999)

Sunshine, C, _The Caribbean: survival, struggle and sovereignty_ (Washington D.C., 1985)

Chapter 18

Beckles, H & Shepherd, V (eds.), *Caribbean freedom* (Kingston, 1993) See articles by Beckles, Belle, Hart, Lasserre and Mabileau, Lewis, Nettleford, Ruiz, Stubbs, Suchlicki and Wallace

Beckles, H, *History of Barbados* (Cambridge, 1990)

Brathwaite, K & Phillips, A, *The people who came, Bk 3* (Trinidad and Jamaica, 1972)

Brereton, B, *A history of modern Trinidad, 1783–1962* (Kingston, 1981)

Bryan, P, *The Haitian revolution and its effects* (Kingston, 1984)

Carnegie, J, *Some aspects of Jamaican politics, 1918–1938* (Kingston, 1973)

Césaire, A, *Discourse on colonialism* (New York, 1972)

Duncan, N, *Women and politics in Barbados* (Kingston, 1983)

Duncker, S, *A visual history of the West Indies* (London, 1965)

Ferguson, J, *The story of the Caribbean people* (Kingston, 1999)

Fraser, L M, *History of Trinidad. 2 vols.* (London, 1971)

Hart, R, *From occupation to independence: a short history of the English-speaking Caribbean region* (London, 1998)

Harvey, W W, *Sketches of Haiti: from the expulsion of the French to the death of Christophe* (London, n.d.)

Henry, P & Stone, C (eds.), *The new Caribbean: decolonisation, democracy and development* (Philadelphia, 1983)

Knight, F, 'Political protest and organisation in Cuba during the 19th century', in *Political protest and political organisation in the Caribbean from the late 19th century*, Vol 1, papers presented at the 5th Annual Conference of the Association of Caribbean Historians, UWI, St Augustine, 9–13 April, 1973

Sedoe-Dahlberg, B (ed.), *The Dutch Caribbean: prospects for democracy* (New York, 1990)

Shepherd, V (ed.), *Women in Caribbean history* (Kingston, 1999)

Sunshine, C, *The Caribbean: survival, struggle and sovereignty* (Washington D.C., 1985)

Weinstein, B, *The French island possessions: evolving status and continuing tensions* (Washington D.C., 1978)

Williams, E, *History of the people of Trinidad and Tobago* (London, 1962)

Williams, N, *A history of the Cayman Islands* (Grand Cayman, 1970)

Websites consulted

http://centrelink.org

http://www.cubanfineart.com/images/k_pictografia_20.jpg

http://www.geocites.com/ronemrit/pofiles/cazabon.jpg

http://www.cubanfineart.com

http://linrary.ucf.edu/SpecialCollections/Exhibits/past/OurIslandHomesExhibits.htm

www.aragornsstudio.com/CaribCrafts/DSC_0137.jpg

dreadeye@surfbvi.com

www.playjouvert.com

http://www.guyanaundersiege.com/Cultural/Chutney%Music%20.htm

http://davidrudder.co.tt/

http://bbc.co.uk

http://www.kaiso.net

http://www.calypsoworld.org

www.oecsathlete.com/main/printer_friendly.php?news_id=587&team_id=&sport_i

www.grenadines.net/carriacou/carriacouartist.htm

appendix | *References and sources for further research*

Glossary and abbreviations

A.C.S.	Association of Caribbean States
anthropology	the study of the cultures of different peoples
Apprenticeship	the transitional period between 1834 and 1838 when full freedom was granted in the British-colonised Caribbean
arbitration	the hearing and settlement by a third party of a legal dispute between two parties
ateliers de discipline	workhouses in the French Caribbean
bounty system	the system whereby Caribbean governments imported labourers at public expense, through taxes
campesinos	a term used for peasants in the Spanish Caribbean
CARICOM	Caribbean Community (an organization of Caribbean countries working to achieve economic and political co-operation/integration)
cartel	a number of companies that come together to keep up prices and kill competition
caudrillas	work gangs
code rural	a labour code introduced by Dessalines in Haiti in the post-slavery period
Colonial Development and Welfare Act	an Act passed after the 1930s labour protests in the British-colonised Caribbean to help fund economic and social programmes
Dance of the Millions	the unprecedented economic boom in Cuba in 1920 as a result of the high price of Cuban sugar on the world market
Deane Commission	a Commission sent out to investigate the social conditions of the British-colonised Caribbean after 1939
dockers	wharf workers
elective principle	the principle that government representatives should be elected by the people, not selected or nominated by a governor or monarch
Encumbered Estates Court Act	an Act approved by the British parliament in 1854, and adopted in some Caribbean territories, to hasten the sale and transfer of land held by insolvent landowners
E.U.	European Union (a common market area of Europe)
feminist	a person who believes in gender equality and who is an activist for women's rights
free birth/free womb	the name given to the system in the Danish Caribbean whereby, after 1847, no African-descended woman could give birth to unfree children. In other words, all African children were born free after 1847
freehold	legal ownership of land, not rented land
G.A.T.T.	General Agreement on Trade and Tariffs (now replaced by the W.T.O.)
gender roles	the roles that society assigns to men and women
Gladstone Experiment	the experimental importation of Indians to colonial Guyana by John Gladstone in 1838
Great Depression	the economic crisis in the industrial world in 1929 and its consequences
higgler	a market seller in an urban area
iconography	literally, the writing of images; the study of symbols used in painting; the art of illustration
intra-Caribbean migration	the movement of people from one Caribbean territory to another
intransigent	uncooperative, rebellious
isthmus	a narrow strip of land connecting two larger bits of land
liquidate	to close down a business and divide its value among its creditors; to pay off and settle a debt
Lome Convention	preferential trade agreement extended by Europe to former European colonies

manumission	a process by which enslaved people and apprentices could buy their freedom
Masters and Servants Act	an Act passed in several Caribbean territories to regulate the relationship between labourers and employers and to control the freedom of movement of labourers
metaire/metayage	a system of share-cropping used in some Caribbean territories, especially in the Windward Islands
monocultural	dependence on one crop or commodity
Moret Law	the 1870 partial abolition law passed in Puerto Rico to facilitate a gradual move to abolition
N.A.F.T.A.	North American Free Trade Area
nationalisation	a process whereby a government removes control of a business from private hands and transfers it to state control
negritude	assertion of African people's rights and African pride by African-descended people; an idea and movement most associated with Aimé Césaire
nett	the value of something after all necessary deductions
non-praedial	the name used to describe apprentices who were not agricultural field workers; as opposed to praedial apprentices who were attached to plantations or other agricultural units in the British colonies
Norman Commission	an 1896 Commission appointed by Joseph Chamberlain and headed by Sir Henry Norman. Its purpose was to investigate and report on causes of British Caribbean economic problems
N.W.S.C.A.	Negro Welfare Cultural and Social Association (Formed by Elma François)
O.A.S.	Organisation of American States
O.E.C.S.	Organisation of Eastern Caribbean States
ordinances	laws sent down by the Crown to be implemented in the colonies, especially the Crown Colonies like Trinidad and St Lucia. These colonies did not have local law-making bodies like the colonies with the Old Representative System
patented	placing a copyright on an invention so that another person cannot claim that he/she invented it
patriarchal domination	a society in which men dominate politics, the economy and society, while women are treated as if they are second-class citizens
patrifocal	centred on the father
patrocinados	the name given to those under the Patronato system
Patronato	the transitional period between slavery and freedom introduced in Cuba in 1880
per capita	average income earned by each person (or head) in a population
perches of land	28 perches = 0.175 acre of land
plural society	according to some sociologists, a society in which there are different ethnic groups that lack a common social will and are kept together only through external forces
polyandry	keeping several male partners at the same time
rations	allowances in kind provided by employers under the metayage system
recaptives	the name given to 'Liberated' Africans
rent-free tenant system	labourers who worked on estates were allowed to occupy estate land without paying
repatriation	the provision of free passage to immigrants who want to return home
republicanism	a form of government without a monarch (king or queen) in which power is vested in the people or their representatives
revenue income earned;	receipts or return from any source
serfs	workers who were legally tied to a particular property and who could not leave the land to which they were attached, even if the property changed hands

share-cropping	a semi-contractual agreement between landlord and labourer to work on the estate. The landlord would provide land, seed and machinery, while the labourer provided labour and, in return, received a portion of the profits
Staatstoezicht	state supervision of the Apprenticeship System in the Dutch colonies
Standing Closer Association	a body established in 1947 to study the possibility of a British Caribbean federation and to draft a federal constitution
Statuut (of 1954)	charter (of political unity) of the kingdom of the Netherlands, Suriname and the Dutch Antilles
Uncle Sam	a popular name for the United States of America
U.N.I.A.	Universal Negro Improvement Association (formed by Marcus Garvey)
United Nations	an organization formed in 1945 (currently headed by Kofi Annan) to promote world peace and international co-operation among world nations
universal adult suffrage	the right of all adults to vote
U.N.R.	Union Nationale Radicale (a political party in the French Caribbean)
Wood Commission	a 1921 Commission headed by EFC Wood (Lord Halifax) to investigate the structure of government in the British Caribbean
W.T.O.	World Trade Organisation (replaced the G.A.T.T.); aims to promote free trade and scrap preferential trade agreements

Index

Logwood industry: in the British-colonised Caribbean, 117
Lomé Convention: and the sugar industry, 108
Longbridge, Gladys (Lady Bustamante): and Jamaica's labour movement, 181
Lord Kitchener: T&T Calypsonian, 233
L'Ouverture, Toussaint: agricultural policy, 37; and the Haitian revolution, vii, 2–4
Love, Dr Robert (Jamaica): and Garvey, 172
Lumber industry, 213

Ma Lou: Jamaican ceramist, 230
Magloire, General Panul (Haiti): and US occupation, 157
Mahogany industry: in Belize, 117–118
Malcolm X (USA), 142
Management: of regional sugar industry, 45
Manifest destiny, 146, 148
Manley, Edna: and Jamaican art, 228; and Jamaica's labour movement, 181
Manley, Norman Washington (Jamaica): and federation, 250; and the labour movement, 184–185; and the PNM, 250
Manley, Prime Minister Michael (Jamaica), 251; and the imposition of a bauxite levy, 128; and US intervention, 161
Manning, Prime Minister Patrick (T&T), 251
Manpower and Citizens' Association (Guyana), 173, 179
Manufacturing industry: in Jamaica, 127–128
Markets: for non-traditional crops, 121
Marriage patterns, 89
Marryshow, T. Albert: and political representation, 183, 247
Marson, Una (Jamaica): and Caribbean theatre, 241; and socio-economic conditions, 166, 171, 181
Martinique: industrialisation in, 129; peasant development in, 41; socio-economic conditions in, 191; sugar industry, 109; tourist industry, 131; worker migration in, 26–27, 28

Masters and Servants Act: and working conditions, 169, 189
McIntosh, George: and political representation, 247; and the St Vincent labour movement, 187
Mechanisation: of the sugar industry, 29
Mendieta, Carlos (Cuba): leadership of, 191
Mento: Jamaican, 233
Metaire system: as labour incentive, 28
Metayage (Metaire) system: terms of the, 29–30
Military intervention: by the USA, 147–163
Migration: intra-Caribbean, 24–25; of workers from plantations, 22–24. See also Emigration and Immigrant labour
Minot, John: arrest of, 11
Missionaries, 88–89. See also individual denominations
Moise, General: and rebellion of Haitian workers (1801), 3
Molasses, 43
Monroe, President James (USA): Caribbean policy, 147–148
Monroe Doctrine, 146–148
Montserrat: Apprenticeship in, 10; peasant development in, 43; political development of, 257; response to Apprenticeship in, 10
Montserrat Trade and Labour Union: women in the, 190
Morant Bay Rebellion, 244–246
Moret Law: and abolition of slavery in, 19
Morton, Rev. John: and education in T&T, 92
Moslem festivals, 205, 207
Mott, Bertha: and the St Vincent labour movement, 187
Moyne Commission of Enquiry: in the British-colonised Caribbean, 187–188, 212; women and the, 188
Multinationals: in the British-colonised Caribbean, 161
Music: Caribbean, 230–236
Myal: African-based ritual, 200

National Club: and Garvey's, 170
National Dance Theatre Company (Jamaica): and traditional dance, 237
National Institute of Agrarian Reform (INRA): and land reform in Cuba, 154
National Workers' Union (NWU, Jamaica): and the ICFTU, 161; and political office, 190
Natural disasters: impact on agriculture, 122
New Jewel Movement (NJM): and Grenada's political development, 255; and US intervention in Grenada, 162
News media, 224
Negro Welfare Cultural and Social Association (NWCSA): Elma François and the, 182
Nevis: independence of, 256–257; peasant development in, 42; response to Apprenticeship in, 10
Nixon, President (USA): and Haiti, 157
North American immigration scheme: and labour supply, 52–53

Obeah, 200
Occupations: in the Caribbean, 212 215
Oil industry, 126; in Dutch-colonised Caribbean, 128–129; strike in T&T oil industry, 177; in T&T, 127
Oilfield Workers trade Union (OWTU, T&T), 190
Olivier, Lord Sydney: conditions in Jamaica, 171; and the trade union movement, 172
Ogoe, Theresa: and the T&T labour movement, 182
O'Neil, Charles Duncan: and the DL, 252
Operation Bootstrap: in Puerto Rico, 124-126
Orde-Browne, Major: report on Belize (1939), 187
Organisation of American States (OAS): US and the, 161
Organisation of Eastern Caribbean States (OECS), 259
Orisha, 200

Trinidad Asphalt Company, 127
Trinidad Dramatic Club, 240
Trinidad Labour Party (TLP): and
    Cipriani, 251; establishment of
    the, 172
Trinidad Oil Company, 127
Trinidad Oilfields Limited, 127
Trinidad and Tobago (T&T):
    Apprenticeship in, 10; art in, 230;
    coffee industry, 115; church
    schools in, 85; drama in, 240;
    education of Indians in, 93; and
    federation, 249–250; freed people
    in, 25; immigrant laws in, 64–65;
    Indian resistance in, 68; labour
    shortage in, 10; oil industry in,
    127; peasant development in , 37,
    46-47; political development in,
    251–252; racial conflict in, 197;
    strikes in, 177; sugar production
    costs, 46; theatre in, 221; tourist
    industry, 130; US military bases in,
    122, 160; wages in, 167; women
    and strikes in, 182–183
Trinidad Workingmen's Association
    (TWA), 172; strike, 176–177, 179,
    182
Truck system: and post-slavery labour,
    23; protests against the, 172
Trujillo massacre, 137
Tourist industry: British-colonised
    Caribbean, 130–131; Cuban
    (1920s), 153; Spanish-colonised
    Caribbean, 130–131
Tyson, JD: and the Moyne Commission,
    188

United British Oilfields Limited
    (UBOT), 127
United Fruit Company, 116
United National Congress (UNC, T&T),
    251
United States of America (USA):
    Caribbean policy, 152–153; civil
    war, 149; independence, 148;
    migration to the, 141–143; military
    intervention of the, 145–165; naval
    bases in T&T, 122; and the
    Panama Canal, 149–151; and
    Puerto Rico, 155–156

Universal Adult Suffrage, 250, 251; in
    Barbados, 252; in Belize, 256
Universal Negro Improvement
    Association (UNIA), 145, 170, 171
University Drama Society: and
    Caribbean Theatre, 239
US architecture, 227
US occupation: of Haiti, 156-158
United Bahamian Party (UBP): and
    Bahamas political development,
    254
United States Virgin Islands (USVI):
    creation of the, 160–161; tourist
    industry, 130–131
USA-Cuba relations, 126
USA-Guyana relations, 254
USA War of Independence, 149–150

Vagrancy Acts (1837), 9
Valdez, José Bordas: and US
    intervention in Santo Domingo,
    159
Van Scholten, Governor: and full
    freedom (St Croix), 17
Varieties: introduction of new sugar
    cane, 108
Vaz, Noel: Jamaican dramatist, 239
Verteuil, Dr Louis de: and crown
    colony government, 171
Victoria, Eladia: and US intervention in
    Santo Domingo, 159
Vincent, President Stenio (Haiti): and
    US occupation, 157
Visa requirements: for Caribbean
    immigrants, 140
Vote: women's right to, 96

Waddell, Rev Hope: on post-slavery
    labour supply, 25
Wages: of agricultural labourers
    (1930s), 212-213; in the British-
    colonised Caribbean, 167; in Cuba,
    190; immigrant, 90; as incentive
    for workers, 28
Walcott, Derek, 239
War Food Programme, 122
Ward schools: in T&T, 86, 92
Water Riots (T&T), 171, 247
Water transportation, 223
Waterfront workers': strike in Jamaica,
    179

Weddings, 206–207
West Indian Department of
    Agriculture, 123
West Indian Regiment: and racism,
    168
West Indies Federation: proposals for
    a, 247–250
White, Cleopatra: and strikes in Belize,
    180
Williams, Dr Eric: and federation, 250;
    and the PNM, 251
Wilson, President Woodrow (USA):
    Caribbean policy, 152; and Haiti,
    156
Windward islands: banana farming in,
    116, 117; peasant development in,
    42
Women: Apprenticeship and the
    enslaved, vii-viii; in cricket, 218;
    and industrialisation, 132-133;
    housing for immigrant, 90; and
    migration, 143; and the Moyne
    Commission, 188; protest against
    Apprenticeship, 17; and strikes,
    180, 181–183
Women Workers' Trade Union
    (WWTU), 190
Worker migration: in British-colonised
    Caribbean, 22–25; in Dutch-
    colonised Caribbean, 27–28; in
    French-colonised Caribbean,
    26–27; in Guadeloupe, 26–27, 28; in
    Guyana, 27; in Martinique, 26–27,
    28; in post-slavery Cuba, 28; in
    Spanish-colonised Caribbean,
    25–26
Workers' Rebellion (1801): in Haiti, 3
Workhouses: and post-slavery labour,
    23
Working conditions: and the British-
    colonised Caribbean, 167–192
World depression: impact on socio-
    economic conditions, 167
World Sugar Council, 112
World Trade Agreement on Tariffs and
    Trade (GATT): and the sugar
    industry, 109
World Trade Organisation (WTO): and
    the banana trade, 123; and the
    sugar industry, 109